한국의 토익 수험자 여러분께,

토익 시험은 세계적인 직무 영어능력 평가 시험으로, 지난 ⟶ 현장에서 필요한 영어능력 평가의 기준을 제시해 왔습니다. 토익 시험 및 토익스피킹, ⟶ 라이팅 시험은 세계에서 가장 널리 통용되는 영어능력 검증 시험으로, 160여 개국 14,000여 기관이 토익 성적을 의사결정에 활용하고 있습니다.

YBM은 한국의 토익 시험을 주관하는 ETS 독점 계약사입니다.

ETS는 한국 수험자들의 효과적인 토익 학습을 돕고자 YBM을 통하여 'ETS 토익 공식 교재'를 독점 출간하고 있습니다. 또한 'ETS 토익 공식 교재' 시리즈에 기출문항을 제공해 한국의 다른 교재들에 수록된 기출을 복제하거나 변형한 문항으로 인하여 발생할 수 있는 수험자들의 혼동을 방지하고 있습니다.

복제 및 변형 문항들은 토익 시험의 출제의도를 벗어날 수 있기 때문에 기출문항을 수록한 'ETS 토익 공식 교재'만큼 시험에 잘 대비할 수 없습니다.

'ETS 토익 공식 교재'를 통하여 수험자 여러분의 영어 소통을 위한 노력에 큰 성취가 있기를 바랍니다.

감사합니다.

Dear TOEIC Test Takers in Korea,

The TOEIC program is the global leader in English-language assessment for the workplace. It has set the standard for assessing English-language skills needed in the workplace for more than 40 years. The TOEIC tests are the most widely used English language assessments around the world, with 14,000+ organizations across more than 160 countries trusting TOEIC scores to make decisions.

YBM is the ETS Country Master Distributor for the TOEIC program in Korea and so is the exclusive distributor for TOEIC Korea.

To support effective learning for TOEIC test-takers in Korea, ETS has authorized YBM to publish the only Official TOEIC prep books in Korea. These books contain actual TOEIC items to help prevent confusion among Korean test-takers that might be caused by other prep book publishers' use of reproduced or paraphrased items.

Reproduced or paraphrased items may fail to reflect the intent of actual TOEIC items and so will not prepare test-takers as well as the actual items contained in the ETS TOEIC Official prep books published by YBM.

We hope that these ETS TOEIC Official prep books enable you, as test-takers, to achieve great success in your efforts to communicate effectively in English.

Thank you.

입문부터 실전까지 수준별 학습을 통해 최단기 목표점수 달성!

ETS TOEIC® 공식수험서
스마트 학습 지원

www.ybmbooks.com에서도 무료 MP3를 다운로드 받을 수 있습니다.

ETS 토익 모바일 학습 플랫폼!
ETS 토익기출 수험서 [어플]

구글플레이   앱스토어

교재 학습 지원
- 교재 해설 강의
- LC 음원 MP3
- 교재/부록 모의고사 채점 분석
- 단어 암기장

부가 서비스
- 데일리 학습(토익 기출문제 풀이)
- 토익 최신 경향 무료 특강
- 토익 타이머

모의고사 결과 분석
- 파트별/문항별 정답률
- 파트별/유형별 취약점 리포트
- 전체 응시자 점수 분포도

ETS 토익 학습 전용 온라인 커뮤티니!
ETS TOEIC® Book [공식카페]

etstoeicbook.co.kr

강사진의 학습 지원   토익 대표강사들의 학습 지원과 멘토링

교재 학습관 운영   교재별 학습게시판을 통해 무료 동영상 강의 등 학습 지원

학습 콘텐츠 제공   토익 학습 콘텐츠와 정기시험 예비특강 업데이트

✳toeic®

토익® 정기시험
기출문제집 4
1000 LC

토익˚정기시험
기출문제집 4
1000 LC

발행인	허문호
발행처	YBM

편집	윤경림, 정유상, 이진열
디자인	강상문, 이미화, 이현숙
마케팅	정연철, 박천산, 고영노, 김동진, 박찬경, 김윤하

초판발행	2023년 12월 18일
5쇄발행	2024년 10월 10일

신고일자	1964년 3월 28일
신고번호	제 1964-000003호
주소	서울시 종로구 종로 104
전화	(02) 2000-0515 [구입문의] / (02) 2000-0304 [내용문의]
팩스	(02) 2285-1523
홈페이지	www.ybmbooks.com

ISBN	978-89-17-23949-2

*toeic®

토익® 정기시험 기출문제집 4

1000

PREFACE

Dear test taker,

English-language proficiency has become a vital tool for success. It can help you excel in business, travel the world, and communicate effectively with friends and colleagues. The TOEIC® test measures your ability to function effectively in English in these types of situations. Because TOEIC scores are recognized around the world as evidence of your English-language proficiency, you will be able to confidently demonstrate your English skills to employers and begin your journey to success.

The test developers at ETS are excited to help you achieve your personal and professional goals through the use of the TOEIC® 정기시험 기출문제집 1000 Vol. 4. This book contains test questions taken from actual, official TOEIC tests. These questions will help you become familiar with the content and the format of the TOEIC test. This book also contains detailed explanations of the question types and language points contained in the TOEIC test. These test questions and explanations have all been prepared by the same test specialists who develop the actual TOEIC test, so you can be confident that you will receive an authentic test-preparation experience.

Features of the TOEIC® 정기시험 기출문제집 1000 Vol. 4 include the following.

- · Ten full-length test forms all accompanied by answer keys and official scripts
- · Specific and easy to understand explanations for learners
- · The very same ETS voice actors that you will hear in an official TOEIC test

By using the TOEIC® 정기시험 기출문제집 1000 Vol. 4 to prepare for the TOEIC test, you can be assured that you have a professionally prepared resource that will provide you with accurate guidance so that you are more familiar with the tasks, content, and format of the test and that will help you maximize your TOEIC test score. With your official TOEIC score certificate, you will be ready to show the world what you know!

We are delighted to assist you on your TOEIC journey with the TOEIC® 정기시험 기출문제집 1000 Vol. 4 and wish you the best of success.

최신 기출문제 전격 공개!

유일무이

출제기관이 독점 제공한 기출문제가 담긴 유일한 교재!
이 책에는 정기시험 기출문제 10세트가 수록되어 있다. 시험에 나온
최신 기출문제로 실전 감각을 키워 시험에 확실하게 대비하자!

국내최고

정기시험 성우 음성으로 실전 대비!
이 책에 수록된 10세트의 LC 음원은 모두 실제 시험에서 나온 정기 시험
성우의 음원이다. 시험장에서 듣게 될 음성으로 공부하면 까다로운
영국·호주발음도 걱정 없다.

독점제공

ETS 제공 표준점수 환산표!
출제기관 ETS가 독점 제공하는 표준점수 환산표를 수록했다. 채점
후 환산표를 통해 자신의 실력이 어느 정도인지 가늠해 보자!

스마트 학습

동영상 강의, 단어장, 채점서비스 무료 제공!
ETS 토익기출 수험서 어플 다운로드 및 실행 ▶ 토익(상단 메뉴)
▶ 실전서(좌측 메뉴) ▶ ETS 토익 정기시험 기출문제집 1000 Vol. 4
LC를 클릭해 무료 제공하는 자료로 스마트하게 학습하자!

* ybmbooks.com에서도 단어장 MP3파일, 단어장 PDF, 정답 PDF,
토익 연습용 답안지 PDF 제공

TOEIC 소개

Test of English for International Communication(국제적 의사소통을 위한 영어 시험)의 약자로, 영어가 모국어가 아닌 사람들이 일상생활 또는 비즈니스 현장에서 꼭 필요한 실용적 영어 구사 능력을 갖추었는가를 평가하는 시험이다.

시험 구성

구성	PART		유형	문항 수	시간	배점
Listening	Part 1		사진 묘사	6	45분	495점
	Part 2		질의 응답	25		
	Part 3		짧은 대화	39		
	Part 4		짧은 담화	30		
Reading	Part 5		단문 빈칸 채우기	30	75분	495점
	Part 6		장문 빈칸 채우기	16		
	Part 7	독해	단일 지문	29		
			이중 지문	10		
			삼중 지문	15		
Total	7 Parts			200문항	120분	990점

평가 항목

LC	RC
단문을 듣고 이해하는 능력	읽은 글을 통해 추론해 생각할 수 있는 능력
짧은 대화체 문장을 듣고 이해하는 능력	장문에서 특정한 정보를 찾을 수 있는 능력
비교적 긴 대화체에서 주고받은 내용을 파악할 수 있는 능력	글의 목적, 주제, 의도 등을 파악하는 능력
장문에서 핵심이 되는 정보를 파악할 수 있는 능력	뜻이 유사한 단어들의 정확한 용례를 파악하는 능력
구나 문장에서 화자의 목적이나 함축된 의미를 이해하는 능력	문장 구조를 제대로 파악하는지, 문장에서 필요한 품사, 어구 등을 찾는 능력

※ 성적표에는 전체 수험자의 평균과 해당 수험자가 받은 성적이 백분율로 표기되어 있다.

수험 정보

시험 접수 방법

한국 토익 위원회 사이트(www.toeic.co.kr)에서 시험일 약 2개월 전부터
온라인으로 접수 가능

시험장 준비물

신분증	규정 신분증만 가능 (주민등록증, 운전면허증, 기간 만료 전의 여권, 공무원증)
필기구	연필, 지우개 (볼펜이나 사인펜은 사용 금지)

시험 진행 시간

09:20	입실 (9:50 이후 입실 불가)
09:30 ~ 09:45	답안지 작성에 관한 오리엔테이션
09:45 ~ 09:50	휴식
09:50 ~ 10:05	신분증 확인
10:05 ~ 10:10	문제지 배부 및 파본 확인
10:10 ~ 10:55	듣기 평가 (LISTENING TEST)
10:55 ~ 12:10	독해 평가 (READING TEST)

**TOEIC
성적 확인**

시험일로부터 약 10-11일 후, 인터넷 홈페이지와 어플리케이션을 통해 성적을 확인할 수 있다.
TOEIC 성적표는 우편이나 온라인으로 발급받을 수 있다(시험 접수 시 양자택일).
우편으로 발급받을 경우는 성적 발표 후 대략 일주일이 소요되며, 온라인 발급을 선택하면
유효기간 내에 홈페이지에서 본인이 직접 1회에 한해 무료 출력할 수 있다. TOEIC 성적은
시험일로부터 2년간 유효하다.

토익 점수

TOEIC 점수는 듣기 영역(LC)과 읽기 영역(RC)을 합계한 점수로 5점 단위로 구성되며 총점은
990점이다. TOEIC 성적은 각 문제 유형의 난이도에 따른 점수 환산표에 의해 결정된다.

토익 경향 분석

PART 1 사진 묘사 Photographs

1인 등장 사진

주어는 He/She, A man/woman 등이며 주로 앞부분에 나온다.

2인 이상 등장 사진

주어는 They, Some men/women/people, One of the men/women 등이며 주로 중간부분에 나온다.

사물/배경 사진

주어는 A car, Some chairs 등이며 주로 뒷부분에 나온다.

사람 또는 사물 중심 사진

주어가 일부는 사람, 일부는 사물이며 주로 뒷부분에 나온다.

사람 또는 사물 중심 사진 **33%**

1인 등장 사진 **33%**

PART 1 최신 출제 경향

사물/배경 사진 **17%**

2인 이상 등장 사진 **17%**

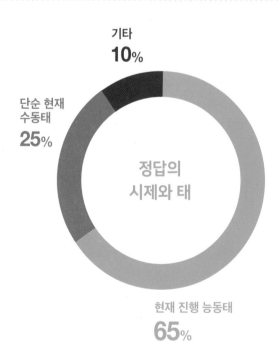

기타 **10%**

단순 현재 수동태 **25%**

정답의 시제와 태

현재 진행 능동태 **65%**

현재 진행 능동태

\<is/are + 현재분사\> 형태이며 주로 사람이 주어이다.

단순 현재 수동태

\<is/are + 과거분사\> 형태이며 주로 사물이 주어이다.

기타

\<is/are + being + 과거분사\> 형태의 현재 진행 수동태, \<has/have + been + 과거분사\> 형태의 현재 완료 수동태, '타동사 + 목적어' 형태의 단순 현재 능동태, There is/are와 같은 단순 현재도 나온다.

평서문

질문이 아니라 객관적인 사실이나 화자의 의견 등을 나타내는 문장이다.

의문사 의문문

각 의문사마다 1~2개씩 나온다. 의문사가 단독으로 나오기도 하지만 What time ~?, How long ~?, Which room ~? 등에서처럼 다른 명사나 형용사와 같이 나오기도 한다.

명령문

동사원형이나 Please 등으로 시작한다.

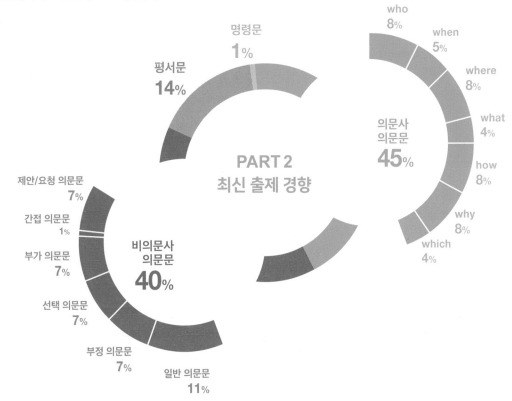

비의문사 의문문

일반(Yes/No) 의문문 적게 나올 때는 1~2개, 많이 나올 때는 3~4개씩 나오는 편이다.

부정 의문문 Don't you ~?, Isn't he ~? 등으로 시작하는 문장이며 일반 긍정 의문문보다는 약간 더 적게 나온다.

선택 의문문 A or B 형태로 나오며 A와 B의 형태가 단어, 구, 절일 수 있다. 구나 절일 경우 문장이 길어져서 어려워진다.

부가 의문문 ~ don't you?, ~ isn't he? 등으로 끝나는 문장이며, 일반 부정 의문문과 비슷하다고 볼 수 있다.

간접 의문문 의문사가 문장 처음 부분이 아니라 문장 중간에 들어 있다.

제안/요청 의문문 정보를 얻기보다는 상대방의 도움이나 동의 등을 얻기 위한 목적이 일반적이다.

- 3인 대화의 경우 남자 화자 두 명과 여자 화자
  한 명 또는 남자 화자 한 명과 여자 화자 두 명이
  나온다. 따라서 문제에서는 2인 대화에서와 달리
  the man이나 the woman이 아니라 the men이나
  the women 또는 특정한 이름이 언급될 수 있다.

- 대화 & 시각 정보는 항상 파트의 뒷부분에 나온다.

- 시각 정보의 유형으로 chart, map, floor plan,
  schedule, table, weather forecast, directory,
  list, invoice, receipt, sign, packing slip 등
  다양한 자료가 골고루 나온다.

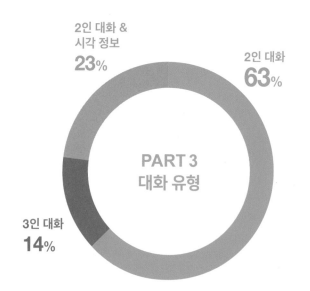

2인 대화 &
시각 정보
23%

2인 대화
63%

PART 3
대화 유형

3인 대화
14%

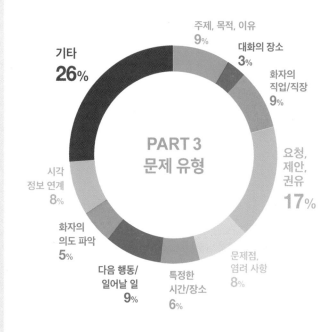

주제, 목적, 이유
9%

대화의 장소
3%

화자의
직업/직장
9%

기타
26%

PART 3
문제 유형

요청,
제안,
권유
17%

시각
정보 연계
8%

화자의
의도 파악
5%

다음 행동/
일어날 일
9%

특정한
시간/장소
6%

문제점,
염려 사항
8%

- 주제, 목적, 이유, 대화의 장소, 화자의 직업/직장
  등과 관련된 문제는 주로 대화의 첫 번째 문제로
  나오며 다음 행동/일어날 일 등과 관련된 문제는
  주로 대화의 세 번째 문제로 나온다.

- 화자의 의도 파악 문제는 주로 2인 대화에
  나오지만, 가끔 3인 대화에 나오기도 한다. 시각
  정보 연계 대화에는 나오지 않고 있다.

- Part 3에서 화자의 의도 파악 문제는 2개가
  나오고 시각 정보 연계 문제는 3개가 나온다.

PART 4 짧은 담화 Short Talks

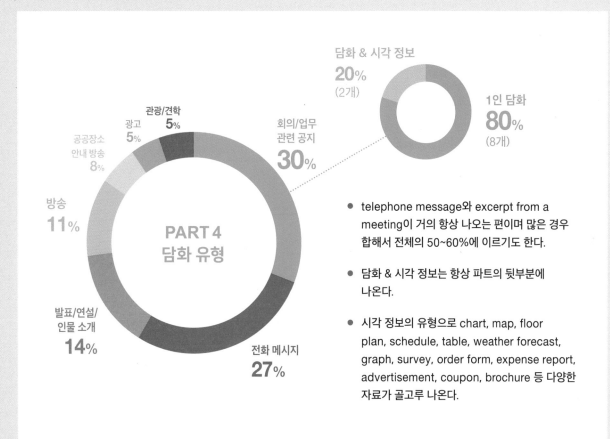

- telephone message와 excerpt from a meeting이 거의 항상 나오는 편이며 많은 경우 합해서 전체의 50~60%에 이르기도 한다.

- 담화 & 시각 정보는 항상 파트의 뒷부분에 나온다.

- 시각 정보의 유형으로 chart, map, floor plan, schedule, table, weather forecast, graph, survey, order form, expense report, advertisement, coupon, brochure 등 다양한 자료가 골고루 나온다.

- 문제 유형은 기본적으로 Part 3과 거의 비슷하다.

- 주제, 목적, 이유, 담화의 장소, 화자의 직업/직장 등과 관련된 문제는 주로 담화의 첫 번째 문제로 나오며 다음 행동/일어날 일 등과 관련된 문제는 주로 담화의 세 번째 문제로 나온다.

- Part 4에서 화자의 의도 파악 문제는 3개가 나오고 시각 정보 연계 문제는 2개가 나온다.

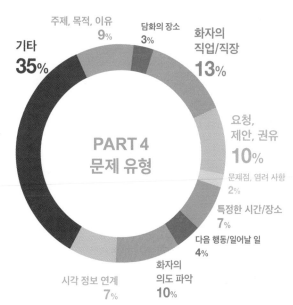

문법 문제

시제와 대명사와 관련된 문법 문제가 2개씩, 한정사와 분사와 관련된 문법 문제가 1개씩 나온다. 시제 문제의 경우 능동태/수동태나 수의 일치와 연계되기도 한다. 그 밖에 한정사, 능동태/수동태, 부정사, 동명사 등과 관련된 문법 문제가 나온다.

어휘 문제

동사, 명사, 형용사, 부사와 관련된 어휘 문제가 각각 2~3개씩 골고루 나온다. 전치사 어휘 문제는 3개씩 꾸준히 나오지만, 접속사나 어구와 관련된 어휘 문제는 나오지 않을 때도 있고 3개가 나올 때도 있다.

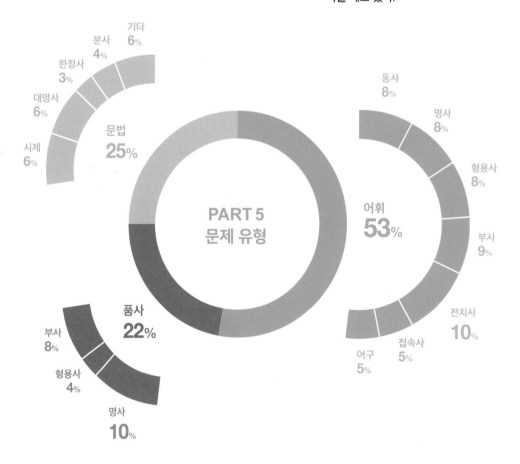

품사 문제

명사와 부사와 관련된 품사 문제가 2~3개씩 나오며, 형용사와 관련된 품사 문제가 상대적으로 적은 편이다.

PART 6 장문 빈칸 채우기 Text Completion

총 4지문 16문제 (지문당 4문제)

한 지문에 4문제가 나오며 평균적으로 어휘 문제가 2개, 품사나 문법 문제가 1개, 문맥에 맞는 문장 고르기 문제가 1개 들어간다. 문맥에 맞는 문장 고르기 문제를 제외하면 문제 유형은 기본적으로 파트 5와 거의 비슷하다.

어휘 문제

동사, 명사, 부사, 어구와 관련된 어휘 문제는 매번 1~2개씩 나온다. 부사 어휘 문제의 경우 therefore(그러므로)나 however(하지만)처럼 문맥의 흐름을 자연스럽게 연결해 주는 부사가 자주 나온다.

문맥에 맞는 문장 고르기

문맥에 맞는 문장 고르기 문제는 지문당 한 문제씩 나오는데, 나오는 위치의 확률은 4문제 중 두 번째 문제, 세 번째 문제, 네 번째 문제, 첫 번째 문제 순으로 높다.

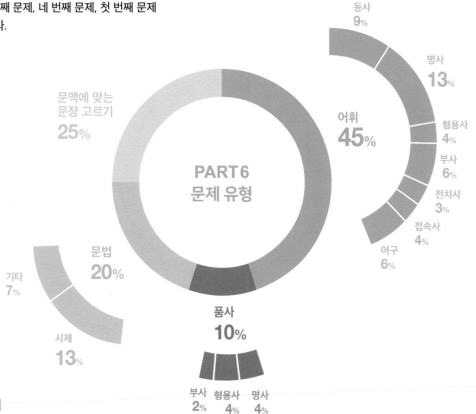

PART 6
문제 유형

문맥에 맞는 문장 고르기 **25%**

어휘 **45%**

동사 9%
명사 **13%**
형용사 4%
부사 6%
전치사 3%
접속사 4%
어구 6%

품사 **10%**
부사 2% 형용사 4% 명사 4%

문법 **20%**
시제 **13%**
기타 7%

문법 문제

문맥의 흐름과 밀접하게 관련이 있는 시제 문제가 2개 정도 나오며, 능동태/수동태나 수의 일치와 연계되기도 한다. 그 밖에 대명사, 능동태/수동태, 부정사, 접속사/전치사 등과 관련된 문법 문제가 나온다.

품사 문제

명사나 형용사 문제가 부사 문제보다 좀 더 자주 나온다.

PART 7 독해 Reading Comprehension

지문 유형	지문당 문제 수	지문 개수	비중 %
단일 지문	2문항	4개	약 15%
	3문항	3개	약 16%
	4문항	3개	약 22%
이중 지문	5문항	2개	약 19%
삼중 지문	5문항	3개	약 28%

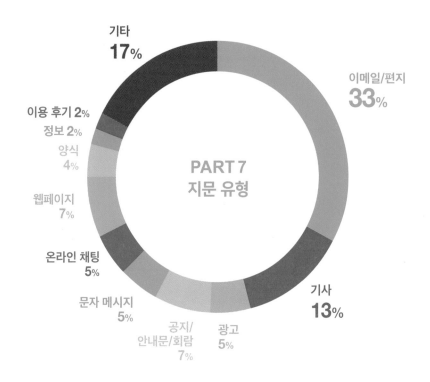

- 이메일/편지, 기사 유형 지문은 거의 항상 나오는 편이며 많은 경우 합해서 전체의 50~60%에 이르기도 한다.

- 기타 지문 유형으로 agenda, brochure, comment card, coupon, flyer, instructions, invitation, invoice, list, menu, page from a catalog, policy statement, report, schedule, survey, voucher 등 다양한 자료가 골고루 나온다.

(이중 지문과 삼중 지문 속의 지문들을 모두 낱개로 계산함 – 총 23지문)

총 15지문 54문제 (지문당 2~5문제)

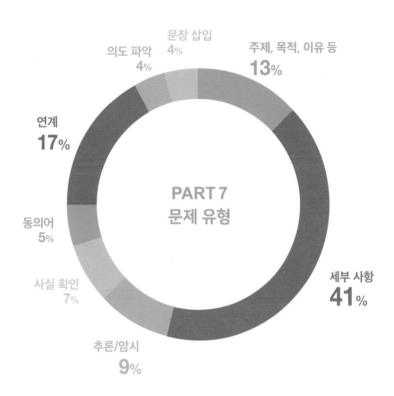

문장 삽입
4%

의도 파악
4%

주제, 목적, 이유 등
13%

연계
17%

동의어
5%

PART 7
문제 유형

세부 사항
41%

사실 확인
7%

추론/암시
9%

- 동의어 문제는 주로 이중 지문이나 삼중 지문에 나온다.
- 연계 문제는 일반적으로 이중 지문에서 한 문제, 삼중 지문에서 두 문제가 나온다.
- 의도 파악 문제는 문자 메시지(text-message chain)나 온라인 채팅(online chat discussion) 지문에서 출제되며 두 문제가 나온다.
- 문장 삽입 문제는 주로 기사, 이메일, 편지, 회람 지문에서 출제되며 두 문제가 나온다.

점수 환산표 및 산출법

점수 환산표 이 책에 수록된 각 Test를 풀고 난 후, 맞은 개수를 세어 점수를 환산해 보세요.

LISTENING Raw Score (맞은 개수)	LISTENING Scaled Score (환산 점수)	READING Raw Score (맞은 개수)	READING Scaled Score (환산 점수)
96-100	475-495	96-100	460-495
91-95	435-495	91-95	425-490
86-90	405-470	86-90	400-465
81-85	370-450	81-85	375-440
76-80	345-420	76-80	340-415
71-75	320-390	71-75	310-390
66-70	290-360	66-70	285-370
61-65	265-335	61-65	255-340
56-60	240-310	56-60	230-310
51-55	215-280	51-55	200-275
46-50	190-255	46-50	170-245
41-45	160-230	41-45	140-215
36-40	130-205	36-40	115-180
31-35	105-175	31-35	95-150
26-30	85-145	26-30	75-120
21-25	60-115	21-25	60-95
16-20	30-90	16-20	45-75
11-15	5-70	11-15	30-55
6-10	5-60	6-10	10-40
1-5	5-50	1-5	5-30
0	5-35	0	5-15

점수 산출 방법 아래의 방식으로 점수를 산출할 수 있다.

STEP 1

자신의 답안을 수록된 정답과 대조하여 채점한다. 각 Section의 맞은 개수가 본인의 Section별 '실제 점수(통계 처리하기 전의 점수, raw score)'이다. Listening Test와 Reading Test의 정답 수를 세어, 자신의 실제 점수를 아래의 해당란에 기록한다.

	맞은 개수	환산 점수대
LISTENING		
READING		
총점		

Section별 실제 점수가 그대로 Section별 TOEIC 점수가 되는 것은 아니다. TOEIC은 시행할 때마다 별도로 특정한 통계 처리 방법을 사용하며 이러한 실제 점수를 환산 점수(converted[scaled] score)로 전환하게 된다. 이렇게 전환함으로써, 매번 시행될 때마다 문제는 달라지지만 그 점수가 갖는 의미는 같아지게 된다. 예를 들어 어느 한 시험에서 총점 550점의 성적을 받는 실력이라면 다른 시험에서도 거의 550점대의 성적을 받게 되는 것이다.

STEP 2

실제 점수를 위 표에 기록한 후 왼쪽 페이지의 점수 환산표를 보도록 한다. TOEIC이 시행될 때마다 대개 이와 비슷한 형태의 표가 작성되는데, 여기 제시된 환산표는 본 교재에 수록된 Test용으로 개발된 것이다. 이 표를 사용하여 자신의 실제 점수를 환산 점수로 전환하도록 한다. 즉, 예를 들어 Listening Test의 실제 정답 수가 61~65개이면 환산 점수는 265점에서 335점 사이가 된다. 여기서 실제 정답 수가 61개이면 환산 점수가 265점이고, 65개이면 환산 점수가 335점임을 의미하는 것은 아니다. 본 책의 Test를 위해 작성된 이 점수 환산표가 자신의 영어 실력이 어느 정도인지 대략적으로 파악하는 데 도움이 되긴 하지만, 이 표가 실제 TOEIC 성적 산출에 그대로 사용된 적은 없다는 사실을 밝혀 둔다.

토익®정기시험
기출문제집4
1000

TEST 01
무료 동영상 강의

LC

기출 TEST

01

LISTENING TEST

In the Listening test, you will be asked to demonstrate how well you understand spoken English. The entire Listening test will last approximately 45 minutes. There are four parts, and directions are given for each part. You must mark your answers on the separate answer sheet. Do not write your answers in your test book.

PART 1

Directions: For each question in this part, you will hear four statements about a picture in your test book. When you hear the statements, you must select the one statement that best describes what you see in the picture. Then find the number of the question on your answer sheet and mark your answer. The statements will not be printed in your test book and will be spoken only one time.

Statement (C), "They're sitting at a table," is the best description of the picture, so you should select answer (C) and mark it on your answer sheet.

1.

2.

GO ON TO THE NEXT PAGE

3.

4.

5.

6.

GO ON TO THE NEXT PAGE

PART 2

Directions: You will hear a question or statement and three responses spoken in English. They will not be printed in your test book and will be spoken only one time. Select the best response to the question or statement and mark the letter (A), (B), or (C) on your answer sheet.

7. Mark your answer on your answer sheet.

8. Mark your answer on your answer sheet.

9. Mark your answer on your answer sheet.

10. Mark your answer on your answer sheet.

11. Mark your answer on your answer sheet.

12. Mark your answer on your answer sheet.

13. Mark your answer on your answer sheet.

14. Mark your answer on your answer sheet.

15. Mark your answer on your answer sheet.

16. Mark your answer on your answer sheet.

17. Mark your answer on your answer sheet.

18. Mark your answer on your answer sheet.

19. Mark your answer on your answer sheet.

20. Mark your answer on your answer sheet.

21. Mark your answer on your answer sheet.

22. Mark your answer on your answer sheet.

23. Mark your answer on your answer sheet.

24. Mark your answer on your answer sheet.

25. Mark your answer on your answer sheet.

26. Mark your answer on your answer sheet.

27. Mark your answer on your answer sheet.

28. Mark your answer on your answer sheet.

29. Mark your answer on your answer sheet.

30. Mark your answer on your answer sheet.

31. Mark your answer on your answer sheet.

PART 3

Directions: You will hear some conversations between two or more people. You will be asked to answer three questions about what the speakers say in each conversation. Select the best response to each question and mark the letter (A), (B), (C), or (D) on your answer sheet. The conversations will not be printed in your test book and will be spoken only one time.

32. What event does the woman mention?

(A) A job fair
(B) A cooking class
(C) A fund-raiser
(D) A company picnic

33. What does the woman ask for?

(A) A guest list
(B) A dessert recipe
(C) A business card
(D) A promotional code

34. What does the man recommend doing?

(A) Returning some merchandise
(B) Watching a video
(C) Creating an account
(D) Reading a review

35. What department do the speakers most likely work in?

(A) Accounting
(B) Research and development
(C) Maintenance
(D) Marketing

36. What problem does the woman mention?

(A) A report has not been submitted.
(B) An invoice is not accurate.
(C) A policy has not been followed.
(D) An order has not been delivered.

37. What does the man say he will do?

(A) Delete an electronic file
(B) Authorize a reimbursement
(C) Set up a sales meeting
(D) Review a spreadsheet

38. What industry do the speakers most likely work in?

(A) Shipping
(B) Manufacturing
(C) Hospitality
(D) Meteorology

39. What is the reason for a delay?

(A) A schedule was written incorrectly.
(B) Some equipment is not properly set up.
(C) Weather conditions are poor.
(D) Several staff members are absent.

40. What does the man say he will do?

(A) Update a shift schedule
(B) Clear a work space
(C) Complete a checklist
(D) Place a call

41. Why is the woman at the restaurant?

(A) To celebrate a retirement
(B) To perform an inspection
(C) To meet with some clients
(D) To write an article

42. What does the woman mean when she says, "it's very hot today"?

(A) She is unable to accept an invitation.
(B) A cooling system is not working.
(C) A meeting will end soon.
(D) She wants to change a seating request.

43. What does the man say about a parking garage?

(A) It is free for customers.
(B) It is under construction.
(C) It closes soon.
(D) It offers monthly contracts.

GO ON TO THE NEXT PAGE

44. Where does the woman most likely work?

    (A) At a university
    (B) At a publishing company
    (C) At an electronics store
    (D) At a grocery store

45. What does Murat ask about?

    (A) How much an item costs
    (B) When an event will begin
    (C) How many people will participate
    (D) Where to set up some equipment

46. What does the woman suggest doing?

    (A) Offering a discount
    (B) Displaying informational materials
    (C) Holding a contest
    (D) Visiting a registration table

47. What type of industry do the speakers most likely work in?

    (A) Textile manufacturing
    (B) Food production
    (C) Health care
    (D) Hospitality

48. What business challenge are the speakers discussing?

    (A) Lack of qualified personnel
    (B) Rising production costs
    (C) Changes in consumer preferences
    (D) Increased competition

49. What does the man say he will do?

    (A) Research more information
    (B) Negotiate a discount
    (C) Upgrade some machinery
    (D) Train a new employee

50. Why is the man calling?

    (A) To explain a business merger
    (B) To describe a new company policy
    (C) To offer the woman a work assignment
    (D) To invite the woman to speak at a conference

51. What does the man say a client is interested in doing?

    (A) Purchasing another business
    (B) Finding a new office space
    (C) Revising a budget proposal
    (D) Creating a marketing campaign

52. What does the woman ask the man to send?

    (A) A project description
    (B) An event invitation
    (C) Some social media links
    (D) Some contact information

53. What problem does the woman mention?

    (A) A vehicle is out of service.
    (B) An employee is late.
    (C) A shipment was damaged.
    (D) Traffic is heavy.

54. Where do the speakers most likely work?

    (A) At a recording studio
    (B) At a catering company
    (C) At a radio station
    (D) At a car dealership

55. What does the man say he will do next?

    (A) Arrange for a car repair
    (B) Order some kitchen supplies
    (C) Carry some items
    (D) Offer a refund

56. Why is the man calling the woman?

    (A) To plan a company event
    (B) To confirm a work deadline
    (C) To discuss a career path
    (D) To accept a job offer

57. Who most likely is the woman?

    (A) A newspaper editor
    (B) A university professor
    (C) A delivery person
    (D) A professional actor

58. What will the woman most likely do next?

    (A) Negotiate a contract
    (B) Explain an office policy
    (C) Review a résumé
    (D) Describe a work schedule

59. What are the speakers mainly discussing?

    (A) A new transportation route
    (B) A company merger
    (C) A public relations initiative
    (D) A medical facility design

60. Why does the woman say, "they also talked about it last year"?

    (A) To express doubt
    (B) To explain a process
    (C) To make a recommendation
    (D) To update some information

61. What does the woman want to avoid?

    (A) Paying a certification fee
    (B) Training additional staff
    (C) Upgrading some technology
    (D) Relocating to another city

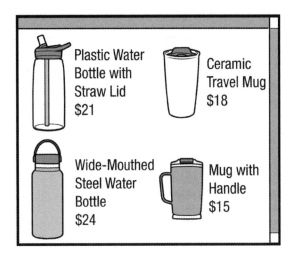

Plastic Water Bottle with Straw Lid $21

Ceramic Travel Mug $18

Wide-Mouthed Steel Water Bottle $24

Mug with Handle $15

62. Who is a gift for?

    (A) Donors
    (B) Volunteers
    (C) Employees
    (D) Clients

63. Look at the graphic. What is the price of the item the man recommends?

    (A) $21
    (B) $18
    (C) $24
    (D) $15

64. What is the woman going to send to the man?

    (A) A graphic file
    (B) A list of names
    (C) A delivery address
    (D) An account number

GO ON TO THE NEXT PAGE

Title	Artist
A Careful Glance	So-Jin Park
Promises	Vivek Madan
Stormy Sea	Claudia Hoffman
The Moment	Adisa Rotimi

65. What type of art will be displayed in an exhibit?

(A) Clay sculptures
(B) Oil paintings
(C) Black-and-white photographs
(D) Pencil drawings

66. Look at the graphic. Which piece of artwork will no longer be included?

(A) *A Careful Glance*
(B) *Promises*
(C) *Stormy Sea*
(D) *The Moment*

67. What does the woman say she will do right away?

(A) Speak with an artist
(B) Edit a recording
(C) Clean a gallery space
(D) Greet some visitors

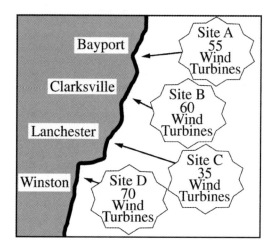

68. Who most likely are the speakers?

(A) Urban planners
(B) Journalists
(C) Engineers
(D) Environmental scientists

69. Look at the graphic. Which site has already been completed?

(A) Site A
(B) Site B
(C) Site C
(D) Site D

70. What does the man suggest focusing on?

(A) Work opportunities
(B) Wind turbine costs
(C) Supply chain issues
(D) Power capacity

PART 4

Directions: You will hear some talks given by a single speaker. You will be asked to answer three questions about what the speaker says in each talk. Select the best response to each question and mark the letter (A), (B), (C), or (D) on your answer sheet. The talks will not be printed in your test book and will be spoken only one time.

71. Who has recorded the message?
    (A) A city mayor's office
    (B) A maintenance department
    (C) An automobile dealership
    (D) A building management office

72. What are the listeners asked to do?
    (A) Move their vehicles
    (B) Pay their parking fines
    (C) Use an alternate entrance
    (D) Participate in a meeting

73. What does the speaker say was mailed last week?
    (A) An election ballot
    (B) A maintenance plan
    (C) A map
    (D) A coupon

74. What is the topic of the episode?
    (A) Garden landscaping
    (B) Window installation
    (C) Roof maintenance
    (D) Kitchen renovations

75. What does the speaker emphasize about some tools?
    (A) They should be cleaned regularly.
    (B) They should be of high quality.
    (C) They were recently invented.
    (D) They can be easily stored.

76. What does the speaker recommend doing every year?
    (A) Treating some wood
    (B) Consulting an electrician
    (C) Taking some photos
    (D) Draining some water

77. Who most likely is the speaker?
    (A) A radio show host
    (B) A tour guide
    (C) A sales associate
    (D) A professor

78. What will happen at two o'clock?
    (A) A lecture will begin.
    (B) A demonstration will be given.
    (C) An interview will be conducted.
    (D) A park will close.

79. What is *Orchid Caretakers*?
    (A) A book
    (B) An album
    (C) A film
    (D) A magazine

80. What event is taking place?
    (A) A fund-raising concert
    (B) A sports competition
    (C) A play rehearsal
    (D) An awards ceremony

81. What does the organization plan to do?
    (A) Change a policy
    (B) Repair a building
    (C) Select a winner
    (D) Sponsor a team

82. What does the speaker encourage the listeners to do?
    (A) Order tickets early
    (B) Visit a community center
    (C) Purchase refreshments
    (D) Donate clothing

GO ON TO THE NEXT PAGE

83. What is the topic of the workshop?

    (A) Time management
    (B) Public speaking
    (C) Leadership skills
    (D) Professional networking

84. What does the speaker imply when he says, "Erina's at the back of the room"?

    (A) A guest speaker has just arrived.
    (B) Assistance is available.
    (C) Attendees should speak clearly and loudly.
    (D) An extra chair should be provided.

85. What will the listeners do next?

    (A) Sign their names on a list
    (B) Take a break
    (C) Participate in an introductory activity
    (D) Fill out a questionnaire

86. What is a historical site famous for?

    (A) Its defensive walls
    (B) Its royal inhabitants
    (C) An event that happened there
    (D) Some artwork

87. Why does the speaker apologize?

    (A) The listeners cannot take pictures.
    (B) An area is closed to the listeners.
    (C) There is no gift shop.
    (D) A tour started late.

88. What does the speaker ask the listeners to do?

    (A) Show their tickets
    (B) Put on protective clothing
    (C) Use some handrails
    (D) Speak quietly

89. What is the speaker mainly discussing?

    (A) An advertising campaign
    (B) A market expansion
    (C) Some contract negotiations
    (D) Some audit procedures

90. What does the speaker imply when he says, "this is a priority"?

    (A) Overtime pay has been approved.
    (B) A deadline must be met.
    (C) A client expressed concern.
    (D) A supervisor will be observing closely.

91. What will the listeners do next?

    (A) View a presentation
    (B) Review a budget
    (C) Revise some work
    (D) Do some research

92. Where do the listeners most likely work?

    (A) At a hospital
    (B) At a restaurant
    (C) At a grocery store
    (D) At an electronics store

93. What is the main purpose of the talk?

    (A) To make a request
    (B) To address staff complaints
    (C) To present a new schedule
    (D) To explain a technical process

94. What does the speaker imply when she says, "That will require management approval"?

    (A) A process has not been followed.
    (B) The listeners may be asked to work extra shifts.
    (C) The listeners should contact a manager.
    (D) A change will not be immediate.

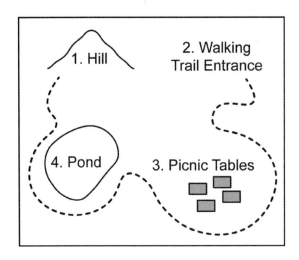

Soil Sampling Timeline		
Time of Year	Type of Crop	Depth
September–October	All plants	12 inches
November–August	Flowers	4 inches
	Vegetables	6 inches
	Trees and shrubs	8 inches

95. According to the speaker, what was recently completed?

    (A) A company reorganization
    (B) A park renovation
    (C) A volunteer training
    (D) A conservation project

96. Look at the graphic. Where does the speaker say refreshments will be served?

    (A) Location 1
    (B) Location 2
    (C) Location 3
    (D) Location 4

97. What are the listeners reminded to do?

    (A) Complete a survey
    (B) Donate some money
    (C) Join an organization
    (D) Post some photographs

98. What is the topic of today's lecture?

    (A) When to harvest crops
    (B) Where to plant trees
    (C) How to grow vegetables
    (D) Which flowers need more sun

99. Look at the graphic. At what depth should samples be collected this month?

    (A) 12 inches
    (B) 4 inches
    (C) 6 inches
    (D) 8 inches

100. What does the speaker encourage the listeners to do?

    (A) Turn off mobile phones
    (B) Have some refreshments
    (C) Purchase some seeds
    (D) Sign up for a mailing list

This is the end of the Listening test.

토익®정기시험
기출문제집 4
1000

TEST 02
무료 동영상 강의

LC

기출 TEST
02

LISTENING TEST

In the Listening test, you will be asked to demonstrate how well you understand spoken English. The entire Listening test will last approximately 45 minutes. There are four parts, and directions are given for each part. You must mark your answers on the separate answer sheet. Do not write your answers in your test book.

PART 1

Directions: For each question in this part, you will hear four statements about a picture in your test book. When you hear the statements, you must select the one statement that best describes what you see in the picture. Then find the number of the question on your answer sheet and mark your answer. The statements will not be printed in your test book and will be spoken only one time.

Statement (C), "They're sitting at a table," is the best description of the picture, so you should select answer (C) and mark it on your answer sheet.

1.

2.

GO ON TO THE NEXT PAGE

3.

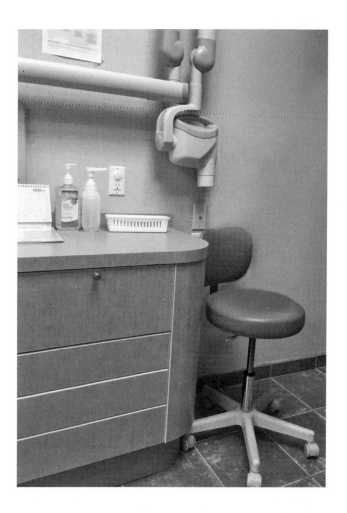

4.

5.

6.

GO ON TO THE NEXT PAGE ➡

PART 2

Directions: You will hear a question or statement and three responses spoken in English. They will not be printed in your test book and will be spoken only one time. Select the best response to the question or statement and mark the letter (A), (B), or (C) on your answer sheet.

7. Mark your answer on your answer sheet.

8. Mark your answer on your answer sheet.

9. Mark your answer on your answer sheet.

10. Mark your answer on your answer sheet.

11. Mark your answer on your answer sheet.

12. Mark your answer on your answer sheet.

13. Mark your answer on your answer sheet.

14. Mark your answer on your answer sheet.

15. Mark your answer on your answer sheet.

16. Mark your answer on your answer sheet.

17. Mark your answer on your answer sheet.

18. Mark your answer on your answer sheet.

19. Mark your answer on your answer sheet.

20. Mark your answer on your answer sheet.

21. Mark your answer on your answer sheet.

22. Mark your answer on your answer sheet.

23. Mark your answer on your answer sheet.

24. Mark your answer on your answer sheet.

25. Mark your answer on your answer sheet.

26. Mark your answer on your answer sheet.

27. Mark your answer on your answer sheet.

28. Mark your answer on your answer sheet.

29. Mark your answer on your answer sheet.

30. Mark your answer on your answer sheet.

31. Mark your answer on your answer sheet.

PART 3

Directions: You will hear some conversations between two or more people. You will be asked to answer three questions about what the speakers say in each conversation. Select the best response to each question and mark the letter (A), (B), (C), or (D) on your answer sheet. The conversations will not be printed in your test book and will be spoken only one time.

32. Where does the conversation most likely take place?
    (A) On a train
    (B) On a boat
    (C) At a factory
    (D) At an airport

33. What caused a delay?
    (A) An electrical failure occurred.
    (B) A worker was unavailable.
    (C) Some information was incorrect.
    (D) The weather was bad.

34. What will the man do next?
    (A) Confirm a schedule
    (B) Speak to a coworker
    (C) Check some machinery
    (D) Clean a storage room

35. Where does the woman most likely work?
    (A) At a sports stadium
    (B) At a fitness center
    (C) At a doctor's office
    (D) At a library

36. What does the man ask about?
    (A) A discount
    (B) A form
    (C) A business location
    (D) A parking policy

37. What will the woman do next?
    (A) Post a sign
    (B) Confirm an account number
    (C) Provide a tour
    (D) Look at a schedule

38. Who most likely are the speakers?
    (A) Art restorers
    (B) Event planners
    (C) Photographers
    (D) Interior designers

39. What does the woman say she will do?
    (A) Hire an intern
    (B) Review a contract
    (C) Take some measurements
    (D) Investigate a problem

40. Why does the man suggest beginning a project quickly?
    (A) Payment has already been made.
    (B) Staff will be on vacation.
    (C) An important event is approaching.
    (D) A client is in town for a limited time.

41. What is the woman preparing?
    (A) A slide presentation
    (B) A travel itinerary
    (C) A guest list
    (D) A sales contract

42. What kind of business is Smith Incorporated?
    (A) A law firm
    (B) A construction company
    (C) A pharmaceutical manufacturer
    (D) A bookstore chain

43. What do the men agree about?
    (A) A subscription should be canceled.
    (B) An advertising campaign should be delayed.
    (C) A training session should be mandatory.
    (D) A meeting should be casual.

GO ON TO THE NEXT PAGE

44. Why does the woman congratulate the man?

(A) He finished a road race.
(B) He won a publishing award.
(C) His experiment was successful.
(D) His research funding was extended.

45. What does the man imply when he says, "Esra's leaving the company next week"?

(A) He needs assistance planning a party for Esra.
(B) He will not submit a report to Esra.
(C) He will apply for a new position.
(D) A larger office has become available.

46. What does the man hope to do next quarter?

(A) Receive a research grant
(B) Publish a book
(C) Replace some furniture
(D) Gain management experience

47. Where most likely are the speakers?

(A) At a sporting goods store
(B) At a television studio
(C) At a sports arena
(D) At a gym

48. What does the man say he recently did?

(A) He retired from his job.
(B) He designed a Web site.
(C) He opened a new facility.
(D) He competed in a sports event.

49. What does the woman ask the man to talk about?

(A) His career path
(B) His mentors
(C) His future goals
(D) His hobbies

50. What has the woman been hired to do?

(A) Write articles
(B) Update some software
(C) Organize a fund-raiser
(D) Manage office staff

51. According to the director, what is the organization's goal?

(A) To hire professionals in the field
(B) To create educational programs
(C) To collect data from other scientific institutes
(D) To protect aquatic environments

52. What does Roberto say is exciting?

(A) The use of some equipment
(B) The results of a survey
(C) The public response to a project
(D) A recent donation to the institute

53. What does the man say about some contacts in China?

(A) They submitted some preliminary results.
(B) They requested help with a presentation.
(C) They are celebrating a holiday.
(D) They are coming to visit soon.

54. What does the woman imply when she says, "we didn't allocate funds for a project leader"?

(A) She thinks a project deadline should be extended.
(B) She is surprised by a suggestion.
(C) A scheduled meeting should take place.
(D) A project leader will not be hired.

55. What does the woman say about some travel expenses?

(A) They are unnecessary.
(B) They have been refunded.
(C) They require receipts.
(D) They were charged to the company credit card.

56. Where is the woman calling from?

(A) A clothing store
(B) A furniture store
(C) A restaurant supply company
(D) A graphic design firm

57. What is some software being used for?

(A) Inventory management
(B) Employee performance reviews
(C) Sales forecasting
(D) Web site design

58. What does the man help the woman do?

(A) Return a purchase
(B) Customize a setting
(C) Repair an engine
(D) Inspect a shipment

59. Where are the speakers most likely working?

(A) At a flower shop
(B) At a botanical garden
(C) At a fruit orchard
(D) At a hardware store

60. What have the speakers been asked to do?

(A) Arrange some flowers
(B) Deliver some tools
(C) Install a watering system
(D) Repair a lawn mower

61. What does the man offer to do?

(A) Look for some materials
(B) Train an assistant
(C) Transplant some trees
(D) Work extra hours

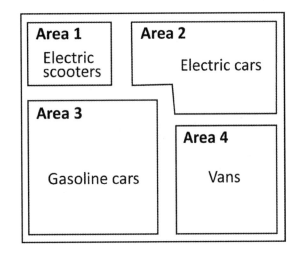

62. Why does the man apologize?

(A) He lost a key.
(B) He arrived late.
(C) He turned off some equipment.
(D) He forgot an instruction manual.

63. According to the woman, why will the speakers be very busy today?

(A) The agency is offering a discount.
(B) A new rental office is opening.
(C) There is a conference in town.
(D) A sporting event will take place.

64. Look at the graphic. Where will the man go first?

(A) Area 1
(B) Area 2
(C) Area 3
(D) Area 4

GO ON TO THE NEXT PAGE

Tree	Average Height
Eastern redbud	9 meters
Japanese maple	7 meters
White fringe tree	6 meters
Panicle hydrangea	4.5 meters

65. Where do the speakers most likely work?

(A) At a landscaping company
(B) At a local government office
(C) At a garden store
(D) At a lumber yard

66. What does the woman say will take place next month?

(A) A seasonal promotion
(B) A product demonstration
(C) A poster contest
(D) A lecture series

67. Look at the graphic. What kind of seedlings will be given away?

(A) Eastern redbud
(B) Japanese maple
(C) White fringe tree
(D) Panicle hydrangea

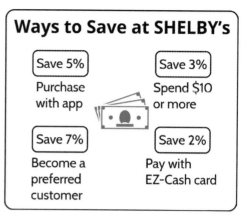

Ways to Save at SHELBY's

Save 5% — Purchase with app

Save 3% — Spend $10 or more

Save 7% — Become a preferred customer

Save 2% — Pay with EZ-Cash card

68. Where does the conversation most likely take place?

(A) At a café
(B) At an electronics shop
(C) At a stationery store
(D) At a clothing store

69. Look at the graphic. How much will the man save on his purchase?

(A) 5%
(B) 3%
(C) 7%
(D) 2%

70. What does the man say he will do later today?

(A) Call a business
(B) Return some merchandise
(C) Fill out an online survey
(D) Hang up some posters

PART 4

Directions: You will hear some talks given by a single speaker. You will be asked to answer three questions about what the speaker says in each talk. Select the best response to each question and mark the letter (A), (B), (C), or (D) on your answer sheet. The talks will not be printed in your test book and will be spoken only one time.

71. Who most likely is the speaker?

    (A) An art gallery owner
    (B) A hairstylist
    (C) A clothing designer
    (D) A jewelry maker

72. Why did the speaker include a special gift?

    (A) Because the listener is a new customer
    (B) Because the listener is celebrating a special occasion
    (C) Because the listener is a loyal customer
    (D) Because the listener placed a large order

73. Why is the listener asked to return a phone call?

    (A) To give feedback
    (B) To confirm receipt of an order
    (C) To update a payment method
    (D) To provide an address

74. What does the listener want to do?

    (A) Hire a caterer
    (B) Purchase a painting
    (C) Have a printer repaired
    (D) Have a photograph framed

75. What does the speaker expect the listener to do on a Web site?

    (A) View a list of prices
    (B) Place an order
    (C) Schedule a time to meet
    (D) Read customer reviews

76. What is included for an extra fee?

    (A) Shipping
    (B) An artist's signature
    (C) A newsletter
    (D) A warranty

77. Who are the listeners?

    (A) Hotel receptionists
    (B) Health-care staff
    (C) Customer-service representatives
    (D) Fitness trainers

78. What has the speaker prepared?

    (A) Activities
    (B) Food
    (C) Certificates
    (D) A video

79. What does the speaker imply when he says, "I must leave at noon"?

    (A) He would like permission to leave.
    (B) He cannot join a luncheon.
    (C) A colleague will fill in for him.
    (D) Some material will not be covered today.

80. What is the purpose of the advertisement?

    (A) To announce a contest
    (B) To promote an upcoming sale
    (C) To introduce new services
    (D) To recruit employees

81. How is the speaker's company different from its competitors?

    (A) It is dependable.
    (B) It produces innovative products.
    (C) It offers flexible schedules.
    (D) It pays employees well.

82. What does the speaker encourage the listeners to do?

    (A) Complete a survey
    (B) Fill out an application
    (C) Place an order
    (D) Get more information

GO ON TO THE NEXT PAGE

83. What is the message mainly about?

    (A) Revising a restaurant menu
    (B) Filming for a television show
    (C) Launching an advertising campaign
    (D) Renovating a kitchen

84. What does the speaker ask the listener to do on Wednesday?

    (A) Come to work early
    (B) Experiment with new ingredients
    (C) Train an employee
    (D) Prepare for a safety inspection

85. Where will the speaker go next week?

    (A) To a food festival
    (B) To a cooking class
    (C) To a farmers market
    (D) To a bakery opening

86. What is the speaker mainly discussing?

    (A) A job fair
    (B) A factory
    (C) Some traffic patterns
    (D) A prototype electric vehicle

87. What does the speaker imply when he says, "No one made any comments"?

    (A) Few people were in attendance.
    (B) Another meeting will be scheduled.
    (C) A project has community support.
    (D) A public comment period has ended.

88. What can the public view at the city hall building?

    (A) An official contract
    (B) Some images
    (C) A list of companies
    (D) Some facts about local politicians

89. What type of product is being advertised?

    (A) A floor lamp
    (B) A bookshelf
    (C) An office chair
    (D) A desk organizer

90. What special feature does the speaker emphasize?

    (A) It is durable.
    (B) It is adjustable.
    (C) It is easy to assemble.
    (D) It is available in many colors.

91. How can the listeners receive a discount?

    (A) By calling within a time limit
    (B) By entering an e-mail address
    (C) By referring a product to a friend
    (D) By using a mobile phone application

92. According to the speaker, what is the purpose of the podcast?

    (A) To discuss the restaurant industry
    (B) To review new cooking equipment
    (C) To share information about nutrition
    (D) To showcase individual ingredients

93. Why does the speaker say, "this product line will not be available for long"?

    (A) To encourage the listeners to place an order
    (B) To apologize to the listeners for a product shortage
    (C) To justify a high price
    (D) To criticize a business decision

94. According to the speaker, what did Rebecca Murray recently do?

    (A) She published a cookbook.
    (B) She launched a culinary training course.
    (C) She opened a restaurant.
    (D) She traveled abroad.

Train 133	
City	Arrival Time
New York	9:30 A.M.
Philadelphia	10:45 A.M.
Wilmington	12:05 P.M.
Baltimore	1:00 P.M.
Washington, D.C.	1:30 P.M.

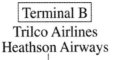

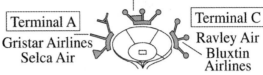

95. Why does the speaker apologize?

(A) There is construction noise at the station.
(B) There are no more seats available on a train.
(C) A printed schedule has incorrect information.
(D) A train service has been delayed.

96. According to the speaker, why may some listeners need to see an agent?

(A) To ask for a refund
(B) To request baggage service
(C) To purchase a monthly pass
(D) To arrange a transfer

97. Look at the graphic. When is Train 133 scheduled to arrive at its next stop?

(A) At 10:45 A.M.
(B) At 12:05 P.M.
(C) At 1:00 P.M.
(D) At 1:30 P.M.

98. Who most likely are the listeners?

(A) Civil engineers
(B) Urban planners
(C) News reporters
(D) Safety inspectors

99. Look at the graphic. Which of the following companies will be affected by a delay?

(A) Selca Air
(B) Trilco Airlines
(C) Heathson Airways
(D) Bluxtin Airlines

100. What does the speaker invite the listeners to do?

(A) Download some designs
(B) Look at a model
(C) Take a site tour
(D) View a Webcam

This is the end of the Listening test.

토익® 정기시험
기출문제집 4
1000

TEST 03
무료 동영상 강의

LC

기출 TEST

03

LISTENING TEST

In the Listening test, you will be asked to demonstrate how well you understand spoken English. The entire Listening test will last approximately 45 minutes. There are four parts, and directions are given for each part. You must mark your answers on the separate answer sheet. Do not write your answers in your test book.

PART 1

Directions: For each question in this part, you will hear four statements about a picture in your test book. When you hear the statements, you must select the one statement that best describes what you see in the picture. Then find the number of the question on your answer sheet and mark your answer. The statements will not be printed in your test book and will be spoken only one time.

Statement (C), "They're sitting at a table," is the best description of the picture, so you should select answer (C) and mark it on your answer sheet.

1.

2.

GO ON TO THE NEXT PAGE ➡

3.

4.

5.

6.

GO ON TO THE NEXT PAGE ➡

PART 2

Directions: You will hear a question or statement and three responses spoken in English. They will not be printed in your test book and will be spoken only one time. Select the best response to the question or statement and mark the letter (A), (B), or (C) on your answer sheet.

7. Mark your answer on your answer sheet.

8. Mark your answer on your answer sheet.

9. Mark your answer on your answer sheet.

10. Mark your answer on your answer sheet.

11. Mark your answer on your answer sheet.

12. Mark your answer on your answer sheet.

13. Mark your answer on your answer sheet.

14. Mark your answer on your answer sheet.

15. Mark your answer on your answer sheet.

16. Mark your answer on your answer sheet.

17. Mark your answer on your answer sheet.

18. Mark your answer on your answer sheet.

19. Mark your answer on your answer sheet.

20. Mark your answer on your answer sheet.

21. Mark your answer on your answer sheet.

22. Mark your answer on your answer sheet.

23. Mark your answer on your answer sheet.

24. Mark your answer on your answer sheet.

25. Mark your answer on your answer sheet.

26. Mark your answer on your answer sheet.

27. Mark your answer on your answer sheet.

28. Mark your answer on your answer sheet.

29. Mark your answer on your answer sheet.

30. Mark your answer on your answer sheet.

31. Mark your answer on your answer sheet.

PART 3

Directions: You will hear some conversations between two or more people. You will be asked to answer three questions about what the speakers say in each conversation. Select the best response to each question and mark the letter (A), (B), (C), or (D) on your answer sheet. The conversations will not be printed in your test book and will be spoken only one time.

32. What change is a company making?

    (A) It is lowering some prices.
    (B) It is hiring more staffers.
    (C) It is moving to a new location.
    (D) It is expanding a product line.

33. What suggestion does the woman make?

    (A) Updating a handbook
    (B) Donating some furniture
    (C) Creating a schedule
    (D) Downloading a software program

34. What will the speakers most likely do next?

    (A) Train a new employee
    (B) Review an application
    (C) Check a list
    (D) Talk to some directors

35. Who most likely are the women?

    (A) Company executives
    (B) Journalists
    (C) Health-care professionals
    (D) Safety inspectors

36. What does the man say he is pleased about?

    (A) The number of event participants
    (B) The amount of money raised
    (C) The quality of vendors
    (D) The variety of presentations

37. What will the women do next?

    (A) Watch a demonstration
    (B) Get some refreshments
    (C) Register for an event
    (D) Take a photograph

38. What most likely is the woman's job?

    (A) Professional chef
    (B) Bank executive
    (C) Administrative assistant
    (D) Web designer

39. What will the man most likely do?

    (A) Buy some materials from the woman
    (B) Check the woman's work
    (C) List investment options
    (D) Update some client information

40. What will the woman most likely send to the man?

    (A) A cost estimate
    (B) A revised schedule
    (C) A building plan
    (D) A list of changes

41. Why is a train platform closed?

    (A) Safety inspections are being conducted.
    (B) New escalators are being installed.
    (C) Tracks are being repaired.
    (D) Waiting areas are being remodeled.

42. What does the man say he is upset about?

    (A) Misunderstanding some instructions
    (B) Being late for an appointment
    (C) Losing a travel pass
    (D) Boarding the wrong train

43. What will the man most likely do next?

    (A) Purchase a snack
    (B) Take a shuttle bus
    (C) File a complaint
    (D) Download a map

GO ON TO THE NEXT PAGE

44. Why does the man call the woman?

    (A) To provide an update on his project

    (B) To get approval on some design changes

    (C) To receive the woman's feedback on a prototype

    (D) To persuade the woman to invest in his business

45. According to the man, what is unique about a product?

    (A) It is inexpensive.

    (B) It is easy to assemble.

    (C) It is adjustable.

    (D) It is lightweight.

46. Why does the woman request some documents?

    (A) To open a customer account

    (B) To issue a certificate

    (C) To make some copies

    (D) To evaluate a proposal

47. What are the speakers preparing for?

    (A) A construction-site visit

    (B) A safety inspection

    (C) An interview

    (D) A film festival

48. What is the woman concerned about?

    (A) A lighting issue

    (B) A script mistake

    (C) A material shortage

    (D) A revenue decrease

49. Who is Marcel Lambert?

    (A) A company accountant

    (B) A possible client

    (C) A supervisor

    (D) An intern

50. What does the woman thank the man for?

    (A) Distributing some fliers

    (B) Completing some calculations

    (C) Placing a catering order

    (D) Preparing some paper copies

51. Why is a gathering being planned?

    (A) A colleague was promoted.

    (B) The company won an award.

    (C) A colleague will be retiring.

    (D) The company will be training employees.

52. What does the man imply when he says, "I booked conference room B"?

    (A) A room is too small.

    (B) An invitation is incorrect.

    (C) No other conference rooms were available.

    (D) Another administrative assistant was too busy.

53. What type of event is the man planning?

    (A) A retirement banquet

    (B) A company retreat

    (C) A press conference

    (D) A fund-raiser

54. Why was Ms. Ishikawa delayed?

    (A) She was stuck in traffic.

    (B) She was at lunch.

    (C) She was setting up a room.

    (D) She was on the phone.

55. What does the man inquire about?

    (A) An airport shuttle

    (B) Late checkout

    (C) A fitness center

    (D) Internet capabilities

56. Where does the conversation most likely take place?

(A) At a restaurant
(B) At a shipping dock
(C) At a farm
(D) At a supermarket

57. What does the man say is popular?

(A) A colorful package design
(B) A self-service machine
(C) A same-day delivery service
(D) A television advertisement

58. What does the man suggest doing?

(A) Waiting for some data
(B) Issuing a refund
(C) Hiring more staff
(D) Rearranging some merchandise

59. What are the speakers discussing?

(A) Relocating their office
(B) Attracting new patients
(C) Scheduling appointments
(D) Finding qualified staff

60. Why does the man say, "You just have to check a box"?

(A) To request some performance feedback
(B) To express concern about a procedure
(C) To correct a misunderstanding
(D) To support a suggestion

61. What does the woman offer to do this afternoon?

(A) Investigate options
(B) Revise a budget
(C) Contact a patient
(D) Update a Web site

Basic small mug $15	Night Sky small mug $20
Desert Roaming medium mug $23	Under the Sea large mug $25

62. Who will the man give some gifts to?

(A) Conference participants
(B) Employees
(C) Contest winners
(D) Visitors

63. Look at the graphic. How much is the mug that the woman likes?

(A) $15
(B) $20
(C) $23
(D) $25

64. What does the man say he will do?

(A) Submit a registration form
(B) Adjust a work schedule
(C) Approve an order
(D) Ask for a bulk-pricing rate

GO ON TO THE NEXT PAGE

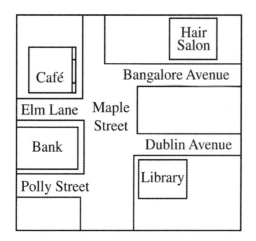

The Treasure Search	
Level name	**Level number**
Jungle Adventure	1
Ocean Kingdom	2
Desert Sands	3
Outer Space	4

65. What industry do the speakers most likely work in?

(A) Tourism
(B) Film
(C) Engineering
(D) Transportation

66. Why does the woman want to make a change?

(A) Some equipment is not available.
(B) A new business is opening.
(C) A process will be easier.
(D) Costs will be lower.

67. Look at the graphic. Which road should be closed?

(A) Bangalore Avenue
(B) Dublin Avenue
(C) Polly Street
(D) Elm Lane

68. What are the speakers preparing for?

(A) A video-game convention
(B) An in-store demonstration
(C) A product launch
(D) A focus-group session

69. Look at the graphic. Which level is the woman concerned about?

(A) Level 1
(B) Level 2
(C) Level 3
(D) Level 4

70. What does the woman suggest doing?

(A) Contacting a colleague
(B) Postponing an event
(C) Working over the weekend
(D) Making travel arrangements

PART 4

Directions: You will hear some talks given by a single speaker. You will be asked to answer three questions about what the speaker says in each talk. Select the best response to each question and mark the letter (A), (B), (C), or (D) on your answer sheet. The talks will not be printed in your test book and will be spoken only one time.

71. What kind of business is being advertised?

(A) A health-care clinic
(B) A computer service store
(C) An auto repair shop
(D) A real estate agency

72. Why is a business celebrating?

(A) It has been operating for ten years.
(B) It has doubled its customer base.
(C) It has won an award.
(D) It has opened a new location.

73. What do the listeners need to do to obtain a discount?

(A) Make an appointment
(B) Print out a coupon
(C) Attend an open house
(D) Refer a friend

74. What is the podcast episode about?

(A) Marketing strategies
(B) Commercial real estate
(C) Customer loyalty
(D) Staff management

75. What does the speaker say Ms. Bertrand is good at?

(A) Designing billboard ads
(B) Solving budget problems
(C) Explaining complicated ideas
(D) Creating training programs

76. What will the speaker discuss next?

(A) Breaking news
(B) Survey results
(C) Upcoming contests
(D) Future episode topics

77. What will be delivered next Wednesday?

(A) Office furniture
(B) Color printers
(C) Potted plants
(D) Framed artwork

78. What does the speaker say about productivity?

(A) It has been improving recently.
(B) It is higher in other departments.
(C) It can be improved by office surroundings.
(D) It can be increased by working in groups.

79. According to the speaker, what is available in the staff room?

(A) A catalog
(B) A vending machine
(C) Staff uniforms
(D) Exercise equipment

80. According to the speaker, what happened three years ago?

(A) A council member was elected.
(B) A local tax law changed.
(C) A train station opened.
(D) A business relocated.

81. Who is Matthew Hughes?

(A) A banker
(B) A real estate developer
(C) A government official
(D) A store owner

82. What will the listeners hear about next?

(A) A sporting event
(B) Street closures
(C) The weather
(D) Parking fines

GO ON TO THE NEXT PAGE

83. What is the speaker discussing?

(A) The renovation of a train station
(B) The construction of a tunnel
(C) The replacement of a bridge
(D) The repaving of a bicycle trail

84. Why does the speaker say, "this is just one of our many projects"?

(A) To propose a change of topic
(B) To explain a delay
(C) To praise some employees
(D) To ask for help

85. What does the speaker suggest doing?

(A) Organizing an opening ceremony
(B) Scheduling a television interview
(C) Revising a design
(D) Meeting with the press

86. According to the speaker, what will be different about today's session?

(A) It will take place outside.
(B) It will be recorded.
(C) Participants will work in pairs.
(D) Participants will deliver presentations.

87. What is the topic of today's session?

(A) Improving communication skills
(B) Updating accounting practices
(C) Managing company finances
(D) Recruiting qualified job candidates

88. What does the speaker say about the lunch?

(A) It has been donated.
(B) It is vegetarian.
(C) It will arrive late.
(D) It will include a dessert.

89. Where does the speaker most likely work?

(A) At a car-rental company
(B) At an appliance-repair shop
(C) At a car wash
(D) At an auto-mechanic shop

90. What does the speaker imply when he says, "we'll have to take a look"?

(A) A schedule may be changed.
(B) A supervisor should be consulted.
(C) A cost cannot be determined yet.
(D) A new policy must be followed.

91. What does the speaker say about tomorrow?

(A) Some machinery will be serviced.
(B) The business will close early.
(C) Some new employees will start work.
(D) An appointment will probably become available.

92. What type of business does the speaker most likely work at?

(A) A car dealership
(B) An electronics store
(C) A clothing boutique
(D) A furniture store

93. What does the speaker imply when he says, "that day will probably not be a profitable day for us anyway"?

(A) Reduced profits have prevented salary increases.
(B) A new sales strategy will have to be developed.
(C) The listeners will be able to attend an event.
(D) The listeners have been keeping accurate records.

94. What does the speaker expect the listeners to do?

(A) Submit an order form
(B) Provide some feedback
(C) Sign a contract
(D) Check a display area

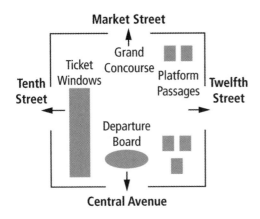

Market Street

Grand Concourse

Ticket Windows

Tenth Street

Platform Passages

Twelfth Street

Departure Board

Central Avenue

Conference Schedule		
Introduction	8:00 A.M.	Dr. Bajaj
"The Truth About Fruit"	8:15 A.M.	Dr. Novikova
Coffee break	9:00 A.M.	
"Daily Mineral Recommendations"	9:15 A.M.	Dr. Ivanda
"Talking to Patients About Hydration"	10:00 A.M.	Dr. Shimizu

95. Who most likely is the speaker?

(A) A rideshare driver
(B) A tour guide
(C) A ticket agent
(D) A baggage handler

96. Look at the graphic. Where does the speaker want to meet?

(A) On Market Street
(B) On Twelfth Street
(C) On Central Avenue
(D) On Tenth Street

97. How can a change be confirmed?

(A) By sending an e-mail
(B) By providing an e-signature
(C) By using an app
(D) By returning a call

98. Look at the graphic. Who is the speaker?

(A) Dr. Bajaj
(B) Dr. Novikova
(C) Dr. Ivanda
(D) Dr. Shimizu

99. What did the speaker do last year?

(A) She started her own medical practice.
(B) She received an award.
(C) She published a study.
(D) She developed a fitness application.

100. According to the speaker, where can the listeners test a product?

(A) In a lobby
(B) In an auditorium
(C) In a gift shop
(D) In a dining area

This is the end of the Listening test.

토익®정기시험
기출문제집 4
1000

TEST 04
무료 동영상 강의

LC

기출 TEST

04

LISTENING TEST

In the Listening test, you will be asked to demonstrate how well you understand spoken English. The entire Listening test will last approximately 45 minutes. There are four parts, and directions are given for each part. You must mark your answers on the separate answer sheet. Do not write your answers in your test book.

PART 1

Directions: For each question in this part, you will hear four statements about a picture in your test book. When you hear the statements, you must select the one statement that best describes what you see in the picture. Then find the number of the question on your answer sheet and mark your answer. The statements will not be printed in your test book and will be spoken only one time.

Statement (C), "They're sitting at a table," is the best description of the picture, so you should select answer (C) and mark it on your answer sheet.

1.

2.

GO ON TO THE NEXT PAGE

3.

4.

5.

6.

GO ON TO THE NEXT PAGE

PART 2

Directions: You will hear a question or statement and three responses spoken in English. They will not be printed in your test book and will be spoken only one time. Select the best response to the question or statement and mark the letter (A), (B), or (C) on your answer sheet.

7. Mark your answer on your answer sheet.

8. Mark your answer on your answer sheet.

9. Mark your answer on your answer sheet.

10. Mark your answer on your answer sheet.

11. Mark your answer on your answer sheet.

12. Mark your answer on your answer sheet.

13. Mark your answer on your answer sheet.

14. Mark your answer on your answer sheet.

15. Mark your answer on your answer sheet.

16. Mark your answer on your answer sheet.

17. Mark your answer on your answer sheet.

18. Mark your answer on your answer sheet.

19. Mark your answer on your answer sheet.

20. Mark your answer on your answer sheet.

21. Mark your answer on your answer sheet.

22. Mark your answer on your answer sheet.

23. Mark your answer on your answer sheet.

24. Mark your answer on your answer sheet.

25. Mark your answer on your answer sheet.

26. Mark your answer on your answer sheet.

27. Mark your answer on your answer sheet.

28. Mark your answer on your answer sheet.

29. Mark your answer on your answer sheet.

30. Mark your answer on your answer sheet.

31. Mark your answer on your answer sheet.

PART 3

Directions: You will hear some conversations between two or more people. You will be asked to answer three questions about what the speakers say in each conversation. Select the best response to each question and mark the letter (A), (B), (C), or (D) on your answer sheet. The conversations will not be printed in your test book and will be spoken only one time.

32. Where most likely are the speakers?

(A) At a ferry terminal
(B) At a swimming area
(C) At a shopping mall
(D) At a restaurant

33. What problem does the man mention?

(A) Some repairs are needed.
(B) A business is understaffed.
(C) The weather is bad.
(D) Some tickets are sold out.

34. What will the woman do next?

(A) Read a book
(B) Get a meal
(C) Watch a movie
(D) Go to a hotel

35. Who most likely is the woman?

(A) An author
(B) A librarian
(C) A bookseller
(D) An event organizer

36. What does the man say happened this morning?

(A) He received an e-mail notification.
(B) He applied for a job online.
(C) He lost a receipt.
(D) He made a delivery.

37. What does the woman offer to do?

(A) Attend an event
(B) Fill out an online form
(C) Place an order
(D) Search for an item

38. What type of business does the man most likely work for?

(A) A moving company
(B) A furniture manufacturer
(C) A painting company
(D) A catering service

39. What point does the man emphasize?

(A) A deposit is required before work can begin.
(B) A price may be higher than expected.
(C) A discount is available for a limited time.
(D) A schedule cannot be changed easily.

40. What does the woman ask about?

(A) Signing a contract
(B) Purchasing specialized tools
(C) Moving some furniture
(D) Seeing some samples

41. Where does the man work?

(A) At a community park
(B) At a fitness center
(C) At a public beach
(D) At a sports equipment store

42. What is the purpose of the woman's visit?

(A) She is applying for a job.
(B) She has a complaint.
(C) She needs specific directions.
(D) She is interested in a membership.

43. What will the woman most likely do next?

(A) Join a team
(B) Go on a tour
(C) Make a phone call
(D) Fill out an application

GO ON TO THE NEXT PAGE

44. Who most likely is the man?

(A) A janitor
(B) A property manager
(C) A carpenter
(D) An interior designer

45. What does the woman say recently happened?

(A) She earned a degree.
(B) She won an award.
(C) She got a promotion.
(D) She transferred to a new location.

46. What will the man do next?

(A) Make a phone call
(B) Prepare a contract
(C) Drop off a key
(D) Log some work hours

47. According to the woman, what has recently happened at her business?

(A) Customers have complained.
(B) Inspections have been conducted.
(C) Online orders have increased.
(D) Shipments have been incomplete.

48. What can the man's company do?

(A) Provide safety training
(B) Post demonstration videos
(C) Acquire more warehouse space
(D) Create customer surveys

49. What does the woman say she could offer her customers?

(A) A discount
(B) Expedited shipping
(C) Free product samples
(D) A personal consultation

50. Where most likely are the speakers?

(A) At a farm
(B) At a landscaping company
(C) At a hotel
(D) At a catering firm

51. What type of event is going to take place?

(A) A wedding
(B) A flower exposition
(C) A grand opening
(D) A birthday party

52. What does the woman say she will do?

(A) Sign a receipt
(B) Adjust a schedule
(C) Add items to an order
(D) Call a supervisor

53. What kind of business do the men most likely work for?

(A) A fencing company
(B) A landscaping service
(C) A roofing company
(D) An auto repair shop

54. Why is the woman relieved?

(A) Some damage is minor.
(B) A delivery arrived early.
(C) Customer reviews are positive.
(D) The weather forecast is good.

55. What will the woman do on Tuesday?

(A) Wash her car
(B) Close her store
(C) Take some measurements
(D) Look at some material samples

56. Why does the man apologize?

(A) He missed a meeting.
(B) He has a poor Internet connection.
(C) He failed to complete an assignment.
(D) He lost his employee badge.

57. Why does the woman say, "Well, there is a rapid-transit bus service"?

(A) To praise improvements to a system
(B) To correct a mistaken assumption
(C) To express dissatisfaction
(D) To justify a decision

58. What will the woman do next?

(A) Download a ticket
(B) Pick up some clients
(C) Activate a key card
(D) Forward some Web-site links

59. Who is the woman?

(A) An architect
(B) A clothing designer
(C) A construction manager
(D) A department store director

60. Why does the woman say, "They usually market to a younger clientele"?

(A) To reject a suggestion
(B) To justify a decision
(C) To express disappointment
(D) To ask for clarification

61. What does the man say he will give the woman?

(A) An area map
(B) A list of businesses
(C) Some photographs
(D) Some measurements

Directory	
Liliana Flores	Set designer
Svetlana Popova	Director
Lauren Campbell	Actor
So-Jin Park	Costume designer

62. Look at the graphic. Who is the woman?

(A) Liliana Flores
(B) Svetlana Popova
(C) Lauren Campbell
(D) So-Jin Park

63. What problem do the speakers discuss?

(A) Some equipment is not working.
(B) Some costumes are not ready.
(C) Some music is distracting.
(D) An actor is late.

64. What will happen next week?

(A) A playwright will attend a show.
(B) Publicity photos will be taken.
(C) A play will open.
(D) A dress rehearsal will be held.

GO ON TO THE NEXT PAGE

Adventure awaits you!

Kayaking led by Ketan Bora

Fly-Fishing led by Beatriz Romero

Trail Biking led by Arnaud Fournier

Hiking led by Brandon Murray

Quadrant 1 Garden	Quadrant 2 Kitchen
Tower Quadrant 3	Great Hall Quadrant 4

65. Why is the man surprised?

(A) A new vacation policy was announced.
(B) A group is larger than expected.
(C) A price has increased.
(D) A date has been changed.

66. What does the woman like about a venue?

(A) The comfortable rooms
(B) The food selection
(C) The views
(D) The fitness center

67. Look at the graphic. Who will lead the activity the man is interested in?

(A) Ketan Bora
(B) Beatriz Romero
(C) Arnaud Fournier
(D) Brandon Murray

68. What is the conversation mostly about?

(A) Organizing an exhibit
(B) Arranging a public tour
(C) Filming a documentary
(D) Requesting financial support

69. Look at the graphic. Which part of the castle is being excavated today?

(A) The garden
(B) The kitchen
(C) The tower
(D) The great hall

70. According to the man, why has some work been delayed?

(A) An archaeological team is very small.
(B) Weather conditions have been poor.
(C) A source of funding was unavailable.
(D) New volunteers required special training.

PART 4

Directions: You will hear some talks given by a single speaker. You will be asked to answer three questions about what the speaker says in each talk. Select the best response to each question and mark the letter (A), (B), (C), or (D) on your answer sheet. The talks will not be printed in your test book and will be spoken only one time.

71. What kind of business recorded the message?

   (A) A city planning office
   (B) A cybersecurity firm
   (C) A utility company
   (D) An electronics repair shop

72. What does the speaker say will happen this afternoon?

   (A) A problem will be resolved.
   (B) A shipment will be delivered.
   (C) Some software will be updated.
   (D) Some refreshments will be offered.

73. What does the speaker say is available on a Web site?

   (A) Customer reviews
   (B) Work order forms
   (C) Business hours
   (D) Product manuals

74. According to the speaker, why is a change being made?

   (A) To keep track of expenses
   (B) To help a business expand
   (C) To improve security
   (D) To attract job applicants

75. What are the listeners asked to do?

   (A) Shut down their computers
   (B) Reduce their expenses
   (C) Consult with their department managers
   (D) Create an equipment inventory

76. What department does Marta Fuentes most likely work in?

   (A) Legal
   (B) Marketing
   (C) Human Resources
   (D) Information Technology

77. According to the speaker, what will begin on Monday?

   (A) A seasonal internship program
   (B) Road construction
   (C) Landscaping maintenance
   (D) An equipment upgrade

78. What will the company provide for the listeners?

   (A) Free lunch
   (B) New identification badges
   (C) Parking passes
   (D) Transportation

79. Why should the listeners visit a Web site?

   (A) To download a map
   (B) To post feedback
   (C) To fill out a registration form
   (D) To read project updates

80. What is the speaker preparing for?

   (A) A client visit
   (B) A branch opening
   (C) A job fair
   (D) An equipment upgrade

81. Why does the speaker say, "there is one on Jefferson Avenue"?

   (A) To express surprise
   (B) To correct some information
   (C) To complain about a decision
   (D) To recommend an alternative

82. What additional service is mentioned?

   (A) A catered meal
   (B) A shuttle bus
   (C) Technical support
   (D) Secure storage

GO ON TO THE NEXT PAGE

83. According to the speaker, why are some changes needed?

(A) To retain employees
(B) To attract investors
(C) To satisfy customers
(D) To increase productivity

84. What additional service does the company plan to offer?

(A) Free product returns
(B) Expedited bulk shipping
(C) Pickup at self-service kiosks
(D) Real-time package tracking

85. According to the speaker, what will begin next month?

(A) A workshop series
(B) A new corporate policy
(C) A land development project
(D) A business collaboration

86. What industry does the speaker most likely work in?

(A) Civil service
(B) Hospitality
(C) Media
(D) Architecture

87. What is planned for next month?

(A) A retirement luncheon
(B) An employee-performance review
(C) A computer-system upgrade
(D) A tour of a facility

88. Who should send the speaker an e-mail?

(A) Those going on vacation
(B) Those willing to volunteer
(C) Those wishing to provide feedback
(D) Those presenting at a conference

89. What does the speaker's company most likely sell?

(A) Beauty supplies
(B) Kitchen appliances
(C) Books
(D) Sporting goods

90. What event does the speaker invite the listeners to?

(A) A sales workshop
(B) A product demonstration
(C) A celebratory dinner
(D) A concert

91. What does the speaker mean when he says, "there's a sports event that night"?

(A) The office will be closed.
(B) Parking will be limited.
(C) A meeting will be rescheduled.
(D) The listeners should buy some tickets.

92. Who most likely is the speaker?

(A) An artist
(B) A business owner
(C) A local journalist
(D) A government official

93. Why does the speaker say, "art isn't only inside the walls of a museum"?

(A) To apologize for an exhibit closure
(B) To disagree with an online review
(C) To motivate the listeners to take another tour
(D) To recommend a building renovation

94. What does the speaker give to the listeners?

(A) City maps
(B) Gift cards
(C) Name badges
(D) Informational brochures

Proposal	Projected Cost
Plan A	$200 million
Plan B	$450 million
Plan C	$300 million
Plan D	$250 million

95. What is the broadcast mainly about?

(A) A renovated airport terminal
(B) A redesigned city hall
(C) A new train station
(D) A new bridge

96. Look at the graphic. Which proposal was chosen?

(A) Plan A
(B) Plan B
(C) Plan C
(D) Plan D

97. According to the speaker, what will residents be able to vote on?

(A) Parking options
(B) Food vendors
(C) Public artwork
(D) Park ideas

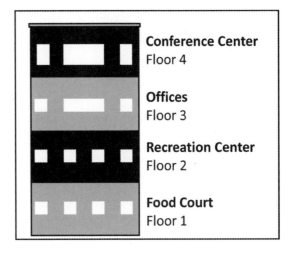

Conference Center
Floor 4

Offices
Floor 3

Recreation Center
Floor 2

Food Court
Floor 1

98. Who is the speaker?

(A) A structural engineer
(B) A journalist
(C) A tour guide
(D) A city official

99. Why is a building special?

(A) It was constructed in a short time.
(B) It has a technologically advanced security system.
(C) It has environmentally friendly features.
(D) It was designed by a famous architect.

100. Look at the graphic. Which floor of the building is not open yet?

(A) Floor 4
(B) Floor 3
(C) Floor 2
(D) Floor 1

This is the end of the Listening test.

토익®정기시험
기출문제집 4
1000

TEST 05
무료 동영상 강의

LC

기출 TEST

05

LISTENING TEST

In the Listening test, you will be asked to demonstrate how well you understand spoken English. The entire Listening test will last approximately 45 minutes. There are four parts, and directions are given for each part. You must mark your answers on the separate answer sheet. Do not write your answers in your test book.

PART 1

Directions: For each question in this part, you will hear four statements about a picture in your test book. When you hear the statements, you must select the one statement that best describes what you see in the picture. Then find the number of the question on your answer sheet and mark your answer. The statements will not be printed in your test book and will be spoken only one time.

Statement (C), "They're sitting at a table," is the best description of the picture, so you should select answer (C) and mark it on your answer sheet.

1.

2.

GO ON TO THE NEXT PAGE

3.

4.

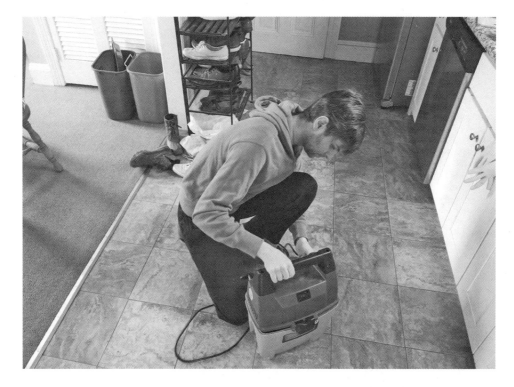

5.

6.

GO ON TO THE NEXT PAGE

PART 2

Directions: You will hear a question or statement and three responses spoken in English. They will not be printed in your test book and will be spoken only one time. Select the best response to the question or statement and mark the letter (A), (B), or (C) on your answer sheet.

7. Mark your answer on your answer sheet.

8. Mark your answer on your answer sheet.

9. Mark your answer on your answer sheet.

10. Mark your answer on your answer sheet.

11. Mark your answer on your answer sheet.

12. Mark your answer on your answer sheet.

13. Mark your answer on your answer sheet.

14. Mark your answer on your answer sheet.

15. Mark your answer on your answer sheet.

16. Mark your answer on your answer sheet.

17. Mark your answer on your answer sheet.

18. Mark your answer on your answer sheet.

19. Mark your answer on your answer sheet.

20. Mark your answer on your answer sheet.

21. Mark your answer on your answer sheet.

22. Mark your answer on your answer sheet.

23. Mark your answer on your answer sheet.

24. Mark your answer on your answer sheet.

25. Mark your answer on your answer sheet.

26. Mark your answer on your answer sheet.

27. Mark your answer on your answer sheet.

28. Mark your answer on your answer sheet.

29. Mark your answer on your answer sheet.

30. Mark your answer on your answer sheet.

31. Mark your answer on your answer sheet.

PART 3

Directions: You will hear some conversations between two or more people. You will be asked to answer three questions about what the speakers say in each conversation. Select the best response to each question and mark the letter (A), (B), (C), or (D) on your answer sheet. The conversations will not be printed in your test book and will be spoken only one time.

32. What problem does the woman describe?

(A) A room is not available.
(B) A window will not open.
(C) A projector is not working.
(D) The weather has changed suddenly.

33. What does the man suggest doing?

(A) Moving to a different room
(B) Calling a technician
(C) Canceling an event
(D) Ordering some supplies

34. What does the man hand to the woman?

(A) An umbrella
(B) Some keys
(C) A cable
(D) Some printouts

35. What industry does Amanda Hoffman work in?

(A) Hospitality
(B) Healthcare
(C) Publishing
(D) Information technology

36. According to the man, what is included in the registration packet?

(A) A map
(B) A gift card
(C) A schedule of events
(D) A certificate of attendance

37. What does the man tell the woman to do?

(A) Arrive early
(B) Pay a fee
(C) Wear a name badge
(D) Choose a menu option

38. What event will the woman attend this weekend?

(A) A wedding
(B) A birthday party
(C) A retirement dinner
(D) A graduation celebration

39. What does the man offer to do?

(A) Authorize free shipping
(B) Apply a discount
(C) Provide a sample
(D) Make a recommendation

40. What does the woman ask about?

(A) An expiration date
(B) A manufacturer's guarantee
(C) The origin of a product
(D) The cost of a product

41. Why is the woman visiting?

(A) To promote a product
(B) To sign a contract
(C) To tour a facility
(D) To inspect some equipment

42. What did the woman's company design?

(A) A digital security system
(B) A device to lift heavy objects
(C) An application to monitor machines
(D) Protective clothing for workers

43. What does the woman say her company can provide?

(A) A new client discount
(B) A training video
(C) An extended warranty
(D) Customer testimonials

GO ON TO THE NEXT PAGE

44. Who most likely is the man?

(A) A theater employee
(B) A taxi driver
(C) A train conductor
(D) A construction worker

45. What is causing a problem?

(A) A truck is too heavy.
(B) An event has been delayed.
(C) A parking area is full.
(D) A road is closed.

46. What does the man say he will do?

(A) Ask for a refund
(B) Take a different route
(C) Postpone a trip
(D) File a complaint

47. Why does the woman say, "Last year we sent only two representatives"?

(A) To explain a delay
(B) To compliment a team
(C) To point out that an event was unsuccessful
(D) To question a decision

48. According to the man, what do some clients want to do?

(A) Increase their online offerings
(B) Obtain additional financing
(C) Open a new office
(D) Recruit more employees

49. According to the man, what is the Renova Hotel offering this month?

(A) A new shuttle service
(B) A discount for businesses
(C) A flexible cancellation policy
(D) Complimentary meals

50. What problem does the woman mention?

(A) A decrease in ticket sales
(B) A lack of exhibition space
(C) A colleague's resignation
(D) A damaged painting

51. What does the man suggest doing?

(A) Relocating an exhibit
(B) Consulting a specialist
(C) Adding security measures
(D) Introducing a new activity

52. What will the man most likely do next?

(A) Write a press release
(B) Attend a budget meeting
(C) Make a list of supplies
(D) Plan a site visit

53. Where most likely are the speakers?

(A) At a clothing factory
(B) At a bookstore
(C) At a tailor's shop
(D) At a furniture store

54. According to the man, why will a product cost more?

(A) It includes an extended warranty.
(B) It is a custom order.
(C) A rebate has expired.
(D) Shipping will be expedited.

55. What does the man request?

(A) A purchase receipt
(B) A delivery address
(C) A form of identification
(D) An account number

56. Where most likely are the speakers?

(A) At a hotel
(B) At a factory
(C) At a retail store
(D) At a trade show

57. What feature does the man emphasize about some chairs?

(A) The color
(B) The price
(C) The shape
(D) The durability

58. What does the man say he will do later?

(A) Modify a design
(B) E-mail a contract
(C) Create an invoice
(D) Send a photo

---

59. What will happen next month?

(A) An award will be given.
(B) A new product will launch.
(C) A colleague will retire.
(D) An office will relocate.

60. What department do the speakers work in?

(A) Sales
(B) Human Resources
(C) Legal
(D) Accounting

61. What does the man imply when he says, "we need someone with experience"?

(A) The team has grown very quickly.
(B) The woman should apply for a job.
(C) A job description should be revised.
(D) A new manager is not experienced enough.

Line	Destination	Next Train
Red	Shady Grove	7 minutes
Yellow	Braddock Bay	9 minutes
Blue	Largo	14 minutes
Silver	Ashburn	11 minutes

62. Why are the speakers in New York?

(A) They saw a play.
(B) They attended a conference.
(C) They met with some clients.
(D) They viewed some real estate.

63. What does the woman ask the man about?

(A) Locating some information
(B) Applying for a position
(C) Opening a branch office
(D) Making a reservation

64. Look at the graphic. Where will the man travel to next?

(A) Shady Grove
(B) Braddock Bay
(C) Largo
(D) Ashburn

GO ON TO THE NEXT PAGE

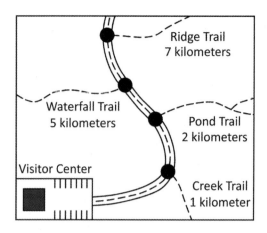

65. What does the woman ask the man about?

(A) Whether a coupon is valid
(B) Whether a food is spicy
(C) Whether a drink is included
(D) Whether any seats are available

66. Look at the graphic. Which special does the woman order?

(A) Special 1
(B) Special 2
(C) Special 3
(D) Special 4

67. What will the woman most likely do next?

(A) Move her car
(B) Go to a patio
(C) Make a reservation
(D) Meet some friends

68. What is the woman happy about?

(A) She happened to meet some friends.
(B) The weather is perfect for an activity.
(C) The park was closer than expected.
(D) There are few people in the park.

69. Look at the graphic. How far will the speakers hike?

(A) 7 kilometers
(B) 5 kilometers
(C) 2 kilometers
(D) 1 kilometer

70. What can the speakers do while waiting for the shuttle?

(A) Buy some snacks
(B) Watch a video
(C) Visit a gift shop
(D) Rent some equipment

PART 4

Directions: You will hear some talks given by a single speaker. You will be asked to answer three questions about what the speaker says in each talk. Select the best response to each question and mark the letter (A), (B), (C), or (D) on your answer sheet. The talks will not be printed in your test book and will be spoken only one time.

71. What did the listener do yesterday?

(A) She placed an order.
(B) She scheduled an event.
(C) She called a manager.
(D) She painted some rooms.

72. What problem does the speaker mention?

(A) A price has increased.
(B) A machine needs to be repaired.
(C) A product is not available.
(D) A performance has been canceled.

73. What does the speaker offer the listener?

(A) Expedited shipping
(B) A full refund
(C) A free consultation
(D) A discount

74. According to the speaker, what is special about Osterwind Estate?

(A) It houses many historic paintings.
(B) It was designed by its owner.
(C) It includes a botanical garden.
(D) It is used as a museum.

75. Why are the listeners at Osterwind Estate?

(A) To attend an awards ceremony
(B) To apply for landscaping jobs
(C) To take a tour of a building
(D) To clean up some gardens

76. What will the listeners receive?

(A) Gift-shop coupons
(B) Free passes
(C) Lunch boxes
(D) T-shirts

77. Who most likely is the listener?

(A) A travel agent
(B) An administrative assistant
(C) A flight attendant
(D) A security guard

78. Why does the speaker say, "I know this is inconvenient"?

(A) To suggest a deadline extension
(B) To report on an additional cost
(C) To offer an alternative solution
(D) To apologize for a request

79. What will the speaker do when he arrives in San Diego?

(A) Retrieve his messages
(B) Check in to a hotel
(C) Change a flight reservation
(D) Visit a company office

80. What does the speaker say her videos are usually about?

(A) How to plan trips
(B) How to reuse items
(C) How to organize closets
(D) How to draw landscapes

81. What first step does the speaker mention?

(A) Writing a list
(B) Finding coupons
(C) Gathering supplies
(D) Looking at images online

82. According to the speaker, what can the listeners do on a Web site?

(A) Enter a contest
(B) Subscribe to a video channel
(C) Submit some photographs
(D) Download some instructions

GO ON TO THE NEXT PAGE

83. What is the speech mainly about?

   (A) A financial report
   (B) A round of promotions
   (C) A product prototype
   (D) A construction project

84. Why does the speaker say, "all required studies were conducted a year ago"?

   (A) To correct a timeline error
   (B) To provide reassurance
   (C) To deny responsibility for a problem
   (D) To argue that a new study is needed

85. What will the next speaker discuss?

   (A) A job fair
   (B) A school opening
   (C) A ceremony
   (D) A sporting event

86. Who most likely is the speaker?

   (A) A salesperson
   (B) A government official
   (C) An interior designer
   (D) A building manager

87. Why does the speaker say, "It's been ten days"?

   (A) To explain an expense
   (B) To point out a problem
   (C) To make an offer
   (D) To thank a colleague

88. What does the speaker offer to do?

   (A) Open the door to a room
   (B) Reset a password
   (C) Send a copy of a document
   (D) Refund a payment

89. What is mentioned about Ferndale Valley?

   (A) It is heavily forested.
   (B) It attracts many tourists.
   (C) It is developing quickly.
   (D) It is very windy.

90. Who will participate in a project?

   (A) Biologists
   (B) Farmers
   (C) Airline pilots
   (D) Real estate agents

91. What will the participants receive?

   (A) Tickets to an industry event
   (B) Technical assistance
   (C) Financial compensation
   (D) Advertising advice

92. What kind of business does the speaker work for?

   (A) A construction firm
   (B) A landscaping service
   (C) A storage company
   (D) An auto repair shop

93. Why is the speaker calling?

   (A) To apologize for a cancellation
   (B) To confirm a delivery
   (C) To share a price quote
   (D) To update some contact information

94. What does the speaker ask the listener to do?

   (A) Purchase a warranty
   (B) Complete a survey
   (C) Clean up an area
   (D) Apply for a permit

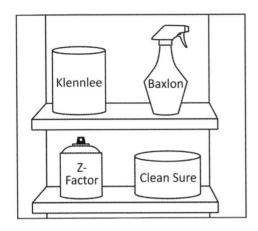

95. What is the purpose of the talk?

(A) To discuss a schedule
(B) To consider changing suppliers
(C) To train employees
(D) To develop an inventory system

96. Look at the graphic. Which product does the speaker say is new?

(A) Klennlee
(B) Baxlon
(C) Z-Factor
(D) Clean Sure

97. What happens at one o'clock on Tuesdays?

(A) An expense report is due.
(B) A work shift begins.
(C) A staff meeting is held.
(D) A delivery arrives.

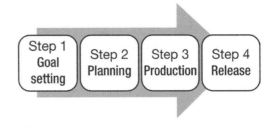

98. What is the topic of the course?

(A) Marketing
(B) Investing
(C) Documentary filmmaking
(D) Software development

99. Look at the graphic. Which step will be discussed today?

(A) Step 1
(B) Step 2
(C) Step 3
(D) Step 4

100. What will the listeners do next?

(A) Read a handout
(B) Watch a video
(C) Take a coffee break
(D) Listen to a guest speaker

This is the end of the Listening test.

토익®정기시험
기출문제집 4
1000

TEST 06
무료 동영상 강의

LC

기출 TEST
06

LISTENING TEST

In the Listening test, you will be asked to demonstrate how well you understand spoken English. The entire Listening test will last approximately 45 minutes. There are four parts, and directions are given for each part. You must mark your answers on the separate answer sheet. Do not write your answers in your test book.

PART 1

Directions: For each question in this part, you will hear four statements about a picture in your test book. When you hear the statements, you must select the one statement that best describes what you see in the picture. Then find the number of the question on your answer sheet and mark your answer. The statements will not be printed in your test book and will be spoken only one time.

Statement (C), "They're sitting at a table," is the best description of the picture, so you should select answer (C) and mark it on your answer sheet.

1.

2.

GO ON TO THE NEXT PAGE

3.

4.

5.

6.

GO ON TO THE NEXT PAGE ➤

PART 2

Directions: You will hear a question or statement and three responses spoken in English. They will not be printed in your test book and will be spoken only one time. Select the best response to the question or statement and mark the letter (A), (B), or (C) on your answer sheet.

7. Mark your answer on your answer sheet.

8. Mark your answer on your answer sheet.

9. Mark your answer on your answer sheet.

10. Mark your answer on your answer sheet.

11. Mark your answer on your answer sheet.

12. Mark your answer on your answer sheet.

13. Mark your answer on your answer sheet.

14. Mark your answer on your answer sheet.

15. Mark your answer on your answer sheet.

16. Mark your answer on your answer sheet.

17. Mark your answer on your answer sheet.

18. Mark your answer on your answer sheet.

19. Mark your answer on your answer sheet.

20. Mark your answer on your answer sheet.

21. Mark your answer on your answer sheet.

22. Mark your answer on your answer sheet.

23. Mark your answer on your answer sheet.

24. Mark your answer on your answer sheet.

25. Mark your answer on your answer sheet.

26. Mark your answer on your answer sheet.

27. Mark your answer on your answer sheet.

28. Mark your answer on your answer sheet.

29. Mark your answer on your answer sheet.

30. Mark your answer on your answer sheet.

31. Mark your answer on your answer sheet.

PART 3

Directions: You will hear some conversations between two or more people. You will be asked to answer three questions about what the speakers say in each conversation. Select the best response to each question and mark the letter (A), (B), (C), or (D) on your answer sheet. The conversations will not be printed in your test book and will be spoken only one time.

32. What are the speakers mainly discussing?

(A) Theater renovations
(B) Changes to a performance schedule
(C) Selection of a new lighting director
(D) A promotional gift

33. What does the man say about a musical production?

(A) It was based on a book.
(B) It has been successful.
(C) It will be performed overseas.
(D) Some casting changes were made.

34. What event are the speakers planning?

(A) A press conference
(B) A fund-raiser
(C) An audition
(D) An autograph session

35. What did the speakers recently do?

(A) They launched a new product.
(B) They chose a job candidate.
(C) They moved to a different city.
(D) They renovated a space.

36. What do the speakers like about a building?

(A) It provides 24-hour access.
(B) It has an outdoor space.
(C) It is near public transportation.
(D) It uses renewable energy.

37. What is the woman worried about?

(A) A new competitor
(B) A longer commute
(C) A high price
(D) An upcoming deadline

38. What event is the woman planning?

(A) A retirement party
(B) A birthday party
(C) A science fair
(D) A school festival

39. Who most likely is the man?

(A) A baker
(B) A musician
(C) A gardener
(D) A teacher

40. Why does the man apologize?

(A) Some tools cannot be found.
(B) Some invitations were sent late.
(C) A store is closed for a holiday.
(D) A request cannot be fulfilled.

41. What did the man try to do online?

(A) Purchase a new phone
(B) Make an appointment
(C) Order a part
(D) Cancel a contract

42. What does the man say is wrong with his mobile phone?

(A) It has a short battery life.
(B) The screen is damaged.
(C) A cable is missing.
(D) It has limited storage space.

43. What will the man most likely do next?

(A) Speak with a manager
(B) Call technical support
(C) Visit a store
(D) Restart a device

GO ON TO THE NEXT PAGE

44. Where do the speakers most likely work?

    (A) At a bank
    (B) At a research laboratory
    (C) At a newspaper company
    (D) At a legal firm

45. Why has the woman been unable to finish a task?

    (A) She needs a manager's signature.
    (B) She cannot access her files.
    (C) She cannot get the necessary information.
    (D) Some data are incorrect.

46. What solution does the man propose?

    (A) Changing a deadline
    (B) Scheduling a meeting
    (C) Asking a colleague for help
    (D) Reviewing some documents

47. What kind of work does the man do?

    (A) Appliance repair
    (B) Painting
    (C) Landscaping
    (D) Roofing

48. What does the woman imply when she says, "I don't want to have to make repairs"?

    (A) She is not qualified for a task.
    (B) She prefers durable materials.
    (C) She will buy a new appliance.
    (D) She is not happy with a cost estimate.

49. What will the man show to the woman?

    (A) A list of prices
    (B) A license
    (C) Some references
    (D) Some photographs

50. Why is the man calling?

    (A) To track a shipment
    (B) To ask about a payment
    (C) To close an account
    (D) To request computer help

51. According to the woman, what caused a delay?

    (A) An employee was out of the office.
    (B) A software program was updated.
    (C) A document was mislabeled.
    (D) A new policy was implemented.

52. What information will the woman most likely provide later?

    (A) A cost breakdown
    (B) An account number
    (C) A time estimate
    (D) A phone number

53. Where does the conversation take place?

    (A) At a game arcade
    (B) At a grocery store
    (C) At an auto repair shop
    (D) At a parking garage

54. What type of product does the woman mention?

    (A) Some videos
    (B) Some brochures
    (C) A price scanner
    (D) A mobile phone application

55. What do the men want to do?

    (A) Extend business hours
    (B) Enter a local contest
    (C) Include customized content
    (D) Upgrade some equipment

56. What industry do the speakers most likely work in?

(A) Fashion photography
(B) Information technology
(C) Filmmaking
(D) Marketing

57. What does the man imply when he says, "I want it to be less than an hour"?

(A) He is very busy.
(B) He approves an itinerary.
(C) A route has a lot of traffic.
(D) Some revisions are needed.

58. Why does the man need to contact a team?

(A) To explain a permit procedure
(B) To confirm equipment availability
(C) To introduce a colleague
(D) To devise a safety plan

59. What did the man review yesterday?

(A) A budget
(B) A weather report
(C) Some test results
(D) Some hiring plans

60. What do the speakers hope to do?

(A) Improve the condition of a sports field
(B) Expand the city's athletic programs
(C) Plan a fund-raising event
(D) Acquire more public land

61. What will Melissa send by e-mail?

(A) A summary of work tasks
(B) A letter of appreciation
(C) A news article
(D) A cost estimate

League Schedule	
Junior League (ages 9–12)	
Monday	5:30 P.M.
Teen League (ages 13–17)	
Tuesday	6:00 P.M.
Wednesday	7:00 P.M.
Adult League	
Thursday	6:00 P.M.

62. Where do the speakers work?

(A) At a bowling alley
(B) At a swimming pool
(C) At an ice-skating rink
(D) At a baseball field

63. Look at the graphic. On which day will the Junior League meet starting next month?

(A) Monday
(B) Tuesday
(C) Wednesday
(D) Thursday

64. What does the woman say she will do?

(A) Hang a poster
(B) Send an e-mail
(C) Deliver a package
(D) Process a payment

GO ON TO THE NEXT PAGE

TEST 6

Monday	2 P.M.	Children's Story Time
Tuesday	3 P.M.	Computer Class
Wednesday	6 P.M.	Book Signing: Sumit Mehta
Thursday	7 P.M.	Movie: Red Sunrise
Friday	Closed	

Color	Price
Garden Green	$23
Misty Blue	$27
Sunrise Peach	$19
Antique White	$16

65. According to the woman, why will the library be closed on Friday?

(A) An election will be held there.
(B) Some renovations will take place.
(C) Bad weather is expected.
(D) A national holiday will be observed.

66. What schedule conflict does the man mention?

(A) He has a family obligation.
(B) His car will be at a mechanic's shop.
(C) He will be attending a performance.
(D) He has a business meeting.

67. Look at the graphic. When will the man most likely attend a library event?

(A) On Monday
(B) On Tuesday
(C) On Wednesday
(D) On Thursday

68. What is the conversation about?

(A) Extending a fence
(B) Building a storage shed
(C) Repairing a bridge
(D) Updating an entrance area

69. According to the woman, how is a project being funded?

(A) With donations from visitors
(B) With money from a grant
(C) With revenue from ticket sales
(D) With proceeds from a charity auction

70. Look at the graphic. Which color does the woman select?

(A) Garden Green
(B) Misty Blue
(C) Sunrise Peach
(D) Antique White

PART 4

Directions: You will hear some talks given by a single speaker. You will be asked to answer three questions about what the speaker says in each talk. Select the best response to each question and mark the letter (A), (B), (C), or (D) on your answer sheet. The talks will not be printed in your test book and will be spoken only one time.

71. Where does the talk most likely take place?

    (A) At a medical clinic
    (B) At an airport
    (C) At a fitness center
    (D) At a bank

72. What is mainly being discussed?

    (A) A hiring decision
    (B) A marketing campaign
    (C) A customer satisfaction survey
    (D) An electronic check-in system

73. What will happen next Tuesday?

    (A) A new security system will be installed.
    (B) A branch location will open.
    (C) A training session will take place.
    (D) A product will be delivered.

74. Who is the podcast intended for?

    (A) Party organizers
    (B) Travel agents
    (C) Technology enthusiasts
    (D) Carpenters

75. According to the speaker, what will some listeners need?

    (A) An insurance policy
    (B) A letter of recommendation
    (C) An event venue
    (D) A license

76. What information will the speaker share?

    (A) Application instructions
    (B) Retail locations
    (C) Names of instructors
    (D) User reviews

77. Who are the listeners?

    (A) Mechanical engineers
    (B) Trade show participants
    (C) Government officials
    (D) Laboratory assistants

78. What does the speaker request that the listeners do?

    (A) Take safety precautions
    (B) Sign a registration sheet
    (C) Wear name tags
    (D) Move their vehicles

79. What will take place in the evening?

    (A) A debate
    (B) An award ceremony
    (C) A film screening
    (D) A reception

80. Who most likely is the speaker?

    (A) A customer service representative
    (B) A software developer
    (C) A podcast host
    (D) An event coordinator

81. According to the speaker, what can a software application be used for?

    (A) Making travel reservations
    (B) Uploading documents
    (C) Managing subscriptions
    (D) Searching for discounts

82. How can the listeners receive some free tickets?

    (A) By clicking on a link
    (B) By signing up for a newsletter
    (C) By buying a product in-store
    (D) By writing a review

GO ON TO THE NEXT PAGE

83. Who is the speaker most likely calling?

    (A) A store owner
    (B) A property manager
    (C) A delivery driver
    (D) A restaurant supplier

84. What problem does the speaker have?

    (A) Some appliances have not arrived.
    (B) Some boxes have been damaged.
    (C) A water cooler is not working.
    (D) A sink is not draining.

85. Why does the speaker say, "I think I've done all I can do"?

    (A) To request that the listener give her a refund
    (B) To indicate that she needs the listener's assistance
    (C) To explain why she enrolled in a training course
    (D) To confirm that a task has been completed

---

86. What will the listeners do next Tuesday?

    (A) Renew their contracts
    (B) Clean their offices
    (C) Visit a recycling center
    (D) Greet new clients

87. What does the speaker thank Rajeev for doing?

    (A) Paying for refreshments
    (B) Reserving a meeting room
    (C) Arranging transportation
    (D) Renting some equipment

88. Why does the speaker say, "the south corner of the office has a lot of empty file cabinets"?

    (A) To suggest a location for some desks
    (B) To indicate where some files should be stored
    (C) To explain that a task has already been completed
    (D) To ask for more office supplies to be ordered

---

89. What does Ziegler Incorporated sell?

    (A) Office paper
    (B) Gardening tools
    (C) Computers
    (D) Car parts

90. According to the speaker, what problem is the company experiencing?

    (A) Staffing shortages
    (B) Shipping delays
    (C) Limited warehouse space
    (D) Insufficient inventory

91. What will arrive in an e-mail?

    (A) Some contact information
    (B) An order form
    (C) A discount code
    (D) A price list

---

92. What has the mayor decided to do?

    (A) Run for election again
    (B) Redevelop an area of the city
    (C) Host an art festival
    (D) Provide public art classes

93. What is the goal of a survey?

    (A) To decide on a theme
    (B) To raise money for a project
    (C) To educate the public about a problem
    (D) To recruit some volunteers

94. Why does the speaker say, "I think Alvaro Gomez has won several awards"?

    (A) To correct some information
    (B) To praise a museum exhibit
    (C) To recommend a suitable candidate
    (D) To congratulate a colleague

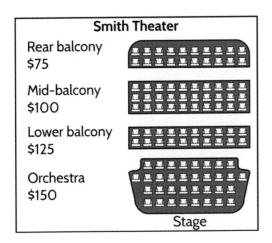

Smith Theater

Rear balcony
$75

Mid-balcony
$100

Lower balcony
$125

Orchestra
$150

Stage

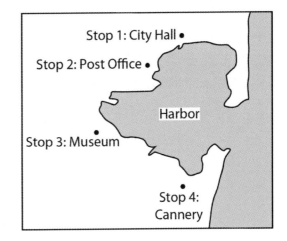

Stop 1: City Hall •

Stop 2: Post Office •

Harbor

Stop 3: Museum

Stop 4:
Cannery

95. Who most likely is the speaker?

(A) A seating usher
(B) A band director
(C) A stage actor
(D) A sales agent

96. Look at the graphic. How much do tickets in the available section cost?

(A) $75
(B) $100
(C) $125
(D) $150

97. What does the listener need to do within 24 hours?

(A) Make a phone call
(B) Send in a payment
(C) Pick up an item
(D) Fill out a form

98. Look at the graphic. Which stop has been canceled?

(A) Stop 1
(B) Stop 2
(C) Stop 3
(D) Stop 4

99. Why has a stop been canceled?

(A) A guest speaker is unavailable.
(B) A building is undergoing maintenance.
(C) An area has closed for a festival.
(D) A private event has been scheduled.

100. What will the listeners receive?

(A) A refund
(B) A souvenir
(C) A printed map
(D) Meal vouchers

This is the end of the Listening test.

토익® 정기시험
기출문제집 4
1000

TEST 07
무료 동영상 강의

LC

기출 TEST
07

LISTENING TEST

In the Listening test, you will be asked to demonstrate how well you understand spoken English. The entire Listening test will last approximately 45 minutes. There are four parts, and directions are given for each part. You must mark your answers on the separate answer sheet. Do not write your answers in your test book.

PART 1

Directions: For each question in this part, you will hear four statements about a picture in your test book. When you hear the statements, you must select the one statement that best describes what you see in the picture. Then find the number of the question on your answer sheet and mark your answer. The statements will not be printed in your test book and will be spoken only one time.

Statement (C), "They're sitting at a table," is the best description of the picture, so you should select answer (C) and mark it on your answer sheet.

1.

2.

GO ON TO THE NEXT PAGE

3.

4.

5.

6.

GO ON TO THE NEXT PAGE ➡

Directions: You will hear a question or statement and three responses spoken in English. They will not be printed in your test book and will be spoken only one time. Select the best response to the question or statement and mark the letter (A), (B), or (C) on your answer sheet.

7. Mark your answer on your answer sheet.

8. Mark your answer on your answer sheet.

9. Mark your answer on your answer sheet.

10. Mark your answer on your answer sheet.

11. Mark your answer on your answer sheet.

12. Mark your answer on your answer sheet.

13. Mark your answer on your answer sheet.

14. Mark your answer on your answer sheet.

15. Mark your answer on your answer sheet.

16. Mark your answer on your answer sheet.

17. Mark your answer on your answer sheet.

18. Mark your answer on your answer sheet.

19. Mark your answer on your answer sheet.

20. Mark your answer on your answer sheet.

21. Mark your answer on your answer sheet.

22. Mark your answer on your answer sheet.

23. Mark your answer on your answer sheet.

24. Mark your answer on your answer sheet.

25. Mark your answer on your answer sheet.

26. Mark your answer on your answer sheet.

27. Mark your answer on your answer sheet.

28. Mark your answer on your answer sheet.

29. Mark your answer on your answer sheet.

30. Mark your answer on your answer sheet.

31. Mark your answer on your answer sheet.

PART 3

Directions: You will hear some conversations between two or more people. You will be asked to answer three questions about what the speakers say in each conversation. Select the best response to each question and mark the letter (A), (B), (C), or (D) on your answer sheet. The conversations will not be printed in your test book and will be spoken only one time.

32. What is the woman preparing to do?
    (A) Conduct an inspection
    (B) Film a cooking demonstration
    (C) Offer some product samples
    (D) Make a purchase

33. Where is the conversation most likely taking place?
    (A) At a restaurant
    (B) At a factory
    (C) At an organic farm
    (D) At a grocery store

34. What does the man offer to help with?
    (A) Scheduling an interview
    (B) Mixing some ingredients
    (C) Carrying some supplies
    (D) Assembling some equipment

35. Who most likely is the man?
    (A) A bank teller
    (B) A librarian
    (C) A mail carrier
    (D) A truck driver

36. What does the woman ask about?
    (A) A method of payment
    (B) A type of delivery service
    (C) A way to fill out a form
    (D) A schedule change

37. What does the man say he will do?
    (A) Look up some information
    (B) Print a document
    (C) Check on a machine
    (D) Update an account

38. What does the woman say she has finished doing?
    (A) Organizing a luncheon
    (B) Preparing some materials
    (C) Submitting a purchase order
    (D) Reviewing some résumés

39. Why was a change made at the last minute?
    (A) An area is too noisy.
    (B) Some participants are delayed.
    (C) A room was already taken.
    (D) Some revisions were requested.

40. What is the woman concerned about?
    (A) The security of an Internet connection
    (B) The amount of approved funding
    (C) The feedback from some colleagues
    (D) The availability of some equipment

41. What problem do the speakers discuss?
    (A) A parking garage is full.
    (B) A street is closed.
    (C) Some equipment is broken.
    (D) Some items are damaged.

42. What does the man say customers will have to do?
    (A) Visit an online store
    (B) Present a receipt
    (C) Park in a different area
    (D) Schedule a delivery

43. What will the woman do next?
    (A) Cancel her plans for the weekend
    (B) Close the shop early
    (C) Drive slowly
    (D) Post an update on social media

GO ON TO THE NEXT PAGE

44. Where do the speakers most likely work?

(A) At a nature preserve
(B) At a vegetable farm
(C) At a garden supply store
(D) At a construction site

45. What will the speakers do with some samples?

(A) Display them in a window
(B) Send them to a laboratory
(C) Distribute them to customers
(D) Donate them to a university

46. What does the woman volunteer to do?

(A) Lead a training session
(B) Take some photographs
(C) Order some supplies
(D) Organize a tour

47. Who are the speakers?

(A) Executive assistants
(B) Maintenance supervisors
(C) Postal workers
(D) Food delivery drivers

48. What was announced in a flyer?

(A) Some computer software will be replaced.
(B) A building will be sold.
(C) A route will be added.
(D) Some vehicles will be replaced.

49. What is the man concerned about?

(A) How long a battery will last
(B) How expensive a purchase will be
(C) How accurate a weather forecast is
(D) How current a training program is

50. What does Ms. Park ask the man to do?

(A) Assist a new employee
(B) Book an event
(C) Meet with a vendor
(D) Prepare a presentation

51. Where does the conversation most likely take place?

(A) At a museum
(B) At a technology firm
(C) At an airport
(D) At a hotel

52. What will the man do next?

(A) Provide some feedback
(B) Check a calendar
(C) Demonstrate a computer program
(D) Help a coworker find some supplies

53. What do the speakers find surprising about a restaurant?

(A) Its prices
(B) Its popularity
(C) Its menu options
(D) Its decor

54. Why are the speakers in a hurry?

(A) They need to catch a train.
(B) They will be conducting an interview.
(C) They will be leading a training session.
(D) A business is about to close.

55. What will the speakers most likely do next?

(A) Go to another restaurant
(B) Try a free sample
(C) Order food to go
(D) Pay a bill

56. Where do the speakers most likely work?

   (A) At a sporting goods store
   (B) At a campground
   (C) At a footwear factory
   (D) At a fitness center

57. Why does the man say, "this is a densely populated area"?

   (A) To complain that traffic is heavy
   (B) To suggest changes in regulations
   (C) To explain a decision
   (D) To request a review of property values

58. What does the woman think a business should do?

   (A) Hire more employees
   (B) Place a large order
   (C) Revise an employee handbook
   (D) Advertise on social media

59. What is the conversation about?

   (A) Organizing an event
   (B) Preparing for a renovation
   (C) Updating some software
   (D) Selecting a caterer

60. What does the woman imply when she says, "Nearly a third of our staff will be participating remotely"?

   (A) Travel expenses should be refunded.
   (B) Some workers may feel excluded.
   (C) A venue is not the correct size.
   (D) A workshop should be postponed.

61. What will the woman do next?

   (A) Review an agenda
   (B) Reserve an event space
   (C) Research some online activities
   (D) Check a budget

Woodlands Store	
Floor	**Department**
1	Customer Service
2	Jewelry
3	Furniture
4	Appliances
5	Clothing

62. Look at the graphic. Which floor will the man visit?

   (A) Floor 1
   (B) Floor 2
   (C) Floor 3
   (D) Floor 4

63. Why is the man calling the store?

   (A) To complain about receiving a faulty product
   (B) To point out an error in an invoice
   (C) To ask about seeing some merchandise
   (D) To request delivery of a catalog

64. What does the woman assure the man about?

   (A) An online payment system is secure.
   (B) A building is wheelchair accessible.
   (C) A product is eligible for a refund.
   (D) A food court is open daily.

TEST 7

GO ON TO THE NEXT PAGE

Flights to Kyoto		
From	**Airline**	**Departure Time**
Newark	Sky Air	6:02 A.M.
New York	Alpha Star	8:15 A.M.
New York	Blue Jet	9:07 A.M.
Newark	High Wings	10:20 A.M.

65. Why does the woman need to go to Kyoto?

(A) To attend a conference
(B) To sign a contract
(C) To find investors
(D) To report on a project

66. Look at the graphic. What time will the woman depart for Kyoto?

(A) At 6:02 A.M.
(B) At 8:15 A.M.
(C) At 9:07 A.M.
(D) At 10:20 A.M.

67. What does the man say he will do?

(A) Drive the woman to the airport
(B) Reserve a hotel
(C) E-mail some information
(D) Print out a boarding pass

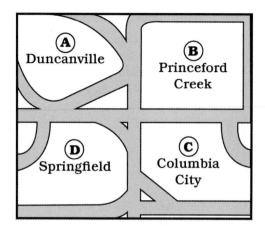

68. Who most likely are the speakers?

(A) Architects
(B) Government officials
(C) News reporters
(D) Contractors

69. What does the woman say she had access to?

(A) Uniform designs
(B) Sporting event tickets
(C) A company vehicle
(D) Bid proposals

70. Look at the graphic. According to the woman, where will a stadium most likely be located?

(A) At site A
(B) At site B
(C) At site C
(D) At site D

PART 4

Directions: You will hear some talks given by a single speaker. You will be asked to answer three questions about what the speaker says in each talk. Select the best response to each question and mark the letter (A), (B), (C), or (D) on your answer sheet. The talks will not be printed in your test book and will be spoken only one time.

71. What is being advertised?
    (A) An accounting firm
    (B) A real estate office
    (C) A trucking company
    (D) A community college

72. What happened last month?
    (A) A Web site was launched.
    (B) A company merger was finalized.
    (C) A new location was opened.
    (D) A new director was hired.

73. What are the listeners invited to do?
    (A) Join an online group
    (B) Participate in a study
    (C) Attend a workshop
    (D) Submit an application

74. What is scheduled for April 16 ?
    (A) An awards banquet
    (B) A software demonstration
    (C) A company celebration
    (D) A national holiday

75. What does the speaker thank Sung-Hee for doing?
    (A) Presenting her research
    (B) Approving a budget
    (C) E-mailing an agenda
    (D) Reserving some space

76. Why does the speaker say, "Everyone has my e-mail address"?
    (A) To discourage the listeners from calling his phone
    (B) To complain that he receives too many e-mails
    (C) To explain how he learned about an opportunity
    (D) To encourage the listeners to make suggestions

77. Why is the speaker calling?
    (A) To obtain a copy of his medical records
    (B) To express interest in a job
    (C) To complain about a service
    (D) To request an appointment

78. What event did the speaker recently participate in?
    (A) An art festival
    (B) An athletic competition
    (C) A career fair
    (D) A walking tour

79. What does the speaker say he will be doing this morning?
    (A) Picking up supplies
    (B) Holding interviews
    (C) Giving a demonstration
    (D) Touring a facility

80. What does the listener produce?
    (A) Furniture
    (B) Electronics
    (C) Food
    (D) Vehicles

81. What does the speaker say he will send the listener?
    (A) A contract
    (B) A delivery schedule
    (C) Some display ideas
    (D) Some coupons

82. What does the speaker recommend doing?
    (A) Lowering a price
    (B) Advertising in a newspaper
    (C) Developing new flavors
    (D) Sending plenty of inventory

GO ON TO THE NEXT PAGE

83. What type of product has the team developed?

(A) A robot for household tasks
(B) A mobile application for weather updates
(C) A satellite dish for Internet access
(D) A smartwatch for fitness tracking

84. What has caused a problem for some users?

(A) Limited screen options
(B) A short battery life
(C) Unclear instructions
(D) Poor weather conditions

85. What will the listeners most likely do next?

(A) Take a break
(B) Work in small groups
(C) Visit a production facility
(D) Take some measurements

86. Why does the speaker say, "Unfortunately, some of the microphones aren't working"?

(A) To suggest purchasing new equipment
(B) To recommend changing a venue
(C) To ask the listeners to remain silent
(D) To apologize for a delay

87. What are the listeners invited to do?

(A) Upgrade their tickets
(B) Become volunteers
(C) Participate in a contest
(D) Ask the performers some questions

88. Where does the speaker say some information can be found?

(A) On a posted sign
(B) At the box office
(C) In a program booklet
(D) On a Web site

89. What is the focus of the training?

(A) Using some software
(B) Processing customer complaints
(C) Securing sensitive documents
(D) Creating advertisements

90. Where do the listeners most likely work?

(A) At a conference center
(B) At a factory
(C) At a warehouse
(D) At a department store

91. What does the speaker ask the listeners to do?

(A) Create an account
(B) Open a manual
(C) Fill out a form
(D) Take out an electronic device

92. What is the topic of the talk?

(A) Customer satisfaction
(B) Career development
(C) Energy efficiency
(D) Time management

93. Why does the speaker say, "There's a lot of combined knowledge at this meeting"?

(A) To encourage participation
(B) To indicate an agenda change
(C) To stress the importance of leadership
(D) To correct a misconception

94. What does the speaker say will happen after the talk?

(A) Refreshments will be served.
(B) Payment will be collected.
(C) A group photograph will be taken.
(D) A recording will be shared.

Load Description	Load Length
Propane	10 meters
Automobiles	13 meters
Lumber	20 meters
Steel beams	25 meters

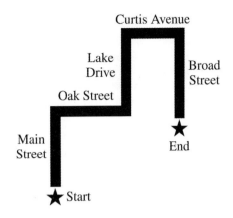

95. Who most likely are the listeners?

(A) Warehouse supervisors
(B) Construction workers
(C) Safety inspectors
(D) Truck drivers

96. What does the speaker remind Yasushi to do?

(A) Park in a different location
(B) Follow a checklist
(C) Contact a customer
(D) Check a schedule

97. Look at the graphic. Which load length is the speaker concerned about?

(A) 10 meters
(B) 13 meters
(C) 20 meters
(D) 25 meters

98. What will begin at 10 A.M. on Saturday?

(A) A holiday parade
(B) A bicycle race
(C) A new bus route
(D) Some road construction

99. Look at the graphic. Which road will be excluded?

(A) Oak Street
(B) Lake Drive
(C) Curtis Avenue
(D) Broad Street

100. What will the listeners hear after a commercial break?

(A) A financial report
(B) A weather forecast
(C) An interview with a government official
(D) A live musical performance

TEST 7

This is the end of the Listening test.

토익® 정기시험
기출문제집 4
1000

TEST 08
무료 동영상 강의

LC

기출 TEST
08

LISTENING TEST

In the Listening test, you will be asked to demonstrate how well you understand spoken English. The entire Listening test will last approximately 45 minutes. There are four parts, and directions are given for each part. You must mark your answers on the separate answer sheet. Do not write your answers in your test book.

PART 1

Directions: For each question in this part, you will hear four statements about a picture in your test book. When you hear the statements, you must select the one statement that best describes what you see in the picture. Then find the number of the question on your answer sheet and mark your answer. The statements will not be printed in your test book and will be spoken only one time.

Statement (C), "They're sitting at a table," is the best description of the picture, so you should select answer (C) and mark it on your answer sheet.

1.

2.

GO ON TO THE NEXT PAGE

3.

4.

5.

6.

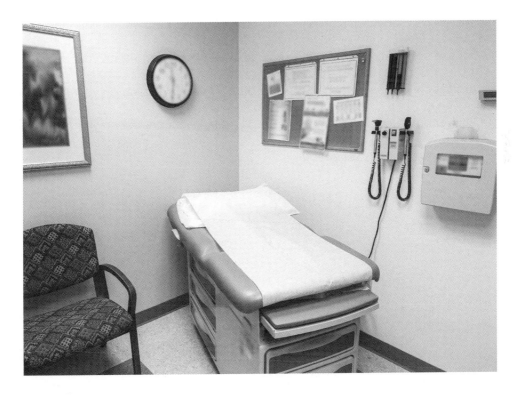

GO ON TO THE NEXT PAGE

TEST 8

Directions: You will hear a question or statement and three responses spoken in English. They will not be printed in your test book and will be spoken only one time. Select the best response to the question or statement and mark the letter (A), (B), or (C) on your answer sheet.

7. Mark your answer on your answer sheet.

8. Mark your answer on your answer sheet.

9. Mark your answer on your answer sheet.

10. Mark your answer on your answer sheet.

11. Mark your answer on your answer sheet.

12. Mark your answer on your answer sheet.

13. Mark your answer on your answer sheet.

14. Mark your answer on your answer sheet.

15. Mark your answer on your answer sheet.

16. Mark your answer on your answer sheet.

17. Mark your answer on your answer sheet.

18. Mark your answer on your answer sheet.

19. Mark your answer on your answer sheet.

20. Mark your answer on your answer sheet.

21. Mark your answer on your answer sheet.

22. Mark your answer on your answer sheet.

23. Mark your answer on your answer sheet.

24. Mark your answer on your answer sheet.

25. Mark your answer on your answer sheet.

26. Mark your answer on your answer sheet.

27. Mark your answer on your answer sheet.

28. Mark your answer on your answer sheet.

29. Mark your answer on your answer sheet.

30. Mark your answer on your answer sheet.

31. Mark your answer on your answer sheet.

Directions: You will hear some conversations between two or more people. You will be asked to answer three questions about what the speakers say in each conversation. Select the best response to each question and mark the letter (A), (B), (C), or (D) on your answer sheet. The conversations will not be printed in your test book and will be spoken only one time.

32. According to the woman, what will happen next week?
    (A) A renovation project will begin.
    (B) A company will move to a new location.
    (C) Some technology will be updated.
    (D) Some new employees will be trained.

33. What does the man recommend?
    (A) Ordering some equipment
    (B) Printing some instructions
    (C) Donating some furniture
    (D) Arranging a catered meal

34. What does the woman say she will do?
    (A) Meet a client
    (B) Research some options
    (C) Make a presentation
    (D) Sign a contract

35. Where do the speakers most likely work?
    (A) At a restaurant
    (B) At a farm
    (C) On a fishing boat
    (D) At a public park

36. What does Brian give to Liam?
    (A) Some gloves
    (B) Some bags
    (C) A plastic bucket
    (D) A clipboard

37. According to Brian, what is important?
    (A) Using sunscreen lotion
    (B) Labeling some items
    (C) Following a schedule
    (D) Drinking water

38. Who most likely is the man?
    (A) An event coordinator
    (B) A book publisher
    (C) A city official
    (D) A podcast host

39. What does the woman say is special about a flower?
    (A) It is resistant to insects.
    (B) It has an unusual color.
    (C) It can bloom for a long time.
    (D) It has a unique smell.

40. What will happen next month?
    (A) A botanical show will be held.
    (B) A public garden will open.
    (C) An experiment will be conducted.
    (D) A gardening class will be offered.

41. What does the woman propose doing?
    (A) Hiring a computer technician
    (B) Using a training application
    (C) Replacing some printers
    (D) Changing business hours

42. What is the man concerned about?
    (A) Scheduling delays
    (B) Employee satisfaction
    (C) The cost of a product
    (D) The quality of a product

43. According to the woman, what can be found on a Web site?
    (A) A company address
    (B) Customer reviews
    (C) A chat feature
    (D) Discount coupons

TEST 8

GO ON TO THE NEXT PAGE

44. What are the speakers mainly discussing?

(A) A presenter at an event
(B) End-of-year bonuses
(C) Vacation requests
(D) An applicant for a new role

45. According to the speakers, what has Amanda Diop accomplished?

(A) She secured a business deal.
(B) She completed a professional certification.
(C) She won an industry award.
(D) She reduced production costs.

46. What does the woman say she will do?

(A) Submit some documents
(B) Reserve a venue
(C) Calculate a budget
(D) Check some references

47. What is the topic of the conversation?

(A) A hiring initiative
(B) A tax proposal
(C) A volunteer opportunity
(D) A community festival

48. What is Ms. Haddad excited about?

(A) Attracting international visitors
(B) Increasing employment opportunities
(C) Installing bicycle lanes
(D) Improving a health-care facility

49. What concern does the man point out?

(A) Some equipment is missing.
(B) A project may be understaffed.
(C) Some safety guidelines are unclear.
(D) Some parking spaces may be lost.

50. Who is the woman scheduled to meet with?

(A) A company lawyer
(B) A senior partner
(C) A prospective employee
(D) A potential customer

51. What does the man remind the woman about?

(A) A luggage restriction
(B) A required signature
(C) An online guidebook
(D) A refund policy

52. What does the man agree to do?

(A) Look up a phone number
(B) Arrange for a car rental
(C) File an expense report
(D) Forward an e-mail

53. Where are the speakers?

(A) At an electronics store
(B) At a trade show
(C) At a seminar
(D) At an award ceremony

54. What does the woman mean when she says, "we have about 200 employees"?

(A) A product would not be useful for her company.
(B) She is looking to hire a manager.
(C) Her business has recently become successful.
(D) Employees will need to be trained.

55. What does the man give to the woman?

(A) A regional map
(B) A name tag
(C) A résumé
(D) A chart

56. Who most likely are the speakers?

(A) Plumbers
(B) Commercial architects
(C) Road repair contractors
(D) Landscapers

57. Why will a project be rescheduled?

(A) Rainy weather is expected.
(B) A design requires revisions.
(C) Some supplies have not arrived.
(D) A crew member is not available.

58. What will the speakers most likely do on Monday?

(A) Finalize a contract
(B) Train some employees
(C) Move some vehicles
(D) Provide some consultations

---

59. Where do the speakers most likely work?

(A) At a bookstore
(B) At a dry cleaning business
(C) At a bakery
(D) At a factory

60. What does the man imply when he says, "employees have to carry the batches across the room"?

(A) A machine is malfunctioning.
(B) A process is time-consuming.
(C) Salaries should be increased.
(D) More workers should be hired.

61. What will the man show the woman?

(A) A cost estimate
(B) A floor plan
(C) A schedule
(D) A catalog

Product Code	Item	Quantity
XPFN	Computer mouse	20
KDQV	Ballpoint pen	35
LMTS	Microfiber cloth	15
ZUEH	Webcam	10

62. What department do the speakers work in?

(A) Legal
(B) Engineering
(C) Human Resources
(D) Information Technology

63. Look at the graphic. Which quantity needs to be changed?

(A) 20
(B) 35
(C) 15
(D) 10

64. What does the woman ask about?

(A) A refund
(B) A signature
(C) A meeting location
(D) A delivery date

GO ON TO THE NEXT PAGE

TEST 8

Flowers	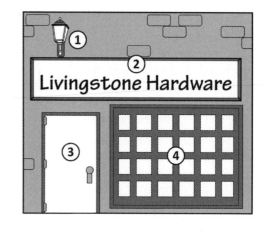

Flower Type	Price per Stem
Lilies	$4.50
Tulips	$4.75
Roses	$6.25
Orchids	$8.00

65. What type of event are the speakers discussing?

(A) A retirement party
(B) A wedding
(C) A garden show
(D) A grand opening

66. According to the woman, what has caused a problem?

(A) An invoice error
(B) A rainstorm
(C) A supply shortage
(D) A reservation cancellation

67. Look at the graphic. Which flowers will be used in the arrangements?

(A) Lilies
(B) Tulips
(C) Roses
(D) Orchids

68. What is the man most likely planning to do?

(A) Sell a shop
(B) Expand warehouse space
(C) Replace a sign
(D) Install air-conditioning

69. Look at the graphic. Which part of the storefront does the man say is historic?

(A) Part 1
(B) Part 2
(C) Part 3
(D) Part 4

70. What will the woman do next?

(A) Recommend a paint color
(B) Inspect some lighting
(C) Measure a wall
(D) Take some photographs

Directions: You will hear some talks given by a single speaker. You will be asked to answer three questions about what the speaker says in each talk. Select the best response to each question and mark the letter (A), (B), (C), or (D) on your answer sheet. The talks will not be printed in your test book and will be spoken only one time.

71. What product is being advertised?

(A) A desk
(B) A bed
(C) A bookcase
(D) A chair

72. What advantage of the product does the speaker mention?

(A) It helps save space.
(B) It is guaranteed to last.
(C) It comes in multiple sizes.
(D) It is environmentally friendly.

73. How can the listeners receive a gift?

(A) By filling out a survey
(B) By going into a store
(C) By entering a code on a Web site
(D) By subscribing to a newsletter

74. What is the broadcast mainly about?

(A) The weather
(B) Traffic updates
(C) An outdoor festival
(D) A city cleanup initiative

75. What does the speaker recommend?

(A) Filling out a form
(B) Wearing appropriate clothing
(C) Checking a map
(D) Using public transportation

76. What will the listeners hear next?

(A) An interview
(B) An advertisement
(C) Some sports updates
(D) Some newly released songs

77. Why is the speaker calling?

(A) To provide a cost estimate
(B) To confirm some warranty information
(C) To report that a service has been completed
(D) To recommend that another business be contacted

78. What does the speaker suggest the listener do?

(A) Schedule regular maintenance
(B) Wait for a sale price
(C) Call the manufacturer
(D) Ask for a second opinion

79. Why will a business be closed tomorrow?

(A) Some renovations will be done.
(B) The owner will be on vacation.
(C) An inspection will be conducted.
(D) It will be a national holiday.

80. What is the purpose of the speech?

(A) To present an award
(B) To announce a job promotion
(C) To introduce a new product
(D) To celebrate a retirement

81. What does the company produce?

(A) Cookware
(B) Shoes
(C) Cameras
(D) Light fixtures

82. What will the listeners most likely do next?

(A) Watch a video
(B) Ask questions
(C) Eat a meal
(D) Take a group photograph

TEST 8

GO ON TO THE NEXT PAGE

83. What does the speaker say will happen tomorrow?

(A) A roof will be repaired.
(B) A pipe will be replaced.
(C) A payment will be processed.
(D) An application will be submitted.

84. Why does the speaker say, "they'll be using loud machinery"?

(A) To reject a proposal
(B) To explain a delay
(C) To provide a warning
(D) To make a complaint

85. What does the speaker say about a permit?

(A) It has been mailed to the listener.
(B) It has been denied.
(C) It cost a lot of money.
(D) It was granted sooner than expected.

86. Where is the meeting taking place?

(A) At an office building
(B) At a museum
(C) At a hospital
(D) At a hotel

87. What problem does the speaker mention?

(A) A door to a room is locked.
(B) There is a staff shortage.
(C) A delivery has been delayed.
(D) Wireless Internet is not available.

88. What does the speaker remind the listeners to do?

(A) Submit their time sheets
(B) Limit their mobile phone usage
(C) Share some information
(D) Use an alternate product

89. What is the speaker mainly discussing?

(A) Updating a menu
(B) Organizing a health fair
(C) Planting a vegetable garden
(D) Reviewing some survey results

90. Why does the speaker mention a recent study?

(A) To support her opinion
(B) To suggest a process
(C) To request a guest speaker
(D) To publicize an event

91. Why does the speaker say, "small changes can have surprising results"?

(A) To agree with a decision
(B) To reassure the listeners
(C) To congratulate the listeners
(D) To request some assistance

92. What type of service does the speaker's company provide?

(A) Travel planning
(B) Online advertising
(C) Staff recruitment
(D) Inventory management

93. What does the speaker mean when he says, "40 percent of our business comes from two clients"?

(A) His team should be rewarded.
(B) He has time to develop more projects.
(C) The clients are major corporations.
(D) The company needs more clients.

94. What incentive does the company plan to offer?

(A) A discount for referrals
(B) A subscription to an online magazine
(C) A satisfaction guarantee
(D) A certification course

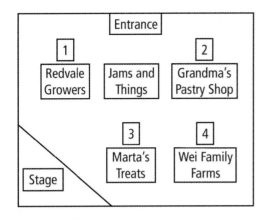

SESSION	TIME	PLACE
Remote Workforces	9:00–10:00	Sky Room
Team Collaboration	10:00–11:00	Landmark Room
Lunch	11:00–12:15	Cafeteria
Innovation Tools	12:30–1:30	Orion Room
Problem-Solving	1:30–2:30	Vista Room

95. What does the speaker say about the vendors?

(A) They use sustainable practices.
(B) They are offering free samples.
(C) Their goods are homemade.
(D) Their prices are reasonable.

96. Look at the graphic. Where can the listeners purchase concert tickets?

(A) At location 1
(B) At location 2
(C) At location 3
(D) At location 4

97. According to the speaker, what can be found on the festival Web site?

(A) A job listing
(B) An event program
(C) Safety regulations
(D) Names of sponsors

98. What does the speaker encourage the listeners to do?

(A) Pick up refreshments
(B) Purchase a book
(C) Exchange contact details
(D) Volunteer for an activity

99. What does the speaker say happened as a result of attendee feedback?

(A) Registration was conducted online.
(B) A more diverse range of speakers were invited.
(C) Extra charging stations were provided.
(D) Another conference day was added.

100. Look at the graphic. Which session's location has changed?

(A) Remote Workforces
(B) Team Collaboration
(C) Innovation Tools
(D) Problem-Solving

This is the end of the Listening test.

TEST 8

토익®정기시험
기출문제집 4
1000

TEST 09
무료 동영상 강의

LC

기출 TEST

09

LISTENING TEST

In the Listening test, you will be asked to demonstrate how well you understand spoken English. The entire Listening test will last approximately 45 minutes. There are four parts, and directions are given for each part. You must mark your answers on the separate answer sheet. Do not write your answers in your test book.

PART 1

Directions: For each question in this part, you will hear four statements about a picture in your test book. When you hear the statements, you must select the one statement that best describes what you see in the picture. Then find the number of the question on your answer sheet and mark your answer. The statements will not be printed in your test book and will be spoken only one time.

Statement (C), "They're sitting at a table," is the best description of the picture, so you should select answer (C) and mark it on your answer sheet.

1.

2.

GO ON TO THE NEXT PAGE

3.

4.

5.

6.

GO ON TO THE NEXT PAGE

TEST 9

PART 2

Directions: You will hear a question or statement and three responses spoken in English. They will not be printed in your test book and will be spoken only one time. Select the best response to the question or statement and mark the letter (A), (B), or (C) on your answer sheet.

7. Mark your answer on your answer sheet.

8. Mark your answer on your answer sheet.

9. Mark your answer on your answer sheet.

10. Mark your answer on your answer sheet.

11. Mark your answer on your answer sheet.

12. Mark your answer on your answer sheet.

13. Mark your answer on your answer sheet.

14. Mark your answer on your answer sheet.

15. Mark your answer on your answer sheet.

16. Mark your answer on your answer sheet.

17. Mark your answer on your answer sheet.

18. Mark your answer on your answer sheet.

19. Mark your answer on your answer sheet.

20. Mark your answer on your answer sheet.

21. Mark your answer on your answer sheet.

22. Mark your answer on your answer sheet.

23. Mark your answer on your answer sheet.

24. Mark your answer on your answer sheet.

25. Mark your answer on your answer sheet.

26. Mark your answer on your answer sheet.

27. Mark your answer on your answer sheet.

28. Mark your answer on your answer sheet.

29. Mark your answer on your answer sheet.

30. Mark your answer on your answer sheet.

31. Mark your answer on your answer sheet.

PART 3

Directions: You will hear some conversations between two or more people. You will be asked to answer three questions about what the speakers say in each conversation. Select the best response to each question and mark the letter (A), (B), (C), or (D) on your answer sheet. The conversations will not be printed in your test book and will be spoken only one time.

32. Where is the conversation taking place?
    (A) At an athletic club
    (B) At a hospital
    (C) At a shipping company
    (D) At an accounting firm

33. What was the man's previous job?
    (A) Receptionist
    (B) Custodian
    (C) Tour guide
    (D) Bus driver

34. What does the woman emphasize about the job being offered?
    (A) It demands long hours.
    (B) It requires a lot of experience.
    (C) It offers a competitive salary.
    (D) It involves a lot of walking.

35. What kind of business will the men open?
    (A) An electronics repair shop
    (B) A car dealership
    (C) A restaurant
    (D) A clothing store

36. How did the men learn about the woman's consulting service?
    (A) From a local business owner
    (B) From a marketing course
    (C) From a friend who works in retail
    (D) From a newspaper advertisement

37. What does the woman say should be emphasized about a business?
    (A) That it will provide many jobs
    (B) That it will be run by family members
    (C) That its owners have a lot of experience
    (D) That its owners live in the neighborhood

38. What are the speakers excited about?
    (A) An upcoming holiday
    (B) A staff training session
    (C) Some new equipment
    (D) Some staff discounts

39. Where most likely do the speakers work?
    (A) At a train station
    (B) At a grocery store
    (C) At an electronics store
    (D) At a medical center

40. What will the woman tell her manager?
    (A) She can work extra hours.
    (B) She needs more supplies.
    (C) She stocked some shelves.
    (D) She completed a project.

41. What type of business do the women work at?
    (A) A furniture store
    (B) A hardware store
    (C) A construction company
    (D) A landscaping service

42. According to the man, what may be surprising about a product?
    (A) Its weight
    (B) Its durability
    (C) Its cost
    (D) Its color

43. What will Ms. Taylor most likely ask the man for?
    (A) Some samples
    (B) A software demonstration
    (C) Some equipment
    (D) Free delivery

GO ON TO THE NEXT PAGE

44. Who most likely is the man?

(A) A history professor
(B) A mechanic
(C) A lawyer
(D) A journalist

45. What does the man say he read about the company?

(A) It was started by the woman's father.
(B) It manufactures automobile parts.
(C) It was recently purchased by a competitor.
(D) It is the area's largest employer.

46. Why does the woman say, "We export to fifty-nine countries around the world"?

(A) To correct an error
(B) To justify a decision
(C) To confirm an assumption
(D) To explain a delay

47. Who most likely are the speakers?

(A) Artists
(B) Engineers
(C) Accountants
(D) Lawyers

48. What does the woman ask the man to do?

(A) Lead part of a meeting
(B) Revise a cost estimate
(C) Contact a client
(D) Perform an inspection

49. What will the man send the woman?

(A) An itinerary
(B) A contract
(C) Some driving directions
(D) Some calculations

50. What products are the speakers discussing?

(A) Software programs
(B) Screen protectors
(C) Computer keyboards
(D) Wireless printers

51. According to the man, how are the products currently being advertised?

(A) On television
(B) On a Web site
(C) In magazines
(D) By direct mail

52. What topic will the speakers discuss at a meeting?

(A) Budget changes
(B) Design modifications
(C) Production delays
(D) Open job positions

53. What project are the speakers mainly discussing?

(A) The demolition of a shopping center
(B) The construction of a skyscraper
(C) The replacement of a bridge
(D) The redesign of a train station

54. What does the woman imply when she says, "steel costs per ton are in the thousands for every bid"?

(A) A coworker's calculations are incorrect.
(B) The man's concern is justified.
(C) A contractor should be replaced.
(D) A new construction method will be used.

55. What will the speakers do this afternoon?

(A) Take some photographs
(B) Organize a site visit
(C) Create a spreadsheet
(D) Speak to an accountant

56. Why was the man in Vancouver?

(A) To attend a trade show
(B) To meet with a client
(C) To take a vacation
(D) To facilitate a workshop

57. What does the woman say about a hotel?

(A) It was a suitable venue for an event.
(B) It was reserved by a professional organization.
(C) It is environmentally friendly.
(D) It is convenient to public transportation.

58. Why will the hotel close temporarily?

(A) To allow staff to conduct a training session
(B) To be subject to an inspection
(C) To accommodate an expansion
(D) To ensure movers have access to the rooms

59. What did the woman apply for?

(A) A professional license
(B) A job at a bank
(C) A business loan
(D) A credit card

60. What information does the man ask the woman to verify?

(A) Her income
(B) Her account number
(C) Her phone number
(D) Her address

61. What will the woman most likely do next?

(A) Sign some documents
(B) Download some software
(C) Speak with a friend
(D) Make an appointment

Cabin Rates	
North cabin (2 people)	$100
East cabin (3 people)	$120
South cabin (4 people)	$135
West cabin (5–7 people)	$150

62. When will the man stay at the resort?

(A) On Monday night
(B) On Tuesday night
(C) On Wednesday night
(D) On Thursday night

63. Look at the graphic. Which cabin does the man agree to reserve?

(A) North cabin
(B) East cabin
(C) South cabin
(D) West cabin

64. What can cabin guests receive free of charge?

(A) Shuttle rides
(B) Swimming pool access
(C) A hot breakfast
(D) A guided tour

GO ON TO THE NEXT PAGE

TEST 9

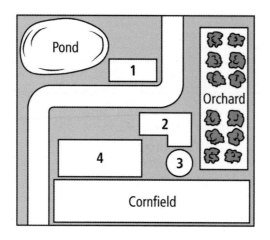

Job Number	Time Received	Business Name
15	9:30 A.M.	Larkston Hotel
16	10:00 A.M.	Trissler Hotel
17	11:30 A.M.	Benchlal Restaurant
18	12:00 P.M.	Cho Fine Dining

65. What problem does the man mention?

(A) A worker has not yet arrived.
(B) Some tools have been misplaced.
(C) A tractor is not working.
(D) Some crops are damaged.

66. Look at the graphic. Where does the woman tell the man to go?

(A) To building 1
(B) To building 2
(C) To building 3
(D) To building 4

67. What does the woman offer to do?

(A) Complete the man's work shift
(B) Go with the man
(C) Move some boxes
(D) Unlock a gate

68. Where do the speakers most likely work?

(A) At a fabric store
(B) At an employee staffing service
(C) At a health-inspection department
(D) At a commercial laundry facility

69. Look at the graphic. Which business did the man receive a request from?

(A) Larkston Hotel
(B) Trissler Hotel
(C) Benchlal Restaurant
(D) Cho Fine Dining

70. How does the woman suggest resolving an issue?

(A) By issuing a refund
(B) By consulting with a supervisor
(C) By explaining a policy to a customer
(D) By adjusting the order of some work

PART 4

Directions: You will hear some talks given by a single speaker. You will be asked to answer three questions about what the speaker says in each talk. Select the best response to each question and mark the letter (A), (B), (C), or (D) on your answer sheet. The talks will not be printed in your test book and will be spoken only one time.

71. Where is the announcement most likely being made?

    (A) At a clothing shop
    (B) At a bookstore
    (C) At a hardware store
    (D) At an auto dealership

72. What does the speaker say is happening this week?

    (A) Discounts are being offered.
    (B) An area is being remodeled.
    (C) New merchandise is arriving.
    (D) Interviews are being conducted.

73. What does the speaker remind the listeners about?

    (A) A return policy
    (B) A rewards program
    (C) An updated Web site
    (D) An additional location

74. What is the speaker discussing?

    (A) A vacation schedule
    (B) A professional-development opportunity
    (C) A department's social event
    (D) A marketing campaign

75. Why does the speaker say, "there's a bank across the street"?

    (A) To request assistance
    (B) To make a suggestion
    (C) To provide driving directions
    (D) To complain about a location

76. What does the speaker ask the listeners to do?

    (A) Fill out a sign-up sheet
    (B) E-mail agenda items
    (C) Attend an additional meeting
    (D) Complete an evaluation form

77. Why is Malton Supermarket hosting a party?

    (A) To welcome a new manager
    (B) To celebrate an anniversary
    (C) To thank local suppliers
    (D) To promote new products

78. According to Antonella Lambert, why is Malton Supermarket successful?

    (A) It is open 24 hours a day.
    (B) It is near public transportation.
    (C) It offers international products.
    (D) It provides friendly service.

79. Why is Antonella Lambert raising funds?

    (A) To open additional locations
    (B) To remodel a space
    (C) To increase advertising
    (D) To support a charity

80. What is not working properly?

    (A) The lighting
    (B) The plumbing
    (C) A payment portal
    (D) An Internet connection

81. According to the speaker, what will happen in the next few hours?

    (A) A technician will come in.
    (B) A complaint will be filed.
    (C) A Web site will be updated.
    (D) An office will close.

82. What does the speaker mean when he says, "I've talked to your team leads about the issue"?

    (A) The team leads will take over a project.
    (B) A deadline will be adjusted.
    (C) New teams will be formed.
    (D) An extra expense will be approved.

GO ON TO THE NEXT PAGE

83. What type of business does the speaker own?

(A) A tea shop
(B) A childcare center
(C) A pottery studio
(D) A party supply store

84. What does the speaker imply when she says, "you've worked here for five months now"?

(A) The listener is capable of doing a task.
(B) The listener should apply for a promotion.
(C) The speaker is ready to retire.
(D) A training period is too short.

85. What does the speaker say is located in the back room?

(A) Some decorations
(B) A video projector
(C) Some furniture
(D) Some dishes

86. What industry does the speaker most likely work in?

(A) Transportation
(B) Health care
(C) Hospitality
(D) Entertainment

87. What does the speaker say is a priority?

(A) Upgrading some equipment
(B) Promoting an industry event
(C) Hiring more staff
(D) Increasing inventory

88. What change does the speaker mention?

(A) A shuttle bus will be provided.
(B) Free meals will be available.
(C) A work schedule will be reduced.
(D) An additional branch has opened.

89. Where do the listeners most likely work?

(A) At a jewelry store
(B) At a security company
(C) At a factory
(D) At a university

90. Why does the speaker apologize?

(A) A wait time increased.
(B) A hiring was delayed.
(C) A new rule may be unpopular.
(D) Some items cannot be stored on-site.

91. What are the listeners reminded to do?

(A) Secure their belongings
(B) Verify their appointment time
(C) Provide detailed information
(D) Arrive early

92. What is the speaker announcing?

(A) A security update
(B) A menu adjustment
(C) A mandatory uniform
(D) A schedule change

93. Where do the listeners most likely work?

(A) At a farm
(B) At a restaurant
(C) At a public park
(D) At an electronics store

94. What does the speaker reassure the listeners about?

(A) They will be paid overtime.
(B) They will receive annual bonuses.
(C) Their paycheck mistake will be corrected.
(D) There will still be work available.

Cooking Class	June 2
Starting a Garden	June 9
Music with Larry Bowen	June 16
Harvest Festival	June 23

95. According to the speaker, what has changed at the farm?

(A) The prices
(B) The type of crops
(C) The management
(D) The hours of operation

96. Look at the graphic. When does the mentioned activity take place?

(A) On June 2
(B) On June 9
(C) On June 16
(D) On June 23

97. What are visitors to the business advised to do?

(A) Come on weekdays
(B) Park in a designated area
(C) Bring reusable containers
(D) Use an alternate entrance

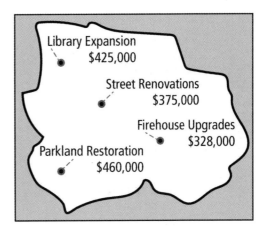

98. What does the speaker say residents have noticed?

(A) Rising fuel prices
(B) Limited housing options
(C) Traffic congestion
(D) Increased taxes

99. Look at the graphic. What is the cost of the project currently being worked on?

(A) $425,000
(B) $375,000
(C) $328,000
(D) $460,000

100. What is scheduled for Wednesday?

(A) A fund-raiser
(B) A festival
(C) An election
(D) A debate

This is the end of the Listening test.

토익˚정기시험
기출문제집 4
1000

TEST 10
무료 동영상 강의

LC

기출 TEST
10

LISTENING TEST

In the Listening test, you will be asked to demonstrate how well you understand spoken English. The entire Listening test will last approximately 45 minutes. There are four parts, and directions are given for each part. You must mark your answers on the separate answer sheet. Do not write your answers in your test book.

PART 1

Directions: For each question in this part, you will hear four statements about a picture in your test book. When you hear the statements, you must select the one statement that best describes what you see in the picture. Then find the number of the question on your answer sheet and mark your answer. The statements will not be printed in your test book and will be spoken only one time.

Statement (C), "They're sitting at a table," is the best description of the picture, so you should select answer (C) and mark it on your answer sheet.

1.

2.

GO ON TO THE NEXT PAGE →

TEST 10

3.

4.

5.

6.

GO ON TO THE NEXT PAGE

TEST 10

PART 2

Directions: You will hear a question or statement and three responses spoken in English. They will not be printed in your test book and will be spoken only one time. Select the best response to the question or statement and mark the letter (A), (B), or (C) on your answer sheet.

7. Mark your answer on your answer sheet.

8. Mark your answer on your answer sheet.

9. Mark your answer on your answer sheet.

10. Mark your answer on your answer sheet.

11. Mark your answer on your answer sheet.

12. Mark your answer on your answer sheet.

13. Mark your answer on your answer sheet.

14. Mark your answer on your answer sheet.

15. Mark your answer on your answer sheet.

16. Mark your answer on your answer sheet.

17. Mark your answer on your answer sheet.

18. Mark your answer on your answer sheet.

19. Mark your answer on your answer sheet.

20. Mark your answer on your answer sheet.

21. Mark your answer on your answer sheet.

22. Mark your answer on your answer sheet.

23. Mark your answer on your answer sheet.

24. Mark your answer on your answer sheet.

25. Mark your answer on your answer sheet.

26. Mark your answer on your answer sheet.

27. Mark your answer on your answer sheet.

28. Mark your answer on your answer sheet.

29. Mark your answer on your answer sheet.

30. Mark your answer on your answer sheet.

31. Mark your answer on your answer sheet.

Directions: You will hear some conversations between two or more people. You will be asked to answer three questions about what the speakers say in each conversation. Select the best response to each question and mark the letter (A), (B), (C), or (D) on your answer sheet. The conversations will not be printed in your test book and will be spoken only one time.

32. What did the woman forget to do?
    (A) Ask about menu choices
    (B) Reserve a table
    (C) Invite a colleague
    (D) Bring a parking permit

33. What does the man say about the restaurant?
    (A) There are more customers than usual.
    (B) There is an upstairs area for parties.
    (C) The business hours are different today.
    (D) The waitstaff is new.

34. What does the woman request?
    (A) A group discount
    (B) A special menu item
    (C) To be seated in a quiet area
    (D) To be seated near a window

35. What is the conversation mainly about?
    (A) A company training initiative
    (B) A factory relocation plan
    (C) A business collaboration
    (D) An upcoming press conference

36. What does the man emphasize about some products?
    (A) They have a low price point.
    (B) They can easily be customized.
    (C) They are designed to be durable.
    (D) They are made of recycled materials.

37. Why has Vedika joined the meeting?
    (A) To discuss sales results
    (B) To take some photographs
    (C) To conduct an interview
    (D) To go over customer feedback

38. What event are the speakers discussing?
    (A) An annual sales promotion
    (B) A company picnic
    (C) An office health fair
    (D) A charity bike race

39. What does the man suggest doing this year?
    (A) Hiring a caterer
    (B) Donating a prize
    (C) Changing a location
    (D) Updating a logo

40. What concern does the woman express?
    (A) A proposal may be too costly.
    (B) An employee needs further training.
    (C) A guest speaker is not available.
    (D) A shipment has been delayed.

41. Who is the man?
    (A) A security guard
    (B) A photographer
    (C) An engineer
    (D) A safety inspector

42. What product does the company manufacture?
    (A) Drones
    (B) Sound systems
    (C) Car engines
    (D) Vacuum cleaners

43. What will the woman most likely do next?
    (A) Report a lost badge
    (B) Tour a facility
    (C) Work on an assigned task
    (D) Fill out some paperwork

TEST 10

GO ON TO THE NEXT PAGE

44. What was the man hoping to do this weekend?

(A) Go on a camping trip
(B) Perform in a local band
(C) Attend a sports competition
(D) Volunteer at a community center

45. Why does the man need to cancel his plans?

(A) A client has made a request.
(B) An event has been postponed.
(C) A coworker is unavailable.
(D) A flight was canceled.

46. What does the woman offer to do?

(A) Change a reservation
(B) Check some products
(C) Speak to the man's supervisor
(D) Give the man a ride

---

47. What was the man asked to do in preparation for a conference?

(A) Choose a caterer
(B) Book the conference rooms
(C) Find a keynote speaker
(D) Make travel arrangements

48. Who is the conference intended for?

(A) Baseball coaches
(B) Medical doctors
(C) Accountants
(D) Publishers

49. What does the woman want to hand out to conference attendees?

(A) Books
(B) Tote bags
(C) Tickets to a sports event
(D) Copies of a speech

---

50. Who is the woman?

(A) A truck driver
(B) A plumber
(C) A furniture maker
(D) A mechanic

51. What does the man highlight about a work space?

(A) It has a loading dock.
(B) It is close to the city center.
(C) It has an assigned parking space.
(D) It has fast Internet service.

52. What does the man offer to do for the woman?

(A) Print out a contract
(B) Activate a utility
(C) Replace some lights
(D) Apply a discount

---

53. What are the speakers preparing for?

(A) A seminar
(B) A trade show
(C) A client meeting
(D) A book launch

54. What does the man imply when he says, "The workbook's already been printed"?

(A) He is not sure enough copies were ordered.
(B) He is expecting a delivery.
(C) A change cannot be made.
(D) A task was completed on schedule.

55. What does the man suggest?

(A) Contacting a presenter
(B) Using a catering service
(C) Adding a page to a book
(D) Revising an invitation

---

56. Who most likely is the woman?

(A) A career counselor
(B) A sales representative
(C) A factory supervisor
(D) A computer programmer

57. Why does the woman say, "we've had a lot of requests for that lately"?

(A) To express doubt about a possibility
(B) To request assistance with a task
(C) To explain a delay
(D) To compliment a colleague

58. What does the woman say she will do?

(A) Attend a meeting
(B) Check a schedule
(C) Take inventory
(D) Hire more employees

59. What news does the woman share?

(A) A colleague will be late to work.
(B) An item cannot be found.
(C) A form has a mistake in it.
(D) An order has been canceled.

60. Who are the men?

(A) Auto mechanics
(B) Factory workers
(C) Boat captains
(D) Tour guides

61. Why is Rajeev nervous?

(A) He made a mistake on his paperwork.
(B) He recently asked for a salary increase.
(C) He cannot reach someone by mobile phone.
(D) He has not completed his training yet.

Lane 1	Lane 2	Lane 3	Lane 4
Inner Shoulder	Passing Lane	Travel Lane	Outer Shoulder

62. Where has the woman just come from?

(A) A manager's office
(B) A police station
(C) A rental facility
(D) An equipment storage area

63. Look at the graphic. Which lane will stay open today?

(A) Lane 1
(B) Lane 2
(C) Lane 3
(D) Lane 4

64. What does the woman say she will ask for?

(A) A pay raise
(B) Extra supplies
(C) More personnel
(D) A safety barricade

GO ON TO THE NEXT PAGE

Oliver's Orchard: Picking Dates

Strawberries: May

Black Cherries: June, July

Blueberries: August

Green Apples: September, October

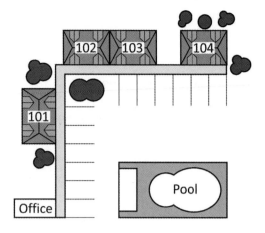

65. What does the woman suggest about an event location?

(A) It should be outdoors.
(B) It should be inexpensive.
(C) It should be local.
(D) It should offer lunch.

66. Look at the graphic. Which fruit will be picked during the event?

(A) Strawberries
(B) Black cherries
(C) Blueberries
(D) Green apples

67. What does the woman say she will do?

(A) Contact a business
(B) Draft an invitation
(C) Recruit some volunteers
(D) Prepare a budget

68. Who most likely is the woman?

(A) A landscape worker
(B) A taxi driver
(C) An apartment manager
(D) An interior decorator

69. Look at the graphic. Which location is the woman referring to?

(A) 101
(B) 102
(C) 103
(D) 104

70. What might the man pay extra for?

(A) A pool membership
(B) A reserved parking space
(C) Monthly maintenance
(D) Laundry facilities

PART 4

Directions: You will hear some talks given by a single speaker. You will be asked to answer three questions about what the speaker says in each talk. Select the best response to each question and mark the letter (A), (B), (C), or (D) on your answer sheet. The talks will not be printed in your test book and will be spoken only one time.

71. What is the purpose of a meeting?

(A) To prepare staff for a special event
(B) To review some closing procedures
(C) To introduce some staff members
(D) To resolve an issue with inventory

72. What type of business do the listeners most likely work for?

(A) A restaurant
(B) A library
(C) An appliance store
(D) A manufacturing facility

73. What does the speaker say he will do?

(A) Sign a contract
(B) Mail an invoice
(C) Edit a document
(D) Change a schedule

74. What topic did the listener write an article about?

(A) Forest conservation
(B) Travel recommendations
(C) Bird-watching
(D) Social media usage

75. What does the speaker like about the article?

(A) The descriptions
(B) The photographs
(C) The organization
(D) The use of statistics

76. Who does the speaker want the listener to interview?

(A) Restaurant chefs
(B) Park rangers
(C) Biologists
(D) Government officials

77. What does the speaker imply when she says, "we have a lot of speakers on the schedule"?

(A) The listeners should check the schedule.
(B) An advertisement was popular.
(C) An event will begin right away.
(D) More refreshments will be needed.

78. What industry does Dr. Adachi most likely work in?

(A) Filmmaking
(B) Interior design
(C) Construction
(D) Computer science

79. What does the speaker encourage the listeners to do?

(A) Complete a survey
(B) Ask questions
(C) Introduce themselves
(D) Work in small groups

80. What type of event is most likely taking place?

(A) A trade show
(B) A museum exhibit
(C) A food festival
(D) A gardening workshop

81. What are exhibitors asked to do?

(A) Wear identification badges
(B) Distribute samples
(C) Obtain parking passes
(D) Arrive at a location early

82. What does the speaker say attendees can do with their tickets?

(A) Receive a discount
(B) Enter a contest
(C) Access a special area
(D) Purchase refreshments

GO ON TO THE NEXT PAGE

83. What industry does the speaker most likely work in?

(A) Hospitality
(B) Finance
(C) Advertising
(D) Technology

84. What does the speaker mean when she says, "this is your first account"?

(A) She is impressed by some work.
(B) She is available to answer questions.
(C) A mistake is understandable.
(D) A process will take a long time.

85. What does the speaker ask the listener to send?

(A) A timeline
(B) An address
(C) Some sales figures
(D) Some meeting notes

86. Where do the listeners most likely work?

(A) At a public park
(B) At a landscaping company
(C) At a farm
(D) At a supermarket

87. What is the speaker mainly discussing?

(A) Purchasing some tools
(B) Training cleaning staff
(C) Repairing some equipment
(D) Arranging transportation

88. What solution does the speaker suggest?

(A) Contacting a manufacturer
(B) Decreasing a budget
(C) Renting some tents
(D) Extending hours of operation

89. Who is Johann Weber?

(A) A musician
(B) A librarian
(C) A painter
(D) A journalist

90. What will take place momentarily?

(A) A director will give a talk.
(B) A facility tour will begin.
(C) A group photo will be taken.
(D) A meal will be served.

91. According to the speaker, what can the listeners do at the information desk?

(A) Pick up a newsletter
(B) Sign up for a membership
(C) Enter a contest
(D) Register for a workshop

92. Where does the speaker most likely work?

(A) At a dental office
(B) At a commercial bank
(C) At an equipment rental company
(D) At an employment agency

93. What does the speaker imply when she says, "we haven't looked at other suppliers recently"?

(A) She is unfamiliar with a task.
(B) She is asking for volunteers.
(C) More affordable options may be available.
(D) Some information needs to be corrected.

94. What will most likely be discussed next?

(A) A relocation plan
(B) A staff-recruitment drive
(C) Some changes to a work policy
(D) Some marketing ideas

Backpack Features

	Laptop Sleeve	Water Bottle Pocket	Padded Straps
The Outsider		✓	✓
Modern Traveler			✓
Road Bound	✓	✓	
Elite Pro	✓		✓

Hours of Operation

Monday–Wednesday: 9:30 A.M.–7:00 P.M.

Thursday: 9:30 A.M.–9:00 P.M.

Friday: 9:30 A.M.–9:00 P.M.

Saturday: 10:00 A.M.–5:00 P.M.

Sunday: Closed

---

95. Why does the speaker want to purchase backpacks?

    (A) To make a donation to a local school
    (B) To give to clients as gifts
    (C) To help employees carry materials at conferences
    (D) To advertise a company logo

96. Look at the graphic. Which backpack fits the speaker's needs?

    (A) The Outsider
    (B) Modern Traveler
    (C) Road Bound
    (D) Elite Pro

97. What does the speaker ask about?

    (A) Photographs
    (B) Expedited shipping
    (C) A return policy
    (D) A discount

98. What type of business does the speaker run?

    (A) A hair salon
    (B) A bookstore
    (C) A grocery store
    (D) An appliance store

99. According to the speaker, what did the business receive?

    (A) A loan
    (B) An award
    (C) Some sample products
    (D) Good customer reviews

100. Look at the graphic. Which day will the business hours change?

    (A) Thursday
    (B) Friday
    (C) Saturday
    (D) Sunday

This is the end of the Listening test.

TEST 10

토익 정기시험 기출문제집 4 1000

ANSWERS

기출 TEST 1

동영상 강의

1 (A)	2 (B)	3 (B)	4 (D)	5 (C)
6 (C)	7 (B)	8 (C)	9 (C)	10 (A)
11 (C)	12 (C)	13 (C)	14 (B)	15 (A)
16 (A)	17 (A)	18 (C)	19 (B)	20 (C)
21 (A)	22 (B)	23 (C)	24 (A)	25 (C)
26 (A)	27 (B)	28 (A)	29 (C)	30 (C)
31 (B)	32 (D)	33 (B)	34 (B)	35 (A)
36 (C)	37 (B)	38 (A)	39 (C)	40 (D)
41 (C)	42 (D)	43 (A)	44 (C)	45 (D)
46 (B)	47 (B)	48 (C)	49 (A)	50 (C)
51 (D)	52 (A)	53 (A)	54 (B)	55 (C)
56 (C)	57 (A)	58 (D)	59 (B)	60 (A)
61 (D)	62 (C)	63 (C)	64 (A)	65 (D)
66 (C)	67 (B)	68 (B)	69 (D)	70 (A)
71 (D)	72 (A)	73 (C)	74 (C)	75 (B)
76 (C)	77 (B)	78 (A)	79 (C)	80 (A)
81 (B)	82 (C)	83 (A)	84 (B)	85 (C)
86 (D)	87 (A)	88 (C)	89 (A)	90 (B)
91 (C)	92 (A)	93 (B)	94 (D)	95 (B)
96 (A)	97 (D)	98 (C)	99 (A)	100 (D)

기출 TEST 2

동영상 강의

1 (A)	2 (B)	3 (C)	4 (D)	5 (C)
6 (D)	7 (A)	8 (A)	9 (B)	10 (B)
11 (C)	12 (C)	13 (B)	14 (A)	15 (B)
16 (B)	17 (A)	18 (C)	19 (B)	20 (C)
21 (A)	22 (A)	23 (B)	24 (A)	25 (C)
26 (C)	27 (B)	28 (A)	29 (C)	30 (A)
31 (A)	32 (B)	33 (D)	34 (C)	35 (B)
36 (A)	37 (C)	38 (A)	39 (D)	40 (C)
41 (A)	42 (D)	43 (D)	44 (C)	45 (B)
46 (D)	47 (B)	48 (C)	49 (A)	50 (A)
51 (D)	52 (A)	53 (C)	54 (C)	55 (A)
56 (C)	57 (B)	58 (B)	59 (B)	60 (C)
61 (A)	62 (B)	63 (C)	64 (B)	65 (B)
66 (C)	67 (A)	68 (A)	69 (B)	70 (A)
71 (D)	72 (C)	73 (A)	74 (D)	75 (B)
76 (D)	77 (B)	78 (A)	79 (B)	80 (B)
81 (C)	82 (D)	83 (B)	84 (A)	85 (A)
86 (B)	87 (B)	88 (B)	89 (B)	90 (B)
91 (A)	92 (B)	93 (C)	94 (C)	95 (A)
96 (B)	97 (B)	98 (C)	99 (A)	100 (B)

기출 TEST 3

동영상 강의

1 (D)	2 (C)	3 (D)	4 (B)	5 (B)
6 (D)	7 (A)	8 (A)	9 (C)	10 (B)
11 (B)	12 (A)	13 (C)	14 (B)	15 (A)
16 (A)	17 (B)	18 (B)	19 (A)	20 (C)
21 (C)	22 (A)	23 (C)	24 (A)	25 (B)
26 (C)	27 (B)	28 (C)	29 (C)	30 (B)
31 (C)	32 (C)	33 (B)	34 (D)	35 (B)
36 (A)	37 (D)	38 (D)	39 (B)	40 (D)
41 (C)	42 (B)	43 (B)	44 (D)	45 (C)
46 (D)	47 (C)	48 (A)	49 (D)	50 (D)
51 (C)	52 (A)	53 (B)	54 (D)	55 (D)
56 (D)	57 (B)	58 (A)	59 (C)	60 (D)
61 (A)	62 (B)	63 (C)	64 (C)	65 (B)
66 (C)	67 (A)	68 (C)	69 (B)	70 (C)
71 (C)	72 (C)	73 (A)	74 (A)	75 (C)
76 (B)	77 (C)	78 (C)	79 (A)	80 (D)
81 (B)	82 (C)	83 (C)	84 (B)	85 (D)
86 (C)	87 (A)	88 (A)	89 (D)	90 (C)
91 (B)	92 (D)	93 (C)	94 (A)	95 (A)
96 (A)	97 (C)	98 (B)	99 (C)	100 (D)

기출 TEST 4

동영상 강의

1 (C)	2 (D)	3 (A)	4 (B)	5 (C)
6 (D)	7 (A)	8 (B)	9 (B)	10 (A)
11 (C)	12 (A)	13 (C)	14 (C)	15 (A)
16 (C)	17 (B)	18 (A)	19 (C)	20 (C)
21 (A)	22 (A)	23 (C)	24 (C)	25 (C)
26 (B)	27 (C)	28 (A)	29 (C)	30 (B)
31 (B)	32 (A)	33 (C)	34 (B)	35 (B)
36 (A)	37 (D)	38 (C)	39 (B)	40 (C)
41 (B)	42 (C)	43 (B)	44 (B)	45 (C)
46 (A)	47 (C)	48 (D)	49 (A)	50 (C)
51 (A)	52 (C)	53 (C)	54 (A)	55 (B)
56 (A)	57 (B)	58 (D)	59 (B)	60 (A)
61 (B)	62 (B)	63 (A)	64 (C)	65 (D)
66 (A)	67 (A)	68 (C)	69 (B)	70 (B)
71 (C)	72 (A)	73 (B)	74 (C)	75 (A)
76 (B)	77 (B)	78 (A)	79 (D)	80 (A)
81 (D)	82 (B)	83 (C)	84 (D)	85 (D)
86 (C)	87 (B)	88 (B)	89 (D)	90 (C)
91 (B)	92 (D)	93 (D)	94 (D)	95 (C)
96 (D)	97 (D)	98 (D)	99 (C)	100 (C)

기출 TEST 5 동영상 강의

1 (D)	2 (A)	3 (C)	4 (D)	5 (A)
6 (B)	7 (A)	8 (C)	9 (C)	10 (B)
11 (B)	12 (A)	13 (B)	14 (C)	15 (B)
16 (A)	17 (B)	18 (A)	19 (B)	20 (C)
21 (B)	22 (A)	23 (B)	24 (C)	25 (C)
26 (B)	27 (C)	28 (C)	29 (A)	30 (A)
31 (A)	32 (C)	33 (A)	34 (C)	35 (C)
36 (B)	37 (A)	38 (B)	39 (D)	40 (A)
41 (A)	42 (C)	43 (B)	44 (B)	45 (D)
46 (B)	47 (D)	48 (A)	49 (B)	50 (A)
51 (D)	52 (C)	53 (D)	54 (B)	55 (C)
56 (B)	57 (C)	58 (D)	59 (C)	60 (A)
61 (B)	62 (B)	63 (A)	64 (C)	65 (B)
66 (C)	67 (B)	68 (D)	69 (B)	70 (B)
71 (A)	72 (C)	73 (D)	74 (B)	75 (D)
76 (B)	77 (B)	78 (D)	79 (A)	80 (B)
81 (C)	82 (D)	83 (D)	84 (B)	85 (C)
86 (D)	87 (B)	88 (A)	89 (D)	90 (B)
91 (C)	92 (C)	93 (B)	94 (B)	95 (C)
96 (D)	97 (D)	98 (A)	99 (C)	100 (D)

기출 TEST 6 동영상 강의

1 (B)	2 (A)	3 (D)	4 (B)	5 (C)
6 (A)	7 (A)	8 (A)	9 (A)	10 (C)
11 (B)	12 (C)	13 (A)	14 (C)	15 (A)
16 (B)	17 (B)	18 (B)	19 (B)	20 (C)
21 (A)	22 (A)	23 (C)	24 (A)	25 (C)
26 (B)	27 (C)	28 (A)	29 (A)	30 (A)
31 (A)	32 (A)	33 (B)	34 (B)	35 (B)
36 (D)	37 (C)	38 (B)	39 (A)	40 (D)
41 (B)	42 (A)	43 (C)	44 (C)	45 (C)
46 (A)	47 (B)	48 (B)	49 (D)	50 (B)
51 (A)	52 (C)	53 (C)	54 (A)	55 (C)
56 (C)	57 (D)	58 (B)	59 (C)	60 (A)
61 (D)	62 (A)	63 (D)	64 (B)	65 (A)
66 (D)	67 (C)	68 (C)	69 (B)	70 (B)
71 (A)	72 (D)	73 (C)	74 (C)	75 (D)
76 (A)	77 (B)	78 (A)	79 (D)	80 (C)
81 (D)	82 (A)	83 (B)	84 (D)	85 (B)
86 (B)	87 (D)	88 (A)	89 (A)	90 (B)
91 (C)	92 (B)	93 (A)	94 (C)	95 (D)
96 (C)	97 (A)	98 (C)	99 (B)	100 (D)

기출 TEST 7 동영상 강의

1 (D)	2 (D)	3 (A)	4 (B)	5 (C)
6 (C)	7 (A)	8 (C)	9 (B)	10 (C)
11 (A)	12 (A)	13 (C)	14 (B)	15 (C)
16 (C)	17 (A)	18 (A)	19 (A)	20 (B)
21 (A)	22 (A)	23 (B)	24 (B)	25 (C)
26 (A)	27 (A)	28 (B)	29 (B)	30 (A)
31 (A)	32 (C)	33 (D)	34 (C)	35 (B)
36 (A)	37 (C)	38 (B)	39 (C)	40 (D)
41 (B)	42 (C)	43 (D)	44 (A)	45 (B)
46 (B)	47 (C)	48 (D)	49 (A)	50 (A)
51 (D)	52 (C)	53 (B)	54 (C)	55 (C)
56 (D)	57 (C)	58 (A)	59 (A)	60 (B)
61 (C)	62 (C)	63 (C)	64 (B)	65 (D)
66 (C)	67 (C)	68 (C)	69 (D)	70 (C)
71 (D)	72 (C)	73 (D)	74 (C)	75 (D)
76 (D)	77 (B)	78 (B)	79 (B)	80 (C)
81 (A)	82 (D)	83 (C)	84 (D)	85 (B)
86 (D)	87 (B)	88 (C)	89 (A)	90 (A)
91 (D)	92 (C)	93 (A)	94 (D)	95 (D)
96 (B)	97 (C)	98 (A)	99 (D)	100 (B)

기출 TEST 8 동영상 강의

1 (D)	2 (B)	3 (D)	4 (C)	5 (B)
6 (A)	7 (B)	8 (A)	9 (B)	10 (B)
11 (C)	12 (B)	13 (B)	14 (B)	15 (A)
16 (C)	17 (A)	18 (B)	19 (C)	20 (A)
21 (B)	22 (C)	23 (B)	24 (B)	25 (A)
26 (A)	27 (C)	28 (A)	29 (C)	30 (C)
31 (B)	32 (A)	33 (C)	34 (B)	35 (B)
36 (A)	37 (D)	38 (B)	39 (C)	40 (A)
41 (B)	42 (C)	43 (B)	44 (D)	45 (A)
46 (A)	47 (B)	48 (C)	49 (D)	50 (D)
51 (A)	52 (B)	53 (B)	54 (A)	55 (D)
56 (C)	57 (A)	58 (D)	59 (D)	60 (B)
61 (A)	62 (B)	63 (A)	64 (D)	65 (B)
66 (C)	67 (B)	68 (A)	69 (D)	70 (D)
71 (B)	72 (A)	73 (C)	74 (A)	75 (B)
76 (B)	77 (C)	78 (A)	79 (D)	80 (D)
81 (B)	82 (A)	83 (B)	84 (C)	85 (D)
86 (C)	87 (B)	88 (C)	89 (C)	90 (A)
91 (B)	92 (B)	93 (D)	94 (A)	95 (A)
96 (C)	97 (B)	98 (B)	99 (D)	100 (C)

기출 TEST 9

동영상 강의

1 (C)	2 (D)	3 (C)	4 (B)	5 (A)
6 (C)	7 (C)	8 (A)	9 (B)	10 (A)
11 (A)	12 (C)	13 (A)	14 (A)	15 (B)
16 (B)	17 (A)	18 (C)	19 (B)	20 (A)
21 (C)	22 (B)	23 (A)	24 (A)	25 (C)
26 (B)	27 (A)	28 (A)	29 (A)	30 (C)
31 (C)	32 (B)	33 (A)	34 (D)	35 (D)
36 (C)	37 (B)	38 (C)	39 (B)	40 (A)
41 (C)	42 (C)	43 (A)	44 (D)	45 (A)
46 (C)	47 (B)	48 (A)	49 (D)	50 (C)
51 (B)	52 (A)	53 (C)	54 (B)	55 (C)
56 (A)	57 (C)	58 (C)	59 (C)	60 (D)
61 (A)	62 (A)	63 (D)	64 (D)	65 (C)
66 (A)	67 (B)	68 (D)	69 (C)	70 (D)
71 (B)	72 (A)	73 (D)	74 (C)	75 (B)
76 (A)	77 (B)	78 (C)	79 (A)	80 (D)
81 (A)	82 (B)	83 (A)	84 (A)	85 (C)
86 (A)	87 (C)	88 (B)	89 (C)	90 (C)
91 (A)	92 (D)	93 (B)	94 (D)	95 (C)
96 (A)	97 (D)	98 (D)	99 (C)	100 (D)

기출 TEST 10

동영상 강의

1 (D)	2 (B)	3 (C)	4 (A)	5 (C)
6 (A)	7 (A)	8 (B)	9 (C)	10 (A)
11 (C)	12 (C)	13 (A)	14 (C)	15 (C)
16 (A)	17 (A)	18 (A)	19 (B)	20 (B)
21 (A)	22 (C)	23 (B)	24 (C)	25 (C)
26 (A)	27 (B)	28 (C)	29 (A)	30 (B)
31 (C)	32 (B)	33 (C)	34 (C)	35 (C)
36 (D)	37 (B)	38 (D)	39 (B)	40 (A)
41 (C)	42 (D)	43 (C)	44 (C)	45 (A)
46 (B)	47 (C)	48 (B)	49 (A)	50 (C)
51 (A)	52 (B)	53 (A)	54 (C)	55 (C)
56 (C)	57 (A)	58 (B)	59 (A)	60 (D)
61 (D)	62 (A)	63 (B)	64 (C)	65 (A)
66 (B)	67 (A)	68 (C)	69 (D)	70 (B)
71 (B)	72 (A)	73 (C)	74 (A)	75 (A)
76 (D)	77 (C)	78 (D)	79 (B)	80 (A)
81 (D)	82 (B)	83 (C)	84 (A)	85 (A)
86 (C)	87 (C)	88 (A)	89 (C)	90 (A)
91 (B)	92 (A)	93 (C)	94 (D)	95 (B)
96 (A)	97 (D)	98 (C)	99 (A)	100 (D)

ANSWER SHEET

토익® 정기시험 기출문제집

수험번호						

응시일자 : 20 년 월 일

성명	한 글	
	한 자	
	영 자	

Test 01 (Part 1~4)

1	ⓐ ⓑ ⓒ ⓓ	21	ⓐ ⓑ ⓒ	41	ⓐ ⓑ ⓒ ⓓ	61	ⓐ ⓑ ⓒ ⓓ	81	ⓐ ⓑ ⓒ ⓓ
2	ⓐ ⓑ ⓒ ⓓ	22	ⓐ ⓑ ⓒ	42	ⓐ ⓑ ⓒ ⓓ	62	ⓐ ⓑ ⓒ ⓓ	82	ⓐ ⓑ ⓒ ⓓ
3	ⓐ ⓑ ⓒ ⓓ	23	ⓐ ⓑ ⓒ	43	ⓐ ⓑ ⓒ ⓓ	63	ⓐ ⓑ ⓒ ⓓ	83	ⓐ ⓑ ⓒ ⓓ
4	ⓐ ⓑ ⓒ ⓓ	24	ⓐ ⓑ ⓒ	44	ⓐ ⓑ ⓒ ⓓ	64	ⓐ ⓑ ⓒ ⓓ	84	ⓐ ⓑ ⓒ ⓓ
5	ⓐ ⓑ ⓒ ⓓ	25	ⓐ ⓑ ⓒ	45	ⓐ ⓑ ⓒ ⓓ	65	ⓐ ⓑ ⓒ ⓓ	85	ⓐ ⓑ ⓒ ⓓ
6	ⓐ ⓑ ⓒ ⓓ	26	ⓐ ⓑ ⓒ	46	ⓐ ⓑ ⓒ ⓓ	66	ⓐ ⓑ ⓒ ⓓ	86	ⓐ ⓑ ⓒ ⓓ
7	ⓐ ⓑ ⓒ	27	ⓐ ⓑ ⓒ	47	ⓐ ⓑ ⓒ ⓓ	67	ⓐ ⓑ ⓒ ⓓ	87	ⓐ ⓑ ⓒ ⓓ
8	ⓐ ⓑ ⓒ	28	ⓐ ⓑ ⓒ	48	ⓐ ⓑ ⓒ ⓓ	68	ⓐ ⓑ ⓒ ⓓ	88	ⓐ ⓑ ⓒ ⓓ
9	ⓐ ⓑ ⓒ	29	ⓐ ⓑ ⓒ	49	ⓐ ⓑ ⓒ ⓓ	69	ⓐ ⓑ ⓒ ⓓ	89	ⓐ ⓑ ⓒ ⓓ
10	ⓐ ⓑ ⓒ	30	ⓐ ⓑ ⓒ	50	ⓐ ⓑ ⓒ ⓓ	70	ⓐ ⓑ ⓒ ⓓ	90	ⓐ ⓑ ⓒ ⓓ
11	ⓐ ⓑ ⓒ	31	ⓐ ⓑ ⓒ	51	ⓐ ⓑ ⓒ ⓓ	71	ⓐ ⓑ ⓒ ⓓ	91	ⓐ ⓑ ⓒ ⓓ
12	ⓐ ⓑ ⓒ	32	ⓐ ⓑ ⓒ ⓓ	52	ⓐ ⓑ ⓒ ⓓ	72	ⓐ ⓑ ⓒ ⓓ	92	ⓐ ⓑ ⓒ ⓓ
13	ⓐ ⓑ ⓒ	33	ⓐ ⓑ ⓒ ⓓ	53	ⓐ ⓑ ⓒ ⓓ	73	ⓐ ⓑ ⓒ ⓓ	93	ⓐ ⓑ ⓒ ⓓ
14	ⓐ ⓑ ⓒ	34	ⓐ ⓑ ⓒ ⓓ	54	ⓐ ⓑ ⓒ ⓓ	74	ⓐ ⓑ ⓒ ⓓ	94	ⓐ ⓑ ⓒ ⓓ
15	ⓐ ⓑ ⓒ	35	ⓐ ⓑ ⓒ ⓓ	55	ⓐ ⓑ ⓒ ⓓ	75	ⓐ ⓑ ⓒ ⓓ	95	ⓐ ⓑ ⓒ ⓓ
16	ⓐ ⓑ ⓒ	36	ⓐ ⓑ ⓒ ⓓ	56	ⓐ ⓑ ⓒ ⓓ	76	ⓐ ⓑ ⓒ ⓓ	96	ⓐ ⓑ ⓒ ⓓ
17	ⓐ ⓑ ⓒ	37	ⓐ ⓑ ⓒ ⓓ	57	ⓐ ⓑ ⓒ ⓓ	77	ⓐ ⓑ ⓒ ⓓ	97	ⓐ ⓑ ⓒ ⓓ
18	ⓐ ⓑ ⓒ	38	ⓐ ⓑ ⓒ ⓓ	58	ⓐ ⓑ ⓒ ⓓ	78	ⓐ ⓑ ⓒ ⓓ	98	ⓐ ⓑ ⓒ ⓓ
19	ⓐ ⓑ ⓒ	39	ⓐ ⓑ ⓒ ⓓ	59	ⓐ ⓑ ⓒ ⓓ	79	ⓐ ⓑ ⓒ ⓓ	99	ⓐ ⓑ ⓒ ⓓ
20	ⓐ ⓑ ⓒ	40	ⓐ ⓑ ⓒ ⓓ	60	ⓐ ⓑ ⓒ ⓓ	80	ⓐ ⓑ ⓒ ⓓ	100	ⓐ ⓑ ⓒ ⓓ

Test 02 (Part 1~4)

1	ⓐ ⓑ ⓒ ⓓ	21	ⓐ ⓑ ⓒ	41	ⓐ ⓑ ⓒ ⓓ	61	ⓐ ⓑ ⓒ ⓓ	81	ⓐ ⓑ ⓒ ⓓ
2	ⓐ ⓑ ⓒ ⓓ	22	ⓐ ⓑ ⓒ	42	ⓐ ⓑ ⓒ ⓓ	62	ⓐ ⓑ ⓒ ⓓ	82	ⓐ ⓑ ⓒ ⓓ
3	ⓐ ⓑ ⓒ ⓓ	23	ⓐ ⓑ ⓒ	43	ⓐ ⓑ ⓒ ⓓ	63	ⓐ ⓑ ⓒ ⓓ	83	ⓐ ⓑ ⓒ ⓓ
4	ⓐ ⓑ ⓒ ⓓ	24	ⓐ ⓑ ⓒ	44	ⓐ ⓑ ⓒ ⓓ	64	ⓐ ⓑ ⓒ ⓓ	84	ⓐ ⓑ ⓒ ⓓ
5	ⓐ ⓑ ⓒ ⓓ	25	ⓐ ⓑ ⓒ	45	ⓐ ⓑ ⓒ ⓓ	65	ⓐ ⓑ ⓒ ⓓ	85	ⓐ ⓑ ⓒ ⓓ
6	ⓐ ⓑ ⓒ ⓓ	26	ⓐ ⓑ ⓒ	46	ⓐ ⓑ ⓒ ⓓ	66	ⓐ ⓑ ⓒ ⓓ	86	ⓐ ⓑ ⓒ ⓓ
7	ⓐ ⓑ ⓒ	27	ⓐ ⓑ ⓒ	47	ⓐ ⓑ ⓒ ⓓ	67	ⓐ ⓑ ⓒ ⓓ	87	ⓐ ⓑ ⓒ ⓓ
8	ⓐ ⓑ ⓒ	28	ⓐ ⓑ ⓒ	48	ⓐ ⓑ ⓒ ⓓ	68	ⓐ ⓑ ⓒ ⓓ	88	ⓐ ⓑ ⓒ ⓓ
9	ⓐ ⓑ ⓒ	29	ⓐ ⓑ ⓒ	49	ⓐ ⓑ ⓒ ⓓ	69	ⓐ ⓑ ⓒ ⓓ	89	ⓐ ⓑ ⓒ ⓓ
10	ⓐ ⓑ ⓒ	30	ⓐ ⓑ ⓒ	50	ⓐ ⓑ ⓒ ⓓ	70	ⓐ ⓑ ⓒ ⓓ	90	ⓐ ⓑ ⓒ ⓓ
11	ⓐ ⓑ ⓒ	31	ⓐ ⓑ ⓒ	51	ⓐ ⓑ ⓒ ⓓ	71	ⓐ ⓑ ⓒ ⓓ	91	ⓐ ⓑ ⓒ ⓓ
12	ⓐ ⓑ ⓒ	32	ⓐ ⓑ ⓒ ⓓ	52	ⓐ ⓑ ⓒ ⓓ	72	ⓐ ⓑ ⓒ ⓓ	92	ⓐ ⓑ ⓒ ⓓ
13	ⓐ ⓑ ⓒ	33	ⓐ ⓑ ⓒ ⓓ	53	ⓐ ⓑ ⓒ ⓓ	73	ⓐ ⓑ ⓒ ⓓ	93	ⓐ ⓑ ⓒ ⓓ
14	ⓐ ⓑ ⓒ	34	ⓐ ⓑ ⓒ ⓓ	54	ⓐ ⓑ ⓒ ⓓ	74	ⓐ ⓑ ⓒ ⓓ	94	ⓐ ⓑ ⓒ ⓓ
15	ⓐ ⓑ ⓒ	35	ⓐ ⓑ ⓒ ⓓ	55	ⓐ ⓑ ⓒ ⓓ	75	ⓐ ⓑ ⓒ ⓓ	95	ⓐ ⓑ ⓒ ⓓ
16	ⓐ ⓑ ⓒ	36	ⓐ ⓑ ⓒ ⓓ	56	ⓐ ⓑ ⓒ ⓓ	76	ⓐ ⓑ ⓒ ⓓ	96	ⓐ ⓑ ⓒ ⓓ
17	ⓐ ⓑ ⓒ	37	ⓐ ⓑ ⓒ ⓓ	57	ⓐ ⓑ ⓒ ⓓ	77	ⓐ ⓑ ⓒ ⓓ	97	ⓐ ⓑ ⓒ ⓓ
18	ⓐ ⓑ ⓒ	38	ⓐ ⓑ ⓒ ⓓ	58	ⓐ ⓑ ⓒ ⓓ	78	ⓐ ⓑ ⓒ ⓓ	98	ⓐ ⓑ ⓒ ⓓ
19	ⓐ ⓑ ⓒ	39	ⓐ ⓑ ⓒ ⓓ	59	ⓐ ⓑ ⓒ ⓓ	79	ⓐ ⓑ ⓒ ⓓ	99	ⓐ ⓑ ⓒ ⓓ
20	ⓐ ⓑ ⓒ	40	ⓐ ⓑ ⓒ ⓓ	60	ⓐ ⓑ ⓒ ⓓ	80	ⓐ ⓑ ⓒ ⓓ	100	ⓐ ⓑ ⓒ ⓓ

ANSWER SHEET

토익 정기시험 기출문제집

수험번호

응시일자 : 20 년 월 일

한 글	성
한 자	명
영 자	

Test 03 (Part 1~4)

| 1 | 2 | 3 | 4 | 5 | 6 | 7 | 8 | 9 | 10 | 11 | 12 | 13 | 14 | 15 | 16 | 17 | 18 | 19 | 20 |

Test 04 (Part 1~4)

ANSWER SHEET

토익® 정기시험 기출문제집

수험번호

응시일자 : 20_____ 년_____ 월_____ 일

성명 | 한글 |
| 한자 |
| 영자 |

Test 05 (Part 1~4)

| 1 | 2 | 3 | 4 | ... 20 |
| 21 ... 40 |
| 41 ... 60 |
| 61 ... 80 |
| 81 ... 100 |

Test 06 (Part 1~4)

| 1 ... 20 |
| 21 ... 40 |
| 41 ... 60 |
| 61 ... 80 |
| 81 ... 100 |

ANSWER SHEET

토익® 정기시험 기출문제집

수험번호

응시일자 : 20 ____ 년 ____ 월 ____ 일

	성명
한글	
한자	
영자	

Test 07 (Part 1~4)

1–20	21–40	41–60	61–80	81–100
1	21	41	61	81
2	22	42	62	82
3	23	43	63	83
4	24	44	64	84
5	25	45	65	85
6	26	46	66	86
7	27	47	67	87
8	28	48	68	88
9	29	49	69	89
10	30	50	70	90
11	31	51	71	91
12	32	52	72	92
13	33	53	73	93
14	34	54	74	94
15	35	55	75	95
16	36	56	76	96
17	37	57	77	97
18	38	58	78	98
19	39	59	79	99
20	40	60	80	100

Test 08 (Part 1~4)

1–20	21–40	41–60	61–80	81–100
1	21	41	61	81
2	22	42	62	82
3	23	43	63	83
4	24	44	64	84
5	25	45	65	85
6	26	46	66	86
7	27	47	67	87
8	28	48	68	88
9	29	49	69	89
10	30	50	70	90
11	31	51	71	91
12	32	52	72	92
13	33	53	73	93
14	34	54	74	94
15	35	55	75	95
16	36	56	76	96
17	37	57	77	97
18	38	58	78	98
19	39	59	79	99
20	40	60	80	100

*toeic.

토익 정기시험 기출문제집 4
1000 LC

정답 및 해설

1 (A)	**2** (B)	**3** (B)	**4** (D)	**5** (C)
6 (C)	**7** (B)	**8** (C)	**9** (C)	**10** (A)
11 (C)	**12** (C)	**13** (C)	**14** (B)	**15** (A)
16 (A)	**17** (A)	**18** (C)	**19** (B)	**20** (C)
21 (A)	**22** (B)	**23** (C)	**24** (A)	**25** (C)
26 (A)	**27** (B)	**28** (A)	**29** (C)	**30** (C)
31 (B)	**32** (D)	**33** (B)	**34** (B)	**35** (A)
36 (C)	**37** (B)	**38** (A)	**39** (C)	**40** (D)
41 (C)	**42** (D)	**43** (A)	**44** (C)	**45** (D)
46 (B)	**47** (B)	**48** (C)	**49** (A)	**50** (C)
51 (D)	**52** (A)	**53** (A)	**54** (B)	**55** (C)
56 (C)	**57** (A)	**58** (D)	**59** (B)	**60** (A)
61 (D)	**62** (C)	**63** (C)	**64** (A)	**65** (D)
66 (C)	**67** (B)	**68** (B)	**69** (D)	**70** (A)
71 (D)	**72** (A)	**73** (C)	**74** (C)	**75** (B)
76 (C)	**77** (B)	**78** (A)	**79** (C)	**80** (A)
81 (B)	**82** (C)	**83** (A)	**84** (B)	**85** (C)
86 (D)	**87** (A)	**88** (C)	**89** (A)	**90** (B)
91 (C)	**92** (A)	**93** (B)	**94** (D)	**95** (B)
96 (A)	**97** (D)	**98** (C)	**99** (A)	**100** (D)

PART 1

1 M-Au

(A) She's eating in a picnic area.
(B) She's waiting in line at a food truck.
(C) She's wiping off a bench.
(D) She's throwing away a plate.

(A) 여자가 피크닉 구역에서 음식을 먹고 있다.
(B) 여자가 푸드 트럭에 줄을 서서 기다리고 있다.
(C) 여자가 벤치를 닦아내고 있다.
(D) 여자가 접시를 버리고 있다.

어휘 wait in line 줄을 서서 기다리다 wipe off 닦아내다 throw away 버리다

해설 1인 등장 사진 – 사람의 동작/상태 묘사
(A) 정답. 여자가 피크닉 구역에서 음식을 먹고 있는(is eating in a picnic area) 모습이므로 정답.
(B) 동사 오답. 여자가 푸드 트럭에 줄을 서서 기다리고 있는(is waiting in line at a food truck) 모습이 아니므로 오답.
(C) 동사 오답. 여자가 벤치를 닦아내고 있는(is wiping off a bench) 모습이 아니므로 오답.

(D) 동사 오답. 여자가 접시를 버리고 있는(is throwing away a plate) 모습이 아니므로 오답.

2 W-Br

(A) The man is brushing snow off the roof of a car.
(B) The man is standing in the snow beside a car.
(C) The man is shoveling snow from a walkway.
(D) The man is running through the snow.

(A) 남자가 차 지붕의 눈을 털어내고 있다.
(B) 남자가 자동차 옆 눈 속에 서 있다.
(C) 남자가 삽으로 보도의 눈을 치우고 있다.
(D) 남자가 눈 속을 달리고 있다.

어휘 brush ~ off ~을 털어내다 beside ~ 옆에 shovel 삽질하다, 삽으로 옮기다 walkway 보도, 통로

해설 1인 등장 사진 – 사람의 동작/상태 묘사
(A) 동사 오답. 남자가 차 지붕의 눈을 털어내고 있는(is brushing snow off the roof of a car) 모습이 아니므로 오답.
(B) 정답. 남자가 자동차 옆 눈 속에 서 있는(is standing in the snow beside a car) 모습이므로 정답.
(C) 동사 오답. 남자가 삽으로 눈을 치우고 있는(is shoveling snow) 모습이 아니므로 오답.
(D) 동사 오답. 남자가 눈 속을 달리고 있는(is running through the snow) 모습이 아니므로 오답.

3 M-Cn

(A) Some workers are hanging art in a gallery.
(B) Two of the people are having a conversation.
(C) One of the men is rearranging cushions on a sofa.
(D) One of the men is painting a picture.

(A) 인부들이 화랑에 그림을 걸고 있다.
(B) 사람들 중 두 명이 대화를 하고 있다.
(C) 남자들 중 한 명이 소파 위 쿠션들을 재배치하고 있다.
(D) 남자들 중 한 명이 그림을 그리고 있다.

어휘 gallery 화랑 have a conversation 대화하다 rearrange 재배치하다

해설 2인 이상 등장 사진 – 사람의 동작/상태 묘사

(A) 동사 오답. 화랑에 그림을 걸고 있는(are hanging art in a gallery) 인부들의 모습이 보이지 않으므로 오답.

(B) 정답. 왼쪽에 서 있는 두 사람이 대화를 하고 있는(are having a conversation) 모습이므로 정답.

(C) 사진에 없는 명사를 이용한 오답. 사진에 쿠션들(cushions)의 모습이 보이지 않으므로 오답.

(D) 동사 오답. 그림을 그리고 있는(is painting a picture) 남자의 모습이 보이지 않으므로 오답.

---

4 W-Am

▶ 동영상 강의

(A) Vehicles are entering a parking garage.
(B) Clothes hangers are scattered on the ground.
(C) Empty racks are lined up next to a building.
(D) Clothing is being displayed under a tent.

(A) 차들이 주차장으로 들어가고 있다.
(B) 옷걸이들이 땅에 흩어져 있다.
(C) 빈 옷걸이들이 건물 옆에 줄지어 있다.
(D) 천막 아래 의류가 진열되어 있다.

어휘 vehicle 차량 parking garage 주차장 be scattered 흩어지다 rack 선반

해설 사물/풍경 사진 – 사물 묘사

(A) 동사 오답. 차들(Vehicles)이 주차장으로 들어가고 있는(are entering a parking garage) 모습이 아니므로 오답.

(B) 동사 오답. 옷걸이들(Clothes hangers)이 땅에 흩어져 있는(are scattered on the ground) 모습이 아니므로 오답.

(C) 사진에 없는 명사를 이용한 오답. 옷걸이들이 비어 있지 않으며, 건물(a building)의 모습이 보이지 않으므로 오답.

(D) 정답. 의류(Clothing)가 천막 아래 진열되어 있는(is being displayed under a tent) 모습이므로 정답. be being displayed는 진열하고 있는 동작이 아니라 진열되어 있는 상태를 뜻한다. 사물/풍경 사진에서 정답으로 잘 등장하니 유의하자!

---

5 W-Br

(A) Potted plants have been suspended from a ceiling.
(B) Chairs have been stacked in front of an entryway.
(C) A computer station has been set up on a desk.
(D) A rug has been rolled up against a wall.

(A) 화분에 심은 식물들이 천장에 매달려 있다.
(B) 의자들이 입구 통로 앞에 쌓여 있다.
(C) 책상에 컴퓨터 자리가 마련되어 있다.
(D) 양탄자가 말려서 벽에 기대어 있다.

어휘 potted plant 화분에 심은 식물 be suspended from ~에 매달려 있다 stack 쌓다, 포개다 entryway 입구의 통로 set up 마련하다, 설치하다 roll up 말다

해설 사물/풍경 사진 – 사물 묘사

(A) 동사 오답. 화분에 심은 식물들(Potted plants)이 천장에 매달려 있는(have been suspended from a ceiling) 모습이 아니므로 오답.

(B) 동사 오답. 의자들(Chairs)이 입구 통로 앞에 쌓여 있는(have been stacked in front of an entryway) 모습이 아니므로 오답.

(C) 정답. 컴퓨터 자리(A computer station)가 책상 위에 마련되어 있는(has been set up on a desk) 모습이므로 정답.

(D) 동사 오답. 양탄자(A rug)가 말려서 벽에 기대어 있는(has been rolled up against a wall) 모습이 아니므로 오답.

---

6 M-Cn

(A) One of the men is sweeping a patio.
(B) One of the men is replacing some flooring.
(C) A door has been taken off its frame.
(D) A light fixture has been left on the ground.

(A) 남자들 중 한 명이 테라스를 쓸고 있다.
(B) 남자들 중 한 명이 바닥재를 교체하고 있다.
(C) 문이 문틀에서 떨어져 있다.
(D) 조명 기구가 바닥에 놓여 있다.

어휘 sweep 쓸다 replace 교체하다 flooring 바닥재 frame 틀 light fixture 조명 기구

해설 혼합 사진 – 사람/사물/풍경 혼합 묘사

(A) 사진에 없는 명사를 이용한 오답. 사진에 테라스(a patio)의 모습이 보이지 않으므로 오답.

(B) 동사 오답. 바닥재를 교체하고 있는(is replacing some flooring) 남자의 모습이 보이지 않으므로 오답.

(C) 정답. 문(A door)이 문틀에서 떨어져 있는(has been taken off its frame) 모습이므로 정답.

(D) 위치 오답. 조명 기구(A light fixture)가 바닥에 놓여 있는(has been left on the ground) 모습이 아니므로 오답.

PART 2

7

W-Br How old is this building?

M-Au (A) To ship some materials.
(B) About ten years old.
(C) Company offices, I think.

이 건물은 얼마나 오래됐나요?

(A) 자재를 수송하려고요.

(B) 10년 정도요.

(C) 회사 사무실인 것 같아요.

어휘 ship 수송하다, 운송하다   material 자재, 재료

해설 건물의 나이를 묻는 How 의문문

(A) 연상 단어 오답. 질문의 building에서 연상 가능한 some materials 를 이용한 오답.

(B) 정답. 건물의 나이를 묻는 질문에 10년 정도라고 구체적으로 응답하고 있으므로 정답.

(C) 연상 단어 오답. 질문의 building에서 연상 가능한 company offices를 이용한 오답.

8

W-Am Can you come to my jazz performance tonight?

M-Cn (A) I'm sorry I was late for the meeting.
(B) Mostly just local musicians.
(C) Sure, I'll be there!

오늘 밤 제 재즈 공연에 오실 수 있어요?

(A) 회의에 늦어서 죄송합니다.

(B) 대부분 지역 음악가예요.

(C) 물론이죠, 갈게요!

어휘 performance 공연   mostly 대부분   local 지역의, 현지의

해설 부탁/요청의 의문문

(A) 연상 단어 오답. 질문의 come to my jazz performance에서 연상 가능한 late를 이용한 오답.

(B) 연상 단어 오답. 질문의 jazz performance에서 연상 가능한 local musicians를 이용한 오답.

(C) 정답. 오늘 밤 재즈 공연에 와 달라는 요청에 물론이죠(Sure)라고 수락한 뒤, 가겠다며 긍정 답변과 일관된 내용을 덧붙이고 있으므로 정답.

9

W-Br Which apartment submitted a work order?

W-Am (A) It's what you did for a living.
(B) Submit your assignment here.
(C) It came from the tenants in B23.

어떤 아파트가 작업 지시서를 제출했죠?

(A) 그게 당신이 생계를 위해 한 일이군요.

(B) 과제를 여기에 제출하세요.

(C) B23 세입자들에게서 왔어요.

어휘 submit 제출하다   work order 작업 지시서   do for a living 생계를 위해 일하다   assignment 과제   tenant 세입자

해설 작업 지시서를 제출한 아파트를 묻는 Which 의문문

(A) 연상 단어 오답. 질문의 apartment에서 연상 가능한 living을 이용한 오답.

(B) 파생어 오답. 질문의 submitted와 파생어 관계인 submit을 이용한 오답.

(C) 정답. 작업 지시서를 제출한 아파트를 묻는 질문에 B23 세입자들이라고 구체적인 출처를 밝히고 있으므로 정답.

10

M-Cn Will you contact the vendor about changing our delivery date?

W-Br (A) Of course, I'll take care of it.
(B) An e-mail receipt.
(C) Could I get change for a dollar?

저희 배송일 변경에 관해 판매업체에 연락하실 건가요?

(A) 물론이죠, 제가 처리할게요.

(B) 이메일 영수증이요.

(C) 1달러를 잔돈으로 바꿀 수 있을까요?

어휘 vendor 판매업체   receipt 영수증   change 잔돈, 거스름돈

해설 판매업체에 연락할 건지 계획을 묻는 조동사(Will) 의문문

(A) 정답. 배송일 변경에 관해 판매업체에 연락할 건지 계획을 묻는 질문에 물론이죠(Of course)라고 대답한 뒤, 자신이 처리하겠다며 긍정 답변과 일관된 내용을 덧붙이고 있으므로 정답.

(B) 연상 단어 오답. 질문의 contact에서 연상 가능한 e-mail을 이용한 오답.

(C) 파생어 오답. 질문의 changing과 파생어 관계인 change를 이용한 오답.

11

M-Au Why was the maintenance worker here?

W-Am (A) No, he didn't.
(B) From three o'clock until four.
(C) Because a light needed to be fixed.

유지보수 인부가 왜 여기 왔었나요?

(A) 아니요, 그는 하지 않았어요.

(B) 3시부터 4시까지요.

(C) 조명을 수리해야 했어요.

어휘 maintenance 관리, 보수   fix 수리하다, 바로잡다

해설 유지보수 인부가 왔던 이유를 묻는 Why 의문문

(A) Yes/No 불가 오답. Why 의문문에는 Yes/No 응답이 불가능하므로 오답.

(B) 질문과 상관없는 오답. How long 의문문에 대한 응답이므로 오답.

(C) 정답. 유지보수 인부가 왔던 이유를 묻는 질문에 조명을 수리해야 했기 때문이라고 이유를 제시하고 있으므로 정답.

12

W-Am Did management make a hiring decision yet?

M-Cn (A) Put it on the highest shelf.
(B) The personnel department.
(C) Yes, they chose Jacob Borgman.

경영진이 이제 채용 결정을 내렸나요?
(A) 그것을 맨 위 선반에 두세요.
(B) 인사부요.
(C) 네, 제이콥 보그먼을 선택했어요.

어휘 management 경영진, 운영진   make a decision 결정하다
hiring 채용   personnel (조직의) 인원, 인사과   department
부서

해설 경영진의 채용 결정 여부를 묻는 조동사(Did) 의문문
(A) 유사 발음 오답. 질문의 hiring과 부분적으로 발음이 유사한 highest
를 이용한 오답.
(B) 연상 단어 오답. 질문의 a hiring decision에서 연상 가능한 the
personnel department를 이용한 오답.
(C) 정답. 경영진이 채용 결정을 내렸는지 여부를 묻는 질문에 네(Yes)라
고 대답한 뒤, 제이콥 보그먼을 선택했다며 긍정 답변과 일관된 내용
을 덧붙였으므로 정답.

13

M-Cn Do you want to eat here in our cafeteria or go
out?

W-Am (A) He went there yesterday.
(B) Well, maybe a sandwich.
(C) Let's eat here.

여기 구내식당에서 먹고 싶으세요, 아니면 나가서 먹고 싶으세
요?
(A) 그는 어제 거기 갔어요.
(B) 음, 아마 샌드위치요.
(C) 여기서 먹죠.

어휘 cafeteria 구내식당

해설 식사 장소를 묻는 선택 의문문
(A) 연상 단어 오답. 질문의 here에서 연상 가능한 there를 이용한 오답.
(B) 연상 단어 오답. 질문의 cafeteria에서 연상 가능한 a sandwich를
이용한 오답.
(C) 정답. 여기와 밖 중 원하는 식사 장소를 묻는 질문에 여기서 먹자며 둘
중 하나를 선택해 응답하고 있으므로 정답.

14

M-Au Didn't you e-mail the employment contract to
Mr. Patel yesterday?

W-Br (A) Yes, I would agree.
(B) No, I'll send it now.
(C) Check the employee manual.

어제 파텔 씨에게 이메일로 고용 계약서를 보내지 않으셨어요?
(A) 네, 동의해요.
(B) 아니요, 지금 보낼 거예요.
(C) 직원 수칙을 확인하세요.

어휘 employment 고용   contract 계약, 계약서   agree 동의하다
employee 직원

해설 고용 계약서의 이메일 송부 여부를 확인하는 부정 의문문
(A) 질문과 상관없는 오답.
(B) 정답. 어제 파텔 씨에게 이메일로 고용 계약서를 보냈는지 여부를 묻
는 질문에 아니요(No)라고 대답한 뒤, 지금 보낼 것이라며 부정 답변
과 일관된 내용을 덧붙이고 있으므로 정답.
(C) 파생어 오답. 질문의 employment와 파생어 관계인 employee를
이용한 오답.

15

▶ 동영상 강의

M-Au Our division's picnic is this Saturday, right?

M-Cn (A) There's a lot of rain in the forecast.
(B) Sure, I like salad.
(C) At the end of this corridor.

우리 부서 야유회가 이번 주 토요일이죠, 그렇죠?
(A) 예보에서는 많은 비가 온대요.
(B) 물론이죠, 저는 샐러드가 좋아요.
(C) 이 복도 끝에요.

어휘 division 부서   forecast 예보   corridor 복도

해설 부서 야유회가 토요일인지 확인하는 부가 의문문
(A) 정답. 부서 야유회가 이번 주 토요일인지를 확인하는 질문에 예보에는
많은 비가 온다며 토요일에 열리지만 날씨 때문에 우려된다는 것을 우
회적으로 나타내고 있으므로 정답.
(B) 질문의 picnic에서 연상 가능한 salad를 이용한 오답.
(C) 연상 단어 오답. 질문의 division에서 연상 가능한 At the end of
this corridor를 이용한 오답.

16

W-Br Would you like coffee or tea?

W-Am (A) Just water, please.
(B) For a few dollars more.
(C) A fifteen-minute break.

커피 드릴까요, 차를 드릴까요?
(A) 그냥 물 주세요.
(B) 몇 달러 더 내면요.
(C) 15분 휴식 시간이요.

어휘 break 휴식 시간

해설 선호하는 음료를 묻는 선택 의문문
(A) 정답. 커피와 차 중 원하는 음료를 묻는 질문에 물을 달라고 두 선택지
를 제외한 제3의 답변을 제시하고 있는 정답.
(B) 질문과 상관없는 오답.
(C) 연상 단어 오답. 질문의 coffee와 tea에서 연상 가능한 break를 이용
한 오답.

17

W-Am We achieved our sales targets this month.

M-Cn (A) That's excellent news!
(B) A few times a day.
(C) To the end of April.

우리는 이번 달 판매 목표를 달성했어요.
(A) 좋은 소식이네요!
(B) 하루에 몇 번이요.
(C) 4월 말까지요.

어휘 achieve 달성하다, 성취하다   sales target 판매 목표

해설 정보 전달의 평서문
(A) 정답. 이번 달 판매 목표를 달성했다는 평서문에 좋은 소식이라며 호응하고 있으므로 정답.
(B) 평서문과 상관없는 오답. How often 의문문에 대한 응답이므로 오답.
(C) 평서문과 상관없는 오답. When 의문문에 대한 응답이므로 오답.

18

M-Au How often do you travel for your job?

W-Br (A) It turned out well.
(B) Yes, I did find one.
(C) About once a month.

출장을 얼마나 자주 가세요?
(A) 일이 잘 풀렸어요.
(B) 네, 저는 하나 찾았어요.
(C) 한 달에 한 번 정도요.

어휘 turn out (일, 결과가) 되다, 되어 가다

해설 출장 빈도를 묻는 How often 의문문
(A) 연상 단어 오답. 질문의 How에서 연상 가능한 부사 well을 이용한 오답.
(B) Yes/No 불가 오답. How often 의문문에는 Yes/No 응답이 불가능하므로 오답.
(C) 정답. 출장을 얼마나 자주 가는지 묻는 질문에 한 달에 한 번 정도라고 구체적인 빈도를 제시하고 있으므로 정답.

19

W-Br We should hike the Wildflower Trail today.

M-Cn (A) This seat is available.
(B) I didn't bring boots.
(C) At the visitors' center.

우리 오늘 야생화길 하이킹하면 좋겠어요.
(A) 이 좌석은 이용 가능합니다.
(B) 저는 부츠를 안 가져왔어요.
(C) 방문자 센터에서요.

어휘 available 이용할 수 있는   bring 가져오다

해설 제안/권유의 평서문
(A) 연상 단어 오답. 평서문의 trail을 train으로 잘못 들었을 경우 연상 가능한 seat를 이용한 오답.

(B) 정답. 야생화길을 하이킹하면 좋겠다고 권유하는 평서문에 부츠를 안 가져왔다는 이유를 들어 권유를 간접적으로 거절하고 있으므로 정답.
(C) 평서문과 상관없는 오답. Where 의문문에 대한 응답이므로 오답.

20

M-Au You've booked a hotel in London, haven't you?

W-Am (A) Very enjoyable, thanks.
(B) He usually takes the train.
(C) Yes, I made a reservation last week.

런던에 호텔을 예약하셨죠, 그렇죠?
(A) 매우 즐거워요. 감사합니다.
(B) 그는 보통 기차를 타요.
(C) 네, 지난주에 예약했어요.

어휘 book 예약하다   enjoyable 즐거운   usually 대개, 보통   make a reservation 예약하다

해설 호텔 예약 여부를 확인하는 부가 의문문
(A) 연상 단어 오답. 질문의 hotel에서 연상 가능한 enjoyable을 이용한 오답.
(B) 질문과 상관없는 오답. 질문에 3인칭 대명사 He로 지칭할 인물이 언급된 적이 없으므로 오답.
(C) 정답. 런던에 호텔을 예약했는지 여부를 확인하는 질문에 네(Yes)라고 대답한 뒤, 지난주에 예약했다며 긍정 답변과 일관된 내용을 덧붙였으므로 정답.

21

W-Am Are there any tickets left for tonight's concert?

M-Au (A) It's sold out.
(B) He's a concert violinist.
(C) They already left.

오늘 밤 음악회 입장권 남은 거 있나요?
(A) 매진됐어요.
(B) 그는 연주회 바이올리니스트예요.
(C) 그들은 이미 떠났어요.

어휘 sold out 매진된, 품절된

해설 음악회 입장권이 남아 있는지 묻는 Be동사 의문문
(A) 정답. 오늘 밤 음악회 입장권이 남아 있는지 묻는 질문에 매진됐다며 부정하는 대답을 우회적으로 표현하고 있으므로 정답.
(B) 단어 반복 오답. 질문의 concert를 반복 이용한 오답.
(C) 단어 반복 오답. 질문의 left를 반복 이용한 오답.

22

W-Br Haven't you used this software before?

M-Cn (A) Can I take your order?
(B) I haven't had the chance.
(C) About 40 dollars.

이 소프트웨어를 전에 사용해 본 적 없으신가요?
(A) 주문하시겠습니까?
(B) 저는 기회가 없었어요.
(C) 약 40달러요.

어휘 take an order 주문을 받다   chance 기회

해설 소프트웨어 사용 여부를 확인하는 부정 의문문
(A) 질문과 상관없는 오답.
(B) 정답. 소프트웨어 사용 여부를 묻는 질문에 기회가 없었다며 부정하는 대답을 우회적으로 표현하고 있으므로 정답.
(C) 질문과 상관없는 오답. How much 의문문에 대한 응답이므로 오답.

23

M-Au When is the new blender going to be released?

W-Br (A) Only with fruits and vegetables.
(B) In the kitchen cabinet.
(C) The prototype is still being tested.

새 믹서기는 언제 출시될 예정이죠?
(A) 과일과 채소만요.
(B) 주방 캐비닛이에요.
(C) 시제품이 아직 시험 중이에요.

어휘 blender 믹서기   release 출시하다   prototype 시제품, 원형

해설 새 믹서기 출시 시기를 묻는 When 의문문
(A) 연상 단어 오답. 질문의 blender에서 연상 가능한 fruits와 vegetables를 이용한 오답.
(B) 질문과 상관없는 오답. Where 의문문에 대한 응답이므로 오답.
(C) 정답. 새 믹서기 출시 시기를 묻는 질문에 시제품이 아직 시험 중이라 출시 시기를 알 수 없음을 우회적으로 나타내고 있으므로 정답.

24

M-Au Who's picking up our clients at the airport?

W-Am (A) They decided to drive.
(B) At terminal 2.
(C) It's a marketing position.

누가 공항에서 우리 고객을 모셔올 예정이죠?
(A) 그들은 운전해서 오기로 했어요.
(B) 제2터미널에서요.
(C) 마케팅 직책이에요.

어휘 pick up 차로 태우러 가다   decide 결정하다   position 직위, 직책

해설 공항에서 고객을 모셔올 사람을 묻는 Who 의문문
(A) 정답. 공항에서 고객을 모셔올 사람이 누구인지 묻는 질문에 그들이 운전해서 오기로 했다면서 고객을 모셔오지 않아도 됨을 우회적으로 알려 주고 있으므로 정답.
(B) 연상 단어 오답. 질문의 airport에서 연상 가능한 terminal을 이용한 오답.
(C) 연상 단어 오답. 질문의 Who에서 연상 가능한 직책 a marketing position을 이용한 오답.

25

 동영상 강의

M-Cn Where are the red roses that came in this morning?

M-Au (A) About three liters of water.
(B) No, I didn't check out the sale.
(C) I needed some for a large bouquet.

오늘 오전에 온 빨간 장미꽃은 어디 있어요?
(A) 물 3리터쯤요.
(B) 아니요, 세일을 확인하지 않았어요.
(C) 대형 부케를 만들 때 좀 필요했어요.

어휘 come in (제품 등이) 들어오다

해설 빨간 장미의 위치를 묻는 Where 의문문
(A) 연상 단어 오답. 질문의 red roses에서 연상 가능한 water를 이용한 오답.
(B) Yes/No 불가 오답. Where 의문문에는 Yes/No 응답이 불가능하므로 오답.
(C) 정답. 오전에 온 빨간 장미꽃의 위치를 묻는 질문에 대형 부케를 만들 때 좀 필요했다며 그 장미를 사용했음을 간접적으로 알려 주고 있으므로 정답.

26

 동영상 강의

M-Au This film has been nominated for several awards.

W-Am (A) Why don't we go see it?
(B) After the announcement.
(C) He made a great speech.

이 영화는 여러 수상 후보에 올랐어요.
(A) 보러 가면 어때요?
(B) 발표 후에요.
(C) 그는 훌륭한 연설을 했어요.

어휘 nominate (후보자로) 지명하다   award 상   announcement 발표   make a speech 연설하다

해설 정보 전달의 평서문
(A) 정답. 이 영화는 여러 수상 후보에 올랐다는 평서문에 보러 가면 어떤지를 물으며 수상 후보에 오른 영화와 관련된 내용을 묻고 있으므로 정답.
(B) 연상 단어 오답. 평서문의 awards에서 연상 가능한 announcement를 이용한 오답.
(C) 평서문과 상관없는 오답. 평서문에 3인칭 대명사 He로 지칭할 인물이 언급된 적이 없으므로 오답.

27

M-Cn Who's interested in starting a car pool program?

W-Br (A) Thanks, but I can't swim.
(B) Clara's already organizing one.
(C) It's a very interesting article.

누가 카풀 프로그램을 시작하는 데 관심이 있죠?
(A) 감사합니다만, 저는 수영을 못해요.
(B) 클라라가 이미 하나 만들고 있어요.
(C) 아주 흥미로운 기사예요.

어휘 be interested in ~에 흥미가 있다, 관심이 있다 organize
조직하다, 준비하다 article 기사

해설 카풀 프로그램을 시작하는 데 관심 있는 사람을 묻는 Who 의문문
(A) 연상 단어 오답. 질문의 pool을 swimming pool로 잘못 이해했을
경우 연상 가능한 swim을 이용한 오답.
(B) 정답. 카풀 프로그램을 시작하는 데 관심 있는 사람을 묻는 질문에 클
라라가 이미 하나 만들고 있다고 알려 주고 있으므로 정답.
(C) 파생어 오답. 질문의 interested와 파생어 관계인 interesting을 이
용한 오답.

28

W-Br Where will I teach my workshop this month?

M-Cn (A) We just sent an e-mail to all instructors.
(B) Five to seven months.
(C) Yes, it's a beautiful building.

저는 이번 달에 어디서 워크숍을 진행하죠?
(A) 저희가 방금 모든 강사들께 이메일을 보냈습니다.
(B) 5~7개월요.
(C) 네, 멋진 건물이에요.

어휘 instructor 강사

해설 이번 달 워크숍 진행 장소를 묻는 Where 의문문
(A) 정답. 이번 달 워크숍 진행 장소를 묻는 질문에 방금 모든 강사들께 이
메일을 보냈다고 워크숍 장소가 이메일에 나와 있음을 우회적으로 알
려 주고 있으므로 정답.
(B) 파생어 오답. 질문의 month와 파생어 관계인 months를 이용한 오답.
(C) Yes/No 불가 오답. Where 의문문에는 Yes/No 응답이 불가능하므
로 오답.

29

M-Cn Why are we moving these sweaters to the back
of the store?

W-Am (A) In the new shopping mall.
(B) Yes, they come in other colors.
(C) Our spring merchandise is arriving soon.

왜 이 스웨터들을 매장 뒤편으로 옮기는 건가요?
(A) 새 쇼핑몰에서요.
(B) 네, 그것들은 다른 색상이 있어요.
(C) 봄 상품이 곧 도착해요.

어휘 merchandise 상품

해설 스웨터들을 매장 뒤편으로 옮기는 이유를 묻는 Why 의문문
(A) 연상 단어 오답. 질문의 store에서 연상 가능한 shopping mall을 이
용한 오답.
(B) Yes/No 불가 오답. Why 의문문에는 Yes/No 응답이 불가능하므로
오답.
(C) 정답. 스웨터들을 매장 뒤편으로 옮기는 이유를 묻는 질문에 봄 상품

이 곧 도착해서라고 구체적인 이유를 제시하고 있으므로 정답.

30

W-Br Would you be interested in working on some of
these contracts?

M-Au (A) Thank you for meeting me.
(B) A contact lens prescription.
(C) I have very limited time.

이러한 계약 중 일부를 맡아서 하실 의향이 있나요?
(A) 만나 주셔서 감사합니다.
(B) 콘택트렌즈 처방전이요.
(C) 저는 시간이 정말 없어요.

어휘 contract 계약 prescription 처방전, 처방약 limited 제한된,
한정된

해설 제안/권유의 의문문
(A) 질문과 상관없는 오답.
(B) 유사 발음 오답. 질문의 contracts와 부분적으로 발음이 유사한
contact를 이용한 오답.
(C) 정답. 계약 중 일부를 맡아서 할 의향이 있는지 묻는 질문에 시간이 정
말 없다는 이유를 들어 의향이 없음을 우회적으로 표현하고 있으므로
정답.

31

M-Cn What type of job are you looking for?

W-Am (A) No, at ten A.M.
(B) I really like working with computers.
(C) Just a résumé is needed.

어떤 종류의 일을 찾고 계세요?
(A) 아니요, 오전 10시에요.
(B) 저는 컴퓨터로 작업하는 것을 무척 좋아합니다.
(C) 이력서만 필요해요.

어휘 look for ~을 찾다 résumé 이력서

해설 찾고 있는 일 종류를 묻는 What 의문문
(A) Yes/No 불가 오답. What 의문문에는 Yes/No 응답이 불가능하므로
오답.
(B) 정답. 찾고 있는 일 종류를 묻는 질문에 컴퓨터로 작업하는 것을 무척 좋
아한다고 컴퓨터 관련 일이라고 간접적으로 알려 주고 있으므로 정답.
(C) 연상 단어 오답. 질문의 job에서 연상 가능한 résumé를 이용한 오답.

PART 3

32-34

W-Am	**32 Thank you so much for organizing the annual company picnic,** Jingdao. Everybody seemed to enjoy it.
M-Au	Well, we deserved it after working so hard this year.
W-Am	I agree. **33 The food was great, by the way. Especially the peach pie you made. Would you mind sharing the recipe?** It was delicious.
M-Au	**34 I found the recipe online. I'll send you a link to the Web page. There's a really helpful video that walks you through all the steps. I recommend you watch it first.**
W-Am	All right, thanks.

여	**연례 회사 야유회를 준비해 주셔서 정말 고마워요,** 징다오 씨. 모두가 즐거워하는 것 같았어요.
남	음, 올해 정말 열심히 일했으니 그럴 자격이 있죠.
여	맞아요. **그리고 음식도 훌륭했어요. 특히 당신이 만든 복숭아 파이요. 조리법을 알려 주실 수 있나요?** 맛있었어요.
남	**조리법은 온라인에서 찾았어요. 웹페이지 링크를 보내 드릴게요. 모든 단계를 보여주는 정말 유용한 동영상이 있어요. 그걸 먼저 보시는 걸 권해요.**
여	알겠어요. 감사합니다.

어휘	organize 준비하다, 조직하다 annual 연례의, 매년의 deserve ~을 누릴 자격이 있다, ~을 받을 만하다 especially 특히 share 나누다, 공유하다 recipe 조리법 walk ~ through … ~에게 …을 안내하다, 보여주다

32

What event does the woman mention?
(A) A job fair
(B) A cooking class
(C) A fund-raiser
(D) A company picnic

여자는 어떤 행사를 언급하는가?
(A) 취업 박람회
(B) 요리 강좌
(C) 모금 행사
(D) 회사 야유회

해설 세부 사항 관련 – 여자가 언급한 행사
여자가 첫 대사에서 연례 회사 야유회를 준비해 줘서 정말 고맙다(Thank you so much for organizing the annual company picnic)고 말하고 있으므로 정답은 (D)이다.

33

What does the woman ask for?
(A) A guest list
(B) A dessert recipe
(C) A business card
(D) A promotional code

여자는 무엇을 요청하는가?
(A) 손님 명단
(B) 후식 조리법
(C) 명함
(D) 쿠폰 번호

해설 세부 사항 관련 – 여자가 요청한 것
여자가 두 번째 대사에서 음식도 훌륭했는데 특히 남자가 만든 복숭아 파이가 훌륭했다(The food was great ~. Especially the peach pie you made)고 하면서 조리법을 알려줄 수 있는지(Would you mind sharing the recipe?) 묻고 있으므로 정답은 (B)이다.

> **Paraphrasing** 대화의 peach pie → 정답의 dessert

34

What does the man recommend doing?
(A) Returning some merchandise
(B) Watching a video
(C) Creating an account
(D) Reading a review

남자는 무엇을 하라고 권하는가?
(A) 일부 상품 반품하기
(B) 동영상 시청하기
(C) 계정 만들기
(D) 후기 읽기

어휘 merchandise 상품 account 계정, 계좌 review 후기

해설 세부 사항 관련 – 남자의 권유 사항
남자가 마지막 대사에서 조리법은 온라인에서 찾았는데 웹페이지 링크를 보내 주겠다(I found the recipe online. I'll send you a link to the Web page)고 말하고 나서, 모든 단계를 보여주는 정말 유용한 동영상이 있으니 그걸 먼저 보는 걸 권한다(There's a really helpful video that walks you through all the steps. I recommend you watch it first)고 했으므로 정답은 (B)이다.

35-37

M-Cn	**35 I'd like to finish calculating the company's expense reports for the month. Have you finished reviewing the travel reimbursement forms from all the departments?**
W-Br	**35 I'm almost done,** but I have a question about a hotel receipt from one of our employees.

M-Cn	What's the problem?
W-Br	Well, ³⁶**our policy is for employees to stay at a hotel that's on our list of approved accommodations. This one isn't on the list.**
M-Cn	Who submitted the receipt?
W-Br	Moritz Ziegler, one of our sales representatives.
M-Cn	Hmm. He's a new employee and may have forgotten the policy. ³⁷**As a supervisor, I can approve the expense this one time.**

남	이번 달 회사 경비 보고서 계산을 마무리하고 싶어요. 모든 부서에서 온 출장비 환급 서류 검토는 다 하셨나요?
여	거의 다 됐어요. 그런데 직원 한 명에게서 받은 호텔 영수증에 관해 질문이 있어요.
남	어떤 문제인가요?
여	우리 정책은 직원들이 승인된 숙소 목록에 있는 호텔에 투숙하기로 되어 있잖아요. 이 호텔은 목록에 없네요.
남	누가 영수증을 제출했죠?
여	영업사원인 모리츠 지글러예요.
남	음… 그는 신입 사원인데 정책을 잊어버렸을지도 몰라요. **관리자로서 제가 이번 한 번은 해당 지출을 승인해 줄 수 있어요.**

어휘	calculate 계산하다 expense report 경비 보고서 reimbursement 상환, 변상 department 부서 receipt 영수증 policy 정책 approved 승인된 accommodation 숙소 sales representative 영업사원 supervisor 감독관, 관리자

35

What department do the speakers most likely work in?
(A) Accounting
(B) Research and development
(C) Maintenance
(D) Marketing

화자들은 어떤 부서에서 일하겠는가?
(A) 회계
(B) 연구 개발
(C) 유지보수
(D) 마케팅

해설 전체 내용 관련 – 화자들의 근무 부서
남자가 첫 대사에서 이번 달 회사 경비 보고서 계산을 마무리하고 싶은데 모든 부서에서 온 출장비 환급 서류 검토는 다 했는지(I'd like to finish calculating the company's expense reports for the month. Have you finished reviewing the travel reimbursement forms from all the departments?)를 묻자 여자가 거의 다 됐다(I'm almost done)고 대답하고 있는 것으로 보아 화자들은 회계 부서에서 근무하고 있다는 것을 알 수 있다. 따라서 정답은 (A)이다.

36

What problem does the woman mention?
(A) A report has not been submitted.
(B) An invoice is not accurate.
(C) A policy has not been followed.
(D) An order has not been delivered.

여자는 어떤 문제를 언급하는가?
(A) 보고서가 제출되지 않았다.
(B) 청구서가 정확하지 않다.
(C) 정책이 준수되지 않았다.
(D) 주문품이 배달되지 않았다.

어휘 invoice 송장, 청구서 accurate 정확한

해설 세부 사항 관련 – 여자가 언급하는 문제점
여자가 두 번째 대사에서 정책상 직원들은 승인된 숙소 목록에 있는 호텔에 투숙하기로 되어 있다(our policy is for employees to stay at a hotel that's on our list of approved accommodations)고 하면서 이 호텔은 목록에 없다(This one isn't on the list)고 말하고 있으므로 정답은 (C)이다.

37

What does the man say he will do?
(A) Delete an electronic file
(B) Authorize a reimbursement
(C) Set up a sales meeting
(D) Review a spreadsheet

남자는 무엇을 하겠다고 말하는가?
(A) 전자 파일 삭제하기
(B) 환급 승인하기
(C) 영업 회의 준비하기
(D) 스프레드시트 검토하기

어휘 delete 삭제하다 electronic 전자의 authorize 승인하다 set up 준비하다

해설 세부 사항 관련 – 남자가 할 일
남자가 마지막 대사에서 관리자로서 이번 한 번은 해당 지출을 승인해 줄 수 있다(As a supervisor, I can approve the expense this one time)고 말하고 있으므로 정답은 (B)이다.

> Paraphrasing 대화의 approve → 정답의 Authorize

38-40

M-Au	Good morning, Damilola. How's everything up here on deck?
W-Br	Hi, Pedro. It was an uneventful night, and ³⁸**our cargo ship still hasn't moved yet.**
M-Au	Hmm, I hope the fog over the harbor lifts soon.
W-Br	Yeah, me too. ³⁹**The ship won't be able to leave until the weather improves.**

M-Au I hope we won't get too far behind schedule. ⁴⁰I'll be sure to call the port authority soon for an update on when we'll be cleared to leave.

W-Br Sounds good.

남	안녕하세요, 다밀롤라. 여기 갑판은 어때요?
여	안녕하세요, 페드로. 밤엔 별일 없었고, **화물선은 아직 움직이지 않았어요.**
남	음… 항구의 안개가 빨리 걷히면 좋겠네요.
여	네, 저도요. **날씨가 좋아지기 전엔 배가 떠나지 못할 거예요.**
남	예정보다 너무 늦어지지 않았으면 좋겠어요. **우리가 언제 출발할 수 있는지 최신 소식을 알려 달라고 항만 당국에 곧 전화할게요.**
여	좋아요.

어휘	deck 갑판 uneventful 특별한 일이 없는 cargo ship 화물선 fog 안개 harbor 항구 improve 나아지다, 개선되다 behind schedule 예정보다 늦게 port authority 항만 당국

38

What industry do the speakers most likely work in?
(A) Shipping
(B) Manufacturing
(C) Hospitality
(D) Meteorology

화자들은 어떤 업계에서 일하겠는가?
(A) 운송
(B) 제조
(C) 접객 서비스
(D) 기상학

해설 전체 내용 관련 – 화자들의 근무 업계
여자가 첫 대사에서 우리 화물선은 아직 움직이지 않았다(our cargo ship still hasn't moved yet)고 말하는 것으로 보아 정답은 (A)이다.

39

What is the reason for a delay?
(A) A schedule was written incorrectly.
(B) Some equipment is not properly set up.
(C) Weather conditions are poor.
(D) Several staff members are absent.

지연된 이유는 무엇인가?
(A) 일정표가 잘못 작성되었다.
(B) 장비가 제대로 설치되어 있지 않다.
(C) 기상 상황이 좋지 않다.
(D) 직원 여러 명이 결근했다.

어휘 incorrectly 잘못, 부정확하게 equipment 장비 properly 제대로, 적절히 condition 상태 absent 결석한, 결근한

해설 세부 사항 관련 – 지연 이유
여자가 두 번째 대사에서 날씨가 좋아지기 전엔 배가 떠나지 못할 것(The ship won't be able to leave until the weather improves)이라고 말하고 있으므로 정답은 (C)이다.

40

What does the man say he will do?
(A) Update a shift schedule
(B) Clear a work space
(C) Complete a checklist
(D) Place a call

남자는 무엇을 하겠다고 말하는가?
(A) 교대 근무 일정 업데이트하기
(B) 업무 공간 치우기
(C) 체크리스트 작성하기
(D) 전화 걸기

어휘 shift 교대 근무 complete 작성하다, 기입하다 place a call 전화를 걸다

해설 세부 사항 관련 – 남자가 할 일
남자가 마지막 대사에서 항만 당국에 곧 전화하겠다(I'll be sure to call the port authority soon ~)고 말하고 있으므로 정답은 (D)이다.

Paraphrasing 대화의 call → 정답의 Place a call

41-43

W-Br Hi. ⁴¹I've made a reservation to meet with some clients for lunch today. It's under Cohen.

M-Au Oh, yes. I see your reservation. Welcome, Ms. Cohen.

W-Br ⁴²I know I asked to be seated on your beautiful terrace, but it's very hot today.

M-Au Hmm. ⁴²I can seat you at table four inside. Do you mind waiting a few minutes?

W-Br Not at all. By the way, your parking area's nearly full. Where can I tell my clients to park?

M-Au ⁴³Our customers can park for free in the garage across the street. Our cashier will stamp their parking tickets.

W-Br Oh, great. Thanks. I'll call them and let them know.

여	안녕하세요. **오늘 고객과 만나 점심 식사를 하려고 예약했어요.** 코헨 이름으로 되어 있어요.
남	아, 네. 예약 확인했습니다. 어서 오세요, 코헨 씨.

여	멋진 테라스에 앉겠다고 요청했는데 오늘 굉장히 덥네요.
남	음… 안쪽 4번 테이블을 드릴 수 있습니다. 몇 분간 기다려 주시겠습니까?
여	좋아요. 그런데 주차 구역이 거의 꽉 찼네요. 고객들에게 어디에 주차하라고 하면 될까요?
남	**저희 식당 손님은 길 건너 주차장에 무료로 주차하실 수 있습니다.** 저희 출납원이 주차권에 도장을 찍어드려요.
여	아, 좋네요. 감사합니다. 고객들에게 전화해서 알릴게요.

어휘	make a reservation 예약하다 garage 차고, 주차장 cashier 출납원 stamp 도장을 찍다

41

Why is the woman at the restaurant?
(A) To celebrate a retirement
(B) To perform an inspection
(C) To meet with some clients
(D) To write an article

여자는 왜 음식점에 갔는가?
(A) 은퇴를 기념하려고
(B) 점검을 실시하려고
(C) 고객을 만나려고
(D) 기사를 작성하려고

어휘 celebrate 축하하다, 기념하다   retirement 은퇴   perform 수행하다, 실시하다   inspection 점검, 순찰   article 기사

해설 세부 사항 관련 – 여자가 음식점에 간 이유
여자가 첫 대사에서 오늘 고객과 만나 점심 식사를 하려고 예약했다(I've made a reservation to meet with some clients for lunch today)고 말하고 있으므로 정답은 (C)이다.

42

What does the woman mean when she says, "it's very hot today"?
(A) She is unable to accept an invitation.
(B) A cooling system is not working.
(C) A meeting will end soon.
(D) She wants to change a seating request.

여자가 "오늘 굉장히 덥네요"라고 말하는 의도는 무엇인가?
(A) 초청을 수락할 수 없다.
(B) 냉방 시스템이 작동하지 않는다.
(C) 회의가 곧 끝난다.
(D) 좌석 요청을 변경하고 싶다.

어휘 accept 수락하다   invitation 초대, 초청

해설 화자의 의도 파악 – 오늘 굉장히 덥다는 말의 의도
앞에서 여자가 멋진 테라스에 앉겠다고 요청했지만(I know I asked to be seated on your beautiful terrace, but ~)이라고 말한 뒤 인용문을 언급하고 있으며, 남자가 안쪽 4번 테이블을 줄 수 있다(I can seat you at table four inside)며 실내 좌석을 추천하는 것으로 보아 여자는 좌석 변경을 요청하려는 의도로 한 말임을 알 수 있다. 따라서 정답은 (D)이다.

43

What does the man say about a parking garage?
(A) It is free for customers.
(B) It is under construction.
(C) It closes soon.
(D) It offers monthly contracts.

남자는 주차장에 대해 뭐라고 말하는가?
(A) 고객에게 무료다.
(B) 공사 중이다.
(C) 곧 문을 닫는다.
(D) 월간 계약을 제공한다.

어휘 under construction 공사 중인   contract 계약

해설 세부 사항 관련 – 남자가 주차장에 대해 하는 말
남자가 마지막 대사에서 식당 손님은 길 건너 주차장에 무료로 주차할 수 있다(Our customers can park for free in the garage across the street)고 말하고 있으므로 정답은 (A)이다.

44-46 3인 대화

W-Am	Thank you both for coming here today to demonstrate your company's new compact printer. **44I know the store will be busy because we're having a big sale on laptop computers and tablets.**
M-Cn	We're happy to be here. Our printers are perfect for students or people with home offices who may have limited space. **45My partner, Murat, will be setting up the printer station.**
M-Au	**45Yes—where can I put our demonstration table?**
W-Am	I'll show you the area. Also, **46if you brought any brochures with you, it'll be helpful to put those out for people to take.**

여	두 분 모두 오늘 귀사의 새 소형 프린터를 시연하러 와 주셔서 감사합니다. **노트북 컴퓨터와 태블릿이 대대적인 할인에 들어가서 매장이 바쁠 거예요.**
남1	오게 되어 기쁩니다. 저희 프린터는 학생이나 공간이 한정된 홈오피스를 이용하는 분들께 딱 맞아요. **제 동료 무라트가 프린터를 설치할 거예요.**
남2	네. 시연 테이블을 어디에 두면 될까요?
여	자리를 안내해 드릴게요. 그리고 **안내책자를 가져오셨으면 사람들이 가져갈 수 있도록 꺼내 놓는 게 도움이 될 겁니다.**

어휘	demonstrate 시연하다, 보여주다 compact 소형의 limited 한정된, 제한된 set up 설치하다, 준비하다 brochure 안내책자

44

Where does the woman most likely work?
(A) At a university
(B) At a publishing company
(C) At an electronics store
(D) At a grocery store

여자는 어디서 일하겠는가?
(A) 대학교
(B) 출판사
(C) 전자 제품 매장
(D) 식료품점

어휘 publishing 출판 electronics 전자 장치

해설 전체 내용 관련 – 여자의 근무지
여자가 첫 대사에서 노트북 컴퓨터와 태블릿이 대대적인 할인에 들어가서 매장이 바쁠 것(I know the store will be busy because we're having a big sale on laptop computers and tablets)이라고 말하는 것으로 보아 여자는 전자 제품 매장에서 근무하고 있다는 것을 알 수 있다. 따라서 정답은 (C)이다.

> **Paraphrasing** 대화의 laptop computers and tablets
> → 정답의 electronics

45

What does Murat ask about?
(A) How much an item costs
(B) When an event will begin
(C) How many people will participate
(D) Where to set up some equipment

무라트는 무엇에 대해 질문하는가?
(A) 물품 가격
(B) 행사 시작 시기
(C) 참가 인원
(D) 장비 설치 장소

어휘 cost 비용이 들다 participate 참가하다 equipment 장비

해설 세부 사항 관련 – 무라트가 질문하는 것
첫 번째 남자가 첫 대사에서 무라트가 프린터를 설치할 것(My partner, Murat, will be setting up the printer station)이라고 말하자 무라트가 시연 테이블을 어디에 두면 될지(where can I put our demonstration table?)를 묻고 있으므로 정답은 (D)이다.

> **Paraphrasing** 대화의 printer → 정답의 equipment

46

What does the woman suggest doing?
(A) Offering a discount
(B) Displaying informational materials
(C) Holding a contest
(D) Visiting a registration table

여자는 무엇을 하라고 제안하는가?
(A) 할인 제공
(B) 정보를 담은 자료 전시
(C) 대회 개최
(D) 등록 테이블 방문

어휘 informational 정보를 제공하는 material 자료 hold 열다, 개최하다 registration 등록

해설 세부 사항 관련 – 여자의 제안 사항
여자가 마지막 대사에서 안내책자를 가져왔으면 사람들이 가져갈 수 있도록 꺼내 놓는 게 도움이 될 것(if you brought any brochures with you, it'll be helpful to put those out for people to take)이라고 말하고 있으므로 정답은 (B)이다.

> **Paraphrasing** 대화의 brochures
> → 정답의 informational materials

47-49 3인 대화

W-Am	Gizem and Hector, **47 I'm very pleased with the sales of our brands of cakes, pies, and cookies this past holiday season.** Any thoughts on what we should be concentrating on going forward?
W-Br	The biggest trend right now is the reduction of sugar. **48 The public wants healthier products, but the same great taste. That'll be our biggest challenge.**
M-Cn	One of our ingredient suppliers recently started offering a sweetener made entirely from natural ingredients.
W-Am	Are there similar ones on the market? And how do they compare?
M-Cn	**49 I'd have to do some investigation to find out more about that.** I have some time available tomorrow afternoon.

여1	기젬, 헥터. **지난 휴가 시즌 우리 브랜드의 케이크, 파이, 쿠키 판매량이 매우 만족스러워요.** 앞으로 우리가 무엇에 집중해야 하는지에 대한 의견이 있으십니까?
여2	지금 가장 크게 유행하는 건 설탕을 줄이는 거예요. **대중은 건강에 더 좋지만 똑같이 맛있는 제품을 원해요. 그게 가장 큰 문제일 겁니다.**
남	최근에 우리 재료 공급업체 중 한 곳이 완전히 천연 재료로만 만든 감미료를 제공하기 시작했어요.
여1	시장에 비슷한 상품들이 나와 있나요? 비교하면 어때요?
남	**더 알아보려면 조사를 좀 해 봐야겠어요.** 저는 내일 오후에 시간이 있어요.

어휘	thought 생각, 사고 concentrate on ~에 집중하다, 전념하다 going forward 앞으로 reduction 감소

public 대중 challenge 도전, 시험대 ingredient 재료, 성분 recently 최근 entirely 전적으로, 완전히 similar 비슷한, 유사한 compare 비교하다 investigation 조사 available 시간이 되는

47

What type of industry do the speakers most likely work in?
(A) Textile manufacturing
(B) Food production
(C) Health care
(D) Hospitality

화자들은 어떤 종류의 업계에서 일하겠는가?
(A) 직물 제조
(B) 식품 생산
(C) 의료
(D) 접객 서비스

어휘 textile 직물, 옷감 manufacturing 제조 production 생산

해설 전체 내용 관련 – 화자들의 근무 업종
첫 번째 여자가 첫 대사에서 지난 휴가 시즌 케이크, 파이, 쿠키 판매량이 매우 만족스럽다(I'm very pleased with the sales of our brands of cakes, pies, and cookies this past holiday season)고 말하는 것으로 보아 화자들은 식품 제조 업계에 종사하고 있다는 것을 알 수 있다. 따라서 정답은 (B)이다.

> **Paraphrasing** 대화의 cakes, pies, and cookies
> → 정답의 Food

48

What business challenge are the speakers discussing?
(A) Lack of qualified personnel
(B) Rising production costs
(C) Changes in consumer preferences
(D) Increased competition

화자들은 어떤 사업상의 어려움에 대해 이야기하는가?
(A) 자질을 갖춘 직원의 부족
(B) 생산 비용 상승
(C) 고객 선호 변화
(D) 경쟁 증가

어휘 lack 부족, 결핍 qualified 자격이 있는, 자질을 갖춘 personnel 직원 rise 오르다 consumer 소비자 preference 선호 competition 경쟁

해설 세부 사항 관련 – 화자들이 이야기하는 사업상의 어려움
두 번째 여자가 첫 대사에서 대중은 건강에 더 좋지만 똑같이 맛있는 제품을 원한다(The public wants healthier products, but the same great taste)면서 그게 가장 큰 문제일 것(That'll be our biggest challenge)이라고 말하고 있으므로 정답은 (C)이다.

> **Paraphrasing** 대화의 The public wants healthier products
> → 정답의 Changes in consumer preferences

49

What does the man say he will do?
(A) Research more information
(B) Negotiate a discount
(C) Upgrade some machinery
(D) Train a new employee

남자는 무엇을 할 것이라고 말하는가?
(A) 더 많은 정보 조사하기
(B) 할인 협상하기
(C) 기계 업그레이드하기
(D) 신입 사원 교육하기

어휘 research 조사하다 negotiate 협상하다 machinery 기계(류)

해설 세부 사항 관련 – 남자가 할 일
남자가 마지막 대사에서 더 알아보려면 조사를 좀 해 봐야겠다(I'd have to do some investigation to find out more about that)고 말하고 있으므로 정답은 (A)이다.

> **Paraphrasing** 대화의 do some investigation
> → 정답의 Research

50-52

M-Au Hi, Bianca. **⁵⁰I'm calling to see if you'd have time to work on a project for my marketing firm.** We've expanded a lot in the past year, and we need some help.

W-Am Thanks for thinking of me. What type of work would I be doing?

M-Au Well, **⁵¹we have a new client in Brazil who's interested in creating a marketing campaign for social media sites.** You'd be overseeing the campaign.

W-Am Oh, I have experience with that. **⁵²Why don't you send me a detailed description of the work?** That'll give me an idea of how much time this project will take.

남 안녕하세요, 비앙카. **제 마케팅 회사의 프로젝트를 진행해 주실 시간이 되시는지 알아보려고 전화 드렸어요.** 지난해에 크게 확장을 해서 도움이 필요하거든요.

여 저를 떠올려 주셔서 감사합니다. 제가 어떤 종류의 일을 하게 되나요?

남 **브라질에 신규 고객이 있는데 소셜미디어 사이트용 마케팅 캠페인을 만들고 싶어 해요.** 그 캠페인을 관리 감독하게 될 겁니다.

여	아, 그쪽에 경험이 있어요. **그 일에 대한 상세한 설명서를 보내주시겠어요?** 이 프로젝트에 시간이 얼마나 걸릴지 제가 짐작할 수 있을 거예요.
어휘	expand 확장하다, 확대하다 be interested in ~에 관심이 있다 oversee 감독하다 experience 경험 detailed 상세한 description 설명, 기술

50

Why is the man calling?
(A) To explain a business merger
(B) To describe a new company policy
(C) To offer the woman a work assignment
(D) To invite the woman to speak at a conference

남자가 전화한 이유는?
(A) 업체 합병에 대해 설명하려고
(B) 새로운 회사 정책을 말하려고
(C) 여자에게 업무 할당을 제안하려고
(D) 여자에게 학회 연설을 요청하려고

어휘 merger 합병 policy 정책 assignment 배정, 할당
conference 회의, 학회

해설 전체 내용 관련 – 남자가 전화하는 이유

남자가 첫 대사에서 본인의 마케팅 회사의 프로젝트를 진행해 줄 시간이 되는지 알아보려고 전화했다(I'm calling to see if you'd have time to work on a project for my marketing firm)고 말하고 있으므로 정답은 (C)이다.

51

What does the man say a client is interested in doing?
(A) Purchasing another business
(B) Finding a new office space
(C) Revising a budget proposal
(D) Creating a marketing campaign

남자는 고객이 무엇을 하는 데 관심이 있다고 말하는가?
(A) 다른 업체 매입하기
(B) 새로운 사무 공간 찾기
(C) 예산 제안서 수정하기
(D) 마케팅 캠페인 만들기

어휘 space 공간 revise 변경하다, 수정하다 budget 예산
proposal 제안, 제안서

해설 세부 사항 관련 – 고객이 관심 있는 일

남자가 두 번째 대사에서 브라질에 신규 고객이 있는데 소셜미디어 사이트용 마케팅 캠페인을 만들고 싶어 한다(we have a new client in Brazil who's interested in creating a marketing campaign for social media sites)고 말하고 있으므로 정답은 (D)이다.

52

What does the woman ask the man to send?
(A) A project description
(B) An event invitation
(C) Some social media links
(D) Some contact information

여자는 남자에게 무엇을 보내 달라고 요청하는가?
(A) 프로젝트 설명서
(B) 행사 초청장
(C) 소셜미디어 링크
(D) 연락처

어휘 invitation 초대, 초대장 contact information 연락처

해설 세부 사항 관련 – 여자가 남자에게 보내 달라고 요청하는 것
여자가 마지막 대사에서 그 일에 대한 상세한 설명서를 보내줄 것(Why don't you send me a detailed description of the work?)을 요청하고 있으므로 정답은 (A)이다.

> Paraphrasing 대화의 a detailed description of the work
> → 정답의 A project description

53-55

W-Br	Hey, Koji? [53] **We were about to pack van number five for the music festival when we noticed it's got a flat tire.**
M-Au	Oh. That's not good.
W-Br	We're supposed to get there by eleven to set up lunch for the performers. Is there another van we can take?
M-Au	Let me see what's available. [54] **We've got a lot of catering jobs today.** Ah, yes—we can use van number three. Do you need help loading?
W-Br	Yes, thanks. [55] **The food's already in coolers, but everything's in the kitchen with the serving utensils and napkins. It all needs to be brought to the parking area.**
M-Au	[55] **All right; I can help with that.**

여	안녕하세요, 코지? **음악 축제에 가려고 5번 밴에 짐을 채우려는 참인데요. 타이어에 펑크가 난 것을 알았어요.**
남	아, 안타깝네요.
여	연주자들을 위한 점심 식사를 준비하러 11시까지 도착해야 해요. 저희가 탈 수 있는 다른 밴이 있나요?
남	어떤 밴을 이용할 수 있는지 확인해 볼게요. **오늘은 케이터링 일감이 많군요.** 아, 있어요. 3번 밴을 쓰면 돼요. 짐을 싣는 걸 도와드릴까요?

여	네, 감사합니다. **음식은 이미 아이스 박스에 담겨 있는데, 모든 것이 식기류와 냅킨과 함께 주방에 있어요. 주차장으로 모두 가져와야 해요.**
남	**알겠습니다. 도와드릴게요.**

어휘	**pack** (짐을) 꾸리다, 채우다 **notice** 알다 **get a flat tire** 타이어에 펑크가 나다 **be supposed to** ~하기로 되어 있다 **performer** 연주자, 연기자 **available** 이용할 수 있는 **catering** 출장 요리, 음식 공급(업) **load** 싣다 **utensil** (가정에서 사용하는) 기구, 도구

53

What problem does the woman mention?
(A) A vehicle is out of service.
(B) An employee is late.
(C) A shipment was damaged.
(D) Traffic is heavy.

여자는 어떤 문제를 언급하는가?
(A) 차량이 고장 났다.
(B) 직원이 늦었다.
(C) 수송품이 훼손됐다.
(D) 교통이 혼잡하다.

어휘 **vehicle** 차량   **out of service** 작동되지 않는, 고장 난   **damage** 훼손시키다, 손상을 주다   **traffic** 교통

해설 세부 사항 관련 – 여자가 언급하는 문제점
여자가 첫 대사에서 음악 축제에 가려고 5번 밴에 짐을 채우려는 참인데 타이어에 펑크가 난 것을 알았다(We were about to pack van number five for the music festival when we noticed it's got a flat tire)고 말하고 있으므로 정답은 (A)이다.

Paraphrasing	대화의 van → 정답의 A vehicle 대화의 got a flat tire → 정답의 is out of service

54

Where do the speakers most likely work?
(A) At a recording studio
(B) At a catering company
(C) At a radio station
(D) At a car dealership

화자들은 어디서 일하겠는가?
(A) 녹음 스튜디오
(B) 출장 요리 업체
(C) 라디오 방송국
(D) 자동차 대리점

어휘 **recording** 녹음, 녹화   **station** 방송국   **dealership** 대리점

해설 전체 내용 관련 – 화자들의 근무지
남자가 두 번째 대사에서 오늘은 케이터링 일감이 많다(We've got a lot of catering jobs today)고 말하고 있으므로 정답은 (B)이다.

55

What does the man say he will do next?
(A) Arrange for a car repair
(B) Order some kitchen supplies
(C) Carry some items
(D) Offer a refund

남자는 다음으로 무엇을 하겠다고 말하는가?
(A) 차량 수리 준비하기
(B) 주방용품 주문하기
(C) 일부 물품 옮기기
(D) 환불해 주기

어휘 **arrange** 마련하다, 주선하다   **supply** 물품   **offer a refund** 환불해 주다

해설 세부 사항 관련 – 남자가 다음에 할 일
여자가 마지막 대사에서 음식은 이미 아이스 박스에 담겨 있는데, 모든 것이 식기류와 냅킨과 함께 주방에 있다(The food's already in coolers, but everything's in the kitchen with the serving utensils and napkins)면서 주차장으로 모두 가져와야 한다(It all needs to be brought to the parking area)고 말하자, 남자가 알겠다(All right)고 답하면서 도와주겠다(I can help with that)고 말하고 있으므로 정답은 (C)이다.

Paraphrasing	대화의 everything, the serving utensils and napkins → 정답의 some items

56-58

M-Cn	Thanks for taking my call. As I mentioned in my e-mail, **56 I'm interested in working in your field. But I'm talking to some professionals first so I can find out more about it.**
W-Am	Happy to help.
M-Cn	**57 So how did you get your start?**
W-Am	Oh, my family always subscribed to three newspapers. So I always thought the news was important. **57 At my university, I joined the newspaper and eventually worked my way up to being an editor.**
M-Cn	Wow. Is it true that people in the news business work very long hours? **58 So what's your schedule like?**

남	전화 받아 주셔서 고맙습니다. 이메일에서 언급한 것처럼 **이 분야에서 일하는 데 관심이 있어요. 그런데 이에 대해 더 자세히 알아보기 위해 먼저 전문가들과 이야기를 나누고 있습니다.**
여	도울 수 있어 기뻐요.
남	**어떻게 일을 시작하게 되었나요?**

여　　아, 저희 가족은 항상 신문 세 종류를 구독했어요. 그래서 언제나 뉴스가 중요하다고 생각했죠. **대학 시절에 신문사에 들어가 결국 편집자까지 된 겁니다.**

남　　우와! 뉴스 업계 직원들이 굉장히 긴 시간을 일한다는 게 사실인가요? **일정은 어떻게 되세요?**

어휘　mention 언급하다　professional 전문직 종사자
subscribe 구독하다　eventually 결국　work one's way 끝까지 해내다, 노력하며 나아가다　editor 편집자

56

Why is the man calling the woman?
(A) To plan a company event
(B) To confirm a work deadline
(C) To discuss a career path
(D) To accept a job offer

남자가 여자에게 전화한 이유는?
(A) 회사 행사를 계획하려고
(B) 업무 마감 기한을 확인하려고
(C) 진로를 의논하려고
(D) 일자리 제안을 수락하려고

어휘　confirm 확인하다, 확정하다　deadline 마감 기한　career path 진로　accept 수락하다, 받아들이다　job offer 일자리 제안

해설　전체 내용 관련 – 남자가 여자에게 전화를 건 이유
남자가 첫 대사에서 이 분야에서 일하는 데 관심이 있다(I'm interested in working in your field)고 하면서 더 자세히 알아보기 위해 먼저 전문가들과 이야기를 나누고 있다(But I'm talking to some professionals first so I can find out more about it)고 말하고 있으므로 정답은 (C)이다.

> **Paraphrasing**　대화의 talking → 정답의 discuss

57

Who most likely is the woman?
(A) A newspaper editor
(B) A university professor
(C) A delivery person
(D) A professional actor

여자는 누구이겠는가?
(A) 신문 편집자
(B) 대학교수
(C) 배달원
(D) 전문 배우

어휘　professor 교수

해설　전체 내용 관련 – 여자의 직업
남자가 두 번째 대사에서 어떻게 일을 시작하게 됐는지(how did you get your start?) 묻자 여자는 대학 시절에 신문사에 들어가 결국 편집자까지 되었다(At my university, I joined the newspaper and eventually worked my way up to being an editor)고 답하고 있으므로 정답은 (A)이다.

58

What will the woman most likely do next?
(A) Negotiate a contract
(B) Explain an office policy
(C) Review a résumé
(D) Describe a work schedule

여자는 다음으로 무엇을 하겠는가?
(A) 계약 협상하기
(B) 사무실 정책 설명하기
(C) 이력서 검토하기
(D) 업무 일정 설명하기

어휘　negotiate 협상하다　contract 계약　policy 정책　review 검토하다　résumé 이력서

해설　세부 사항 관련 – 여자가 다음에 할 일
남자가 마지막 대사에서 일정은 어떻게 되는지(what's your schedule like?) 묻고 있으므로 정답은 (D)이다.

59-61

M-Au　Hi, Karen! **59I just read the article on the company Web site about the proposed merger with QZ Corporation. 60It looks like we're going ahead with it.**

W-Br　**60There would be a lot of advantages to merging operations, although they also talked about it last year.**

M-Au　I remember that. But there were a lot of details to work out—like whether our offices would stay in Chicago. **61Now it looks like we won't be relocating.**

W-Br　Well, **61I really don't want to move,** so that's a relief.

남　　안녕하세요, 카렌! **회사 웹사이트에서 QZ 코퍼레이션과의 합병 제안에 관한 기사를 방금 읽었어요. 추진될 것 같네요.**

여　　**합병하면 많은 이점이 있겠지만 그 얘기는 작년에도 있었어요.**

남　　기억나요. 하지만 사무실이 시카고에 계속 남아있을지 여부 등 해결해야 할 세부 사항이 많았어요. **이제 우리가 이전하진 않을 것 같네요.**

여　　음, **저는 정말 옮기고 싶지 않아요.** 그래서 안심이 돼요.

어휘　article 기사　propose 제안하다　merger 합병　go ahead with ~을 추진하다　advantage 이점, 유리한 점　merge 합병하다　operation 사업, 사업체　relocate 이전하다　relief 안도

59

What are the speakers mainly discussing?
(A) A new transportation route
(B) A company merger
(C) A public relations initiative
(D) A medical facility design

화자들은 주로 무엇에 관해 이야기하는가?
(A) 새로운 운송 경로
(B) 회사 합병
(C) 홍보 계획
(D) 의료 시설 설계

어휘 transportation 운송, 수송 public relations 홍보 initiative
 (새로운) 계획 facility 시설

해설 전체 내용 관련 – 대화의 주제
남자가 첫 대사에서 회사 웹사이트에서 QZ 코퍼레이션과의 합병 제안에 관한 기사를 방금 읽었다(I just read the article on the company Web site about the proposed merger with QZ Corporation)고 말하며 대화를 시작했고, 화자들이 회사 합병에 관한 대화를 이어 가고 있으므로 정답은 (B)이다.

60

Why does the woman say, "they also talked about it last year"?
(A) To express doubt
(B) To explain a process
(C) To make a recommendation
(D) To update some information

여자가 "그 얘기는 작년에도 있었어요"라고 말하는 이유는?
(A) 의심을 나타내려고
(B) 절차를 설명하려고
(C) 추천하려고
(D) 최신 정보를 주려고

어휘 express doubt 의심을 나타내다 process 과정, 절차
 recommendation 추천, 권장

해설 화자의 의도 파악 – 그 얘기는 작년에도 있었다는 말의 의도
앞에서 남자가 합병이 추진될 것 같다(It looks like we're going ahead with it)고 말하자 여자가 합병하면 많은 이점이 있겠지만(There would be a lot of advantages to merging operations, although)이라고 말하며 인용문을 언급한 것으로 보아, 작년에도 합병 얘기는 있었지만 성사되지 않아서 합병 추진에 대해 의심을 나타내려는 의도로 한 말임을 알 수 있다. 따라서 정답은 (A)이다.

61

What does the woman want to avoid?
(A) Paying a certification fee
(B) Training additional staff
(C) Upgrading some technology
(D) Relocating to another city

여자는 무엇을 피하고 싶어 하는가?
(A) 증명서 발급비 지불
(B) 추가 직원 교육
(C) 기술 업그레이드
(D) 다른 도시로 이전

어휘 avoid 피하다 certification 증명서 (교부) additional 추가의

해설 세부 사항 관련 – 여자가 피하고 싶은 것
남자가 마지막 대사에서 이전하진 않을 것 같다(Now it looks like we won't be relocating)고 말하자, 여자가 정말 옮기고 싶지 않다(I really don't want to move)고 말하고 있으므로 정답은 (D)이다.

> **Paraphrasing** 대화의 really don't want
> → 질문의 want to avoid

62-64 대화 + 웹사이트

M-Au Thanks for calling Customized Concepts. How can I help you?

W-Am **62 My company wants to give every employee a gift**, something useful but not too big. Since we're about to host our annual staff basketball tournament, I thought a water bottle might be good.

M-Au We carry a few drink containers. If you're at our Web site, you'll see them under the Lifestyle tab.

W-Am Let me pull it up now... All right.

M-Au **63 I recommend the metal bottle with the wide-mouthed lid.** It's easier to clean than the one with the straw.

W-Am OK, thanks. And you could put our company logo on it, right?

M-Au Yes. **64 You'll just need to send me the graphic file.**

W-Am **64 I can do that.**

남 커스터마이즈 컨셉에 전화 주셔서 감사합니다. 무엇을 도와드릴까요?

여 **저희 회사에서 모든 직원들에게 선물을 주려고 합니다.** 유용한데 그리 크지 않은 걸로요. 연례 직원 농구 대회를 주최할 참이라서 물병이 좋을 것 같다고 생각했어요.

남 저희는 몇 가지 음료 용기를 취급합니다. 저희 웹사이트를 방문하시면 라이프스타일 탭 아래에서 보실 수 있습니다.

여 지금 열어 볼게요… 됐어요.

남 **뚜껑 입구가 큰 금속병을 추천해요.** 빨대가 있는 것보다 닦기 쉽습니다.

여 좋아요, 감사합니다. 저희 회사 로고를 넣어 주실 수 있죠, 그렇죠?

남 네. **저에게 그래픽 파일만 보내주시면 됩니다.**

여 **보내드릴게요.**

어휘 useful 유용한 annual 연례의, 매년의 carry (가게에서 품목을) 취급하다 container 용기 pull up (컴퓨터 화면에서 창을) 열다 metal 금속의 wide-mouthed 입이 큰 lid 뚜껑 straw 빨대

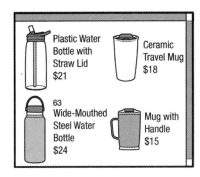

62

Who is a gift for?
(A) Donors
(B) Volunteers
(C) Employees
(D) Clients

누구를 위한 선물인가?
(A) 기증자
(B) 자원봉사자
(C) 직원
(D) 고객

해설 세부 사항 관련 – 선물을 받을 사람
여자가 첫 대사에서 회사에서 모든 직원들에게 선물을 주려고 한다(My company wants to give every employee a gift)고 말하고 있으므로 정답은 (C)이다.

63

Look at the graphic. What is the price of the item the man recommends?
(A) $21
(B) $18
(C) $24
(D) $15

시각 정보에 의하면, 남자가 추천하는 물품의 가격은?
(A) 21달러
(B) 18달러
(C) 24달러
(D) 15달러

해설 시각 정보 연계 – 남자가 추천하는 물품의 가격
남자가 세 번째 대사에서 뚜껑 입구가 큰 금속병을 추천한다(I recommend the metal bottle with the wide-mouthed lid)고 말하고 있고, 웹사이트에 따르면 뚜껑 입구가 큰 금속병은 24달러이므로 정답은 (C)이다.

64

What is the woman going to send to the man?
(A) A graphic file
(B) A list of names
(C) A delivery address
(D) An account number

여자는 남자에게 무엇을 보낼 것인가?
(A) 그래픽 파일
(B) 명단
(C) 배송 주소
(D) 계좌 번호

해설 세부 사항 관련 – 여자가 남자에게 보낼 것
남자가 마지막 대사에서 그래픽 파일만 보내주면 된다(You'll just need to send me the graphic file)고 그래픽 파일을 요청하자 여자가 보내겠다(I can do that)고 대답하고 있으므로 정답은 (A)이다.

65-67 대화 + 목록

W-Br Yun, **65 I just finished recording the audio guide for the pencil drawings that'll be included in our modern art exhibit next week.** The files'll be loaded onto the audio devices tomorrow.

M-Cn That's great. But, unfortunately, we have to make one change. **66 The drawing by Claudia Hoffman will no longer be in the exhibit.** There was a scheduling mix-up, and it was promised to another museum starting next week.

W-Br Oh, that's too bad. That was one of my favorite pieces. Will you put anything in its place?

M-Cn No. We'll just remove it.

W-Br OK, **67 then I'll make that change to the audio-guide recording. I'll do that right away.**

여	윤, 다음 주에 있을 현대 미술전에 포함될 연필화의 오디오 가이드 녹음을 막 마쳤어요. 파일은 내일 오디오 기기에 로딩될 거예요.
남	좋아요. 그런데 안타깝게도 한 가지 바꿀 게 있습니다. **클라우디아 호프만의 그림은 이제 전시되지 않을 거예요.** 일정 혼동이 있었고, 다음 주부터 다른 미술관과 약속되어 있어요.
여	아, 너무 아쉽네요. 제가 가장 좋아하는 작품 중 하나였거든요. 그 자리에 다른 작품을 넣으실 건가요?
남	아니요, 그냥 없앨 거예요.
여	네, **그러면 오디오 가이드 녹음을 그렇게 바꿀게요. 지금 바로 할게요.**

어휘	drawing 그림 include 포함시키다 modern art 현대 미술, 근대 미술 exhibit 전시 device 장치, 기기 unfortunately 안타깝게도, 유감스럽게도 no longer 더 이상 ~ 아닌 mix-up 혼동 promise 약속하다 museum 박물관, 미술관 favorite 가장 좋아하는 remove 없애다, 제거하다

Title	Artist
A Careful Glance	So-Jin Park
Promises	Vivek Madan
66 *Stormy Sea*	Claudia Hoffman
The Moment	Adisa Rotimi

제목	화가
〈조심스러운 시선〉	소진 박
〈약속〉	비벡 마단
66 **〈폭풍의 바다〉**	**클라우디아 호프만**
〈순간〉	아디사 로티미

어휘 careful 조심스러운 glance 흘낏 봄 stormy 폭풍우가 몰아치는 moment 순간

65

What type of art will be displayed in an exhibit?
(A) Clay sculptures
(B) Oil paintings
(C) Black-and-white photographs
(D) Pencil drawings

전시회에 어떤 종류의 작품이 전시될 것인가?
(A) 점토 조각
(B) 유화
(C) 흑백 사진
(D) **연필화**

어휘 clay 점토, 진흙 sculpture 조각

해설 세부 사항 관련 – 전시회에 전시될 작품
여자가 첫 대사에서 다음 주에 있을 현대 미술전에 포함될 연필화의 오디오 가이드 녹음을 막 마쳤다(I just finished recording the audio guide for the pencil drawings that'll be included in our modern art exhibit next week)고 말하고 있으므로 정답은 (D)이다.

66

Look at the graphic. Which piece of artwork will no longer be included?
(A) *A Careful Glance*
(B) *Promises*
(C) *Stormy Sea*
(D) *The Moment*

시각 정보에 의하면, 어떤 작품이 더 이상 포함되지 않을 것인가?
(A) 〈조심스러운 시선〉
(B) 〈약속〉
(C) **〈폭풍의 바다〉**
(D) 〈순간〉

해설 시각 정보 연계 – 더 이상 포함되지 않을 작품
남자가 첫 대사에서 클라우디아 호프만의 그림은 이제 전시되지 않을 것(The drawing by Claudia Hoffman will no longer be in the exhibit)이라고 말하고 있고, 목록에 의하면 클라우디아 호프만의 그림은 *Stormy Sea*라고 표기되어 있으므로 정답은 (C)이다.

67

What does the woman say she will do right away?
(A) Speak with an artist
(B) Edit a recording
(C) Clean a gallery space
(D) Greet some visitors

여자는 무엇을 바로 하겠다고 말하는가?
(A) 화가와 이야기하기
(B) **녹음 수정하기**
(C) 미술품 전시 공간 청소하기
(D) 방문객 맞이하기

어휘 edit 수정하다, 편집하다 gallery 미술관, 화랑 greet 맞다, 환영하다

해설 세부 사항 관련 – 여자가 바로 할 일
여자가 마지막 대사에서 오디오 가이드 녹음을 바꾸겠다(then I'll make that change to the audio-guide recording)면서 지금 바로 하겠다(I'll do that right away)고 말하고 있으므로 정답은 (B)이다.

> **Paraphrasing** 대화의 make that change → 정답의 Edit

68-70 대화 + 지도

M-Cn	68 **I'm glad we were assigned to cover the press conference earlier today.** I counted seven other major media networks there, in addition to ours.
W-Am	Well, the offshore wind industry is going to transform the way this region gets its power.
M-Cn	Agreed. Let's compare our facts before we start writing.

W-Am **69** So the largest cluster of wind turbines—off the coast of Winston—is already built. The other sites are at different stages of construction, though Lanchester is also close to being done.

M-Cn Right. **70** And I think it's crucial for us to focus on how many new jobs related to assembling and maintaining the turbines are opening up in the area as a result of this.

남 아까 우리가 기자회견 취재를 맡아서 기뻐요. 세어 보니 우리 외에도 7개의 주요 방송국이 참석했어요.

여 해상 풍력 산업이 이 지역이 전력을 얻는 방식을 완전히 바꿔 놓을 거예요.

남 맞아요. 기사를 쓰기 전에 사실과 비교해 봅시다.

여 풍력 발전용 터빈이 가장 많이 설치되는 곳은 윈스턴 앞바다인데 이미 지어졌어요. 다른 현장들도 각기 다른 공사 단계에 있지만 란체스터는 거의 완공 단계이고요.

남 네. 그 결과로 지역 내에서 터빈 조립 및 관리와 관련된 새 일자리가 얼마나 많이 생기고 있는지에 초점을 맞추는 것이 정말 중요할 것 같아요.

어휘 assign 배정하다 cover 취재하다 press conference 기자회견 count 세다 in addition to ~에 더하여 offshore wind 해상 풍력 transform 탈바꿈하다, 완전히 바꿔 놓다 region 지역 compare 비교하다 cluster 무리 coast 해안 stage 단계 construction 건설, 공사 crucial 중대한, 결정적인 related to ~에 관련된 assemble 조립하다 maintain 관리하다

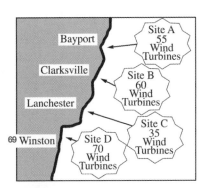

68

Who most likely are the speakers?
(A) Urban planners
(B) Journalists
(C) Engineers
(D) Environmental scientists

화자들은 누구이겠는가?
(A) 도시 계획자
(B) 기자
(C) 엔지니어
(D) 환경 과학자

어휘 urban 도시의   environmental 환경의

해설 전체 내용 관련 – 화자들의 직업

남자가 첫 대사에서 아까 기자회견 취재를 맡아서 기쁘다(I'm glad we were assigned to cover the press conference earlier today)고 말하는 것으로 보아 화자들은 기자임을 알 수 있다. 따라서 정답은 (B)이다.

69

Look at the graphic. Which site has already been completed?
(A) Site A
(B) Site B
(C) Site C
(D) Site D

시각 정보에 의하면, 어떤 현장이 이미 완공됐는가?
(A) 현장 A
(B) 현장 B
(C) 현장 C
(D) 현장 D

해설 시각 정보 연계 – 이미 완공된 현장

여자가 풍력 발전용 터빈이 가장 많이 설치되는 곳은 윈스턴 앞바다인데 이미 지어졌다(So the largest cluster of wind turbines—off the coast of Winston—is already built)고 말하고 있고, 지도에 의하면 윈스턴은 현장 D이므로 정답은 (D)이다.

70

What does the man suggest focusing on?
(A) Work opportunities
(B) Wind turbine costs
(C) Supply chain issues
(D) Power capacity

남자는 무엇에 초점을 맞추자고 제안하는가?
(A) 일자리 기회
(B) 풍력 발전용 터빈 비용
(C) 공급망 문제
(D) 전력 용량

어휘 opportunity 기회 supply chain 공급망 capacity 용량, 능력

해설 세부 사항 관련 – 남자가 초점을 맞추자고 제안하는 것

남자가 마지막 대사에서 그 결과로 지역 내에서 터빈 조립 및 관리와 관련된 새 일자리가 얼마나 많이 생기고 있는지에 초점을 맞추는 것이 정말 중요할 것 같다(I think it's crucial for us to focus on how many new jobs related to assembling and maintaining the turbines are opening up in the area as a result of this)고 말하고 있으므로 정답은 (A)이다.

> **Paraphrasing**   대화의 how many new jobs ~ are opening up in the area
> → 정답의 Work opportunities

PART 4

71-73 녹음 메시지

> M-Au   **71 You have reached the information line for the Cranbury Apartments management office.** On Monday, April twelfth, maintenance work will begin to repave the entire parking area adjacent to our building's main entrance. **72 All Cranbury residents should move their vehicles from their designated parking spots before eight A.M. on Monday.** Any vehicle still in its spot after eight A.M. will be towed at the owner's expense. **73 A map of alternate parking sites was mailed to residents last week and is also posted in the building lobby.**

> 크랜버리 아파트 관리 사무소 안내 전화입니다. 4월 12일 월요일에는 건물 정문에 인접한 주차 구역 전체를 재포장하는 보수 작업이 시작됩니다. **모든 크랜버리 주민께서는 월요일 오전 8시 전까지 지정 주차 구역에서 차량을 옮겨 주셔야 합니다.** 오전 8시 이후 주차 구역에 그대로 있는 차량은 소유자 부담으로 견인될 것입니다. 지난주에 주민 여러분께 대체 주차장 약도를 우편으로 보냈으며 건물 로비에도 게시되어 있습니다.

> 어휘 reach (전화로) 연락하다   management 관리   maintenance 유지보수, 관리   repave 재포장하다   entire 전체의   adjacent to ~에 인접한   main entrance 정문   resident 주민   designated 지정된   tow 견인하다   at one's expense 자신의 비용으로, 자비로   alternate 대체하는

71

Who has recorded the message?
(A) A city mayor's office
(B) A maintenance department
(C) An automobile dealership
(D) A building management office

누가 메시지를 녹음했는가?
(A) 시장실
(B) 유지보수 부서
(C) 자동차 대리점
(D) 건물 관리 사무소

어휘 mayor 시장   department 부서   dealership 대리점

해설 전체 내용 관련 – 메시지 녹음을 한 곳

화자가 도입부에 크랜버리 아파트 관리 사무소 안내 전화(You have reached the information line for the Cranbury Apartments management office)라고 했으므로 메시지 녹음은 관리 사무소에서 한 것임을 알 수 있다. 따라서 정답은 (D)이다.

> **Paraphrasing**   담화의 the Cranbury Apartments management office
> → 정답의 A building management office

72

What are the listeners asked to do?
(A) Move their vehicles
(B) Pay their parking fines
(C) Use an alternate entrance
(D) Participate in a meeting

청자들은 무엇을 하라고 요청받는가?
(A) 차량 이동하기
(B) 주차 위반 벌금 납부하기
(C) 다른 출입구 이용하기
(D) 회의 참석하기

어휘 fine 벌금   participate in ~에 참가하다

해설 세부 사항 관련 – 청자들이 요청받는 일

화자가 중반부에 모든 크랜버리 주민은 월요일 오전 8시 전까지 지정 주차 구역에서 차량을 옮겨야 한다(All Cranbury residents should move their vehicles from their designated parking spots ~)고 했으므로 정답은 (A)이다.

73

What does the speaker say was mailed last week?
(A) An election ballot
(B) A maintenance plan
(C) A map
(D) A coupon

화자는 지난주에 무엇을 우편으로 보냈다고 말하는가?
(A) 선거 투표용지
(B) 유지보수 계획
(C) 약도
(D) 쿠폰

어휘 election 선거   ballot 투표용지

해설 세부 사항 관련 – 화자가 지난주에 우편으로 보낸 것

화자가 후반부에 지난주에 주민들에게 대체 주차장 약도를 우편으로

보냈다(A map of alternate parking sites was mailed to residents last week ~)고 했으므로 정답은 (C)이다.

74-76 방송

W-Am Welcome to *Your House Works.* **⁷⁴On today's episode, we'll go over how you can maintain and make minor repairs to the roof of your home. ⁷⁵The first thing to do is to invest in a few special tools, like a trowel and crowbar. It's important to choose some that are high quality because you'll use them for many years.** With your trowel and some roof cement, you can seal any cracks or chips. The crowbar will help you remove loose shingles that you can then replace. Now, **⁷⁶I highly recommend you take photos of your roof every year so that you can track its overall condition.**

〈유어 하우스 웍스〉입니다. 오늘 에피소드에서는 여러분의 집 지붕을 유지보수하고 사소한 수리를 하는 방법을 살펴볼 예정입니다. 첫 번째 할 일은 모종삽이나 쇠지레 같은 특수 도구에 투자하는 겁니다. 몇 년 쓰실 테니 질 좋은 물건을 선택하는 것이 중요합니다. 모종삽과 지붕 시멘트가 있으면 어떤 금이 가거나 깨진 곳도 메꿀 수 있습니다. 쇠지레는 헐거워진 지붕널을 제거하고 교체할 수 있게 해 줍니다. 이제, 전반적인 상태를 추적할 수 있도록 매년 지붕 사진을 찍으실 것을 적극 추천합니다.

어휘 maintain 유지하다 minor 작은, 사소한 invest 투자하다 trowel 모종삽 crowbar 쇠지레 seal 봉인하다, 밀봉하다 crack 금 chip 이가 빠진 흔적 remove 제거하다, 없애다 loose 헐거워진 shingle 지붕널 replace 교체하다 track 추적하다 overall 전체의

74

What is the topic of the episode?
(A) Garden landscaping
(B) Window installation
(C) Roof maintenance
(D) Kitchen renovations

에피소드 주제는 무엇인가?
(A) 정원 조경
(B) 창문 설치
(C) 지붕 유지보수
(D) 주방 개조

어휘 landscaping 조경 installation 설치 renovation 개조, 보수

해설 전체 내용 관련 – 에피소드 주제
화자가 초반부에서 오늘 에피소드에서는 집 지붕을 유지보수하고 사소한 수리를 하는 방법을 살펴볼 예정(On today's episode, we'll go over how you can maintain and make minor repairs to the roof of your home)이라고 했으므로 정답은 (C)이다.

> **Paraphrasing** 담화의 maintain and make minor repairs to the roof → 정답의 Roof maintenance

75

What does the speaker emphasize about some tools?
(A) They should be cleaned regularly.
(B) They should be of high quality.
(C) They were recently invented.
(D) They can be easily stored.

화자는 도구에 대해 어떤 점을 강조하는가?
(A) 정기적으로 닦아야 한다.
(B) 품질이 좋아야 한다.
(C) 최근 발명됐다.
(D) 쉽게 보관할 수 있다.

어휘 regularly 정기적으로 recently 최근 invent 발명하다 store 보관하다, 저장하다

해설 세부 사항 관련 – 화자가 도구에 대해 강조하는 점
화자가 중반부에 첫 번째 할 일은 모종삽이나 쇠지레 같은 특수 도구에 투자하는 것(The first thing to do is to invest in a few special tools, like a trowel and crowbar)이라고 하면서 몇 년 쓸 테니 질 좋은 물건을 선택하는 것이 중요하다(It's important to choose some that are high quality because you'll use them for many years)고 했으므로 정답은 (B)이다.

76

What does the speaker recommend doing every year?
(A) Treating some wood
(B) Consulting an electrician
(C) Taking some photos
(D) Draining some water

화자는 매년 무엇을 하라고 권장하는가?
(A) 나무에 화학 처리를 하기
(B) 전기 기사에게 상담하기
(C) 사진 찍기
(D) 물 빼내기

어휘 treat (화학 물질을 써서) 처리하다 consult 상담하다 electrician 전기 기사 drain 물을 빼내다

해설 세부 사항 관련 – 화자가 매년 하라고 권장하는 일
화자가 마지막에 매년 지붕 사진을 찍을 것을 적극 추천한다(I highly recommend you take photos of your roof every year ~)고 했으므로 정답은 (C)이다.

77-79 담화

W-Br **77 Thanks again for joining me on today's tour of the beautiful Wallingford Conservatory.** I hope you enjoyed seeing and learning about the many species of plants and flowers we care for here. As I mentioned at the beginning of the tour, **78 world-renowned botanist Samantha Hughes will be giving a lecture on the care of flowering orchid plants at two o'clock in the community room.** I recommend attending. **79 Samantha's work has also been featured in a documentary film called *Orchid Caretakers*,** which you can purchase through the conservatory's online gift shop. I watched it recently and learned many new things about the orchid species we have right here at the conservatory.

오늘 아름다운 월링포드 온실 견학을 함께해 주셔서 다시 한번 감사드립니다. 이곳에서 가꾸는 많은 종의 식물과 꽃을 보고 배우는 것이 즐거우셨기를 바랍니다. 견학 시작 때 말씀드렸듯이, **2시에 커뮤니티룸에서 세계적으로 유명한 식물학자 사만다 휴스 씨가 꽃을 피우는 난초 관리에 대해 강연할 예정인데요.** 참석을 권장합니다. **사만다 씨의 작품은 〈난초를 가꾸는 사람들〉이라는 다큐멘터리 영화에도 등장한 바 있습니다.** 온실의 온라인 기념품점에서 구입하실 수 있습니다. 저는 최근에 시청했는데 이곳 온실에 있는 난초 종에 대해 새로운 사실을 많이 배웠어요.

어휘 conservatory 온실 species 종 mention 언급하다 world-renowned 세계적으로 유명한 botanist 식물학자 give a lecture 강연하다 orchid plant 난초 feature 특별히 포함하다 recently 최근

77

Who most likely is the speaker?
(A) A radio show host
(B) A tour guide
(C) A sales associate
(D) A professor

화자는 누구이겠는가?
(A) 라디오 프로그램 진행자
(B) 투어 가이드
(C) 영업사원
(D) 교수

해설 전체 내용 관련 – 화자의 직업
화자가 도입부에 아름다운 월링포드 온실 견학을 함께해 주셔서 다시 한번 감사드린다(Thanks again for joining me on today's tour of the beautiful Wallingford Conservatory)고 말하는 것으로 보아 화자는 투어 가이드일 가능성이 높다. 따라서 정답은 (B)이다.

78

What will happen at two o'clock?
(A) A lecture will begin.
(B) A demonstration will be given.
(C) An interview will be conducted.
(D) A park will close.

2시에 어떤 일이 있을 것인가?
(A) 강연이 시작된다.
(B) 시연이 진행된다.
(C) 인터뷰가 진행된다.
(D) 공원이 문을 닫는다.

어휘 demonstration 설명, 시연 conduct 하다

해설 세부 사항 관련 – 2시에 있을 일
화자가 중반부에 2시에 세계적으로 유명한 식물학자 사만다 휴스 씨가 난초 관리에 대해 강연할 예정(world-renowned botanist Samantha Hughes will be giving a lecture on the care of flowering orchid plants at two o'clock ~)이라고 말하고 있으므로 정답은 (A)이다.

79

What is *Orchid Caretakers*?
(A) A book
(B) An album
(C) A film
(D) A magazine

〈난초를 가꾸는 사람들〉은 무엇인가?
(A) 책
(B) 앨범
(C) 영화
(D) 잡지

해설 세부 사항 관련 – 〈난초를 가꾸는 사람들〉의 종류
화자가 후반부에 사만다 씨의 작품은 〈난초를 가꾸는 사람들〉이라는 다큐멘터리 영화에도 등장한 바 있다(Samantha's work has also been featured in a documentary film called *Orchid Caretakers*)고 했으므로 정답은 (C)이다.

80-82 연설

M-Au **80 Before the benefit concert begins, I want to thank all of you for supporting the Hillcaster Community Center.** As you know, **81 our facilities have been in need of some repairs for quite a while.** So far, we've raised 5,000 dollars in ticket sales, but we haven't quite reached our goal yet. **82 So during the concert, I want to encourage you to buy food and drinks from the concession stand. 81 Eighty percent of the proceeds will go to construction at the Hillcaster Community Center.** Enjoy the music!

자선 음악회를 시작하기 전에 힐캐스터 커뮤니티 센터를 지원해 주신 여러분께 감사의 말씀을 전하고 싶습니다. 아시다시피 **저희 시설은 꽤 오랫동안 수리가 필요했어요.** 지금까지 표 판매로 5천 달러를 모금했지만 아직 목표에 채 미치지 못했습니다. 그래서 여러분께 음악회 도중 매점에서 음식과 음료를 사 달라고 말씀드리고 싶어요. 수익금의 80%는 힐캐스터 커뮤니티 센터 공사에 쓰입니다. 즐겁게 음악 감상하세요!

어휘 benefit concert 자선 음악회 support 지원하다, 지지하다 facility 시설 in need of ~이 필요한 quite a while 꽤 오랫동안 reach 도달하다 encourage 격려하다, 권장하다 concession stand 구내 매점 proceeds 수익금 construction 공사

80

What event is taking place?
(A) A fund-raising concert
(B) A sports competition
(C) A play rehearsal
(D) An awards ceremony

어떤 행사가 열리는가?
(A) 모금 음악회
(B) 스포츠 대회
(C) 연극 리허설
(D) 시상식

어휘 fund-raising 모금 competition 대회, 경쟁

해설 전체 내용 관련 – 열리고 있는 행사
화자가 도입부에 자선 음악회를 시작하기 전(Before the benefit concert begins, ~)이라고 말하고 있으므로 정답은 (A)이다.

Paraphrasing	담화의 the benefit concert → 정답의 A fund-raising concert

81

What does the organization plan to do?
(A) Change a policy
(B) Repair a building
(C) Select a winner
(D) Sponsor a team

해당 단체는 무엇을 할 계획인가?
(A) 정책 변경
(B) 건물 수리
(C) 우승자 선정
(D) 팀 후원

어휘 policy 정책 select 선택하다 sponsor 후원하다

해설 세부 사항 관련 – 해당 단체가 계획하는 일
화자가 중반부에 시설이 꽤 오랫동안 수리가 필요했다(our facilities have been in need of some repairs for quite a while)며 모금 현황을 알리고, 후반부에 행사의 수익금은 힐캐스터 커뮤니티 센터 공사에 쓰인다(Eighty percent of the proceeds will go to construction at the Hillcaster Community Center)고 했으므로 시설 수리를 계획하고

있음을 알 수 있다. 따라서 정답은 (B)이다.

Paraphrasing	담화의 facilities → 정답의 a building

82

What does the speaker encourage the listeners to do?
(A) Order tickets early
(B) Visit a community center
(C) Purchase refreshments
(D) Donate clothing

화자는 청자들에게 무엇을 하라고 권하는가?
(A) 표를 일찍 주문하기
(B) 커뮤니티 센터 방문하기
(C) 다과 구입하기
(D) 의류 기부하기

어휘 refreshments 다과 donate 기부하다

해설 세부 사항 관련 – 화자가 청자들에게 권하는 것
화자가 후반부에 음악회 도중 매점에서 음식과 음료를 사 달라고 말씀드리고 싶다(So during the concert, I want to encourage you to buy food and drinks from the concession stand)고 했으므로 정답은 (C)이다.

Paraphrasing	담화의 buy food and drinks → 정답의 Purchase refreshments

83-85 연설

M-Cn Thank you all for attending today's workshop. Erina Kimura and I will be conducting the session, and **[83]we'll be focusing on using time efficiently as a business owner.** Planning and spending your time wisely is a key factor to business success. **[84]During the presentation, I'll be referring to documents from the packet you were handed as you arrived. If you don't have one yet,** Erina's at the back of the room. OK then, **[85]to start off, we'll do an exercise to get to know one another better.**

오늘 워크숍에 참석해 주신 모든 분들께 감사드립니다. 에리나 키무라와 제가 세션을 진행할 예정이며, **사업주로서 시간을 효율적으로 활용하는 부분에 중점을 둘 것입니다.** 시간을 현명하게 계획하고 사용하는 것은 사업 성공의 핵심 요소입니다. 발표 중에 여러분이 도착했을 때 받은 봉투에 있는 서류를 참조할 것입니다. 아직 없으시다면 에리나가 회의실 뒤쪽에 있습니다. 자, 그럼 먼저 서로 더 잘 알아갈 수 있는 활동을 해 보겠습니다.

어휘 conduct 하다 focus on ~에 중점을 두다 efficiently 효율적으로 key factor 핵심 요소 presentation 발표 refer to ~을 참조하다 packet 꾸러미, 봉투

83

What is the topic of the workshop?
(A) Time management
(B) Public speaking
(C) Leadership skills
(D) Professional networking

워크숍의 주제는 무엇인가?
(A) 시간 관리
(B) 대중 연설
(C) 리더십 기술
(D) 직업적 인맥 쌓기

어휘 management 관리 professional 직업의, 전문적인

해설 전체 내용 관련 – 워크숍의 주제
화자가 초반부에 사업주로서 시간을 효율적으로 활용하는 부분에 중점을 둘 것(we'll be focusing on using time efficiently as a business owner)이라고 했으므로 정답은 (A)이다.

> Paraphrasing 담화의 using time efficiently
> → 정답의 Time management

84

What does the speaker imply when he says, "Erina's at the back of the room"?
(A) A guest speaker has just arrived.
(B) Assistance is available.
(C) Attendees should speak clearly and loudly.
(D) An extra chair should be provided.

화자가 "에리나가 회의실 뒤쪽에 있습니다"라고 말하는 의도는 무엇인가?
(A) 객원 연설자가 막 도착했다.
(B) 도움을 받을 수 있다.
(C) 참석자들은 명확하고 크게 이야기해야 한다.
(D) 여분의 의자가 제공되어야 한다.

어휘 guest speaker 객원 연설자 assistance 도움 available 이용할 수 있는 attendee 참석자

해설 화자의 의도 파악 – 에리나가 회의실 뒤쪽에 있다는 말의 의도
앞에서 발표 중에 도착할 때 받은 봉투에 있는 서류를 참조할 것(During the presentation, I'll be referring to documents from the packet you were handed as you arrived)이라고 하면서 아직 없다면(If you don't have one yet)이라고 말한 뒤 인용문을 언급한 것으로 보아, 서류가 없다면 에리나에게 요청하면 받을 수 있다는 의미로 한 말임을 알 수 있다. 따라서 정답은 (B)이다.

85

What will the listeners do next?
(A) Sign their names on a list
(B) Take a break
(C) Participate in an introductory activity
(D) Fill out a questionnaire

청자들은 다음으로 무엇을 할 것인가?
(A) 목록에 서명하기
(B) 휴식 취하기
(C) 소개하는 활동에 참가하기
(D) 설문지 작성하기

어휘 take a break 휴식을 취하다 participate in ~에 참가하다 introductory 소개하는, 서두의 fill out a questionnaire 설문지를 작성하다

해설 세부 사항 관련 – 청자들이 다음에 할 일
화자가 마지막에 먼저 서로 더 잘 알아갈 수 있는 활동을 해 보겠다(to start off, we'll do an exercise to get to know one another better)고 말하고 있으므로 정답은 (C)이다.

> Paraphrasing 담화의 an exercise to get to know one another better
> → 정답의 an introductory activity

86-88 여행 정보

W-Br **86At this site, archaeologists have uncovered the remains of a fifth-century marketplace with colorful mosaic tiles on the walls.** You'll notice how vibrant the colors are, even after all these centuries. **86This is what the ruins are most famous for.** You can still see intricate details in the artists' pictures of scenes from daily life. Now, to protect the mosaics, a roof has been constructed over the area, and the lights are dim. And **87I'm sorry, but taking photos is not allowed**, as the flash would damage the tiles. **88As we proceed, please hold on to the handrails on either side.** They'll help you stay on the path and protect the ruins around us.

이곳에서 고고학자들은 벽에 다채로운 모자이크 타일이 붙어 있는 5세기 장터 유적을 찾아냈습니다. 몇 세기가 지났음에도 불구하고 색깔이 얼마나 선명한지 확인하실 수 있을 거예요. 이 유적은 바로 이것으로 가장 유명합니다. 일상 생활의 모습을 담은 화가들의 그림에서 복잡한 디테일을 보실 수 있을 겁니다. 지금은 모자이크를 보호하기 위해 이 구역 위에 지붕이 세워져 있고 조명은 어둡습니다. 플래시가 타일을 손상시킬 수 있어서 죄송하지만 사진 촬영은 허용되지 않습니다. 이동하면서 한쪽 난간을 꼭 잡아주세요. 통로를 벗어나지 않게 해줄 것이고 주변 유적을 보호할 수 있도록 해 줄 겁니다.

어휘 archaeologist 고고학자 uncover 알아내다 remains 유적 marketplace 장터, 시장 mosaic 모자이크 vibrant 강렬한, 선명한 ruins 폐허, 유적, 잔해 intricate 복잡한 protect 보호하다 construct 건설하다 dim 어둑한, 흐릿한 allow 허용하다 proceed (특정 방향으로) 나아가다, 이동하다 hold on to ~을 꼭 잡다, ~에 의지하다 handrail 난간

86

What is a historical site famous for?
(A) Its defensive walls
(B) Its royal inhabitants
(C) An event that happened there
(D) Some artwork

사적지는 무엇으로 유명한가?
(A) 방어벽
(B) 왕실 사람들
(C) 그곳에서 있었던 행사
(D) 예술 작품

어휘 historical site 사적지 defensive 방어의 inhabitant 주민

해설 세부 사항 관련 – 사적지에서 유명한 것
화자가 도입부에 이곳에서 고고학자들은 벽에 다채로운 모자이크 타일이 붙어 있는 5세기 장터 유적을 찾아냈다(At this site, archaeologists have uncovered the remains of a fifth-century marketplace with colorful mosaic tiles on the walls)고 하면서 몇 세기가 지났는데도 색깔이 선명한 것을 확인할 수 있는데 이것으로 가장 유명하다(This is what the ruins are most famous for)고 말하고 있으므로 정답은 (D)이다.

> **Paraphrasing**   담화의 colorful mosaic tiles
> → 정답의 Some artwork

87

Why does the speaker apologize?
(A) The listeners cannot take pictures.
(B) An area is closed to the listeners.
(C) There is no gift shop.
(D) A tour started late.

화자가 사과하는 이유는?
(A) 청자들이 사진을 찍을 수 없다.
(B) 청자들에게 구역이 폐쇄되었다.
(C) 기념품점이 없다.
(D) 투어가 늦게 시작됐다.

해설 세부 사항 관련 – 화자가 사과하는 이유
화자가 중반부에 죄송하지만 사진 촬영은 허용되지 않는다(I'm sorry, but taking photos is not allowed)고 했으므로 정답은 (A)이다.

> **Paraphrasing**   담화의 taking photos is not allowed
> → 정답의 cannot take pictures

88

What does the speaker ask the listeners to do?
(A) Show their tickets
(B) Put on protective clothing
(C) Use some handrails
(D) Speak quietly

화자는 청자들에게 무엇을 하라고 요청하는가?
(A) 표 제시하기
(B) 보호복 착용하기
(C) 난간 이용하기
(D) 조용히 말하기

어휘 protective 보호용의

해설 세부 사항 관련 – 화자의 요청 사항
화자가 후반부에 이동하면서 한쪽 난간을 꼭 잡으라(As we proceed, please hold on to the handrails on either side)고 요청하고 있으므로 정답은 (C)이다.

> **Paraphrasing**   담화의 hold on to the handrails
> → 정답의 Use some handrails

89-91 회의 발췌

M-Cn **89 As you all know, our agency's just won an important contract with Parker Auto Parts Company. 89,90 We'll be developing two 30-second ads for local radio stations to be released next month and two additional 20-second ads for the following month.** Now, **90 I know it's a tight schedule**, but this is a priority. The client has actually started trying to work on this internally, **91 so there's a rough ad we can start editing. Let's work on that now.**

모두 아시는 것처럼, 우리 대행사가 파커 자동차 부품회사와의 중요한 계약을 따냈습니다. 우리는 다음 달 지역 라디오 방송국에서 공개될 30초짜리 광고 두 편과 그 다음 달에 공개될 20초짜리 추가 광고 두 편을 개발할 예정입니다. 자, 빡빡한 일정이라는 것은 알지만 이것이 우선입니다. 사실 고객이 내부에서 이 건을 작업하기 시작해서 우리가 편집 작업을 시작할 수 있는 광고 초안이 있습니다. 지금 그것을 작업해 봅시다.

어휘 contract 계약 develop 개발하다 ad 광고 local 지역의 station 방송국 release 발표하다, 공개하다 additional 추가의 tight schedule 빡빡한 일정 priority 우선 사항 internally 내부적으로, 내부에서 rough 초고 edit 편집하다

89

What is the speaker mainly discussing?
(A) An advertising campaign
(B) A market expansion
(C) Some contract negotiations
(D) Some audit procedures

화자는 주로 무엇에 대해 이야기하는가?
(A) 광고 캠페인
(B) 시장 확대
(C) 계약 협상
(D) 감사 절차

어휘 advertising 광고 expansion 확대, 확장 negotiation 협상
audit 회계 감사 procedure 절차

해설 전체 내용 관련 – 담화의 주제
화자가 도입부에 파커 자동차 부품회사와의 중요한 계약을 따냈다
(~ our agency's just won an important contract with Parker
Auto Parts Company)고 하면서 다음 달 지역 라디오 방송국에서
공개될 30초짜리 광고 두 편과 그 다음 달에 공개될 20초짜리 추가 광고
두 편을 개발할 예정(We'll be developing two 30-second ads ~ two
additional 20-second ads for the following month)이라고 했으므로
정답은 (A)이다.

90

What does the speaker imply when he says, "this is a
priority"?
(A) Overtime pay has been approved.
(B) A deadline must be met.
(C) A client expressed concern.
(D) A supervisor will be observing closely.

화자가 "이것이 우선입니다"라고 말하는 의도는 무엇인가?
(A) 초과 근무 수당이 승인됐다.
(B) 마감 기한을 맞춰야 한다.
(C) 고객이 우려를 표했다.
(D) 관리자가 면밀히 관찰할 것이다.

어휘 overtime pay 초과 근무 수당 approve 승인하다 deadline
기한, 마감 시간 express concern 우려를 표하다 observe
관찰하다, 주시하다

해설 화자의 의도 파악 – 이것이 우선이라는 말의 의도
앞에서 다음 달 지역 라디오 방송국에서 공개될 30초짜리 광고 두 편과
그 다음 달에 공개될 20초짜리 추가 광고 두 편을 개발할 예정(We'll be
developing two 30-second ads for local radio stations to be
released next month and two additional 20-second ads for the
following month)이라고 하면서 빡빡한 일정이라는 것은 안다(I know
it's a tight schedule)고 한 뒤 인용문을 언급한 것으로 보아, 빡빡한
일정이지만 마감 기한을 맞춰야 한다는 의도로 한 말임을 알 수 있다.
따라서 정답은 (B)이다.

91

What will the listeners do next?
(A) View a presentation
(B) Review a budget
(C) Revise some work
(D) Do some research

청자들은 다음으로 무엇을 할 것인가?
(A) 발표 보기
(B) 예산 검토하기
(C) 작업물 수정하기
(D) 조사하기

어휘 presentation 발표 budget 예산 revise 수정하다, 변경하다
do research 조사하다, 연구하다

해설 세부 사항 관련 – 청자들이 다음에 할 일
화자가 마지막에 우리가 편집 작업을 시작할 수 있는 광고 초안이 있다
(there's a rough ad we can start editing)고 하면서 지금 그것을 작
업해 보자(Let's work on that now)고 말하고 있으므로 정답은 (C)이다.

> **Paraphrasing** 담화의 editing → 정답의 Revise

92-94 회의 발췌

> W-Am ⁹²Excuse me, nurses. Your attention please.
> ⁹³I've been receiving complaints about the free
> snacks in the hospital break rooms. Some people
> have mentioned that they don't like the selection
> of snacks, and some have said that they don't
> get to eat them at all because they're gone by the
> time the evening shift starts. ⁹⁴So I was thinking
> about putting some money into each of your staff
> spending accounts every month so that you can
> buy the snacks you want at the hospital cafeteria.
> That will require management approval, but I'll
> keep you posted.

> 잠시만요, 간호사 여러분. 주목해 주세요. 병원 휴게실에 있는 무료 간
> 식에 대한 불만이 계속 접수되고 있습니다. 어떤 분들은 간식 종류가 마
> 음에 들지 않는다고 하고, 어떤 분들은 저녁 교대 근무를 시작할 때쯤엔
> 다 사라지고 없어서 먹지 못한다고 합니다. 그래서 병원 매점에서 원하
> 는 간식을 살 수 있도록 매달 각 직원의 지출 계좌에 일정 금액을 입금
> 해 드리는 것을 생각 중입니다. 경영진의 승인이 필요합니다. 계속 소
> 식을 전해 드리겠습니다.

> 어휘 attention 주목, 주의 집중 complaint 불만, 불평
> break room 휴게실 selection 선발(된 것들) shift 교대 근무
> spending 지출 account 계좌 management 경영진
> approval 승인 keep ~ posted ~에게 정보를 알리다

92

Where do the listeners most likely work?
(A) At a hospital
(B) At a restaurant
(C) At a grocery store
(D) At an electronics store

청자들은 어디서 일하겠는가?
(A) 병원
(B) 음식점
(C) 식료품점
(D) 전자 제품 매장

해설 전체 내용 관련 – 청자들의 근무지
화자가 도입부에 간호사 여러분(Excuse me, nurses)이라고 말하고
있는 것으로 보아 화자들의 근무 장소는 병원임을 알 수 있다. 따라서
정답은 (A)이다.

93

What is the main purpose of the talk?
(A) To make a request
(B) To address staff complaints
(C) To present a new schedule
(D) To explain a technical process

담화의 주 목적은?
(A) 요청하는 것
(B) 직원 불만 사항을 해결하는 것
(C) 새 일정을 제시하는 것
(D) 기술적 절차를 설명하는 것

어휘 make a request 요청하다   address 다루다, 고심하다
present 제시하다, 보여주다   process 과정, 절차

해설 전체 내용 관련 – 담화의 목적
화자가 초반부에 병원 휴게실에 있는 무료 간식에 대한 불만이 계속 접수되고 있다(I've been receiving complaints about the free snacks in the hospital break rooms)고 직원들의 불만에 대해 언급하고 있으므로 정답은 (B)이다.

94

What does the speaker imply when she says, "That will require management approval"?
(A) A process has not been followed.
(B) The listeners may be asked to work extra shifts.
(C) The listeners should contact a manager.
(D) A change will not be immediate.

화자가 "경영진의 승인이 필요합니다"라고 말하는 의도는 무엇인가?
(A) 절차를 따르지 않았다.
(B) 청자들에게 추가 교대 근무를 요청할 수도 있다.
(C) 청자들은 관리자에게 연락해야 한다.
(D) 변경은 즉시 이뤄지지 않을 것이다.

어휘 follow 따르다   contact 연락하다   immediate 즉각적인

해설 화자의 의도 파악 – 경영진의 승인이 필요하다는 말의 의도
앞에서 화자가 병원 매점에서 원하는 간식을 살 수 있도록 매달 각 직원의 지출 계좌에 일정 금액을 입금하는 것을 생각 중(So I was thinking about putting some money ~ you can buy the snacks you want at the hospital cafeteria)이라고 한 뒤 인용문을 언급하고 있으므로, 경영진의 승인이 필요하므로 시간이 걸린다는 의도로 한 말임을 알 수 있다. 따라서 정답은 (D)이다.

95-97 연설 + 지도

M-Cn As mayor of Lakeville, **⁹⁵I'm pleased to welcome you to the celebration for our town's newly renovated Lakeville Park.** There are a lot of new areas to explore, so we've planned a short hike. We'll be walking around the pond and along the renovated walking trail. **⁹⁶We'll end our walk**

on the hill on the north side of the park. There we'll be having some free snacks and ice cream. **⁹⁷For those of you taking photos, don't forget to post them on the city's Web site.** We'd like to commemorate this special day.

레이크빌 시장으로서 **새롭게 보수한 레이크빌 공원의 기념 행사에 여러분을 초대하게 되어 기쁘게 생각합니다.** 답사할 새 구역이 많아서 간단한 하이킹을 계획해 보았습니다. 연못 근처와 보수한 산책로를 따라 걸을 예정입니다. **산책은 공원 북쪽 언덕에서 끝납니다.** 거기서 무료 간식과 아이스크림을 먹습니다. 사진을 찍는 분들은 잊지 말고 시 웹사이트에 게시해 주세요. 이 특별한 날을 기념하고자 합니다.

어휘 mayor 시장   celebration 기념 행사, 축하 행사   renovate 개조하다, 보수하다   explore 답사하다, 탐험하다   trail 산길, 오솔길   post 게시하다   commemorate 기념하다

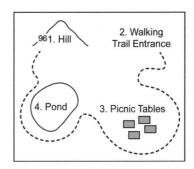

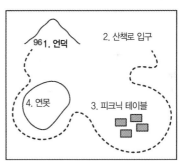

95

According to the speaker, what was recently completed?
(A) A company reorganization
(B) A park renovation
(C) A volunteer training
(D) A conservation project

화자에 따르면, 최근 무엇이 완료됐는가?
(A) 회사 조직 개편
(B) 공원 보수
(C) 자원봉사자 교육
(D) 자연 보호 프로젝트

어휘 reorganization 재편성, 개편   volunteer 자원봉사자
conservation (자연 환경) 보호

해설 세부 사항 관련 – 최근에 완료된 것

화자가 도입부에 새롭게 보수한 레이크빌 공원의 기념 행사에 여러분을 초대하게 되어 기쁘게 생각한다(I'm pleased to welcome you to the celebration for our town's newly renovated Lakeville Park)고 말하고 있으므로 정답은 (B)이다.

Paraphrasing	담화의 newly renovated Lakeville Park → 정답의 A park renovation

96

Look at the graphic. Where does the speaker say refreshments will be served?
(A) Location 1
(B) Location 2
(C) Location 3
(D) Location 4

시각 정보에 의하면, 화자는 어디서 다과를 제공할 것이라고 말하는가?
(A) 1번 장소
(B) 2번 장소
(C) 3번 장소
(D) 4번 장소

어휘 refreshments 다과

해설 시각 정보 연계 – 다과를 제공할 장소

화자가 중반부에 산책은 공원 북쪽 언덕에서 끝난다(We'll end our walk on the hill on the north side of the park)고 하면서 거기서 무료 간식과 아이스크림을 먹는다(There we'll be having some free snacks and ice cream)고 말하고 있고, 지도에 따르면 공원 북쪽 언덕은 1번 장소이므로 정답은 (A)이다.

Paraphrasing	담화의 snacks and ice cream → 질문의 refreshments

97

What are the listeners reminded to do?
(A) Complete a survey
(B) Donate some money
(C) Join an organization
(D) Post some photographs

청자들에게 무엇을 하라고 상기시키는가?
(A) 설문 작성하기
(B) 돈 기부하기
(C) 단체 가입하기
(D) 사진 게시하기

어휘 complete 작성하다, 완료하다 survey 조사 donate 기부하다 organization 단체, 기관

해설 세부 사항 관련 – 청자들에게 상기시키는 것

화자가 후반부에 사진을 찍는 사람은 잊지 말고 시 웹사이트에 게시해 달라(For those of you taking photos, don't forget to post them on the city's Web site)고 말하고 있으므로 정답은 (D)이다.

Paraphrasing	담화의 photos → 정답의 photographs

98-100 담화 + 표

W-Br **98 Thanks, everyone, for attending today's free public lecture, sponsored by the Springfield Farmers' Association. So, we've received lots of requests for information on growing a vegetable garden.** People want to know how to keep their garden healthy and get the vegetables they want. The first thing we recommend is regular soil testing. **99 Since this is September, all soil samples in the next six weeks should be taken from the same depth, as seen on this chart.** Oh, and before you leave today, **100 please sign up for our mailing list to stay informed of future lectures.**

여러분, 스프링필드 농부 협회에서 후원하는 오늘의 무료 공개 강의에 참석해 주셔서 감사합니다. 자, 텃밭 가꾸기에 관한 정보를 달라는 요청을 많이 받았는데요. 사람들은 텃밭을 건강하게 유지하고 원하는 채소를 얻는 방법을 알고 싶어 합니다. 추천하는 첫 번째 방법은 정기적인 토양 검사인데요. 지금이 9월이니 앞으로 6주간 모든 토양 시료는 이 도표에 보이는 것처럼 같은 깊이에서 채취해야 해요. 아, 오늘 가시기 전에 우편물 수신을 신청해서 향후 강의 정보를 계속 받으시기 바랍니다.

어휘 lecture 강의 sponsor 후원하다 association 협회 vegetable garden 텃밭 regular 정기적인, 규칙적인 soil 토양 depth 깊이 sign up for ~을 신청하다 stay informed of ~의 정보를 계속 얻다

Soil Sampling Timeline		
Time of Year	Type of Crop	Depth
99 September-October	All plants	12 inches
November-August	Flowers	4 inches
	Vegetables	6 inches
	Trees and shrubs	8 inches

토양 시료 추출 일정		
연중 시기	작물 유형	깊이
99 9월-10월	**모든 식물**	**12인치**
11월-8월	꽃	4인치
	채소	6인치
	나무 및 관목	8인치

어휘 timeline 시각표 crop 작물 shrub 관목

98

What is the topic of today's lecture?

(A) When to harvest crops

(B) Where to plant trees

(C) How to grow vegetables

(D) Which flowers need more sun

오늘 강의의 주제는 무엇인가?

(A) 작물 수확 시기

(B) 나무 심을 장소

(C) 채소 기르는 방법

(D) 햇빛이 더 많이 필요한 꽃

어휘 harvest 수확하다

해설 전체 내용 관련 – 오늘 강의의 주제

화자가 도입부에 오늘의 무료 공개 강의에 참석해 줘서 감사하다(Thanks, everyone, for attending today's free public lecture, ~)고 하면서 텃밭 가꾸기에 관한 정보를 달라는 요청을 많이 받았다(So, we've received lots of requests for information on growing a vegetable garden)고 말하는 것으로 보아, 오늘 강의 주제는 텃밭 가꾸기에 관련된 내용임을 알 수 있다. 따라서 정답은 (C)이다.

99

Look at the graphic. At what depth should samples be collected this month?

(A) 12 inches

(B) 4 inches

(C) 6 inches

(D) 8 inches

시각 정보에 의하면, 이번 달은 어떤 깊이로 시료를 수집해야 하는가?

(A) 12인치

(B) 4인치

(C) 6인치

(D) 8인치

어휘 collect 수집하다, 모으다

해설 시각 정보 연계 – 이번 달 수집해야 할 시료의 깊이

화자가 중반부에 지금이 9월이니 앞으로 6주간 모든 토양 시료는 이 도표에서 보이는 것처럼 같은 깊이에서 채취해야 한다(Since this is September, all soil samples in the next six weeks should be taken from the same depth, as seen on this chart)고 말하고 있고, 표에 따르면 9월-10월에는 견본의 깊이가 12인치이므로 정답은 (A)이다.

100

What does the speaker encourage the listeners to do?

(A) Turn off mobile phones

(B) Have some refreshments

(C) Purchase some seeds

(D) Sign up for a mailing list

화자는 청자들에게 무엇을 하라고 권하는가?

(A) 휴대전화 끄기

(B) 다과 즐기기

(C) 종자 구매하기

(D) 우편물 수신 신청하기

어휘 turn off 끄다 refreshments 다과 seed 씨앗, 종자

해설 세부 사항 관련 – 화자가 청자들에게 권장하는 것

화자가 마지막에 우편물 수신을 신청해서 향후 강의 정보를 계속 받기 바란다(please sign up for our mailing list to stay informed of future lectures)고 하므로 정답은 (D)이다.

1 (A)	**2** (B)	**3** (C)	**4** (D)	**5** (C)
6 (D)	**7** (A)	**8** (A)	**9** (B)	**10** (B)
11 (C)	**12** (C)	**13** (B)	**14** (A)	**15** (B)
16 (B)	**17** (A)	**18** (C)	**19** (B)	**20** (C)
21 (B)	**22** (A)	**23** (B)	**24** (A)	**25** (B)
26 (C)	**27** (B)	**28** (A)	**29** (C)	**30** (A)
31 (A)	**32** (B)	**33** (D)	**34** (C)	**35** (B)
36 (A)	**37** (C)	**38** (A)	**39** (D)	**40** (C)
41 (A)	**42** (D)	**43** (D)	**44** (C)	**45** (B)
46 (D)	**47** (B)	**48** (C)	**49** (A)	**50** (A)
51 (D)	**52** (A)	**53** (C)	**54** (C)	**55** (A)
56 (C)	**57** (A)	**58** (B)	**59** (B)	**60** (C)
61 (A)	**62** (B)	**63** (C)	**64** (B)	**65** (B)
66 (C)	**67** (A)	**68** (A)	**69** (D)	**70** (A)
71 (D)	**72** (C)	**73** (A)	**74** (D)	**75** (B)
76 (D)	**77** (B)	**78** (A)	**79** (D)	**80** (D)
81 (C)	**82** (D)	**83** (B)	**84** (A)	**85** (A)
86 (B)	**87** (C)	**88** (B)	**89** (D)	**90** (B)
91 (A)	**92** (D)	**93** (A)	**94** (C)	**95** (A)
96 (B)	**97** (B)	**98** (C)	**99** (A)	**100** (B)

Part 1

1 M-Cn

(A) She's inserting a cord into an outlet.
(B) She's pressing a button on a machine.
(C) She's gripping the handle of a drawer.
(D) She's tacking a notice onto the wall.

(A) 여자가 콘센트에 코드를 꽂고 있다.
(B) 여자가 기계의 버튼을 누르고 있다.
(C) 여자가 서랍 손잡이를 잡고 있다.
(D) 여자가 압정으로 벽에 안내문을 붙이고 있다.

어휘 insert 끼우다, 넣다 outlet 콘센트 grip 꽉 잡다, 움켜쥐다 tack 압정으로 고정하다

해설 혼합 사진 – 사람의 동작/상태 묘사

(A) 정답. 여자가 콘센트에 코드를 꽂고 있는(is inserting a cord into an outlet) 모습이므로 정답.
(B) 동사 오답. 여자가 기계의 버튼을 누르고 있는(is pressing a button on a machine) 모습이 아니므로 오답.

(C) 동사 오답. 여자가 서랍 손잡이를 잡고 있는(is gripping the handle of a drawer) 모습이 아니므로 오답.
(D) 동사 오답. 여자가 압정으로 벽에 안내문을 붙이고 있는(is tacking a notice onto the wall) 모습이 아니므로 오답.

2 W-Am

(A) Some window shutters are being replaced.
(B) A pillow is being arranged on a seat.
(C) An outdoor table is being cleared off.
(D) Some wooden boards are being painted.

(A) 덧창들이 교체되고 있다.
(B) 쿠션이 좌석에 정리되고 있다.
(C) 야외 테이블이 치워지고 있다.
(D) 널빤지들이 도색되고 있다.

어휘 shutter 덮개 arrange 정리하다 wooden board 널빤지

해설 혼합 사진 – 사람/사물/풍경 혼합 묘사

(A) 동사 오답. 덧창들(Some window shutters)이 교체되고 있는(are being replaced) 모습이 아니므로 오답.
(B) 정답. 쿠션(A pillow)이 좌석에 정리되고 있는(is being arranged on a seat) 모습이므로 정답.
(C) 동사 오답. 야외 테이블(An outdoor table)이 치워지고 있는(is being cleared off) 모습이 아니므로 오답.
(D) 동사 오답. 널빤지들(Some wooden boards)이 도색되고 있는(are being painted) 모습이 아니므로 오답.

3 M-Cn

▶ 동영상 강의

(A) Some utensils have been discarded in a bin.
(B) Some bottles are being emptied into a sink.
(C) A rolling chair has been placed next to a counter.
(D) Some drawers have been left open.

(A) 기구들이 쓰레기통에 버려져 있다.
(B) 병들이 싱크대에 비워지고 있다.
(C) 바퀴 달린 의자가 카운터 옆에 놓여 있다.
(D) 서랍들이 열려 있다.

어휘 utensil 기구, 도구 discard 버리다, 폐기하다 empty 비우다 rolling chair 바퀴 달린 의자

해설 사물/풍경 사진 – 사물 묘사
(A) 사진에 없는 명사를 이용한 오답. 사진에 기구들(Some utensils)과 쓰레기통(a bin)의 모습이 보이지 않으므로 오답.
(B) 사진에 없는 명사를 이용한 오답. 사진에 싱크대(a sink)의 모습이 보이지 않으므로 오답.
(C) 정답. 바퀴 달린 의자(A rolling chair)가 카운터 옆에 놓여 있는(has been placed next to a counter) 모습이므로 정답.
(D) 동사 오답. 서랍들(Some drawers)이 열려 있는(have been left open) 모습이 아니므로 오답.

4 W-Am

(A) A man is chopping some wood into pieces.
(B) Leaves are scattered across the grass.
(C) A man is closing a window.
(D) Wood is piled near a fence.

(A) 남자가 나무를 여러 조각으로 자르고 있다.
(B) 풀밭에 나뭇잎이 흩어져 있다.
(C) 남자가 창문을 닫고 있다.
(D) 울타리 근처에 나무가 쌓여 있다.

어휘 chop (장작 같은 것을) 패다, 찍어서 자르다   scatter 흩어지게 만들다, 흩뿌리다   pile 쌓다

해설 혼합 사진 – 사람/사물/풍경 혼합 묘사
(A) 동사 오답. 남자가 나무를 여러 조각으로 자르고 있는(is chopping some wood into pieces) 모습이 아니므로 오답.
(B) 동사 오답. 나뭇잎(Leaves)이 풀밭에 흩어져 있는(are scattered across the grass) 모습이 아니므로 오답.
(C) 동사 오답. 남자가 창문을 닫고 있는(is closing a window) 모습이 아니므로 오답.
(D) 정답. 나무(Wood)가 울타리 근처에 쌓여 있는(is piled near a fence) 모습이므로 정답.

5 W-Br

(A) People are standing in line in a lobby.
(B) Items are being loaded into shopping bags.
(C) Tents have been set up in a parking area.
(D) A worker is putting up a canopy.

(A) 사람들이 로비에 일렬로 서 있다.
(B) 물건들이 쇼핑백에 담기고 있다.
(C) 주차장에 천막들이 설치되어 있다.
(D) 인부가 덮개를 치고 있다.

어휘 load 싣다, 적재하다   set up 세우다, 설치하다   canopy 덮개

해설 혼합 사진 – 사람/사물/풍경 혼합 묘사
(A) 사진에 없는 명사를 이용한 오답. 사진에 로비(a lobby)의 모습이 보이지 않으므로 오답.
(B) 동사 오답. 물건들(Items)이 쇼핑백에 담기고 있는(are being loaded into shopping bags) 모습이 아니므로 오답.
(C) 정답. 천막들(Tents)이 주차장에 설치되어 있는(have been set up in a parking area) 모습이므로 정답.
(D) 동사 오답. 인부(A worker)가 덮개를 치고 있는(is putting up a canopy) 모습이 아니므로 오답.

6 W-Am

(A) Some luggage is stacked next to an escalator.
(B) A suitcase is being lifted onto a shuttle bus.
(C) Some suitcases are displayed in a shop window.
(D) A luggage rack has two levels.

(A) 에스컬레이터 옆에 수하물들이 쌓여 있다.
(B) 셔틀버스에 여행 가방이 들어올려지고 있다.
(C) 쇼윈도에 여행 가방들이 진열되어 있다.
(D) 수하물 선반이 2층으로 되어 있다.

어휘 luggage 수하물, 짐   stack 쌓다   display 진열하다, 전시하다   rack 선반

해설 사물/풍경 사진 – 사물 묘사
(A) 사진에 없는 명사를 이용한 오답. 사진에 에스컬레이터(an escalator)의 모습이 보이지 않으므로 오답.
(B) 사진에 없는 명사를 이용한 오답. 사진에 셔틀버스(a shuttle bus)의 모습이 보이지 않으므로 오답.
(C) 사진에 없는 명사를 이용한 오답. 사진에 쇼윈도(a shop window)의 모습이 보이지 않으므로 오답.
(D) 정답. 수하물 선반(A luggage rack)이 2층으로 되어 있는(has two levels) 모습이므로 정답.

PART 2

7

M-Au Have the machines on the factory floor been cleaned?

W-Am (A) No, not yet.
(B) It's in the shipping container.
(C) I just put it in the trash bin.

작업 현장의 기계들은 청소가 되어 있나요?
(A) 아니요, 아직이요.
(B) 그것은 선적 컨테이너에 있어요.
(C) 막 쓰레기통에 넣었어요.

어휘 factory floor (공장의) 작업 현장   shipping container 선적 컨테이너   trash bin 쓰레기통

해설 작업 현장 기계들이 청소되어 있는지 여부를 묻는 조동사(Have) 의문문

(A) 정답. 작업 현장의 기계들이 청소되어 있는지 여부를 묻는 질문에 아니요(No)라고 대답한 뒤, 아직이라며 부정 답변과 일관된 내용을 덧붙이고 있으므로 정답.

(B) 연상 단어 오답. 질문의 factory에서 연상 가능한 shipping container를 이용한 오답.

(C) 연상 단어 오답. 질문의 cleaned에서 연상 가능한 trash bin을 이용한 오답.

8

M-Au How much will the budget increase next year?

W-Br (A) About 10 percent.
(B) Three hours, I think.
(C) At the bank's main branch.

내년에 예산이 얼마나 오를까요?
(A) 10퍼센트 정도요.
(B) 세 시간일 것 같아요.
(C) 은행 본점에서요.

어휘 budget 예산   main branch 본점

해설 내년 예산 증가율을 묻는 How much 의문문

(A) 정답. 내년 예산 증가율을 묻는 질문에 10퍼센트 정도라며 구체적인 숫자로 응답하고 있으므로 정답.

(B) 질문과 상관없는 오답. How long 의문문에 대한 응답이므로 오답.

(C) 질문과 상관없는 오답. Where 의문문에 대한 응답이므로 오답.

9

W-Br You're going to water the plants before you leave, aren't you?

M-Cn (A) I walked the whole way.
(B) Yes, right after lunch.
(C) In the breakroom.

가기 전에 식물에 물을 주실 거죠, 그렇죠?
(A) 저는 내내 걸었어요.
(B) 네, 점심 식사 직후예요.
(C) 휴게실에서요.

어휘 the whole way 내내, 끝까지   break room 휴게실

해설 가기 전에 식물에 물을 줄 건지 의사를 확인하는 부가 의문문

(A) 연상 단어 오답. 질문의 going에서 연상 가능한 walked를 이용한 오답.

(B) 정답. 가기 전에 식물에 물을 줄 건지 의사를 확인하는 질문에 네(Yes)라고 대답한 뒤, 점심 식사 직후라며 긍정 답변과 일관된 내용을 덧붙였으므로 정답.

(C) 질문과 상관없는 오답. Where 의문문에 대한 응답이므로 오답.

10

W-Am Aren't you going to schedule an eye doctor appointment?

M-Cn (A) Those glasses look nice on you.
(B) I already scheduled one.
(C) The seminar is three days long.

안과 예약 일정을 잡으실 것 아닌가요?
(A) 그 안경이 잘 어울리시네요.
(B) 이미 예약을 잡았어요.
(C) 세미나는 3일간이에요.

어휘 schedule 일정을 잡다   appointment 약속, 예약

해설 안과 예약 진행 여부를 확인하는 부정 의문문

(A) 연상 단어 오답. 질문의 eye에서 연상 가능한 glasses를 이용한 오답.

(B) 정답. 안과 예약 일정을 잡을 건지 묻는 질문에 이미 예약을 잡았다며 아니요(No)를 생략한 부정 답변을 하고 있으므로 정답.

(C) 질문과 상관없는 오답.

11

W-Am I'm going to try to fix this printer.

M-Au (A) You're right, it doesn't fit.
(B) Double-sided copies.
(C) Are you sure it can be repaired?

이 프린터를 수리해 보려고 해요.
(A) 그래요, 맞지 않아요.
(B) 양면 복사요.
(C) 수리가 될까요?

어휘 fit 맞다   double-sided 양면의

해설 의사 전달의 평서문

(A) 유사 발음 오답. 평서문의 fix와 부분적으로 발음이 유사한 fit을 이용한 오답.

(B) 연상 단어 오답. 평서문의 printer에서 연상 가능한 copies를 이용한 오답.

(C) 정답. 이 프린터를 수리해 보려고 한다는 평서문에 수리가 될지를 되물으며 의구심을 표현하고 있으므로 정답.

12

W-Am What should we do with these brochures?

M-Cn (A) A trip to the seashore.
(B) Yes, I found it already.
(C) I'll leave them at the front desk.

이 안내 책자들을 어떻게 할까요?
(A) 해안 여행이요.
(B) 네, 이미 찾았어요.
(C) 제가 프런트 데스크에 둘게요.

어휘 brochure 안내 책자   seashore 해안

해설 안내 책자의 처리 방법을 묻는 What 의문문

(A) 연상 단어 오답. 질문의 brochures에서 연상 가능한 trip을 이용한 오답.

(B) Yes/No 불가 오답. What 의문문에는 Yes/No 응답이 불가능하므로 오답.

(C) 정답. 안내 책자의 처리 방법을 묻는 질문에 프런트 데스크에 둘 것이라며 처리 방법을 구체적으로 알려 주고 있으므로 정답.

13

M-Au Has the policy meeting been rescheduled?

W-Br (A) We have lots of desk calendar designs.
(B) Yes, it's happening tomorrow instead.
(C) This soup I ordered is delicious.

정책 회의 일정이 변경됐나요?
(A) 책상 달력 디자인이 많이 있어요.
(B) 네, 대신 내일 열려요.
(C) 제가 주문한 수프가 맛있네요.

어휘 reschedule 일정을 변경하다

해설 정책 회의 일정의 변경 여부를 묻는 조동사(Has) 의문문
(A) 연상 단어 오답. 질문의 rescheduled에서 연상 가능한 calendar를 이용한 오답.
(B) 정답. 정책 회의 일정의 변경 여부를 묻는 질문에 네(Yes)라고 대답한 뒤, 내일 열린다며 긍정 답변과 일관된 내용을 덧붙이고 있으므로 정답.
(C) 질문과 상관없는 오답.

14

W-Am Why don't we stop by the office cafeteria on our way to the workshop?

M-Cn (A) Sure, we have time for that.
(B) A full-service buffet.
(C) The topic is professional networking.

워크숍 가는 길에 사내 카페에 잠깐 들르면 어때요?
(A) 좋아요, 그럴 시간이 있어요.
(B) 풀서비스 뷔페예요.
(C) 주제는 직업상 인맥 쌓기입니다.

어휘 stop by 잠깐 들르다   networking 인적 네트워크 형성

해설 제안/권유의 의문문
(A) 정답. 워크숍 가는 길에 사내 카페테리아에 잠깐 들릴 것을 제안하는 질문에 좋아요(Sure)라고 제안을 받아들인 뒤, 그럴 시간이 있다며 긍정 답변과 일관된 내용을 덧붙였으므로 정답.
(B) 연상 단어 오답. 질문의 cafeteria에서 연상 가능한 buffet를 이용한 오답.
(C) 연상 단어 오답. 질문의 workshop에서 연상 가능한 topic을 이용한 오답.

15

M-Cn Have you tried our famous pasta dish?

W-Br (A) We need a table for five.
(B) Yes, it was delicious.
(C) I'll try to make it on time.

저희 유명한 파스타 요리를 드셔 보셨나요?

(A) 다섯 명 자리가 필요해요.
(B) 네, 맛있었어요.
(C) 제시간에 가도록 해 볼게요.

어휘 make it 시간 맞춰 가다   on time 제시간에, 늦지 않게

해설 파스타 요리 식사 경험 유무를 묻는 조동사(Have) 의문문
(A) 연상 단어 오답. 질문의 dish에서 연상 가능한 table을 이용한 오답.
(B) 정답. 파스타 요리 식사 경험 유무를 묻는 질문에 네(Yes)라고 대답한 뒤, 맛있었다며 긍정 답변과 일관된 내용을 덧붙이고 있으므로 정답.
(C) 파생어 오답. 질문의 tried와 파생어 관계인 try를 이용한 오답.

16

M-Au Who's the opening act at tonight's concert?

W-Br (A) Could you turn up the volume?
(B) A jazz singer from France.
(C) The position has been filled.

오늘 밤 음악회의 개막 공연은 누가 하죠?
(A) 볼륨 좀 높여 주시겠어요?
(B) 프랑스 출신의 재즈 가수요.
(C) 그 자리는 충원됐어요.

어휘 opening act 개막 공연   fill the position 충원하다

해설 음악회의 개막 공연자를 묻는 Who 의문문
(A) 연상 단어 오답. 질문의 concert에서 연상 가능한 volume을 이용한 오답.
(B) 정답. 오늘 밤 음악회 개막 공연을 할 사람을 묻는 질문에 프랑스 출신의 재즈 가수라고 알려 주고 있으므로 정답.
(C) 연상 단어 오답. 질문의 opening을 '공석'으로 잘못 이해했을 경우 연상 가능한 position을 이용한 오답.

17

M-Au When do the product demonstrations start?

W-Am (A) The schedule was e-mailed last Friday.
(B) Some innovative features.
(C) In room 202, I think.

제품 시연은 언제 시작하나요?
(A) 지난 금요일에 일정표가 이메일로 발송됐어요.
(B) 획기적인 기능들이요.
(C) 202호인 것 같아요.

어휘 demonstration 시연, 시범 설명   innovative 획기적인, 혁신적인   feature 특징, 기능

해설 제품 시연의 시작 시기를 묻는 When 의문문
(A) 정답. 제품 시연의 시작 시기를 묻는 질문에 지난 금요일에 일정표가 이메일로 발송됐다며 알 수 있는 방법을 간접적으로 제시하고 있으므로 정답.
(B) 연상 단어 오답. 질문의 product에서 연상 가능한 features를 이용한 오답.
(C) 질문과 상관없는 오답. Where 의문문에 대한 응답이므로 오답.

18

M-Au I tried updating the Web site, but it didn't work.

W-Br (A) That date works for me.
(B) Usually our online reviews.
(C) Just send me the changes you want.

웹사이트를 업데이트해 봤는데, 안 됐어요.
(A) 저는 그날 괜찮아요.
(B) 보통 저희 온라인 후기요.
(C) 원하시는 변경 사항을 저에게 보내주세요.

해설 문제점 전달의 평서문
(A) 파생어 오답. 평서문의 work와 파생어 관계인 works를 이용한 오답.
(B) 연상 단어 오답. 평서문의 Web site에서 연상 가능한 online을 이용한 오답.
(C) 정답. 웹사이트를 업데이트해 봤는데, 안 됐다는 평서문에 원하는 변경 사항을 보내 달라며 문제점에 대한 해결책을 제시하고 있으므로 정답.

19

▶ 동영상 강의

W-Am Did you hire a new welding specialist?

M-Au (A) The part's back-ordered.
(B) Yes, he starts tomorrow.
(C) No, it should be higher.

용접 전문가를 새로 고용했나요?
(A) 그 부품은 주문이 밀려 있어요.
(B) 네, 내일부터 일을 시작해요.
(C) 아니요, 더 높아야 해요.

어휘 welding 용접 back-ordered 주문이 밀려 있는

해설 용접 전문가 고용 여부를 묻는 조동사(Did) 의문문
(A) 질문과 상관없는 오답.
(B) 정답. 용접 전문가 고용 여부를 묻는 질문에 네(Yes)라고 대답한 뒤, 내일부터 일을 시작한다며 긍정 답변과 일관된 내용을 덧붙였으므로 정답.
(C) 유사 발음 오답. 질문의 hire와 발음이 유사한 higher를 이용한 오답.

20

W-Br How was the color palette for the lobby chosen?

M-Au (A) Blue and orange.
(B) It was fine, thanks.
(C) I wasn't involved.

로비의 색상 조합은 어떻게 선택됐나요?
(A) 파란색과 오렌지색이요.
(B) 좋았어요, 감사합니다.
(C) 저는 관여하지 않았는데요.

어휘 be involved 관여하다

해설 로비 색상 선택 방식을 묻는 How 의문문
(A) 연상 단어 오답. 질문의 color에서 연상 가능한 blue와 orange를 이용한 오답.
(B) 연상 단어 오답. 질문의 How를 의견을 묻는 것으로 이해했을 경우 연상 가능한 fine을 이용한 오답.
(C) 정답. 로비 색상 조합이 어떤 방식으로 선택됐는지 묻는 질문에 자신은 관여하지 않았다며 모른다는 사실을 우회적으로 표현하고 있으므로 정답.

21

W-Br When are we ordering more supplies for the office?

M-Cn (A) In the storage closet.
(B) Next week on Monday.
(C) The new desk looks great!

사무실 용품은 언제 더 주문해요?
(A) 수납장에요.
(B) 다음 주 월요일에요.
(C) 새 책상이 멋지네요!

어휘 supply 용품 storage closet 수납장

해설 사무실 용품의 추가 주문 시점을 묻는 When 의문문
(A) 연상 단어 오답. 질문의 supplies에서 연상 가능한 storage closet을 이용한 오답.
(B) 정답. 사무실 용품 추가 주문 시점을 묻는 질문에 다음 주 월요일이라고 구체적인 시점을 알려 주고 있으므로 정답.
(C) 연상 단어 오답. 질문의 office에서 연상 가능한 desk를 이용한 오답.

22

▶ 동영상 강의

W-Am The battery for the water pump is going to be solar powered, right?

M-Cn (A) We're still in the planning stages.
(B) A hundred and forty dollars per year.
(C) Yes, I'd love a glass of water.

양수기 배터리는 태양열로 작동되겠죠, 그렇죠?
(A) 아직 기획 단계에 있어요.
(B) 1년에 140달러요.
(C) 네, 물 한 잔 주세요.

어휘 solar powered 태양열로 움직이는, 태양열 발전의

해설 양수기 배터리가 태양열로 작동될 것인지 확인하는 부가 의문문
(A) 정답. 양수기 배터리가 태양열로 작동될 것인지 묻는 질문에 아직 기획 단계에 있다며 결정되지 않았음을 간접적으로 알려 주고 있으므로 정답.
(B) 질문과 상관없는 오답. How much 의문문에 대한 응답이므로 오답.
(C) 단어 반복 오답. 질문의 water를 반복 이용한 오답.

23

M-Au Where can I buy a charger for this laptop?

W-Br (A) Around three o'clock.
(B) I can order one for you.
(C) A limited return policy.

이 노트북 충전기는 어디서 살 수 있나요?

(A) 3시쯤요.

(B) 제가 주문해 드릴 수 있어요.

(C) 제한적인 반품 규정이요.

어휘 charger 충전기 limited 한정된, 제한된

해설 노트북 충전기 구매 가능 장소를 묻는 Where 의문문

(A) 질문과 상관없는 오답. When 의문문에 대한 응답이므로 오답.

(B) 정답. 노트북 충전기 구매 가능 장소를 묻는 질문에 주문해 줄 수 있다며 도와주겠다는 의사를 표현하고 있으므로 정답.

(C) 연상 단어 오답. 질문의 buy에서 연상 가능한 return을 이용한 오답.

24

M-Cn Do I need to reserve a meeting room?

W-Am (A) Yes, let me show you how.

(B) The service is good.

(C) My slide presentation.

회의실을 예약해야 할까요?

(A) 네, 방법을 알려 드릴게요.

(B) 서비스가 좋네요.

(C) 제 슬라이드 발표요.

해설 회의실을 예약해야 하는지 묻는 조동사(Do) 의문문

(A) 정답. 회의실 예약을 해야 하는지 묻는 질문에 네(Yes)라고 대답한 뒤, 방법을 알려 주겠다며 긍정 답변과 일관된 내용을 덧붙였으므로 정답.

(B) 질문과 상관없는 오답.

(C) 연상 단어 오답. 질문의 meeting에서 연상 가능한 presentation을 이용한 오답.

25

M-Cn When's the new department director supposed to start?

W-Br (A) It's an hour long.

(B) Ms. Pavlova isn't retiring for several weeks.

(C) No, that department's upstairs.

신임 부서장은 언제 일을 시작하기로 되어 있나요?

(A) 한 시간 걸려요.

(B) 파블로바 씨가 몇 주간 퇴직하지 않을 거예요.

(C) 아니요, 그 부서는 위층에 있어요.

어휘 be supposed to ~하기로 되어 있다 retire 은퇴하다, 퇴직하다

해설 신임 부서장의 직무 시작 시점을 묻는 When 의문문

(A) 질문과 상관없는 오답. How long 의문문에 대한 응답이므로 오답.

(B) 정답. 신임 부서장의 직무 시작 시점을 묻는 질문에 파블로바 씨가 몇 주간 퇴직하지 않을 거라며 몇 주 후에야 신임 부서장이 직무를 시작할 수 있음을 간접적으로 알려 주고 있으므로 정답.

(C) Yes/No 불가 오답. When 의문문에는 Yes/No 응답이 불가능하므로 오답.

26

W-Br Should I deliver these pizzas, or will you?

M-Au (A) No thanks—I'm not hungry.

(B) Ten dollars for two.

(C) They're being picked up.

제가 이 피자들을 배달해야 하나요, 아니면 당신이 하시겠어요?

(A) 괜찮아요. 배가 고프지 않아서요.

(B) 두 개에 10달러입니다.

(C) 가지러 올 거예요.

해설 피자 배달할 사람을 묻는 선택 의문문

(A) 연상 단어 오답. 질문의 pizzas에서 연상 가능한 hungry를 이용한 오답.

(B) 질문과 상관없는 오답. How much 의문문에 대한 응답이므로 오답.

(C) 정답. 두 사람 중 누가 피자를 배달할지 묻는 질문에 가지러 올 거라며 두 선택지를 제외한 제3의 안을 제시하고 있는 정답.

27

M-Au This month's shipment schedule has been revised.

W-Br (A) I couldn't find them either.

(B) Which dates have been changed?

(C) Two dollars per pound.

이번 달 수송 일정이 변경됐어요.

(A) 저도 찾을 수 없었어요.

(B) 어떤 날짜가 변경됐죠?

(C) 파운드당 2달러입니다.

어휘 shipment 수송, 운송 revise 변경하다, 수정하다

해설 정보 전달의 평서문

(A) 평서문과 상관없는 오답. 평서문에 3인칭 대명사 them으로 지칭할 복수 명사가 언급된 적이 없으므로 오답.

(B) 정답. 이번 달 수송 일정이 변경됐다는 평서문에 어떤 날짜가 변경됐는지 일정 변경과 관련된 내용을 묻고 있으므로 정답.

(C) 평서문과 상관없는 오답. How much 의문문에 대한 응답이므로 오답.

28

M-Cn How much will the repairs cost?

W-Br (A) The work is covered under the warranty plan.

(B) Yes, it's also available in red.

(C) In about two weeks.

수리 비용은 얼마나 들까요?

(A) 그 작업은 품질 보증서 보장 범위 안에 있습니다.

(B) 네, 빨간색도 있습니다.

(C) 대략 2주 후예요.

어휘 warranty 품질 보증서 available 이용 가능한, 구할 수 있는

해설 수리 비용을 묻는 How much 의문문

(A) 정답. 수리 비용을 묻는 질문에 그 작업은 품질 보증서 보장 범위 안에 있다며 비용이 발생하지 않음을 간접적으로 알려 주고 있으므로 정답.

（B) Yes/No 불가 오답. How much 의문문에는 Yes/No 응답이 불가능하므로 오답.
(C) 질문과 상관없는 오답. When 의문문에 대한 응답이므로 오답.

29

W-Br　Why don't we provide more samples of the wallpaper patterns?

M-Au　(A) The newspaper is delivered daily.
　　　(B) An interior design course.
　　　(C) There are plenty in the binders.

벽지 무늬 견본을 더 제공하면 어때요?
(A) 신문은 매일 배달됩니다.
(B) 실내 디자인 강의요.
(C) 바인더에 많이 있어요.

어휘 wallpaper 벽지　plenty 풍부한 양

해설 제안/권유의 의문문
(A) 유사 발음 오답. 질문의 wallpaper와 부분적으로 발음이 유사한 newspaper를 이용한 오답.
(B) 연상 단어 오답. 질문의 samples와 patterns에서 연상 가능한 design을 이용한 오답.
(C) 정답. 벽지 무늬 견본 추가 제공을 제안하는 질문에 바인더에 많이 있다며 제안에 대한 거절 의사를 우회적으로 표현하고 있으므로 정답.

30

W-Am　Can you give me a tour of the property this afternoon?

M-Cn　(A) Sorry, I won't have time until tomorrow.
　　　(B) It has a very modern design.
　　　(C) A house on Maple Street.

오늘 오후에 그 건물을 견학시켜 주실 수 있나요?
(A) 죄송하지만 내일까지 시간이 없어요.
(B) 굉장히 현대적인 디자인입니다.
(C) 메이플 가에 있는 집이요.

어휘 property 건물, 부동산

해설 부탁/요청의 의문문
(A) 정답. 오늘 오후에 건물을 견학시켜 달라는 요청에 죄송하다(Sorry)라고 거절한 뒤, 내일까지 시간이 없다며 부정 답변과 일관된 내용을 덧붙이고 있으므로 정답.
(B) 연상 단어 오답. 질문의 property에서 연상 가능한 modern design을 이용한 오답.
(C) 연상 단어 오답. 질문의 property에서 연상 가능한 house를 이용한 오답.

31

W-Br　Who's scheduled to test the product today?

M-Au　(A) We're waiting for confirmation.
　　　(B) It's a great album, right?
　　　(C) About six weeks ago.

오늘 제품 테스트는 누가 할 예정인가요?
(A) 확정되길 기다리고 있어요.
(B) 멋진 앨범이네요, 그렇죠?
(C) 약 6주 전에요.

어휘 be scheduled to ~할 예정이다　confirmation 획정, 확인

해설 제품을 테스트할 사람을 묻는 Who 의문문
(A) 정답. 제품을 테스트할 사람을 묻는 질문에 확정되길 기다리고 있다며 아직 정해지지 않았음을 우회적으로 알려 주고 있으므로 정답.
(B) 질문과 상관없는 오답.
(C) 질문과 상관없는 오답. When 의문문에 대한 응답이므로 오답.

PART 3

32-34

M-Cn　[32]Good morning, captain. We'll be docking at the port in Kolkata this evening, right?

W-Am　[33]Actually, we had to change course overnight to avoid a storm, so we're running behind schedule. But we should arrive early tomorrow.

M-Cn　Well, that's not too bad.

W-Am　Oh, Hector has the day off today, so [34]I'll need you to do the morning rounds—starting with checking the machinery in the engine room.

M-Cn　[34]Of course—I'll head there now.

남　안녕하세요, 선장님. 오늘 저녁 콜카타 항구에 정박할 예정이죠, 그렇죠?
여　실은 폭풍우를 피하기 위해 밤새 경로를 변경해야 했어요. 그래서 예정보다 늦어지고 있습니다. 하지만 내일 일찍 도착할 거예요.
남　뭐, 그렇게 나쁘진 않네요.
여　아, 헥터가 오늘 휴무라서 오전 일과를 해 주셔야 해요. 기관실 기계 확인부터요.
남　네, 지금 그리로 갈게요.

어휘　dock 부두에 대다　avoid 피하다　behind schedule 예정보다 늦게　machinery 기계　engine room (선박의) 기관실　head 향하다

32

Where does the conversation most likely take place?
(A) On a train
(B) On a boat
(C) At a factory
(D) At an airport

대화는 어디서 이루어지겠는가?

(A) 기차
(B) 배
(C) 공장
(D) 공항

해설 전체 내용 관련 – 대화의 장소

남자가 첫 대사에서 선장인 여자에게 인사(Good morning, captain)하며 오늘 저녁 콜카타 항구에 정박할 예정인지(We'll be docking at the port in Kolkata this evening, right?)를 묻고 있으므로 배 위에서 이루어지는 대화임을 알 수 있다. 따라서 정답은 (B)이다.

33

What caused a delay?
(A) An electrical failure occurred.
(B) A worker was unavailable.
(C) Some information was incorrect.
(D) The weather was bad.

지연된 이유는 무엇인가?
(A) 정전이 발생했다.
(B) 인부를 구할 수 없었다.
(C) 정보가 정확하지 않았다.
(D) 날씨가 나빴다.

어휘 electrical failure 정전 occur 발생하다 unavailable 구할 수 없는, 이용할 수 없는 incorrect 부정확한, 맞지 않는

해설 세부 사항 관련 – 지연된 이유

여자가 첫 대사에서 폭풍우를 피하기 위해 밤새 경로를 변경해야 했기 때문에 예정보다 늦어지고 있다(Actually, we had to change course overnight to avoid a storm, so we're running behind schedule)고 말하고 있으므로 정답은 (D)이다.

> Paraphrasing 대화의 behind schedule → 질문의 a delay
> 대화의 a storm → 정답의 The weather was bad.

34

What will the man do next?
(A) Confirm a schedule
(B) Speak to a coworker
(C) Check some machinery
(D) Clean a storage room

남자는 다음으로 무엇을 할 것인가?
(A) 일정 확인
(B) 동료에게 이야기
(C) 기계 확인
(D) 보관실 청소

어휘 confirm 확인해 주다, 확정하다 coworker 동료 storage 보관

해설 세부 사항 관련 – 남자가 다음에 할 일

여자가 두 번째 대사에서 남자에게 기관실 기계 확인부터 시작해 줄 것(I'll need you ~ starting with checking the machinery in the engine room)을 요청하자 남자가 물론(Of course)이라고 대답하며 지금 그리로

가겠다(I'll head there now)고 덧붙이고 있으므로 정답은 (C)이다.

35-37

M-Cn	Hi. ³⁵**I'm here to schedule some personal training sessions.**
W-Br	OK. ³⁵**What are your fitness goals?**
M-Cn	I'd like to lift weights and build strength.
W-Br	I can work with you on that. Are you currently a member here?
M-Cn	No, I'll also need to sign up for a membership. ³⁶**I saw online that you're running a special for new members—fifty percent off the first month's membership. Can I sign up for that?**
W-Br	Absolutely. ³⁷**But before I get you signed up, let me show you around our facility.**

남	안녕하세요. **PT 일정을 잡으러 왔어요.**
여	네. **운동 목표가 무엇인가요?**
남	웨이트 트레이닝으로 근력을 키우고 싶어요.
여	제가 도와드릴 수 있어요. 현재 이곳 회원이세요?
남	아니요, 회원 가입도 해야 해요. **온라인에서 봤는데, 신규 회원에게 특별히 첫 달 회비를 50% 할인해 준다고 하던데요. 신청할 수 있나요?**
여	그럼요, **그런데 신청하시기 전에 저희 시설을 안내해 드릴게요.**

어휘	personal 개인의 sign up for ~을 신청하다 absolutely 전적으로, 틀림없이 facility 시설

35

Where does the woman most likely work?
(A) At a sports stadium
(B) At a fitness center
(C) At a doctor's office
(D) At a library

여자는 어디서 일하겠는가?
(A) 경기장
(B) 피트니스 센터
(C) 병원
(D) 도서관

해설 전체 내용 관련 – 여자의 근무지

남자가 첫 대사에서 PT 일정을 잡으러 왔다(I'm here to schedule some personal training sessions)고 하자 여자가 운동 목표가 무엇인지(What are your fitness goals?)를 묻는 것으로 보아 여자는 피트니스 센터에서 근무 중임을 알 수 있다. 따라서 정답은 (B)이다.

36

What does the man ask about?
(A) A discount
(B) A form
(C) A business location
(D) A parking policy

남자는 무엇에 대해 물어보는가?
(A) 할인
(B) 서식
(C) 업체 위치
(D) 주차 정책

해설 세부 사항 관련 – 남자의 문의 사항

남자가 세 번째 대사에서 신규 회원은 첫 달 회비를 50% 할인해 준다는 것을 온라인에서 봤다(I saw online that you're running a special for new members—fifty percent off the first month's membership)고 했고 신청할 수 있는지(Can I sign up for that?)를 묻고 있으므로 정답은 (A)이다.

> **Paraphrasing** 대화의 fifty percent off → 정답의 A discount

37

What will the woman do next?
(A) Post a sign
(B) Confirm an account number
(C) Provide a tour
(D) Look at a schedule

여자는 다음으로 무엇을 하겠는가?
(A) 표지판 게시하기
(B) 계좌 번호 확인하기
(C) 견학 제공하기
(D) 일정표 보기

어휘 post 게시하다 account number 계좌 번호

해설 세부 사항 관련 – 여자가 다음에 할 일

여자가 마지막 대사에서 시설을 안내해 주겠다(~ let me show you around our facility)고 말하고 있으므로 정답은 (C)이다.

> **Paraphrasing** 대화의 show you around our facility
> → 정답의 Provide a tour

38-40

W-Am	As you can see, this Renaissance landscape painting we acquired is in bad condition. We can't display it yet.
M-Cn	Hmm, yes. ³⁸**This painting will need significant restoration work.**
W-Am	³⁸, ³⁹**I'll begin by investigating the artist's color palette and style to see how we should repair the damaged areas.**

M-Cn	You know, ⁴⁰**this would be a stunning piece to unveil at our anniversary dinner in June. And, since it's a big project to finish by then, we should get started right away.**

여	보시다시피 우리가 구한 이 르네상스 풍경화는 상태가 좋지 않아요. 아직 전시할 수 없습니다.
남	음… 네. 이 그림은 상당한 복원 작업이 필요하겠어요.
여	우선 화가의 색채와 화풍부터 조사해 손상된 부분을 어떻게 복구해야 하는지 살펴볼 것입니다.
남	자, 6월에 있을 기념일 만찬에서 공개하기에 아주 멋진 작품이 될 거예요. 그때까지 끝내야 하는 큰 프로젝트이니 당장 시작해야 합니다.

어휘	landscape painting 풍경화 acquire 획득하다, 얻다 condition 상태 significant 중요한, 커다란 restoration 복원 investigate 조사하다 stunning 굉장히 아름다운, 아주 멋진 unveil 공개하다, 발표하다 anniversary 기념일

38

Who most likely are the speakers?
(A) Art restorers
(B) Event planners
(C) Photographers
(D) Interior designers

화자들은 누구이겠는가?
(A) 예술품 복원가
(B) 행사 기획자
(C) 사진작가
(D) 실내 디자이너

어휘 restorer 복원가

해설 전체 내용 관련 – 화자들의 직업

남자가 첫 대사에서 이 그림은 상당한 복원 작업이 필요하겠다(This painting will need significant restoration work)고 했고, 여자가 손상된 곳을 어떻게 수리할 것인지(~ to see how we should repair the damaged areas)에 대해 언급하는 것으로 보아 화자들은 그림 복원가임을 알 수 있다. 따라서 정답은 (A)이다.

> **Paraphrasing** 대화의 painting → 정답의 Art

39

What does the woman say she will do?
(A) Hire an intern
(B) Review a contract
(C) Take some measurements
(D) Investigate a problem

여자는 무엇을 하겠다고 말하는가?
(A) 인턴 고용하기
(B) 계약 검토하기
(C) 치수 재기
(D) 문제 조사하기

어휘 contract 계약　take a measurement 치수를 재다

해설 세부 사항 관련 – 여자가 할 일

여자가 두 번째 대사에서 화가의 색채와 화풍부터 조사해 손상된 부분을 어떻게 복구해야 하는지 살펴볼 것(I'll begin by investigating the artist's color palette and style to see how we should repair the damaged areas)이라고 말하고 있으므로 정답은 (D)이다.

40

Why does the man suggest beginning a project quickly?
(A) Payment has already been made.
(B) Staff will be on vacation.
(C) An important event is approaching.
(D) A client is in town for a limited time.

남자는 왜 프로젝트를 빨리 시작하자고 제안하는가?
(A) 이미 지불이 완료돼서
(B) 직원들이 휴가를 갈 것이라서
(C) 중요한 행사가 다가오고 있어서
(D) 고객이 한정된 시간 동안만 있을 것이라서

어휘 payment 지불, 결제　on vacation 휴가 중인　approach 다가오다　limited 한정된, 제한된

해설 세부 사항 관련 – 남자가 프로젝트를 빨리 시작하자고 제안하는 이유

남자가 마지막 대사에서 6월에 있을 기념일 만찬에서 공개하기에 아주 멋진 작품이 될 것(this would be a stunning piece to unveil at our anniversary dinner in June)이라며, 그때까지 끝내야 하는 큰 프로젝트이니 당장 시작해야 한다(since it's a big project to finish by then, we should get started right away)고 말하고 있으므로 정답은 (C)이다.

> Paraphrasing　대화의 our anniversary dinner in June
> → 정답의 An important event

41-43 3인 대화

W-Br	Hi, Ozan. **⁴¹Do you have time to review some slides I'm presenting at a meeting on Thursday?**
M-Au	Oh. **⁴²Is that the meeting with Smith Incorporated?**
W-Br	**⁴²Yes. I'm presenting them with our updated marketing plan for their chain of bookstores.**

M-Au	You know, **⁴³Smith Incorporated prefers informal meetings.** I think just a handout highlighting how our marketing plan will positively impact their book sales would be enough.
W-Br	Really? Thilo, you've worked with this client before. What do you think?
M-Cn	**⁴³Ozan is right. I think they'd prefer a meeting that was more of a conversation than a presentation.**

여	안녕하세요, 오잔. **제가 목요일 회의 때 발표할 슬라이드를 검토해 주실 시간이 있나요?**
남1	아, **스미스 주식회사와의 회의인가요?**
여	네. 그들의 서점 체인점을 위해 업데이트한 마케팅 계획을 발표할 거예요.
남1	저, **스미스 주식회사는 편안한 회의를 선호해요.** 제 생각엔 우리 마케팅 계획이 그들의 책 판매에 어떻게 긍정적인 영향을 줄 것인지 강조한 유인물만으로 충분할 것 같은데요.
여	정말요? 틸로, 전에 이 고객과 일해본 적이 있으시잖아요. 어떻게 생각하세요?
남2	**오잔 말이 맞아요. 발표보다는 대화에 가까운 회의를 더 좋아할 거예요.**

어휘	incorporated 주식회사　informal 편안한, 격식에 얽매이지 않는　handout 인쇄물, 유인물　highlight 강조하다　positively 긍정적으로　impact 영향

41

What is the woman preparing?
(A) A slide presentation
(B) A travel itinerary
(C) A guest list
(D) A sales contract

여자는 무엇을 준비하는가?
(A) 슬라이드 발표
(B) 여행 일정
(C) 손님 명단
(D) 판매 계약

어휘 itinerary 여행 일정표

해설 세부 사항 관련 – 여자가 준비 중인 일

여자가 첫 대사에서 목요일 회의 때 발표할 슬라이드를 검토해 줄 시간이 있는지(Do you have time to review some slides I'm presenting at a meeting on Thursday?) 묻고 있으므로 정답은 (A)이다.

> Paraphrasing　대화의 some slides I'm presenting
> → 정답의 A slide presentation

42

What kind of business is Smith Incorporated?
(A) A law firm
(B) A construction company
(C) A pharmaceutical manufacturer
(D) A bookstore chain

스미스 주식회사는 어떤 종류의 업체인가?
(A) 법률 사무소
(B) 건설 회사
(C) 제약 회사
(D) 서점 체인

어휘 construction 건설　pharmaceutical 제약의　manufacturer
제조사, 생산 회사

해설 세부 사항 관련 – 스미스 주식회사 업종
첫 번째 남자가 첫 대사에서 스미스 주식회사와의 회의인지(Is that the
meeting with Smith Incorporated?)를 묻자 여자가 그렇다(Yes)고
대답한 뒤, 그들의 서점 체인점을 위해 업데이트한 마케팅 계획을 발표할
것(I'm presenting them with our updated marketing plan for
their chain of bookstores)이라고 말하고 있으므로 정답은 (D)이다.

43

What do the men agree about?
(A) A subscription should be canceled.
(B) An advertising campaign should be delayed.
(C) A training session should be mandatory.
(D) A meeting should be casual.

남자들은 무엇에 대해 동의하는가?
(A) 구독이 취소되어야 한다.
(B) 광고 캠페인이 연기되어야 한다.
(C) 교육을 의무로 해야 한다.
(D) 회의는 격식에 얽매이지 않는 것이 좋다.

어휘 subscription 구독　mandatory 의무적인　casual 격식을
차리지 않는

해설 세부 사항 관련 – 남자들이 동의하는 것
첫 번째 남자가 두 번째 대사에서 스미스 주식회사는 편안한 회의를 선호
한다(Smith Incorporated prefers informal meetings)고 말했고, 두
번째 남자가 오잔 말이 맞다(Ozan is right)면서 발표보다는 대화에 가
까운 회의를 더 좋아할 것(I think they'd prefer a meeting that was
more of a conversation than a presentation)이라고 말하고 있으므
로 정답은 (D)이다.

> **Paraphrasing**　대화의 informal → 정답의 casual

44-46

W-Am	**⁴⁴I heard that the results of your experiment were better than you expected. Congratulations!**

M-Au	Thanks! I thought we'd have to run that reaction ten times before we got a positive result. But we got it on the third try.
W-Am	**⁴⁵You'll have to write up your results and submit them to the research director. That's Esra, right?**
M-Au	Oh, Esra's leaving the company next week.
W-Am	Oh, I didn't know that. I wonder if you'll be promoted to fill her position.
M-Au	I don't think so. **⁴⁶I've never managed an entire research group. I hope to get some experience doing that next quarter.**

여	**실험 결과가 예상하신 것보다 좋다고 들었어요. 축하해요!**
남	감사합니다! 반응 실험을 열 번은 해야 긍정적인 결과를 얻을 거라고 생각했는데요. 세 번째 시도에서 됐어요.
여	**결과를 적어서 연구소장에게 제출하셔야 할 거예요. 에스라죠, 그렇죠?**
남	아, 에스라는 다음 주에 회사를 그만둬요.
여	아, 몰랐어요. 당신이 승진해서 그 자리로 갈지 궁금하네요.
남	아닐 것 같은데요. **연구실 전체를 관리해 본 적이 없거든요. 다음 분기에는 그런 경험을 해봤으면 좋겠네요.**

어휘 experiment 실험　reaction 반응　positive 긍정적인
be promoted 승진하다　fill the position 충원하다
entire 전체의　quarter 분기

44

Why does the woman congratulate the man?
(A) He finished a road race.
(B) He won a publishing award.
(C) His experiment was successful.
(D) His research funding was extended.

여자는 왜 남자에게 축하를 전하는가?
(A) 도로 경주를 끝마쳤다.
(B) 출판상을 수상했다.
(C) 실험이 성공을 거뒀다.
(D) 연구 기금이 확대됐다.

어휘 funding 기금, 자금　extend 확대하다, 연장하다

해설 세부 사항 관련 – 여자가 남자에게 축하를 전한 이유
여자가 첫 대사에서 실험 결과가 예상했던 것보다 좋다고 들었다(I
heard that the results of your experiment were better than you
expected)며 축하한다(Congratulations!)고 말하고 있으므로 정답은
(C)이다.

> **Paraphrasing**　대화의 better than you expected
> → 정답의 successful

45

What does the man imply when he says, "Esra's leaving the company next week"?

(A) He needs assistance planning a party for Esra.
(B) He will not submit a report to Esra.
(C) He will apply for a new position.
(D) A larger office has become available.

남자가 "에스라는 다음 주에 회사를 그만둬요"라고 말하는 의도는 무엇인가?

(A) 에스라를 위한 파티를 계획하는 데 도움이 필요하다.
(B) 에스라에게 보고서를 제출하지 않을 것이다.
(C) 새로운 직책에 지원할 것이다.
(D) 더 큰 사무실을 구할 수 있게 됐다.

어휘 assistance 도움 apply for ~에 지원하다 available 구할 수 있는, 이용할 수 있는

해설 화자의 의도 파악 – 에스라는 다음 주에 회사를 그만둔다는 말의 의도

앞에서 여자가 결과를 연구소장에게 제출해야 할 것(You'll have to write up your results and submit them to the research director)이라며 에스라가 맞는지(That's Esra, right?) 확인하자 남자가 인용문을 언급하고 있는 것으로 보아, 에스라가 회사를 그만두기에 보고서를 그녀에게 제출하지 않겠다는 의도로 한 말임을 알 수 있다. 따라서 정답은 (B)이다.

46

What does the man hope to do next quarter?

(A) Receive a research grant
(B) Publish a book
(C) Replace some furniture
(D) Gain management experience

남자는 다음 분기에 무엇을 하고 싶어 하는가?

(A) 연구 지원금 받기
(B) 책 출간하기
(C) 가구 교체하기
(D) 관리 경험 얻기

어휘 grant 지원금 gain 얻다

해설 세부 사항 관련 – 남자가 다음 분기에 하고 싶은 일

남자가 마지막 대사에서 연구실 전체를 관리해 본 적이 없다(I've never managed an entire research group)며 다음 분기에는 그런 경험을 해봤으면 좋겠다(I hope to get some experience doing that next quarter)고 말하고 있으므로 정답은 (D)이다.

Paraphrasing 대화의 get → 정답의 Gain

47-49

W-Am Now we'll move on to a special segment of our news program where we highlight new local businesses for our viewers. Today I'm talking with Dhruv Bajaj—a personal trainer and gym owner. ⁴⁷**Thanks for coming into the studio today, Dhruv!**

M-Cn Thanks for having me! ⁴⁸**I'm excited to tell you about the gym I just opened last month.** It has state-of-the-art equipment, and my trainers can work with clients at any stage in their fitness journey.

W-Am Sounds great. ⁴⁹**How did you get started in this line of work?**

M-Cn Well, I was an athlete in school, and when I stopped competing, I wanted to continue doing something fitness-related. So I started working as a trainer.

여 이제 시청자들을 위해 신규 지역 업체를 집중 조명해 알려주는 뉴스 프로그램의 특별 코너로 넘어가겠습니다. 오늘은 개인 트레이너이자 체육관 소유주인 드루브 바자즈 씨와 얘기를 나누겠습니다. **오늘 스튜디오에 나와 주셔서 감사합니다, 드루브 씨!**

남 불러 주셔서 감사합니다! **지난달 문을 연 체육관에 대해 이야기하게 되어 기쁩니다.** 최첨단 장비를 갖추고 있고요. 저희 트레이너들은 운동 여정의 모든 단계에서 고객과 함께할 수 있어요.

여 훌륭하군요. **이 일을 어떻게 시작하게 되셨나요?**

남 저는 학창 시절에 선수였는데요. 시합 출전을 그만뒀을 때 운동 관련 일을 계속하고 싶었어요. 그래서 트레이너로 일하기 시작했죠.

어휘 segment 부분 highlight 강조하다, 집중 조명하다 local 지역의 owner 소유주 state-of-the-art 최신의, 최첨단의 equipment 장비 journey 여정 athlete 운동 선수 compete 경쟁하다, 시합에 참가하다

47

Where most likely are the speakers?

(A) At a sporting goods store
(B) At a television studio
(C) At a sports arena
(D) At a gym

화자들은 어디에 있겠는가?

(A) 스포츠 용품점
(B) TV 스튜디오
(C) 경기장
(D) 체육관

해설 전체 내용 관련 – 대화의 장소

여자가 첫 대사에서 스튜디오에 나와 줘서 감사하다(Thanks for coming into the studio today, Dhruv!)고 말하는 것으로 보아 대화의 장소가 스튜디오라는 것을 알 수 있다. 따라서 정답은 (B)이다.

48

What does the man say he recently did?
(A) He retired from his job.
(B) He designed a Web site.
(C) He opened a new facility.
(D) He competed in a sports event.

남자는 최근 무엇을 했다고 말하는가?
(A) 퇴직했다.
(B) 웹사이트를 디자인했다.
(C) 새 시설을 열었다.
(D) 스포츠 경기에 출전했다.

어휘 retire 은퇴하다, 퇴직하다　facility 시설

해설 세부 사항 관련 – 남자가 최근에 한 일

남자가 첫 대사에서 지난달 문을 연 체육관에 대해 이야기하게 되어 기쁘다(I'm excited to tell you about the gym I just opened last month)고 말하고 있으므로 정답은 (C)이다.

> **Paraphrasing**　대화의 last month → 질문의 recently
> 대화의 the gym I just opened
> → 정답의 a new facility

49

What does the woman ask the man to talk about?
(A) His career path
(B) His mentors
(C) His future goals
(D) His hobbies

여자는 남자에게 무엇에 대해 이야기해 달라고 요청하는가?
(A) 이력
(B) 멘토
(C) 향후 목표
(D) 취미

해설 세부 사항 관련 – 여자가 남자에게 요청한 이야기 주제

여자가 두 번째 대사에서 이 일을 어떻게 시작하게 되었는지(How did you get started in this line of work?) 묻고 있으므로 정답은 (A)이다.

50-52 3인 대화

M-Au	**51 As director, I'm delighted to welcome you to the Redmond Aquatic Institute.** We're happy you'll be producing content for our Web site.
W-Br	**50 I'm looking forward to writing about Redmond's initiatives in marine biology.**
M-Au	Yes, the more articles the public can read about threats to aquatic ecosystems, the

better. **51 Public awareness will help us get funding to meet our aim of preserving these ecosystems.** This is Roberto. He's working on our mangrove research project, which is the first one you'll cover.

M-Cn　It's an interesting project. And **52 what's exciting is that we've started using drones to photograph the area with the mangroves.** So we have some great images you could use.

남1	협회장으로서 레드몬드 수상 협회에 오신 것을 환영합니다. 저희 웹사이트 콘텐츠를 만들어 주신다니 기쁩니다.
여	레드몬드가 해양 생물학과 관련해서 진행하는 프로젝트들에 대해 글을 쓰게 돼 무척 기대돼요.
남1	네, 수중 생태계 위협에 대해 대중이 읽을 수 있는 기사가 많을수록 좋습니다. 대중의 인식이 생태계 보존이라는 우리의 목표를 달성하기 위한 기금을 확보하는 데 도움이 될 거예요. 이쪽은 로베르토입니다. 맹그로브 연구 프로젝트를 맡고 있죠. 처음으로 취재하실 내용입니다.
남2	그건 흥미로운 프로젝트예요. 흥미로운 점은 맹그로브가 있는 지역을 촬영하기 위해 드론을 사용하기 시작한 것입니다. 그래서 사용하실 수 있는 멋진 사진들이 있습니다.

어휘 delighted 아주 기뻐하는　aquatic 물과 관련된　institute 기관, 협회　look forward to ~을 고대하다　initiative 계획, 진취성　marine biology 해양 생물학　ecosystem 생태계　public awareness 대중의 인식　aim 목표　preserve 보존하다　cover 취재하다

50

What has the woman been hired to do?
(A) Write articles
(B) Update some software
(C) Organize a fund-raiser
(D) Manage office staff

여자는 무엇을 하도록 고용되었는가?
(A) 기사 작성
(B) 소프트웨어 업데이트
(C) 모금 행사 준비
(D) 사무실 직원 관리

어휘 organize 준비하다, 조직하다　fund-raiser 모금 행사

해설 세부 사항 관련 – 여자가 고용되어 할 일

여자가 첫 대사에서 레드몬드가 해양 생물학과 관련해서 진행하는 프로젝트들에 대해 글을 쓰게 돼 무척 기대된다(I'm looking forward to writing about Redmond's initiatives in marine biology)고 말하고 있으므로 정답은 (A)이다.

> **Paraphrasing**　대화의 writing about Redmond's initiatives in marine biology → 정답의 Write articles

51

According to the director, what is the organization's goal?

(A) To hire professionals in the field
(B) To create educational programs
(C) To collect data from other scientific institutes
(D) To protect aquatic environments

협회장에 따르면, 기관의 목표는 무엇인가?

(A) 해당 분야의 전문가 고용
(B) 교육 프로그램 제작
(C) 다른 과학 협회로부터 자료 수집
(D) 수중 환경 보호

어휘 organization 기관, 단체   collect 수집하다   scientific 과학의

해설 세부 사항 관련 – 협회장이 기관의 목표라고 말하는 것
첫 번째 남자가 첫 대사에서 자신을 협회장(As director, I'm ~)이라고 소개하고 있고, 두 번째 대사에서 생태계 보존이라는 목표(~ our aim of preserving these ecosystems)를 언급하고 있으므로 정답은 (D)이다.

> Paraphrasing   대화의 preserving these ecosystems
> → 정답의 protect aquatic environments

52

What does Roberto say is exciting?

(A) The use of some equipment
(B) The results of a survey
(C) The public response to a project
(D) A recent donation to the institute

로베르토는 무엇이 흥미롭다고 말하는가?

(A) 장비 이용
(B) 조사 결과
(C) 프로젝트에 대한 대중의 반응
(D) 최근 협회 기부

어휘 equipment 장비   donation 기부, 기증

해설 세부 사항 관련 – 로베르토가 흥미롭다고 말하는 것
두 번째 남자가 마지막 대사에서 흥미로운 점은 맹그로브가 있는 지역을 촬영하기 위해 드론을 사용하기 시작한 것(what's exciting is that we've started using drones to photograph the area with the mangroves)이라고 말하고 있으므로 정답은 (A)이다.

> Paraphrasing   대화의 using drones
> → 정답의 The use of some equipment

53-55

> W-Am Matthew, ⁵⁴**you're not planning to cancel Wednesday's budget meeting, are you?**

M-Au I haven't sent out the cancellation yet, but ⁵³**our research partners in China are off this week for a national holiday,** so there's no point in meeting. Why?

W-Am Well, ⁵⁴**I've been looking at the draft budget,** and we didn't allocate funds for a project leader.

M-Au Uh-oh. I wonder how that happened. You're right. ⁵⁵**We need to discuss how to fix that.**

W-Am You know, ⁵⁵**we allocated money for a trip to Singapore to present our preliminary findings. We don't really need to do that.**

여 매튜, 수요일 예산 회의를 취소할 계획은 아니시죠, 그렇죠?

남 아직 취소 소식을 보내진 않았는데, **중국에 있는 협력 연구자들이 이번 주에 국경일이라 쉬거든요.** 회의를 하는 의미가 없죠. 왜요?

여 음, 예산 초안을 보고 있는데 프로젝트 리더를 위한 예산을 할당하지 않았더라고요.

남 저런. 어쩌다 그렇게 됐는지 모르겠네요. 당신 말이 맞아요. **어떻게 바로잡을지 논의해야 해요.**

여 있잖아요, **예비 결과를 발표하러 싱가포르로 출장 갈 예산을 할당했잖아요. 꼭 그러지 않아도 돼요.**

어휘 budget 예산   there is no point 의미가 없다, 무의미하다   draft 초안, 원고   allocate 할당하다   fund 기금, 돈   preliminary 예비의   findings 연구 결과

53

What does the man say about some contacts in China?

(A) They submitted some preliminary results.
(B) They requested help with a presentation.
(C) They are celebrating a holiday.
(D) They are coming to visit soon.

남자는 중국에 있는 인맥에 대해 뭐라고 말하는가?

(A) 예비 결과를 제출했다.
(B) 발표에 도움을 요청했다.
(C) 국경일을 기념할 것이다.
(D) 곧 방문하러 올 것이다.

어휘 contact 인맥, (업무상) 연락하는 사람   celebrate 기념하다

해설 세부 사항 관련 – 남자가 중국 쪽 인맥에 대해 말하는 것
남자가 첫 대사에서 중국에 있는 협력 연구자들이 이번 주에 국경일이라 쉰다(our research partners in China are off this week for a national holiday)고 말하고 있으므로 정답은 (C)이다.

> Paraphrasing   대화의 are off this week for a national holiday → 정답의 are celebrating a holiday

54

What does the woman imply when she says, "we didn't allocate funds for a project leader"?
(A) She thinks a project deadline should be extended.
(B) She is surprised by a suggestion.
(C) A scheduled meeting should take place.
(D) A project leader will not be hired.

여자가 "프로젝트 리더를 위한 예산을 할당하지 않았더라고요"라고 말하는 의도는 무엇인가?
(A) 프로젝트 기한이 연장되어야 한다고 생각한다.
(B) 제안을 듣고 놀랐다.
(C) 예정된 회의가 열려야 한다.
(D) 프로젝트 리더는 고용되지 않을 것이다.

어휘 deadline 마감, 기한   extend 연장하다   suggestion 제안

해설 화자의 의도 파악 – 프로젝트 리더를 위한 예산을 할당하지 않았다는 말의 의도

앞에서 여자가 수요일 예산 회의를 취소할 계획은 아닌지(you're not planning to cancel Wednesday's budget meeting, are you?) 확인했고, 예산 초안을 보고 있다(I've been looking at the draft budget)고 한 뒤, 인용문을 언급했으므로 여자는 수요일 예산 회의가 필요하다는 의도로 한 말임을 알 수 있다. 따라서 정답은 (C)이다.

55

What does the woman say about some travel expenses?
(A) They are unnecessary.
(B) They have been refunded.
(C) They require receipts.
(D) They were charged to the company credit card.

여자는 출장비에 대해 뭐라고 말하는가?
(A) 불필요하다.
(B) 환불됐다.
(C) 영수증이 필요하다.
(D) 법인 신용카드로 청구됐다.

어휘 travel expense 출장비   unnecessary 불필요한   refund 환불해 주다   receipt 영수증   charge 청구하다

해설 세부 사항 관련 – 여자가 출장비에 대해 말하는 것

남자가 두 번째 대사에서 예산을 어떻게 바로잡을지 논의해야 한다(We need to discuss how to fix that)고 하자 여자가 싱가포르로 출장 갈 예산을 할당했다(we allocated money for a trip to Singapore ~)며 꼭 그러지 않아도 된다(We don't really need to do that)고 대답하는 것으로 보아 정답은 (A)이다.

56-58

 동영상 강의

M-Cn Hello, you've reached tech support.

W-Br ⁵⁶**I'm calling from Rubin Restaurant Equipment.** ⁵⁷**I recently purchased your**

software to keep track of my warehouse inventory, and I have a question about setting alerts.

M-Cn Sure. How can I help?

W-Br Well, we've been getting an alert whenever the inventory for our deep fryers drops below ten. But we usually don't stock many of those because restaurants don't often need to replace them. So, can I lower the alert level for just those items?

M-Cn Yes. ⁵⁸**In the system, if you click on that product, you'll see a link that says, "Set Custom Alert."** And you can set it to any number from there.

W-Br I see it. Thanks for your help.

남 안녕하세요, 기술 지원팀입니다.

여 **루빈 식당 장비인데요. 창고 재고 현황을 지속적으로 파악하려고 최근 귀사의 소프트웨어를 구입했는데,** 알림 설정에 관해 질문이 있어서요.

남 네. 어떻게 도와드릴까요?

여 음, 튀김기 재고가 10개 미만이 될 때마다 알림을 받았는데요. 그런데 보통 그 제품을 많이 갖춰 두진 않아요. 음식점들은 이걸 자주 교체할 필요가 별로 없거든요. 그래서 그 항목만 알림 수준을 낮출 수 있을까요?

남 네. **시스템에서 해당 제품을 클릭하시면 "맞춤형 알림 설정"이라고 된 링크가 보일 거예요. 거기서 어떤 숫자로든 설정하실 수 있습니다.**

여 알겠습니다. 도와주셔서 감사합니다.

어휘 reach (전화로) 연결하다   keep track of ~을 계속 파악하다   warehouse 창고   inventory 재고   alert 알림, 경계 경보   deep fryer 튀김기   stock (판매할 상품을 갖춰 두고) 있다   custom 주문 제작

56

Where is the woman calling from?
(A) A clothing store
(B) A furniture store
(C) A restaurant supply company
(D) A graphic design firm

여자는 어디서 전화하는가?
(A) 의류 매장
(B) 가구점
(C) 식당 용품 업체
(D) 그래픽 디자인 회사

해설 전체 내용 관련 – 여자의 전화 장소

여자가 첫 대사에서 루빈 식당 장비(I'm calling from Rubin Restaurant Equipment)라고 말하고 있으므로 정답은 (C)이다.

Paraphrasing   대화의 Rubin Restaurant Equipment
→ 정답의 A restaurant supply company

57

What is some software being used for?

(A) Inventory management
(B) Employee performance reviews
(C) Sales forecasting
(D) Web site design

소프트웨어는 무엇에 사용되고 있는가?

(A) 재고 관리
(B) 직원 인사 고과
(C) 판매 예측
(D) 웹사이트 디자인

어휘 management 관리 performance review 인사 고과
　　 forecasting 예측

해설 세부 사항 관련 – 소프트웨어가 사용되는 곳
여자가 첫 대사에서 창고 재고 현황을 지속적으로 파악하려고 소프트웨어를 구입했다(I recently purchased your software to keep track of my warehouse inventory ~)고 말하고 있으므로 정답은 (A)이다.

> Paraphrasing 대화의 keep track of my warehouse
> inventory → 정답의 Inventory management

58

What does the man help the woman do?

(A) Return a purchase
(B) Customize a setting
(C) Repair an engine
(D) Inspect a shipment

남자는 여자가 무엇을 하도록 돕는가?

(A) 구매 물건 반품하기
(B) 설정 바꾸기
(C) 엔진 수리하기
(D) 수송품 검사하기

어휘 customize 원하는 대로 바꾸다 inspect 검사하다, 점검하다

해설 세부 사항 관련 – 남자가 여자가 하도록 돕는 일
남자가 마지막 대사에서 "맞춤형 알림 설정"이라고 된 링크가 보일 것(~ you'll see a link that says, "Set Custom Alert.")이라며 거기서 어떤 숫자로든 설정할 수 있다(And you can set it to any number from there)고 말하고 있으므로 정답은 (B)이다.

> Paraphrasing 대화의 set it to any number
> → 정답의 Customize a setting

59-61

M-Au ⁵⁹**I just spoke to the garden director.**
^{59,60}He wants us to install an irrigation
system in the rose garden as well as the
magnolia grove. He wants to be sure the
flowers get plenty of water during the hot
summer months.

W-Br OK, let's walk over there now and take
some measurements. Then we can figure
out what materials we'll need.

M-Au Sure. ⁶¹**We have some extra parts left over**
from when we worked on the cherry trees.
I'll check what we have left after we finish
measuring the rose garden.

남 정원 관리자와 방금 얘기했어요. 그는 우리가 목련 숲뿐만 아니라 장미 정원에도 급수 시스템을 설치해 주길 원하네요. 꽃들이 무더운 여름철에 충분한 물을 얻었으면 해서요.

여 좋아요. 지금 가서 측량해 보죠. 그러면 어떤 재료가 필요한지 알 수 있을 거예요.

남 그래요. 체리나무 작업을 할 때 남은 여분의 부품이 좀 있어요. 장미 정원의 측량을 마치고 나면 남은 것들을 확인해 볼게요.

어휘 install 설치하다 irrigation 관개, 급수 magnolia 목련
　　 grove 숲 take measurements 치수를 재다 figure
　　 out 알아내다, 생각해 내다 material 재료 extra 여분의
　　 part 부품 left over 남은

59

Where are the speakers most likely working?

(A) At a flower shop
(B) At a botanical garden
(C) At a fruit orchard
(D) At a hardware store

화자들은 어디서 일하고 있겠는가?

(A) 꽃 가게
(B) 식물원
(C) 과수원
(D) 철물점

해설 전체 내용 관련 – 화자들의 작업 장소
남자가 첫 대사에서 정원 관리자와 방금 얘기했는데(I just spoke to the garden director) 목련 숲뿐만 아니라 장미 정원에도 급수 시스템을 설치해 주길 원한다(He wants us to install an irrigation system in the rose garden as well as the magnolia grove)고 말하는 것으로 보아 화자들은 식물원에서 작업 중이라는 것을 알 수 있다. 따라서 정답은 (B)이다.

> Paraphrasing 대화의 the rose garden as well as the
> magnolia grove
> → 정답의 a botanical garden

60

What have the speakers been asked to do?

(A) Arrange some flowers
(B) Deliver some tools
(C) Install a watering system
(D) Repair a lawn mower

화자들은 무엇을 하라고 요청받았는가?

(A) 꽃꽂이
(B) 연장 배달
(C) 급수 시스템 설치
(D) 잔디 깎는 기계 수리

어휘 arrange flowers 꽃꽂이하다   watering 급수   lawn mower 잔디 깎는 기계

해설 세부 사항 관련 – 화자들이 요청받은 일

남자가 첫 대사에서 정원 관리자는 우리가 급수 시스템을 설치해 주길 원한다(He wants us to install an irrigation system ~)고 말하고 있으므로 정답은 (C)이다.

> **Paraphrasing** 대화의 an irrigation system
> → 정답의 a watering system

61

What does the man offer to do?

(A) Look for some materials
(B) Train an assistant
(C) Transplant some trees
(D) Work extra hours

남자는 무엇을 하겠다고 제안하는가?

(A) 자재 찾기
(B) 조수 교육
(C) 나무 옮겨 심기
(D) 초과 근무

어휘 assistant 조수   transplant 이식하다, 옮겨 심다

해설 세부 사항 관련 – 남자의 제안 사항

남자가 마지막 대사에서 체리나무 작업을 할 때 남은 여분의 부품이 좀 있다(We have some extra parts left over from when we worked on the cherry trees)며 장미 정원의 측량을 마치고 나면 남은 것들을 확인해 보겠다(I'll check what we have left after we finish measuring the rose garden)고 말하고 있으므로 정답은 (A)이다.

> **Paraphrasing** 대화의 check what we have left
> → 정답의 Look for some materials

62-64 대화 + 배치도

> **M-Au** Good morning, Ms. Aljohani. ⁶²**Sorry I'm a little late.** Traffic was terrible.
>
> **W-Am** That's OK, but ⁶³ **our rental office will be very busy this morning. There's a big education convention in town starting today,** and a lot of attendees from out of town have reserved cars to get to the conference center.
>
> **M-Au** Right. ⁶⁴**What do you want me to do first?**
>
> **W-Am** ⁶⁴**I'd like you to start by checking the batteries in our electric cars.** We want to be sure they're all fully charged.

<hr/>

> 남   안녕하세요, 알조하니 씨. **좀 늦어서 죄송해요.** 교통 체증이 심했어요.
>
> 여   괜찮아요. 그런데 **우리 렌터카 사무실이 오늘 오전에 굉장히 바쁠 거예요. 오늘부터 대규모 교육 협의회가 시내에서 열리거든요.** 다른 도시에서 온 많은 참석자들이 학회장으로 가기 위해 차를 예약했어요.
>
> 남   알겠습니다. **먼저 뭘 할까요?**
>
> 여   **전기차 배터리를 확인하는 것부터 해 주셨으면 해요.** 모두 완전히 충전되어 있어야 해요.

어휘 education 교육   convention 협의회, 대회   attendee 참석자   electric 전기의   fully charged 완전히 충전된

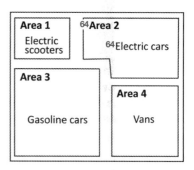

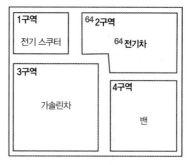

62

Why does the man apologize?

(A) He lost a key.
(B) He arrived late.
(C) He turned off some equipment.
(D) He forgot an instruction manual.

남자가 사과하는 이유는?

(A) 열쇠를 잃어버렸다.
(B) 늦게 도착했다.
(C) 장비를 껐다.
(D) 취급 설명서를 잊어버렸다.

어휘 apologize 사과하다   equipment 장비   instruction manual 취급 설명서, 사용 안내서

해설 세부 사항 관련 – 남자가 사과하는 이유

남자가 첫 대사에서 좀 늦어서 죄송하다(Sorry I'm a little late)고 사과하고 있으므로 정답은 (B)이다.

63

According to the woman, why will the speakers be very busy today?
(A) The agency is offering a discount.
(B) A new rental office is opening.
(C) There is a conference in town.
(D) A sporting event will take place.

여자에 따르면, 화자들은 오늘 왜 무척 바쁠 것인가?
(A) 업체가 할인을 제공한다.
(B) 새 렌터카 사무실을 연다.
(C) 시내에 학회가 있다.
(D) 스포츠 행사가 열린다.

해설 세부 사항 관련 – 여자가 오늘 바쁠 것이라고 말하는 이유
여자가 첫 대사에서 오늘 오전에 굉장히 바쁠 것(our rental office will be very busy this morning)이라며 오늘부터 대규모 교육 협의회가 시내에서 열린다(There's a big education convention in town starting today)고 말하고 있으므로 정답은 (C)이다.

> **Paraphrasing** 대화의 a big education convention
> → 정답의 a conference

64

Look at the graphic. Where will the man go first?
(A) Area 1
(B) Area 2
(C) Area 3
(D) Area 4

시각 정보에 의하면, 남자는 어디로 먼저 갈 것인가?
(A) 1구역
(B) 2구역
(C) 3구역
(D) 4구역

해설 시각 정보 연계 – 남자가 먼저 갈 곳
남자가 마지막 대사에서 먼저 뭘 할지(What do you want me to do first?) 묻자 여자가 전기차 배터리를 확인하는 것부터 해 줄 것(I'd like you to start by checking the batteries in our electric cars)을 요청했다. 배치도에 따르면 전기차는 2구역이므로 정답은 (B)이다.

65-67 대화 + 표

M-Au	I've been on vacation, so I missed our department's meeting. Can you give me an update?
W-Br	Well, 65 **all our public programs and community events are on schedule.**
M-Au	Great! How about the Jannis Park project? We're still planning on planting trees best suited for residential areas, right?

W-Br	That's right. I'm working on the public education part now. 66 **There'll be a children's poster competition next month,** which the city mayor will judge.
M-Au	Interesting. Is there a prize?
W-Br	The winner will get a ribbon. But all participants will get a seedling to plant at home. 67 **We'll be giving away the tallest of these four varieties,** since it was the most popular in a survey of our residents.

남	휴가를 다녀와서 부서 회의를 놓쳤어요. 새로운 사항을 알려 주실 수 있나요?
여	**우리 공익 프로그램과 지역 사회 행사가 일정대로 진행되고 있어요.**
남	좋군요! 재니스 공원 프로젝트는요? 여전히 주거 지역에 가장 적합한 나무를 심을 계획이죠, 그렇죠?
여	맞아요. 저는 지금 공공 교육 부문을 맡고 있어요. **다음 달에 어린이 포스터 대회가 있을 텐데** 시장님이 심사하실 거예요.
남	흥미롭네요. 상도 있나요?
여	우승자는 리본을 받아요. 하지만 모든 참가자는 집에 심을 묘목을 받을 거예요. **이 네 가지 종류 중 가장 키가 큰 걸로 나눠줄 겁니다.** 주민 설문 조사에서 가장 인기가 많았거든요.

어휘	be on schedule 일정대로 되어 가다 plant 심다 suited for ~에 적당한 residential 주택지의, 거주하기 좋은 education 교육 competition 경쟁, 대회 mayor 시장 judge 판정하다, 심판을 보다 participant 참가자 seedling 묘목 variety 종류 resident 주민

Tree	Average Height
67 Eastern redbud	9 meters
Japanese maple	7 meters
White fringe tree	6 meters
Panicle hydrangea	4.5 meters

나무	평균 키
67 캐나다 박태기	**9미터**
일본 단풍나무	7미터
이팝나무	6미터
나무수국	4.5미터

어휘 average 평균 height 높이, 키

65

Where do the speakers most likely work?
(A) At a landscaping company
(B) At a local government office
(C) At a garden store
(D) At a lumber yard

화자들은 어디서 일하겠는가?
(A) 조경 회사
(B) 지역 관공서
(C) 원예 용품점
(D) 목재 저장소

해설 전체 내용 관련 – 화자들의 근무지

여자가 첫 대사에서 공익 프로그램과 지역 사회 행사(all our public programs and community events)를 언급하고 있는 것으로 보아 정답은 (B)이다.

66

What does the woman say will take place next month?
(A) A seasonal promotion
(B) A product demonstration
(C) A poster contest
(D) A lecture series

여자는 다음 달에 무슨 일이 있을 것이라고 말하는가?
(A) 계절성 판촉 행사
(B) 제품 시연
(C) 포스터 대회
(D) 강좌 시리즈

어휘 seasonal 계절적인 promotion 홍보, 판촉 demonstration 시연, 설명 contest 대회 lecture 강의

해설 세부 사항 관련 – 다음 달에 있을 일

여자가 두 번째 대사에서 다음 달에 어린이 포스터 대회가 있을 것 (There'll be a children's poster competition next month)이라고 말하고 있으므로 정답은 (C)이다.

> **Paraphrasing** 대화의 a children's poster competition
> → 정답의 A poster contest

67

Look at the graphic. What kind of seedlings will be given away?
(A) Eastern redbud
(B) Japanese maple
(C) White fringe tree
(D) Panicle hydrangea

시각 정보에 의하면, 어떤 종류의 묘목을 나눠줄 것인가?
(A) 캐나다 박태기
(B) 일본 단풍나무
(C) 이팝나무
(D) 나무수국

해설 시각 정보 연계 – 나눠줄 묘목

여자가 마지막 대사에서 이 네 가지 종류 중 가장 키가 큰 걸로 나눠줄 것(We'll be giving away the tallest of these four varieties)이라고 했고, 표에 따르면 가장 키가 큰 나무는 캐나다 박태기이므로 정답은 (A)이다.

68-70 대화 + 표지판

M-Cn Hi, ⁶⁸ **I'd like a large black coffee and an egg-and-cheese croissant, please.**

W-Am Sure. That'll be eight dollars. Are you a Shelby's preferred customer?

M-Cn Uh, no I'm not. But ⁶⁹ **I do have an EZ-Cash card.**

W-Am ⁶⁹ **Great. Let me ring that up for you.**

M-Cn By the way, I'd like to order breakfast for my team tomorrow morning. Can I place that order ahead of time?

W-Am Sure. Would you like to do that now?

M-Cn No, ⁷⁰ **I'll call you later today** when I know what everyone wants. Thanks for the information.

남 안녕하세요. **블랙 커피 라지하고 에그 앤 치즈 크루아상 주세요.**

여 네. 8달러입니다. 쉘비 우대 고객이신가요?

남 아, 아니요, 하지만 **EZ-캐시 카드가 있어요.**

여 **좋아요. 입력할게요.**

남 그런데 내일 아침에 저희 팀 아침 식사를 주문하고 싶은데요. 미리 주문해도 되나요?

여 그럼요, 지금 하시겠어요?

남 아니요, 모두가 원하는 것을 알아보고 **이따가 전화할게요.** 알려주셔서 감사합니다.

어휘 preferred customer 우대 고객 ring ~ up (금전 등록기에 상품 가격을) 입력하다 ahead of time 미리

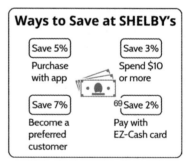

Ways to Save at SHELBY's

Save 5%	Save 3%
Purchase with app	Spend $10 or more
Save 7%	⁶⁹Save 2%
Become a preferred customer	Pay with EZ-Cash card

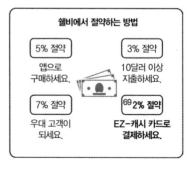

쉘비에서 절약하는 방법

5% 절약	3% 절약
앱으로 구매하세요.	10달러 이상 지출하세요.
7% 절약	⁶⁹2% 절약
우대 고객이 되세요.	EZ-캐시 카드로 결제하세요.

68

Where does the conversation most likely take place?
(A) At a café
(B) At an electronics shop
(C) At a stationery store
(D) At a clothing store

대화는 어디서 이루어지겠는가?
(A) 카페
(B) 전자 제품 매장
(C) 문구점
(D) 의류 매장

해설 전체 내용 관련 – 대화의 장소
남자가 첫 대사에서 블랙 커피 라지하고 에그 앤 치즈 크루아상을 주문(I'd like a large black coffee and an egg-and-cheese croissant, please)하는 것으로 보아 대화 장소는 카페라는 것을 알 수 있다. 따라서 정답은 (A)이다.

69

Look at the graphic. How much will the man save on his purchase?
(A) 5%
(B) 3%
(C) 7%
(D) 2%

시각 정보에 의하면, 남자는 구매 시 얼마를 절약할 수 있는가?
(A) 5%
(B) 3%
(C) 7%
(D) 2%

해설 시각 정보 연계 – 남자가 절약할 수 있는 비용
남자가 두 번째 대사에서 EZ-캐시 카드가 있다(I do have an EZ-Cash card)고 하자 여자가 좋아요(Great)라고 하면서 입력하겠다(Let me ring that up for you)고 말하고 있으며, 표시판에 따르면 EZ-캐시 카드로 결제 시 2%를 절약할 수 있으므로 정답은 (D)이다.

70

What does the man say he will do later today?
(A) Call a business
(B) Return some merchandise
(C) Fill out an online survey
(D) Hang up some posters

남자는 이따가 무엇을 하겠다고 말하는가?
(A) 업체에 전화하기
(B) 물건 반품하기
(C) 온라인 설문 작성하기
(D) 포스터 걸기

어휘 merchandise 상품 fill out 작성하다 hang up 내걸다

해설 세부 사항 관련 – 남자가 이따가 할 일
남자가 마지막 대사에서 이따가 전화하겠다(I'll call you later today)고 말하고 있으므로 정답은 (A)이다.

PART 4

71-73 전화 메시지

W-Br Hi, Amina. This is Sabine calling from Blue Drop Creations. **71I just put the earrings and necklaces that you ordered from me in the mail. 72Because you've been a customer for over ten years, I've also included a special gift in the package for you.** It's a case for your jewelry. This is a new product that I'm starting to offer, **73so please call me back after you receive it. I'd really like to hear your thoughts on it.**

안녕하세요, 아미나. 블루 드롭 크리에이션즈의 사빈입니다. **주문하신 귀걸이와 목걸이를 방금 우편으로 부쳤습니다. 10년 넘게 고객이 되어 주셨기에 소포에 특별 선물도 넣었는데요.** 보석함입니다. 새롭게 선보이기 시작한 신제품이에요. **받으신 후에 전화 주세요. 어떻게 생각하시는지 무척 알고 싶습니다.**

어휘 include 포함시키다 jewelry 보석 thought 생각

71

Who most likely is the speaker?
(A) An art gallery owner
(B) A hairstylist
(C) A clothing designer
(D) A jewelry maker

화자는 누구이겠는가?
(A) 화랑 소유주
(B) 헤어스타일리스트
(C) 의류 디자이너
(D) 보석 제작자

해설 전체 내용 관련 – 화자의 직업
화자가 초반부에 청자가 주문한 귀걸이와 목걸이를 방금 우편으로 부쳤다(I just put the earrings and necklaces that you ordered from me in the mail)고 말하고 있으므로 보석과 관련된 일을 한다는 것을 알 수 있다. 따라서 정답은 (D)이다.

Paraphrasing 담화의 earrings, necklaces → 정답의 jewelry

72

Why did the speaker include a special gift?
(A) Because the listener is a new customer
(B) Because the listener is celebrating a special occasion
(C) Because the listener is a loyal customer
(D) Because the listener placed a large order

화자는 왜 특별 선물을 넣었는가?
(A) 청자가 신규 고객이어서
(B) 청자가 특별한 날을 기념하고 있어서
(C) 청자가 단골 고객이어서
(D) 청자가 대량 주문을 넣어서

어휘 special occasion 특별한 경우   loyal customer 단골 고객

해설 세부 사항 관련 – 화자가 특별 선물을 넣은 이유

화자가 중반부에 10년 넘게 고객이 되어 주었기에 소포에 특별 선물도 넣었다(Because you've been a customer for over ten years, I've also included a special gift in the package for you)고 말하고 있으므로 정답은 (C)이다.

> Paraphrasing   담화의 a customer for over ten years
> → 정답의 a loyal customer

73

Why is the listener asked to return a phone call?
(A) To give feedback
(B) To confirm receipt of an order
(C) To update a payment method
(D) To provide an address

청자는 왜 전화 회신 요청을 받는가?
(A) 피드백을 달라고
(B) 주문 접수를 확인해 달라고
(C) 결제 방식을 업데이트해 달라고
(D) 주소를 제공해 달라고

어휘 receipt 영수증   payment method 결제 방식

해설 세부 사항 관련 – 청자가 전화 회신 요청을 받는 이유

화자가 후반부에 소포를 받은 후에 전화 줄 것(please call me back after you receive it)을 요청하면서 어떻게 생각하는지 무척 알고 싶다(I'd really like to hear your thoughts on it)고 말하고 있으므로 정답은 (A)이다.

> Paraphrasing   담화의 your thoughts → 정답의 feedback

74-76 전화 메시지

> **M-Au** Good morning, this is Brandon from Dakota Framing Company, returning your call. [74]**We received your voicemail about wanting to frame a wedding picture.** There is no need to print the photo yourself. We prefer that you e-mail us a digital copy. So, to answer your question, [75]**you can complete the whole order online**. Just visit our Web site, where you'll fill in your choices for photo size and the frame and upload your photo. And [76]**for a small extra cost, we'll guarantee to replace your frame in case of damage.** Please be sure to check that box when you order.

> 안녕하세요. 다코타 액자 회사의 브랜든인데요. 회신 전화 드립니다. **결혼 사진을 액자에 넣고 싶으시다는 음성 메시지 잘 받았습니다.** 직접 사진을 출력하실 필요는 없어요. 저희에게 디지털 사본을 이메일로 보내주시는 것이 더 좋습니다. 질문에 답변 드리자면 **모든 주문을 온라인으로 완료하실 수 있습니다.** 저희 웹사이트를 방문하셔서 사진 크기와 액자를 선택하고 사진을 업로드하시면 됩니다. **비용을 조금 더 지불하시면 액자 손상 시 교체를 보증합니다.** 주문하실 때 체크박스를 꼭 확인해 주세요.

> 어휘 voicemail 음성 메시지   frame 틀, 액자   whole 전체의
> fill in 작성하다   guarantee 보증하다   replace 교체하다
> in case of ~의 경우   damage 손상

74

What does the listener want to do?
(A) Hire a caterer
(B) Purchase a painting
(C) Have a printer repaired
(D) Have a photograph framed

청자는 무엇을 하고 싶어 하는가?
(A) 케이터링 업체 고용하기
(B) 그림 구매하기
(C) 프린터 수리하기
(D) 사진을 액자에 넣기

해설 세부 사항 관련 – 청자가 하고 싶어 하는 일

화자가 초반부에 결혼 사진을 액자에 넣고 싶다는 청자의 음성 메시지 잘 받았다(We received your voicemail about wanting to frame a wedding picture)고 말하고 있으므로 정답은 (D)이다.

> Paraphrasing   담화의 frame a wedding picture
> → 정답의 Have a photograph framed

75

What does the speaker expect the listener to do on a Web site?
(A) View a list of prices
(B) Place an order
(C) Schedule a time to meet
(D) Read customer reviews

화자는 청자가 웹사이트에서 무엇을 하기를 기대하는가?
(A) 가격 목록 확인하기
(B) 주문 넣기
(C) 만날 시간 잡기
(D) 고객 후기 읽기

어휘 review 후기, 논평

해설 세부 사항 관련 – 청자가 웹사이트에서 하기를 기대하는 것
화자가 중반부에 모든 주문을 온라인으로 완료할 수 있다(you can complete the whole order online)며 주문 방법을 설명하고 있으므로 정답은 (B)이다.

76

What is included for an extra fee?
(A) Shipping
(B) An artist's signature
(C) A newsletter
(D) A warranty

추가 요금에는 무엇이 포함되는가?
(A) 배송
(B) 화가 사인
(C) 소식지
(D) 품질 보증서

어휘 signature 서명

해설 세부 사항 관련 – 추가 요금에 포함되는 것
화자가 후반부에 비용을 조금 더 지불하면 액자 손상 시 교체를 보증한다 (for a small extra cost, we'll guarantee to replace your frame in case of damage)고 말하고 있으므로 정답은 (D)이다.

Paraphrasing 담화의 guarantee to replace your frame
→ 정답의 A warranty

77-79 담화

M-Cn 77 **Welcome all to this week's training in our series of patient care programs.** Our physical therapy center is known for the excellent care we provide to our patients, and that's because of you, our staff. The training today will be about ways to engage the patients who reside in our facility through playing games. 78,79 **I've prepared different types of activities for us to try out**, including some games that involve mental stimulation as well as physical exercises. But, I have to let you know that today I must leave at noon. 79 **Next week we'll try out more of the games.**

이번 주 환자 치료 프로그램 교육에 와 주신 여러분을 환영합니다. 저희 물리치료 센터는 환자에게 탁월한 치료를 제공하는 것으로 잘 알려져 있는데요. 직원 여러분 덕분입니다. 오늘 교육은 게임을 통해 시설 내에 거주하는 환자들을 사로잡는 방법에 관한 것입니다. **여러분이 시도해 볼 수 있는 다양한 종류의 활동을 준비했어요.** 신체 운동뿐 아니라 정신적 자극도 수반하는 게임이 포함됩니다. 그런데 오늘 제가 정오에 떠나야 해요. 다음 주에 게임을 더 많이 해 볼 겁니다.

어휘 patient 환자 physical therapy 물리치료 engage 사로잡다, 참여시키다 reside 거주하다, 살다 activity 활동 try out 시도해 보다 involve 수반하다 stimulation 자극

77

Who are the listeners?
(A) Hotel receptionists
(B) Health-care staff
(C) Customer-service representatives
(D) Fitness trainers

청자들은 누구이겠는가?
(A) 호텔 접수 담당자
(B) 의료 서비스 직원
(C) 고객 서비스 직원
(D) 헬스 트레이너

어휘 health-care 의료 서비스 representative 대표, 대리인

해설 전체 내용 관련 – 청자들의 직업
화자가 도입부에 이번 주 환자 치료 프로그램 교육에 온 것을 환영한다(Welcome all to this week's training in our series of patient care programs)고 말하고 있으므로 정답은 (B)이다.

78

What has the speaker prepared?
(A) Activities
(B) Food
(C) Certificates
(D) A video

화자는 무엇을 준비했는가?
(A) 활동
(B) 음식
(C) 자격증
(D) 동영상

해설 세부 사항 관련 – 화자가 준비한 것
화자가 중반부에 시도해 볼 수 있는 다양한 종류의 활동을 준비했다(I've prepared different types of activities for us to try out)고 했으므로 정답은 (A)이다.

79

What does the speaker imply when he says, "I must leave at noon"?
(A) He would like permission to leave.
(B) He cannot join a luncheon.
(C) A colleague will fill in for him.
(D) Some material will not be covered today.

화자가 "제가 정오에 떠나야 해요"라고 말하는 의도는 무엇인가?
(A) 자리를 떠날 허가를 받고 싶다.
(B) 오찬에 참석할 수 없다.
(C) 동료가 그의 자리를 대신할 것이다.
(D) 일부 자료는 오늘 다루지 못할 것이다.

어휘 permission 허가, 승인 luncheon 오찬 colleague 동료
fill in for ~을 대신하다 material 자료

해설 화자의 의도 파악 – 정오에 떠나야 한다는 말의 의도
앞서 다양한 종류의 활동을 준비했다(I've prepared different types of activities ~)고 언급하였고, 인용문을 언급한 뒤 다음 주에 게임을 더 많이 해 볼 것(Next week we'll try out more of the games)이라고 말하는 것으로 보아, 게임을 많이 준비했지만 오늘 다 할 수는 없을 것이라는 의도로 한 말임을 알 수 있다. 따라서 정답은 (D)이다.

80-82 광고

 동영상 강의

> **M-Au** Are you a certified commercial truck driver? **80 Hoffman Oversized Haulers is currently looking for experienced truck drivers to join our team.** As our name suggests, we transport oversized cargo throughout the region. **81 With Hoffman, drivers enjoy flexible scheduling. In fact, we're the only company in the region that allows employees to determine their own work hours.** If you don't have experience working with oversized loads, training is available. **82 Please check out our Web site to learn more about our open positions.** We can't wait to work with you.

> 면허증이 있는 영업용 트럭 운전기사이십니까? **호프만 특대 화물 운송업체는 현재 저희 팀에 합류할 숙련된 트럭 운전기사를 찾고 있습니다.** 이름에서 암시하듯, 저희는 지역 전체에 특대형 화물을 운송합니다. **호프만에 오시면 운전기사들은 근무 일정을 유연하게 조절할 수 있습니다. 사실 저희는 이 지역에서 직원들에게 각자 근무 시간을 정하게 하는 유일한 업체입니다.** 특대형 짐을 다룬 경력이 없으시면 교육을 해 드립니다. **저희 웹사이트에서 공석을 더 확인해 보세요.** 어서 함께 일하고 싶습니다.

> 어휘 certified 면허증이 있는 commercial 상업의 currently 현재 transport 수송하다 oversized 특대의 cargo 화물 region 지역 flexible 유연한 determine 결정하다 load 짐 available 이용할 수 있는 open position 공석

80

What is the purpose of the advertisement?
(A) To announce a contest
(B) To promote an upcoming sale
(C) To introduce new services
(D) To recruit employees

광고의 목적은 무엇인가?
(A) 대회를 알리는 것
(B) 다가오는 할인을 홍보하는 것
(C) 새로운 서비스를 소개하는 것
(D) 직원을 모집하는 것

어휘 promote 홍보하다 upcoming 다가오는, 곧 있을 recruit 모집하다

해설 전체 내용 관련 – 광고의 목적
화자가 초반부에 호프만 특대 화물 운송업체는 현재 팀에 합류할 숙련된 트럭 운전기사를 찾고 있다(Hoffman Oversized Haulers is currently looking for experienced truck drivers to join our team)고 말하고 있으므로 직원을 모집하기 위한 구인 광고임을 알 수 있다. 따라서 정답은 (D)이다.

81

How is the speaker's company different from its competitors?
(A) It is dependable.
(B) It produces innovative products.
(C) It offers flexible schedules.
(D) It pays employees well.

화자의 회사는 경쟁업체와 어떻게 다른가?
(A) 믿을 수 있다.
(B) 획기적인 제품을 생산한다.
(C) 유연한 일정을 제공한다.
(D) 직원들에게 보수를 많이 준다.

어휘 competitor 경쟁자 dependable 믿을 수 있는 innovative 획기적인 flexible 유연한

해설 세부 사항 관련 – 회사가 경쟁업체와 다른 점
화자가 중반부에 호프만에 오면 운전기사들은 근무 일정을 유연하게 조절할 수 있다(With Hoffman, drivers enjoy flexible scheduling)며 이 지역에서 직원들에게 각자 근무 시간을 정하게 하는 유일한 업체(In fact, we're the only company in the region that allows employees to determine their own work hours)라고 말하는 것으로 보아 화자의 회사가 유연한 일정을 제공하는 것이 경쟁업체와 다른 점이라는 것을 알 수 있다. 따라서 정답은 (C)이다.

82

What does the speaker encourage the listeners to do?
(A) Complete a survey
(B) Fill out an application
(C) Place an order
(D) Get more information

화자는 청자들에게 무엇을 하라고 장려하는가?
(A) 설문 조사 작성하기
(B) 지원서 기입하기
(C) 주문 넣기
(D) 추가 정보 얻기

어휘 complete 작성하다 fill out 기입하다 application 지원서

해설 세부 사항 관련 – 화자가 청자들에게 권장하는 것
화자가 후반부에 웹사이트에서 공석을 더 확인해 볼 것(Please check out our Web site to learn more about our open positions)을 권하고 있으므로 정답은 (D)이다.

> Paraphrasing 담화의 learn more about our open positions → 정답의 Get more information

83-85 전화 메시지

W-Am Hi, Jinyu. I have some exciting news! **83 *The Farmer's Table* television program wants to feature our restaurant in an upcoming episode. 84 They'll be coming on Wednesday to film everyone at work in the kitchen during our dinner service. Since you're the executive chef, I'll need you to come in earlier than usual to get everything prepped and set up.** And just as a reminder, **85 I'm still planning to be out of town next week for the Springdale Pastry and Dessert Festival.** Thanks!

안녕하세요, 진유. 좋은 소식이 있어요! TV 프로그램 〈농부의 식탁〉에서 곧 있을 에피소드에 우리 식당을 소개하고 싶어 해요. 수요일에 와서 저녁 시간 동안 주방에서 근무하는 모두를 촬영할 거예요. 총주방장이시니 평소보다 빨리 와서 모든 준비를 마쳐 주셨으면 합니다. 다시 알려 드리자면 저는 여전히 다음 주에 스프링데일 페이스트리 앤 디저트 축제 때문에 자리를 비울 계획이에요. 감사합니다!

어휘 feature 특별히 포함하다 upcoming 다가오는, 곧 있을 executive chef 총주방장 prep 준비하다 set up 준비하다 reminder 상기시키는 것

83

What is the message mainly about?
(A) Revising a restaurant menu
(B) Filming for a television show
(C) Launching an advertising campaign
(D) Renovating a kitchen

메시지는 주로 무엇에 관한 것인가?
(A) 식당 메뉴 변경
(B) TV 프로그램 촬영
(C) 광고 캠페인 개시
(D) 주방 개조

어휘 revise 변경하다, 수정하다 launch 개시, 착수, 시작 renovate 보수하다, 개조하다

해설 전체 내용 관련 – 메시지의 주제
화자가 초반부에 TV 프로그램 〈농부의 식탁〉에서 곧 있을 에피소드에 우리 식당을 소개하고 싶어 한다(*The Farmer's Table* television program wants to feature our restaurant in an upcoming episode)고 말하는 것으로 보아, TV 프로그램 촬영에 대해 이야기하고 있음을 알 수 있다. 따라서 정답은 (B)이다.

84

What does the speaker ask the listener to do on Wednesday?
(A) Come to work early
(B) Experiment with new ingredients
(C) Train an employee
(D) Prepare for a safety inspection

화자는 청자에게 수요일에 무엇을 하라고 요청하는가?
(A) 일찍 출근하기
(B) 새로운 재료로 시험해 보기
(C) 직원 교육하기
(D) 안전 점검 대비하기

어휘 experiment 실험하다, 시험해 보다 ingredient 성분, 재료 inspection 점검

해설 세부 사항 관련 – 화자가 청자에게 수요일에 하라고 요청하는 일
화자가 중반부에 수요일에 촬영할 것(They'll be coming on Wednesday to film everyone ~)이라며 평소보다 빨리 와서 모든 준비를 마쳐 줬으면 한다(~ I'll need you to come in earlier than usual to get everything prepped and set up)고 하므로 정답은 (A)이다.

> Paraphrasing 담화의 come in earlier than usual
> → 정답의 Come to work early

85

Where will the speaker go next week?
(A) To a food festival
(B) To a cooking class
(C) To a farmers market
(D) To a bakery opening

화자는 다음 주 어디에 갈 것인가?
(A) 음식 축제
(B) 요리 강좌
(C) 농산물 직판장
(D) 제과점 개업식

해설 세부 사항 관련 – 화자가 다음 주에 갈 곳
화자가 후반부에 다음 주에 스프링데일 페이스트리 앤 디저트 축제 때문에 자리를 비울 계획(I'm still planning to be out of town next week for the Springdale Pastry and Dessert Festival)이라고 말하고 있으므로 정답은 (A)이다.

> Paraphrasing 담화의 the Springdale Pastry and Dessert Festival → 정답의 a food festival

86-88 방송

M-Cn Good evening and thank you for watching Channel Four News. I'm here in Rockville, a suburb in the metropolitan area. **86 Rockville was recently chosen as the site of a multimillion-dollar electric vehicle battery factory.** This project promises to bring thousands of jobs, both directly and indirectly, to the surrounding community. **87 At a recent well-attended public comment meeting, residents had a chance to voice any opposition to the project.** No one made any comments. To learn more about this exciting development, **88 artist-rendered images of the project are on display at the city hall building.**

안녕하십니까? 채널 4 뉴스를 시청해 주셔서 감사합니다. 저는 대도시 교외에 있는 록빌에 나와 있습니다. **록빌은 최근 수백만 달러 규모의 전기차 배터리 공장 부지로 선정됐는데요.** 이 프로젝트는 인근 지역 사회에 수천 개의 직, 간접적인 일자리를 약속합니다. **많은 사람들이 참석한 최근 공개 논평회에서 주민들은 프로젝트에 반대하는 목소리를 낼 기회가 있었는데요.** 아무도 의견을 내지 않았습니다. 이 흥미로운 개발에 대해 더 자세히 알아보시려면 **아티스트에 의해 제작된 이 프로젝트의 이미지가 시청 건물에 전시되어 있습니다.**

> **어휘** suburb 교외 metropolitan 대도시의 indirectly 간접적으로 surrounding 인근의, 주위의 well-attended 많은 사람들이 참석한 comment 논평 resident 주민 voice (말로) 표하다 opposition 반대 render 만들다, 하다

86

What is the speaker mainly discussing?
(A) A job fair
(B) A factory
(C) Some traffic patterns
(D) A prototype electric vehicle

화자는 주로 무엇에 대해 이야기하는가?
(A) 취업 박람회
(B) 공장
(C) 교통 패턴
(D) 전기차 시제품

어휘 prototype 원형, 시제품

해설 전체 내용 관련 – 담화의 주제
화자가 초반부에 록빌은 최근 수백만 달러 규모의 전기차 배터리 공장 부지로 선정됐다(Rockville was recently chosen as the site of a multimillion-dollar electric vehicle battery factory)며 이 프로젝트에 대한 이야기를 이어가고 있으므로 정답은 (B)이다.

87

What does the speaker imply when he says, "No one made any comments"?
(A) Few people were in attendance.
(B) Another meeting will be scheduled.
(C) A project has community support.
(D) A public comment period has ended.

화자가 "아무도 의견을 내지 않았습니다"라고 말하는 의도는 무엇인가?
(A) 참석한 사람이 거의 없었다.
(B) 다른 회의 일정이 잡힐 것이다.
(C) 프로젝트가 지역 사회의 지지를 받는다.
(D) 공개 논평 기간이 끝났다.

어휘 in attendance 참석한 period 기간

해설 화자의 의도 파악 – 아무도 의견을 내지 않았다는 말의 의도
화자가 많은 사람들이 참석한 최근 공개 논평회에서 주민들은 프로젝트에 반대하는 목소리를 낼 기회가 있었다(At a recent well-attended public comment meeting, residents had a chance to voice any

opposition to the project)고 한 뒤 인용문을 언급한 것으로 보아, 프로젝트에 반대하는 사람이 아무도 없으며 지지를 받는다는 것을 나타낼 의도로 한 말임을 알 수 있다. 따라서 정답은 (C)이다.

88

What can the public view at the city hall building?
(A) An official contract
(B) Some images
(C) A list of companies
(D) Some facts about local politicians

대중은 시청 건물에서 무엇을 볼 수 있는가?
(A) 공식 계약서
(B) 그림
(C) 업체 목록
(D) 지역 정치인들에 대한 사실

어휘 politician 정치인

해설 세부 사항 관련 – 대중이 시청 건물에서 볼 수 있는 것
화자가 후반부에 아티스트에 의해 제작된 이 프로젝트의 이미지가 시청 건물에 전시되어 있다(~ artist-rendered images of the project are on display at the city hall building)고 말하고 있으므로 정답은 (B)이다.

89-91 광고

W-Br Tired of losing things on your desk because it's too cluttered? If so, [89]**the Optimum Space Organizer is the perfect product for you.** Designed with office employees like you in mind, [89]**this product can make even the messiest of desks look neat again.** [90]**Best of all, the organizer adjusts to any sized space you may have on your desk.** It can be as narrow or as wide as you need it to be—within seconds! [91]**If you call in the next ten minutes, you'll receive a 30 percent discount!**

책상이 너무 어수선해서 물건을 잃어버리는 거에 지치셨나요? 그렇다면 **옵티멈 스페이스 오거나이저가 딱 맞는 제품입니다.** 여러분과 같은 사무실 직원을 염두에 두고 디자인된 **이 제품은 가장 지저분한 책상도 다시 깔끔해 보일 수 있도록 해 줍니다. 무엇보다도 이 정리함은 책상 위 어떤 크기의 공간에도 맞출 수 있죠.** 몇 초 만에 필요에 따라 좁거나 넓게 만들 수 있어요. **앞으로 10분 안에 전화하시면 30퍼센트 할인을 받습니다!**

> **어휘** tired of ~에 진저리가 나는 cluttered 어수선한 organizer 정리함 messy 지저분한 neat 깔끔한 adjust 조정하다 narrow 좁은

89

What type of product is being advertised?
(A) A floor lamp
(B) A bookshelf
(C) An office chair
(D) A desk organizer

어떤 종류의 제품을 광고하는가?
(A) 스탠드
(B) 책장
(C) 사무용 의자
(D) 책상 정리함

해설 전체 내용 관련 – 광고되고 있는 제품
화자가 초반부에 옵티멈 스페이스 오거나이저라는 이름의 제품을 언급했고(the Optimum Space Organizer is the perfect product for you), 중반부에 이 제품은 가장 지저분한 책상도 다시 깔끔해 보일 수 있도록 해 준다(this product can make even the messiest of desks look neat again)고 말하는 것에서 책상 정리와 관련된 제품을 광고하고 있다는 것을 알 수 있다. 따라서 정답은 (D)이다.

90

What special feature does the speaker emphasize?
(A) It is durable.
(B) It is adjustable.
(C) It is easy to assemble.
(D) It is available in many colors.

화자는 어떤 특징을 강조하는가?
(A) 내구성이 있다.
(B) 조절이 가능하다.
(C) 조립하기 쉽다.
(D) 여러 색상으로 나온다.

어휘 durable 내구성이 있는 adjustable 조절 가능한 assemble 조립하다 available 구할 수 있는, 이용 가능한

해설 세부 사항 관련 – 화자가 강조하는 특징
화자가 중반부에 무엇보다도 이 정리함은 책상 위 어떤 크기의 공간에도 맞출 수 있다(Best of all, the organizer adjusts to any sized space you may have on your desk)고 말하고 있으므로 정답은 (B)이다.

> Paraphrasing 담화의 adjusts to any sized space
> → 정답의 adjustable

91

How can the listeners receive a discount?
(A) By calling within a time limit
(B) By entering an e-mail address
(C) By referring a product to a friend
(D) By using a mobile phone application

청자들은 어떻게 할인을 받을 수 있는가?
(A) 제한 시간 내에 전화해서
(B) 이메일 주소를 입력해서
(C) 제품을 친구에게 추천해서
(D) 휴대전화 앱을 이용해서

어휘 limit 제한, 한도 enter 입력하다 refer 언급하다, 참조하게 하다

해설 세부 사항 관련 – 청자가 할인을 받을 수 있는 방법
화자가 후반부에 앞으로 10분 안에 전화하면 30퍼센트 할인을 받는다(If you call in the next ten minutes, you'll receive a 30 percent discount!)고 말하고 있으므로 정답은 (A)이다.

> Paraphrasing 담화의 in the next ten minutes
> → 정답의 within a time limit

92-94 팟캐스트   동영상 강의

W-Am Thanks for listening to this episode of *Fabulous Foods*. [92]**Every week, we discuss a different vegetable and ways to cook with it to maximize flavor.** Now, before we get started, [93]**I'm excited to announce that I've been collaborating with Cartwell Kitchen Supplies to develop a new line of cookware. It'll be released in November, but it's available for preorder right now.** Keep in mind, this product line will not be available for long. OK, let's move on to our program. With us today is renowned chef Rebecca Murray to talk about this week's vegetable: eggplant! [94]**Rebecca recently launched a vegetarian restaurant in New York that is getting rave reviews so far.**

〈광장한 요리〉 이번 에피소드를 청취해 주셔서 감사합니다. 저희는 매주 다양한 채소와 이를 이용해 맛을 극대화하는 요리법에 대해 이야기 나누고 있는데요. 시작하기에 앞서, 제가 카트웰 주방용품과 협력해 새로운 취사도구 제품을 개발했다는 사실을 알려 드리게 되어 기쁩니다. 11월에 출시되지만 현재 선주문이 가능합니다. 기억해 두세요. 이 제품은 오랫동안 구입할 수 있진 않을 겁니다. 자, 프로그램으로 넘어가 보죠. 오늘은 유명 요리사인 레베카 머레이 씨가 함께해 이번 주 채소인 가지에 대해 이야기해 주시겠습니다! 레베카 씨는 최근 뉴욕에 채식 식당을 열었는데 지금까지 극찬을 받고 있습니다.

어휘 fabulous 광장한, 아주 멋진 maximize 극대화하다 flavor 맛, 풍미 collaborate 협력하다, 공동으로 작업하다 kitchen supply 주방용품 cookware 취사도구 release 출시하다, 공개하다 available 이용 가능한, 구할 수 있는 preorder 선주문 renowned 유명한 eggplant 가지 launch 개시하다, 시작하다 rave review 극찬, 호평

92

According to the speaker, what is the purpose of the podcast?
(A) To discuss the restaurant industry
(B) To review new cooking equipment
(C) To share information about nutrition
(D) To showcase individual ingredients

화자에 따르면, 팟캐스트의 목적은 무엇인가?
(A) 요식업계에 대해 이야기하는 것
(B) 새로운 조리기구를 평가하는 것
(C) 영양 관련 정보를 공유하는 것
(D) 개별 재료 소개하는 것

어휘 equipment 장비, 도구　share 공유하다　nutrition 영양
　　showcase 소개하다, 공개하다　individual 개개의, 각각의
　　ingredient 성분, 재료

해설 전체 내용 관련 – 팟캐스트의 목적

화자가 초반부에 매주 다양한 채소와 이를 이용해 맛을 극대화하는 요리법에 대해 이야기 나눈다(Every week, we discuss a different vegetable and ways to cook with it to maximize flavor)고 팟캐스트를 설명하고 있으므로 정답은 (D)이다.

> **Paraphrasing**　담화의 discuss a different vegetable
> → 정답의 showcase individual ingredients

93

Why does the speaker say, "this product line will not be available for long"?
(A) To encourage the listeners to place an order
(B) To apologize to the listeners for a product shortage
(C) To justify a high price
(D) To criticize a business decision

화자가 "이 제품은 오랫동안 구입할 수 있진 않을 겁니다"라고 말하는 이유는?
(A) 청자들에게 주문을 장려하려고
(B) 청자들에게 제품 부족에 대해 사과하려고
(C) 높은 가격에 대해 해명하려고
(D) 사업상의 결정을 비판하려고

어휘 encourage 장려하다, 권장하다　apologize 사과하다　shortage
　　결핍, 부족　justify 정당화하다, 해명하다　criticize 비판하다
　　decision 결심, 결정

해설 화자의 의도 파악 – 이 제품은 오랫동안 구입할 수 있진 않을 거라는 말의 의도

화자가 초반부에 카트웰 주방용품과 협력해 새로운 취사도구 제품을 개발했다는 사실을 알리게 되어 기쁘다(I'm excited to announce that I've been collaborating with Cartwell Kitchen Supplies to develop a new line of cookware)고 하면서 11월에 출시되지만 현재 선주문이 가능하다(It'll be released in November, but it's available for preorder right now)고 말한 뒤 인용문을 언급하고 있으므로, 청자들에게 제품 주문을 장려하는 의도로 한 말임을 알 수 있다. 따라서 정답은 (A)이다.

94

According to the speaker, what did Rebecca Murray recently do?
(A) She published a cookbook.
(B) She launched a culinary training course.
(C) She opened a restaurant.
(D) She traveled abroad.

화자에 따르면, 레베카 머레이는 최근 무엇을 했는가?
(A) 요리책을 출간했다.
(B) 요리 강좌를 시작했다.
(C) 식당을 열었다.
(D) 해외 여행을 했다.

어휘 publish 출판하다　culinary 요리의

해설 세부 사항 관련 – 레베카 머레이가 최근에 한 일

화자가 후반부에 레베카 씨는 최근 뉴욕에 채식 식당을 열었다(Rebecca recently launched a vegetarian restaurant in New York ~)고 했으므로 정답은 (C)이다.

> **Paraphrasing**　담화의 launched a vegetarian restaurant
> → 정답의 opened a restaurant

95-97 공지 + 시간표

W-Br Attention passengers. **95Renovation work to upgrade and modernize our train station is underway. We apologize for the inconvenience the construction noise may cause.** Please note that regional train schedules are not affected. Train 133 with service to Washington, D.C., will be arriving shortly. All passengers to Washington, please proceed to Track 26B. **96If you need assistance handling your baggage, please speak to a ticket agent immediately. 97Train 133's next stop will be Wilmington,** followed by Baltimore and then Washington, D.C.

승객 여러분께 알려드립니다. **저희 기차역을 업그레이드하고 현대화하는 보수 작업이 진행 중입니다. 공사 소음으로 불편을 드려 죄송합니다.** 지역 열차 시간표는 영향이 없습니다. 워싱턴 D.C.행 133번 열차가 곧 도착하겠습니다. 워싱턴으로 가시는 승객께서는 26B 트랙으로 이동하시기 바랍니다. **짐을 옮기는 데 도움이 필요하시면 즉시 매표원에게 말씀해 주세요. 133번 열차의 다음 역은 윌밍턴이며,** 이후 볼티모어를 거쳐 워싱턴 D.C로 이동합니다.

어휘 attention 알립니다, 주목하세요　passenger 승객
　　renovation 개조, 보수　modernize 현대화하다　underway
　　진행 중인　apologize 사과하다　inconvenience 불편
　　construction 공사　regional 지역의　affect 영향을 주다
　　proceed to ~로 향하다, 나아가다　handle 들다, 옮기다
　　baggage 짐, 수하물　immediately 즉시

Train 133	
City	Arrival Time
New York	9:30 A.M.
Philadelphia	10:45 A.M.
97Wilmington	12:05 P.M.
Baltimore	1:00 P.M.
Washington, D.C.	1:30 P.M.

133번 열차	
도시	도착 시간
뉴욕	오전 9시 30분
필라델피아	오전 10시 45분
97월밍턴	오후 12시 5분
볼티모어	오후 1시
워싱턴 D.C.	오후 1시 30분

95

Why does the speaker apologize?
(A) There is construction noise at the station.
(B) There are no more seats available on a train.
(C) A printed schedule has incorrect information.
(D) A train service has been delayed.

화자는 왜 사과하는가?
(A) 역에 공사 소음이 있다.
(B) 열차에 이용 가능한 좌석이 더 이상 없다.
(C) 출력된 일정표에 틀린 정보가 있다.
(D) 열차 운행이 지연됐다.

어휘 available 이용 가능한, 구할 수 있는 incorrect 부정확한, 틀린 delay 지연시키다

해설 세부 사항 관련 – 화자가 사과하는 이유
화자가 초반부에 기차역을 업그레이드하고 현대화하는 보수 작업이 진행 중(Renovation work to upgrade and modernize our train station is underway)이며 공사 소음으로 불편을 드려 죄송하다(We apologize for the inconvenience the construction noise may cause)고 공사 소음에 대해 사과하고 있으므로 정답은 (A)이다.

96

According to the speaker, why may some listeners need to see an agent?
(A) To ask for a refund
(B) To request baggage service
(C) To purchase a monthly pass
(D) To arrange a transfer

화자에 따르면, 일부 청자들은 왜 매표원을 만나야 하는가?
(A) 환불을 요청하려고
(B) 수하물 서비스를 요청하려고
(C) 월 정기권을 구매하려고
(D) 환승을 하려고

어휘 refund 환불 monthly pass 월 정기권 arrange 마련하다, 주선하다 transfer 환승, 이동

해설 세부 사항 관련 – 일부 청자들이 매표원을 만나야 하는 이유
화자가 중반부에 짐을 옮기는 데 도움이 필요하면 즉시 매표원에게 말해 달라(If you need assistance handling your baggage, please speak to a ticket agent immediately)고 했으므로 정답은 (B)이다.

> Paraphrasing 담화의 assistance handling your baggage
> → 정답의 baggage service

97

Look at the graphic. When is Train 133 scheduled to arrive at its next stop?
(A) At 10:45 A.M.
(B) At 12:05 P.M.
(C) At 1:00 P.M.
(D) At 1:30 P.M.

시각 정보에 의하면, 133번 열차는 언제 다음 역에 도착하는가?
(A) 오전 10시 45분
(B) 오후 12시 5분
(C) 오후 1시
(D) 오후 1시 30분

해설 시각 정보 연계 – 133번 열차가 다음 역에 도착하는 시간
화자가 후반부에 133번 다음 역은 윌밍턴(Train 133's next stop will be Wilmington)이라고 말하고 있고, 시간표에 따르면 윌밍턴은 오후 12시 5분에 도착하므로 정답은 (B)이다.

98-100 연설 + 공항 지도

W-Am Hello, everyone. I'm Carmen Salazar, the airport operations director, 98and I wanted to thank you for attending this press conference. As of this week, construction on the new regional airport is proceeding on schedule for two of the three terminals. 99Minor design adjustments to terminal A have put the project slightly behind schedule, and we anticipate about two months will be added to the construction time frame as a result. 100I'd also like to mention that we now have a 3-D printed model of this project! Please feel free to visit our Web site so you can view it.

안녕하세요, 여러분. 공항 운영 책임자인 카르멘 살라자르입니다. **기자 회견에 참석해 주셔서 감사합니다.** 이번 주를 기준으로 새로운 지역 공항의 세 개의 터미널 중 두 곳에서 공사가 예정대로 진행됩니다. **A 터미널은 작은 설계 수정으로 인해 프로젝트가 예정보다 약간 늦어졌습니다.** 결과적으로 약 2개월 정도 공사 기간이 길어질 것으로 예상합니다. **또한 이 프로젝트의 3D 프린팅 모형도 있음을 말씀드리고자 합니다. 저희 웹사이트를 방문하면 보실 수 있습니다.**

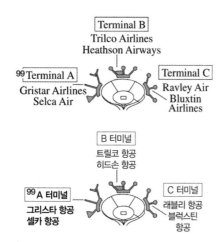

98

Who most likely are the listeners?
(A) Civil engineers
(B) Urban planners
(C) News reporters
(D) Safety inspectors

청자들은 누구이겠는가?
(A) 토목 기사
(B) 도시 계획자
(C) 취재 기자
(D) 안전 검사관

어휘 urban 도시의 inspector 검사관

해설 전체 내용 관련 – 청자들의 직업

화자가 초반부에 기자회견에 참석해 주셔서 감사하다(I wanted to thank you for attending this press conference)고 말하고 있으므로 청자들은 기자들임을 알 수 있다. 따라서 정답은 (C)이다.

99

Look at the graphic. Which of the following companies will be affected by a delay?
(A) Selca Air
(B) Trilco Airlines
(C) Heathson Airways
(D) Bluxtin Airlines

시각 정보에 의하면, 다음 중 지연에 영향을 받는 업체는?
(A) 셀카 항공
(B) 트릴코 항공
(C) 히드손 항공
(D) 블럭스틴 항공

어휘 affect 영향을 주다

해설 시각 정보 연계 – 지연에 영향을 받는 업체

화자가 중반부에 A 터미널은 작은 설계 수정으로 인해 프로젝트가 예정보다 약간 늦어진다(Minor design adjustments to terminal A have put the project slightly behind schedule ~)고 말하고 있고, 공항 지도에 따르면 A 터미널에는 셀카 항공이 있으므로 정답은 (A)이다.

> **Paraphrasing** 담화의 behind schedule → 질문의 a delay

100

What does the speaker invite the listeners to do?
(A) Download some designs
(B) Look at a model
(C) Take a site tour
(D) View a Webcam

화자는 청자들에게 무엇을 하라고 요청하는가?
(A) 디자인 다운로드하기
(B) 모형 보기
(C) 현장 견학하기
(D) 웹캠 보기

어휘 site tour 현장 견학

해설 세부 사항 관련 – 청자들에게 요청하는 일

화자가 마지막에 프로젝트의 3D 프린팅 모형도 있다(I'd also like to mention that we now have a 3-D printed model of this project!)며 웹사이트를 방문하면 볼 수 있다(Please feel free to visit our Web site so you can view it)고 말하고 있으므로 정답은 (B)이다.

> **Paraphrasing** 담화의 view → 정답의 Look at

1 (D)	**2** (C)	**3** (D)	**4** (B)	**5** (B)
6 (D)	**7** (A)	**8** (A)	**9** (C)	**10** (B)
11 (B)	**12** (A)	**13** (C)	**14** (B)	**15** (A)
16 (A)	**17** (B)	**18** (B)	**19** (A)	**20** (C)
21 (C)	**22** (A)	**23** (C)	**24** (A)	**25** (B)
26 (C)	**27** (B)	**28** (C)	**29** (C)	**30** (B)
31 (C)	**32** (C)	**33** (B)	**34** (D)	**35** (B)
36 (A)	**37** (D)	**38** (D)	**39** (B)	**40** (D)
41 (C)	**42** (B)	**43** (B)	**44** (D)	**45** (C)
46 (D)	**47** (C)	**48** (A)	**49** (D)	**50** (D)
51 (C)	**52** (A)	**53** (B)	**54** (D)	**55** (D)
56 (D)	**57** (B)	**58** (A)	**59** (C)	**60** (D)
61 (A)	**62** (B)	**63** (C)	**64** (C)	**65** (B)
66 (C)	**67** (A)	**68** (C)	**69** (B)	**70** (C)
71 (C)	**72** (C)	**73** (A)	**74** (A)	**75** (C)
76 (B)	**77** (C)	**78** (C)	**79** (A)	**80** (D)
81 (B)	**82** (C)	**83** (C)	**84** (B)	**85** (D)
86 (C)	**87** (A)	**88** (A)	**89** (D)	**90** (C)
91 (B)	**92** (D)	**93** (C)	**94** (A)	**95** (A)
96 (A)	**97** (C)	**98** (B)	**99** (C)	**100** (D)

PART 1

1 M-Au

▶ 동영상 강의

(A) She's cleaning an oven.
(B) She's moving a pot.
(C) She's opening a cabinet.
(D) She's holding a towel.

(A) 여자가 오븐을 청소하고 있다.
(B) 여자가 냄비를 옮기고 있다.
(C) 여자가 캐비닛을 열고 있다.
(D) 여자가 수건을 잡고 있다.

어휘 hold 잡다, 쥐다

해설 1인 등장 사진 – 사람의 동작/상태 묘사
(A) 동사 오답. 여자가 오븐을 청소하고 있는(is cleaning an oven) 모습
이 아니므로 오답.
(B) 동사 오답. 여자가 냄비를 옮기고 있는(is moving a pot) 모습이 아
니므로 오답.

(C) 동사 오답. 여자가 캐비닛을 열고 있는(is opening a cabinet) 모습
이 아니므로 오답.
(D) 정답. 여자가 수건을 잡고 있는(is holding a towel) 모습이므로 정답.

2 M-Cn

(A) They're putting trash in a bag.
(B) They're taking off their jackets.
(C) They're facing a shelving unit.
(D) They're painting a room.

(A) 사람들이 쓰레기를 봉지에 넣고 있다.
(B) 사람들이 재킷을 벗고 있다.
(C) 사람들이 선반을 마주보고 있다.
(D) 사람들이 방을 칠하고 있다.

어휘 trash 쓰레기 take off 벗다 face 마주보다 shelving unit
선반

해설 2인 이상 등장 사진 – 사람의 동작/상태 묘사
(A) 동사 오답. 사람들이 쓰레기를 봉지에 넣고 있는(are putting trash
in a bag) 모습이 아니므로 오답.
(B) 동사 오답. 사람들이 재킷을 벗고 있는(are taking off their
jackets) 모습이 아니므로 오답.
(C) 정답. 사람들이 선반을 마주보고 있는(are facing a shelving unit)
모습이므로 정답.
(D) 동사 오답. 사람들이 방을 칠하고 있는(are painting a room) 모습
이 아니므로 오답.

3 M-Cn

(A) One of the men is removing his hat.
(B) A line of customers extends out a door.
(C) Some workers are installing a sign.
(D) Musicians have gathered in a circle.

(A) 남자들 중 한 명이 모자를 벗고 있다.
(B) 줄지어 선 손님들이 문 밖까지 이어져 있다.
(C) 몇몇 인부들이 표지판을 설치하고 있다.
(D) 음악가들이 원을 이루어 모여 있다.

어휘 remove (옷 등을) 벗다 extend 늘이다, 늘리다 install 설치하다
sign 표지판 gather 모이다 in a circle 원형을 이루어

해설 2인 이상 등장 사진 – 사람의 동작/상태 묘사
(A) 동사 오답. 모자를 벗고 있는(is removing his hat) 남자의 모습이
보이지 않으므로 오답.

(B) 사진에 없는 명사를 이용한 오답. 사진에 줄지어 선 손님들(A line of customers)의 모습이 보이지 않으므로 오답.

(C) 사진에 없는 명사를 이용한 오답. 사진에 표지판(a sign)의 모습이 보이지 않으므로 오답.

(D) 정답. 음악가들(Musicians)이 원을 이루어 모여 있는(have gathered in a circle) 모습이므로 정답.

4 W-Br

(A) Some tools have been left on a chair.
(B) Some tool sets have been laid out.
(C) A cup of coffee has spilled.
(D) A table leg is being repaired.

(A) 연장들이 의자에 놓여 있다.
(B) 공구 세트들이 펼쳐져 있다.
(C) 커피 컵이 쏟아졌다.
(D) 탁자 다리가 수리되고 있다.

어휘 tool 연장, 도구 lay out 펼치다 spill 쏟아지다, 흘리다 repair 수리하다

해설 사물/풍경 사진 – 사물 묘사

(A) 사진에 없는 명사를 이용한 오답. 사진에 의자(a chair)의 모습이 보이지 않으므로 오답.

(B) 정답. 공구 세트들(Some tool sets)이 펼쳐져 있는(have been laid out) 모습이므로 정답.

(C) 동사 오답. 커피 컵(A cup of coffee)이 쏟아져 있는(has spilled) 모습이 아니므로 오답.

(D) 동사 오답. 탁자 다리(A table leg)가 수리되고 있는(is being repaired) 모습이 아니므로 오답.

5 W-Am

(A) A railing is being removed.
(B) A roof is under construction.
(C) Some workers are carrying a ladder.
(D) Some workers are holding sheets of metal.

(A) 난간이 제거되고 있다.
(B) 지붕이 공사 중이다.
(C) 몇몇 인부들이 사다리를 옮기고 있다.
(D) 몇몇 인부들이 금속판을 들고 있다.

어휘 railing 철책, 난간 remove 제거하다, 없애다 under construction 공사 중인 ladder 사다리 metal 금속

해설 혼합 사진 – 사람/사물/풍경 혼합 묘사

(A) 동사 오답. 난간(A railing)이 제거되고 있는(is being removed) 모습이 아니므로 오답.

(B) 정답. 지붕(A roof)이 공사 중인(is under construction) 모습이므로 정답.

(C) 동사 오답. 사다리를 옮기고 있는(are carrying a ladder) 인부들의 모습이 보이지 않으므로 오답.

(D) 사진에 없는 명사를 이용한 오답. 사진에 금속판(sheets of metal)의 모습이 보이지 않으므로 오답.

6 M-Cn

(A) A ladder has been leaned against a tree.
(B) There are piles of tree branches discarded in a field.
(C) Wooden benches have been arranged in a circle.
(D) A wooden structure has been built near some trees.

(A) 사다리가 나무에 기대어 있다.
(B) 들판에 버려진 나뭇가지 더미가 있다.
(C) 나무 벤치가 원형으로 배열되어 있다.
(D) 나무로 된 구조물이 나무 근처에 지어져 있다.

어휘 lean 기대 놓다 pile 더미, 포개 놓은 것 discard 버리다, 폐기하다 arrange 정리하다, 배열하다 structure 구조물

해설 사물/풍경 사진 – 사물 묘사

(A) 동사 오답. 사다리(A ladder)가 나무에 기대어 있는(has been leaned against a tree) 모습이 아니므로 오답.

(B) 사진에 없는 명사를 이용한 오답. 사진에 버려진 나뭇가지 더미(piles of tree branches discarded)의 모습이 보이지 않으므로 오답.

(C) 사진에 없는 명사를 이용한 오답. 사진에 나무 벤치(Wooden benches)의 모습이 보이지 않으므로 오답.

(D) 정답. 나무로 된 구조물(A wooden structure)이 나무 근처에 지어져 있는(has been built near some trees) 모습이므로 정답.

PART 2

7

M-Au Why is there no flour on the shelf?

W-Br (A) Because it's out of stock.
(B) Those roses smell nice.
(C) No, the other cake.

왜 선반에 밀가루가 없죠?
(A) 재고가 없어서요.
(B) 그 장미는 향기가 좋아요.
(C) 아니요, 다른 케이크요.

어휘 flour 밀가루 shelf 선반 out of stock 품절된, 재고가 없는

해설 선반에 밀가루가 없는 이유를 묻는 Why 의문문

(A) 정답. 선반에 밀가루가 없는 이유를 묻는 질문에 재고가 없어서라고 구체적인 이유를 제시하고 있으므로 정답.

(B) 연상 단어 오답. 질문의 flour를 flower로 잘못 이해했을 경우 연상 가능한 roses를 이용한 오답.

(C) Yes/No 불가 오답. Why 의문문에는 Yes/No 응답이 불가능하므로 오답.

8

M-Au When will the catering company arrive?

W-Am (A) At four o'clock.
(B) That's a delicious flavor.
(C) Many vegetarian options.

케이터링 업체가 언제 도착할까요?

(A) 4시에요.
(B) 맛이 좋아요.
(C) 채식 식단이 많아요.

어휘 delicious 맛있는 flavor 맛, 풍미 vegetarian 채식주의자

해설 케이터링 업체의 도착 시간을 묻는 When 의문문

(A) 정답. 케이터링 업체의 도착 시간을 묻는 질문에 4시라고 구체적인 시간으로 응답하고 있으므로 정답.

(B) 연상 단어 오답. 질문의 catering에서 연상 가능한 delicious를 이용한 오답.

(C) 연상 단어 오답. 질문의 catering에서 연상 가능한 vegetarian options를 이용한 오답.

9

W-Am When's the meeting scheduled to start?

M-Cn (A) At a networking event.
(B) I started this job six years ago.
(C) Right after lunch.

회의는 언제 시작될 예정인가요?

(A) 교류 행사에서요.
(B) 저는 6년 전에 이 일을 시작했어요.
(C) 점심 식사 직후에요.

어휘 be scheduled to ~할 예정이다 networking 인적 네트워크 형성

해설 회의 시작 시간을 묻는 When 의문문

(A) 질문과 상관없는 오답. Where 의문문에 대한 응답이므로 오답.

(B) 파생어 오답. 질문의 start와 파생어 관계인 started를 이용한 오답.

(C) 정답. 회의 시작 시간을 묻는 질문에 점심 식사 직후라고 응답하고 있으므로 정답.

10

W-Am How much will the repairs cost?

M-Cn (A) I have two pairs of shoes.
(B) Around 200 dollars.
(C) The restaurant downtown.

수리하는 데 비용이 얼마나 들까요?

(A) 저는 신발 두 켤레가 있어요.
(B) 200달러 정도요.
(C) 시내 음식점이요.

어휘 pair 쌍, 짝

해설 수리 비용을 묻는 How much 의문문

(A) 유사 발음 오답. 질문의 repairs와 부분적으로 발음이 유사한 pairs를 이용한 오답.

(B) 정답. 수리 비용을 묻는 질문에 200달러 정도라고 구체적인 액수로 응답하고 있으므로 정답.

(C) 질문과 상관없는 오답.

11

M-Au You went to the dentist this morning, didn't you?

W-Br (A) Oh, I've already had breakfast.
(B) Yes, for an annual checkup.
(C) Let's take the bus.

오늘 오전에 치과에 갔죠, 그렇죠?

(A) 아, 저는 이미 아침 식사를 했어요.
(B) 네, 연례 검진 때문에요.
(C) 버스를 타죠.

어휘 dentist 치과 의사 annual 연례의, 매년의 checkup 점검, 건강 검진

해설 오늘 오전에 치과에 갔는지 여부를 확인하는 부가 의문문

(A) 연상 단어 오답. 질문의 morning에서 연상 가능한 breakfast를 이용한 오답.

(B) 정답. 오늘 오전에 치과에 갔는지 여부를 확인하는 질문에 네(Yes)라고 대답한 뒤, 연례 검진 때문이라고 긍정 답변과 일관된 내용을 덧붙였으므로 정답.

(C) 질문과 상관없는 오답.

12

W-Am Where should we put the new printer?

M-Cn (A) In the corner by the stairs.
(B) The third page of the document.
(C) A reusable ink cartridge.

새 프린터를 어디에 둬야 하나요?

(A) 계단 옆 모퉁이에요.
(B) 서류 세 번째 장이요.
(C) 재사용할 수 있는 잉크 카트리지요.

어휘 document 문서, 서류 reusable 재사용할 수 있는

해설 새 프린터를 둘 위치를 묻는 Where 의문문
(A) 정답. 새 프린터를 둘 위치를 묻는 질문에 계단 옆 모퉁이라고 구체적인 위치로 응답하고 있으므로 정답.
(B) 질문과 상관없는 오답.
(C) 연상 단어 오답. 질문의 printer에서 연상 가능한 ink cartridge를 이용한 오답.

13

M-Cn What type of plant do you have in your office?

W-Am (A) Whenever I sit at my desk.
(B) Thanks—I just bought it.
(C) One that doesn't require much water.

사무실에 어떤 종류의 식물이 있나요?
(A) 책상에 앉을 때마다요.
(B) 고마워요. 이제 막 샀어요.
(C) 물을 많이 필요로 하지 않는 거요.

어휘 plant 식물 whenever ~할 때마다 require 필요로 하다

해설 사무실에 있는 식물 종류를 묻는 What 의문문
(A) 연상 단어 오답. 질문의 office에서 연상 가능한 desk를 이용한 오답.
(B) 질문과 상관없는 오답.
(C) 정답. 사무실에 있는 식물 종류를 묻는 질문에 물을 많이 필요로 하지 않는 거라고 응답하고 있으므로 정답.

14

M-Au There was a sale at the furniture store.

W-Am (A) No, it wasn't in storage.
(B) Did you buy anything?
(C) Some old receipts.

가구점에서 할인을 했어요.
(A) 아니요, 그건 보관소에 없었어요.
(B) 뭐라도 샀나요?
(C) 오래된 영수증이요.

어휘 furniture 가구 storage 보관소, 저장고 receipt 영수증

해설 정보 전달의 평서문
(A) 유사 발음 오답. 평서문의 store와 부분적으로 발음이 유사한 storage를 이용한 오답.
(B) 정답. 가구점에서 할인을 했다고 말하는 평서문에 뭐라도 샀는지 관련된 내용을 묻고 있으므로 정답.
(C) 연상 단어 오답. 평서문의 sale에서 연상 가능한 receipts를 이용한 오답.

15

M-Au Can you show me how to submit a tech help ticket?

W-Br (A) Let me send you the link.
(B) A broken power cable.
(C) No, over ten minutes.

기술 지원 티켓을 어떻게 제출하는지 알려 주실 수 있나요?
(A) 링크를 보내 드릴게요.
(B) 고장 난 전원 케이블이요.
(C) 아니요, 10분 이상이요.

어휘 submit 제출하다 broken 고장 난

해설 기술 지원 티켓의 제출 방법을 묻는 간접 의문문
(A) 정답. 기술 지원 티켓의 제출 방법을 묻는 질문에 링크를 보내 주겠다고 제출 방법을 제시하고 있으므로 정답.
(B) 질문과 상관없는 오답. What 의문문에 대한 응답이므로 오답.
(C) 질문과 상관없는 오답.

16

M-Cn Where is the power button on this device?

M-Au (A) I've never used that model before.
(B) Ten euros per hour.
(C) We charge more for color photographs.

이 기기의 전원 버튼은 어디 있죠?
(A) 전에 그 모델을 써 본 적이 없어요.
(B) 시간당 10유로입니다.
(C) 컬러 사진은 돈을 더 받습니다.

어휘 device 장치, 기구 charge 청구하다, 비용을 달라고 하다

해설 전원 버튼의 위치를 묻는 Where 의문문
(A) 정답. 기기의 전원 버튼의 위치를 묻는 질문에 전에 그 모델을 써 본 적이 없다며 알지 못함을 우회적으로 알려 주고 있으므로 정답.
(B) 질문과 상관없는 오답. How much 의문문에 대한 응답이므로 오답.
(C) 질문과 상관없는 오답.

17

 동영상 강의

W-Am Do you want to take a walk now, or would later be better?

W-Br (A) A nearby lake.
(B) I'm free to walk now.
(C) No, I don't use a fitness tracker.

지금 산책하고 싶으세요, 아니면 나중이 더 나을까요?
(A) 근처 호수요.
(B) 지금 산책할 시간이 있어요.
(C) 아니요, 저는 피트니스 트래커를 사용하지 않아요.

어휘 take a walk 산책하다 nearby 인근의, 가까운 곳의 fitness tracker 건강 지표 추적기

해설 원하는 산책 시간을 묻는 선택 의문문
(A) 연상 단어 오답. 질문의 take a walk에서 연상 가능한 lake를 이용한 오답.
(B) 정답. 지금과 나중 중 원하는 산책 시간을 묻는 질문에 지금 산책할 시간이 있다며 지금을 선택해 응답하고 있으므로 정답.
(C) 연상 단어 오답. 질문의 take a walk에서 연상 가능한 a fitness tracker를 이용한 오답.

18

M-Cn I ordered some new equipment for the factory.

W-Am (A) The news program on Channel Ten.
(B) Great—I can't wait to use it.
(C) The car dealership.

공장에서 쓸 새 장비를 주문했어요.
(A) 10번 채널 뉴스 프로그램이요.
(B) 좋아요. 어서 쓰고 싶네요.
(C) 자동차 대리점이요.

어휘 equipment 장비 car dealership 자동차 영업소, 대리점

해설 정보 전달의 평서문
(A) 유사 발음 오답. 평서문의 new와 부분적으로 발음이 유사한 news를 이용한 오답.
(B) 정답. 공장에서 쓸 새 장비를 주문했다고 말하는 평서문에 좋다 (Great)고 대답한 뒤, 어서 쓰고 싶다며 새 장비에 대한 의견을 덧붙였으므로 정답.
(C) 평서문과 상관없는 오답.

19

M-Cn There's a nice place to rent on Mercer Street.

W-Am (A) I just renewed my current lease.
(B) It was a great show.
(C) A standard rental application.

머서 가에 임대하기에 좋은 곳이 있어요.
(A) 저는 현재 임대차 계약을 막 연장했어요.
(B) 멋진 공연이었어요.
(C) 일반 임대 신청서요.

어휘 rent 임대하다, 임차하다 renew 갱신하다, 연장하다 current 현재의 lease 임대차 계약 rental application 임대 신청서

해설 정보 전달의 평서문
(A) 정답. 머서 가에 임대하기에 좋은 곳이 있다는 평서문에 현재 임대차 계약을 막 연장했다며 새로 임대를 찾을 필요가 없음을 우회적으로 알려 주고 있으므로 정답.
(B) 연상 단어 오답. 평서문의 nice place에서 연상 가능한 great를 이용한 오답.
(C) 파생어 오답. 평서문의 rent와 파생어 관계인 rental을 이용한 오답.

20

W-Br Is the heating system working?

M-Cn (A) Yes, that's my Web site.
(B) A five-kilometer run.
(C) I just called maintenance.

난방 장치가 작동되나요?
(A) 네, 그건 제 웹사이트예요.
(B) 5킬로미터 달리기요.
(C) 방금 유지보수 부서에 전화했어요.

어휘 heating system 난방 장치, 난방 설비 maintenance 유지보수

해설 난방 장치가 작동되는지 묻는 Be동사 의문문
(A) 질문과 상관없는 오답.
(B) 질문과 상관없는 오답.
(C) 정답. 난방 장치가 작동되는지 묻는 질문에 방금 유지보수 부서에 전화했다며 난방 장치가 작동되지 않음을 우회적으로 알려 주고 있으므로 정답.

21

M-Au Isn't the roadwork in front of city hall finished yet?

M-Cn (A) I just finished my conference presentation.
(B) A lot of traffic in the evening.
(C) No, they still have another month to go.

시청 앞 도로 공사가 아직 안 끝났나요?
(A) 저는 학술 발표를 막 끝냈어요.
(B) 저녁에 교통량이 많아요.
(C) 아니요, 아직 한 달 더 해야 해요.

어휘 roadwork 도로 공사 city hall 시청 conference presentation 학술 발표 traffic 교통(량)

해설 시청 앞 도로 공사가 끝났는지 확인하는 부정 의문문
(A) 단어 반복 오답. 질문의 finished를 반복 이용한 오답.
(B) 연상 단어 오답. 질문의 roadwork에서 연상 가능한 traffic을 이용한 오답.
(C) 정답. 시청 앞 도로 공사가 끝났는지 확인하는 질문에 아니요(No)라고 대답한 뒤, 아직 한 달 더 해야 한다며 부정 답변과 일관된 내용을 덧붙이고 있으므로 정답.

22

W-Br Who will lead the new-employee training today?

M-Au (A) We're using a recorded video.
(B) Yes, right after lunch.
(C) Classroom 124.

오늘 신입 사원 교육은 누가 진행해요?
(A) 저희는 녹화된 영상을 활용하고 있어요.
(B) 네, 점심 식사 직후예요.
(C) 124호 강의실이요.

어휘 recorded 녹화된, 녹음된

해설 신입 사원 교육 진행자를 묻는 Who 의문문
(A) 정답. 신입 사원 교육을 진행할 사람이 누구인지 묻는 질문에 녹화된 영상을 활용하고 있다며 진행자가 따로 없음을 우회적으로 알려 주고 있으므로 정답.
(B) Yes/No 불가 오답. Who 의문문에는 Yes/No 응답이 불가능하므로 오답.
(C) 연상 단어 오답. 질문의 training에서 연상 가능한 classroom을 이용한 오답.

23

M-Au Is the safety inspection scheduled for this month or next month?

W-Br (A) I thought I saved the file.
(B) The factory supervisor.
(C) It's this Wednesday.

안전 점검은 이번 달로 예정되어 있나요, 아니면 다음 달인가요?
(A) 저는 파일을 저장했다고 생각했어요.
(B) 공장 관리자요.
(C) 이번 주 수요일이에요.

어휘 be scheduled for ~로 예정되다   safety inspection 안전 점검
save 저장하다   supervisor 감독관, 관리자

해설 안전 점검 예정 시기에 대해 묻는 선택 의문문
(A) 유사 발음 오답. 질문의 safety와 부분적으로 발음이 유사한 saved를 이용한 오답.
(B) 연상 단어 오답. 질문의 safety inspection에서 연상 가능한 supervisor를 이용한 오답.
(C) 정답. 안전 점검 예정 시기에 대해 묻는 질문에 이번 주 수요일이라며 정확한 시기를 알려 주고 있으므로 정답.

24

W-Br When is the harvest festival taking place?

M-Au (A) It's a week from tomorrow.
(B) Sure, I can take it.
(C) The park next to the art museum.

추수 감사제는 언제 열리나요?
(A) 내일부터 1주일 후요.
(B) 물론이죠, 제가 가져갈 수 있어요.
(C) 미술관 옆 공원이요.

어휘 harvest 수확, 추수   take place 열리다   art museum 미술관

해설 추수 감사제가 열리는 시기를 묻는 When 의문문
(A) 정답. 추수 감사제가 열리는 시기를 묻는 질문에 내일부터 1주일 후라고 구체적인 시점으로 응답하고 있으므로 정답.
(B) Yes/No 불가 오답. When 의문문에는 Yes/No 응답이 불가능한데, Sure도 일종의 Yes 응답이라고 볼 수 있으므로 오답.
(C) 질문과 상관없는 오답. Where 의문문에 대한 응답이므로 오답.

25

M-Cn Was your new laptop expensive?

M-Au (A) Do you have a new password?
(B) I had a discount coupon.
(C) On top of the cabinet.

당신의 새 노트북 컴퓨터는 비쌌나요?
(A) 새 비밀번호가 있어요?
(B) 할인 쿠폰이 있었어요.
(C) 캐비닛 위요.

어휘 expensive 비싼   password 비밀번호   discount 할인

해설 새 노트북 컴퓨터가 비쌌는지 묻는 Be동사 의문문
(A) 단어 반복 오답. 질문의 new를 반복 이용한 오답.
(B) 정답. 새 노트북 컴퓨터가 비쌌는지 묻는 질문에 할인 쿠폰이 있었다며 할인을 받아 그다지 비싸지 않았음을 우회적으로 알려 주고 있으므로 정답.
(C) 유사 발음 오답. 질문의 laptop과 부분적으로 발음이 유사한 top을 이용한 오답.

26

▶ 동영상 강의

W-Br Why don't we go on our camping trip next weekend?

W-Am (A) Yes, that table lamp is quite nice.
(B) Should we go left or right?
(C) I have a performance scheduled with my band.

다음 주 주말에 캠핑 여행을 가는 게 어때요?
(A) 네, 그 테이블 램프는 꽤 괜찮아요.
(B) 왼쪽으로 가야 해요, 오른쪽으로 가야 해요?
(C) 밴드와 함께 예정된 공연이 있어요.

어휘 performance 공연   scheduled 예정된

해설 제안/권유의 의문문
(A) 질문과 상관없는 오답.
(B) 단어 반복 오답. 질문의 go를 반복 이용한 오답.
(C) 정답. 다음 주 주말에 캠핑 여행을 가자고 제안하는 질문에 밴드와 함께 예정된 공연이 있다며 제안을 거절하는 의사를 우회적으로 표현하고 있으므로 정답.

27

M-Cn The workshop for this afternoon was postponed, wasn't it?

M-Au (A) At the post office.
(B) I haven't checked my e-mail.
(C) A ticket for two o'clock, please.

오늘 오후 워크숍은 연기됐죠, 그렇죠?
(A) 우체국에서요.
(B) 이메일 확인을 안 했는데요.
(C) 두 시 표 주세요.

어휘 postpone 연기하다

해설 오늘 오후 워크숍의 연기 여부를 확인하는 부가 의문문
(A) 유사 발음 오답. 질문의 postponed와 부분적으로 발음이 유사한 post office를 이용한 오답.
(B) 정답. 오늘 오후 워크숍이 연기됐는지 여부를 확인하는 질문에 이메일 확인을 안 했다며 자신도 모름을 우회적으로 표현하고 있으므로 정답.
(C) 연상 단어 오답. 질문의 workshop에서 연상 가능한 ticket을 이용한 오답.

28

▶ 동영상 강의

W-Am How were our production figures last month?

M-Au (A) They produce electric cars.
(B) Nine o'clock in the morning.
(C) We were closed down for a week.

우리 지난달 생산량은 어땠어요?
(A) 그들은 전기차를 생산해요.
(B) 오전 9시요.
(C) 1주간 폐쇄됐잖아요.

어휘 production 생산(량)　figure 수치　electric car 전기차
be closed down 폐쇄되다

해설 지난달 생산량에 대해 묻는 How 의문문
(A) 파생어 오답. 질문의 production과 파생어 관계인 produce를 이용한 오답.
(B) 질문과 상관없는 오답. When 의문문에 대한 응답이므로 오답.
(C) 정답. 지난달 생산량에 대해 묻는 질문에 1주간 폐쇄됐다며 생산량이 줄었을 것임을 우회적으로 알려 주고 있으므로 정답.

29

W-Br When can I see the speech therapist?

M-Cn (A) A one-hour session.
(B) Just a microphone.
(C) How about tomorrow afternoon?

언어 치료사를 언제 만날 수 있어요?
(A) 한 시간 세션입니다.
(B) 그냥 마이크예요.
(C) 내일 오후 어때요?

어휘 speech therapist 언어 치료사

해설 언어 치료사를 만날 시기를 묻는 When 의문문
(A) 연상 단어 오답. 질문의 speech에서 연상 가능한 session을 이용한 오답.
(B) 연상 단어 오답. 질문의 speech에서 연상 가능한 microphone을 이용한 오답.
(C) 정답. 언어 치료사를 만날 시기를 묻는 질문에 내일 오후가 어떤지 구체적인 시간으로 묻고 있으므로 정답.

30

W-Am Aren't you picking up the clients from the airport?

M-Cn (A) A product demonstration.
(B) No, I believe Tomoko is doing that.
(C) He prefers an aisle seat.

당신이 공항에서 고객들을 모셔올 예정 아닌가요?
(A) 제품 시연이요.
(B) 아니요, 토모코 씨가 하는 걸로 알고 있어요.
(C) 그는 통로 쪽 좌석을 좋아해요.

어휘 pick up ~을 차에 태우러 가다　client 고객　demonstration 설명, 시연　prefer 선호하다　aisle 통로

해설 공항에서 고객들을 모셔올지 여부를 확인하는 부정 의문문
(A) 질문과 상관없는 오답.
(B) 정답. 공항에서 고객들을 모셔올 예정인지 묻는 질문에 아니요(No)라고 대답한 뒤, 토모코 씨가 하는 걸로 알고 있다고 부정 답변과 일관된 내용을 덧붙였으므로 정답.
(C) 질문과 상관없는 오답. 질문에 3인칭 대명사 He로 지칭할 인물이 언급된 적이 없으므로 오답.

31

W-Am How was your morning client meeting?

M-Au (A) It's great to meet you.
(B) No, over in conference room two.
(C) The contract is now officially signed.

오전 고객 회의는 어땠어요?
(A) 만나서 반갑습니다.
(B) 아니요, 2번 회의실에서요.
(C) 계약이 이제 공식 체결됐어요.

어휘 conference room 회의실　officially 공식적으로
sign a contract 계약을 맺다

해설 오전 고객 회의에 대해 묻는 How 의문문
(A) 파생어 오답. 질문의 meeting과 파생어 관계인 meet를 이용한 오답.
(B) Yes/No 불가 오답. How 의문문에는 Yes/No 응답이 불가능하므로 오답.
(C) 정답. 오전 고객 회의에 대해 묻는 질문에 계약이 공식 체결됐다며 회의의 결과가 좋았다는 것을 우회적으로 알려 주고 있으므로 정답.

PART 3

32-34

M-Cn ³²**The company's making a big change this year by moving offices.** It's exciting that the new space will be much bigger.

W-Am Yes. Do you know what the company's planning to do with our meeting tables and chairs?

M-Cn Well, ³³**the new location already has furniture, so we don't need them.**

W-Am ³³**Why don't we donate them?** The Jebreen Foundation is a local organization that picks up old furniture for donation.

M-Cn That's a good idea. ³⁴**Let's talk to our directors to see what they think.**

남 회사에서 올해 사무실 이전으로 큰 변화를 꾀하고 있어요. 새로운 공간은 훨씬 더 넓어질 예정이라 기대돼요.

여 네. 회사에서 우리 회의 탁자와 의자를 어떻게 할 계획인지 아세요?

남	음… 새로운 곳에는 이미 가구가 있으니 필요 없어요.
여	**기부하는 건 어때요?** 제브린 재단은 낡은 가구를 가져가서 기부하는 지역 단체예요.
남	좋은 생각이네요. **임원들이 어떻게 생각하는지 얘기해 보죠.**

어휘	make a change 변화를 주다 location 장소, 곳 furniture 가구 donate 기부하다 foundation 재단 local 지역의 organization 단체, donation 기부 director 임원, 관리자

32

What change is a company making?
(A) It is lowering some prices.
(B) It is hiring more staffers.
(C) It is moving to a new location.
(D) It is expanding a product line.

회사는 어떤 변화를 꾀하고 있는가?
(A) 가격을 낮추고 있다.
(B) 직원을 더 고용하고 있다.
(C) 새로운 장소로 이전하려고 한다.
(D) 제품군을 확대하고 있다.

어휘 lower 낮추다 staffer 직원 expand 확대하다, 확장하다 product 제품

해설 세부 사항 관련 – 회사가 꾀하고 있는 변화
남자가 첫 대사에서 회사에서 올해 사무실 이전으로 큰 변화를 꾀하고 있다(The company's making a big change this year by moving offices)고 했으므로 정답은 (C)이다.

Paraphrasing	대화의 moving offices → 정답의 moving to a new location

33

What suggestion does the woman make?
(A) Updating a handbook
(B) Donating some furniture
(C) Creating a schedule
(D) Downloading a software program

여자는 어떤 제안을 하는가?
(A) 안내서 업데이트하기
(B) 가구 기부하기
(C) 일정표 만들기
(D) 소프트웨어 프로그램 다운로드하기

어휘 suggestion 제안 handbook 편람, 안내서 create 만들다

해설 세부 사항 관련 – 여자의 제안 사항
남자가 두 번째 대사에서 새로운 곳에는 이미 가구가 있으니 필요 없다(the new location already has furniture, so we don't need them)고 말하자, 여자가 기부하는 게 어떤지(Why don't we donate them?) 제안하고 있으므로 정답은 (B)이다.

34

What will the speakers most likely do next?
(A) Train a new employee
(B) Review an application
(C) Check a list
(D) Talk to some directors

화자들은 다음에 무엇을 하겠는가?
(A) 신입 사원 교육하기
(B) 지원서 검토하기
(C) 목록 확인하기
(D) 임원에게 얘기하기

어휘 train 교육하다 review 검토하다 application 지원, 지원서

해설 세부 사항 관련 – 화자들이 다음에 할 일
남자가 마지막 대사에서 임원들이 어떻게 생각하는지 얘기해 보자(Let's talk to our directors to see what they think)고 말하는 것으로 보아 임원에게 얘기할 것임을 알 수 있다. 따라서 정답은 (D)이다.

35-37 3인 대화

M-Au	Welcome! I'm excited to show you both around the Southeast Medical Trade Show.
W-Am	³⁵**Thanks for allowing us to cover the event for our newspaper. We really wanted to interview you as the organizer.**
W-Br	Yes. How many people are you expecting to attend this trade show?
M-Au	³⁶**I'm pleased to report that registration has increased this year.** We have over 2,000 participants.
W-Br	That's impressive.
M-Au	It's our best turnout yet.
W-Am	Actually, ³⁷**before we go into the main room, can we get a photo of you in front of the poster for the show?** The one on that wall?
M-Au	³⁷**Certainly!**

남	환영합니다! 두 분께 사우스이스트 의학 박람회를 소개하게 되어 기쁩니다.
여1	**저희 신문사에서 이 행사를 취재할 수 있게 해 주셔서 감사합니다. 주최자이신 당신을 꼭 인터뷰하고 싶었거든요.**
여2	네. 이번 박람회에 얼마나 많이 참석할 것으로 예상하세요?
남	**올해 등록이 증가했음을 알리게 되어 기쁘네요.** 참가자가 2천 명이 넘습니다.
여2	인상적이군요.
남	지금껏 가장 높은 참가자 수입니다.
여1	저, **주 회의장으로 가기 전에 박람회 포스터 앞에서 당신의 사진을 찍어도 될까요?** 벽에 있는 포스터요.
남	**물론이죠!**

어휘 medical trade show 의학 박람회 allow 허락하다,
허용하다 cover 취재하다 organizer 주최인, 주최측
registration 등록 increase 증가하다, 늘다
participant 참가자 impressive 인상적인, 인상 깊은
turnout 참가자의 수 actually 실은, 저 certainly 물론

35

Who most likely are the women?
(A) Company executives
(B) Journalists
(C) Health-care professionals
(D) Safety inspectors

여자들은 누구이겠는가?
(A) 회사 임원
(B) 기자
(C) 의료 전문가
(D) 안전 검사관

어휘 executive 간부, 경영진 health-care 보건, 의료 서비스
professional 전문직 종사자 safety 안전 inspector 검사관

해설 전체 내용 관련 – 여자들의 직업
첫 번째 여자가 첫 대사에서 남자에게 우리 신문사(our newspaper)에서
이 행사를 취재할 수 있게 해 주셔서 감사하다고 한 후, 꼭 인터뷰하고
싶었다(We really wanted to interview you as the organizer)고
말하는 것으로 보아 여자들은 기자임을 알 수 있다. 따라서 정답은
(B)이다.

36

What does the man say he is pleased about?
(A) The number of event participants
(B) The amount of money raised
(C) The quality of vendors
(D) The variety of presentations

남자는 무엇에 대해 기쁘다고 말하는가?
(A) 행사 참가자 수
(B) 모금액
(C) 판매 업체 자질
(D) 발표의 다양성

어휘 raise money 모금하다 vendor 판매 회사 variety 다양성
presentation 발표

해설 세부 사항 관련 – 남자가 기쁘다고 말하는 것
남자가 두 번째 대사에서 올해 등록이 증가했음을 알리게 되어 기쁘다(I'm
pleased to report that registration has increased this year)고
말하고 있으므로 정답은 (A)이다.

37

What will the women do next?
(A) Watch a demonstration
(B) Get some refreshments
(C) Register for an event
(D) Take a photograph

여자들은 다음에 무엇을 할 것인가?
(A) 시연 보기
(B) 다과 먹기
(C) 행사 등록하기
(D) 사진 찍기

어휘 demonstration 시범 설명, 시연 refreshments 다과
register for ~에 등록하다

해설 세부 사항 관련 – 여자들이 다음에 할 일
첫 번째 여자가 마지막 대사에서 주 회의장으로 가기 전에 박람회 포스터
앞에서 사진을 찍어도 되는지(~ can we get a photo of you in front
of the poster for the show?) 물었고, 남자가 물론(Certainly!)이라고
수락의 답변을 하고 있으므로 정답은 (D)이다.

> Paraphrasing 대화의 get a photo
> → 정답의 Take a photograph

38-40

W-Am	Murad, I need your help. Can you spare 30 minutes?
M-Cn	I have some time after lunch. How can I help?
W-Am	As you know, **38 I've been redesigning Ace Bancorp's Web site to add new online banking functions**.
M-Cn	This is the client that wanted streamlined menus on their home page too, right?
W-Am	Yes. **39 I wonder whether you could test out the redeveloped site for me**.
M-Cn	**39 I can do that. 40 Why don't you send me a list of the specific updates you made?** I'll make sure I check those.

여	무라드, 당신의 도움이 필요해요. 30분만 시간을 내 주실 수 있나요?
남	점심 시간 이후에 시간이 있어요. 어떻게 도와드릴까요?
여	아시다시피, **제가 새로운 온라인 뱅킹 기능을 추가하기 위해 에이스 반코프의 웹사이트를 다시 디자인하고 있잖아요.**
남	홈페이지에도 간소화된 메뉴를 원한 고객이죠, 그렇죠?
여	네. **다시 개발한 사이트를 테스트해 주실 수 있으신지요.**
남	**해 드릴 수 있어요. 진행하신 구체적인 업데이트 목록을 보내 주시겠어요?** 그것들을 확인할게요.

어휘 spare (시간을) 할애하다, 내어 주다 add 추가하다
function 기능 streamline 간소화하다, 능률화하다
redevelop 재개발하다 specific 특정한, 구체적인

38

What most likely is the woman's job?
(A) Professional chef
(B) Bank executive
(C) Administrative assistant
(D) Web designer

여자의 직업은 무엇이겠는가?
(A) 전문 요리사
(B) 은행 임원
(C) 행정 보조원
(D) 웹 디자이너

어휘 executive 간부, 경영진   administrative 관리상의, 행정의

해설 전체 내용 관련 – 여자의 직업

여자가 두 번째 대사에서 새로운 온라인 뱅킹 기능을 추가하기 위해 에이스 반코프의 웹사이트를 다시 디자인하고 있다(I've been redeveloping Ace Bancorp's Web site)고 말하는 것으로 보아 여자는 웹 디자이너임을 알 수 있다. 따라서 정답은 (D)이다.

39

What will the man most likely do?
(A) Buy some materials from the woman
(B) Check the woman's work
(C) List investment options
(D) Update some client information

남자는 무엇을 하겠는가?
(A) 여자에게서 재료 구입
(B) 여자의 작업 확인
(C) 투자 옵션 목록 작성
(D) 고객 정보 업데이트

어휘 material 재료, 자료   investment 투자

해설 세부 사항 관련 – 남자가 할 일

여자가 마지막 대사에서 다시 개발한 사이트를 테스트해 줄 수 있는지(I wonder whether you could test out the redeveloped site for me) 묻자 남자가 해 줄 수 있다(I can do that)고 답변하는 것으로 보아 남자는 여자가 작업한 것을 확인해 줄 것임을 알 수 있다. 따라서 정답은 (B)이다.

> **Paraphrasing** 대화의 test out the redeveloped site for me
> → 정답의 Check the woman's work

40

What will the woman most likely send to the man?
(A) A cost estimate
(B) A revised schedule
(C) A building plan
(D) A list of changes

여자는 남자에게 무엇을 보내겠는가?
(A) 견적서
(B) 수정된 일정표
(C) 건축 계획
(D) 변경 사항 목록

어휘 cost estimate 견적서   revise 변경하다, 수정하다

해설 세부 사항 관련 – 여자가 남자에게 보낼 것

남자가 마지막 대사에서 여자에게 구체적인 업데이트 목록을 보내줄 것(Why don't you send me a list of the specific updates you made?)을 요청하고 있는 것으로 보아 여자가 변경 사항 목록을 보낼 것임을 알 수 있다. 따라서 정답은 (D)이다.

> **Paraphrasing** 대화의 a list of the specific updates
> → 정답의 A list of changes

41-43

M-Cn	Excuse me. I'm trying to catch a train from this platform, but I've been waiting, and no train has arrived.
W-Br	Oh, yes. **41 Unfortunately, some tracks are being repaired, so no trains are departing from this platform.**
M-Cn	I see. I had no idea this was happening. And **42 I'm upset that now I'm late for an appointment.**
W-Br	Well, they're providing free bus service to the next few stations. **43 You can catch a shuttle bus from the south side of the station.**

남	실례합니다. 이 승강장에서 기차를 타려고 하는데요. 계속 기다리고 있는데 기차가 한 대도 오지 않네요.
여	아, 네. **안타깝게도 일부 철로가 수리 중이라서 이 승강장에서는 기차가 출발하지 않습니다.**
남	알겠습니다. 이런 일이 있는 줄 몰랐어요. **지금 약속에 늦어서 기분이 좋지 않네요.**
여	음… 다음 몇 개의 역까지 무료 버스를 제공하고 있습니다. **역 남쪽에서 셔틀버스를 타시면 됩니다.**

어휘	unfortunately 유감스럽게도, 안타깝게도 repair 수리하다 depart 출발하다 upset 속상한 appointment 약속 provide 제공하다

41

Why is a train platform closed?
(A) Safety inspections are being conducted.
(B) New escalators are being installed.
(C) Tracks are being repaired.
(D) Waiting areas are being remodeled.

열차 승강장이 폐쇄된 이유는?
(A) 안전 점검이 진행되고 있다.
(B) 에스컬레이터가 새로 설치되고 있다.
(C) 철로가 수리되고 있다.
(D) 대기 구역을 개조하고 있다.

어휘 safety inspection 안전 점검   conduct 하다   install 설치하다
    remodel 개조하다

해설 세부 사항 관련 – 열차 승강장이 폐쇄된 이유
여자가 첫 대사에서 안타깝게도 일부 철로가 수리 중이라서 이 승강장에서는 기차가 출발하지 않는다(Unfortunately, some tracks are being repaired, so no trains are departing from this platform)고 말하고 있으므로 정답은 (C)이다.

42

What does the man say he is upset about?
(A) Misunderstanding some instructions
(B) Being late for an appointment
(C) Losing a travel pass
(D) Boarding the wrong train

남자는 무엇 때문에 기분이 좋지 않다고 말하는가?
(A) 일부 설명을 오해한 것
(B) 약속에 늦은 것
(C) 기차표를 잃어버린 것
(D) 기차를 잘못 탄 것

어휘 misunderstand 오해하다   instruction 설명, 지시   lose
    잃어버리다   board 승차하다, 탑승하다

해설 세부 사항 관련 – 남자가 기분이 좋지 않은 이유
남자가 두 번째 대사에서 지금 약속에 늦어서 기분이 좋지 않다(I'm upset that now I'm late for an appointment)고 말하고 있으므로 정답은 (B)이다.

43

What will the man most likely do next?
(A) Purchase a snack
(B) Take a shuttle bus
(C) File a complaint
(D) Download a map

남자는 다음에 무엇을 하겠는가?
(A) 간식 구입하기
(B) 셔틀버스 타기
(C) 민원 넣기
(D) 지도 다운로드하기

어휘 file a complaint 불만을 제기하다, 민원을 넣다

해설 세부 사항 관련 – 남자가 다음에 할 일
여자가 마지막 대사에서 역 남쪽에서 셔틀버스를 타면 된다(You can catch a shuttle bus from the south side of the station)고 안내하고 있는 것으로 보아 남자가 셔틀버스를 탈 것임을 알 수 있다. 따라서 정답은 (B)이다.

Paraphrasing   대화의 catch a shuttle bus
          → 정답의 Take a shuttle bus

44-46

M-Cn	Thanks for taking my call, Ms. Hazarika.
W-Br	**44I understand from your e-mail that you're looking for investors in your business.**
M-Cn	Yes. Storing bikes in small apartments is tough. That's why I've developed this space-saving bicycle rack.
W-Br	I've seen other indoor bike racks-what's unique about yours?
M-Cn	Most indoor racks are one size. But not all bikes are the same. 45**My product can be adjusted to suit different types of bicycles.**
W-Br	That's interesting. Send me your business model. 46**I need to determine if you have a reasonable plan for expanding production and increasing sales before I make any decisions.**

남	전화 받아 주셔서 감사합니다, 하자리카 씨.
여	**보내주신 이메일을 보니 사업 투자자를 찾고 계신다고요.**
남	네. 소형 아파트에 자전거를 보관하기가 어렵잖아요. 그래서 이 공간 절약형 자전거 보관대를 개발한 겁니다.
여	다른 실내 자전거 보관대도 본 적이 있는데요. 이건 어떤 점이 특별하죠?
남	대부분의 실내 보관대는 사이즈가 하나입니다. 하지만 모든 자전거의 크기가 같지는 않잖아요. **저희 제품은 다양한 종류의 자전거에 맞춰 조절할 수 있어요.**
여	흥미롭네요. 비즈니스 모델을 저에게 보내주세요. **제가 결정을 내리기 전에 귀사에 생산 확대 및 판매 증가를 위한 합리적인 계획이 있는지 파악해야 하니까요.**

어휘 investor 투자자   store 보관하다, 저장하다   develop 개발하다   space-saving 공간이 절약되는, 공간을 적게 차지하는   rack 받침대, 선반   indoor 실내의   adjust 조절하다, 조정하다   suit 맞다   determine 알아내다, 밝히다   reasonable 합리적인, 합당한   expand 확장하다, 확대하다   production 생산   increase 늘리다, 증가시키다   make a decision 결정하다

44

Why does the man call the woman?
(A) To provide an update on his project
(B) To get approval on some design changes
(C) To receive the woman's feedback on a prototype
(D) To persuade the woman to invest in his business

남자가 여자에게 전화한 이유는?

(A) 프로젝트 최신 정보를 제공하려고
(B) 디자인 변경에 관한 승인을 받으려고
(C) 시제품에 대한 여자의 피드백을 받으려고
(D) 여자가 사업에 투자하도록 설득하려고

어휘 provide 제공하다 approval 승인 prototype 원형, 시제품 persuade 설득하다

해설 전체 내용 관련 – 남자가 전화하는 이유

여자가 첫 대사에서 남자의 이메일을 보고 사업 투자자를 찾고 있는 걸 알고 있다(I understand from your e-mail that you're looking for investors in your business)고 말하고 있으므로 정답은 (D)이다.

45

According to the man, what is unique about a product?
(A) It is inexpensive.
(B) It is easy to assemble.
(C) It is adjustable.
(D) It is lightweight.

남자에 따르면, 제품의 어떤 점이 특별한가?
(A) 비싸지 않다.
(B) 조립이 쉽다.
(C) 조절 가능하다.
(D) 가볍다.

어휘 inexpensive 비싸지 않은 assemble 조립하다 adjustable 조절 가능한 lightweight 가벼운, 경량의

해설 세부 사항 관련 – 제품의 특별한 점

남자가 마지막 대사에서 이 제품은 다양한 종류의 자전거에 맞춰 조절할 수 있다(My product can be adjusted to suit different types of bicycles)고 말하고 있으므로 정답은 (C)이다.

> **Paraphrasing** 대화의 can be adjusted
> → 정답의 is adjustable

46

Why does the woman request some documents?
(A) To open a customer account
(B) To issue a certificate
(C) To make some copies
(D) To evaluate a proposal

여자가 서류를 요청한 이유는?
(A) 고객 계정을 개설하려고
(B) 증명서를 발급하려고
(C) 복사하려고
(D) 제안을 평가하려고

어휘 open an account 계정을 만들다, 계좌를 개설하다 issue 발급하다 certificate 증명서, 자격증 evaluate 평가하다 proposal 제안, 제안서

해설 세부 사항 관련 – 여자가 서류를 요청한 이유

여자가 마지막 대사에서 결정을 내리기 전에 귀사에 생산 확대와 판매 증가를 위한 합리적인 계획이 있는지 파악해야 한다(I need to determine if you have a reasonable plan for expanding production and increasing sales before I make any decisions)고 말하고 있으므로 정답은 (D)이다.

> **Paraphrasing** 대화의 to determine if you have a reasonable plan
> → 정답의 To evaluate a proposal

47-49

W-Am Alberto, [47]**it's time to leave the studio and head over to the central bank for our interview with the director.**

M-Cn Yes, I have all the cameras we'll need today.

W-Am Great. And make sure you have the special low-light lenses. [48]**I'm concerned about the poor lighting at the bank.** It's pretty dark in there, and that can ruin our key interview shots.

M-Cn Oh, yes. I have those. And by the way, [49]**our new intern Marcel Lambert is interested in joining us.**

W-Am That's a good idea. It'll be a good experience for him.

여 알베르토, **스튜디오에서 출발해 임원을 인터뷰하러 중앙 은행으로 갈 시간이에요.**

남 네, 오늘 필요한 카메라는 제가 다 챙겼어요.

여 좋아요. 특수 저조도 렌즈를 꼭 챙기도록 하세요. **은행의 조명이 안 좋아서 걱정이네요.** 그곳이 꽤 어두워서 중요한 인터뷰 사진을 망칠 수도 있거든요.

남 아, 네, 챙겼습니다. 그런데 **새 인턴 마셀 램버트가 함께 가고 싶어 해요.**

여 좋은 생각이군요. 좋은 경험이 될 거예요.

어휘 head over to ~로 향하다, ~로 가다 director 관리자, 임원 low-light 저조도의 ruin 망치다, 엉망으로 만들다 experience 경험

47

What are the speakers preparing for?
(A) A construction-site visit
(B) A safety inspection
(C) An interview
(D) A film festival

화자들은 무엇을 준비하고 있는가?
(A) 건설 현장 방문
(B) 안전 점검
(C) 인터뷰
(D) 영화제

어휘 construction site 공사 현장 safety inspection 안전 점검

해설 세부 사항 관련 – 화자들이 준비하고 있는 것

여자가 첫 대사에서 임원을 인터뷰하러(our interview with the director) 중앙 은행으로 갈 시간이라고 말하고 있으므로 정답은 (C)이다.

48

What is the woman concerned about?
(A) A lighting issue
(B) A script mistake
(C) A material shortage
(D) A revenue decrease

여자는 무엇을 걱정하는가?

(A) 조명 문제
(B) 대본 오류
(C) 자료 부족
(D) 수익 감소

어휘 script 대본 material 자료, 재료 shortage 부족 revenue 수익, 수입 decrease 감소

해설 세부 사항 관련 – 여자가 걱정하는 것

여자가 두 번째 대사에서 은행의 조명이 안 좋아서 걱정이 된다(I'm concerned about the poor lighting at the bank)고 말하고 있으므로 정답은 (A)이다.

> **Paraphrasing** 대화의 the poor lighting
> → 정답의 A lighting issue

49

Who is Marcel Lambert?
(A) A company accountant
(B) A possible client
(C) A supervisor
(D) An intern

마셀 램버트는 누구인가?

(A) 회사 회계원
(B) 예비 고객
(C) 감독관
(D) 인턴

어휘 accountant 회계원 possible 가능성 있는

해설 세부 사항 관련 – 마셀 램버트의 직업

남자가 마지막 대사에서 새 인턴 마셀 램버트가 함께 가고 싶어 한다(our new intern Marcel Lambert is interested in joining us)고 말하고 있으므로 정답은 (D)이다.

50-52

W-Am Waseem, I know you've been very busy this morning, but ⁵⁰**did you have time to take care of the photocopies I asked for?**

M-Au ⁵⁰**Oh, yes, those are all ready.**

W-Am Excellent! ⁵⁰**Thanks.** By the way, ⁵¹**how are the preparations coming along for Sabine Hoffman's retirement party?**

M-Au Great. I've booked a room and invited everyone on our team to the event. I'll call the caterer next.

W-Am You know, ⁵²**I'm sure she would love to celebrate with her former colleagues from other teams as well**, if it's not too much trouble to invite them.

M-Au Sure. I booked conference room B,⁵²**but I'll go ahead and change that.**

여 와심, 오늘 오전에 굉장히 바쁘셨던 건 아는데, **제가 요청한 복사를 처리해 주실 시간이 있었나요?**

남 **아, 네, 모두 준비해 뒀습니다.**

여 **훌륭해요! 감사합니다.** 그런데 **사빈 호프만의 은퇴 기념 파티 준비는 어떻게 되어 가나요?**

남 잘되고 있어요. 회의실을 예약했고 우리 팀 전원을 행사에 초대했어요. 다음으로 케이터링 업체에 전화할 겁니다.

여 **그녀는 분명 다른 팀의 이전 동료들과도 함께 기념하고 싶어 할 거예요.** 그들을 초대하는 것이 너무 수고스럽지만 않다면요.

남 물론이에요. B회의실을 예약했는데, **가서 변경할게요.**

어휘 take care of ~을 처리하다 photocopy 복사 preparation 준비 come along 되어 가다 retirement 은퇴 book 예약하다 celebrate 기념하다, 축하하다 former 이전의 colleague 동료 conference room 회의실

50

What does the woman thank the man for?
(A) Distributing some fliers
(B) Completing some calculations
(C) Placing a catering order
(D) Preparing some paper copies

여자는 남자에게 무엇에 대해 고마워하는가?

(A) 전단을 배포한 것
(B) 계산을 완료한 것
(C) 케이터링 주문을 넣은 것
(D) 복사물을 준비한 것

어휘 distribute 배포하다, 나눠주다 flier(flyer) 전단 complete 완료하다 calculation 계산

해설 세부 사항 관련 – 여자가 남자에게 고마워하는 일

여자가 첫 대사에서 요청한 복사를 처리할 시간이 있었는지(did you have time to take care of the photocopies I asked for?) 묻자 남자는 모두 준비해 뒀다(Oh, yes, those are all ready)고 답하고, 이에 여자가 감사하다(Thanks)고 말하고 있으므로 정답은 (D)이다.

> **Paraphrasing** 대화의 take care of the photocopies
> → 정답의 Preparing some paper copies

51

Why is a gathering being planned?
(A) A colleague was promoted.
(B) The company won an award.
(C) A colleague will be retiring.
(D) The company will be training employees.

왜 모임을 계획하는가?
(A) 동료가 승진했다.
(B) 회사가 상을 받았다.
(C) 동료가 은퇴할 예정이다.
(D) 회사가 직원들을 교육시킬 것이다.

어휘 colleague 동료 be promoted 승진하다 win an award 상을 받다 train 교육시키다, 훈련시키다

해설 세부 사항 관련 – 모임을 계획하는 이유

여자가 두 번째 대사에서 사빈 호프만의 은퇴 기념 파티 준비는 어떻게 되어 가는지(how are the preparations coming along for Sabine Hoffman's retirement party?) 묻고 있으므로 정답은 (C)이다.

> **Paraphrasing** 대화의 Sabine Hoffman's retirement party
> → 정답의 A colleague will be retiring.

52

What does the man imply when he says, "I booked conference room B"?
(A) A room is too small.
(B) An invitation is incorrect.
(C) No other conference rooms were available.
(D) Another administrative assistant was too busy.

남자가 "B회의실을 예약했는데"라고 말하는 의도는 무엇인가?
(A) 회의실이 너무 작다.
(B) 초대가 잘못됐다.
(C) 이용할 수 있는 다른 회의실이 없었다.
(D) 다른 행정 보조 직원이 너무 바빴다.

어휘 incorrect 맞지 않는, 부정확한 available 이용할 수 있는 administrative 행정의, 관리의

해설 화자의 의도 파악 – B회의실을 예약했다는 말의 의도

앞에서 여자가 그녀는 분명 다른 팀의 이전 동료들과도 함께 기념하고 싶어 할 것(I'm sure she would love to celebrate with her former colleagues from other teams as well)이라고 했고, 남자가 인용문을 언급하고 나서 변경하겠다(I'll go ahead and change that)고 말한 것으로 보아 사람들을 더 초대하기에는 예약한 회의실이 작다는 의미로 한 말임을 알 수 있다. 따라서 정답은 (A)이다.

53-55 3인 대화

M-Cn	Hi. I'm Kota Ogawa from Langston Limited. I have an appointment with Ms. Ishikawa to view your hotel facilities **53for my company's upcoming retreat.**
W-Am	**54I know that she's been expecting you, and she just wrapped up an urgent phone call.** She's on her way now.
W-Br	Hi. You must be Mr. Ogawa. I'm Hikaru Ishikawa. Why don't we see our largest conference room first?
M-Cn	Great. And I'd also like to look at the guest rooms. **55All the rooms have a high-speed Internet connection, right**?
W-Br	Yes, and we have a fully equipped recreation area as well.

남	안녕하세요. 랭스턴 유한회사의 코타 오가와입니다. **곧 있을 저희 회사 수련회를 위해** 호텔 시설을 둘러보려고 이시카와 씨와 약속을 했어요.
여1	**이시카와 씨가 기다리고 계시는 걸로 아는데요, 막 급한 전화 통화를 마치셨어요.** 이제 오고 계십니다.
여2	안녕하세요. 오가와 씨죠? 저는 히카루 이시카와입니다. 가장 큰 회의실을 먼저 보시는 게 어때요?
남	좋습니다. 객실도 보고 싶어요. **모든 객실에 초고속 인터넷이 연결되어 있죠, 그렇죠?**
여2	네, 그리고 시설이 완비된 레크리에이션 공간도 있습니다.

어휘	appointment 약속 upcoming 다가오는, 곧 있을 retreat (평상시의 생활에서 벗어날 수 있는) 조용한 곳, 수련회 expect (오기로 되어 있는 대상을) 기다리다 wrap up 마치다, 마무리하다 urgent 급한 connection 연결 fully equipped 시설이 완비된

53

What type of event is the man planning?
(A) A retirement banquet
(B) A company retreat
(C) A press conference
(D) A fund-raiser

남자는 어떤 종류의 행사를 계획하는가?
(A) 은퇴 기념 연회
(B) 회사 수련회
(C) 기자회견
(D) 모금 행사

해설 전체 내용 관련 – 남자가 계획하는 행사

남자가 첫 대사에서 곧 있을 회사 수련회를 위해(for my company's upcoming retreat) 호텔 시설을 둘러보기로 했다고 말하고 있으므로 정답은 (B)이다.

> **Paraphrasing** 대화의 my company's upcoming retreat
> → 정답의 A company retreat

54

Why was Ms. Ishikawa delayed?
(A) She was stuck in traffic.
(B) She was at lunch.
(C) She was setting up a room.
(D) She was on the phone.

이시카와 씨는 왜 늦었는가?
(A) 교통 체증에 갇혔다.
(B) 점심을 먹고 있었다.
(C) 회의실을 준비하고 있었다.
(D) 통화 중이었다.

어휘 delay 지연시키다, 지체시키다　be stuck in traffic 교통 체증에
갇히다　set up 준비하다

해설 세부 사항 관련 - 이시카와 씨가 늦은 이유
첫 번째 여자가 첫 대사에서 이시카와 씨가 기다리고 있었고, 막 급한 전화
통화를 마쳤다(I know that she's been expecting you, and she just
wrapped up an urgent phone call)고 말하고 있으므로 정답은 (D)이다.

55

What does the man inquire about?
(A) An airport shuttle
(B) Late checkout
(C) A fitness center
(D) Internet capabilities

남자는 무엇에 대해 문의하는가?
(A) 공항 셔틀
(B) 늦은 체크아웃
(C) 피트니스 센터
(D) 인터넷 성능

어휘 capability 능력, 성능

해설 세부 사항 관련 - 남자의 문의 사항
남자가 마지막 대사에서 모든 객실에 초고속 인터넷이 연결되어
있는지(All the rooms have a high-speed Internet connection,
right?) 묻고 있으므로 정답은 (D)이다.

56-58

W-Br　Look at these results! ⁵⁶**Sales of
pineapples have gone up a lot this month
at our store.**

M-Au　⁵⁷**It must be the pineapple-peeling
machine we installed in the fruit aisle.
Customers like watching it peel and slice
their pineapple for them.**

W-Br　It is a unique experience. I think we should
install one in our other two store branches.

M-Au　I'm not sure about that. I think the novelty
will wear off in a few weeks. ⁵⁸**Let's wait
to see if sales numbers stay high before
we invest in any more.**

여　이 결과 좀 보세요! **이번 달 우리 매장에서 파인애플 판매량이
많이 늘었어요.**

남　분명 과일 통로에 설치한 파인애플 껍질 벗기는 기계 덕분일
거예요. 고객들은 그 기계가 파인애플 껍질을 벗겨서 잘라
주는 걸 보고 좋아해요.

여　특별한 경험이죠. 다른 두 지점에도 설치해야겠어요.

남　그건 잘 모르겠네요. 몇 주 후면 참신함이 사라질 거예요.
**더 투자하기 전에 판매 수치가 계속 높게 유지되는지 기다려
봅시다.**

어휘　peel 껍질을 벗기다　install 설치하다　aisle 통로　slice
썰다, 얇게 자르다　unique 특별한, 독특한　branch
지사, 분점　novelty 참신함, 새로움　wear off 사라지다
invest 투자하다

56

Where does the conversation most likely take place?
(A) At a restaurant
(B) At a shipping dock
(C) At a farm
(D) At a supermarket

대화는 어디에서 이루어지겠는가?
(A) 음식점
(B) 하역장
(C) 농장
(D) 슈퍼마켓

해설 전체 내용 관련 - 대화의 장소
여자가 첫 대사에서 이번 달 우리 매장에서 파인애플 판매량이 많이
늘었다(Sales of pineapples have gone up a lot this month at our
store)고 말하는 것으로 보아 대화 장소는 파인애플을 판매하는 매장임을
알 수 있다. 따라서 정답은 (D)이다.

57

What does the man say is popular?
(A) A colorful package design
(B) A self-service machine
(C) A same-day delivery service
(D) A television advertisement

남자는 무엇이 인기 있다고 말하는가?
(A) 다채로운 포장 디자인
(B) 셀프 서비스 기계
(C) 당일 배송 서비스
(D) 텔레비전 광고

어휘 package 포장　delivery 배달　advertisement 광고

해설 세부 사항 관련 – 남자가 인기 있다고 말하는 것

남자가 첫 대사에서 과일 통로에 설치한 파인애플 껍질 벗기는 기계 덕분일 것(It must be the pineapple-peeling machine we installed in the fruit aisle)이라며 고객들은 그 기계가 파인애플 껍질을 벗겨서 잘라주는 걸 보고 좋아한다(Customers like watching it peel and slice their pineapple for them)고 말하고 있으므로 정답은 (B)이다.

> **Paraphrasing** 대화의 Customers like → 질문의 is popular

58

What does the man suggest doing?
(A) Waiting for some data
(B) Issuing a refund
(C) Hiring more staff
(D) Rearranging some merchandise

남자는 무엇을 제안하는가?
(A) 데이터 기다리기
(B) 환불해 주기
(C) 직원 추가 고용하기
(D) 상품 재배치하기

어휘 issue a refund 환불해 주다   rearrange 재배치하다, 재배열하다   merchandise 상품

해설 세부 사항 관련 – 남자의 제안 사항

남자가 마지막 대사에서 더 투자하기 전에 판매 수치가 계속 높게 유지되는지 기다려 보자(Let's wait to see if sales numbers stay high before we invest in any more)고 제안하고 있으므로 정답은 (A)이다.

> **Paraphrasing** 대화의 wait to see if sales numbers stay high → 정답의 Waiting for some data

59-61

 동영상 강의

M-Cn	Ingrid, ⁵⁹**we've had three patients this week who had to cancel their dental appointments at the last minute.**
W-Am	⁵⁹**Yes, that's a problem. Other patients might have taken those available appointments if we'd been able to contact them in time.**
M-Cn	You know, I have an idea. ⁶⁰**I recently scheduled a doctor's visit online, and there was an option to receive a text-message notification if an earlier slot became available.** You just have to check a box. What do you think about something like that?
W-Am	That would be helpful. ⁶¹**I have some time this afternoon. I'll look into software packages that include that feature.**

남 잉그리드, **이번 주에 예약 시간 직전에 치과 예약을 취소한 환자가 세 명 있었어요.**

여 네, 그게 문제예요. 우리가 제때 연락할 수 있었다면 다른 환자들이 그 시간대를 이용할 수 있었을 텐데요.

남 저에게 좋은 생각이 있어요. **최근 온라인으로 병원 방문을 예약했는데, 더 이른 시간대를 이용할 수 있게 되면 문자 메시지 알림을 받는 옵션이 있었어요. 박스에 체크하기만 하면 돼요.** 그런 건 어떻게 생각하세요?

여 유용할 것 같아요. 제가 오늘 오후에 시간이 좀 있어요. 그 기능을 포함하는 소프트웨어 패키지를 알아볼게요.

어휘 dental 치과의 appointment 약속, 예약 at the last minute 마지막 순간에, 임박해서 available 이용 가능한 in time 제때에 recently 최근 notification 알림 look into ~을 조사하다 include 포함하다 feature 기능, 특징

59

What are the speakers discussing?
(A) Relocating their office
(B) Attracting new patients
(C) Scheduling appointments
(D) Finding qualified staff

화자들은 무엇에 관해 이야기하는가?
(A) 사무실 이전하기
(B) 신규 환자 유치하기
(C) 예약 일정 잡기
(D) 자격을 갖춘 직원 찾기

어휘 relocate 이전하다 attract 끌다 qualified 자격이 있는

해설 전체 내용 관련 – 대화의 주제

남자가 첫 대사에서 이번 주에 예약 시간 직전에 치과 예약을 취소한 환자가 세 명 있었다(we've had three patients this week who had to cancel their dental appointments at the last minute)고 말하자, 여자가 긍정(Yes)의 답변과 함께 그것이 문제(that's a problem)라면서 제때 연락할 수 있었다면 다른 환자들이 그 시간대를 이용할 수 있었을 것(Other patients might have taken those available appointments if we'd been able to contact them in time)이라고 예약 잡는 것에 대해 이야기하고 있으므로 정답은 (C)이다.

60

Why does the man say, "You just have to check a box"?
(A) To request some performance feedback
(B) To express concern about a procedure
(C) To correct a misunderstanding
(D) To support a suggestion

남자가 "박스에 체크하기만 하면 돼요"라고 말하는 이유는?
(A) 성과 피드백을 요청하려고
(B) 절차에 관한 우려를 표하려고
(C) 오해를 바로잡으려고
(D) 제안을 뒷받침하려고

어휘 performance 실적, 성과 express concern 우려를 표하다
procedure 절차 correct 바로잡다 misunderstanding 오해
suggestion 제안

해설 화자의 의도 파악 – 박스에 체크하기만 하면 된다는 말의 의도
앞에서 남자가 최근 온라인으로 병원 방문을 예약했는데, 더 이른
시간대를 이용할 수 있게 되면 문자 메시지 알림을 받는 옵션이 있었다(I
recently scheduled a doctor's visit online, and there was an
option to receive a text-message notification if an earlier slot
became available)고 말한 뒤, 인용문을 언급한 것으로 보아 남자는 그
옵션에 대해 자신이 말한 것을 뒷받침하려고 한 말임을 알 수 있다. 따라서
정답은 (D)이다.

61

What does the woman offer to do this afternoon?

(A) Investigate options
(B) Revise a budget
(C) Contact a patient
(D) Update a Web site

여자는 오늘 오후 무엇을 하겠다고 제안하는가?

(A) 옵션 조사
(B) 예산 수정
(C) 환자에게 연락
(D) 웹사이트 업데이트

어휘 investigate 조사하다, 살피다 revise 변경하다, 수정하다
budget 예산

해설 세부 사항 관련 – 여자가 오후에 할 일
여자가 마지막 대사에서 오늘 오후에 시간이 있다(I have some time
this afternoon)며 그 기능을 포함하는 소프트웨어 패키지를 알아보겠다
(I'll look into software packages that include that feature)고 말하
고 있으므로 정답은 (A)이다.

> **Paraphrasing** 대화의 look into software packages
> → 정답의 Investigate options

62-64 대화 + 제품 목록

M-Cn Hi, Raquel. ⁶²**Have you had a chance
to look for something I could buy the
employees for the New Year**? I want to be
sure I thank everyone for their hard work.

W-Am Well, a good quality travel mug would be
appreciated.

M-Cn Interesting. Which one would you
recommend?

W-Am Take a look at this brochure. This company
has a variety of designs—sea animals, sky
scenes. ⁶³**I like the medium mug with the
Desert Roaming design.**

M-Cn That is nice. ⁶⁴**I'll sign off on that order
request once you fill out the paperwork.**

남 안녕하세요, 라켈. **새해를 맞아 직원들에게 사줄 만한 것을
찾아볼 기회가 있었나요?** 제가 모두의 노고에 감사한다는
것을 확실히 하고 싶어요.

여 음, 품질 좋은 여행용 머그잔을 좋아할 것 같아요.

남 흥미롭군요. 어떤 걸 추천하세요?

여 이 안내 책자를 보세요. 이 업체는 해양 동물, 하늘 풍경 등
다양한 디자인을 갖추고 있어요. **사막 여행 디자인의 중간
크기 머그잔이 마음에 드네요.**

남 그거 좋네요. **서류를 작성해 주시면 주문 요청서에
서명할게요.**

어휘 appreciate 감사하다, 진가를 알아보다 take a look at
~을 한번 보다 a variety of 다양한 roaming 방랑,
배회 sign off 서명하여 승인하다 fill out 작성하다,
기입하다

62

Who will the man give some gifts to?

(A) Conference participants
(B) Employees
(C) Contest winners
(D) Visitors

남자는 누구에게 선물을 줄 것인가?

(A) 회의 참가자들
(B) 직원들
(C) 대회 우승자들
(D) 방문객들

어휘 conference 회의 participant 참여자 contest 대회

해설 세부 사항 관련 – 남자의 선물 대상
남자가 첫 대사에서 새해를 맞아 직원들에게 사줄 만한 것을 찾아볼
기회가 있었는지(Have you had a chance to look for something
I could buy the employees for the New Year?) 묻고 있으므로
직원들에게 선물하려는 것임을 알 수 있다. 따라서 정답은 (B)이다.

63

Look at the graphic. How much is the mug that the woman likes?
(A) $15
(B) $20
(C) $23
(D) $25

시각 정보에 의하면, 여자가 마음에 들어 하는 머그잔은 얼마인가?
(A) 15달러
(B) 20달러
(C) 23달러
(D) 25달러

해설 시각 정보 연계 – 여자가 마음에 들어 하는 머그잔의 가격

여자가 두 번째 대사에서 사막 여행 디자인의 중간 크기 머그잔이 마음에 든다(I like the medium mug with the Desert Roaming design)고 말하고 있으며, 제품 목록에 따르면 사막 여행 중형 머그잔이 23달러라고 나와 있으므로 정답은 (C)이다.

64

What does the man say he will do?
(A) Submit a registration form
(B) Adjust a work schedule
(C) Approve an order
(D) Ask for a bulk-pricing rate

남자는 무엇을 할 것이라고 말하는가?
(A) 신청서 제출
(B) 업무 일정 조정
(C) 주문 승인
(D) 대량 주문 금액 요청

어휘 registration form 신청서, 등록 서류   adjust 조정하다, 조절하다   approve 승인하다   bulk 대량, 대규모

해설 세부 사항 관련 – 남자가 할 일

남자가 마지막 대사에서 서류를 작성해 주면 주문 요청서에 서명하겠다(I'll sign off on that order request once you fill out the paperwork)고 말하고 있으므로 정답은 (C)이다.

> **Paraphrasing**   대화의 sign off on that order request
> → 정답의 Approve an order

65-67 대화 + 지도   동영상 강의

M-Au   **⁶⁵Here's the map that you requested for next week's shoot, for the driving scene.**

W-Br   Great—let's see. **⁶⁵The actors will be driving north on Maple Street.** Hmm...

M-Au   Is something wrong?

W-Br   **⁶⁶We may need to alter the route so it'll be less difficult for our camera operators to follow the action.**

M-Au   OK. What are you thinking?

W-Br   **⁶⁷Instead of turning left on Elm Lane, let's have them turn right and park in front of the hair salon.**

M-Au   OK. **⁶⁷I'll arrange for that road to be closed while we're working and alert the business owners.**

남   다음 주 운전 장면 촬영을 위해 요청하신 지도가 여기 있습니다.

여   좋아요, 한번 보죠. 배우들이 메이플 가에서 북쪽으로 운전할 예정이죠. 음…

남   뭐가 잘못됐나요?

여   촬영 기사들이 액션을 따라가기 덜 어렵게 경로를 변경해야 할 수도 있겠네요.

남   좋아요. 어떻게 하실 생각인가요?

여   엘름 길에서 좌회전하지 말고 우회전해서 미용실 앞에 주차하도록 하죠.

남   알겠습니다. 작업하는 동안 해당 도로가 봉쇄될 수 있도록 하고 사업주들에게 알려 둘게요.

어휘   shoot 촬영   alter 변경하다   route 경로, 길   camera operator 촬영 기사, 촬영 감독   instead of ~ 대신   arrange 주선하다, 마련하다   alert 알리다

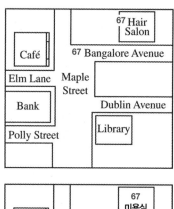

65

What industry do the speakers most likely work in?
(A) Tourism
(B) Film
(C) Engineering
(D) Transportation

화자들은 어떤 업계에서 일하겠는가?
(A) 관광
(B) 영화
(C) 공학
(D) 운송

해설 전체 내용 관련 – 화자들의 근무 업계

남자가 첫 대사에서 다음 주 운전 장면 촬영을 위해 요청한 지도가 여기 있다(Here's the map that you requested for next week's shoot, for the driving scene)고 말하자 여자가 배우들이 메이플 가에서 북쪽으로 운전할 예정(The actors will be driving north on Maple Street)이라고 대화를 이어 가고 있으므로 화자들은 영화 업계에 종사함을 알 수 있다. 따라서 정답은 (B)이다.

66

Why does the woman want to make a change?
(A) Some equipment is not available.
(B) A new business is opening.
(C) A process will be easier.
(D) Costs will be lower.

여자는 왜 변경하고 싶어 하는가?
(A) 일부 장비를 이용할 수 없다.
(B) 새 업체가 문을 연다.
(C) 과정이 더 쉬워진다.
(D) 비용이 줄어든다.

어휘 equipment 장비 available 이용할 수 있는 process 과정, 절차 cost 비용

해설 세부 사항 관련 – 여자가 변경하고 싶어 하는 이유

여자가 두 번째 대사에서 촬영 기사들이 덜 어렵게 액션을 따라갈 수 있도록 경로를 변경해야 할 수도 있겠다(We may need to alter the route so it'll be less difficult for our camera operators to follow the action)고 말하고 있으므로 정답은 (C)이다.

> **Paraphrasing** 대화의 alter → 질문의 make a change
> 대화의 it'll be less difficult for our camera operators to follow the action
> → 정답의 A process will be easier.

67

Look at the graphic. Which road should be closed?
(A) Bangalore Avenue
(B) Dublin Avenue
(C) Polly Street
(D) Elm Lane

시각 정보에 의하면, 어떤 도로가 봉쇄되는가?
(A) 방갈로르 가
(B) 더블린 가
(C) 폴리 가
(D) 엘름 길

해설 시각 정보 연계 – 봉쇄되는 도로

여자가 세 번째 대사에서 엘름 길에서 좌회전하지 말고 우회전해서

미용실 앞에 주차하자(~ let's have them turn right and park in front of the hair salon)고 제안하자 남자가 작업하는 동안 해당 도로가 봉쇄될 수 있도록 하고 사업주들에게 알려 두겠다(I'll arrange for that road to be closed while we're working and alert the business owners)고 말하고 있으므로 미용실 앞 도로가 봉쇄될 것임을 알 수 있다. 지도에 따르면 미용실 앞 도로는 방갈로르 가이므로 정답은 (A)이다.

68-70 대화 + 표

W-Br	Hi, Pablo. **68 I wanted to talk to you about the video game we designed—the one we're launching soon.**
M-Cn	Sure. Did something come up?
W-Br	Well, I think the jungle level looks great. **69 But in the underwater level, there's a problem with the part where the characters discover the lost city in the ocean.** As I was going over the layout, I found a glitch in the game play.
M-Cn	Oh, OK. We still have time to fix it.
W-Br	Yes, but **70 we should work on it as soon as possible. I could put some extra time in over the weekend. How about you**?
M-Cn	Probably—just let me check my calendar.

여	안녕하세요, 파블로. **우리가 디자인한 비디오 게임에 대해 얘기하고 싶어요. 곧 출시할 게임이요.**
남	네. 무슨 일이 생겼나요?
여	음, 정글 레벨은 좋아 보여요. **그런데 수중 레벨에서 캐릭터들이 바닷속 잃어버린 도시를 발견하는 부분에 문제가 있네요.** 레이아웃을 검토하다가 게임 플레이에 결함이 있는 것을 발견했어요.
남	아, 알겠습니다. 아직 고칠 시간이 있어요.
여	네, 하지만 **가능한 한 빨리 작업을 해야 돼요. 난 주말 동안 시간을 좀 더 낼 수 있어요. 파블로 씨는 어때요?**
남	아마도요. 일정을 확인해 볼게요.

어휘	launch 출시하다, 개시하다 discover 발견하다 go over 검토하다 layout 배치 glitch 작은 문제 fix 바로잡다, 수리하다 as soon as possible 가능한 한 빨리

The Treasure Search	
Level name	**Level number**
Jungle Adventure	1
69 Ocean Kingdom	2
Desert Sands	3
Outer Space	4

보물을 찾아서	
레벨명	레벨 번호
정글 모험	1
69 바다 왕국	2
모래 사막	3
우주	4

어휘 treasure 보물 adventure 모험 kingdom 왕국 desert 사막 outer space 우주

68

What are the speakers preparing for?
(A) A video-game convention
(B) An in-store demonstration
(C) A product launch
(D) A focus-group session

화자들은 무엇을 준비하고 있는가?
(A) 비디오 게임 대회
(B) 매장 내 시연
(C) 제품 출시
(D) 포커스 그룹 시간

어휘 convention 대회, 협의회 in-store 매장 내의 demonstration 시범 설명, 시연 focus group 포커스 그룹 (시장 조사나 여론 조사를 위해 각 계층을 대표하도록 뽑은 소수의 사람들로 이뤄진 그룹)

해설 세부 사항 관련 – 화자들이 준비하고 있는 일
여자가 첫 대사에서 우리가 디자인한 비디오 게임에 대해 얘기하고 싶다면서 곧 출시할 게임(I wanted to talk to you about the video game we designed—the one we're launching soon)이라고 덧붙이고 있으므로 정답은 (C)이다.

> Paraphrasing 대화의 the video game ~ the one we're launching soon → 정답의 A product launch

69

Look at the graphic. Which level is the woman concerned about?
(A) Level 1
(B) Level 2
(C) Level 3
(D) Level 4

시각 정보에 의하면 여자는 어떤 레벨에 대해 우려하는가?
(A) 레벨 1
(B) 레벨 2
(C) 레벨 3
(D) 레벨 4

어휘 be concerned about ~에 대해 우려하다

해설 시각 정보 연계 – 여자가 우려하는 레벨
여자가 두 번째 대사에서 수중 레벨에서 문제가 있다(But in the underwater level, there's a problem)고 말하고 있고, 표에 따르면 수중 레벨은 레벨 2이므로 정답은 (B)이다.

70

What does the woman suggest doing?
(A) Contacting a colleague
(B) Postponing an event
(C) Working over the weekend
(D) Making travel arrangements

여자는 무엇을 제안하는가?
(A) 동료에게 연락하기
(B) 행사 연기하기
(C) 주말 동안 일하기
(D) 여행 준비하기

어휘 contact 연락하다 colleague 동료 postpone 연기하다 travel arrangement 여행 준비

해설 세부 사항 관련 – 여자의 제안 사항
여자가 마지막 대사에서 가능한 한 빨리 작업을 해야 된다(we should work on it as soon as possible)며 주말 동안 시간을 좀 더 낼 수 있다(I could put some extra time in over the weekend)고 한 후 상대방에게 어떤지(How about you?) 묻고 있으므로 정답은 (C)이다.

PART 4

71-73 광고

M-Cn 71 At Volkov Tire and Auto Service, we're proud to serve the Livingstone Valley area. 71 We offer quality automotive maintenance and repairs at affordable prices. Our mechanics are the best in the industry, and our dedication to customer service shows. Once again, 72 readers of the *Livingstone Valley Chronicle* have awarded us with the title of Best in the Valley. That's five years in a row! And to celebrate, we're offering ten percent off all oil changes in July. 73 To get this deal, you must schedule an appointment, either by phone or online. Appointments are filling up fast!

저희 볼코브 타이어 앤 오토 서비스는 리빙스톤 밸리 지역에 서비스를 제공하게 되어 자랑스럽습니다. 저희는 양질의 자동차 유지보수 및 수리 서비스를 적정한 가격에 제공해 드립니다. 저희 정비사들은 업계 최고이며, 고객 서비스에 대한 저희의 헌신적인 노력도 보여드립니다. 다시 한번 〈리빙스톤 밸리 크로니클〉 독자들이 저희 업체에 밸리 최고 업체라는 타이틀의 상을 주었습니다. 5년 연속입니다! 이를 기념하기 위해 7월에 모든 오일 교환 건에 대해 10퍼센트 할인을 제공합니다. 할인을 받으시려면 전화나 온라인으로 예약 일정을 잡으셔야 합니다. 예약은 금세 찹니다!

어휘 quality 양질의, 우수한 automotive 자동차의 maintenance 유지보수 affordable (가격 등이) 적정한, 알맞은 mechanic 정비공 industry 산업, 업계 dedication 헌신, 전념 award 수여하다 in a row 잇달아, 계속해서, 연이어 celebrate 기념하다, 축하하다 appointment 약속 fill up 가득 차다

71

What kind of business is being advertised?
(A) A health-care clinic
(B) A computer service store
(C) An auto repair shop
(D) A real estate agency

어떤 종류의 업체를 광고하는가?
(A) 병원
(B) 컴퓨터 서비스 매장
(C) 자동차 수리점
(D) 부동산 중개업소

어휘 advertise 광고하다   health care 의료, 보건   real estate 부동산

해설 전체 내용 관련 – 광고되고 있는 업체
화자가 초반부에서 볼코브 타이어 앤 오토 서비스(At Volkov Tire and Auto Service)라고 소개하고 양질의 자동차 유지보수 및 수리 서비스를 적정한 가격에 제공한다(We offer quality automotive maintenance and repairs at affordable prices)고 했으므로 정답은 (C)이다.

72

Why is a business celebrating?
(A) It has been operating for ten years.
(B) It has doubled its customer base.
(C) It has won an award.
(D) It has opened a new location.

업체는 왜 축하하는가?
(A) 10년간 운영해 왔다.
(B) 고객층이 두 배가 늘었다.
(C) 상을 받았다.
(D) 새 지점을 열었다.

어휘 operate 운영하다, 운용하다   double 두 배가 되다   customer base 고객층   win an award 상을 받다

해설 세부 사항 관련 – 업체가 축하하는 이유
화자가 중반부에서 〈리빙스톤 밸리 크로니클〉 독자들이 업체에 밸리 최고 업체라는 타이틀의 상을 주었다(readers of the *Livingstone Valley Chronicle* have awarded us with the title of Best in the Valley)고 했으므로 정답은 (C)이다.

> **Paraphrasing**   담화의 have awarded ~ with the title of Best in the Valley → 정답의 has won an award

73

What do the listeners need to do to obtain a discount?
(A) Make an appointment
(B) Print out a coupon
(C) Attend an open house
(D) Refer a friend

청자들은 할인을 받기 위해 무엇을 해야 하는가?
(A) 예약하기
(B) 쿠폰 출력하기
(C) 공개 행사 참석하기
(D) 친구를 소개하기

어휘 obtain 얻다, 구하다   open house 공개 행사   refer 소개하다

해설 세부 사항 관련 – 청자들이 할인을 받기 위해 해야 할 일
화자가 후반부에서 할인을 받으려면 전화나 온라인으로 예약 일정을 잡아야 한다(To get this deal, you must schedule an appointment, either by phone or online)고 했으므로 정답은 (A)이다.

> **Paraphrasing**   담화의 schedule an appointment → 정답의 Make an appointment

74-76 방송

> M-Cn **⁷⁴Today's episode of the *Financial Parade Podcast* is about the possibilities and limitations of marketing on social media.** How can businesses improve on their marketing efforts and do a better job of reaching their target audience? To help us answer this, we are joined by Magali Bertrand, Marketing director at Blue Lane Consulting. **⁷⁵Ms. Bertrand is a frequent guest on the show because she is good at taking complex business principles and breaking them down to offer clear, simple advice.** But first, **⁷⁶I'd like to discuss the results of my recent survey where you all shared your approaches to product placement.**

> 〈파이낸셜 퍼레이드 팟캐스트〉의 오늘 에피소드는 소셜 미디어 마케팅의 가능성과 한계에 관한 내용입니다. 업체들은 어떻게 하면 마케팅 활동을 개선해서 광고 대상 고객에게 더 잘 다가갈 수 있을까요? 질문에 대답하기 위해 블루 레인 컨설팅의 마케팅 관리자인 매갈리 버트런드 씨가 나와 주셨습니다. 버트런드 씨는 저희 프로그램에서 자주 모시는 게스트이신데요, 복잡한 비즈니스 원리를 이용하여 그것을 분해해 명확하고 간결한 조언을 제공하는 데 능숙한 분이기 때문입니다. 하지만 우선, 여러분이 제품 간접 광고에 대한 접근 방법을 공유해 주신 최근 조사 결과를 먼저 얘기하고 싶습니다.

> 어휘 possibility 가능성   limitation 한계   improve 개선하다, 향상시키다   reach 도달하다   target audience 광고 대상자, 광고 타깃   frequent 잦은, 빈번한   complex 복잡한   principle 원리   break down 분해하다, 부수다   recent 최근의   survey 조사   approach 접근, 접근법   product placement (영화나 TV 프로그램을 이용한) 간접 광고(PPL)

74

What is the podcast episode about?
(A) Marketing strategies
(B) Commercial real estate
(C) Customer loyalty
(D) Staff management

팟캐스트 에피소드는 무엇에 관한 것인가?

(A) 마케팅 전략
(B) 상업용 부동산
(C) 고객 충성도
(D) 직원 관리

어휘 strategy 전략 commercial 상업의 real estate 부동산 customer loyalty 고객 충성도 management 관리

해설 전체 내용 관련 – 팟캐스트 에피소드의 주제

화자가 도입부에서 〈파이낸셜 퍼레이드 팟캐스트〉의 오늘 에피소드는 소셜 미디어 마케팅의 가능성과 한계에 관한 내용(Today's episode of the *Financial Parade Podcast* is about the possibilities and limitations of marketing on social media)이라고 했으므로 정답은 (A)이다.

> **Paraphrasing** 담화의 the possibilities and limitations of marketing → 정답의 Marketing strategies

75

What does the speaker say Ms. Bertrand is good at?
(A) Designing billboard ads
(B) Solving budget problems
(C) Explaining complicated ideas
(D) Creating training programs

화자는 버트런드 씨가 무엇에 능숙하다고 말하는가?
(A) 옥외 광고 디자인
(B) 예산 문제 해결
(C) 복잡한 개념 설명
(D) 교육 프로그램 제작

어휘 billboard 옥외 광고판 budget 예산 complicated 복잡한

해설 세부 사항 관련 – 버트런드 씨가 능숙한 일

화자가 중반부에서 버트런드 씨는 프로그램 단골 게스트인데 복잡한 비즈니스 원리를 이용하여 그것을 분해해 명확하고 간결한 조언을 제공하는 데 능숙하다(Ms. Bertrand ~ is good at taking complex business principles and breaking them down to offer clear, simple advice)고 했으므로 정답은 (C)이다.

> **Paraphrasing** 담화의 taking complex business principles ~ clear, simple advice → 정답의 Explaining complicated ideas

76

What will the speaker discuss next?
(A) Breaking news
(B) Survey results
(C) Upcoming contests
(D) Future episode topics

화자는 다음으로 무엇에 대해 말할 것인가?
(A) 뉴스 속보
(B) 조사 결과
(C) 곧 있을 대회
(D) 향후 에피소드 주제

어휘 breaking news 속보 upcoming 다가오는, 곧 있을

해설 세부 사항 관련 – 화자가 다음에 할 이야기

화자가 마지막에 최근 조사 결과를 먼저 얘기하고 싶다(I'd like to discuss the results of my recent survey ~)고 했으므로 정답은 (B)이다.

> **Paraphrasing** 담화의 the results of my recent survey → 정답의 Survey results

77-79 회의 발췌

> W-Br **77 Next Wednesday, Arlington Landscaping will deliver the potted plants we ordered to brighten up the common areas in our office. 78 Studies have shown that plants are great stress relievers and can increase workplace productivity. We think you'll find that this is a great improvement to our work environment.** If you'd like a small plant for your desk, the company will cover the cost. To choose your plant, **79 please check the catalog in the staff room.** It has photos and care instructions.

> 다음 주 수요일에 알링턴 조경에서 우리 사무실 내 공용 구역의 분위기를 밝게 만들고자 주문한 화분을 배송해 줄 것입니다. 연구 결과를 보면 식물은 스트레스를 크게 덜어주고 직장 생산성을 높일 수 있다고 합니다. 여러분은 이것으로 우리 업무 환경이 상당히 개선되었다고 느낄 것입니다. 책상에 작은 식물을 놓고 싶으시면 회사에서 비용을 부담하겠습니다. 식물을 선택하시려면 **직원실에 있는 카탈로그를 확인해 주세요.** 사진과 관리 설명서가 있습니다.

> **어휘** landscaping 조경 potted plant 화분에 심은 식물 brighten up 분위기를 띄우다 stress reliever 스트레스를 완화시켜 주는 것 increase 높이다, 증가시키다 productivity 생산성 improvement 향상, 개선 environment 환경 cover (돈을) 대다 instruction 설명, 지시

77

What will be delivered next Wednesday?
(A) Office furniture
(B) Color printers
(C) Potted plants
(D) Framed artwork

다음 주 수요일에 무엇이 배송될 것인가?
(A) 사무용 가구
(B) 컬러 프린터
(C) 화분 식물
(D) 그림 액자

어휘 furniture 가구 framed 틀에 끼운

해설 세부 사항 관련 – 다음 주 수요일에 배송되는 것

화자가 초반부에서 다음 주 수요일에 알링턴 조경에서 화분을 배송해 줄 것(Next Wednesday, Arlington Landscaping will deliver the potted plants ~)이라고 했으므로 정답은 (C)이다.

78

What does the speaker say about productivity?
(A) It has been improving recently.
(B) It is higher in other departments.
(C) It can be improved by office surroundings.
(D) It can be increased by working in groups.

화자는 생산성에 대해 뭐라고 말하는가?
(A) 최근 향상됐다.
(B) 다른 부서들이 더 높다.
(C) 사무실 환경에 따라 향상될 수 있다.
(D) 그룹으로 일하면 증가할 수 있다.

어휘 recently 최근   department 부서   surroundings 환경

해설 세부 사항 관련 – 화자가 생산성에 대해 하는 말

화자가 중반부에서 연구 결과를 보면 식물은 직장 생산성을 높일 수 있다(Studies have shown that plants ~ can increase workplace productivity)며 여러분은 이것으로 우리 업무 환경이 상당히 개선되었다고 느낄 것(We think you'll find that this is a great improvement to our work environment)이라고 했으므로 정답은 (C)이다.

> Paraphrasing   담화의 work environment
> → 정답의 office surroundings

79

According to the speaker, what is available in the staff room?
(A) A catalog
(B) A vending machine
(C) Staff uniforms
(D) Exercise equipment

화자에 따르면, 직원실에서 무엇을 이용할 수 있는가?
(A) 카탈로그
(B) 자판기
(C) 직원 유니폼
(D) 운동기구

어휘 available 이용 가능한   equipment 장비, 용품

해설 세부 사항 관련 – 직원실에서 이용 가능한 것

화자가 후반부에서 식물을 선택하려면 직원실에 있는 카탈로그를 확인하라(please check the catalog in the staff room)고 했으므로 정답은 (A)이다.

80-82 방송

> M-Cn In local news, the abandoned shoe factory in the central business district is finally getting a makeover. **80 The building has been empty for three years since the factory moved to its new, larger space south of town.** **81 After hearing many proposals, the town council voted last night to sell the building to developer Matthew Hughes, who will convert it into family housing: ten modern, comfortable units with a parking garage underground.** **82 Up next, it looks like the rain is on the way out, giving way to blue skies this weekend. Samantha is here to tell us all about it.**

지역 뉴스에 따르면, 중심 업무 지구에 있는 버려진 신발 공장이 마침내 새단장을 한다고 합니다. 건물은 공장이 시 남쪽에 있는 더 큰 새 공간으로 이전한 이후 3년간 비어 있었는데요. 시 의회는 많은 제안을 듣고 난 후 어젯밤 투표를 통해 건물을 개발업자 매튜 휴즈에게 매각하기로 했습니다. 매튜 휴즈는 공장을 주택으로 개조할 예정입니다. 지하 주차장을 갖춘 현대식의 편안한 공동주택 10채입니다. 다음으로, 이번 주말 비가 그치고 파란 하늘에 자리를 내줄 것 같습니다. 사만다가 자세히 이야기해 드립니다.

어휘 local 지역의   abandoned 버려진, 유기된   district 지구   makeover 단장   proposal 제안   town council 시 의회   vote 투표하다   convert 전환시키다, 개조하다   underground 지하에   give way to ~에 양보하다, 항복하다

80

According to the speaker, what happened three years ago?
(A) A council member was elected.
(B) A local tax law changed.
(C) A train station opened.
(D) A business relocated.

화자에 따르면, 3년 전에 어떤 일이 있었는가?
(A) 의회 의원이 선출됐다.
(B) 지역 세법이 변경됐다.
(C) 기차역이 문을 열었다.
(D) 한 업체가 이전했다.

어휘 elect 선출하다   tax law 세법   relocate 이전하다

해설 세부 사항 관련 – 3년 전에 있었던 일

화자가 초반부에서 건물은 공장이 시 남쪽에 있는 더 큰 새 공간으로 이전한 이후 3년간 비어 있었다(The building has been empty for three years since the factory moved to its new, larger space south of town)고 했으므로 정답은 (D)이다.

> Paraphrasing   담화의 the factory moved to ~ south of town → 정답의 A business relocated

81

Who is Matthew Hughes?
(A) A banker
(B) A real estate developer
(C) A government official
(D) A store owner

매튜 휴즈는 누구인가?
(A) 은행가
(B) 부동산 개발업자
(C) 공무원
(D) 매장 소유주

어휘 real estate 부동산

해설 세부 사항 관련 – 매튜 휴즈의 직업

화자가 중반부에서 시 의회는 투표를 통해 건물을 개발업자 매튜 휴즈에게 매각하기로 했고 매튜 휴즈는 공장을 주택으로 개조할 예정(the town council voted last night to sell the building to developer Matthew Hughes, who will convert it into family housing)이라고 했으므로 정답은 (B)이다.

> **Paraphrasing** 담화의 developer ~ will convert it into family housing
> → 정답의 A real estate developer

82

What will the listeners hear about next?
(A) A sporting event
(B) Street closures
(C) The weather
(D) Parking fines

청자들은 다음으로 무엇에 대해 들을 것인가?
(A) 스포츠 행사
(B) 도로 폐쇄
(C) 날씨
(D) 주차 위반 벌금

어휘 closure 폐쇄

해설 세부 사항 관련 – 청자들이 다음에 들을 내용

화자가 마지막 부분에서 다음으로, 이번 주말 비가 그치고 파란 하늘에 자리를 내줄 것 같다(Up next, it looks like the rain is on the way out, giving way to blue skies this weekend)며 사만다가 자세히 이야기해 줄 것(Samantha is here to tell us all about it)이라고 했으므로 정답은 (C)이다.

> **Paraphrasing** 담화의 rain, blue skies → 정답의 The weather

83-85 회의 발췌

> **W-Am** Before we end this transportation agency meeting, **83I want to give you an update on the Springdale bridge replacement project.** The project is moving forward. However, **84we are more than six months past the scheduled completion date.** But this is just one of our many projects. Now, this delay is frustrating to residents who are dealing with traffic congestion. Therefore, **85I strongly recommend that we hold a press conference to address specific concerns.**

이번 교통국 회의를 마치기 전에 여러분께 스프링데일 교량 교체 프로젝트의 최신 소식을 알려드리고자 합니다. 프로젝트는 진척되고 있습니다. 하지만 완공 예정일보다 6개월 이상 지났습니다. 그러나 이것은 우리가 진행하는 많은 프로젝트 중 하나일 뿐입니다. 이제, 이 지연은 교통 혼잡을 겪는 주민들에게 불만을 안기고 있습니다. 그러므로 구체적인 우려를 해소하기 위해 기자회견을 개최할 것을 강력히 권고합니다.

어휘 transportation 운송, 교통 replacement 교체 move forward 진전되다 completion 완료 delay 지연, 지체 frustrating 불만스러운, 좌절감을 주는 deal with ~을 다루다 traffic congestion 교통 혼잡 press conference 기자회견 address (문제, 상황 등을) 다루다, 처리하다 specific 특정한, 구체적인 concern 우려

83

What is the speaker discussing?
(A) The renovation of a train station
(B) The construction of a tunnel
(C) The replacement of a bridge
(D) The repaving of a bicycle trail

화자는 무엇에 대해 이야기하는가?
(A) 기차역 보수
(B) 터널 건설
(C) 교량 교체
(D) 자전거 도로 재포장

어휘 renovation 개조, 보수 construction 건설 repave 재포장하다

해설 전체 내용 관련 – 담화의 주제

화자가 초반부에서 스프링데일 교량 교체 프로젝트의 최신 소식을 알려주려고 한다(I want to give you an update on the Springdale bridge replacement project)고 했으므로 정답은 (C)이다.

> **Paraphrasing** 담화의 the Springdale bridge replacement project
> → 정답의 The replacement of a bridge

84

Why does the speaker say, "this is just one of our many projects"?
(A) To propose a change of topic
(B) To explain a delay
(C) To praise some employees
(D) To ask for help

화자가 "우리가 진행하는 많은 프로젝트 중 하나일 뿐입니다"라고 말하는 이유는?

(A) 주제 변경을 제안하려고
(B) 지연의 이유를 설명하려고
(C) 일부 직원을 칭찬하려고
(D) 도움을 청하려고

어휘 propose 제안하다   explain (이유를) 설명하다   praise 칭찬하다

해설 화자의 의도 파악 – 우리가 진행하는 많은 프로젝트 중 하나일 뿐이라는 말의 의도

인용문 바로 앞 문장에서 완공 예정일보다 6개월 이상 지났다(we are more than six months past the scheduled completion date)고 말한 뒤, 인용문을 언급한 것으로 보아 많은 프로젝트를 진행 중이라서 이 프로젝트가 지연된 것이라고 프로젝트의 지연 이유를 설명하려 한 말임을 알 수 있다. 따라서 정답은 (B)이다.

Paraphrasing	담화의 more than six months past the scheduled completion date → 정답의 a delay

85

What does the speaker suggest doing?
(A) Organizing an opening ceremony
(B) Scheduling a television interview
(C) Revising a design
(D) Meeting with the press

화자는 무엇을 제안하는가?
(A) 개통식 준비하기
(B) TV 인터뷰 일정 잡기
(C) 디자인 변경하기
(D) 언론과의 만남

어휘 organize 준비하다, 조직하다   opening ceremony 개업식, 개통식   revise 변경하다   press 언론

해설 세부 사항 관련 – 화자의 제안 사항

화자가 마지막에 구체적인 우려를 해소하기 위해 기자회견을 개최할 것을 강력히 권고한다(I strongly recommend that we hold a press conference to address specific concerns)고 했으므로 정답은 (D)이다.

Paraphrasing	담화의 recommend → 질문의 suggest 담화의 hold a press conference → 정답의 Meeting with the press

86-88 연설

W-Br Attention, everyone. I hope you're enjoying the second day of our weekend workshop on leadership skills for entrepreneurs. During yesterday's session, we conducted a discussion about goal setting, and we did that together as a group. However, **86today I'll be matching you with a partner for a one-on-one discussion.** So, **87start thinking about any improvements you'd like to make to your communication skills, because that's what you'll be sharing with each other.** And **88later this afternoon, we'll enjoy a prepared lunch, which has been generously donated to us by Blue Star Catering Company.** We're grateful to them for their support.

여러분께 알립니다. 기업가를 위한 리더십 기술에 관한 주말 워크숍의 둘째 날을 즐겁게 보내고 계시길 바랍니다. 어제 세션 중에 목표 설정에 관한 토론을 했는데요. 그룹 활동으로 함께 했죠. 그런데 오늘은 일대일 토론을 위해 여러분께 파트너를 정해 드리려고 합니다. 그러니 여러분의 의사소통 능력에서 어떤 점을 개선하고 싶은지 생각해 보세요. 서로 그것에 대해 의견을 나눌 것이니까요. 이후 오후에는 준비된 점심 식사를 합니다. 블루 스타 케이터링에서 아낌없이 기부해 주셨어요. 지원에 감사드립니다.

어휘 attention 알립니다, 주목하세요   skill 기량, 기술   entrepreneur 기업가, 사업가   conduct 하다   goal setting 설정   one-on-one 일대일의   improvement 향상, 개선   share 나누다, 공유하다   generously 후하게, 너그러이   donate 기부하다   grateful 감사하는

86

According to the speaker, what will be different about today's session?
(A) It will take place outside.
(B) It will be recorded.
(C) Participants will work in pairs.
(D) Participants will deliver presentations.

화자에 따르면, 오늘 세션은 어떤 점이 다른가?
(A) 외부에서 열린다.
(B) 녹화될 예정이다.
(C) 참가자가 둘씩 짝을 지어 진행한다.
(D) 참가자가 발표를 할 것이다.

어휘 take place 열리다   record 녹화하다, 녹음하다   participant 참여자   in pairs 둘씩 짝을 지어   presentation 발표

해설 세부 사항 관련 – 오늘 세션이 다른 점

화자가 중반부에서 오늘은 일대일 토론을 위해 파트너를 정해 줄 것(today I'll be matching you with a partner for a one-on-one discussion)이라고 말하고 있으므로 정답은 (C)이다.

Paraphrasing	담화의 for a one-on-one discussion → 정답의 in pairs

87

What is the topic of today's session?
(A) Improving communication skills
(B) Updating accounting practices
(C) Managing company finances
(D) Recruiting qualified job candidates

오늘 세션의 주제는 무엇인가?
(A) 의사소통 능력 향상시키기
(B) 회계 상태 업데이트하기
(C) 회사 재무 관리하기
(D) 자격을 갖춘 구직자 모집하기

어휘 accounting practice 회계 상태, 회계 실무 manage 관리하다
finance 재무, 재정 recruit 모집하다 qualified 자격을 갖춘
job candidate 구직자

해설 세부 사항 관련 – 오늘 세션의 주제
화자가 중반부에서 의사소통 능력에서 어떤 점을 개선하고 싶은지 생각해
보라(start thinking about any improvements you'd like to make
to your communication skills ~)며 그것에 대해 의견을 나눌 것이라
고 말하고 있으므로 정답은 (A)이다.

> **Paraphrasing** 담화의 any improvements you'd like to
> make to your communication skills
> → 정답의 Improving communication skills

88

What does the speaker say about the lunch?
(A) It has been donated.
(B) It is vegetarian.
(C) It will arrive late.
(D) It will include a dessert.

화자는 점심 식사에 대해 뭐라고 말하는가?
(A) 기부를 받았다.
(B) 채식 식단이다.
(C) 늦게 도착할 것이다.
(D) 후식이 포함될 것이다.

어휘 vegetarian 채식주의의 include 포함하다

해설 세부 사항 관련 – 화자가 점심 식사에 대해 하는 말
화자가 마지막에 이후 오후에는 준비된 점심 식사를 하는데 블루 스타
케이터링에서 아낌없이 기부해 줬다(later this afternoon, we'll enjoy
a prepared lunch, which has been generously donated to us by
Blue Star Catering Company)고 했으므로 정답은 (A)이다.

89-91 전화 메시지

> M-Cn [89]**This is Adisa from Car Pro returning your
> call.** In your message, you said your sedan seems
> sluggish and isn't accelerating well. There are a
> number of things that could be causing that, and
> [89]**prices vary with the repair.** [90]**It could be as simple**

[90]**as a clogged oil filter, which is inexpensive to
fix.** But we'll have to take a look. Oh, by the way,
[91]**we're closing early tomorrow**, but we can get
you in the day after. We'll open at eight A. M.

> 저는 카프로의 아디사입니다. 회신 전화 드립니다. 메시지에서 귀하의
> 승용차가 속도가 느리고 가속이 잘 안 된다고 하셨는데요. 이런 문제를
> 일으킬 수 있는 것들이 많습니다. **가격은 수리에 따라 달라집니다.** 오
> 일 필터가 막힌 것처럼 간단한 것일 수도 있는데, 이건 수리 비용이 비
> 싸지 않아요. 하지만 한번 봐야 할 겁니다. 아, 그런데 **내일은 일찍 문
> 을 닫습니다.** 하지만 모레는 오실 수 있어요. 저희는 오전 8시에 문을
> 열 것입니다.

어휘 sluggish 느릿느릿 움직이는, 부진한 accelerate 가속하다
cause 야기하다 vary 달라지다 clogged 막힌 inexpensive
비싸지 않은 fix 수리하다

89

Where does the speaker most likely work?
(A) At a car-rental company
(B) At an appliance-repair shop
(C) At a car wash
(D) At an auto-mechanic shop

화자는 어디서 일하겠는가?
(A) 차량 대여업체
(B) 가전기기 수리점
(C) 세차장
(D) 자동차 정비소

어휘 rental 임대, 대여 appliance 가정용 기기 mechanic 정비공

해설 전체 내용 관련 – 화자의 근무지
화자가 초반부에서 카프로의 아디사(This is Adisa from Car Pro
returning your call)라고 소개하며 자동차 문제에 대해 언급한 뒤
가격은 수리에 따라 달라진다(~ prices vary with the repair)고 하는
것으로 보아 자동차 정비소에서 근무함을 알 수 있다. 따라서 정답은
(D)이다.

90

What does the speaker imply when he says, "we'll
have to take a look"?
(A) A schedule may be changed.
(B) A supervisor should be consulted.
(C) A cost cannot be determined yet.
(D) A new policy must be followed.

화자가 "한번 봐야 할 겁니다"라고 말하는 의도는 무엇인가?
(A) 일정이 변경될 수 있다.
(B) 관리자와 상의해야 한다.
(C) 아직 비용을 결정할 수 없다.
(D) 새 정책을 따라야 한다.

어휘 supervisor 감독관, 관리자 consult 상의하다, 상담하다
determine 결정하다, 알아내다 policy 정책 follow 따르다

해설 화자의 의도 파악 – 한 번 봐야 할 것이라는 말의 의도

앞에서 오일 필터가 막힌 것처럼 간단한 것일 수도 있는데, 이건 수리 비용이 비싸지 않다(It could be as simple as a clogged oil filter, which is inexpensive to fix)고 말한 뒤 인용문을 언급한 것으로 보아, 고장에 따라 수리 비용이 달라질 수 있는데 수리 전이라 확실한 비용을 아직 결정할 수 없다는 의미로 한 말임을 알 수 있다. 따라서 정답은 (C)이다.

91

What does the speaker say about tomorrow?
(A) Some machinery will be serviced.
(B) The business will close early.
(C) Some new employees will start work.
(D) An appointment will probably become available.

화자는 내일에 대해 뭐라고 말하는가?
(A) 일부 기계가 정비를 받을 것이다.
(B) 업체가 일찍 문을 닫을 것이다.
(C) 신입 사원 몇 명이 업무를 시작할 것이다.
(D) 예약이 아마 가능할 것이다.

어휘 machinery 기계 service 정비하다, 점검하다 probably 아마

해설 세부 사항 관련 – 화자가 내일에 대해 하는 말

화자가 후반부에서 내일은 일찍 문을 닫는다(we're closing early tomorrow)고 했으므로 정답은 (B)이다.

92-94 회의 발췌

M-Au **92Thanks, everyone, for helping set up the showroom floor with the displays of the new bedroom and living room sets.** They look great. **93Many of you have asked for time off next Wednesday to attend the town parade. I wasn't sure I could grant those requests,** but after thinking about it, I realized that that day will probably not be a profitable day for us anyway. I'll post a new employee schedule! Oh, and one more quick announcement—**94I need all of you to put in an order for a new uniform.** It's time we replaced them.

여러분, 전시장에 새 침실 및 거실 세트 진열 준비를 도와주셔서 감사합니다. 정말 멋지네요. 많은 분들이 시 퍼레이드 참석을 위해 다음 주 수요일 휴가를 신청하셨는데요. 그 요청을 다 받아줄 수 있을지 확실치 않지만, 생각해보니 그날은 어차피 수익이 안 나는 날이더군요. 새로운 근무 일정표를 게시하겠습니다! 아, 빠르게 전해 드릴 또 하나의 소식은, **여러분 모두 새 유니폼 주문을 넣어 주셔야 합니다.** 교체할 시기가 됐어요.

어휘 set up 준비하다 showroom 전시장 grant 승인하다 request 요청 profitable 수익성이 있는, 이익이 되는 post 게시하다 announcement 발표 put in an order 주문하다 replace 교체하다

92

What type of business does the speaker most likely work at?
(A) A car dealership
(B) An electronics store
(C) A clothing boutique
(D) A furniture store

화자는 어떤 종류의 업체에서 일하겠는가?
(A) 자동차 대리점
(B) 전자 제품 매장
(C) 의류 매장
(D) 가구점

어휘 car dealership 자동차 영업소, 자동차 대리점 electronics 전자 장치 furniture 가구

해설 전체 내용 관련 – 화자의 근무 업종

화자가 초반부에서 전시장에 새 침실 및 거실 세트 진열 준비를 도와주어 감사하다(Thanks, everyone, for helping set up the showroom floor with the displays of the new bedroom and living room sets)고 했으므로 가구점에서 근무하고 있다는 것을 알 수 있다. 따라서 정답은 (D)이다.

> Paraphrasing 담화의 bedroom and living room sets
> → 정답의 furniture

93

What does the speaker imply when he says, "that day will probably not be a profitable day for us anyway"?
(A) Reduced profits have prevented salary increases.
(B) A new sales strategy will have to be developed.
(C) The listeners will be able to attend an event.
(D) The listeners have been keeping accurate records.

화자가 '그날은 어차피 우리가 수익이 안 나는 날이더군요'라고 말하는 의도는 무엇인가?
(A) 수익 감소가 급여 인상을 막았다.
(B) 새 영업 전략이 개발되어야 할 것이다.
(C) 청자들은 행사에 참석할 수 있을 것이다.
(D) 청자들은 정확히 기록해오고 있다.

어휘 reduce 감소하다 prevent 막다 increase 증가, 인상 strategy 전략 keep records 기록하다 accurate 정확한

해설 화자의 의도 파악 – 그날은 어차피 수익이 안 나는 날일 것이라는 말의 의도

인용문 앞에서 많은 사람들이 시 퍼레이드 참석을 위해 휴가를 신청했는데(Many of you have asked for time off next Wednesday to attend the town parade) 그 요청을 다 받아줄 수 있을지 확실치 않았다(I wasn't sure I could grant those requests)고 말하면서 인용문을 언급한 것으로 보아, 그날은 어차피 손님이 적을 테니 휴가를 쓰고 퍼레이드에 참석해도 된다는 의미로 한 말임을 알 수 있다. 따라서 정답은 (C)이다.

94

What does the speaker expect the listeners to do?
(A) Submit an order form
(B) Provide some feedback
(C) Sign a contract
(D) Check a display area

화자는 청자들에게 무엇을 하라고 요청하는가?
(A) 주문서 제출하기
(B) 피드백 제공하기
(C) 계약서에 서명하기
(D) 전시 공간 확인하기

어휘 order form 주문서 sign a contract 계약서에 서명하다

해설 세부 사항 관련 – 화자가 청자들에게 요청하는 일
화자가 후반부에서 모두 새 유니폼 주문을 넣어야 한다(I need all of you to put in an order for a new uniform)고 했으므로 정답은 (A)이다.

> **Paraphrasing** 담화의 put in an order
> → 정답의 Submit an order form

95-97 전화 메시지 + 지도

W-Am Hi. ⁹⁵**This is Emily calling from Speedy Services. I'm picking you up from the central train station today.** I see you selected a pickup location near the ticket windows, but there's heavy traffic on that street. ⁹⁵,⁹⁶**Would it be possible to change your pickup location to right outside the station's grand concourse?** ⁹⁵**It's the designated area for rideshare services.** ⁹⁷**Please let me know if you agree with this change by responding to the prompt within the app.** Thanks!

안녕하세요. 스피디 서비스의 에밀리입니다. 오늘 중앙역으로 귀하를 모시러 갈 텐데요. 픽업 장소를 매표소 근처로 선택하신 것을 확인했는데, 그 거리는 교통이 혼잡합니다. 픽업 장소를 역의 대 중앙 홀 바로 밖으로 변경할 수 있을까요? 거기는 승차 공유 서비스 지정 구역입니다. 앱의 프롬프트 메시지에 응답하셔서 변경에 동의하시는지 알려주세요. 감사합니다!

어휘 pick up 태우러 가다 select 선택하다 location 장소 grand 웅장한 concourse 중앙 홀 designated 지정된 rideshare 승차 공유 respond 응답하다

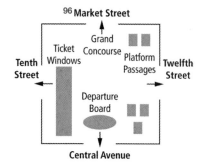

95

Who most likely is the speaker?
(A) A rideshare driver
(B) A tour guide
(C) A ticket agent
(D) A baggage handler

화자는 누구이겠는가?
(A) 승차 공유 운전기사
(B) 투어 가이드
(C) 매표원
(D) 수하물 담당자

어휘 baggage 수하물

해설 전체 내용 관련 – 화자의 직업
화자가 도입부에서 스피디 서비스의 에밀리(This is Emily calling from Speedy Services)라고 소개하며, 오늘 중앙역으로 데리러 갈 것(I'm picking you up from the central train station today)이라고 했고, 중반부에 픽업 장소를 변경할 수 있는지(Would it be possible to change your pickup location ~) 물으면서 승차 공유 서비스 지정 구역(It's the designated area for rideshare services)이라고 말하는 것으로 보아 화자는 승차 공유 운전기사라는 것을 알 수 있다. 따라서 정답은 (A)이다.

96

Look at the graphic. Where does the speaker want to meet?
(A) On Market Street
(B) On Twelfth Street
(C) On Central Avenue
(D) On Tenth Street

시각 정보에 의하면 화자는 어디서 만나고 싶어 하는가?
(A) 마켓 가
(B) 12번 가
(C) 센트럴 가
(D) 10번 가

해설 시각 정보 연계 – 화자가 만나고 싶어 하는 곳
화자가 중반부에서 픽업 장소를 역의 대 중앙 홀 바로 밖으로 변경할 수 있는지(Would it be possible to change your pickup location to right outside the station's grand concourse?) 물었는데, 지도에 따르면 역의 대 중앙 홀 바로 밖은 마켓 가이므로 정답은 (A)이다.

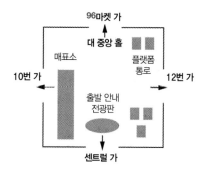

어휘 passage 통로 departure board 출발 안내 전광판

97

How can a change be confirmed?
(A) By sending an e-mail
(B) By providing an e-signature
(C) By using an app
(D) By returning a call

변경은 어떻게 확정될 수 있는가?
(A) 이메일을 보내서
(B) 전자 서명을 제공해서
(C) 앱을 이용해서
(D) 회신 전화를 해서

어휘 e-signature 전자 서명

해설 세부 사항 관련 – 변경을 확정하는 방법

화자가 후반부에서 앱의 프롬프트 메시지에 응답해서 변경에 동의하는지 알려 달라(Please let me know if you agree with this change by responding to the prompt within the app)고 부탁하고 있으므로 정답은 (C)이다.

> **Paraphrasing** 담화의 by responding to the prompt within the app → 정답의 By using an app

98-100 연설 + 학회 일정표

 동영상 강의

W-Br Good morning. ⁹⁸**My presentation will look closely at the nutritional benefits of eating fruit**. Patients often wonder whether the amount of sugar in fruit makes fruit unhealthy, and some even consider limiting it in their diet. But it's more nuanced than that. ⁹⁹**Last year, I published a paper reporting on my research on eating the current recommended serving of fruit each day versus eating less of it for weight-loss purposes.** I'll spend the next 45 minutes going through the results, and then it'll be time for the coffee break. ¹⁰⁰**During the coffee break, feel free to wander to the dining room, where our sponsor has set up a booth to sample a new nutritional beverage.**

안녕하세요. **제 발표에서는 과일 섭취의 영양적 혜택을 면밀히 살펴볼 것입니다.** 환자들은 종종 과일 내 당분의 양 때문에 과일이 건강에 좋지 않은지 궁금해합니다. 어떤 분들은 심지어 식단에서 과일을 제한하는 것도 고려하죠. 하지만 여기에는 좀 더 복잡 미묘한 측면이 있어요. **제가 작년에 연구 보고 논문을 발표했는데요. 매일 권장량의 과일을 섭취하는 것과 체중 감소 목적으로 그보다 적게 섭취하는 것을 대조했어요.** 앞으로 45분간 해당 결과를 말씀드리고, 그 이후에는 휴식 시간을 가질 것입니다. **휴식 시간 동안 식당을 자유롭게 돌아다녀 보세요. 저희 후원업체가 새로운 영양 음료를 시식하실 수 있도록 부스를 설치했습니다.**

어휘 nutritional 영양의   benefit 혜택   unhealthy 건강에 해로운   consider 고려하다   limit 제한하다   nuanced 미묘한 차이가 있는   publish 출판하다, 발표하다   research 연구, 조사   current 현재의   serving 1인분   versus 대   weight loss 체중 감량   purpose 목적   wander 돌아다니다   sponsor 후원자   set up 설치하다   sample 시식하다   beverage 음료

Conference Schedule		
Introduction	8:00 A.M.	Dr. Bajaj
⁹⁸"The Truth About Fruit"	8:15 A.M.	Dr. Novikova
Coffee break	9:00 A.M.	
"Daily Mineral Recommendations"	9:15 A.M.	Dr. Ivanda
"Talking to Patients About Hydration"	10:00 A.M.	Dr. Shimizu

학회 일정표		
소개	오전 8시	바자즈 박사
⁹⁸**"과일에 대한 진실"**	오전 8시 15분	**노비코바 박사**
휴식 시간	오전 9시	
"일일 미네랄 권장"	오전 9시 15분	이반다 박사
"환자들에게 수화 작용에 관해 이야기하기"	오전 10시	시미즈 박사

어휘 introduction 소개   hydration 수화 작용

98

Look at the graphic. Who is the speaker?
(A) Dr. Bajaj
(B) Dr. Novikova
(C) Dr. Ivanda
(D) Dr. Shimizu

시각 정보에 의하면 화자는 누구인가?
(A) 바자즈 박사
(B) 노비코바 박사
(C) 이반다 박사
(D) 시미즈 박사

해설 시각 정보 연계 – 화자의 신분

화자가 초반부에서 본인의 발표에서 과일 섭취의 영양적 혜택을 면밀히 살펴볼 것(My presentation will look closely at the nutritional benefits of eating fruit)이라고 했으며, 학회 일정표에 따르면 노비코바 박사가 "과일에 대한 진실"이라는 주제로 발표할 예정이므로 정답은 (B)이다.

99

What did the speaker do last year?
(A) She started her own medical practice.
(B) She received an award.
(C) She published a study.
(D) She developed a fitness application.

화자는 작년에 무엇을 했는가?
(A) 자신의 의원을 개업했다.
(B) 상을 받았다.
(C) 연구를 발표했다.
(D) 피트니스 앱을 개발했다.

어휘 medical practice 의원, 의료 업무   award 상

해설 세부 사항 관련 – 화자가 작년에 한 일
화자가 중반부에서 작년에 연구 보고 논문을 발표했다(Last year, I published a paper reporting on my research ~)고 했으므로 정답은 (C)이다.

> **Paraphrasing**   담화의 a paper reporting on my research
> → 정답의 a study

100

According to the speaker, where can the listeners test a product?
(A) In a lobby
(B) In an auditorium
(C) In a gift shop
(D) In a dining area

화자에 따르면, 청자들은 어디서 제품을 시험해 볼 수 있는가?
(A) 로비
(B) 강당
(C) 기념품점
(D) 식당

해설 세부 사항 관련 – 청자들이 제품을 시험해 볼 수 있는 곳
화자가 마지막에 휴식 시간 동안 식당을 자유롭게 돌아다녀 보라고 하면서 후원업체가 새로운 영양 음료를 시식할 수 있도록 부스를 설치했다(During the coffee break, feel free to wander to the dining room, ~ to sample a new nutritional beverage)고 했으므로 정답은 (D)이다.

> **Paraphrasing**   담화의 the dining room
> → 정답의 a dining area

1 (C)	2 (D)	3 (A)	4 (B)	5 (C)
6 (D)	7 (A)	8 (B)	9 (B)	10 (A)
11 (C)	12 (A)	13 (C)	14 (C)	15 (A)
16 (C)	17 (B)	18 (A)	19 (C)	20 (C)
21 (A)	22 (A)	23 (C)	24 (C)	25 (C)
26 (B)	27 (C)	28 (A)	29 (C)	30 (B)
31 (B)	32 (A)	33 (C)	34 (B)	35 (B)
36 (A)	37 (D)	38 (C)	39 (B)	40 (C)
41 (B)	42 (D)	43 (B)	44 (B)	45 (C)
46 (A)	47 (C)	48 (D)	49 (A)	50 (C)
51 (A)	52 (D)	53 (C)	54 (A)	55 (B)
56 (A)	57 (B)	58 (D)	59 (B)	60 (A)
61 (B)	62 (B)	63 (A)	64 (C)	65 (D)
66 (A)	67 (A)	68 (C)	69 (B)	70 (B)
71 (C)	72 (A)	73 (B)	74 (C)	75 (A)
76 (D)	77 (B)	78 (D)	79 (D)	80 (A)
81 (D)	82 (B)	83 (C)	84 (D)	85 (D)
86 (C)	87 (D)	88 (B)	89 (B)	90 (C)
91 (B)	92 (B)	93 (C)	94 (D)	95 (C)
96 (D)	97 (D)	98 (D)	99 (C)	100 (C)

PART 1

1 M-Au

(A) He's cleaning the floor.
(B) He's setting a plant on a shelf.
(C) He's pouring some liquid into a cup.
(D) He's ironing a shirt.

(A) 남자가 바닥을 청소하고 있다.
(B) 남자가 선반에 식물을 놓고 있다.
(C) 남자가 컵에 액체를 따르고 있다.
(D) 남자가 셔츠를 다리고 있다.

어휘 floor 바닥 plant 식물 pour 쏟다, 따르다 liquid 액체 iron 다리미질을 하다

해설 1인 등장 사진 – 사람의 동작/상태 묘사
(A) 동사 오답. 남자가 바닥을 청소하고 있는(is cleaning the floor) 모습이 아니므로 오답.
(B) 동사 오답. 남자가 선반에 식물을 놓고 있는(is setting a plant on a shelf) 모습이 아니므로 오답.
(C) 정답. 남자가 컵에 액체를 따르고 있는(pouring some liquid into a cup) 모습이므로 정답.

(D) 동사 오답. 남자가 셔츠를 다리고 있는(is ironing a shirt) 모습이 아니므로 오답.

---

2 W-Br

(A) They're glancing at a monitor.
(B) They're putting pens in a jar.
(C) They're wiping off a desk.
(D) They're examining a document.

(A) 사람들이 모니터를 보고 있다.
(B) 사람들이 병에 펜을 꽂고 있다.
(C) 사람들이 책상을 닦아 내고 있다.
(D) 사람들이 문서를 검토하고 있다.

어휘 glance at ~을 흘끗 보다 wipe off 닦아 내다 examine 조사하다, 검토하다

해설 2인 이상 등장 사진 – 사람의 동작/상태 묘사
(A) 동사 오답. 사람들이 모니터를 보고 있는(are glancing at a monitor) 모습이 아니므로 오답.
(B) 동사 오답. 사람들이 병에 펜을 꽂고 있는(are putting pens in a jar) 모습이 아니므로 오답.
(C) 동사 오답. 사람들이 책상을 닦아 내고 있는(are wiping off a desk) 모습이 아니므로 오답.
(D) 정답. 사람들이 문서를 검토하고 있는(are examining a document) 모습이므로 정답.

---

3 M-Cn

(A) Some people are taking a ride on a boat.
(B) A boat is floating under a bridge.
(C) A boat is being loaded with cargo.
(D) Some people are rowing a boat past a lighthouse.

(A) 사람들이 배를 타고 있다.
(B) 배가 다리 아래 떠 있다.
(C) 배에 화물이 실리고 있다.
(D) 사람들이 배를 저어 등대를 지나고 있다.

어휘 take a ride 타다 float 뜨다 load 싣다 cargo 화물 row 배를 젓다 lighthouse 등대

해설 혼합 사진 – 사람/사물/풍경 혼합 묘사
(A) 정답. 배를 타고 있는(are taking a ride on a boat) 사람들의 모습이 보이므로 정답.
(B) 사진에 없는 명사를 이용한 오답. 사진에 다리(a bridge)의 모습이 보이지 않으므로 오답.

(C) 사진에 없는 명사를 이용한 오답. 사진에 화물(cargo)의 모습이 보이지 않으므로 오답.

(D) 사진에 없는 명사를 이용한 오답. 사진에 등대(a lighthouse)의 모습이 보이지 않으므로 오답.

---

4 W-Am

(A) There's a fire burning in a fireplace.
(B) There's a guitar beside a fireplace.
(C) Some cables have been left on the ground in a pile.
(D) A television is being packed into a box.

(A) 벽난로에 불이 타고 있다.
(B) 벽난로 옆에 기타가 있다.
(C) 바닥에 전선들이 한 무더기 쌓여 있다.
(D) 텔레비전이 상자에 담겨 포장되고 있다.

어휘 fireplace 벽난로   in a pile 무더기로   pack 싸다, 포장하다

해설 사물/풍경 사진 – 사물 묘사
(A) 사진에 없는 명사를 이용한 오답. 사진에 불(a fire)의 모습이 보이지 않으므로 오답.
(B) 정답. 기타(a guitar)가 벽난로 옆에(beside a fireplace) 있는 모습이므로 정답.
(C) 상태 오답. 전선들(Some cables)이 바닥에 한 무더기 쌓여 있는(have been left on the ground in a pile) 모습이 아니므로 오답.
(D) 사진에 없는 명사를 이용한 오답. 사진에 상자(a box)의 모습이 보이지 않으므로 오답.

---

5 W-Au

▶ 동영상 강의

(A) Some people are riding bicycles through a field.
(B) Some people are moving a picnic table.
(C) There are some mountains in the distance.
(D) A bicycle has fallen over on the ground.

(A) 사람들이 들판에서 자전거를 타고 있다.
(B) 사람들이 피크닉 테이블을 옮기고 있다.
(C) 멀리 산이 있다.
(D) 자전거가 땅에 넘어져 있다.

어휘 in the distance 멀리, 먼 곳에

해설 혼합 사진 – 사람/사물/풍경 혼합 묘사
(A) 동사 오답. 들판에서 자전거를 타고 있는(are riding bicycles) 사람들의 모습이 보이지 않으므로 오답.

(B) 동사 오답. 사람들이 피크닉 테이블을 옮기고 있는(are moving a picnic table) 모습이 아니므로 오답.
(C) 정답. 산(some mountains)이 멀리 있는(in the distance) 모습이므로 정답.
(D) 상태 오답. 자전거(A bicycle)가 땅에 넘어져 있는(has fallen over on the ground) 모습이 아니므로 오답.

---

6 M-Cn

(A) Some couches have been pushed against a wall.
(B) Some lights have been hung from the ceiling.
(C) Some cushions have been stacked on the floor.
(D) Some flowers have been arranged in a vase.

(A) 소파들이 벽 쪽으로 밀려 있다.
(B) 전등 몇 개가 천장에 매달려 있다.
(C) 쿠션 몇 개가 바닥에 쌓여 있다.
(D) 꽃병에 꽃이 꽂혀 있다.

어휘 couch 소파   push against ~쪽으로 밀다   be hung from the ceiling 천장에 매달리다   stack 쌓다   arrange flowers 꽃꽂이하다

해설 사물/풍경 사진 – 사물 묘사
(A) 위치 오답. 소파들(Some couches)이 벽 쪽으로 밀려 있는(have been pushed against a wall) 모습이 아니므로 오답.
(B) 위치 오답. 전등 몇 개(Some lights)가 천장에 매달려 있는(have been hung from the ceiling) 모습이 아니므로 오답.
(C) 위치 오답. 쿠션 몇 개(Some cushions)가 바닥에 쌓여 있는(have been stacked on the floor) 모습이 아니므로 오답.
(D) 정답. 꽃(Some flowers)이 꽃병에 꽂혀 있는(have been arranged in a vase) 모습이므로 정답.

PART 2

7

M-Au Does the shop open on Sundays?

W-Am (A) Yes, at one o'clock.
(B) Because we drove.
(C) I'd like to return this item, please.

그 가게는 일요일에 문을 여나요?
(A) 네, 1시에요.
(B) 저희가 운전했거든요.
(C) 이 물건을 반품하고 싶어요.

해설 가게가 일요일에 문을 여는지 여부를 묻는 조동사(Does) 의문문

(A) 정답. 가게가 일요일에 문을 여는지 여부를 묻는 질문에 네(Yes)라고 대답한 뒤, 1시라고 구체적인 시점을 알려 주며 긍정 답변과 일관된 내용을 덧붙이고 있으므로 정답.

(B) 질문과 상관없는 오답. Why 의문문에 대한 응답이므로 오답.

(C) 연상 단어 오답. 질문의 shop에서 연상 가능한 return을 이용한 오답.

8

W-Br Where did these oranges come from?

M-Au (A) Here's a basket you can use.
(B) From a supplier in California.
(C) That umbrella is a nice color.

이 오렌지는 어디에서 왔죠?
(A) 여기 이 바구니를 쓰시면 됩니다.
(B) 캘리포니아의 공급업체에서요.
(C) 저 우산은 색깔이 멋지네요.

어휘 supplier 공급자, 공급 회사

해설 오렌지 공급처를 묻는 Where 의문문

(A) 연상 단어 오답. 질문의 oranges에서 연상 가능한 basket을 이용한 오답.

(B) 정답. 오렌지 공급처를 묻는 질문에 캘리포니아의 공급업체라고 구체적으로 응답하고 있으므로 정답.

(C) 연상 단어 오답. 질문의 oranges를 오렌지 색상으로 잘못 들었을 경우 연상 가능한 color를 이용한 오답.

9

W-Am Should I make the dinner reservation for Friday or Saturday?

W-Br (A) The Beachside Bistro.
(B) Saturday is better.
(C) A large plate of pasta.

저녁 식사 예약을 금요일로 할까요, 토요일로 할까요?
(A) 비치사이드 비스트로요.
(B) 토요일이 더 좋아요.
(C) 파스타 라지요.

어휘 reservation 예약

해설 저녁 식사 예약 요일을 묻는 선택 의문문

(A) 연상 단어 오답. 질문의 dinner에서 연상 가능한 Bistro를 이용한 오답.

(B) 정답. 금요일과 토요일 중 저녁 식사 예약을 언제로 할지 묻는 질문에 토요일이 더 좋다며 둘 중 하나를 선택해 응답하고 있으므로 정답.

(C) 연상 단어 오답. 질문의 dinner에서 연상 가능한 pasta를 이용한 오답.

10

M-Au Will Dr. Ivanova be late today?

W-Br (A) No, you shouldn't have to wait long.
(B) It's just under the desk.
(C) Sure, I can do that for you.

이바노바 박사님은 오늘 늦으시나요?
(A) 아니요, 오래 기다려야 하진 않을 겁니다.
(B) 책상 바로 아래 있어요.
(C) 그럼요, 제가 해 드릴 수 있어요.

해설 이바노바 박사님이 늦을지 여부를 확인하는 조동사(Will) 의문문

(A) 정답. 이바노바 박사님이 늦을지 묻는 질문에 아니요(No)라고 대답한 뒤, 오래 기다려야 하진 않을 거라며 부정 답변과 일관된 내용을 덧붙였으므로 정답.

(B) 질문과 상관없는 오답. Where 의문문에 대한 응답이므로 오답.

(C) 질문과 상관없는 오답.

11

M-Au Aren't there locker rooms at this gym?

M-Cn (A) These socks are quite comfortable.
(B) She teaches an exercise class.
(C) Yes, they're on the lower floor.

이 체육관에 탈의실이 있지 않나요?
(A) 이 양말은 꽤 편해요.
(B) 그녀는 운동 수업을 합니다.
(C) 네, 아래층에 있어요.

어휘 locker room 탈의실 comfortable 편안한 exercise 운동

해설 체육관에 탈의실이 있는지 여부를 확인하는 부정 의문문

(A) 연상 단어 오답. 질문의 rooms에서 연상 가능한 comfortable을 이용한 오답.

(B) 질문과 상관없는 오답. 질문에 3인칭 대명사 She로 지칭할 인물이 언급된 적이 없으므로 오답.

(C) 정답. 체육관에 탈의실이 있는지 묻는 질문에 네(Yes)라고 대답한 뒤, 아래층에 있다고 긍정 답변과 일관된 내용을 덧붙이고 있으므로 정답.

12

M-Cn Who needs a copy of my safety training certificate?

W-Am (A) Maksim does.
(B) You can hang your vest on that hook.
(C) No, I'm certain about that.

누가 제 안전 교육 수료증 사본이 필요하죠?
(A) 막심이요.
(B) 저 옷걸이에 조끼를 걸어 두시면 됩니다.
(C) 아니요, 확실해요.

어휘 certificate 증명서, 수료증, 자격증 hang 걸다 vest 조끼 hook 고리, 걸이

해설 안전 교육 수료증 사본이 필요한 사람을 묻는 Who 의문문

(A) 정답. 안전 교육 수료증 사본이 필요한 사람이 누구인지 묻는 질문에 막심이라고 구체적인 사람 이름으로 알려 주고 있으므로 정답.

(B) 연상 단어 오답. 질문의 safety에서 연상 가능한 vest를 이용한 오답.

(C) Yes/No 불가 오답. Who 의문문에는 Yes/No 응답이 불가능하므로 오답.

13

M-Cn Could you phone Mr. Feras and let him know we're in the hotel lobby?

W-Br (A) Thank you, it was just renovated.
(B) A free continental breakfast.
(C) Yes, of course.

페라스 씨에게 전화해서 우리가 호텔 로비에 있다고 알려 주실 수 있어요?
(A) 감사합니다, 막 개조했어요.
(B) 무료 유럽식 아침 식사요.
(C) 네, 그럼요.

어휘 renovate 개조하다, 보수하다 continental 유럽 대륙의, 유럽식의

해설 부탁/요청의 의문문
(A) 연상 단어 오답. 질문의 hotel lobby에서 연상 가능한 renovated를 이용한 오답.
(B) 연상 단어 오답. 질문의 hotel에서 연상 가능한 breakfast를 이용한 오답.
(C) 정답. 페라스 씨에게 전화해 달라는 요청에 네, 그럼요(Yes, of course)라고 수락하고 있으므로 정답.

14

W-Br Where does she sell her handmade jewelry?

M-Au (A) They'll give you a discount.
(B) A pair of earrings.
(C) At a store in the city center.

그녀는 자신의 수제 보석을 어디서 파나요?
(A) 그들이 할인을 해 줄 거예요.
(B) 귀걸이 한 쌍이요.
(C) 도심에 있는 매장에서요.

어휘 handmade 손으로 만든, 수제의

해설 수제 보석 판매 장소를 묻는 Where 의문문
(A) 연상 단어 오답. 질문의 sell에서 연상 가능한 discount를 이용한 오답.
(B) 연상 단어 오답. 질문의 jewelry에서 연상 가능한 earrings를 이용한 오답.
(C) 정답. 수제 보석 판매 장소를 묻는 질문에 도심에 있는 매장이라고 알려 주고 있으므로 정답.

15

W-Br You're taking a business class in the afternoon, aren't you?

M-Cn (A) Actually, it's in the morning.
(B) That office is on the corner.
(C) I have the train schedule here.

오후에 비즈니스 수업 들으시죠, 그렇지 않나요?
(A) 사실은 오전이에요.
(B) 그 사무실은 모퉁이에 있어요.
(C) 여기 기차 시간표가 있어요.

해설 오후에 비즈니스 수업 수강 여부를 확인하는 부가 의문문
(A) 정답. 오후에 비즈니스 수업 수강 여부를 확인하는 질문에 사실은 오전이라며 관련된 내용으로 응답하고 있으므로 정답.
(B) 연상 단어 오답. 질문의 business에서 연상 가능한 office를 이용한 오답.
(C) 연상 단어 오답. business class를 기차나 비행기의 비즈니스 클래스 좌석으로 잘못 들은 경우 연상 가능한 train을 이용한 오답.

16

M-Au Could I see some sample floral arrangements before I order?

W-Br (A) It's for an award ceremony.
(B) A charge for expedited delivery.
(C) Certainly, I have some right here.

주문하기 전에 꽃꽂이 견본을 좀 볼 수 있을까요?
(A) 시상식에 쓸 거예요.
(B) 빠른 배송 요금이요.
(C) 그럼요, 여기 있어요.

어휘 floral arrangement 꽃꽂이 award ceremony 시상식 charge 요금 expedited delivery 빠른 배송

해설 부탁/요청의 의문문
(A) 연상 단어 오답. 질문의 floral arrangements에서 연상 가능한 award ceremony를 이용한 오답.
(B) 연상 단어 오답. 질문의 order에서 연상 가능한 delivery를 이용한 오답.
(C) 정답. 주문하기 전에 꽃꽂이 견본을 좀 보여 달라는 요청에 그럼요(Certainly)라고 수락한 뒤, 여기 있다며 긍정 답변과 일관된 내용을 덧붙이고 있으므로 정답.

17

M-Cn Don't you want to buy the black sofa?

M-Au (A) Some customer reviews.
(B) We already have one.
(C) I take my coffee with sugar.

검은색 소파를 사고 싶지 않나요?
(A) 고객 후기들이요.
(B) 이미 있어요.
(C) 저는 커피에 설탕을 넣어 마셔요.

해설 검은색 소파 구매 희망 여부를 확인하는 부정 의문문
(A) 연상 단어 오답. 질문의 buy에서 연상 가능한 customer reviews를 이용한 오답.
(B) 정답. 검은색 소파 구매 희망 여부를 묻는 질문에 이미 있다며 거절 의사를 우회적으로 표현하고 있으므로 정답.
(C) 연상 단어 오답. 질문의 black에서 연상 가능한 coffee를 이용한 오답.

18

▶ 동영상 강의

M-Au Do you have this jacket in a larger size?

W-Am (A) Oh, I'm not a sales associate.
(B) I've read the information packet.
(C) A very large uniform.

이 재킷 더 큰 사이즈로 있나요?
(A) 아, 저는 판매원이 아닌데요.
(B) 자료집을 읽었어요.
(C) 아주 큰 유니폼이요.

어휘 sales associate 영업 사원   information packet 자료 묶음

해설 재킷이 더 큰 사이즈가 있는지 여부를 확인하는 조동사(Do) 의문문
(A) 정답. 재킷이 더 큰 사이즈가 있는지 여부를 묻는 질문에 판매원이 아니라며 알지 못함을 우회적으로 알려 주고 있으므로 정답.
(B) 유사 발음 오답. 질문의 jacket과 부분적으로 발음이 유사한 packet을 이용한 오답.
(C) 파생어 오답. 질문의 larger와 파생어 관계인 large를 이용한 오답.

19

W-Am Where did you first learn about the job opening?

M-Au (A) Are there any outdoor tables available?
(B) The door to the building is still open.
(C) I read an online newspaper every morning.

이 구인 건을 어디서 처음 알게 되셨나요?
(A) 쓸 수 있는 야외 테이블이 있나요?
(B) 건물 출입문이 아직 열려 있어요.
(C) 저는 매일 아침 온라인 신문을 읽어요.

어휘 job opening 구인, 공석   available 이용 가능한, 구할 수 있는

해설 구인 건을 알게 된 출처를 묻는 Where 의문문
(A) 질문과 상관없는 오답.
(B) 파생어 오답. 질문의 opening과 파생어 관계인 open을 이용한 오답.
(C) 정답. 구인 건을 알게 된 출처를 묻는 질문에 매일 아침 온라인 신문을 읽는다며 구체적인 정보 출처를 알려 주고 있으므로 정답.

20

W-Br Should I bring anything to the meeting?

M-Cn (A) Probably in the conference room.
(B) They were hired by our manager.
(C) Do we have enough handouts?

회의에 가져가야 할 것이 있나요?
(A) 아마 회의실에서요.
(B) 그들은 우리 관리자가 고용했어요.
(C) 인쇄물이 충분히 있나요?

어휘 conference room 회의실   handout 인쇄물, 유인물

해설 회의에 가져가야 할 것이 있는지 여부를 묻는 조동사(Should) 의문문
(A) 연상 단어 오답. 질문의 meeting에서 연상 가능한 conference room을 이용한 오답.
(B) 질문과 상관없는 오답. 질문에 3인칭 대명사 They로 지칭할 인물이 언급된 적이 없으므로 오답.
(C) 정답. 회의에 가져가야 할 것이 있는지 여부를 묻는 질문에 인쇄물이 충분히 있는지를 물으며 회의에 가져가야 할 것과 관련된 내용을 언급하고 있으므로 정답.

21

W-Am What was the total charge for the hotel stay?

M-Au (A) I'd have to look at the receipt.
(B) The fitness center is across from the reception desk.
(C) I'll be eating breakfast in my room.

호텔 투숙 총 비용이 얼마였죠?
(A) 영수증을 봐야 해요.
(B) 피트니스 센터는 안내 데스크 맞은편에 있어요.
(C) 저는 방에서 아침 식사를 할 거예요.

어휘 charge 요금   receipt 영수증   reception desk 안내 데스크

해설 호텔 투숙 총 비용을 묻는 What 의문문
(A) 정답. 호텔 투숙 총 비용을 묻는 질문에 영수증을 봐야 한다며 현재는 비용을 알지 못함을 간접적으로 알려 주고 있으므로 정답.
(B) 연상 단어 오답. 질문의 hotel에서 연상 가능한 reception desk를 이용한 오답.
(C) 연상 단어 오답. 질문의 hotel에서 연상 가능한 breakfast in my room을 이용한 오답.

22

M-Cn Why did you pursue a career in video game design?

W-Br (A) Because I have a talent for it.
(B) This is my new laptop.
(C) It's on the other shelf.

왜 비디오 게임 디자인 일을 계속하셨나요?
(A) 그쪽에 재능이 있어서요.
(B) 이게 제 새 노트북이에요.
(C) 다른 선반에 있어요.

어휘 pursue 추구하다, 계속해 나가다   talent 재능, 재주

해설 비디오 게임 디자인 일을 계속한 이유를 묻는 Why 의문문
(A) 정답. 비디오 게임 디자인 일을 계속한 이유를 묻는 질문에 그쪽에 재능이 있어서라고 구체적인 이유를 제시하고 있으므로 정답.
(B) 연상 단어 오답. 질문의 game에서 연상 가능한 laptop을 이용한 오답.
(C) 질문과 상관없는 오답. Where 의문문에 대한 응답이므로 오답.

23

W-Br I'd like to attend the job fair next month.

M-Au (A) The speech was inspiring.
(B) Tunji updated the memo.
(C) Registration closed yesterday.

다음 달 취업 박람회에 참석하고 싶어요.
(A) 연설이 고무적이었어요.
(B) 툰지가 메모를 업데이트했어요.
(C) 등록이 어제 끝났는데요.

어휘 job fair 취업 박람회   inspiring 고무적인, 영감을 주는
registration 등록

해설 의사 전달의 평서문
(A) 연상 단어 오답. 평서문의 job fair에서 연상 가능한 speech를 이용한 오답.
(B) 평서문과 상관없는 오답.
(C) 정답. 다음 달 취업 박람회에 참석하고 싶다는 평서문에 등록이 어제 끝났다며 참석할 수 없는 이유를 제시하고 있으므로 정답.

24

W-Br Hasn't anyone called you back for the second interview yet?

M-Cn (A) A new phone number.
(B) Yes, any available position.
(C) I'm still waiting.

아직 2차 면접 전화를 못 받으셨어요?
(A) 새 전화번호요.
(B) 네, 어떤 공석이든지요.
(C) 아직 기다리고 있어요.

어휘 available position 공석

해설 2차 면접 전화를 받았는지 여부를 확인하는 부정 의문문
(A) 연상 단어 오답. 질문의 called에서 연상 가능한 phone number를 이용한 오답.
(B) 연상 단어 오답. 질문의 interview에서 연상 가능한 position을 이용한 오답.
(C) 정답. 2차 면접 전화를 받았는지 여부를 묻는 질문에 아직 기다리고 있다며 전화를 받지 못했음을 우회적으로 응답하고 있으므로 정답.

25

M-Au How many tickets do we need for tonight's concert?

W-Am (A) The theater is on Johnson Avenue.
(B) At seven thirty sharp.
(C) I'll buy mine at the door.

우리 오늘 밤 콘서트 티켓이 몇 장 필요하죠?
(A) 극장은 존슨 가에 있어요.
(B) 7시 30분 정각이요.
(C) 제 것은 입구에서 살게요.

어휘 sharp 정각

해설 필요한 콘서트 티켓 수를 묻는 How many 의문문
(A) 연상 단어 오답. 질문의 concert에서 연상 가능한 theater를 이용한 오답.
(B) 질문과 상관없는 오답. When 의문문에 대한 응답이므로 오답.
(C) 정답. 콘서트 티켓이 몇 장 필요한지 묻는 질문에 자신의 표는 입구에서 사겠다며, 함께 살 필요가 없다고 알려 주고 있으므로 정답.

26

 동영상 강의

W-Am When are they going to decide who to hire?

M-Cn (A) A much higher salary.
(B) A lot of good résumés have come in.
(C) In the building across the street.

그들은 누구를 고용할지 언제 결정할까요?
(A) 훨씬 더 많은 급여요.
(B) 괜찮은 이력서가 많이 들어왔어요.
(C) 길 건너편 건물에서요.

어휘 résumé 이력서

해설 고용 결정 시점을 묻는 When 의문문
(A) 유사 발음 오답. 질문의 hire와 부분적으로 발음이 유사한 higher를 이용한 오답.
(B) 정답. 누구를 고용할지 결정하는 시점을 묻는 질문에 괜찮은 이력서가 많이 들어왔다며, 결정하는 데 시간이 걸린다는 것을 우회적으로 응답하고 있으므로 정답.
(C) 질문과 상관없는 오답. Where 의문문에 대한 응답이므로 오답.

27

M-Au I had a chance to look over the contract this morning.

W-Am (A) Their contact information.
(B) Early next week.
(C) What did you think of it?

오늘 오전에 계약서를 훑어볼 기회가 있었어요.
(A) 그들의 연락처예요.
(B) 다음 주 초요.
(C) 어떻게 생각하시나요?

어휘 look over ~을 훑어보다, 살펴보다   contract 계약, 계약서
contact information 연락처

해설 정보 전달의 평서문
(A) 유사 발음 오답. 평서문의 contract와 부분적으로 발음이 유사한 contact를 이용한 오답.
(B) 연상 단어 오답. 평서문의 this morning에서 연상 가능한 Early next week을 이용한 오답.
(C) 정답. 오늘 오전에 계약서를 훑어볼 기회가 있었다는 말에 어떻게 생각하는지 계약서에 대한 의견을 묻고 있으므로 정답.

28

▶ 동영상 강의

W-Am How are the database updates coming along?

W-Br (A) I've been really busy with the Williams account.
(B) Some customer addresses.
(C) She arrives on Wednesday.

데이터베이스 업데이트는 어떻게 되어 가고 있나요?
(A) 저는 윌리엄스 고객 일로 무척 바빴습니다.
(B) 고객 주소요.
(C) 그녀는 수요일에 도착해요.

어휘 come along 되어 가다 account 고객, 계좌, 계정

해설 데이터베이스 업데이트의 진행 상황을 묻는 How 의문문
(A) 정답. 데이터베이스 업데이트의 진행 상황을 묻는 질문에 자신은 윌리엄스 고객 일로 무척 바빴기 때문에 아직 진행하지 못했음을 우회적으로 응답하고 있으므로 정답.
(B) 연상 단어 오답. 질문의 database에서 연상 가능한 customer addresses를 이용한 오답.
(C) 질문과 상관없는 오답. 질문에 3인칭 대명사 She로 지칭할 인물이 언급된 적이 없으므로 오답.

29

M-Au When can I bring these boxes into the warehouse?

W-Am (A) Ten in a package.
(B) Thanks—I just bought it.
(C) We'll need to clear some space.

언제 이 상자들을 창고로 가져갈 수 있을까요?
(A) 한 상자에 열 개요.
(B) 감사합니다, 막 샀어요.
(C) 자리를 만들어야 할 거예요.

어휘 warehouse 창고 clear 치우다 space 공간

해설 상자들을 창고로 가져갈 수 있는 시점을 묻는 When 의문문
(A) 연상 단어 오답. 질문의 boxes에서 연상 가능한 package를 이용한 오답.
(B) 질문과 상관없는 오답.
(C) 정답. 상자들을 창고로 가져갈 수 있는 시점을 묻는 질문에 자리를 만들어야 한다며, 자리를 만들고 나서야 가능할 것임을 우회적으로 알려 주고 있으므로 정답.

30

M-Cn The market on Fifth Street is closed for a week.

W-Br (A) Some new clothes.
(B) Is there another one nearby?
(C) The price has been marked down.

5번 가 시장은 일주일간 닫아요.
(A) 새 옷이요.
(B) 근처에 다른 시장이 있나요?
(C) 가격이 할인됐어요.

어휘 nearby 근처에 mark down 할인하다

해설 정보 전달의 평서문
(A) 유사 발음 오답. 평서문의 closed와 부분적으로 발음이 유사한 clothes를 이용한 오답.
(B) 정답. 5번 가 시장은 일주일간 닫는다는 말에 근처에 다른 시장이 있는지 관련된 내용을 묻고 있으므로 정답.
(C) 유사 발음 오답. 평서문의 market과 부분적으로 발음이 유사한 marked를 이용한 오답.

31

M-Au Does the company pay for professional-development courses?

W-Br (A) Insook helped develop a new product.
(B) We do have a significant budget surplus.
(C) He's always so professional.

그 회사는 직무 능력 개발 강좌 비용을 지불하나요?
(A) 인숙이 신제품 개발을 도왔어요.
(B) 예산이 많이 남아 있거든요.
(C) 그는 항상 전문가다워요.

어휘 professional development 전문성 개발, 직무 능력 개발 significant 커다란, 상당한 budget 예산 surplus 나머지, 잉여

해설 직무 능력 개발 강좌 비용 지불 여부를 확인하는 조동사(Does) 의문문
(A) 파생어 오답. 질문의 development와 파생어 관계인 develop을 이용한 오답.
(B) 정답. 회사가 직무 능력 개발 강좌 비용을 지불하는지 여부를 묻는 질문에 예산이 많이 남아 있다며 지불할 수 있음을 간접적으로 알려 주고 있으므로 정답.
(C) 단어 반복 오답. 질문의 professional을 반복 이용한 오답.

PART 3

32-34

W-Am Excuse me, but **32 wasn't the ferry to Osaka supposed to leave at ten o'clock?**

M-Cn **32 Yes,** but **33 the port authority has suspended all marine traffic due to rough water.**

W-Am I see. Does that mean ferries are canceled all day?

M-Cn This storm is expected to pass in about three hours. But operations should return to normal after that. Your ticket will be good until midnight.

W-Am OK. **34 Then I guess I'll grab some lunch nearby.**

M-Cn I highly recommend Mary's Café for sandwiches and soup.

여	실례합니다. **오사카행 페리가 10시에 출발하기로 되어 있던 것 아닌가요?**
남	네, 그런데 **항만 당국에서 거친 파도 때문에 모든 해상 교통을 중단시켰어요.**
여	그렇군요. 페리가 종일 취소된다는 뜻인가요?
남	이번 폭풍은 약 3시간 후 지나갈 것으로 예상됩니다. 하지만 운항은 그 이후에 정상화될 겁니다. 표는 자정까지 유효할 거예요.
여	알겠습니다. **그럼 근처에서 잠깐 점심 식사를 해야겠네요.**
남	메리 카페에서 샌드위치와 수프를 드시는 걸 적극 추천해요.
어휘	be supposed to ~하기로 되어 있다 port authority 항만 당국 suspend 중단하다, 유예하다 rough water 격랑, 거친 물결 good 유효한 grab 급히[잠깐] ~하다

32

Where most likely are the speakers?
(A) At a ferry terminal
(B) At a swimming area
(C) At a shopping mall
(D) At a restaurant

화자들은 어디에 있겠는가?
(A) 페리 터미널
(B) 수영 구역
(C) 쇼핑몰
(D) 식당

해설 전체 내용 관련 – 대화의 장소
여자가 첫 대사에서 오사카행 페리가 10시에 출발하기로 되어 있던 것 아닌지(wasn't the ferry to Osaka supposed to leave at ten o'clock?)를 묻자 남자가 네(Yes)라고 대답하는 것으로 보아 대화 장소는 페리 터미널이라는 것을 알 수 있다. 따라서 정답은 (A)이다.

33

What problem does the man mention?
(A) Some repairs are needed.
(B) A business is understaffed.
(C) The weather is bad.
(D) Some tickets are sold out.

남자는 어떤 문제를 언급하는가?
(A) 수리가 필요하다.
(B) 업체에 일손이 부족하다.
(C) 날씨가 궂다.
(D) 표가 매진됐다.

어휘 understaffed 인원이 부족한 sold out 매진된, 품절된

해설 세부 사항 관련 – 남자가 언급하는 문제
남자가 첫 대사에서 항만 당국에서 거친 파도 때문에 모든 해상 교통을 중단시켰다(the port authority has suspended all marine traffic due to rough water)고 했으므로 정답은 (C)이다.

Paraphrasing	대화의 rough water
	→ 정답의 The weather is bad.

34

What will the woman do next?
(A) Read a book
(B) Get a meal
(C) Watch a movie
(D) Go to a hotel

여자는 다음으로 무엇을 할 것인가?
(A) 독서
(B) 식사
(C) 영화 감상
(D) 호텔로 이동

어휘 meal 식사

해설 세부 사항 관련 – 여자가 다음에 할 일
여자가 마지막 대사에서 근처에서 점심 식사를 해야겠다(Then I guess I'll grab some lunch nearby)고 말하고 있으므로 정답은 (B)이다.

Paraphrasing	대화의 grab some lunch
	→ 정답의 Get a meal

35-37

W-Br	Good morning. **35 Are you looking for any particular library book, magazine, or newspaper?**
M-Cn	Actually, no. **36 I'm here because I got an e-mail this morning telling me that I have an overdue book.** But I returned it to the after-hours bin last night.
W-Br	**37 Sometimes a book gets returned and put back on the shelves without being entered into the system first. I can take a look.** Can you tell me the title?

여	안녕하세요. **특정한 도서관 책이나 잡지, 신문을 찾고 계신가요?**
남	실은 그게 아니고요. **오늘 오전에 반납 기한이 지난 책이 있다는 이메일을 받고 왔어요.** 그런데 저는 어젯밤에 운영 시간 이후 반납함에 반납했거든요.
여	**가끔 도서가 반납되면 시스템에 먼저 입력되지 않은 채 책장에 다시 꽂히기도 해요. 제가 한번 볼게요.** 제목을 말씀해 주시겠어요?
어휘	particular 특정한 overdue 기한이 지난 after-hours 영업시간 이후의 enter 입력하다 take a look 보다

35

Who most likely is the woman?
(A) An author
(B) A librarian
(C) A bookseller
(D) An event organizer

여자는 누구이겠는가?
(A) 저자
(B) 사서
(C) 책 판매자
(D) 행사 주최자

해설 전체 내용 관련 – 여자의 직업
여자가 첫 대사에서 특정한 도서관 책이나 잡지, 신문을 찾고 있는지(Are you looking for any particular library book, magazine, or newspaper?)를 묻고 있는 것으로 보아 여자는 도서관 사서임을 알 수 있다. 따라서 정답은 (B)이다.

36

What does the man say happened this morning?
(A) He received an e-mail notification.
(B) He applied for a job online.
(C) He lost a receipt.
(D) He made a delivery.

남자는 오늘 오전 어떤 일이 있었다고 말하는가?
(A) 이메일 알림을 받았다.
(B) 온라인으로 일자리에 지원했다.
(C) 영수증을 잃어버렸다.
(D) 배달을 했다.

어휘 notification 알림, 통지 apply for ~에 지원하다 receipt 영수증

해설 세부 사항 관련 – 오늘 오전에 있었던 일
남자가 첫 대사에서 오늘 오전에 반납 기한이 지난 책이 있다는 이메일을 받고 왔다(I'm here because I got an e-mail this morning telling me that I have an overdue book)고 말하고 있으므로 정답은 (A)이다.

> Paraphrasing 대화의 got an e-mail ~ telling me that ~
> → 정답의 received an e-mail notification

37

What does the woman offer to do?
(A) Attend an event
(B) Fill out an online form
(C) Place an order
(D) Search for an item

여자는 무엇을 하겠다고 제안하는가?
(A) 행사 참석하기
(B) 온라인 서식 작성하기
(C) 주문 넣기
(D) 물건 찾아보기

어휘 fill out 작성하다, 기입하다

해설 세부 사항 관련 – 여자의 제안 사항
여자가 마지막 대사에서 가끔 도서가 반납되면 시스템에 먼저 입력되지 않은 채 책장에 다시 꽂히기도 한다(Sometimes a book gets returned and put back on the shelves without being entered into the system first)며 한번 보겠다(I can take a look)고 말하는 것으로 보아, 여자는 책을 찾아보겠다고 제안하고 있음을 알 수 있다. 따라서 정답은 (D)이다.

> Paraphrasing 대화의 take a look → 정답의 Search

38-40

> M-Au Hi. I'm Malik. [38] **I talked to you this morning on the phone about a price quote for some painting you want done.**
>
> W-Br Oh, hi. Come in. Yes, I want to change the color in the dining room to something lighter.
>
> M-Au Not a problem. But [39] **I do want to stress that the quote may be higher than you expected** because going from a darker color to a lighter one requires more than one coat of paint.
>
> W-Br I understand. And [40] **will you move the table and chairs out of the room before you start?**
>
> M-Au That shouldn't be necessary. We can cover them with a drop cloth.

> 남 안녕하세요, 말릭입니다. **오늘 오전 전화로 원하시는 페인팅 작업의 가격 견적에 대해 말씀드렸죠.**
>
> 여 아, 안녕하세요. 들어오세요. 네, 식사 공간을 더 밝은 색상으로 바꾸고 싶어요.
>
> 남 좋습니다. 그런데 **견적이 예상하시는 것보다 높을 수 있다는 점을 강조하고 싶어요.** 어두운 색상에서 밝은 색상으로 가려면 여러 번의 도색이 필요해서요.
>
> 여 알겠습니다. **시작하시기 전에 탁자와 의자를 방 밖으로 옮길 건가요?**
>
> 남 그럴 필요 없습니다. 덮개 천으로 씌우면 돼요.

> 어휘 price quote 가격 견적 stress 강조하다 coat (페인트 등의) 칠 drop cloth 덮개 천

38

What type of business does the man most likely work for?
(A) A moving company
(B) A furniture manufacturer
(C) A painting company
(D) A catering service

남자는 어떤 종류의 업체에서 일하겠는가?
(A) 이사업체
(B) 가구 제조업체
(C) 페인팅 업체
(D) 케이터링 업체

해설 전체 내용 관련 – 남자의 근무 업종
남자가 첫 대사에서 오늘 오전 전화로 페인팅 작업의 가격 견적에 대해 말했다(I talked to you this morning on the phone about a price quote for some painting you want done)고 말하는 것으로 보아 남자는 페인팅 업체에서 근무하고 있음을 알 수 있다. 따라서 정답은 (C)이다.

39

What point does the man emphasize?
(A) A deposit is required before work can begin.
(B) A price may be higher than expected.
(C) A discount is available for a limited time.
(D) A schedule cannot be changed easily.

남자는 어떤 점을 강조하는가?
(A) 작업이 시작되기 전에 착수금이 필요하다.
(B) 가격이 예상보다 높을 수 있다.
(C) 한시적으로 할인이 된다.
(D) 일정은 쉽게 변경할 수 없다.

어휘 emphasize 강조하다 deposit 착수금, 보증금 available 이용 가능한 for a limited time 한시적으로

해설 세부 사항 관련 – 남자가 강조하는 것
남자가 두 번째 대사에서 견적이 예상보다 높을 수 있다는 점을 강조하고 싶다(I do want to stress that the quote may be higher than you expected)고 말하고 있으므로 정답은 (B)이다.

> **Paraphrasing** 대화의 stress → 질문의 emphasize
> 대화의 the quote → 정답의 A price

40

What does the woman ask about?
(A) Signing a contract
(B) Purchasing specialized tools
(C) Moving some furniture
(D) Seeing some samples

여자는 무엇에 대해 물어보는가?
(A) 계약서 서명
(B) 전문 도구 구매
(C) 가구 이동
(D) 견본 확인

어휘 contract 계약, 계약서 specialized 전문적인

해설 세부 사항 관련 – 여자의 문의 사항
여자가 마지막 대사에서 탁자와 의자를 방 밖으로 옮길 건지(will you move the table and chairs out of the room ～?)를 묻고 있으므로 정답은 (C)이다.

> **Paraphrasing** 대화의 the table and chairs
> → 정답의 some furniture

41-43

> W-Am Hi. This is my first time in here. Nice place! Looks like you've got lots of state-of-the-art equipment.
>
> M-Au Yes, **⁴¹we just opened this week. All the exercise bikes, treadmills, and workout stations that you see are brand-new.**
>
> W-Am Great! **⁴²I'm considering joining.** My office is right around the corner.
>
> M-Au Well, **⁴²here's a brochure with a description of our membership levels.** I'm happy to answer any questions.
>
> W-Am Thanks. I do like to swim a few times a week. Do you have a pool?
>
> M-Au We do. **⁴³Why don't we start by walking around so I can show you all of our facilities?**

> 여 안녕하세요. 여긴 처음 오는데, 멋진 곳이네요! 최신 장비가 많은 것 같아요.
>
> 남 네. **이번 주에 문을 열었어요. 보시는 실내용 자전거, 러닝머신, 운동 기구들이 모두 새것입니다.**
>
> 여 좋네요! **가입할까 생각 중이에요.** 사무실이 아주 가까워서요.
>
> 남 **저희 회원 등급에 대해 설명하는 책자가 여기 있어요.** 어떤 질문이든 해 주세요.
>
> 여 감사합니다. 일주일에 몇 번 수영을 하고 싶어요. 수영장이 있나요?
>
> 남 있습니다. **둘러보면서 저희 시설을 보여 드리면 어떨까요?**

> **어휘** state-of-the-art 최신의 equipment 장비 brand-new 아주 새것의 consider 고려하다 around the corner 아주 가까운 brochure 책자 description 기술, 서술

41

Where does the man work?
(A) At a community park
(B) At a fitness center
(C) At a public beach
(D) At a sports equipment store

남자는 어디서 일하는가?
(A) 근린공원
(B) 피트니스 센터
(C) 공공 해수욕장
(D) 스포츠 장비 매장

남자가 첫 대사에서 이번 주에 문을 열었다(we just opened this week)며, 실내용 자전거, 러닝 머신, 운동 기구들이 모두 새것(All the exercise bikes, treadmills, and workout stations that you see are brand-new)이라고 말하는 것으로 보아 남자는 피트니스 센터에서 근무하고 있음을 알 수 있다. 따라서 정답은 (B)이다.

42

What is the purpose of the woman's visit?
(A) She is applying for a job.
(B) She has a complaint.
(C) She needs specific directions.
(D) She is interested in a membership.

여자가 방문한 목적은?
(A) 일자리에 지원하려고
(B) 불만이 있어서
(C) 구체적인 길 안내가 필요해서
(D) 회원 가입에 관심이 있어서

어휘 apply for ~에 지원하다 complaint 불평, 불만 specific 구체적인, 특정한 directions 길 안내

해설 세부 사항 관련 – 여자의 방문 목적

여자가 두 번째 대사에서 가입할까 생각 중(I'm considering joining)이라고 하자 남자가 회원 등급에 대해 설명하는 책자가 여기 있다(here's a brochure with a description of our membership levels)고 말하는 것으로 보아 여자는 회원 가입에 관심이 있다는 것을 알 수 있다. 따라서 정답은 (D)이다.

43

What will the woman most likely do next?
(A) Join a team
(B) Go on a tour
(C) Make a phone call
(D) Fill out an application

여자는 다음으로 무엇을 하겠는가?
(A) 팀에 합류하기
(B) 견학하기
(C) 전화하기
(D) 지원서 작성하기

어휘 fill out 기입하다, 작성하다 application 지원, 지원서

해설 세부 사항 관련 – 여자가 다음에 할 일

남자가 마지막 대사에서 둘러보면서 시설을 보여 주면 어떨지(Why don't we start by walking around so I can show you all of our facilities?) 시설 견학을 제안하고 있으므로 정답은 (B)이다.

> Paraphrasing 대화의 show you all of our facilities
> → 정답의 Go on a tour

44-46

M-Cn	Hello. ⁴⁴**What brings you into our leasing office today?**
W-Am	Hi. I currently live in unit 217, but I'm wondering if there are any larger units available to rent in the building.
M-Cn	Let me see. Apartment 410 is quite large, and the lease on it ends this November. It's a thousand per month. Does that interest you?
W-Am	⁴⁵**I did just get promoted at work recently**, so I can afford to spend more. So, that won't be a problem.
M-Cn	Great. ⁴⁶**I'll call the current tenant** and we can figure out a time for a viewing.

남	안녕하세요. **오늘 저희 임대 사무소에 무슨 일로 오셨나요?**
여	안녕하세요. 현재 217호에 살고 있는데 건물에 임대 가능한 더 큰 호실이 있는지 궁금해서요.
남	한번 보죠. 410호가 꽤 넓은데, 임대차 계약이 올해 11월에 끝납니다. 한 달에 1,000달러예요. 관심 있으세요?
여	**최근 직장에서 승진을 해서** 더 낼 여력이 있어요. 그러니 괜찮아요.
남	좋습니다. **현재 세입자에게 전화해서** 보러 갈 시간을 알아볼게요.

어휘	leasing office 임대 사무소 currently 현재 available 이용 가능한, 구할 수 있는 rent 세내다, 세놓다 lease 임대차 계약 get promoted 승진하다 afford to ~할 여력이 있다 tenant 세입자 figure out 알아내다

44

Who most likely is the man?
(A) A janitor
(B) A property manager
(C) A carpenter
(D) An interior designer

남자는 누구이겠는가?
(A) 수위
(B) 건물 관리인
(C) 목수
(D) 실내 디자이너

해설 전체 내용 관련 – 남자의 직업

남자가 첫 대사에서 임대 사무소에 무슨 일로 왔는지(What brings you into our leasing office today?)를 묻고 있으므로 남자는 건물 관리인임을 알 수 있다. 따라서 정답은 (B)이다.

45

What does the woman say recently happened?
(A) She earned a degree.
(B) She won an award.
(C) She got a promotion.
(D) She transferred to a new location.

여자는 최근 무슨 일이 있었다고 말하는가?
(A) 학위를 받았다.
(B) 상을 받았다.
(C) 승진했다.
(D) 새로운 곳으로 옮겼다.

어휘 earn a degree 학위를 받다   win an award 상을 받다
transfer 옮기다

해설 세부 사항 관련 – 최근 여자에게 있었던 일

여자가 두 번째 대사에서 최근 직장에서 승진을 했다(I did just get promoted at work recently)고 말하고 있으므로 정답은 (C)이다.

> Paraphrasing   대화의 did just get promoted at work
> → 정답의 got a promotion

46

What will the man do next?
(A) Make a phone call
(B) Prepare a contract
(C) Drop off a key
(D) Log some work hours

남자는 다음으로 무엇을 할 것인가?
(A) 전화하기
(B) 계약서 준비하기
(C) 열쇠 가져다주기
(D) 업무 시간 기록하기

어휘 prepare 준비하다   contract 계약서   drop off 가져다주다
log 일지에 기록하다

해설 세부 사항 관련 – 남자가 다음에 할 일

남자가 마지막 대사에서 현재 세입자에게 전화하겠다(I'll call the current tenant)고 말하고 있으므로 정답은 (A)이다.

> Paraphrasing   대화의 call → 정답의 Make a phone call

47-49

M-Au	Hello, Ms. Bajaj. I'm glad we have a chance to meet today to discuss your business. What's your company's main goal?
W-Br	Well, **47 recently, my craft supply store has started receiving a lot of online orders.** It's important that I get feedback from those customers about the products that I'm selling.
M-Au	**48 We can design an online survey for you.** It's automatically e-mailed out to your customers a week after their order is delivered. We've had a lot of success getting people to respond to those.
W-Br	That's a great idea. **49 Then perhaps I could offer a future discount to any customer who completes the survey.**

남	안녕하세요, 바자즈 씨. 오늘 만나서 당신의 사업에 대해 얘기 나눌 기회가 생겨 기쁩니다. 회사의 주요 목표는 무엇인가요?
여	**최근 제 공예용품점이 온라인 주문을 많이 받기 시작했어요.** 제가 판매하는 제품에 대해 그런 고객들의 의견을 듣는 것이 중요합니다.
남	**저희가 온라인 설문 조사를 설계해 드릴 수 있습니다.** 주문 건이 배송되고 나서 일주일 후, 고객에게 자동으로 이메일이 발송됩니다. 사람들이 조사에 응답하게 한 성공 사례가 많이 있어요.
여	좋은 생각이네요. **그럼 설문 조사를 작성한 고객에게 추후 할인을 제공할 수 있겠네요.**

어휘 goal 목표   craft 공예   automatically 자동으로
respond to ~에 응답하다   perhaps 아마

47

According to the woman, what has recently happened at her business?
(A) Customers have complained.
(B) Inspections have been conducted.
(C) Online orders have increased.
(D) Shipments have been incomplete.

여자에 따르면, 여자의 업체에 최근 어떤 일이 있었는가?
(A) 고객들이 항의했다.
(B) 조사가 이뤄졌다.
(C) 온라인 주문이 증가했다.
(D) 수송품이 불완전했다.

어휘 complain 불평하다, 항의하다   inspection 점검, 조사   conduct 하다   increase 증가하다   shipment 수송, 수송품   incomplete 불완전한, 미완성의

해설 세부 사항 관련 – 여자의 업체에 최근 발생한 일

여자가 첫 대사에서 최근 자신의 공예용품점이 온라인 주문을 많이 받기 시작했다(recently, my craft supply store has started receiving a lot of online orders)고 말하고 있으므로 정답은 (C)이다.

> Paraphrasing   대화의 receiving a lot of online orders
> → 정답의 Online orders have increased.

48

What can the man's company do?
(A) Provide safety training
(B) Post demonstration videos
(C) Acquire more warehouse space
(D) Create customer surveys

남자의 업체는 무엇을 할 수 있는가?
(A) 안전 교육 제공
(B) 시연 동영상 게시
(C) 창고 공간 추가 확보
(D) 고객 설문 조사 개발

어휘 safety 안전 post 게시하다 demonstration (시범) 설명, 시연 acquire 획득하다 warehouse 창고

해설 세부 사항 관련 – 남자의 업체가 할 수 있는 일
남자가 두 번째 대사에서 온라인 설문 조사를 설계해 줄 수 있다(We can design an online survey for you)고 말하고 있으므로 정답은 (D)이다.

> Paraphrasing   대화의 design an online survey
> → 정답의 Create customer surveys

49

What does the woman say she could offer her customers?
(A) A discount
(B) Expedited shipping
(C) Free product samples
(D) A personal consultation

여자는 고객들에게 무엇을 제공할 수 있다고 말하는가?
(A) 할인
(B) 빠른 배송
(C) 무료 제품 견본
(D) 개인 상담

어휘 expedited 더 신속히 처리된, 촉진된 consultation 상담

해설 세부 사항 관련 – 여자가 고객들에게 제공할 수 있다고 말하는 것
여자가 마지막 대사에서 설문 조사를 작성한 고객에게 추후 할인을 제공할 수 있다(I could offer a future discount to any customer who completes the survey)고 말하고 있으므로 정답은 (A)이다.

50-52 3인 대화

M-Au Hello. I'm from District Flower Store, and I have your centerpiece order.

M-Cn ⁵⁰**Let me get the hotel's event manager here; she's the one that ordered. Yuliya?** You have a delivery from District Flower Store at reception.

W-Am Hi! I'm glad you're early. ⁵¹**The wedding's this evening**, but we're already setting up the ballroom.

M-Au I'll need you to acknowledge receipt. Could you sign here? And then, where should I unload your calla lily centerpieces?

W-Am Calla lilies? I ordered lilacs for the wedding centerpieces!

M-Au Oh, I wouldn't know. I just deliver.

W-Am Well, ⁵²**let me call your boss.** We need this sorted out right away.

남1 안녕하세요. 디스트릭트 플라워 스토어인데요. 주문하신 꽃 장식을 가져왔어요.

남2 **호텔 행사 관리자를 부를게요. 주문한 사람이거든요. 율리야?** 디스트릭트 플라워 스토어에서 리셉션에 배달 와 있어요.

여 안녕하세요! 일찍 와 주셔서 좋네요. **결혼식은 오늘 저녁인데** 이미 대연회장을 준비하고 있거든요.

남1 수령을 확인해 주셔야 합니다. 여기 서명해 주시겠어요? 그럼 칼라 꽃 장식을 어디에 내려 드릴까요?

여 칼라요? 저는 결혼식 꽃 장식으로 라일락을 주문했는데요!

남1 아, 저는 모릅니다. 저는 배달만 해요.

여 **사장님께 전화해 볼게요.** 당장 해결해야 해요.

어휘 centerpiece 테이블 중앙에 놓는 꽃 장식물 set up 준비하다 ballroom 대연회장 acknowledge receipt 수령을 확인하다 unload (짐을) 내리다 sort out 문제를 해결하다

50

Where most likely are the speakers?
(A) At a farm
(B) At a landscaping company
(C) At a hotel
(D) At a catering firm

화자들은 어디에 있겠는가?
(A) 농장
(B) 조경업체
(C) 호텔
(D) 케이터링 업체

해설 전체 내용 관련 – 대화의 장소
두 번째 남자가 첫 대사에서 호텔 행사 관리자를 부르겠다(Let me get the hotel's event manager here)면서 그 사람이 주문한 사람(she's the one that ordered)이라며 율리야(Yuliya?)를 부르고 있는 것으로 보아 대화의 장소가 호텔임을 알 수 있다. 따라서 정답은 (C)이다.

51

What type of event is going to take place?
(A) A wedding
(B) A flower exposition
(C) A grand opening
(D) A birthday party

어떤 행사가 열릴 예정인가?

(A) 결혼식
(B) 꽃 박람회
(C) 개업식
(D) 생일 파티

어휘 exposition 박람회, 전시회

해설 세부 사항 관련 – 열릴 예정인 행사

여자가 첫 대사에서 결혼식은 오늘 저녁(The wedding's this evening)이라고 말하고 있으므로 정답은 (A)이다.

52

What does the woman say she will do?
(A) Sign a receipt
(B) Adjust a schedule
(C) Add items to an order
(D) Call a supervisor

여자는 무엇을 할 것이라고 말하는가?
(A) 영수증에 서명하기
(B) 일정 조정하기
(C) 주문에 물품 추가하기
(D) 관리자에게 전화하기

어휘 adjust 조정하다 supervisor 관리자, 감독관

해설 세부 사항 관련 – 여자가 할 일

여자가 마지막 대사에서 사장님께 전화해 보겠다(let me call your boss)고 말하고 있으므로 정답은 (D)이다.

> **Paraphrasing** 대화의 boss → 정답의 supervisor

53-55 3인 대화

M-Cn	Excuse me, Ms. Campbell. **53 My engineer, Adisa, is still on your roof, but I just wanted to let you know we're almost done with the inspection.**
W-Br	How does everything look?
M-Cn	Oh, here's Adisa now. He can answer that.
M-Au	I conducted a thorough inspection. **54 There's no structural damage.** All of the support beams are intact, but **54 we'll have to replace some of the shingles that were blown away in the storm.**
W-Br	Well **54 that's a relief.** I was worried that I'd need major repairs.
M-Au	**55 I'm afraid you'll have to close your store while we replace the shingles.** But we'll be able to finish in one day.
M-Cn	**55 Does Tuesday work for you?**
W-Br	**55 That's fine.**

남1 실례합니다, 캠벨 씨. **저희 기술자 아디사가 아직 지붕 위에 있긴 하지만, 점검을 거의 마쳤다고 알려 드리려고요.**

여 전부 어떤가요?

남1 아, 아디사가 지금 왔네요. 대답해 드릴 수 있을 겁니다.

남2 제가 철저히 점검했는데요. **구조상의 손상은 없습니다.** 지지대는 모두 온전한데요. **폭풍에 날아가 버린 지붕널을 교체해야 할 겁니다.**

여 **그거 다행이네요.** 큰 수리를 해야 할까 봐 걱정했거든요.

남2 **지붕널을 교체하는 동안 가게를 닫으셔야 할 것 같습니다.** 하지만 하루만에 끝낼 수 있어요.

남1 **화요일 괜찮으세요?**

여 **좋아요.**

어휘	inspection 점검 conduct 하다 thorough 철저한, 꼼꼼한 structural 구조상의, 구조적인 support beam 지지대 intact 온전한 shingle 지붕널 blow away 불어 날리다 relief 안도

53

What kind of business do the men most likely work for?
(A) A fencing company
(B) A landscaping service
(C) A roofing company
(D) An auto repair shop

남자들은 어떤 종류의 업체에서 일하겠는가?
(A) 울타리 업체
(B) 조경 서비스 업체
(C) 지붕 공사 업체
(D) 자동차 정비소

어휘 fencing 울타리 landscaping 조경 roofing 지붕 공사

해설 전체 내용 관련 – 남자들의 근무 업종

첫 번째 남자가 첫 대사에서 기술자인 아디사가 아직 지붕 위에 있긴 하지만, 점검을 거의 마쳤다(My engineer, Adisa, is still on your roof, but I just wanted to let you know we're almost done with the inspection)고 말하는 것으로 보아 남자들은 지붕을 수리하는 일을 하고 있음을 알 수 있다. 따라서 정답은 (C)이다.

54

Why is the woman relieved?
(A) Some damage is minor.
(B) A delivery arrived early.
(C) Customer reviews are positive.
(D) The weather forecast is good.

여자는 왜 안심하는가?
(A) 훼손이 경미해서
(B) 택배가 일찍 도착해서
(C) 고객 후기가 긍정적이어서
(D) 일기 예보가 좋아서

어휘 relieved 안도하는 minor 가벼운, 작은 positive 긍정적인
weather forecast 일기 예보

해설 세부 사항 관련 – 여자가 안심하는 이유
두 번째 남자가 첫 대사에서 구조상의 손상은 없다(There's no
structural damage)며 폭풍에 날아가 버린 지붕널을 교체해야 할
것(we'll have to replace some of the shingles that were blown
away in the storm)이라고 하자 여자가 다행(that's a relief)이라고
말하고 있으므로 정답은 (A)이다.

55

What will the woman do on Tuesday?
(A) Wash her car
(B) Close her store
(C) Take some measurements
(D) Look at some material samples

여자는 화요일에 무엇을 할 것인가?
(A) 세차
(B) 가게 문 닫기
(C) 치수 재기
(D) 재료 견본 보기

어휘 take measurements 치수를 재다 material 재료

해설 세부 사항 관련 – 여자가 화요일에 할 일
두 번째 남자가 마지막 대사에서 지붕널을 교체하는 동안 가게를 닫아야
할 것 같다(I'm afraid you'll have to close your store while we
replace the shingles)고 했고, 이어서 첫 번째 남자가 화요일이
괜찮은지(Does Tuesday work for you?)를 묻자 여자가 좋다(That's
fine)고 말하는 것으로 보아 여자는 화요일에 가게 문을 닫을 것이라는
것을 알 수 있다. 따라서 정답은 (B)이다.

56-58

M-Au Hi, Erina. ⁵⁶I'm sorry about missing the
morning meeting! My commute was
horrendous.

W-Am No worries. The meeting notes will be sent
out. What happened?

M-Au ⁵⁷The Metro system's renovating some
station platforms, and it added an extra
half hour to my commute. Trains in both
directions are only using one track, and
⁵⁷the train's my only option!

W-Am Well, there is a rapid-transit bus service.

M-Au I wasn't aware of that. I'm still new to this
city. How do I get more information?

W-Am ⁵⁸I'll send you links to their Web site and
system map.

남 안녕하세요, 에리나. **오전 회의에 못 들어가서 미안해요!**
출근길이 끔찍했어요.

여 괜찮아요. 회의록이 발송될 거예요. 무슨 일이 있었나요?

남 **지하철 일부 역 플랫폼이 보수 공사 중이어서 제 출근 시간이**
30분이나 늘었어요. 단 하나의 선로를 양방향 열차가 모두
쓰고 있는데, **그 열차가 제 유일한 선택지예요!**

여 음, 고속 버스가 있잖아요.

남 몰랐어요. 아직 이 도시는 잘 몰라요. 자세한 정보는 어떻게
알 수 있을까요?

여 **웹사이트와 교통 체계 링크를 보내 드릴게요.**

어휘 miss 놓치다 commute 통근 horrendous 끔찍한,
참혹한 renovate 개조하다, 보수하다 add 더하다
direction 방향 rapid-transit 고속의 be aware of
~에 대해서 알다

56

Why does the man apologize?
(A) He missed a meeting.
(B) He has a poor Internet connection.
(C) He failed to complete an assignment.
(D) He lost his employee badge.

남자는 왜 사과하는가?
(A) 회의에 못 들어가서
(B) 인터넷 연결이 좋지 않아서
(C) 업무를 완료하지 못해서
(D) 사원증을 잃어버려서

어휘 apologize 사과하다 connection 연결 complete 완료하다,
끝마치다 assignment 과제, 업무 employee badge 사원증

해설 세부 사항 관련 – 남자가 사과하는 이유
남자가 첫 대사에서 오전 회의에 못 들어가서 미안하다(I'm sorry about
missing the morning meeting!)고 사과하고 있으므로 정답은 (A)이다.

57

Why does the woman say, "Well, there is a rapid-
transit bus service"?
(A) To praise improvements to a system
(B) To correct a mistaken assumption
(C) To express dissatisfaction
(D) To justify a decision

여자가 "음, 고속 버스가 있잖아요"라고 말하는 이유는?
(A) 제도 개선을 칭찬하려고
(B) 잘못된 추정을 바로잡으려고
(C) 불만을 표시하려고
(D) 결정을 정당화하려고

어휘 praise 칭찬하다 improvement 개선, 향상 correct
바로잡다 mistaken 잘못 알고 있는, 잘못된 assumption 추정
dissatisfaction 불만 justify 정당화하다, 해명하다 decision
결정, 결심

해설 화자의 의도 파악 – 고속 버스가 있다는 말의 의도

앞에서 남자가 지하철 일부 역 플랫폼이 보수 공사 중이어서 출근 시간이 30분이나 늘어났다(The Metro system's renovating some station platforms, and it added an extra half hour to my commute)고 했고 그 열차가 유일한 선택지(the train's my only option!)라고 말하자 여자가 인용문을 언급한 것으로 보아, 지하철이 유일한 선택지가 아니라 다른 교통편도 있다는 것을 알려주려는 의도로 한 말임을 알 수 있다. 따라서 정답은 (B)이다.

58

What will the woman do next?
(A) Download a ticket
(B) Pick up some clients
(C) Activate a key card
(D) Forward some Web-site links

여자는 다음으로 무엇을 할 것인가?
(A) 티켓 다운로드하기
(B) 고객 데리러 가기
(C) 카드키 작동시키기
(D) 웹사이트 링크 보내기

어휘 activate 작동시키다, 활성화시키다 forward 보내다

해설 세부 사항 관련 – 여자가 다음에 할 일
여자가 마지막 대사에서 웹사이트와 교통 체계 링크를 보내 주겠다(I'll send you links to their Web site and system map)고 말하고 있으므로 정답은 (D)이다.

Paraphrasing 대화의 send → 정답의 Forward

59-61

▶ 동영상 강의

M-Cn	Hello, Silvia. Good to see you again. **59My consultancy firm has been working hard to help you grow your clothing company.**
W-Br	Thanks. **59I never expected so much attention for my clothing designs, but I'm so pleased with the reactions.**
M-Cn	OK. **60What do you think about approaching Regents department stores?**
W-Br	They usually market to a younger clientele.
M-Cn	I see. **61Let me get you a list of other stores we also had in mind.**

남 안녕하세요, 실비아. 다시 만나서 반가워요. **저희 자문 회사는 고객님의 의류 회사가 성장하는 데 보탬이 되기 위해 열심히 노력하고 있습니다.**
여 감사합니다. **제 의류 디자인이 그렇게 크게 주목받을지 전혀 예상하지 못했지만 반응에 굉장히 기뻐요.**
남 네. **리젠트 백화점과 접촉하는 건 어떻게 생각하세요?**
여 거긴 보통 더 젊은 고객들을 대상으로 하잖아요.

남 알겠어요. **저희가 또 염두에 둔 다른 매장 목록을 드리죠.**

어휘 consultancy 자문 회사 attention 주목, 주의 reaction 반응 approach 접근하다, 접촉하다 department store 백화점 clientele 모든 고객들 have ~ in mind ~을 염두에 두다

59

Who is the woman?
(A) An architect
(B) A clothing designer
(C) A construction manager
(D) A department store director

여자는 누구인가?
(A) 건축가
(B) 의상 디자이너
(C) 공사 관리자
(D) 백화점 관리자

해설 전체 내용 관련 – 여자의 직업
남자가 첫 대사에서 남자의 자문 회사는 여자의 의류 회사가 성장하는 데 보탬이 되기 위해 열심히 노력하고 있다(My consultancy firm has been working hard to help you grow your clothing company)고 말하자 여자가 자신의 의류 디자인이 그렇게 크게 주목받을지 전혀 예상하지 못했는데 반응에 굉장히 기쁘다(I never expected so much attention for my clothing designs, but I'm so pleased with the reactions)고 말하고 있는 것으로 보아 여자는 의상 디자이너라는 것을 알 수 있다. 따라서 정답은 (B)이다.

60

Why does the woman say, "They usually market to a younger clientele"?
(A) To reject a suggestion
(B) To justify a decision
(C) To express disappointment
(D) To ask for clarification

여자가 "거긴 보통 더 젊은 고객들을 대상으로 하잖아요"라고 말하는 이유는?
(A) 제안을 거절하려고
(B) 결정을 정당화하려고
(C) 실망을 표시하려고
(D) 해명을 요구하려고

어휘 reject 거절하다 justify 정당화하다, 해명하다 disappointment 실망 clarification 해명

해설 화자의 의도 파악 – 거긴 보통 더 젊은 고객들을 대상으로 한다는 말의 의도
앞에서 남자가 리젠트 백화점과 접촉하는 건 어떻게 생각하는지(What do you think about approaching Regents department stores)를 묻자 여자가 인용문을 언급한 것으로 보아 남자가 제안하는 백화점은 고객층이 맞지 않아서 거절하려는 의도로 말한 것임을 알 수 있다. 따라서 정답은 (A)이다.

61

What does the man say he will give the woman?
(A) An area map
(B) A list of businesses
(C) Some photographs
(D) Some measurements

남자는 여자에게 무엇을 주겠다고 말하는가?
(A) 지역 지도
(B) 업체 목록
(C) 사진
(D) 치수

해설 세부 사항 관련 – 남자가 여자에게 주겠다고 하는 것
남자가 마지막 대사에서 또 염두에 둔 다른 매장 목록을 주겠다(Let me get you a list of other stores we also had in mind)고 말하고 있는 것으로 보아 정답은 (B)이다.

Paraphrasing	대화의 a list of other stores → 정답의 A list of businesses

62-64 대화 + 직원 명부

W-Am Luis, **62I noticed something while I was directing yesterday's rehearsal. 63I had a problem while I was trying to give some directions to the actors during act three.** I wanted to ask you about it since you're in charge of lighting.

M-Cn Sure. **63What is it?**

W-Am **63One of the footlights at the front of the stage was flickering**, which was distracting. It made it hard to see the actors' faces and costumes. Can you do something to fix it?

M-Cn Actually, I've already ordered a replacement. It should be here tomorrow.

W-Am Great. Thanks. **64I can't believe opening night is next week.** Everyone has put so much work into the show—it'll be great to have an audience.

여 루이스, **어제 리허설을 감독할 때 뭔가를 알게 됐어요. 3막에서 배우들에게 지시하려고 할 때 문제가 있었어요.** 조명을 맡고 계시니 이것에 관해 여쭤보고 싶었어요.

남 네. **그게 뭐죠?**

여 **무대 앞 바닥 조명 중 하나가 깜박거렸는데,** 집중이 안 되더라고요. 그것 때문에 배우들 얼굴과 의상을 보기가 어려웠어요. 수리를 좀 해 주실 수 있나요?

남 사실은 이미 교체품을 주문했어요. 내일 도착할 겁니다.

여 좋아요. 감사합니다. **첫날 밤 공연이 다음 주라니 믿기지 않네요.** 모두가 이 공연에 정말 많은 노력을 기울였어요. 관객이 들면 정말 좋을 것 같아요.

어휘 direct 감독하다 give directions 지시하다 in charge of ~을 맡고 있는, 담당하는 footlight 바닥 조명 flicker 깜박거리다 distracting 정신을 산만하게 하는 costume 의상 replacement 교체(품) audience 관객, 청중

Directory	
Liliana Flores	Set designer
62Svetlana Popova	Director
Lauren Campbell	Actor
So-Jin Park	Costume designer

명단	
릴리아나 플로레스	세트 디자이너
62스베틀라나 포포바	**감독**
로렌 캠벨	배우
소진 박	의상 디자이너

62

Look at the graphic. Who is the woman?
(A) Liliana Flores
(B) Svetlana Popova
(C) Lauren Campbell
(D) So-Jin Park

시각 정보에 의하면, 여자는 누구인가?
(A) 릴리아나 플로레스
(B) 스베틀라나 포포바
(C) 로렌 캠벨
(D) 소진 박

해설 시각 정보 연계 – 여자의 이름
여자가 첫 대사에서 리허설을 감독할 때 뭔가를 알게 됐다(I noticed something while I was directing yesterday's rehearsal)고 말하고 있고, 표에 따르면 감독은 스베틀라나 포포바이므로 정답은 (B)이다.

63

What problem do the speakers discuss?
(A) Some equipment is not working.
(B) Some costumes are not ready.
(C) Some music is distracting.
(D) An actor is late.

화자들은 어떤 문제를 논의하는가?
(A) 장비가 작동하지 않는다.
(B) 의상이 준비되지 않았다.
(C) 음악이 산만하다.
(D) 배우가 늦는다.

어휘 equipment 장비

해설 세부 사항 관련 – 화자들이 논의하는 문제점
여자가 첫 대사에서 3막에서 배우들에게 지시하려고 할 때 문제가 있었다(I had a problem ~)고 하자 남자가 그게 뭔지(What is it?)를 물었고,

여자가 무대 앞 바닥 조명 중 하나가 깜박거렸다(One of the footlights at the front of the stage was flickering)고 말하고 있으므로 정답은 (A)이다.

64

What will happen next week?
(A) A playwright will attend a show.
(B) Publicity photos will be taken.
(C) A play will open.
(D) A dress rehearsal will be held.

다음 주에 어떤 일이 있을 것인가?
(A) 극작가가 공연에 참석할 것이다.
(B) 홍보 사진을 찍을 것이다.
(C) 연극이 막을 올릴 것이다.
(D) 총연습이 열릴 것이다.

어휘 playwright 극작가, 대본 작가　publicity 홍보　dress rehearsal 총연습

해설 세부 사항 관련 – 다음 주에 일어날 일
여자가 마지막 대사에서 첫날 밤 공연이 다음 주라니 믿기지 않는다(I can't believe opening night is next week)고 말하고 있으므로 정답은 (C)이다.

65-67 대화 + 웹페이지

M-Au	Hey, Hiroko. **⁶⁵I got the e-mail invite to the company retreat. I'm surprised that it's in June this year, instead of September.**
W-Br	Yeah, we changed the dates so we could try out this venue. **⁶⁶I toured it last month and was really impressed. The rooms especially are so comfortable.** There weren't any openings in September, though.
M-Au	I'm sure it'll be worth the change. Your team in Human Resources plans great events.
W-Br	Here, I just pulled up their Web site. Take a look. Staff can choose one of these activities on the second day of the retreat.
M-Au	**⁶⁷I've never been kayaking. This looks like a good chance to try it.**

남	안녕하세요, 히로코 씨. **회사 야유회 이메일 초대장을 받았어요. 올해는 9월이 아니고 6월이라 놀랐어요.**
여	네, 이 장소로 한번 가보려고 날짜를 바꿨어요. **지난달에 돌아봤는데 정말 인상적이었거든요. 특히 객실이**

정말 편안해요. 그런데 9월엔 비는 방이 없더라고요.

남	바꾼 보람이 있을 거예요. 인사팀은 멋진 행사를 기획하시잖아요.
여	여기, 웹사이트를 열었어요. 한번 보세요. 직원들은 야유회 둘째 날 이 활동 중 하나를 선택할 수 있어요.
남	**저는 카약을 해 본 적이 없어요. 한번 해 볼 좋은 기회이겠네요.**

어휘 retreat 수련회, 야유회　venue 장소　impressed 인상 깊게 생각하는, 감명을 받은　especially 특히　comfortable 편안한　opening 빈자리, 공석　be worth ~의 가치가 있다　activity 활동

Adventure awaits you!

⁶⁷Kayaking led by Ketan Bora　　Fly-Fishing led by Beatriz Romero

Trail Biking led by Arnaud Fournier　　Hiking led by Brandon Murray

모험이 여러분을 기다립니다!

⁶⁷케탄 보라가 이끄는 카약　　베아트리츠 로메로가 이끄는 플라이 피싱

아너드 푸르니에가 이끄는 트레일 바이크　　브랜든 머레이가 이끄는 하이킹

어휘 adventure 모험　await 기다리다

65

Why is the man surprised?
(A) A new vacation policy was announced.
(B) A group is larger than expected.
(C) A price has increased.
(D) A date has been changed.

남자가 놀란 이유는?
(A) 새로운 휴가 정책이 발표돼서
(B) 단체가 예상보다 커서
(C) 가격이 올라서
(D) 날짜가 변경돼서

어휘 vacation policy 휴가 정책, 휴가 규정

해설 세부 사항 관련 – 남자가 놀라는 이유
남자가 첫 대사에서 회사 야유회 이메일 초대장을 받았다(I got the e-mail invite to the company retreat)며 올해는 9월이 아니고 6월이라 놀랐다(I'm surprised that it's in June this year, instead of September)고 말하는 것으로 보아, 남자는 회사 야유회 날짜가 변경된

것에 놀라고 있음을 알 수 있다. 따라서 정답은 (D)이다.

66

What does the woman like about a venue?
(A) The comfortable rooms
(B) The food selection
(C) The views
(D) The fitness center

여자는 장소에 대해 어떤 점을 마음에 들어 하는가?
(A) 편안한 객실
(B) 음식 메뉴
(C) 전망
(D) 피트니스 센터

어휘 selection 선택, 선택 가능한 것들의 집합

해설 세부 사항 관련 – 여자가 장소에 대해 마음에 들어 하는 점
여자가 첫 대사에서 지난달에 돌아봤는데 정말 인상적이었다(I toured it last month and was really impressed)며 특히 객실이 정말 편안했다(The rooms especially are so comfortable)고 말하고 있으므로 정답은 (A)이다.

67

Look at the graphic. Who will lead the activity the man is interested in?
(A) Ketan Bora
(B) Beatriz Romero
(C) Arnaud Fournier
(D) Brandon Murray

시각 정보에 의하면, 남자가 관심이 있는 활동은 누가 이끄는가?
(A) 케탄 보라
(B) 베아트리츠 로메로
(C) 아너드 푸르니에
(D) 브랜든 머레이

해설 시각 정보 연계 – 남자가 관심이 있는 활동을 이끄는 사람
남자가 마지막 대사에서 카약을 해 본 적이 없다(I've never been kayaking)며 한번 해 볼 좋은 기회(This looks like a good chance to try it)라고 말하면서 카약에 관심을 보이고 있고, 웹페이지에 따르면 카약을 이끄는 사람은 케탄 보라이므로 정답은 (A)이다.

68-70 대화 + 현장 지도

M-Cn Hi. **68 You must be with the camera crew.** I'm Hector, head archaeologist here at the Arnaud Castle dig site.

W-Am Nice to meet you. I'm Ling. **68 Since it's our first day of filming for our TV documentary special,** we're mainly going to capture general footage of your team at work.

M-Cn Great! **69 We're working in quadrant two today.** We've been finding lots of pottery, so you may capture us unearthing more.

W-Am I see. This excavation has been a lengthy process, right?

M-Cn It has. We'd actually hoped to be further along, but **70 there've been lots of thunderstorms lately, which have slowed things down.**

남	안녕하세요. **촬영팀이시군요.** 저는 이곳 아너드성 발굴지의 수석 고고학자 헥터입니다.
여	만나서 반갑습니다. 저는 링이에요. **저희 TV 특집 다큐멘터리 촬영 첫날이니** 팀이 작업하시는 일반 영상을 주로 담을 겁니다.
남	좋아요! **오늘은 제2사분면에서 작업 중입니다.** 많은 도자기를 발견했으니 저희가 더 파내는 모습을 담을 수 있겠네요.
여	알겠습니다. 이 발굴 작업은 긴 과정이었죠, 그렇죠?
남	맞습니다. 실은 더 진척되길 바랐는데 **최근 뇌우가 많이 발생해서 작업이 늦어졌어요.**

| 어휘 | archaeologist 고고학자 dig site 발굴지, 유적지 capture 담다 footage 영상, 장면 quadrant 사분면 pottery 도자기 unearth 파내다 excavation 발굴 lengthy 너무 긴, 지루한 process 과정, 절차 thunderstorm 뇌우 slow down (속도, 진행을) 늦추다 |

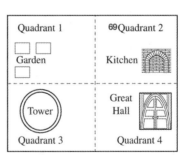

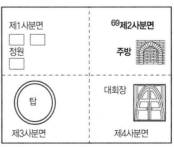

68

What is the conversation mostly about?
(A) Organizing an exhibit
(B) Arranging a public tour
(C) Filming a documentary
(D) Requesting financial support

대화는 주로 무엇에 관한 것인가?
(A) 전시회 준비
(B) 대중 투어 준비
(C) 다큐멘터리 촬영
(D) 재정 지원 요청

어휘 organize 조직하다, 준비하다 arrange 마련하다, 준비하다
　　financial 금융의, 재정의

해설 전체 내용 관련 – 대화의 주제
남자가 첫 대사에서 촬영팀인 것(You must be with the camera crew)을 확인했고, 여자가 TV 특집 다큐멘터리 촬영 첫날(Since it's our first day of filming for our TV documentary special)이라고 말하고 있으므로 정답은 (C)이다.

69

Look at the graphic. Which part of the castle is being excavated today?
(A) The garden
(B) The kitchen
(C) The tower
(D) The great hall

시각 정보에 의하면, 오늘은 성의 어떤 부분을 발굴하는가?
(A) 정원
(B) 주방
(C) 탑
(D) 대회당

해설 시각 정보 연계 – 오늘 발굴하는 성의 부분
남자가 두 번째 대사에서 오늘은 제2사분면에서 작업 중(We're working in quadrant two today)이라고 말하고 있고, 시각 정보에 의하면 제2사분면은 주방이라고 표기되어 있으므로 정답은 (B)이다.

70

According to the man, why has some work been delayed?
(A) An archaeological team is very small.
(B) Weather conditions have been poor.
(C) A source of funding was unavailable.
(D) New volunteers required special training.

남자에 따르면, 일부 작업이 왜 지연됐는가?
(A) 고고학 팀 규모가 너무 작아서
(B) 기상 조건이 좋지 않아서
(C) 자금원을 구할 수 없어서
(D) 새 자원봉사자들에게 특별 교육이 필요해서

어휘 condition 조건 funding 자금, 기금 unavailable 구할 수 없는

해설 세부 사항 관련 – 일부 작업이 지연된 이유
남자가 마지막 대사에서 최근 뇌우가 많이 발생해서 작업이 늦어졌다(there've been lots of thunderstorms lately, which have slowed things down)고 말하고 있으므로 정답은 (B)이다.

> **Paraphrasing**　대화의 there've been lots of thunderstorms
> → 정답의 Weather conditions have been poor.

PART 4

71-73 녹음 메시지

W-Am Hello. **71 You've reached Imperial Electric and Gas, the number one power company in the Northeast region.** Please hold for the next available representative. If you're calling about reported electrical outages in Cedar Springs, **72 rest assured that technicians are on-site now and services will be fully restored this afternoon.** Or **73 if you've recently moved and are calling to either start or stop services, please visit our Web site to fill out a form to have a work order completed.** Thank you.

안녕하세요. **북동부 지역 최고의 전력업체, 임페리얼 전기 가스입니다.** 응대 가능한 다음 상담원을 기다려 주십시오. 보도된 시더 스프링스 정전에 관해 전화하셨다면 **기술자들이 지금 현장에 나가 있으며 오늘 오후면 서비스가 완전히 복구될 것이니 안심하시기 바랍니다.** 혹은 최근 이사를 해서 서비스를 개시하거나 중지하기 위해 전화를 하셨다면, 저희 웹사이트에 방문하셔서 서식을 작성하여 작업 주문서를 완료해 주십시오. 감사합니다.

어휘 reach (전화로) 연락하다 region 지역 hold (전화를 끊지 않고) 기다리다 available 시간이 되는, 이용 가능한 representative 대표, 대리인 electrical outage 정전 rest assured that ~을 믿어도 된다 technician 기술자 on-site 현장에 restore 복구하다, 회복시키다 fill out 기입하다, 작성하다

71

What kind of business recorded the message?
(A) A city planning office
(B) A cybersecurity firm
(C) A utility company
(D) An electronics repair shop

어떤 종류의 업체에서 메시지를 녹음했는가?
(A) 도시 계획 사무소
(B) 사이버 보안 업체
(C) 공익 기업
(D) 전자 제품 수리점

어휘 utility (전기, 수도, 가스 등의) 공익 사업 electronics 전자 장치

해설 전체 내용 관련 – 메시지를 녹음한 업체
화자가 도입부에 북동부 지역 최고의 전력업체, 임페리얼 전기 가스 (You've reached Imperial Electric and Gas, the number one power company in the Northeast region)라고 업체를 소개하고 있으므로 정답은 (C)이다.

> **Paraphrasing** 담화의 power company
> → 정답의 A utility company

72

What does the speaker say will happen this afternoon?
(A) A problem will be resolved.
(B) A shipment will be delivered.
(C) Some software will be updated.
(D) Some refreshments will be offered.

화자는 오늘 오후에 어떤 일이 있을 것이라고 말하는가?
(A) 문제가 해결될 것이다.
(B) 수송품이 배송될 것이다.
(C) 소프트웨어가 업데이트될 것이다.
(D) 다과가 제공될 것이다.

어휘 resolve 해결하다 shipment 수송, 수송품 refreshments 다과

해설 세부 사항 관련 – 오늘 오후에 있을 일
화자가 중반부에 기술자들이 지금 현장에 나가 있으며 오늘 오후면 서비스가 완전히 복구될 것이니 안심하길 바란다(rest assured that technicians are on-site now and services will be fully restored this afternoon)고 말하고 있으므로 오늘 오후에 정전 문제가 해결될 것임을 알 수 있다. 따라서 정답은 (A)이다.

> **Paraphrasing** 담화의 services will be fully restored
> → 정답의 A problem will be resolved.

73

What does the speaker say is available on a Web site?
(A) Customer reviews
(B) Work order forms
(C) Business hours
(D) Product manuals

화자는 웹사이트에서 무엇을 이용할 수 있다고 말하는가?
(A) 고객 후기
(B) 작업 주문서 양식
(C) 운영 시간
(D) 제품 설명서

어휘 business hours 운영 시간, 영업시간 manual 설명서

해설 세부 사항 관련 – 화자가 웹사이트에서 이용할 수 있다고 말하는 것
화자가 마지막에 서비스를 개시하거나 중지하기 위해 전화를 했다면, 웹사이트에 방문해서 서식을 작성하여 작업 주문서를 완료해 달라(~ please visit our Web site to fill out a form to have a work order completed)고 말하고 있으므로 정답은 (B)이다.

W-Br **⁷⁴This weekend, we'll be installing new security software on our internal servers.** This is a little more involved than a routine update—⁷⁴**we need to have an extra layer of protection on our customers' personal data.** So, we're all being asked to help prepare for this event. ⁷⁵**Before we leave the office on Friday, we'll need to shut down our computers to enable the patch.** ⁷⁶**Marta Fuentes is here to explain how we'll finish the installation on our devices when we come in on Monday.**

이번 주말에 내부 서버에 새 보안 소프트웨어를 설치할 예정입니다. 이번은 평상시 업데이트보다 조금 더 복잡합니다. 고객 개인 정보를 보호하는 단계가 추가되어야 하기 때문입니다. 그래서 우리 모두 이 일의 준비를 도와 달라는 요청을 받는 것입니다. 금요일에 사무실을 나서기 전, 패치가 가능하도록 컴퓨터를 꺼야 합니다. 월요일에 출근하면 마르타 푸엔테스가 와서 우리 기기에 설치를 완료하는 방법을 설명해 줄 것입니다.

어휘 install 설치하다 security 보안 internal 내부의 involved 복잡한 routine 일상의, 보통의 layer 층 protection 보호 shut down 문을 닫다, (기계를) 정지시키다 enable 가능하게 하다 device 기기, 장비

74

According to the speaker, why is a change being made?
(A) To keep track of expenses
(B) To help a business expand
(C) To improve security
(D) To attract job applicants

화자에 따르면, 왜 변경이 이뤄지는가?
(A) 경비를 기록하려고
(B) 사업체 확장을 도우려고
(C) 보안을 강화하려고
(D) 구직자를 끌어모으려고

어휘 keep track of ~을 기록하다 expense 경비, 비용 expand 확장시키다, 확대되다 improve 향상시키다, 개선하다 attract 끌어모으다, 이끌다

해설 세부 사항 관련 – 변경이 이뤄지는 이유
화자가 도입부에 이번 주말에 내부 서버에 새 보안 소프트웨어를 설치할 예정(This weekend, we'll be installing new security software on our internal servers)이라고 하면서 고객 개인 정보를 보호하는 단계가 추가되어야 한다(we need to have an extra layer of protection on our customers' personal data)고 말하고 있으므로 정답은 (C)이다.

> **Paraphrasing** 담화의 to have an extra layer of protection on our customers' personal data
> → 정답의 To improve security

75

What are the listeners asked to do?
(A) Shut down their computers
(B) Reduce their expenses
(C) Consult with their department managers
(D) Create an equipment inventory

청자들은 무엇을 하라고 요청받는가?
(A) 컴퓨터 끄기
(B) 비용 줄이기
(C) 부서 관리자와 협의하기
(D) 장비 목록 작성하기

어휘 reduce 줄이다, 축소하다 consult 상의하다, 협의하다
equipment 장비 inventory 물품 목록

해설 세부 사항 관련 – 청자들이 요청받은 일
화자가 중반부에 금요일에 사무실을 나서기 전, 패치가 가능하도록 컴퓨터를 꺼야 한다(~ we'll need to shut down our computers to enable the patch)고 말하고 있으므로 정답은 (A)이다.

76

What department does Marta Fuentes most likely work in?
(A) Legal
(B) Marketing
(C) Human Resources
(D) Information Technology

마르타 푸엔테스는 어떤 부서에서 일하겠는가?
(A) 법무
(B) 마케팅
(C) 인사
(D) 정보 기술

해설 세부 사항 관련 – 마르타 푸엔테스의 근무 부서
화자가 마지막에 월요일에 출근하면 마르타 푸엔테스가 와서 기기에 설치를 완료하는 방법을 설명해 줄 것(Marta Fuentes is here to explain how we'll finish the installation on our devices when we come in on Monday)이라고 말하는 것으로 보아 마르타 푸엔테스는 소프트웨어 설치 업무를 하고 있다는 것을 알 수 있다. 따라서 정답은 (D)이다.

77-79 공지

M-Cn 77 **Let me remind everyone that starting on Monday, the main entrance to the office building will be inaccessible while the road is being widened and repaved.** This also means that our usual parking lot won't be available. But don't worry—there's plenty of space in the parking garage next to the Jay Building. 78 **For your convenience, the company will be providing a van service that will run every fifteen minutes until the project is completed.** The van will operate between seven and nine A.M., and then again between four and six P.M. 79 **We'll be posting project updates on our Web site, so be sure to check it regularly.**

모두에게 다시 알려드립니다. 월요일부터 도로를 넓히고 재포장하는 동안, 사무실 건물 정문을 이용할 수 없습니다. 이는 평상시 주차장을 사용할 수 없다는 뜻이기도 하죠. 하지만 걱정 마세요. 제이 빌딩 옆 주차장에 공간이 많으니까요. **여러분의 편의를 위해, 회사에서는 프로젝트가 종료될 때까지 매 15분마다 운행되는 밴 서비스를 제공할 예정입니다.** 밴은 아침 7시부터 9시까지 운행되며 오후 4시부터 6시까지 다시 운행됩니다. **웹사이트에 프로젝트 최신 소식을 올릴 테니 주기적으로 확인해 주세요.**

어휘 main entrance 정문 inaccessible 접근이 어려운, 접근이 불가능한 widen 넓히다 repave 재포장하다 available 이용 가능한 plenty of 많은 convenience 편리함, 편의 operate 가동시키다, 운용되다 post 게시하다 regularly 주기적으로

77

According to the speaker, what will begin on Monday?
(A) A seasonal internship program
(B) Road construction
(C) Landscaping maintenance
(D) An equipment upgrade

화자에 따르면, 월요일에 무엇이 시작될 것인가?
(A) 계절 인턴십 프로그램
(B) 도로 공사
(C) 조경 유지보수
(D) 장비 업그레이드

어휘 seasonal 계절의 construction 건설, 공사 landscaping 조경
maintenance 유지보수 equipment 장비

해설 세부 사항 관련 – 월요일에 시작될 일
화자가 도입부에 월요일부터 도로를 넓히고 재포장하는 동안, 사무실 건물 정문을 이용할 수 없다(~ starting on Monday, the main entrance to the office building will be inaccessible while the road is being widened and repaved)는 것을 알리고 있으므로 정답은 (B)이다.

Paraphrasing 담화의 the road is being widened and repaved → 정답의 Road construction

78

What will the company provide for the listeners?
(A) Free lunch
(B) New identification badges
(C) Parking passes
(D) Transportation

회사는 청자들에게 무엇을 제공할 것인가?
(A) 무료 점심 식사
(B) 새로운 신분 확인 명찰
(C) 주차권
(D) 교통편

어휘 identification 신분 확인

해설 세부 사항 관련 - 회사가 청자들에게 제공할 것
화자가 중반부에 편의를 위해, 회사에서는 프로젝트가 종료될 때까지 매 15분마다 운행되는 밴 서비스를 제공할 예정(For your convenience, the company will be providing a van service ~)이라고 말하고 있으므로 정답은 (D)이다.

> **Paraphrasing** 담화의 a van service
> → 정답의 Transportation

79

Why should the listeners visit a Web site?
(A) To download a map
(B) To post feedback
(C) To fill out a registration form
(D) To read project updates

청자들은 왜 웹사이트를 방문해야 하는가?
(A) 지도를 다운로드하려고
(B) 피드백을 게시하려고
(C) 등록 서류를 작성하려고
(D) 프로젝트 최신 소식을 읽으려고

해설 세부 사항 관련 - 청자들이 웹사이트를 방문해야 하는 이유
화자가 마지막에 웹사이트에 프로젝트 최신 소식을 올릴 테니 주기적으로 확인할 것(We'll be posting project updates on our Web site, so be sure to check it regularly)을 요청하고 있으므로 정답은 (D)이다.

> **Paraphrasing** 담화의 check → 정답의 read

80-82 전화 메시지

W-Br Hi, Asako. **80 I'm following up about the hotel you asked me to book for our client visiting from India next month.** **81 You wanted to reserve a room for her at the Maple Lodge, but it's fully booked that week. So I've been looking at other hotels in the area**, and there is one on Jefferson Avenue. It's a little farther from our office, but it looks like a nice place. **82 They also have a complimentary shuttle bus that can take our guest back and forth from our office.** Call me and let me know what you think.

안녕하세요, 아사코. **다음 달 인도에서 오시는 고객을 위해 예약해 달라고 요청하신 호텔에 관해 알려드립니다. 메이플 롯지에 객실 예약을 원하셨는데요. 그 주는 예약이 다 찼어요. 그래서 그 지역의 다른 호텔을 보고 있는데** 제퍼슨 가에 하나 있어요. 사무실에서는 좀 더 멀지만 좋은 곳인 것 같습니다. **고객을 태우고 사무실을 오갈 무료 셔틀버스도 있어요.** 전화 주셔서 어떻게 생각하시는지 알려 주세요.

어휘 follow up 덧붙이다, 더 알아보다, 후속 조치를 하다 book 예약하다 reserve 예약하다 fully booked 예약이 다 찬

---

farther 더 먼 complimentary 무료의 back and forth 왔다 갔다, 앞뒤로

80

What is the speaker preparing for?
(A) A client visit
(B) A branch opening
(C) A job fair
(D) An equipment upgrade

화자는 무엇을 준비하는가?
(A) 고객 방문
(B) 지점 개업
(C) 취업 박람회
(D) 장비 업그레이드

어휘 branch 지사, 분점 equipment 장비

해설 세부 사항 관련 - 화자가 준비하고 있는 일
화자가 초반부에 다음 달 인도에서 오는 고객을 위해 예약해 달라고 요청한 호텔에 관해 알린다(I'm following up about the hotel you asked me to book for our client visiting from India next month)고 말하고 있으므로 정답은 (A)이다.

> **Paraphrasing** 담화의 our client visiting from India
> → 정답의 A client visit

81

Why does the speaker say, "there is one on Jefferson Avenue"?
(A) To express surprise
(B) To correct some information
(C) To complain about a decision
(D) To recommend an alternative

화자가 "제퍼슨 가에 하나 있어요"라고 말하는 이유는?
(A) 놀라움을 표현하려고
(B) 정보를 바로잡으려고
(C) 결정에 대해 항의하려고
(D) 대안을 추천하려고

어휘 express 표현하다 correct 바로잡다 complain 불평하다, 항의하다 decision 결심, 결정 alternative 대안

해설 화자의 의도 파악 - 제퍼슨 가에 하나 있다는 말의 의도
앞에서 메이플 롯지에 객실 예약을 원했는데 그 주는 예약이 다 찼다(You wanted to reserve a room for her at the Maple Lodge, but it's fully booked that week)며 그 지역의 다른 호텔을 보고 있다(So I've been looking at other hotels in the area)고 말한 뒤 인용문을 언급한 것으로 보아, 메이플 롯지 대신에 지역 내 다른 호텔을 추천하려는 의도로 한 말임을 알 수 있다. 따라서 정답은 (D)이다.

82

What additional service is mentioned?
(A) A catered meal
(B) A shuttle bus
(C) Technical support
(D) Secure storage

어떤 추가 서비스가 언급되는가?
(A) 케이터링 식사
(B) 셔틀버스
(C) 기술 지원
(D) 안전한 보관 시설

어휘 additional 추가의 support 지원

해설 세부 사항 관련 – 언급된 추가 서비스
화자가 후반부에 고객을 태우고 사무실을 오갈 무료 셔틀버스도
있다(They also have a complimentary shuttle bus that can take
our guest back and forth from our office)고 말하고 있으므로
정답은 (B)이다.

83-85 회의 발췌

> **M-Cn** I'd like to start by giving everyone an update
> on our latest project. As you know, in order to
> stay on top as a leading shipping company, [83]**we
> need to continually make changes to meet our
> customers' expectations.** Since our customers
> prefer doing almost everything digitally, [84]**we're
> going to introduce a new delivery tracking service.
> By using a smartphone application, customers
> will be able to see where their package is in real
> time.** Of course, implementing this will be a major
> project for us and will take place over the coming
> year. So [85]**next month, we'll begin working with
> developers from XKP Software on creating this
> tracking service.**

저희 최근 프로젝트의 최신 소식을 전해 드리면서 시작하겠습니다. 아
시다시피, 앞서가는 배송업체로서 선두를 지키려면, **고객의 기대에 부
응하기 위해 끊임없이 변화할 필요가 있습니다.** 고객이 거의 모든 것을
디지털로 하는 걸 선호하니 **새로운 배송 추적 서비스를 도입하려고 합
니다. 고객들은 스마트폰 앱을 활용해 자신의 소포가 어디에 있는지 실
시간으로 확인할 수 있을 것입니다.** 물론 이를 시행하는 것은 우리에게
중요한 프로젝트로, 내년 한 해 동안 이뤄질 것입니다. **그래서 다음 달
에 XKP 소프트웨어의 개발자들과 협력해 추적 서비스를 만들기 시작
할 것입니다.**

어휘 latest 최신의, 최근의 leading 앞서가는, 선도하는
continually 끊임없이, 부단히 expectation 기대 introduce
소개하다, 도입하다 tracking 추적 in real time 즉시,
실시간으로 implement 시행하다 developer 개발자

83

According to the speaker, why are some changes
needed?
(A) To retain employees
(B) To attract investors
(C) To satisfy customers
(D) To increase productivity

화자에 따르면, 변화가 필요한 이유는?
(A) 직원들을 계속 보유하기 위해
(B) 투자자를 끌어모으기 위해
(C) 고객을 만족시키기 위해
(D) 생산성을 늘리기 위해

어휘 retain 보유하다, 계속 유지하다 attract 이끌다, 끌어모으다
        investor 투자자 satisfy 만족시키다 productivity 생산성

해설 세부 사항 관련 – 변화가 필요한 이유
화자가 초반부에 고객의 기대에 부응하기 위해 끊임없이 변화할 필
요가 있다(we need to continually make changes to meet our
customers' expectations)고 말하고 있으므로 정답은 (C)이다.

> **Paraphrasing** 담화의 to meet our customers'
>   expectations
>   → 정답의 To satisfy customers

84

What additional service does the company plan to
offer?
(A) Free product returns
(B) Expedited bulk shipping
(C) Pickup at self-service kiosks
(D) Real-time package tracking

회사는 어떤 추가 서비스를 제공할 계획인가?
(A) 무료 반품
(B) 신속 대량 배송
(C) 셀프 서비스 주문대에서 수령
(D) 실시간 배송 추적

어휘 expedite 신속히 처리하다 bulk 대량

해설 세부 사항 관련 – 회사가 제공할 계획인 추가 서비스
화자가 중반부에 새로운 배송 추적 서비스를 도입하려고 한다(we're
going to introduce a new delivery tracking service)며 고객들은 스
마트폰 앱을 활용해 자신의 소포가 어디에 있는지 실시간으로 볼 수 있을
것(By using a smartphone application, customers will be able
to see where their package is in real time)이라고 말하고 있으므로
정답은 (D)이다.

> **Paraphrasing** 담화의 see where their package is in real
>   time → 정답의 Real-time package tracking

85

According to the speaker, what will begin next month?
(A) A workshop series
(B) A new corporate policy
(C) A land development project
(D) A business collaboration

화자에 따르면, 다음 달에 무엇이 시작되는가?
(A) 일련의 워크숍
(B) 새 회사 정책
(C) 토지 개발 프로젝트
(D) 업체 협력

어휘 corporate 회사의 policy 정책 development 개발
collaboration 협력

해설 세부 사항 관련 – 다음 달에 시작될 일
화자가 마지막에 다음 달에 XKP 소프트웨어의 개발자들과 협력해 추적 서비스를 만들기 시작할 것(next month, we'll begin working with developers from XKP Software on creating this tracking service)이라고 말하고 있으므로 정답은 (D)이다.

> Paraphrasing 담화의 working with developers from XKP Software
> → 정답의 A business collaboration

86-88 담화

> **W-Br** I'm so happy we got the exclusive video footage of the mayor's response today. **86 We were able to beat the other networks in getting that interview to the public!** I wanted to give you all a heads-up that **87 next month we'll be providing a behind-the-scenes tour for students who are exploring our field as a potential career path.** They'll see things like the assignment coordination desk, our studios, and the control room. **88 I'm looking for a few volunteers who can spare an hour of their time to do this. Please e-mail me if you're interested.**
>
> 오늘 시장의 답변을 담은 독점 영상을 구할 수 있어서 무척 기쁩니다. **다른 방송국을 제치고 그 인터뷰를 대중에게 전할 수 있었어요!** 다음 달 우리 분야를 잠재적인 진로로 생각하고 답사하는 학생들에게 현장 견학을 제공할 것임을 여러분께 알려 드리고 싶습니다. 업무 조정 데스크, 스튜디오, 조정실 같은 것들을 볼 거예요. **이 일에 한 시간을 할애해 줄 수 있는 자원봉사자를 찾고 있습니다. 관심이 있으시면 이메일을 보내주세요.**
>
> 어휘 exclusive 독점적인 video footage 비디오 영상
> response 응답 beat 이기다 network 방송국 heads-up
> 알림 behind-the-scenes 무대 뒤편의, 배후의 explore
> 답사하다, 탐험하다 potential 잠재적인 career path 진로
> volunteer 자원봉사자 spare (시간을) 내다, 할애하다

86

What industry does the speaker most likely work in?
(A) Civil service
(B) Hospitality
(C) Media
(D) Architecture

화자는 어떤 업계에서 일하겠는가?
(A) 공무
(B) 접객 서비스
(C) 미디어
(D) 건축

해설 전체 내용 관련 – 화자의 근무 업계
화자가 초반부에 다른 방송국을 제치고 그 인터뷰를 대중에게 전할 수 있었다(We were able to beat the other networks in getting that interview to the public)며 방송국과 인터뷰에 대해 언급하고 있는 것으로 보아 화자는 미디어 업계에서 근무하고 있다는 것을 알 수 있다. 따라서 정답은 (C)이다.

87

What is planned for next month?
(A) A retirement luncheon
(B) An employee-performance review
(C) A computer-system upgrade
(D) A tour of a facility

다음 달에 무엇이 계획되어 있는가?
(A) 은퇴 기념 오찬
(B) 인사 고과
(C) 컴퓨터 시스템 업그레이드
(D) 시설 견학

어휘 retirement 은퇴, 퇴직 luncheon 오찬

해설 세부 사항 관련 – 다음 달에 계획되어 있는 일
화자가 중반부에 다음 달 학생들에게 현장 견학을 제공할 것(next month we'll be providing a behind-the-scenes tour for students ~)이라고 말하고 있으므로 정답은 (D)이다.

> Paraphrasing 담화의 a behind-the-scenes tour
> → 정답의 A tour of a facility

88

Who should send the speaker an e-mail?
(A) Those going on vacation
(B) Those willing to volunteer
(C) Those wishing to provide feedback
(D) Those presenting at a conference

화자에게 누가 이메일을 보내야 하는가?
(A) 휴가를 가는 사람
(B) 자원봉사를 할 의향이 있는 사람
(C) 피드백을 제공하고 싶은 사람
(D) 회의에 참석하는 사람

어휘 go on vacation 휴가를 가다   be willing to 흔쾌히 ~하다
present 참석하다   conference 회의

해설 세부 사항 관련 – 화자에게 이메일을 발송할 사람

화자가 후반부에 이 일에 한 시간을 할애해 줄 수 있는 자원봉사자를 찾고
있다(I'm looking for a few volunteers who can spare an hour
of their time to do this)며 관심이 있으면 이메일을 보내 달라(Please
e-mail me if you're interested)고 요청하고 있으므로 정답은 (B)이다.

Paraphrasing 담화의 ovens and refrigerators
→ 정답의 Kitchen appliances

89-91 회의 발췌

> M-Au Congratulations on a successful third
> quarter, everyone! **89 You've all done such a great
> job selling our ovens and refrigerators that we've
> already exceeded our sales expectations for the
> year!** **90 To celebrate, we'd like to invite the sales
> team to join us for a company dinner.** The dinner
> will be held on Thursday, December twentieth
> at the Canterbury Restaurant. **91 You might want
> to carpool or take public transportation to the
> event—the restaurant is near the stadium** and
> there's a sports event that night.

> 여러분, 성공적인 3분기를 축하합니다! **모두들 오븐과 냉장고 판매를
> 너무 잘해 주셔서 올해 예상 매출액을 이미 초과했어요!** 축하하기 위해
> **영업팀을 초대해 함께 회식을 했으면 합니다.** 저녁 식사는 12월 20일
> 목요일 캔터베리 레스토랑에서 있을 겁니다. 카풀을 하시거나 대중교통
> 을 이용해 행사장에 오시는 것이 좋을 겁니다. 식당은 경기장 근처로,
> 그날 밤에 스포츠 행사가 있습니다.

> 어휘 successful 성공적인   quarter 분기   refrigerator
> 냉장고   exceed 초과하다   expectation 예상   celebrate
> 축하하다, 기념하다

89

What does the speaker's company most likely sell?
(A) Beauty supplies
(B) Kitchen appliances
(C) Books
(D) Sporting goods

화자의 회사는 무엇을 판매하겠는가?
(A) 미용용품
(B) 주방용 기기
(C) 책
(D) 스포츠 상품

해설 전체 내용 관련 – 화자의 회사가 판매하는 것

화자가 초반부에 모두들 오븐과 냉장고 판매를 너무 잘해 주었다(You've
all done such a great job selling our ovens and refrigerators
~)고 말하고 있으므로 회사가 주방용 기기를 판매한다는 것을 알 수 있다.
따라서 정답은 (B)이다.

90

What event does the speaker invite the listeners to?
(A) A sales workshop
(B) A product demonstration
(C) A celebratory dinner
(D) A concert

화자는 청자들을 어떤 행사에 초대하는가?
(A) 영업 워크숍
(B) 제품 시연
(C) 축하 저녁 식사
(D) 음악회

어휘 demonstration 시연, 시범 설명   celebratory 기념하는,
축하하는

해설 세부 사항 관련 – 화자가 청자들을 초대한 행사

화자가 중반부에 축하하기 위해 영업팀을 초대해 함께 회식을 했으면
한다(To celebrate, we'd like to invite the sales team to join us for
a company dinner)고 말하고 있으므로 정답은 (C)이다.

91

What does the speaker mean when he says, "there's a
sports event that night"?
(A) The office will be closed.
(B) Parking will be limited.
(C) A meeting will be rescheduled.
(D) The listeners should buy some tickets.

남자가 "그날 밤에 스포츠 행사가 있습니다"라고 말하는 의도는 무엇인가?
(A) 사무실을 닫을 것이다.
(B) 주차가 제한될 것이다.
(C) 회의 일정이 변경될 것이다.
(D) 청자들은 표를 사야 한다.

어휘 limited 한정된, 제한된   reschedule 일정을 변경하다

해설 화자의 의도 파악 – 그날 밤에 스포츠 행사가 있다는 말의 의도

앞에서 카풀을 하거나 대중교통을 이용해서 행사장에 오는 것이 좋을
것(You might want to carpool or take public transportation to
the event)이라고 했고 식당은 경기장 근처(the restaurant is near
the stadium)라고 말한 뒤 인용문을 언급한 것으로 보아, 경기 때문에
주차가 어려울 것이라는 의도로 한 말임을 알 수 있다. 따라서 정답은
(B)이다.

92-94 공지

> W-Am I hope you've enjoyed this tour of historic
> homes in Salona City. **92 I founded this tour
> company five years ago,** and I'm happy to

announce that next month my company's expanding its offerings. **93We're launching a new walking tour that will focus on the various murals and statues located throughout the city center. We know tourists like you often visit the exhibitions at our art museum,** but art isn't only inside the walls of a museum. **94Here are some brochures with information, including the times and prices.**

살로나 시의 역사적인 가옥들을 견학하는 시간이 즐거우셨길 바랍니다. 저는 5년 전 이 투어 업체를 설립했는데요. 다음 달 우리 회사가 제공하는 상품을 확대할 것이라는 소식을 알려 드리게 되어 기쁩니다. **도심 전역에 위치한 다양한 벽화와 조각상이 중심이 되는 새로운 도보 투어를 시작할 것입니다. 여러분과 같은 관광객들은 미술관 전시회를 자주 방문한다는 것을 알고 있지만** 예술은 미술관 벽 안에만 있는 것은 아닙니다. 시간과 가격을 포함한 정보가 담긴 안내책자가 여기 있습니다.

어휘 historic 역사적인, 역사적으로 중요한 found 설립하다 offering 제공하는 것 launch 개시하다, 착수하다 focus on ~에 초점을 맞추다 various 다양한 mural 벽화 statue 조각상 throughout 도처에 exhibition 전시 brochure 안내책자

92

Who most likely is the speaker?
(A) An artist
(B) A business owner
(C) A local journalist
(D) A government official

화자는 누구이겠는가?
(A) 화가
(B) 업체 소유주
(C) 지역 기자
(D) 공무원

어휘 local 지역의 journalist 기자

해설 전체 내용 관련 – 화자의 직업
화자가 초반부에 5년 전 이 투어 업체를 설립했다(I founded this tour company five years ago)고 말하고 있으므로 화자는 투어 업체 설립자임을 알 수 있다. 따라서 정답은 (B)이다.

> Paraphrasing 담화의 this tour company
> → 정답의 A business

93

Why does the speaker say, "art isn't only inside the walls of a museum"?
(A) To apologize for an exhibit closure
(B) To disagree with an online review
(C) To motivate the listeners to take another tour
(D) To recommend a building renovation

화자가 "예술은 미술관 벽 안에만 있는 것은 아닙니다"라고 말하는 이유는?
(A) 전시회 폐쇄에 대해 사과하려고
(B) 온라인 후기에 반대하려고
(C) 청자들에게 다른 투어를 하도록 동기를 부여하려고
(D) 건물 보수를 권하려고

어휘 apologize 사과하다 closure 폐쇄 disagree 의견이 다르다, 동의하지 않다 motivate 동기를 부여하다 renovation 개조, 보수

해설 화자의 의도 파악 – 예술은 미술관 벽 안에만 있는 것이 아니라는 말의 의도
앞에서 도심 전역에 위치한 다양한 벽화와 조각상이 중심이 되는 새로운 도보 투어를 시작할 것(We're launching a new walking tour that will focus on the various murals and statues located throughout the city center)이라면서 여러분과 같은 관광객들은 미술관 전시회를 자주 방문한다는 것을 알고 있다(We know tourists like you often visit the exhibitions at our art museum)고 말한 뒤 인용문을 언급하고 있으므로, 청자들에게 도보 투어를 권장하려는 의도로 한 말임을 알 수 있다. 따라서 정답은 (C)이다.

94

What does the speaker give to the listeners?
(A) City maps
(B) Gift cards
(C) Name badges
(D) Informational brochures

화자는 청자들에게 무엇을 주는가?
(A) 도시 지도
(B) 상품권
(C) 이름표
(D) 정보가 담긴 안내책자

어휘 informational 정보를 담은

해설 세부 사항 관련 – 화자가 청자들에게 제공하는 것
화자가 마지막에 시간과 가격을 포함한 정보가 담긴 안내책자가 여기 있다(Here are some brochures with information, including the times and prices)고 말하고 있으므로 정답은 (D)이다.

> Paraphrasing 담화의 brochures with information
> → 정답의 Informational brochures

95-97 방송 + 표

M-Cn In local news, **95the Bayland Transit Agency has announced that construction has begun on the new Alexton train station, which will offer a direct rail connection to the city center.** Spokesperson Claudia Schneider explained that **96the agency initially considered a more elaborate design with a projected cost of 300 million dollars but ultimately decided to go with a more cost-**

effective and straightforward proposal with a price tag of 250 million dollars. Not only is it more economical, but an earlier completion date is expected. ⁹⁷**The building will have an adjacent small park for public use, and beginning in May, residents will be invited to vote on ideas for it.**

지역 소식입니다. 베이랜드 교통국은 새로운 알렉스턴 기차역 공사가 시작됐다고 발표했는데요. 이로써 도심까지 철도가 바로 연결될 것입니다. 클라우디아 슈나이더 대변인의 설명에 따르면, 교통국은 처음에 3억 달러가 예상되는 더 정교한 디자인을 고려했으나 결국 2억 5천만 달러 가격의 보다 비용 효율적이고 간단한 제안으로 결정했다고 합니다. 더 경제적일 뿐 아니라 완공 일자도 더 당겨질 것으로 예상됩니다. 건물 인접한 곳에는 대중들이 이용할 수 있는 작은 공원이 생길 예정인데요. 5월부터 주민들은 그 공원에 대한 아이디어에 투표할 것을 요청받을 것입니다.

어휘 local 지역의 transit agency 교통국 construction 건설, 공사 direct 직접적인 connection 연결 spokesperson 대변인 initially 처음에 elaborate 정교한 projected 예상된 ultimately 결국, 궁극적으로 cost-effective 비용 효율이 높은 straightforward 간단한 proposal 제안 price tag 가격표 economical 경제적인 completion 완료, 완성 adjacent 인접한, 가까운 resident 주민 vote 투표하다

Proposal	Projected Cost
Plan A	$200 million
Plan B	$450 million
Plan C	$300 million
⁹⁶Plan D	$250 million

제안	예상 비용
계획 A	2억 달러
계획 B	4억 5천만 달러
계획 C	3억 달러
⁹⁶계획 D	2억 5천만 달러

95

What is the broadcast mainly about?
(A) A renovated airport terminal
(B) A redesigned city hall
(C) A new train station
(D) A new bridge

방송은 주로 무엇에 관한 것인가?
(A) 개조된 공항 터미널
(B) 재설계된 시청
(C) 새로운 기차역
(D) 새로운 다리

해설 전체 내용 관련 – 방송의 주제
화자가 초반부에 베이랜드 교통국은 새로운 알렉스턴 기차역 공사가 시작됐다고 발표했는데(the Bayland Transit Agency has announced

that construction has begun on the new Alexton train station) 이로써 도심까지 철도가 바로 연결될 것(which will offer a direct rail connection to the city center)이라고 말하고 있으므로 정답은 (C)이다.

96

Look at the graphic. Which proposal was chosen?
(A) Plan A
(B) Plan B
(C) Plan C
(D) Plan D

시각 정보에 의하면, 어떤 제안이 선택됐는가?
(A) 계획 A
(B) 계획 B
(C) 계획 C
(D) 계획 D

해설 시각 정보 연계 – 선택된 제안
화자가 중반부에 교통국은 결국 2억 5천만 달러 가격의 보다 비용 효율적이고 간단한 제안으로 결정했다(the agency ~ ultimately decided to go with a more cost-effective and straightforward proposal with a price tag of 250 million dollars)고 했으며, 표에 따르면 2억 5천만 달러 가격의 제안은 계획 D이므로 정답은 (D)이다.

97

According to the speaker, what will residents be able to vote on?
(A) Parking options
(B) Food vendors
(C) Public artwork
(D) Park ideas

화자에 따르면, 주민들은 무엇에 대해 투표할 수 있는가?
(A) 주차 선택 사항
(B) 음식 노점상
(C) 대중 미술품
(D) 공원 관련 아이디어

어휘 vendor 행상인, 노점상 artwork 미술품

해설 세부 사항 관련 – 주민들이 투표할 내용
화자가 마지막에 건물 인접한 곳에 작은 공원이 생길 예정인데 주민들은 그 공원에 대한 아이디어에 투표할 것을 요청받을 것(The building will have an adjacent small park for public use, ~ residents will be invited to vote on ideas for it)이라고 말하고 있으므로 정답은 (D)이다.

98-100 연설 + 건물 배치도   동영상 강의

W-Am Welcome, everyone, to the grand opening of the Wilton Business Center. ⁹⁸**As the mayor, I'm pleased to see this kind of growth in our city.** And

99 **the environmentally friendly elements incorporated into the design make this building special.** In particular, this building is equipped with a water recycling system and insulation made from repurposed cloth. While today is the grand opening, one part of the building— **100** **the recreation center—will not be available for use until next month, as final touches are still being added to that floor.**

여러분, 월튼 비즈니스 센터 개소식에 오신 것을 환영합니다. **저는 시장으로서 시가 이렇게 성장하는 것을 볼 수 있어 기쁩니다.** 설계에 포함된 환경친화적 요소들이 이 건물을 더 특별하게 합니다. 특히 이 건물은 물 재활용 시스템과 용도를 바꾼 천으로 만든 단열재를 갖추고 있습니다. 오늘이 개소식이지만 건물 일부인 **레크리에이션 센터는 아직 바닥에 마감을 하고 있어서 다음 달까지 이용할 수 없을 것입니다.**

어휘 grand opening 개업식, 개소식   mayor 시장   growth 성장   environmentally friendly 환경친화적   element 요소   incorporate 포함되다   in particular 특히   be equipped with ~을 갖추고 있다   recycling 재활용   insulation 단열재   repurpose 용도를 바꾸다   available 이용 가능한

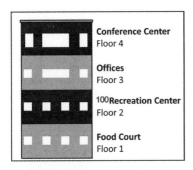

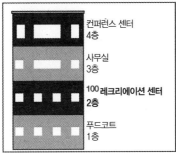

98

Who is the speaker?
(A) A structural engineer
(B) A journalist
(C) A tour guide
(D) A city official

화자는 누구인가?
(A) 구조 공학자
(B) 기자
(C) 투어 가이드
(D) 시 공무원

어휘 structural 구조상의   official 공무원

해설 전체 내용 관련 – 화자의 직업
화자가 초반부에 시장으로서 시가 이렇게 성장하는 것을 볼 수 있어 기쁘다(As the mayor, I'm pleased to see this kind of growth in our city)고 말하고 있으므로 정답은 (D)이다.

> **Paraphrasing**   담화의 the mayor → 정답의 A city official

99

Why is a building special?
(A) It was constructed in a short time.
(B) It has a technologically advanced security system.
(C) It has environmentally friendly features.
(D) It was designed by a famous architect.

건물이 특별한 이유는?
(A) 단기간에 건설됐다.
(B) 기술적으로 앞선 보안 시스템이 있다.
(C) 환경친화적 특징이 있다.
(D) 유명한 건축가가 설계했다.

어휘 technologically 기술적으로   advanced 앞선, 선진의   security 보안   feature 특징   architect 건축가

해설 세부 사항 관련 – 건물이 특별한 이유
화자가 중반부에 설계에 포함된 환경친화적 요소들이 이 건물을 더 특별하게 한다(the environmentally friendly elements incorporated into the design make this building special)고 말하고 있으므로 정답은 (C)이다.

100

Look at the graphic. Which floor of the building is not open yet?
(A) Floor 4
(B) Floor 3
(C) Floor 2
(D) Floor 1

시각 정보에 의하면, 건물 몇 층이 아직 개방되지 못하는가?
(A) 4층
(B) 3층
(C) 2층
(D) 1층

해설 시각 정보 연계 – 아직 개방되지 않은 건물 층
화자가 후반부에 레크리에이션 센터는 다음 달까지 이용할 수 없을 것(the recreation center—will not be available for use until next month)이라고 말하고 있고, 건물 배치도에 따르면 레크리에이션 센터는 2층에 위치하므로 정답은 (C)이다.

1 (D)	2 (A)	3 (C)	4 (D)	5 (A)
6 (B)	7 (A)	8 (C)	9 (C)	10 (B)
11 (B)	12 (A)	13 (B)	14 (C)	15 (B)
16 (A)	17 (B)	18 (A)	19 (B)	20 (C)
21 (B)	22 (A)	23 (B)	24 (C)	25 (C)
26 (B)	27 (C)	28 (C)	29 (A)	30 (A)
31 (A)	32 (C)	33 (A)	34 (C)	35 (C)
36 (B)	37 (A)	38 (B)	39 (D)	40 (A)
41 (A)	42 (C)	43 (B)	44 (B)	45 (D)
46 (B)	47 (D)	48 (A)	49 (B)	50 (A)
51 (D)	52 (C)	53 (D)	54 (B)	55 (C)
56 (B)	57 (C)	58 (D)	59 (C)	60 (A)
61 (B)	62 (B)	63 (A)	64 (C)	65 (B)
66 (C)	67 (B)	68 (D)	69 (B)	70 (B)
71 (A)	72 (C)	73 (D)	74 (B)	75 (D)
76 (B)	77 (B)	78 (D)	79 (A)	80 (B)
81 (C)	82 (D)	83 (D)	84 (B)	85 (C)
86 (D)	87 (B)	88 (A)	89 (D)	90 (B)
91 (C)	92 (C)	93 (B)	94 (B)	95 (C)
96 (D)	97 (D)	98 (A)	99 (C)	100 (D)

PART 1

1 W-Am

(A) The worker is carrying some plants.
(B) The worker is reading a sign.
(C) The worker is pushing a cart.
(D) The worker is writing some notes.

(A) 인부가 식물을 나르고 있다.
(B) 인부가 표지판을 읽고 있다.
(C) 인부가 수레를 밀고 있다.
(D) 인부가 메모를 하고 있다.

어휘 carry 나르다　plant 식물　sign 표지판　note 메모

해설 1인 등장 사진 – 사람의 동작/상태 묘사
(A) 동사 오답. 인부가 식물을 나르고 있는(is carrying some plants) 모습이 아니므로 오답.
(B) 동사 오답. 인부가 표지판을 읽고 있는(is reading a sign) 모습이 아니므로 오답.

(C) 동사 오답. 인부가 수레를 밀고 있는(is pushing a cart) 모습이 아니므로 오답.
(D) 정답. 인부가 메모를 하고 있는(is writing some notes) 모습이므로 정답.

2 M-Cn

(A) Some of the people are pulling suitcases.
(B) Some of the people are relaxing on benches.
(C) Some of the people are putting luggage onto a rack.
(D) Some of the people are waiting in line to purchase a ticket.

(A) 사람들이 여행 가방을 끌고 있다.
(B) 사람들이 벤치에서 쉬고 있다.
(C) 사람들이 수하물을 선반에 놓고 있다.
(D) 사람들이 표를 사기 위해 줄을 서서 기다리고 있다.

어휘 suitcase 여행 가방　relax 휴식을 취하다　luggage 수하물
rack 선반, 받침대　wait in line 줄 서서 기다리다

해설 2인 이상 등장 사진 – 사람의 동작/상태 묘사
(A) 정답. 사람들이 여행 가방을 끌고 있는(are pulling suitcases) 모습이므로 정답.
(B) 동사 오답. 사람들이 벤치에서 쉬고 있는(are relaxing on benches) 모습이 아니므로 오답.
(C) 사진에 없는 명사를 이용한 오답. 사진에 선반(a rack)의 모습이 보이지 않으므로 오답.
(D) 동사 오답. 사람들이 줄을 서서 기다리고 있는(are waiting in line) 모습이 아니므로 오답.

3 W-Br

(A) She's looking into her backpack.
(B) She's tying the laces of her boots.
(C) She's hiking on an outdoor path.
(D) She's walking out of a tunnel.

(A) 여자가 배낭 안을 들여다보고 있다.
(B) 여자가 신발끈을 묶고 있다.
(C) 여자가 야외 길을 걷고 있다.
(D) 여자가 터널 밖으로 걸어 나오고 있다.

어휘 tie 묶다　outdoor 야외의　path 길

해설 1인 등장 사진 – 사람의 동작/상태 묘사
(A) 동사 오답. 여자가 배낭 안을 들여다보고 있는(is looking into her backpack) 모습이 아니므로 오답.
(B) 동사 오답. 여자가 신발끈을 묶고 있는(is tying the laces of her boots) 모습이 아니므로 오답.
(C) 정답. 여자가 야외 길을 걷고 있는(is hiking on an outdoor path) 모습이므로 정답.
(D) 사진에 없는 명사를 이용한 오답. 사진에 터널(a tunnel)의 모습이 보이지 않으므로 오답.

4 M-Au

(A) He's holding the handle of a shopping cart.
(B) He's plugging a cord into a wall outlet.
(C) He's looking into a kitchen cupboard.
(D) He's kneeling down on a tile floor.

(A) 남자가 쇼핑 카트 손잡이를 잡고 있다.
(B) 남자가 벽면 콘센트에 코드를 꽂고 있다.
(C) 남자가 주방 찬장을 들여다보고 있다.
(D) 남자가 타일 바닥에 무릎을 꿇고 있다.

어휘 plug 연결하다, 꽂다   wall outlet 벽면 콘센트   cupboard 찬장   kneel down 무릎을 꿇다

해설 1인 등장 사진 – 사람의 동작/상태 묘사
(A) 사진에 없는 명사를 이용한 오답. 사진에 쇼핑 카트(a shopping cart)의 모습이 보이지 않으므로 오답.
(B) 사진에 없는 명사를 이용한 오답. 사진에 벽면 콘센트(a wall outlet)의 모습이 보이지 않으므로 오답.
(C) 동사 오답. 남자가 주방 찬장을 들여다보고 있는(is looking into a kitchen cupboard) 모습이 아니므로 오답.
(D) 정답. 남자가 타일 바닥에 무릎을 꿇고 있는(is kneeling down on a tile floor) 모습이므로 정답.

5 W-Am

▶ 동영상 강의

(A) Seats have been arranged under some umbrellas.
(B) Some street signs are being taken down.
(C) Some bushes are being trimmed.
(D) Some chairs are being folded and stacked.

(A) 파라솔 아래 의자가 배열되어 있다.
(B) 도로 표지판이 치워지고 있다.
(C) 관목이 다듬어지고 있다.
(D) 의자들이 접혀 쌓이고 있다.

어휘 arrange 정리하다, 배열하다   take down (구조물을 해체하여) 치우다   bush 관목   trim 다듬다   fold 접다   stack 쌓다

해설 혼합 사진 – 사람/사물/풍경 혼합 묘사
(A) 정답. 의자(Seats)가 파라솔 아래 배열되어 있는(have been arranged under some umbrellas) 모습이므로 정답.
(B) 사진에 없는 명사를 이용한 오답. 사진에 도로 표지판(street signs)의 모습이 보이지 않으므로 오답.
(C) 동사 오답. 관목(bushes)이 다듬어지고 있는(are being trimmed) 모습이 아니므로 오답.
(D) 동사 오답. 의자들(chairs)이 접혀 쌓이고 있는(are being folded and stacked) 모습이 아니므로 오답.

6 M-Cn

(A) Some cushions have been laid on the floor.
(B) Books have been piled up by a glass door.
(C) A light fixture is suspended from the ceiling.
(D) A rug has been rolled up against a wall.

(A) 쿠션들이 바닥에 놓여 있다.
(B) 유리문 옆에 책이 쌓여 있다.
(C) 조명 기구가 천장에 매달려 있다.
(D) 깔개가 말려서 벽에 기대어 있다.

어휘 lay 놓다, 두다   pile up 쌓아 올리다   light fixture 조명 기구   be suspended from ~에 매달려 있다   ceiling 천장   roll 말다

해설 사물/풍경 사진 – 사물 묘사
(A) 위치 오답. 쿠션이나 방석(cushions)이 의자에 놓여 있지 바닥에 놓여 있는(have been laid on the floor) 모습이 아니므로 오답.
(B) 정답. 책(Books)이 유리문 옆에 쌓여 있는(have been piled up by a glass door) 모습이므로 정답.
(C) 위치 오답. 조명 기구(A light fixture)가 천장에 매달려 있는(is suspended from the ceiling) 모습이 아니므로 오답.
(D) 동사 오답. 깔개(A rug)가 말려서 벽에 기대어 있는(has been rolled up against a wall) 모습이 아니므로 오답.

PART 2

7

W-Br   There's a meeting in the conference room soon, right?

M-Au   (A) Yes, it's for the whole department.
(B) No, put it in the closet.
(C) The rent is too high.

회의실에서 곧 회의가 있죠?
(A) 네, 부서 전체 회의예요.
(B) 아니요, 벽장에 두세요.
(C) 집세가 너무 비싸요.

어휘 conference room 회의실 whole 전체의 closet 벽장 rent 집세, 임대료

해설 곧 회의가 있는지 확인하는 부가 의문문

(A) 정답. 회의실에서 곧 회의가 있는지 묻는 질문에 네(Yes)라고 대답한 뒤, 부서 전체 회의라며 긍정 답변과 일관된 내용을 덧붙이고 있으므로 정답.
(B) 연상 단어 오답. 질문의 room에서 연상 가능한 closet을 이용한 오답.
(C) 연상 단어 오답. 질문의 room에서 연상 가능한 rent를 이용한 오답.

8

M-Au Why hasn't the mural in the lobby been painted yet?

M-Cn (A) Red and yellow.
(B) Please pick up the ladder.
(C) Because the artist is out of town.

로비 벽화는 왜 아직 칠해지지 않았죠?
(A) 빨간색과 노란색이요.
(B) 사다리를 들어 주세요.
(C) 화가가 지금 여기 없어요.

어휘 mural 벽화 ladder 사다리 out of town (도시를 떠나) 외출 중인

해설 벽화가 아직 칠해지지 않은 이유를 묻는 Why 의문문

(A) 연상 단어 오답. 질문의 painted에서 연상 가능한 Red와 yellow를 이용한 오답.
(B) 연상 단어 오답. 질문의 painted에서 연상 가능한 ladder를 이용한 오답.
(C) 정답. 로비 벽화가 아직 칠해지지 않은 이유를 묻는 질문에 화가가 지금 여기 없어서라고 구체적인 이유를 제시하고 있으므로 정답.

9

M-Cn Do you prefer writing in the morning or the afternoon?

W-Br (A) My publisher requested edits.
(B) Thanks for providing a solution.
(C) Mornings are usually better for me.

글을 오전에 쓰는 걸 선호하세요, 아니면 오후에 쓰는 걸 선호하세요?
(A) 출판사에서 수정을 요청했어요.
(B) 해결책을 제공해 주셔서 감사합니다.
(C) 보통 오전이 더 좋아요.

어휘 publisher 출판사 edit 수정, 편집 solution 해결책, 해답

해설 선호하는 시간을 묻는 선택 의문문

(A) 연상 단어 오답. 질문의 writing에서 연상 가능한 publisher와 edits를 이용한 오답.
(B) 질문과 상관없는 오답.

(C) 정답. 오전과 오후 중 선호하는 시간을 묻는 질문에 오전이라며 둘 중 하나를 선택해 응답하고 있으므로 정답.

10

W-Am I suggest we paint the waiting room light blue.

M-Cn (A) Doctor Park has an opening at three.
(B) That's a good idea.
(C) I prefer the red jacket.

대기실을 하늘색으로 칠할 것을 제안합니다.
(A) 박 박사님은 3시에 비는 시간이 있어요.
(B) 좋은 생각이네요.
(C) 저는 빨간색 재킷이 좋아요.

어휘 waiting room 대기실 have an opening 시간이 있다, 자리가 나다

해설 제안/권유의 평서문

(A) 평서문과 상관없는 오답.
(B) 정답. 대기실을 하늘색으로 칠하자는 제안에 대해 좋은 생각이라며 동조하고 있으므로 정답.
(C) 연상 단어 오답. 평서문의 blue에서 연상 가능한 red를 이용한 오답.

11

M-Au Did you know that the music school is closed on Sundays?

W-Br (A) Forty dollars an hour.
(B) No, I didn't know that.
(C) I saw the piano recital.

음악 학교가 일요일에는 문을 닫는 것을 알고 계셨나요?
(A) 한 시간에 40달러입니다.
(B) 아니요, 몰랐어요.
(C) 저는 피아노 연주회를 봤어요.

어휘 recital 발표회, 연주회

해설 음악 학교가 일요일에 문을 닫는 것을 알았는지 묻는 조동사(Did) 의문문

(A) 질문과 상관없는 오답. How much 의문문에 대한 응답이므로 오답.
(B) 정답. 음악 학교가 일요일에는 문을 닫는 것을 알았는지 묻는 질문에 아니요(No)라고 대답한 뒤, 몰랐다며 부정 답변과 일관된 내용을 덧붙이고 있으므로 정답.
(C) 연상 단어 오답. 질문의 music school에서 연상 가능한 piano recital을 이용한 오답.

12

W-Am How do I find the office manager?

M-Cn (A) The receptionist would know.
(B) Desk lamps and headsets.
(C) Twelve euros.

어떻게 하면 사무실 관리자를 만날 수 있을까요?

(A) 안내 직원이 알 거예요.
(B) 탁상용 스탠드와 헤드셋이요.
(C) 12유로요.

어휘 receptionist 안내 직원, 접수 담당자

해설 사무실 관리자를 만나는 방법을 묻는 How 의문문

(A) 정답. 사무실 관리자를 만나는 방법을 묻는 질문에 안내 직원이 알 거라며 알 만한 사람을 알려 주고 있으므로 정답.
(B) 연상 단어 오답. 질문의 office에서 연상 가능한 Desk lamps를 이용한 오답.
(C) 연상 단어 오답. 질문의 How를 How much로 잘못 들었을 경우 연상 가능한 euros를 이용한 오답.

13

M-Au When did you place the order for the lumber?

W-Br (A) Yes, it's a great place for hiking.
(B) It's out of stock right now.
(C) The warehouse on William Street.

목재 주문을 언제 넣었어요?
(A) 네, 하이킹 하기에 아주 좋은 장소예요.
(B) 지금은 품절이에요.
(C) 윌리엄 가에 있는 창고요.

어휘 place an order 주문을 넣다 lumber 목재 out of stock 품절된, 재고가 없는 warehouse 창고

해설 목재 주문 시점을 묻는 When 의문문

(A) Yes/No 불가 오답. When 의문문에는 Yes/No 응답이 불가능하므로 오답.
(B) 정답. 목재 주문 시점을 묻는 질문에 지금은 품절이라며 주문을 넣을 수 없음을 우회적으로 표현하고 있으므로 정답.
(C) 질문과 상관없는 오답. Where 의문문에 대한 응답이므로 오답.

14

M-Cn Where is the new packaging machine?

W-Br (A) Ten packages a minute.
(B) We met last Thursday.
(C) We decided to keep the old one.

새 포장 기계는 어디 있죠?
(A) 일 분에 상자 열 개요.
(B) 우리는 지난 목요일에 만났어요.
(C) 우리는 예전 것을 계속 쓰기로 했어요.

어휘 packaging 포장 package (포장용) 상자, 포장물

해설 새 포장 기계의 위치를 묻는 Where 의문문

(A) 파생어 오답. 질문의 packaging과 파생어 관계인 packages를 이용한 오답.
(B) 질문과 상관없는 오답.
(C) 정답. 새 포장 기계의 위치를 묻는 질문에 예전 것을 계속 쓰기로 했다며 새 포장 기계가 없음을 우회적으로 알려 주고 있으므로 정답.

15

W-Br I'll be out of the office this afternoon.

M-Au (A) An awfully long commute.
(B) OK—I'll update your schedule.
(C) It's right down the hallway.

저는 오늘 오후에 사무실에 없을 거예요.
(A) 통근 거리가 정말 멀어요.
(B) 알았어요. 일정표를 업데이트할게요.
(C) 복도를 따라가면 바로 있어요.

어휘 awfully 정말, 몹시 commute 통근 (거리) hallway 복도

해설 정보 전달의 평서문

(A) 연상 단어 오답. 평서문의 office에서 연상 가능한 commute를 이용한 오답.
(B) 정답. 오늘 오후에 사무실에 없을 거라는 평서문에 알았다(OK)고 대답한 뒤, 일정표를 업데이트하겠다며 긍정 답변과 일관된 내용을 덧붙이고 있으므로 정답.
(C) 연상 단어 오답. 평서문의 office에서 연상 가능한 hallway를 이용한 오답.

16

W-Am Are you taking a vacation once this project is over?

M-Au (A) Yes—I'm planning a trip to Barcelona.
(B) This is your second time, isn't it?
(C) Blueprints for a high-rise building.

이 프로젝트가 끝나면 휴가를 가실 건가요?
(A) 네. 바르셀로나로 여행 갈 계획이에요.
(B) 이번이 두 번째죠, 그렇지 않나요?
(C) 고층 건물용 청사진입니다.

어휘 take a vacation 휴가 가다 blueprint 청사진 high-rise 고층의

해설 휴가 사용 계획을 묻는 Be동사 의문문

(A) 정답. 이 프로젝트가 끝나면 휴가를 갈 것인지 묻는 질문에 네(Yes)라고 대답한 뒤, 바르셀로나로 여행 갈 계획이라며 긍정 답변과 일관된 내용을 덧붙이고 있으므로 정답.
(B) 연상 단어 오답. 질문의 once에서 연상 가능한 second time을 이용한 오답.
(C) 연상 단어 오답. 질문의 project에서 연상 가능한 Blueprints를 이용한 오답.

17

M-Au Let's post the sales report to our team's Web page.

W-Am (A) We're sharing a taxi to the airport.
(B) I can do that.
(C) A recent hiring decision.

우리 팀 웹페이지에 영업 보고서를 게시합시다.
(A) 우리는 공항까지 택시를 함께 타고 갈 거예요.
(B) 제가 할 수 있어요.
(C) 최근 고용 결정이요.

어휘 post 게시하다 sales report 영업 보고서 share 공유하다
hiring 고용 decision 결정

해설 제안/권유의 평서문
(A) 유사 발음 오답. 평서문의 report와 부분적으로 발음이 유사한 airport를 이용한 오답.
(B) 정답. 팀 웹페이지에 영업 보고서를 게시하자는 제안에 대해 본인이 할 수 있다고 수락의 대답을 하고 있으므로 정답.
(C) 평서문과 상관없는 오답.

18

M-Au Which airline are you planning on using?

W-Br (A) The usual one.
(B) A one-way ticket.
(C) Yes, you can use mine.

어떤 항공사를 이용할 계획이시죠?
(A) 평상시 이용하는 곳이요.
(B) 편도 표요.
(C) 네, 제 걸 쓰시면 돼요.

어휘 airline 항공사

해설 이용할 항공사를 묻는 Which 의문문
(A) 정답. 어느 항공사를 이용할 것인지 묻는 질문에 평상시 이용하는 곳이라고 알려 주고 있으므로 정답. Which 의문문에서는 the ~ one이 정답으로 자주 등장하니 알아 두자.
(B) 연상 단어 오답. 질문의 airline에서 연상 가능한 one-way ticket을 이용한 오답.
(C) Yes/No 불가 오답. Which 의문문에는 Yes/No 응답이 불가능하므로 오답.

19

M-Cn Where's this shipment of parts being sent?

W-Br (A) Around five thirty this evening.
(B) To the assembly plant in Dublin.
(C) Just half the order.

이번 부품 수송은 어디로 보내는 건가요?
(A) 오늘 저녁 5시 30분쯤이요.
(B) 더블린에 있는 조립 공장으로요.
(C) 주문 절반만요.

어휘 shipment 수송, 수송품 assembly 조립 plant 공장

해설 부품 수송 장소를 묻는 Where 의문문
(A) 질문과 상관없는 오답. When 의문문에 대한 응답이므로 오답.
(B) 정답. 부품 수송 장소를 묻는 질문에 더블린에 있는 조립 공장이라고 구체적인 장소를 알려 주고 있으므로 정답.
(C) 연상 단어 오답. 질문의 shipment에서 연상 가능한 order를 이용한 오답.

20

W-Br Who paid for lunch?

M-Cn (A) I just ate.
(B) It closes at five.
(C) Alberto did.

점심값은 누가 냈어요?
(A) 저는 방금 먹었어요.
(B) 그곳은 다섯 시에 닫아요.
(C) 알베르토가 냈어요.

해설 점심값을 낸 사람을 묻는 Who 의문문
(A) 연상 단어 오답. 질문의 lunch에서 연상 가능한 ate를 이용한 오답.
(B) 질문과 상관없는 오답.
(C) 정답. 점심값을 낸 사람이 누구인지 묻는 질문에 알베르토가 냈다고 알려 주고 있으므로 정답.

21

M-Cn How many employees work in your department?

W-Am (A) I don't mind taking notes at the meeting.
(B) A couple dozen, I think.
(C) It's seven meters long.

당신의 부서에서 근무하는 직원은 몇 명인가요?
(A) 회의에서 메모를 해도 괜찮습니다.
(B) 24명 정도 되는 것 같아요.
(C) 길이가 7미터예요.

어휘 take notes 메모하다 a couple dozen 24개 정도

해설 직원 수를 묻는 How many 의문문
(A) 연상 단어 오답. 질문의 department에서 연상 가능한 meeting을 이용한 오답.
(B) 정답. 부서 직원 수를 묻는 질문에 24명 정도 되는 것 같다고 숫자로 응답하고 있으므로 정답.
(C) 연상 단어 오답. How many에서 연상 가능한 숫자 seven을 이용한 오답.

22

M-Cn We should leave for our training course soon, shouldn't we?

W-Br (A) We still have a few minutes.
(B) There's a map on the wall.
(C) Two sessions per day.

이제 곧 교육받으러 가야 하죠?
(A) 아직 몇 분 시간 있어요.
(B) 벽에 지도가 있어요.
(C) 하루에 수업 두 개요.

어휘 session 수업, 기간

해설 곧 교육에 가야 하는지 확인하는 부가 의문문
(A) 정답. 이제 곧 교육받으러 가야 하는지 묻는 질문에 아직 몇 분 시간이 있다며 아직 출발하지 않아도 됨을 우회적으로 표현하고 있으므로 정답.

(B) 질문과 상관없는 오답.
(C) 연상 단어 오답. 질문의 training course에서 연상 가능한 sessions를 이용한 오답.

23

W-Am Isn't there a limit on travel expenses?

M-Au (A) To fix the vending machine.
(B) One hundred dollars per day.
(C) Next to the travel agency.

출장비에 한도가 있지 않나요?
(A) 자판기를 수리하려고요.
(B) 하루 100달러예요.
(C) 여행사 옆에요.

어휘 limit 한계, 한도   travel expense 출장비   fix 수리하다
vending machine 자판기

해설 출장비에 한도가 있는지 확인하는 부정 의문문
(A) 질문과 상관없는 오답. Why 의문문에 대한 응답이므로 오답.
(B) 정답. 출장비에 한도가 있는지 확인하는 질문에 하루 100달러라고 네(Yes)를 생략한 긍정 답변을 하고 있으므로 정답.
(C) 단어 반복 오답. 질문의 travel을 반복 이용한 오답.

24

동영상 강의

M-Cn When should I tell the director that I'm interested in the management position?

W-Br (A) Yes, we're extending our business hours.
(B) Didn't Andrey direct the play?
(C) I'm not on the hiring team.

제가 관리직에 관심이 있다는 걸 책임자에게 언제 말해야 할까요?
(A) 네, 저희는 영업시간을 연장하고 있어요.
(B) 안드레이가 그 연극을 연출하지 않았어요?
(C) 저는 채용팀이 아니에요.

어휘 management position 관리직   extend 연장하다, 늘리다
direct 연출하다, 감독하다

해설 책임자에게 말할 시기를 묻는 When 의문문
(A) Yes/No 불가 오답. When 의문문에는 Yes/No 응답이 불가능하므로 오답.
(B) 파생어 오답. 질문의 director와 파생어 관계인 direct를 이용한 오답.
(C) 정답. 관리직에 관심이 있다는 걸 책임자에게 말할 시기를 묻는 질문에 자신은 채용팀이 아니라며 알지 못함을 우회적으로 표현하고 있으므로 정답.

25

W-Am The layout of the footwear department has changed.

M-Au (A) There's a charging station in the café.
(B) Yes, a three-bedroom apartment.
(C) The store has a new manager.

신발 코너 배치가 바뀌었네요.
(A) 그 카페에는 충전소가 있어요.
(B) 네, 침실 세 개짜리 아파트요.
(C) 매장에 관리자가 새로 왔어요.

어휘 layout 배치   charging station 충전소, 충전기

해설 정보 전달의 평서문
(A) 평서문과 상관없는 오답.
(B) 유사 발음 오답. 평서문의 department와 부분적으로 발음이 유사한 apartment를 이용한 오답.
(C) 정답. 신발 코너 배치가 바뀌었다는 평서문에 매장에 관리자가 새로 왔다며 신발 코너 배치가 바뀐 이유를 알려 주고 있으므로 정답.

26

W-Br Can you look at this month's revenue report?

M-Cn (A) The news program is informative.
(B) I have some free time tomorrow afternoon.
(C) He started that position in July.

이번 달 수익 보고서를 봐 주실 수 있나요?
(A) 그 뉴스 프로그램은 유익해요.
(B) 내일 오후에 시간이 좀 있어요.
(C) 그는 7월에 그 직책을 맡기 시작했어요.

어휘 revenue 수익, 수입   informative 유익한

해설 부탁/요청의 의문문
(A) 연상 단어 오답. 질문의 report를 보도의 의미로 생각할 경우 연상 가능한 news를 이용한 오답.
(B) 정답. 수익 보고서를 봐 달라는 요청에 내일 오후에 시간이 좀 있다며 내일 봐줄 수 있음을 간접적으로 표현하고 있으므로 정답.
(C) 질문과 상관없는 오답. 질문에 3인칭 대명사 He로 지칭할 인물이 언급된 적이 없으므로 오답.

27

W-Am Why haven't the windows been replaced yet?

M-Au (A) Not too much wind, no.
(B) Look in the filing cabinet.
(C) Did you see the cost estimate?

창문을 왜 아직 교체하지 않았죠?
(A) 바람이 그리 많이 불지 않아요.
(B) 문서 보관함을 보세요.
(C) 견적서를 보셨나요?

어휘 replace 교체하다   filing cabinet 문서 보관함   cost estimate 견적서

해설 창문을 교체하지 않은 이유를 묻는 Why 의문문
(A) 유사 발음 오답. 질문의 windows와 부분적으로 발음이 유사한 wind를 이용한 오답.
(B) 질문과 상관없는 오답.
(C) 정답. 창문을 아직 교체하지 않은 이유를 묻는 질문에 견적서를 보았는지 물으면서 견적서에 제시된 비용 때문임을 간접적으로 알려 주고 있으므로 정답.

28

W-Br Isn't your suitcase going to be heavier than the permitted weight?

M-Cn (A) The building permit arrived today.
(B) There are seats in the lobby.
(C) I'll have to pay a little bit extra.

당신의 여행 가방은 허용된 무게보다 무겁지 않을까요?
(A) 건축 허가증이 오늘 도착했어요.
(B) 로비에 좌석이 있어요.
(C) 돈을 조금 더 내야 할 거예요.

어휘 permitted 허용된   weight 무게   building permit 건축 허가

해설 여행 가방이 허용된 무게보다 무거운지 확인하는 부정 의문문
(A) 파생어 오답. 질문의 permitted와 파생어 관계인 permit을 이용한 오답.
(B) 질문과 상관없는 오답.
(C) 정답. 여행 가방이 허용된 무게보다 무거운지 묻는 질문에 돈을 조금 더 내야 할 거라며 허용된 무게보다 무겁다는 것을 우회적으로 표현하고 있으므로 정답.

29

M-Cn Who manufactures the engines for our machines?

W-Am (A) Koji is in charge of supplier contracts.
(B) I'm sorry—the storage room is full.
(C) That's a cargo airplane.

우리 기계 엔진은 누가 제조하나요?
(A) 코지가 공급업체 계약을 담당하고 있어요.
(B) 죄송하지만, 보관실이 꽉 찼어요.
(C) 저건 화물 비행기예요.

어휘 manufacture 제조하다   be in charge of ~을 담당하다
supplier 공급자   contract 계약   storage 보관, 저장   cargo (선박, 비행기의) 화물

해설 기계 엔진 제조업자를 묻는 Who 의문문
(A) 정답. 기계 엔진 제조업자를 묻는 질문에 코지가 공급업체 계약을 담당하고 있다고 그 정보를 알 만한 사람을 알려 주고 있으므로 정답.
(B) 질문과 상관없는 오답.
(C) 연상 단어 오답. 질문의 engines에서 연상 가능한 airplane을 이용한 오답

30

▶ 동영상 강의

W-Br Should we meet at the department store on Fifth Street or the one on Grover Lane?

M-Cn (A) Let's ask Patricia first.
(B) No, I don't mind.
(C) How much does it cost?

우리는 5번 가에 있는 백화점에서 만나는 게 좋을까요, 아니면 그로버 길에 있는 백화점에서 만나는 게 좋을까요?
(A) 패트리샤에게 먼저 물어보죠.
(B) 아니요, 괜찮아요.
(C) 비용이 얼마나 드나요?

어휘 department store 백화점   cost 비용이 들다

해설 만날 장소를 묻는 선택 의문문
(A) 정답. 만날 장소를 묻는 질문에 패트리샤에게 먼저 물어보자며 답변해 줄 수 있는 사람을 알려 주는 제3의 답변을 한 정답.
(B) Yes/No 불가 오답. 문장과 문장을 연결하는 경우를 제외하고는 선택 의문문에는 Yes/No 응답이 불가능하므로 오답.
(C) 연상 단어 오답. 질문의 department store에서 연상 가능한 cost를 이용한 오답.

31

W-Am Which band is playing at the club tonight?

M-Au (A) There's always a comedy show on Thursday nights.
(B) Yes, I've played the piano for many years.
(C) Their number one hit.

오늘 밤 클럽에서 어느 밴드가 연주해요?
(A) 목요일 밤에는 항상 코미디 공연이 있어요.
(B) 네, 저는 수년간 피아노를 쳤어요.
(C) 그들의 최고 히트곡이요.

어휘 number one hit 최고 히트곡

해설 오늘 밤 클럽에서 연주할 밴드를 묻는 Which 의문문
(A) 정답. 오늘 밤 클럽에서 연주할 밴드를 묻는 질문에 목요일에는 코미디 공연이 있다며 오늘 밤은 밴드 공연이 없음을 우회적으로 알리고 있으므로 정답.
(B) Yes/No 불가 오답. Which 의문문에는 Yes/No 응답이 불가능하므로 오답.
(C) 연상 단어 오답. 질문의 band에서 연상 가능한 number one hit를 이용한 오답.

PART 3

32-34

W-Br Hi, Shenchao. **³²I'm practicing my presentation in the conference room across the hall, and the projector in there keeps shutting off.** I think it's overheating. Has this happened to you?

M-Cn Oh, that projector is old. It really needs to be replaced. **³³If I were you, I'd just move to room 204 and practice there.** Also, that room has a window. It's much nicer.

W-Br OK. Thanks.

M-Cn By the way, ³⁴**you'll need a special cable to connect to the control panel in that room. Here, you can use this one.** Just leave it plugged in when you're finished.

여 안녕하세요, 쉔차오. **제가 복도 맞은편 회의실에서 발표 연습을 하고 있는데요. 거기에 있는 프로젝터가 계속 멈추네요.** 과열된 것 같아요. 이런 일이 있었나요?

남 아, 그 프로젝터 낡았어요. 정말로 바꿔야 해요. **제가 당신이라면 204호로 옮겨서 연습하겠어요.** 그리고 그 회의실엔 창문이 있거든요. 훨씬 좋아요.

여 알겠어요. 고마워요.

남 그런데 **그 회의실 제어판에 연결할 특수 케이블이 필요할 거예요. 여기, 이걸 쓰세요.** 다 마치시면 코드를 꽂은 채로 그냥 두세요.

어휘 practice 연습하다 presentation 발표 conference room 회의실 shut off 작동을 멈추다 overheating 과열된 replace 교체하다 connect 연결하다 control panel 제어판 plug in 플러그를 꽂다, 전원을 연결하다

32

What problem does the woman describe?
(A) A room is not available.
(B) A window will not open.
(C) A projector is not working.
(D) The weather has changed suddenly.

여자는 어떤 문제에 대해 설명하는가?
(A) 회의실을 이용할 수 없다.
(B) 창문이 열리지 않는다.
(C) 프로젝터가 작동하지 않는다.
(D) 날씨가 갑자기 바뀌었다.

어휘 available 이용할 수 있는 weather 날씨 suddenly 갑자기

해설 세부 사항 관련 – 여자가 언급하는 문제
여자가 첫 대사에서 복도 맞은편 회의실에서 발표 연습을 하고 있는데 거기에 있는 프로젝터가 계속 멈춘다(I'm practicing my presentation in the conference room across the hall, and the projector in there keeps shutting off)고 말하고 있으므로 정답은 (C)이다.

> Paraphrasing 대화의 keeps shutting off
> → 정답의 is not working

33

What does the man suggest doing?
(A) Moving to a different room
(B) Calling a technician
(C) Canceling an event
(D) Ordering some supplies

남자는 무엇을 하라고 제안하는가?
(A) 다른 방으로 옮기기
(B) 기술자에게 전화하기
(C) 행사 취소하기
(D) 물품 주문하기

어휘 technician 기사 supply 용품

해설 세부 사항 관련 – 남자의 제안 사항
남자가 첫 대사에서 내가 당신이라면 204호로 옮겨서 연습하겠다(If I were you, I'd just move to room 204 and practice there)고 말하며 방을 옮길 것을 제안하고 있으므로 정답은 (A)이다.

> Paraphrasing 대화의 move to room 204
> → 정답의 Moving to a different room

34

What does the man hand to the woman?
(A) An umbrella
(B) Some keys
(C) A cable
(D) Some printouts

남자는 여자에게 무엇을 건네주는가?
(A) 우산
(B) 열쇠
(C) 케이블
(D) 인쇄물

어휘 hand 건네주다

해설 세부 사항 관련 – 남자가 여자에게 건네주는 것
남자가 마지막 대사에서 그 회의실 제어판에 연결할 특수 케이블이 필요할 것(you'll need a special cable to connect to the control panel in that room)이라며 여기, 이걸 쓰라(Here, you can use this one)고 말하고 있으므로 정답은 (C)이다.

35-37

W-Am Hi. ³⁵**I'm Amanda Hoffman, and I'm on the panel of publishing experts.** I was told to check in here at the registration desk.

M-Au Yes, Ms. Hoffman. Welcome to the Portland Literary Conference. ³⁶**Here's your registration packet, which includes a gift card to thank you for participating.**

W-Am Oh, thank you. Just to confirm, the panel discussion begins at three P.M., right?

M-Au Yes, but ³⁷**we do ask that all panel members arrive ten minutes beforehand.** I hope you enjoy the conference!

여	안녕하세요. **아만다 호프만입니다. 출판 전문가 패널인데요.** 이곳 등록 데스크에서 체크인하라고 들었어요.
남	네, 호프만 씨. 포틀랜드 문학 학회에 오신 것을 환영합니다. **여기 등록 안내 패키지가 있어요. 참가해 주셔서 감사하다는 의미의 상품권도 들어 있습니다.**
여	아, 감사합니다. 확인차 여쭤보는데, 패널 토론이 오후 3시에 시작하는 거 맞죠?
남	네, 하지만 **모든 패널 구성원들께 10분 미리 도착해 달라고 요청드리고 있습니다.** 학회에서 좋은 시간 보내세요!

어휘	publishing 출판 registration 등록 literary 문학의 registration packet 등록 안내 패키지 gift card 상품권 participate 참가하다 confirm 확인하다 beforehand 미리, 사전에

35

What industry does Amanda Hoffman work in?
(A) Hospitality
(B) Healthcare
(C) Publishing
(D) Information technology

아만다 호프만은 어떤 업계에서 일하는가?
(A) 접객 서비스
(B) 의료
(C) 출판
(D) 정보 기술

해설 전체 내용 관련 – 아만다 호프만의 근무 업종
여자가 첫 대사에서 자신은 아만다 호프만이며 출판 전문가 패널(I'm Amanda Hoffman, and I'm on the panel of publishing experts)이라고 소개하고 있으므로 정답은 (C)이다.

36

According to the man, what is included in the registration packet?
(A) A map
(B) A gift card
(C) A schedule of events
(D) A certificate of attendance

남자에 따르면, 등록 안내 패키지에 무엇이 포함되어 있는가?
(A) 지도
(B) 상품권
(C) 행사 일정표
(D) 수료증

해설 세부 사항 관련 – 안내 패키지에 포함되어 있는 것
남자가 첫 대사에서 여기 등록 안내 패키지가 있는데 참가해 주셔서 감사하다는 의미의 상품권도 들어 있다(Here's your registration packet, which includes a gift card to thank you for participating)고 말하고 있으므로 정답은 (B)이다.

37

What does the man tell the woman to do?
(A) Arrive early
(B) Pay a fee
(C) Wear a name badge
(D) Choose a menu option

남자는 여자에게 무엇을 하라고 말하는가?
(A) 일찍 도착하기
(B) 요금 지불하기
(C) 명찰 달기
(D) 메뉴 선택하기

어휘 fee 요금, 수수료

해설 세부 사항 관련 – 남자가 여자에게 하라고 한 일
남자가 마지막 대사에서 모든 패널 구성원들에게 10분 미리 도착해 달라고 요청하고 있다(we do ask that all panel members arrive ten minutes beforehand)고 말하고 있으므로 정답은 (A)이다.

> Paraphrasing 대화의 arrive ten minutes beforehand
> → 정답의 Arrive early

38-40

W-Br	**38 I'm looking for a gift for my brother's birthday party this weekend.** He loves teas, and you have so many varieties!
M-Cn	Well, **39 I could recommend a quality brand if you know what type he enjoys.**
W-Br	Oh, I'm not sure. Hmm. Maybe I should get him a gift card so he can choose his own.
M-Cn	That's a good idea.
W-Br	I'll get one for 50 dollars. **40 Do your cards have an expiration date?**
M-Cn	Yes. We ask that they be used within one year of purchase.

여	이번 주말에 있을 남동생 생일 파티 선물을 찾고 있어요. 남동생은 차를 무척 좋아하는데 다양한 종류가 있네요!
남	남동생이 어떤 종류를 즐겨 마시는지 아시면 품질 좋은 브랜드를 추천해 드릴 수 있어요.
여	아, 잘 모르겠네요. 음… 본인이 선택할 수 있게 상품권을 사줘야겠어요.
남	좋은 생각입니다.
여	50달러짜리로 할게요. 카드에 유효 기간이 있나요?
남	네. 구매하고 1년 이내에 사용해 주셔야 해요.

어휘	variety 다양성, 갖가지 choose 선택하다 expiration date 유효 기간

38

What event will the woman attend this weekend?

(A) A wedding
(B) A birthday party
(C) A retirement dinner
(D) A graduation celebration

여자는 이번 주말 어떤 행사에 참석할 것인가?

(A) 결혼식
(B) 생일 파티
(C) 은퇴 기념 저녁 식사
(D) 졸업 기념 행사

어휘 retirement 은퇴   graduation 졸업   celebration 기념 행사

해설 세부 사항 관련 – 여자가 이번 주말 참석할 행사

여자가 첫 대사에서 이번 주말에 있을 남동생 생일 파티 선물을 찾고 있다(I'm looking for a gift for my brother's birthday party this weekend)고 말하고 있으므로 정답은 (B)이다.

39

What does the man offer to do?

(A) Authorize free shipping
(B) Apply a discount
(C) Provide a sample
(D) Make a recommendation

남자는 무엇을 하겠다고 제안하는가?

(A) 무료 배송 승인하기
(B) 할인 적용하기
(C) 샘플 제공하기
(D) 추천하기

어휘 authorize 승인하다   apply 적용하다

해설 세부 사항 관련 – 남자의 제안 사항

남자가 첫 대사에서 여자의 남동생이 어떤 종류의 차를 즐겨 마시는지 알면 품질 좋은 브랜드를 추천해 주겠다(I could recommend a quality brand if you know what type he enjoys)고 말하고 있으므로 정답은 (D)이다.

> **Paraphrasing**   대화의 recommend
> → 정답의 Make a recommendation

40

What does the woman ask about?

(A) An expiration date
(B) A manufacturer's guarantee
(C) The origin of a product
(D) The cost of a product

여자는 무엇에 대해 물어보는가?

(A) 유효 기간
(B) 제조업체 품질 보증서
(C) 제품 원산지
(D) 제품 가격

어휘 manufacturer 제조업체   guarantee 품질 보증서   origin 기원

해설 세부 사항 관련 – 여자가 질문하는 것

여자가 마지막 대사에서 카드에 유효 기간이 있는지(Do your cards have an expiration date?)를 묻고 있으므로 정답은 (A)이다.

41-43 3인 대화

M-Au	Thanks for meeting with us, Ms. Raj. **⁴¹ We're excited to learn about the product your company has developed for factories like ours.**
W-Am	I'm happy to tell you about it. **⁴² It's an application to monitor factory machines.** It identifies problems in operations and generates a report about the efficiency of each machine.
M-Cn	That sounds great! We have about 100 machine operators here. How much training would be involved?
W-Am	About an hour's worth. **⁴³ We provide a video with step-by-step instructions.**
M-Au	Excellent. That's good to know.

남1	만나주셔서 감사합니다, 라즈 씨. **귀사에서 저희 같은 공장을 위해 개발한 제품에 대해 알 수 있어 기쁩니다.**
여	말씀드리게 되어 기뻐요. **공장 기계를 모니터하는 프로그램입니다.** 작동상의 문제를 파악하고 각 기계의 효율성에 관해 보고서를 생성합니다.
남2	아주 좋군요! 이곳에 약 100명의 기계 기사가 있는데요. 교육이 얼마나 필요한가요?
여	약 한 시간 정도요. **단계별 설명이 담긴 동영상을 제공해 드립니다.**
남1	훌륭해요. 좋은 정보네요.

어휘	application 응용 프로그램, 어플 identify 파악하다, 확인하다 operation 작동, 운용 generate 생성하다 efficiency 효율성 involve 필요로 하다, 수반하다 step-by-step 단계적인 instruction 설명, 지시

41

Why is the woman visiting?

(A) To promote a product
(B) To sign a contract
(C) To tour a facility
(D) To inspect some equipment

여자는 왜 방문했는가?

(A) 제품을 홍보하려고
(B) 계약서에 서명하려고
(C) 시설을 견학하려고
(D) 장비를 점검하려고

어휘 sign 서명하다 contract 계약(서) inspect 점검하다, 시찰하다
equipment 장비

해설 세부 사항 관련 – 여자의 방문 이유

첫 번째 남자가 첫 대사에서 귀사에서 저희 같은 공장을 위해 개발한 제품에 대해 알 수 있어 기쁘다(We're excited to learn about the product your company has developed for factories like ours)고 말하고 있으므로 여자는 개발한 제품을 홍보하러 왔다는 것을 알 수 있다. 따라서 정답은 (A)이다.

42

What did the woman's company design?
(A) A digital security system
(B) A device to lift heavy objects
(C) An application to monitor machines
(D) Protective clothing for workers

여자의 회사는 무엇을 설계했는가?
(A) 디지털 보안 시스템
(B) 무거운 물체를 들어 올리는 장비
(C) 기계를 모니터하는 프로그램
(D) 근로자를 위한 보호복

어휘 security 보안 device 장치 protective clothing 보호복

해설 세부 사항 관련 – 여자의 회사가 설계한 것

여자가 첫 대사에서 공장 기계를 모니터하는 프로그램(It's an application to monitor factory machines)이라고 말하고 있으므로 정답은 (C)이다.

43

What does the woman say her company can provide?
(A) A new client discount
(B) A training video
(C) An extended warranty
(D) Customer testimonials

여자는 자신의 회사가 무엇을 제공할 수 있다고 말하는가?
(A) 신규 고객 할인
(B) 교육 동영상
(C) 품질 보증 기간 연장
(D) 고객 추천 글

어휘 extend 연장하다 warranty 품질 보증서 testimonial 추천의 글

해설 세부 사항 관련 – 여자의 회사가 제공할 수 있는 것

여자가 마지막 대사에서 단계별 설명이 담긴 동영상을 제공해 준다(We provide a video with step-by-step instructions)고 말하고 있으므로 정답은 (B)이다.

> **Paraphrasing** 대화의 a video with step-by-step
> instructions → 정답의 A training video

W-Am Hi. **44I'd like to go to the Baldwin Theater.** The address is 91 Circle Drive.

M-Cn **44Sure, 45but did you know they're resurfacing Circle Drive? 44I just dropped someone off in that area.**

W-Am Oh, really? I've got a ticket to a play, and the show starts at seven thirty. They don't let you in if you're late.

M-Cn Well, let me see. **45, 46I can turn onto Felton Street and cut over to Lancaster Drive.** It's a little out of the way, but it'll get you close to the theater.

여 안녕하세요. **볼드윈 극장에 가려고 해요.** 주소는 서클 길 91 입니다.

남 네, 그런데 서클 길은 재포장 공사 중인 걸 알고 계세요? 그 지역에 누구를 막 내려줬거든요.

여 아, 그래요? 연극 표가 있는데 공연이 7시 30분 시작이에요. 늦으면 입장을 시켜주지 않을 거에요.

남 자, 한번 보죠. **펠튼 가로 돌아서 랭커스터 길로 가로질러 갈 수 있어요.** 길을 약간 벗어나긴 하지만 극장 가까이까지 가게 될 거예요.

어휘 resurface 도로를 재포장하다 drop ~ off ~을 내려주다 cut over 횡단하다

44

Who most likely is the man?
(A) A theater employee
(B) A taxi driver
(C) A train conductor
(D) A construction worker

남자는 누구이겠는가?
(A) 극장 직원
(B) 택시 운전사
(C) 열차 승무원
(D) 공사 인부

어휘 conductor (버스나 기차의) 안내원, 승무원 construction 공사

해설 전체 내용 관련 – 남자의 직업

여자가 첫 대사에서 볼드원 극장에 가려고 한다(I'd like to go to the Baldwin Theater)고 하자, 남자가 알겠다(Sure)며, 그 지역에 누구를 막 내려줬다(I just dropped someone off in that area)고 말하고 있는 것으로 보아 남자는 택시 운전사임을 알 수 있다. 따라서 정답은 (B)이다.

45

What is causing a problem?
(A) A truck is too heavy.
(B) An event has been delayed.
(C) A parking area is full.
(D) A road is closed.

무엇 때문에 문제가 발생했는가?
(A) 트럭이 너무 무겁다.
(B) 행사가 지연됐다.
(C) 주차 구역이 꽉 찼다.
(D) 도로가 폐쇄됐다.

어휘 delay 지연시키다

해설 세부 사항 관련 – 문제가 발생한 이유
남자가 첫 대사에서 서클 길은 재포장 공사 중인 걸 알고 있는지(did you know they're resurfacing Circle Drive?) 물었고, 마지막 대사에서 펠튼 가로 돌아서 랭커스터 길로 가로질러 갈 수 있다(I can turn onto Felton Street and cut over to Lancaster Drive)고 말하는 것으로 보아 서클 길이 폐쇄되었음을 알 수 있다. 따라서 정답은 (D)이다.

46

What does the man say he will do?
(A) Ask for a refund
(B) Take a different route
(C) Postpone a trip
(D) File a complaint

남자는 무엇을 하겠다고 말하는가?
(A) 환불 요청
(B) 다른 경로 선택
(C) 여행 연기
(D) 불만 제기

어휘 refund 환불 postpone 연기하다 file a complaint 항의를 제기하다, 민원을 넣다

해설 세부 사항 관련 – 남자가 할 것
남자가 마지막 대사에서 펠튼 가로 돌아서 랭커스터 길로 가로질러 갈 수 있다(I can turn onto Felton Street and cut over to Lancaster Drive)고 말하고 있으므로 정답은 (B)이다.

> Paraphrasing 대화의 turn onto Felton Street and cut over to Lancaster Drive
> → 정답의 Take a different route

47-49

▶ 동영상 강의

| W-Br | Do you have a minute to discuss the budget for the upcoming Vancouver meeting? **[47] I've looked over the travel requests you submitted for your team.** Last year we sent only two representatives. |

M-Au	**[47] Ms. Tamura has just given us approval to send three.** In fact, **[48] the clients are looking to expand their online service options,** and the third representative we're bringing is particularly knowledgeable about that.
W-Br	OK. I guess we'll have to find savings somewhere else, then.
M-Au	I've already looked into some new meeting venues. **[49] The Renova Hotel is offering discounted corporate rates this month.**

여	곧 있을 밴쿠버 회의의 예산에 대해 잠시 논의할 시간 있으세요? 제출하신 팀 출장 요청서를 검토했는데요. 작년에는 대표로 두 명만 보냈잖아요.
남	타무라 씨가 세 명을 보내는 것을 승인해 주셨어요. 사실, 고객이 온라인 서비스 옵션을 확대할 생각을 하고 있어요. 저희가 데려가는 세 번째 직원은 특히 그쪽 지식이 많아요.
여	알겠습니다. 그렇다면 다른 곳에서 절약할 부분을 찾아봐야 할 것 같네요.
남	이미 새로운 회의 장소를 살펴보고 있어요. 레노바 호텔이 이번 달에 기업 할인 요금을 제공해서요.

| 어휘 | budget 예산 upcoming 다가오는, 곧 있을 representative 대표, 대리인 approval 승인 expand 확대하다, 확장하다 option 선택 particularly 특히 knowledgeable 아는 것이 많은 saving 절약 venue 장소 corporate 기업의, 회사의 rate 요금 |

47

Why does the woman say, "Last year we sent only two representatives"?
(A) To explain a delay
(B) To compliment a team
(C) To point out that an event was unsuccessful
(D) To question a decision

여자가 "작년에는 대표로 두 명만 보냈잖아요"라고 말하는 이유는?
(A) 지연에 관해 설명하려고
(B) 팀을 칭찬하려고
(C) 행사가 성공적이지 못했음을 지적하려고
(D) 결정에 이의를 제기하려고

어휘 compliment 칭찬하다 point out 지적하다 unsuccessful 성공하지 못한

해설 화자의 의도 파악 – 작년에는 대표로 두 명만 보냈다는 말의 의도
앞에서 여자가 제출한 팀 출장 요청서를 검토했다(I've looked over the travel requests you submitted for your team)고 말한 뒤 인용문을 언급하자, 남자가 타무라 씨가 세 명을 보내는 것을 승인해 줬다(Ms. Tamura has just given us approval to send three)고 말하는 것으로 보아, 여자가 생각했던 것보다 출장 인원이 많은 것에 대해 이의를 제기하기 위해 한 말임을 알 수 있다. 따라서 정답은 (D)이다.

48

According to the man, what do some clients want to do?

(A) Increase their online offerings
(B) Obtain additional financing
(C) Open a new office
(D) Recruit more employees

남자에 따르면, 고객은 무엇을 하고 싶어 하는가?

(A) 온라인으로 제공하는 것 늘리기
(B) 추가 자금 획득하기
(C) 새 사무실 열기
(D) 직원을 더 채용하기

어휘 obtain 얻다, 획득하다   additional 추가의   financing 자금, 재무   recruit 채용하다

해설 세부 사항 관련 – 고객이 하고 싶어 하는 것
남자가 첫 대사에서 고객이 온라인 서비스 옵션을 확대할 생각을 하고 있다(the clients are looking to expand their online service options)고 말하고 있으므로 정답은 (A)이다.

> Paraphrasing   대화의 expand their online service options
>   → 정답의 Increase their online offerings

49

According to the man, what is the Renova Hotel offering this month?

(A) A new shuttle service
(B) A discount for businesses
(C) A flexible cancellation policy
(D) Complimentary meals

남자에 따르면, 레노바 호텔은 이번 달에 무엇을 제공하는가?

(A) 새로운 셔틀 서비스
(B) 기업 할인
(C) 융통성 있는 취소 정책
(D) 무료 식사

어휘 flexible 융통성 있는, 유연한   complimentary 무료의

해설 세부 사항 관련 – 레노바 호텔이 이번 달에 제공하는 것
남자가 마지막 대사에서 레노바 호텔이 이번 달에 기업 할인 요금을 제공한다(The Renova Hotel is offering discounted corporate rates this month)고 말하고 있으므로 정답은 (B)이다.

> Paraphrasing   대화의 discounted corporate rates
>   → 정답의 A discount for businesses

50-52

W-Am Good morning. ⁵⁰**I wanted to meet today to discuss the recent decline in our museum's ticket sales.** You're the outreach

coordinator, so I'm hoping you might have some ideas on how we can attract more community involvement.

M-Cn Well, ⁵¹**I recently read an article about a museum in Chicago that has a room where visitors can paint on the walls. It's become very popular. We could try it here**—we have that huge room on the third floor that isn't being used.

W-Am That's a great idea. ⁵²**Can you draft a list of the supplies we would need to make sure we have the budget for them?**

여 안녕하세요. 오늘은 최근 우리 박물관 입장권 판매가 감소한 것에 대해 만나서 얘기 나누고 싶었습니다. 봉사 활동 담당자이시니 어떻게 하면 지역 사회 참여를 더 이끌어 낼 수 있을지 의견이 있으실 것 같아요.

남 음, 최근 시카고에 있는 박물관 관련 기사를 읽었는데요. 그곳에는 방문객들이 벽에 그림을 그릴 수 있는 전시실이 있어요. 인기가 굉장히 많아졌죠. 여기서도 시도해 볼 수 있을 것 같습니다. 3층에 사용하지 않는 큰 전시실이 있잖아요.

여 멋진 생각이네요. 예산이 있는지 확인할 수 있도록 필요한 물품 목록 초안을 작성해 주실 수 있나요?

어휘 decline 감소   outreach 봉사 활동   coordinator 조정관, 담당자   attract 끌어들이다, 불러일으키다   involvement 관여, 개입   popular 인기 있는   huge 거대한   draft 초안을 작성하다   budget 예산

50

What problem does the woman mention?

(A) A decrease in ticket sales
(B) A lack of exhibition space
(C) A colleague's resignation
(D) A damaged painting

여자는 어떤 문제를 언급하는가?

(A) 입장권 판매 감소
(B) 전시 공간 부족
(C) 동료의 사직
(D) 그림 훼손

어휘 decrease 감소   lack 부족, 결핍   exhibition 전시   colleague 동료   resignation 사직, 사임

해설 세부 사항 관련 – 여자가 언급하는 문제
여자가 첫 대사에서 오늘은 최근 박물관 입장권 판매가 감소한 것에 대해 만나서 얘기 나누고 싶었다(I wanted to meet today to discuss the recent decline in our museum's ticket sales)고 말하고 있으므로 정답은 (A)이다.

> Paraphrasing   대화의 the recent decline in our museum's ticket sales
>   → 정답의 A decrease in ticket sales

51

What does the man suggest doing?
(A) Relocating an exhibit
(B) Consulting a specialist
(C) Adding security measure
(D) Introducing a new activity

남자는 무엇을 하라고 제안하는가?
(A) 전시회 장소 옮기기
(B) 전문가 자문 구하기
(C) 보안 조치 추가하기
(D) 새로운 활동 도입하기

어휘 relocate 이전하다, 이동하다 exhibit 전시회 consult 상담하다 specialist 전문가 security measure 보안 조치 activity 활동

해설 세부 사항 관련 – 남자의 제안 사항
남자가 첫 대사에서 최근 시카고에 있는 박물관 관련 기사를 읽었는데 그곳에 방문객들이 벽에 그림을 그릴 수 있는 전시실이 있었다(I recently read an article about a museum in Chicago that has a room where visitors can paint on the walls)며 인기가 굉장히 많아졌다(It's become very popular)고 했고, 여기서도 시도해 볼 수 있을 것 같다(We could try it here)고 말하는 것으로 보아 남자는 방문객이 그림을 그리는 것과 같은 새로운 활동을 제안하고 있음을 알 수 있다. 따라서 정답은 (D)이다.

52

What will the man most likely do next?
(A) Write a press release
(B) Attend a budget meeting
(C) Make a list of supplies
(D) Plan a site visit

남자는 다음으로 무엇을 하겠는가?
(A) 보도 자료 작성하기
(B) 예산 회의 참석하기
(C) 물품 목록 작성하기
(D) 현장 방문 계획하기

어휘 press release 보도 자료

해설 세부 사항 관련 – 남자가 다음에 할 일
여자가 마지막 대사에서 필요한 물품 목록 초안을 작성해 줄 수 있는지 (Can you draft a list of the supplies ~?) 묻고 있으므로 정답은 (C)이다.

> Paraphrasing 대화의 draft a list of the supplies
> → 정답의 Make a list of supplies

53-55 3인 대화

W-Br Thilo, [53]**this is Ms. Gao, a new customer. She's purchasing an upholstered sofa.** We just walked around our showroom, and she's decided on our Hudson model.

M-Cn One of our best sellers!

W-Am It is really comfortable.

W-Br Can you assist her with the paperwork for our payment plan?

M-Cn Sure. Happy to help you, Ms. Gao. Are you getting the standard fabric?

W-Am No—I'd like to select a custom fabric.

M-Cn Just so you know, [54]**the price will increase some with a custom order.**

W-Am I think it's worth the extra cost. It'll really brighten up my living room.

M-Cn Wonderful. [55]**Now in order to set up a payment plan, I'll need to see some identification. A driver's license will do.**

여1 틸로, 이쪽은 신규 고객 가오 씨예요. 천을 씌운 소파를 구매하실 거고요. 전시실을 함께 둘러봤는데 허드슨 모델로 결정하셨어요.

남 베스트셀러 상품이죠!

여2 정말 안락해요.

여1 결제 관련 서류를 작성하시는 걸 도와드릴 수 있나요?

남 물론이죠. 도와드리게 되어 기쁩니다, 가오 씨. 일반 천으로 하시나요?

여2 아니요, 주문 제작 천을 선택하려고요.

남 아시겠지만 **주문 제작을 하시면 가격은 올라갑니다.**

여2 추가 비용을 지불할 만한 것 같아요. 거실이 정말 환해 보일 거예요.

남 좋습니다. **결제 방식을 정하려면 신분증을 확인해야 하는데요.** 운전면허증이면 됩니다.

어휘 upholstered (소파 등에) 덮개 천을 씌운 showroom 전시실 assist 돕다 payment plan 결제 방식 standard 일반적인, 보통의 fabric 직물, 천 custom 주문 제작 worth ~의 가치가 있는 brighten 밝히다, 환해 보이게 하다 identification 신원 확인, 신분증

53

Where most likely are the speakers?
(A) At a clothing factory
(B) At a bookstore
(C) At a tailor's shop
(D) At a furniture store

화자들은 어디 있겠는가?
(A) 의류 공장
(B) 서점
(C) 양복점
(D) 가구점

해설 전체 내용 관련 – 대화의 장소
첫 번째 여자가 첫 대사에서 이쪽은 신규 고객 가오 씨(this is Ms. Gao, a new customer)라고 소개하고 천을 씌운 소파를 구매할 것(She's

purchasing an upholstered sofa)이라고 덧붙이고 있는 것으로 보아 화자들은 가구점에서 대화 중임을 알 수 있다. 따라서 정답은 (D)이다.

Paraphrasing 대화의 sofa → 정답의 furniture

54

According to the man, why will a product cost more?
(A) It includes an extended warranty.
(B) It is a custom order.
(C) A rebate has expired.
(D) Shipping will be expedited.

남자에 따르면, 제품은 왜 가격이 더 비쌀 것인가?
(A) 보증 기간 연장을 포함한다.
(B) 주문 제작이다.
(C) 할인이 끝났다.
(D) 빠르게 배송될 것이다.

어휘 extend 연장하다, 늘리다 warranty 품질 보증서 rebate 할인, 환불 expire 만료되다, 끝나다 expedite 더 신속하게 처리하다

해설 세부 사항 관련 – 제품 가격이 더 비싼 이유

남자가 두 번째 대사에서 주문 제작을 하면 가격은 올라간다(the price will increase some with a custom order)고 말하고 있으므로 정답은 (B)이다.

Paraphrasing 대화의 the price will increase
→ 질문의 cost more

55

What does the man request?
(A) A purchase receipt
(B) A delivery address
(C) A form of identification
(D) An account number

남자는 무엇을 요청하는가?
(A) 구매 영수증
(B) 배송지 주소
(C) 신분증
(D) 계좌 번호

어휘 receipt 영수증 account number 계좌 번호

해설 세부 사항 관련 – 남자가 요청하는 것

남자가 마지막 대사에서 결제 방식을 정하려면 신분증을 확인해야 한다(Now in order to set up a payment plan, I'll need to see some identification)고 말하고 있으므로 정답은 (C)이다.

56-58

W-Am Good morning, Mr. Tong. I'm here to check on my order. **56 How are the chairs coming along?**

M-Cn **56 The machines have been assembling them.** They're almost ready. Right over here.

W-Am Wow, they look so nice!

M-Cn **57 Look at the curved shape of the back. The only way you can get that unique shape is by means of the specialized laser we use.**

W-Am Amazing! Can I also see the pullout sofa?

M-Cn Not right now. It's being treated with mineral oil. But **58 later today I should be able to take a photo and send it to you.**

여 안녕하세요, 통 씨. 주문 좀 확인하러 왔어요. **의자들은 어떻게 되어 가나요?**

남 **기계에서 조립하고 있어요.** 준비가 거의 다 됐습니다. 여기 있어요.

여 우와, 정말 멋지네요!

남 **뒷면의 곡선 모양을 보세요. 그렇게 독특한 형태를 얻을 수 있는 방법은 저희가 사용하는 전문 레이저를 쓰는 수밖엔 없어요.**

여 대단해요! 소파베드도 볼 수 있을까요?

남 지금은 안 돼요. 미네랄 오일 처리를 하고 있어요. 하지만 **이따가 사진을 찍어 보내 드릴 수 있을 겁니다.**

어휘 come along 되어 가다 assemble 조립하다 curved 곡선의 by means of ~에 의해, ~을 써서 specialized 전문화된, 전문적인 pullout sofa 소파 베드 treat 처리하다

56

Where most likely are the speakers?
(A) At a hotel
(B) At a factory
(C) At a retail store
(D) At a trade show

화자들은 어디에 있겠는가?
(A) 호텔
(B) 공장
(C) 소매점
(D) 무역 박람회

해설 전체 내용 관련 – 대화의 장소

여자가 첫 대사에서 의자들은 어떻게 되어 가는지(How are the chairs coming along?) 묻자 남자가 기계에서 조립하고 있다(The machines have been assembling them)고 말하는 것으로 보아 화자들은 의자를 생산하는 공장에서 대화 중임을 알 수 있다. 따라서 정답은 (B)이다.

57

What feature does the man emphasize about some chairs?
(A) The color
(B) The price
(C) The shape
(D) The durability

남자는 의자의 어떤 특징을 강조하는가?
(A) 색상
(B) 가격
(C) 모양
(D) 내구성

어휘 feature 특징, 기능 emphasize 강조하다

해설 세부 사항 관련 – 남자가 강조하는 의자 특징
남자가 두 번째 대사에서 뒷면의 곡선 모양을 보라(Look at the curved shape of the back)며, 그렇게 독특한 형태를 얻을 수 있는 방법은 자신들이 사용하는 전문 레이저를 쓰는 수밖엔 없다(The only way you can get that unique shape is by means of the specialized laser we use)고 덧붙이고 있으므로 정답은 (C)이다.

58

What does the man say he will do later?
(A) Modify a design
(B) E-mail a contract
(C) Create an invoice
(D) Send a photo

남자는 나중에 무엇을 하겠다고 말하는가?
(A) 디자인 변경하기
(B) 이메일로 계약서 보내기
(C) 청구서 작성하기
(D) 사진 보내기

어휘 modify 변경하다, 수정하다 contract 계약(서) invoice 청구서

해설 세부 사항 관련 – 남자가 나중에 할 일
남자가 마지막 대사에서 이따가 사진을 찍어 보내 줄 수 있다(later today I should be able to take a photo and send it to you)고 말하고 있으므로 정답은 (D)이다.

59-61

M-Au Hi, So-Jin. **59 I just heard that Ms. Yoon is retiring next month.**

W-Br I'll be sorry to see her go. She was my mentor when I first joined the firm, and we've worked on dozens of projects together.

M-Au **60 It's a bit hard to imagine our sales team without her. 61 Has anybody approached you about leading the team after she's gone?**

W-Br **61 Yes, and I've thought about it. It's a big step up, even for someone like me who's worked in Sales for eight years. And Human Resources hasn't even posted the job description yet.**

M-Au Well, we need someone with experience.

남 안녕하세요, 소진 씨. 방금 들었는데 윤 씨가 다음 달에 퇴직한다면서요.

여 떠나시는 걸 보면 섭섭할 거예요. 제가 처음 입사했을 때 저의 멘토이셨고, 수십 건의 프로젝트를 함께 했거든요.

남 윤 씨가 없는 영업팀은 상상하기 어렵네요. 윤 씨가 떠나고 나면 당신 보고 팀을 이끌어 달라고 누군가 이야기했나요?

여 네, 거기에 대해 생각해 봤어요. 영업팀에서 8년간 일한 저 같은 사람에게도 큰 도약이죠. 인사부에서 아직 직무 기술서를 올리지 않았어요.

남 음, 우린 경력 있는 사람이 필요해요.

어휘 retire 퇴직하다, 은퇴하다 firm 회사 dozens of 수십의 imagine 상상하다 approach (다가와서) 말을 하다, 접근하다 post 게시하다 job description 직무 기술서

59

What will happen next month?
(A) An award will be given.
(B) A new product will launch.
(C) A colleague will retire.
(D) An office will relocate.

다음 달에 무슨 일이 있을 것인가?
(A) 상이 수여된다.
(B) 신제품이 출시된다.
(C) 동료가 퇴직한다.
(D) 사무실을 이전한다.

어휘 award 상 launch 출시되다, 개시하다 colleague 동료 relocate 이전하다

해설 세부 사항 관련 – 다음 달에 발생할 일
남자가 첫 대사에서 윤 씨가 다음 달에 퇴직한다고 방금 들었다(I just heard that Ms. Yoon is retiring next month)고 말하고 있으므로 정답은 (C)이다.

Paraphrasing 대화의 Ms. Yoon is retiring
→ 정답의 A colleague will retire.

60

What department do the speakers work in?
(A) Sales
(B) Human Resources
(C) Legal
(D) Accounting

화자들은 어느 부서에서 일하는가?
(A) 영업부
(B) 인사부
(C) 법무부
(D) 회계부

해설 전체 내용 관련 – 화자들의 근무 부서
남자가 두 번째 대사에서 윤 씨가 없는 영업팀은 상상하기 어렵다(It's a bit hard to imagine our sales team without her)고 말하고 있으므로 화자들은 영업부에서 일하고 있다는 것을 알 수 있다. 따라서 정답은 (A)이다.

61

What does the man imply when he says, "we need someone with experience"?
(A) The team has grown very quickly.
(B) The woman should apply for a job.
(C) A job description should be revised.
(D) A new manager is not experienced enough.

남자가 "우린 경력이 있는 사람이 필요해요"라고 말하는 의도는 무엇인가?
(A) 팀이 매우 빠르게 성장했다.
(B) 여자가 그 자리에 지원해야 한다.
(C) 직무 기술서가 수정되어야 한다.
(D) 신규 관리자는 경력이 충분치 않다.

어휘 apply for ~에 지원하다, 신청하다   revise 변경하다, 수정하다

해설 화자의 의도 파악 – 우린 경력이 있는 사람이 필요하다는 말의 의도
앞에서 남자가 윤 씨가 떠나고 나면 여자에게 팀을 이끌어 달라고 누군가 이야기했는지(Has anybody approached you about leading the team after she's gone?) 묻자 여자가 거기에 대해 생각해 봤다(Yes, and I've thought about it)며 영업팀에서 8년간 일한 자신에게도 큰 도약(It's a big step up, even for someone like me who's worked in Sales for eight years)이라고 했다. 여자가 인사부에서 아직 직무 기술서를 올리지 않았다(And Human Resources hasn't even posted the job description yet)고 덧붙이자 남자가 인용문을 언급하는 것으로 보아 남자는 영업팀에서 8년간 일한 여자가 영업팀 리더 자리에 적합한 사람이므로 지원해야 한다는 의도로 한 말임을 알 수 있다. 따라서 정답은 (B)이다.

62-64 대화 + 시간표

W-Am Rajesh, **62it was nice to see you here in New York again this year.**

M-Cn Same here. **62I look forward to attending the Theater Technology Conference again next year.**

W-Am **63I really enjoyed your talk, especially the information you provided on acoustics. Is it published anywhere?** I'd like to have a closer look.

M-Cn Actually, it is. You can find the article in last November's issue of *Theater Sound*. It's posted online.

W-Am Great. I'll look it up.

M-Cn Oh— **64my train leaves in fourteen minutes.** I have to get going. Safe travels, Camille!

여 라제쉬, 올해도 여기 뉴욕에서 다시 만나게 되어 반가웠어요.

남 저도 그래요. 내년에 다시 극장 기술 학회에 참석할 일이 너무 기다려져요.

여 **말씀하신 내용이 너무 좋았어요. 특히 음향 시설에 관해 제공해 주신 정보가요. 어딘가에 발표됐나요?** 자세히 보고 싶어요.

남 사실 〈극장 음향〉 지난 11월호 기사에서 찾으실 수 있어요. 온라인에 게시됐거든요.

여 좋아요. 찾아볼게요.

남 아, **제가 탈 열차가 14분 후에 출발해요.** 가야겠네요. 조심히 가세요, 카미유!

어휘 look forward to ~을 고대하다   acoustics 음향 시설   publish 출판하다, 발표하다   article 기사   issue 호

Line	Destination	Next Train
Red	Shady Grove	7 minutes
Yellow	Braddock Bay	9 minutes
Blue	64Largo	6414 minutes
Silver	Ashburn	11 minutes

노선	목적지	다음 열차
레드	셰이디 그로브	7분
옐로우	브래독 베이	9분
블루	**64라르고**	**6414분**
실버	애쉬번	11분

62

Why are the speakers in New York?
(A) They saw a play.
(B) They attended a conference.
(C) They met with some clients.
(D) They viewed some real estate.

화자들은 왜 뉴욕에 있는가?
(A) 연극을 보았다.
(B) 학회에 참석했다.
(C) 고객을 만났다.
(D) 부동산을 둘러봤다.

어휘 real estate 부동산

해설 세부 사항 관련 – 화자들이 뉴욕에 있는 이유
여자가 첫 대사에서 올해도 여기 뉴욕에서 다시 만나게 되어 반가웠다(it was nice to see you here in New York again this year)고 하자, 남자가 내년에 다시 극장 기술 학회에 참석할 일이 너무 기다려진다(I look forward to attending the Theater Technology Conference again next year)고 말하고 있으므로 정답은 (B)이다.

63

What does the woman ask the man about?
(A) Locating some information
(B) Applying for a position
(C) Opening a branch office
(D) Making a reservation

여자는 남자에게 무엇에 대해 물어보는가?
(A) 정보 찾기
(B) 일자리 지원하기
(C) 지사 개설하기
(D) 예약하기

어휘 locate 정확한 위치를 찾아내다 apply for ~에 지원하다
branch office 지사

해설 세부 사항 관련 – 여자의 문의 사항
여자가 두 번째 대사에서 음향 시설에 관해 제공해 준 정보가 특히 좋았다(I really enjoyed your talk, especially the information you provided on acoustics)고 하면서 어딘가에 발표됐는지(Is it published anywhere?) 묻고 있으므로 정답은 (A)이다.

64

Look at the graphic. Where will the man travel to next?
(A) Shady Grove
(B) Braddock Bay
(C) Largo
(D) Ashburn

시각 정보에 의하면, 남자는 다음에 어디로 이동할 것인가?
(A) 셰이디 그로브
(B) 브래독 베이
(C) 라르고
(D) 애쉬번

해설 시각 정보 연계 – 남자의 다음 이동 장소
남자가 마지막 대사에서 자신이 탈 열차가 14분 후에 출발한다(my train leaves in fourteen minutes)고 말하고 있고, 시간표에 따르면 14분 후에 오는 열차는 라르고(Largo)행 열차이므로 정답은 (C)이다.

65-67 대화 + 메뉴

M-Cn	Welcome to Orlando's Deli. If you'd like to try one of our daily specials, they're on the board behind me.
W-Br	Wow, that's a great menu. ⁶⁵**The vegetable curry looks good. Is it spicy?**
M-Cn	No, it's very mild—but we just sold out, unfortunately.
W-Br	In that case, ⁶⁶**I'll have the lasagna.**

M-Cn	Great choice. By the way, ⁶⁷**we just opened our new patio this week in case you'd like to sit outside.**
W-Br	Actually, it is a beautiful day. ⁶⁷**And your patio looks lovely.**

남	올랜도 델리입니다. 오늘의 특선 중 하나를 맛보고 싶으시면 제 뒤에 있는 보드에서 보실 수 있습니다.
여	와, 훌륭한 메뉴예요. **채소 카레가 맛있어 보이네요. 맵나요?**
남	아니요, 굉장히 순해요. 하지만 안타깝게도 지금 막 다 팔렸네요.
여	그렇다면 **라자냐를 먹을게요.**
남	잘 고르셨어요. 그런데, **혹시 야외에 앉고 싶으시다면 이번 주에 새 테라스를 열었어요.**
여	사실 날씨가 정말 좋네요. **테라스도 좋아 보이고요.**

어휘 spicy 매운 mild 순한 sold out 다 팔린, 매진된 unfortunately 안타깝게도, 유감스럽게도

Daily Specials
1. Vegetable curry
2. Hamburger platter
⁶⁶3. Lasagna
4. Mushroom pasta

오늘의 특선
1. 채소 카레
2. 햄버거 세트
⁶⁶3. 라자냐
4. 버섯 파스타

65

What does the woman ask the man about?
(A) Whether a coupon is valid
(B) Whether a food is spicy
(C) Whether a drink is included
(D) Whether any seats are available

여자는 남자에게 무엇에 대해 물어보는가?
(A) 쿠폰이 유효한지 여부
(B) 음식이 매운지 여부
(C) 음료가 포함되는지 여부
(D) 좌석이 있는지 여부

어휘 valid 유효한 include 포함시키다 available 이용할 수 있는

해설 세부 사항 관련 – 여자가 남자에게 묻는 것

여자가 첫 번째 대사에서 채소 카레가 맛있어 보인다(The vegetable curry looks good)며 매운지(Is it spicy?)를 묻고 있으므로 정답은 (B)이다.

> **Paraphrasing** 대화의 The vegetable curry → 정답의 a food

66

Look at the graphic. Which special does the woman order?

(A) Special 1
(B) Special 2
(C) Special 3
(D) Special 4

시각 정보에 의하면, 여자는 어떤 특선을 주문하는가?

(A) 특선 1
(B) 특선 2
(C) 특선 3
(D) 특선 4

해설 시각 정보 연계 – 여자가 주문하는 특선

여자가 두 번째 대사에서 라자냐를 먹겠다(I'll have the lasagna)고 말하고 있고, 메뉴를 보면 라자냐는 특선 3이므로 정답은 (C)이다.

67

What will the woman most likely do next?

(A) Move her car
(B) Go to a patio
(C) Make a reservation
(D) Meet some friends

여자는 다음으로 무엇을 하겠는가?

(A) 차량 이동시키기
(B) 테라스로 가기
(C) 예약하기
(D) 친구 만나기

해설 세부 사항 관련 – 여자가 다음에 할 일

남자가 마지막 대사에서 혹시 야외에 앉고 싶다면 이번 주에 새 테라스를 열었다(we just opened our new patio this week in case you'd like to sit outside)고 하자 여자가 테라스도 좋아 보인다(your patio looks lovely)고 말하고 있으므로 정답은 (B)이다.

68-70 대화 + 지도

> W-Am I'm excited about our hike today here at Marina Park. And [68]**I'm so glad we got to the park early before it gets crowded.** Which trail should we hike?
>
> M-Au Let's take a look at the map. We're at the visitor center, and there's a shuttle that

stops at different trailheads.

> W-Am Right. It looks like the Creek Trail and the Pond Trail are fairly short. I'd like to do a more challenging hike.
>
> M-Au OK. [69]**How about the Waterfall Trail?**
>
> W-Am [69]**That sounds good. And look—[70]there's a video about the park. We can watch while we wait.**

> 여 오늘 이곳 마리나 공원에서 하이킹을 하게 되어 정말 신나요. **붐비기 전에 일찍 공원에 도착해서 좋네요.** 우리는 어떤 길에서 하이킹을 하나요?
>
> 남 지도를 봅시다. 우린 지금 방문자 센터에 있는데 여러 기점에 정차하는 셔틀버스가 있어요.
>
> 여 맞아요. 개울길과 연못길이 꽤 짧아 보이네요. 저는 더 어려운 하이킹을 하고 싶어요.
>
> 남 좋아요. **폭포길은 어때요?**
>
> 여 **좋을 것 같아요.** 그리고 자, **공원에 관한 동영상이 있어요. 기다리는 동안 보면 되겠어요.**

> 어휘 crowded 붐비는 trailhead 길의 기점 fairly 꽤 challenging 도전적인, 힘든

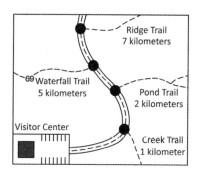

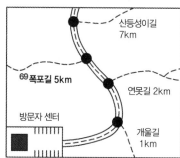

어휘 ridge 산등성이

68

What is the woman happy about?

(A) She happened to meet some friends.
(B) The weather is perfect for an activity.
(C) The park was closer than expected.
(D) There are few people in the park.

여자가 기분이 좋은 이유는?
(A) 우연히 친구들을 만났다.
(B) 활동을 하기에 완벽한 날씨다.
(C) 공원이 예상보다 가깝다.
(D) 공원에 사람이 별로 없다.

해설 세부 사항 관련 – 여자가 기분이 좋은 이유

여자가 첫 대사에서 붐비기 전에 일찍 공원에 도착해서 좋다(I'm so glad we got to the park early before it gets crowded)고 말하고 있으므로 정답은 (D)이다.

Paraphrasing 대화의 glad → 질문의 happy

69

Look at the graphic. How far will the speakers hike?
(A) 7 kilometers
(B) 5 kilometers
(C) 2 kilometers
(D) 1 kilometer

시각 정보에 의하면, 화자들은 얼마나 멀리까지 하이킹을 갈 것인가?
(A) 7km
(B) 5km
(C) 2km
(D) 1km

해설 시각 정보 연계 – 화자들이 하이킹 할 거리

남자가 마지막 대사에서 폭포길은 어떤지(How about the Waterfall Trail?) 묻자, 여자가 좋을 것 같다(That sounds good)고 말하는 것으로 보아 화자들은 폭포길을 하이킹을 할 예정임을 알 수 있다. 지도를 보면 폭포길은 5km이므로 정답은 (B)이다.

70

What can the speakers do while waiting for the shuttle?
(A) Buy some snacks
(B) Watch a video
(C) Visit a gift shop
(D) Rent some equipment

화자들은 셔틀버스를 기다리는 동안 무엇을 할 수 있는가?
(A) 간식 구매
(B) 동영상 시청
(C) 기념품점 방문
(D) 장비 대여

어휘 rent 빌리다, 대여하다   equipment 장비

해설 세부 사항 관련 – 화자들이 셔틀버스를 기다리는 동안 할 일

여자가 마지막 대사에서 공원에 관한 동영상이 있다(there's a video about the park)며 기다리는 동안 보면 되겠다(We can watch while we wait)고 말하고 있으므로 정답은 (B)이다.

PART 4

71-73 전화 메시지

> W-Br Hi, Ms. Cho. I'm calling from Springdale Lights. **71 Yesterday, you ordered 24 of our purple solar lanterns for your upcoming event.** **72 Unfortunately, our supplier won't be able to get us purple lanterns for another three weeks,** so we only have yellow ones in stock. **73 We would like to offer you a ten percent discount on them to apologize for this.** Please call us back to confirm whether you'd like the yellow solar lights, and we'll set them aside for you.

> 안녕하세요, 조 씨. 스프링데일 라이트입니다. 어제 다가오는 행사에 쓸 보라색 태양열 손전등 24개를 주문하셨잖아요. 안타깝게도 공급업체에서 앞으로 3주간 보라색 손전등을 공급하지 못할 거라고 합니다. 그래서 노란색만 재고가 있어요. **사과의 의미로 10퍼센트 할인을 제공해 드리고 싶은데요.** 다시 전화 주셔서 노란색 태양열 손전등을 원하시는지 알려 주시면 따로 준비해 두겠습니다.

> **어휘** solar 태양의, 태양열을 이용한   upcoming 다가오는, 곧 있을   unfortunately 안타깝게도   supplier 공급업자   have ~ in stock ~의 재고가 있다   apologize 사과하다   confirm 확인해 주다, 확정하다   set aside 챙겨 두다, 확보하다

71

What did the listener do yesterday?
(A) She placed an order.
(B) She scheduled an event.
(C) She called a manager.
(D) She painted some rooms.

청자는 어제 무엇을 했는가?
(A) 주문을 했다.
(B) 행사 일정을 잡았다.
(C) 관리자에게 전화했다.
(D) 방을 칠했다.

어휘 schedule 일정을 잡다

해설 세부 사항 관련 – 청자가 어제 한 일

화자가 초반부에 청자가 어제 보라색 태양열 손전등 24개를 주문했다(Yesterday, you ordered 24 of our purple solar lanterns ~)고 말하고 있으므로 정답은 (A)이다.

Paraphrasing 담화의 ordered → 정답의 placed an order

72

What problem does the speaker mention?
(A) A price has increased.
(B) A machine needs to be repaired.
(C) A product is not available.
(D) A performance has been canceled.

화자는 어떤 문제를 언급하는가?
(A) 가격이 올랐다.
(B) 기계를 수리해야 한다.
(C) 제품을 구할 수 없다.
(D) 공연이 취소됐다.

어휘 increase 인상되다, 증가하다   available 이용할 수 있는, 구할 수 있는   performance 공연

해설 세부 사항 관련 – 화자가 언급하는 문제
화자가 중반부에 안타깝게도 공급업체에서 앞으로 3주간 보라색 손전등을 공급하지 못할 것(Unfortunately, our supplier won't be able to get us purple lanterns for another three weeks)이라고 말하고 있으므로 정답은 (C)이다.

73

What does the speaker offer the listener?
(A) Expedited shipping
(B) A full refund
(C) A free consultation
(D) A discount

화자는 청자에게 무엇을 제공하는가?
(A) 신속 배송
(B) 전액 환불
(C) 무료 상담
(D) 할인

어휘 expedite 더 신속히 처리하다   refund 환불   consultation 상담

해설 세부 사항 관련 – 화자가 제공하는 것
화자가 후반부에 사과의 의미로 10퍼센트 할인을 제공하겠다(We would like to offer you a ten percent discount on them to apologize for this)고 말하고 있으므로 정답은 (D)이다.

74-76 담화

M-Au **74 Welcome to Osterwind Estate. The former owner, Ms. Yuping Wei, was a famous painter. What's special about this estate is that Ms. Wei designed it herself, including the landscaping. 75 We're asking volunteers to clear debris from the walkways around the gardens in preparation for the estate's first season as a public park. You can pick up a bag and gloves from the patio area. And remember, be sure to see me as you check out before you leave. 76 All volunteers are eligible for a complimentary visitor pass that you can use to access the estate and attend any events held here all summer long.**

오스터윈드 에스테이트에 오신 것을 환영합니다. 이전 소유주인 유핑 웨이 씨는 유명 화가였습니다. 이 저택의 특별한 점은 웨이 씨가 조경

을 비롯해 직접 설계했다는 것입니다. 공원으로서 첫 시즌을 맞을 준비로 자원봉사자들은 정원 주변 보도에 있는 쓰레기를 치워 주시기 바랍니다. 테라스 구역에서 봉지와 장갑을 가져가시면 됩니다. 가시기 전 체크아웃하실 때 반드시 저에게 와 주세요. 모든 자원봉사자는 무료 방문자 출입증을 받을 수 있으며, 이 패스를 사용하여 여름 내내 이 저택에 입장할 수 있고 이곳에서 열리는 모든 행사에 참석할 수 있습니다.

어휘 estate 저택, 토지   former 이전의   landscaping 조경   volunteer 자원봉사자   debris 쓰레기   walkway 보도, 통로   in preparation for ~의 준비로   be eligible for ~을 받을 자격이 있다   complimentary 무료의   pass 통행증, 출입증   access 접근하다, 이용하다

74

According to the speaker, what is special about Osterwind Estate?
(A) It houses many historic paintings.
(B) It was designed by its owner.
(C) It includes a botanical garden.
(D) It is used as a museum.

화자에 따르면, 오스터윈드 에스테이트의 특별한 점은 무엇인가?
(A) 역사적인 그림을 많이 소장하고 있다.
(B) 소유주가 설계했다.
(C) 식물원이 포함되어 있다.
(D) 박물관으로 이용된다.

어휘 house 소장하다, 수용하다   historic 역사적인   include 포함하다   botanical garden 식물원

해설 세부 사항 관련 – 오스터윈드 에스테이트의 특별한 점
화자가 도입부에 오스터윈드 에스테이트에 오신 것을 환영한다(Welcome to Osterwind Estate)고 하면서 이전 소유주인 유핑 웨이 씨는 유명 화가(The former owner, Ms. Yuping Wei, was a famous painter)였고, 이 저택의 특별한 점은 웨이 씨가 직접 설계한 것(What's special about this estate is that Ms. Wei designed it herself ~)이라고 말하고 있으므로 정답은 (B)이다.

75

Why are the listeners at Osterwind Estate?
(A) To attend an awards ceremony
(B) To apply for landscaping jobs
(C) To take a tour of a building
(D) To clean up some gardens

청자들은 왜 오스터윈드 에스테이트에 갔는가?
(A) 시상식에 참석하려고
(B) 조경 일자리에 지원하려고
(C) 건물을 견학하려고
(D) 정원을 청소하려고

어휘 awards ceremony 시상식   apply for ~에 지원하다

해설 세부 사항 관련 – 청자들이 오스터윈드 에스테이트에 간 이유
화자가 중반부에 자원봉사자들은 정원 주변 보도에 있는 쓰레기를 치워 주기 바란다(We're asking volunteers to clear debris from the

walkways around the gardens ～)며 테라스 구역에서 봉지와 장갑을 가져가면 된다(You can pick up a bag and gloves from the patio area)고 말하고 있으므로 청자들은 자원봉사자들이며 정원을 청소하러 갔다는 것을 알 수 있다. 따라서 정답은 (D)이다.

> **Paraphrasing** 담화의 clear debris from the walkways around the gardens
> → 정답의 clean up some gardens

76

What will the listeners receive?
(A) Gift-shop coupons
(B) Free passes
(C) Lunch boxes
(D) T-shirts

청자들은 무엇을 받을 것인가?
(A) 기념품점 쿠폰
(B) 무료 출입증
(C) 점심 도시락
(D) 티셔츠

해설 세부 사항 관련 – 청자들이 받을 것
화자가 마지막에 모든 자원봉사자들은 무료 방문자 출입증을 받을 수 있다(All volunteers are eligible for a complimentary visitor pass ～)고 말하고 있으므로 정답은 (B)이다.

> **Paraphrasing** 담화의 a complimentary visitor pass
> → 정답의 Free passes

77-79 전화 메시지

M-Cn Good morning, Ms. Espinosa. This is Marcel Fournier. It's Saturday morning, and I'm on my way to the airport. This is a little out of the ordinary, but ⁷⁷**I'm calling because in my haste I left a note with Mr. Hang's mobile phone number on my office desk.** He's picking me up from the airport, and I'll be stuck if I can't reach him. ⁷⁷,⁷⁸**I'll need you to go into the office and text me with the number.** I know this is inconvenient. ⁷⁹**I'll check my messages once I land in San Diego.**

안녕하세요, 에스피노사 씨. 마르셀 푸르니에입니다. 지금은 토요일 아침이고 공항으로 가는 길이에요. 이런 적이 별로 없었는데, **급하게 나오느라 행 씨의 핸드폰 번호가 적힌 쪽지를 사무실 책상에 두고 와서 전화드려요.** 행 씨가 공항으로 저를 픽업하러 나올 텐데 연락이 안 되면 오도가도 못할 겁니다. **사무실로 가서 전화번호를 문자 메시지로 보내주세요.** 불편한 일이라는 거 알아요. 샌디에이고에 착륙하면 메시지를 확인할게요.

> **어휘** out of the ordinary 이색적인, 특이한 in one's haste 서두른 나머지 stuck 꼼짝 못하는, 빠져나갈 수가 없는 reach (전화로) 연락하다 inconvenient 불편한 land 착륙하다, 도착하다

77

Who most likely is the listener?
(A) A travel agent
(B) An administrative assistant
(C) A flight attendant
(D) A security guard

청자는 누구이겠는가?
(A) 여행사 직원
(B) 행정 비서
(C) 항공기 승무원
(D) 보안 요원

어휘 administrative 행정상의, 관리상의

해설 전체 내용 관련 – 청자의 직업
화자가 초반부에서 급하게 나오느라 행 씨의 핸드폰 번호가 적힌 쪽지를 사무실 책상에 두고 와서 전화한다(I'm calling because in my haste I left a note with Mr. Hang's mobile phone number on my office desk)며, 사무실로 가서 전화번호를 문자 메시지로 보내 달라(I'll need you to go into the office and text me with the number)고 말하는 것으로 보아 청자는 비서임을 알 수 있다. 따라서 정답은 (B)이다.

78

Why does the speaker say, "I know this is inconvenient"?
(A) To suggest a deadline extension
(B) To report on an additional cost
(C) To offer an alternative solution
(D) To apologize for a request

화자가 "불편한 일이라는 거 알아요"라고 말하는 이유는?
(A) 기한 연장을 제안하려고
(B) 추가 비용에 대해 보고하려고
(C) 대안이 될 해결책을 제안하려고
(D) 요청한 것에 대해 사과하려고

어휘 deadline 기한, 마감 일자 extension 연장 additional 추가의 alternative 대안이 되는 apologize 사과하다

해설 화자의 의도 파악 – 불편한 일이라는 거 안다는 말의 의도
앞에서 사무실로 가서 전화번호를 문자 메시지로 보내달라(I'll need you to go into the office and text me with the number)고 한 뒤 인용문을 언급하고 있으므로, 요청에 대해 사과하려는 의도로 한 말임을 알 수 있다. 따라서 정답은 (D)이다.

79

What will the speaker do when he arrives in San Diego?
(A) Retrieve his messages
(B) Check in to a hotel
(C) Change a flight reservation
(D) Visit a company office

화자는 샌디에이고에 도착하면 무엇을 할 것인가?
(A) 메시지 확인하기
(B) 호텔에 체크인하기
(C) 항공편 예약 변경하기
(D) 사무실 방문하기

어휘 retrieve (저장된 정보를) 확인하다   reservation 예약

해설 세부 사항 관련 – 화자가 샌디에이고에 도착해서 할 일

화자가 마지막에 샌디에이고에 착륙하면 메시지를 확인하겠다(I'll check my messages once I land in San Diego)고 말하고 있으므로 정답은 (A)이다.

> **Paraphrasing**   담화의 land → 질문의 arrives
> 담화의 check → 정답의 Retrieve

80-82 담화

> **W-Am** Hi, everyone! Thanks for watching today. If you're new to my channel, you should know that **80 my videos focus on ways that we can repurpose common objects so that they don't end up in landfills.** In this video, you'll learn how to make candles from old and leftover crayons. **81 Your first step is to collect the items you'll need.** You may already have some old crayons around the house, or you can ask your friends and neighbors for theirs. I'll be covering a lot of steps, but don't worry, **82 a full written version of the instructions is available on my Web site. I recommend downloading those later for future reference.**

안녕하세요, 여러분! 오늘도 시청해 주셔서 감사합니다. 제 채널을 처음 방문하셨다면, 제 영상은 흔한 물건들의 용도를 변경하여 쓰레기 매립지로 가지 않도록 하는 방법에 초점을 맞추고 있다는 것을 아시면 좋겠습니다. 이번 영상에서는 낡은 크레용 찌꺼기로 양초를 만드는 방법을 배우게 됩니다. 첫 번째 단계는 필요한 물품을 모으는 일입니다. 이미 집에 낡은 크레용이 있을 겁니다. 아니면 친구나 이웃에게 요청해도 돼요. 많은 단계를 다루겠지만 걱정 마세요. 제 웹사이트에 서면으로 된 전체 설명서가 있습니다. 향후에 참고할 수 있도록 다운로드하시는 것을 권장합니다.

어휘 focus on ~에 초점을 맞추다   repurpose 다른 용도에 맞게 고치다   object 물건, 물체   end up in 결국 ~로 끝나다   landfill 쓰레기 매립지   leftover 남은 것, 찌꺼기   collect 모으다, 수집하다

---

neighbor 이웃   cover 다루다   instructions 설명서   available 이용할 수 있는, 구할 수 있는   reference 참고, 참조

80

What does the speaker say her videos are usually about?
(A) How to plan trips
(B) How to reuse items
(C) How to organize closets
(D) How to draw landscapes

화자는 자신의 영상이 보통 무엇에 관한 것이라고 말하는가?
(A) 여행을 계획하는 법
(B) 물건을 재사용하는 법
(C) 벽장을 정리하는 법
(D) 풍경화를 그리는 법

어휘 reuse 재사용하다   organize 정리하다   landscape 풍경, 풍경화

해설 세부 사항 관련 – 영상 주제에 대해 하는 말

화자가 초반부에 자신의 영상은 흔한 물건들의 용도를 변경하여 쓰레기 매립지로 가지 않도록 하는 방법에 초점을 맞추고 있다(my videos focus on ways that we can repurpose common objects so that they don't end up in landfills)고 말하고 있으므로 정답은 (B)이다.

> **Paraphrasing**   담화의 ways that we can repurpose common objects
> → 정답의 How to reuse items

81

What first step does the speaker mention?
(A) Writing a list
(B) Finding coupons
(C) Gathering supplies
(D) Looking at images online

화자가 언급하는 첫 번째 단계는 무엇인가?
(A) 목록 작성하기
(B) 쿠폰 찾기
(C) 물품 모으기
(D) 온라인에서 이미지 보기

어휘 gather 모으다   supply 용품, 물품

해설 세부 사항 관련 – 화자가 언급한 첫 번째 단계

화자가 중반부에 첫 번째 단계는 필요한 물품을 모으는 일(Your first step is to collect the items you'll need)이라고 말하고 있으므로 정답은 (C)이다.

> **Paraphrasing**   담화의 collect the items
> → 정답의 Gathering supplies

82

According to the speaker, what can the listeners do on a Web site?
(A) Enter a contest
(B) Subscribe to a video channel
(C) Submit some photographs
(D) Download some instructions

화자에 따르면, 청자들은 웹사이트에서 무엇을 할 수 있는가?
(A) 대회 참가하기
(B) 영상 채널 구독하기
(C) 사진 제출하기
(D) 설명서 다운로드하기

어휘 enter a contest 대회에 참가하다 subscribe to ~을 구독하다

해설 세부 사항 관련 – 웹사이트에서 할 수 있는 것

화자가 마지막에 웹사이트에 서면으로 된 전체 설명서가 있다(a full written version of the instructions is available on my Web site)고 하면서 향후에 참고할 수 있도록 다운로드하는 것을 권장한다(I recommend downloading those later for future reference)고 말하는 것으로 보아 웹사이트에서 설명서를 다운로드할 수 있다는 것을 알 수 있다. 따라서 정답은 (D)이다.

83-85 연설   동영상 강의

> **W-Br** Thank you all for coming to this press conference. As you know, [83]**the Grand Falls Bridge improvement work has been underway for almost a year.** We're nearing the final stage of sanding and painting the newly built portions. [84]**I know the fishing community has expressed concern over the potential environmental impact of this project on our local marine life.** Well, all required studies were conducted a year ago. I'll take some questions now. [85]**After that, our special-events coordinator will discuss the bridge-opening ceremony that's being planned.**
>
> 기자 회견에 참석해 주신 여러분께 감사드립니다. 아시다시피 **그랜드 폴스 브리지의 개선 공사가 거의 일 년째 진행 중입니다.** 새로 지어진 부분에 사포질과 페인트칠을 하는 마지막 단계에 다다르고 있습니다. **이 프로젝트가 지역 해양 생물에 미칠 수 있는 환경적 영향에 대해 어업계에서 우려를 표하고 있는 것을 알고 있습니다. 일 년 전에 모든 필요한 연구가 시행됐습니다.** 이제 질문을 받겠습니다. **이후 특별 행사 담당자가 계획 중인 다리 개통식에 대해 이야기할 겁니다.**
>
> 어휘 press conference 기자 회견 improvement 개선, 향상 underway 진행 중인 express concern 우려를 표하다 potential 잠재적인 environmental 환경의 impact 영향 local 지역의 conduct 하다 opening ceremony 개소식, 개통식

83

What is the speech mainly about?
(A) A financial report
(B) A round of promotions
(C) A product prototype
(D) A construction project

연설은 주로 무엇에 관한 것인가?
(A) 재무 보고서
(B) 홍보 활동
(C) 시제품
(D) 공사 프로젝트

어휘 financial 재정의, 금융의 promotion 홍보 활동, 판촉 활동 prototype 원형, 시제품 construction 건설, 공사

해설 전체 내용 관련 – 담화의 주제

화자가 초반부에 그랜드 폴스 브리지의 개선 공사가 거의 일 년째 진행 중(the Grand Falls Bridge improvement work has been underway for almost a year)이라고 말하는 것으로 보아 그랜드 폴스 브리지의 개선 공사에 관한 연설임을 알 수 있다. 따라서 정답은 (D)이다.

Paraphrasing	담화의 the Grand Falls Bridge improvement work → 정답의 A construction project

84

Why does the speaker say, "all required studies were conducted a year ago"?
(A) To correct a timeline error
(B) To provide reassurance
(C) To deny responsibility for a problem
(D) To argue that a new study is needed

화자가 "일 년 전에 모든 필요한 연구가 시행됐습니다"라고 말하는 이유는?
(A) 시간표 상의 오류를 바로잡으려고
(B) 안심시키려고
(C) 문제에 대한 책임을 부인하려고
(D) 새로운 연구가 필요하다고 주장하려고

어휘 correct 바로잡다 timeline 시각표 reassurance 안심시키는 말[행동] deny 부인하다 responsibility 책임 argue 주장하다

해설 화자의 의도 파악 – 일 년 전에 모든 필요한 연구가 시행됐다는 말의 의도

앞에서 이 프로젝트가 지역 해양 생물에 미칠 수 있는 환경적 영향에 대해 어업계에서 우려를 표하고 있는 것을 알고 있다(I know the fishing community has expressed concern over the potential environmental impact of this project on our local marine life)고 말한 뒤 인용문을 언급한 것으로 보아, 이미 필요한 연구가 모두 시행되어 어업계의 우려에 대해서는 걱정하지 않아도 된다고 안심시키려고 한 말임을 알 수 있다. 따라서 정답은 (B)이다.

85

What will the next speaker discuss?
(A) A job fair
(B) A school opening
(C) A ceremony
(D) A sporting event

다음 화자는 무엇에 대해 이야기할 것인가?
(A) 취업 박람회
(B) 학교 개교
(C) 의식
(D) 스포츠 행사

해설 세부 사항 관련 – 다음 화자가 이야기할 주제

화자가 마지막에 이후 특별 행사 담당자가 다리 개통식에 대해 이야기할 것(After that, our special-events coordinator will discuss the bridge-opening ceremony)이라고 말하고 있으므로 정답은 (C)이다.

86-88 전화 메시지

W-Am Hello, Mr. Smith. **86 I hope you're getting settled into your office space in our building.** I'm calling about some large packages that arrived for your company last week. We're keeping them for you in the storage room downstairs. **87 The lease agreement says management will hold packages for five days.** It's been ten days. Please give me a call and let me know when you can come down to claim them so **88 I can be there to open the storage room door for you.**

인녕하세요, 스미스 씨. **저희 건물 사무실 공간에 잘 적응하고 계시길 바랍니다.** 지난주 귀사 앞으로 온 큰 소포와 관련해 전화를 드렸습니다. 그것을 아래층 보관실에 맡아 두고 있어요. **임대 계약서에는 관리실에서 소포를 5일간 보관하는 것으로 명시되어 있는데요.** 열흘이 됐어요. 전화 주셔서 언제 가지러 오실 수 있으신지 알려 주세요. **제가 가서 보관실 문을 열어 드릴 수 있게요.**

어휘 settle into ~에 적응하다, 정착하다 storage 보관, 저장 lease agreement 임대차 계약 management 관리 claim 요구하다, 요청하다

86

Who most likely is the speaker?
(A) A salesperson
(B) A government official
(C) An interior designer
(D) A building manager

화자는 누구이겠는가?
(A) 판매원
(B) 공무원
(C) 실내 디자이너
(D) 건물 관리인

해설 전체 내용 관련 – 화자의 직업

화자가 초반부에 건물의 사무실 공간에 잘 적응하고 있길 바란다(I hope you're getting settled into your office space in our building)고 하면서, 소포가 와서 보관하고 있다고 말하는 것으로 보아 화자는 건물 관리인일 가능성이 높다. 따라서 정답은 (D)이다.

87

Why does the speaker say, "It's been ten days"?
(A) To explain an expense
(B) To point out a problem
(C) To make an offer
(D) To thank a colleague

화자가 "열흘이 됐어요"라고 말하는 이유는 무엇인가?
(A) 비용에 대해 설명하려고
(B) 문제를 지적하려고
(C) 제안을 하려고
(D) 동료에게 감사하려고

어휘 expense 비용, 경비 point out 지적하다 colleague 동료

해설 화자의 의도 파악 – 열흘이 됐다는 말의 의도

앞에서 임대 계약서에는 관리실에서 소포를 5일간 보관하는 것으로 명시되어 있다(The lease agreement says management will hold packages for five days)고 한 뒤 인용문을 언급한 것으로 보아, 임대 계약서에 명시된 기간이 초과되었음을 지적하기 위해 한 말임을 알 수 있다. 따라서 정답은 (B)이다.

88

What does the speaker offer to do?
(A) Open the door to a room
(B) Reset a password
(C) Send a copy of a document
(D) Refund a payment

화자는 무엇을 하겠다고 제안하는가?
(A) 보관실 문 열어 주기
(B) 비밀번호 재설정하기
(C) 문서 사본 보내기
(D) 환불해 주기

어휘 reset 재설정하다 refund 환불하다 payment 지불금

해설 세부 사항 관련 – 화자의 제안 사항

화자가 마지막에 언제 가지러 올 수 있는지 알려 주면 보관실 문을 열어 줄 수 있다(~ I can be there to open the storage room door for you)고 말하고 있으므로 정답은 (A)이다.

Paraphrasing 담화의 open the storage room door → 정답의 Open the door to a room

W-Br ⁸⁹**Our next story concerns Ferndale Valley. It's well-known that the area is one of the windiest locations in the region,** and one company would like to take advantage of that natural energy source. Breeze Capture hopes to install dozens of wind turbines by the end of next year. ⁹⁰**The company is looking for local farmers who are interested in leasing some of their land for the project.** ⁹¹**In addition to being paid for the land use, participants will also be compensated for the energy that is generated by the turbines.** For more information, e-mail info@breezecapture.com.

다음 이야기는 펀데일 밸리에 관한 것입니다. 그곳은 그 지역에서 바람이 가장 많이 부는 곳으로 잘 알려져 있는데요. 한 업체에서 그 천연 에너지원을 이용하고 싶어 합니다. 브리즈 캡처는 내년 말까지 수십 개의 풍력 발전용 터빈을 설치하고자 하는데요. 이 업체는 해당 프로젝트를 위해 토지를 임대하는 데 관심 있는 지역 농부들을 찾고 있습니다. 참여하시는 분은 토지 사용료를 받을 뿐 아니라 터빈으로 생성되는 에너지에 대한 보상도 받을 것입니다. 더 자세한 내용은 info@breezecapture.com으로 이메일을 보내 주세요.

어휘 concern ~에 관한 것이다 region 지역 take advantage of ~을 이용하다 install 설치하다 wind turbine 풍력 발전용 터빈 local 지역의 lease 임대하다 participant 참가자 be compensated for ~에 대해 보상받다 generate 발생시키다, 만들어 내다

89
What is mentioned about Ferndale Valley?
(A) It is heavily forested.
(B) It attracts many tourists.
(C) It is developing quickly.
(D) It is very windy.

펀데일 밸리에 대해 무엇을 언급하는가?
(A) 숲이 울창하다.
(B) 많은 관광객을 유치한다.
(C) 빠르게 개발되고 있다.
(D) 바람이 많이 분다.

어휘 forested 숲으로 뒤덮인 attract 유치하다, 끌어모으다

해설 세부 사항 관련 – 펀데일 밸리에 대해 언급하는 것
화자가 도입부에 다음 이야기는 펀데일 밸리에 관한 것(Our next story concerns Ferndale Valley)이라고 하면서 그 지역에서 바람이 가장 많이 부는 곳으로 잘 알려져 있다(It's well-known that the area is one of the windiest locations in the region)고 말하고 있으므로 정답은 (D)이다.

Paraphrasing 담화의 the area is one of the windiest locations → 정답의 It is very windy.

90
Who will participate in a project?
(A) Biologists
(B) Farmers
(C) Airline pilots
(D) Real estate agents

누가 프로젝트에 참여할 것인가?
(A) 생물학자
(B) 농부
(C) 항공기 조종사
(D) 부동산 중개인

해설 세부 사항 관련 – 프로젝트에 참여할 사람
화자가 중반부에 이 업체는 해당 프로젝트를 위해 토지를 임대하는 데 관심 있는 지역 농부들을 찾고 있다(The company is looking for local farmers who are interested in leasing some of their land for the project)고 말하고 있으므로 정답은 (B)이다.

91
What will the participants receive?
(A) Tickets to an industry event
(B) Technical assistance
(C) Financial compensation
(D) Advertising advice

참여자들은 무엇을 받을 것인가?
(A) 업계 행사 입장권
(B) 기술 지원
(C) 재정적 보상
(D) 광고 조언

어휘 technical 기술의 assistance 도움, 지원 advertising 광고

해설 세부 사항 관련 – 참여자들이 받을 것
화자가 후반부에 참여하는 사람들은 토지 사용료를 받을 뿐 아니라 터빈으로 생성되는 에너지에 대한 보상도 받는다(In addition to being paid for the land use, participants will also be compensated for the energy that is generated by the turbines)고 말하고 있으므로 정답은 (C)이다.

Paraphrasing 담화의 being paid → 정답의 Financial compensation

92-94 전화 메시지

M-Cn Hello, Mr. Kimura. ⁹²**I'm calling from Feras Portable Storage. You recently ordered a container to store and move your household belongings in.** ⁹³**I'm calling to confirm that your container will be delivered tomorrow morning at nine o'clock.** The driver will place it in your driveway. After the delivery, if you could, ⁹⁴**please complete the customer feedback survey that we'll e-mail you.** It will help us to improve our service. Thanks.

TEST 5

안녕하세요, 키무라 씨. **페라스 포터블 스토리지입니다. 최근 가재도구를 보관해서 옮길 컨테이너를 주문하셨죠.** 주문하신 컨테이너가 내일 아침 9시에 배송되는 것을 확정하려 전화 드립니다. 기사가 컨테이너를 귀하의 차량 진입로에 둘 겁니다. 배송된 후에 가능하시면 **이메일로 보내 드릴 고객 의견 설문을 작성해 주세요.** 서비스 향상에 도움이 될 것입니다. 감사합니다.

어휘 store 보관하다, 저장하다 household belongings 가재도구 driveway (도로부터 집까지 이르는) 차량 진입로 improve 향상시키다, 개선하다

92

What kind of business does the speaker work for?
(A) A construction firm
(B) A landscaping service
(C) A storage company
(D) An auto repair shop

화자는 어떤 종류의 업체에서 일하는가?
(A) 건설업체
(B) 조경 서비스
(C) 보관업체
(D) 자동차 정비소

어휘 construction 건설 landscaping 조경

해설 전체 내용 관련 – 화자의 근무 업체

화자가 초반부에 페라스 포터블 스토리지(I'm calling from Feras Portable Storage)라고 자신의 업체를 소개하면서 청자가 최근 가재도구를 보관해서 옮길 컨테이너를 주문했다(You recently ordered a container to store and move your household belongings in)고 말하고 있으므로 화자는 보관업체에서 근무 중이라는 것을 알 수 있다. 따라서 정답은 (C)이다.

93

Why is the speaker calling?
(A) To apologize for a cancellation
(B) To confirm a delivery
(C) To share a price quote
(D) To update some contact information

화자는 왜 전화했는가?
(A) 취소에 대해 사과하려고
(B) 배송을 확정하려고
(C) 견적서를 공유하려고
(D) 연락처를 업데이트하려고

어휘 apologize 사과하다 cancellation 취소 price quote 견적서

해설 전체 내용 관련 – 전화 건 이유

화자가 중반부에 주문한 컨테이너가 내일 아침 9시에 배송되는 것을 확정하려고 전화했다(I'm calling to confirm that your container will be delivered tomorrow morning at nine o'clock)고 말하고 있으므로 정답은 (B)이다.

94

What does the speaker ask the listener to do?
(A) Purchase a warranty
(B) Complete a survey
(C) Clean up an area
(D) Apply for a permit

화자는 청자에게 무엇을 해 달라고 요청하는가?
(A) 품질 보증서 구입하기
(B) 설문 작성하기
(C) 구역 청소하기
(D) 허가증 신청하기

어휘 warranty 품질 보증서 apply for ~을 신청하다, 지원하다 permit 허가증

해설 세부 사항 관련 – 화자의 요청 사항

화자가 후반부에 이메일로 보낼 고객 의견 설문을 작성해 달라(~ please complete the customer feedback survey that we'll e-mail you)고 요청하고 있으므로 정답은 (B)이다.

95-97 담화 + 청소용품

W-Am **95 This is the custodial staff's cabinet for cleaning supplies.** As part of your training, you'll be expected to learn which cleaning solutions are used for different surfaces in the hotel, such as carpet and tile flooring. **96 The spray bottle on the top shelf, Baxlon, is for glass surfaces.** The product directly under the spray bottle is brand new. It was just released this month, and it's excellent for polishing furniture. Oh, and **97 every Tuesday at one o'clock, a delivery truck brings any supplies that we're low on.** Don't forget to check that.

이것은 청소 직원들이 청소용품을 두는 캐비닛입니다. 교육의 일환으로, 카펫이나 타일 바닥재 등 호텔 내 다양한 표면에 어떤 청소 용액을 쓰는지 배우셔야 합니다. 맨 위 선반에 있는 스프레이 병, 백슬론은 유리 표면을 위한 것입니다. 그 스프레이 병 바로 아래 제품은 신상품인데요. 이번 달에 출시됐고, 가구 광을 내는 데 아주 좋습니다. 아, 매주 화요일 1시에 배송 트럭이 부족한 용품을 가져옵니다. 잊지 말고 확인하세요.

어휘 custodial staff 청소부 cleaning supplies 청소용품 solution 용액 surface 표면 flooring 바닥재 directly 바로 release 출시하다 polish 윤을 내다, 광을 내다 low on ~이 부족한

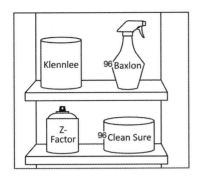

95

What is the purpose of the talk?
(A) To discuss a schedule
(B) To consider changing suppliers
(C) To train employees
(D) To develop an inventory system

담화의 목적은?
(A) 일정 논의
(B) 공급업체 변경 고려
(C) 직원 교육
(D) 재고 관리 시스템 개발

어휘 consider 고려하다   inventory 재고, 물품 목록

해설 전체 내용 관련 – 담화의 목적
화자가 도입부에 이것은 청소 직원들이 청소용품을 두는 캐비닛(This is the custodial staff's cabinet for cleaning supplies)이라며 교육의 일환으로, 다양한 표면에 어떤 청소 용액을 쓰는지 배워야 한다(As part of your training, you'll be expected to learn which cleaning solutions are used different surfaces ~)고 말하고 있으므로 담화의 목적은 청소 직원들을 교육하는 것임을 알 수 있다. 따라서 정답은 (C)이다.

96

Look at the graphic. Which product does the speaker say is new?
(A) Klennlee
(B) Baxlon
(C) Z-Factor
(D) Clean Sure

시각 정보에 의하면, 화자는 어떤 것이 신제품이라고 말하는가?
(A) 클렌리
(B) 백슬론
(C) Z-팩터
(D) 클린 슈어

해설 시각 정보 연계 – 화자가 신제품이라고 말하는 것
화자가 중반부에 맨 위 선반에 있는 스프레이 병은 백슬론(The spray bottle on the top shelf, Baxlon, ~)이고, 그 스프레이 병 바로 아래 제품은 신상품(The product directly under the spray bottle is brand new)이라고 말하고 있다. 청소용품 배치도에 따르면 백슬론 아래 제품은 클린 슈어이므로 정답은 (D)이다.

97

What happens at one o'clock on Tuesdays?
(A) An expense report is due.
(B) A work shift begins.
(C) A staff meeting is held.
(D) A delivery arrives.

매주 화요일 1시에 어떤 일이 있는가?
(A) 지출 품의서를 내야 한다.
(B) 교대 근무가 시작된다.
(C) 직원 회의가 열린다.
(D) 배송이 도착한다.

어휘 expense report 지출 품의서

해설 세부 사항 관련 – 매주 화요일 1시에 있는 일
화자가 후반부에 매주 화요일 1시에 배송 트럭이 부족한 용품을 가져온다(every Tuesday at one o'clock, a delivery truck brings any supplies that we're low on)고 말하고 있으므로 정답은 (D)이다.

> **Paraphrasing**   담화의 a delivery truck brings any supplies → 정답의 A delivery arrives.

98-100 워크숍 발췌 + 순서도

M-Au Welcome back to this professional development workshop. **98 We'll continue from where we left off in our discussion on advertising through social media using videos,** and we'll end today's meeting by performing a group task. **98 Last week, we discussed the planning phase for a video marketing campaign. 99 Today, we'll move on to the production phase.** During this phase, you'll need to ensure that high-quality equipment is used for lighting and camera work and that you have the best video editors you can get for the job. **100 We're very lucky to have an expert here today to talk about her experience with the process. Please give your attention to Usha Madan.**

전문성 개발 워크숍에 다시 오신 것을 환영합니다. **동영상을 활용한 소셜미디어 광고에 대한 논의를 하다가 중단한 부분부터 이어서 하겠습니다.** 그리고 그룹 과제를 수행하는 것으로 오늘 모임을 마치겠습니다. **지난주에 동영상 마케팅 캠페인의 기획 단계에 대해 이야기했는데요.** **오늘은 제작 단계로 넘어가겠습니다.** 이 단계에서는 조명과 카메라 작업에 고품질 장비를 사용하고, 작업에 적합한 최고의 영상 편집자를 확보해야 합니다. **운 좋게도 오늘 이곳에 해당 과정에 대한 경험을 이야기해 줄 전문가를 모셨습니다. 우샤 마단 씨께 귀를 기울여 주세요.**

어휘 development 개발　leave off 멈추다, 중단하다
advertising 광고　perform 수행하다　phase 단계
production 제작　equipment 장비　lighting 조명　editor
편집자　process 과정, 절차　give attention 귀를 기울이다

98

What is the topic of the course?
(A) Marketing
(B) Investing
(C) Documentary filmmaking
(D) Software development

강좌의 주제는?
(A) 마케팅
(B) 투자
(C) 다큐멘터리 영화 제작
(D) 소프트웨어 개발

해설 전체 내용 관련 – 강좌의 주제
화자가 초반부에 동영상을 활용한 소셜미디어 광고에 대한 논의를 하다가 중단한 부분부터 이어서 하겠다(We'll continue from where we left off in our discussion on advertising through social media using videos ~)는 말과 지난주에 동영상 마케팅 캠페인의 기획 단계에 대해 이야기했다(Last week, we discussed the planning phase for a video marketing campaign)는 말을 통해 마케팅에 대한 워크숍임을 알 수 있다. 따라서 정답은 (A)이다.

> Paraphrasing　담화의 advertising → 정답의 Marketing

99

Look at the graphic. Which step will be discussed today?
(A) Step 1
(B) Step 2
(C) Step 3
(D) Step 4

시각 정보에 의하면, 오늘 어떤 단계를 논의할 것인가?
(A) 1단계
(B) 2단계
(C) 3단계
(D) 4단계

해설 시각 정보 연계 – 오늘 논의할 단계
화자가 중반부에 오늘은 제작 단계로 넘어가겠다(Today, we'll move on to the production phase)고 말하고 있고, 순서도에 따르면 제작 단계는 3단계이므로 정답은 (C)이다.

100

What will the listeners do next?
(A) Read a handout
(B) Watch a video
(C) Take a coffee break
(D) Listen to a guest speaker

청자들은 다음으로 무엇을 할 것인가?
(A) 인쇄물 읽기
(B) 동영상 시청하기
(C) 휴식 시간 갖기
(D) 객원 강연자의 강연 듣기

어휘 handout 인쇄물, 유인물　guest speaker 객원 연설자

해설 세부 사항 관련 – 청자들이 다음에 할 일
화자가 후반부에 해당 과정에 대한 경험을 이야기해 줄 전문가를 모셨다(We're very lucky to have an expert here today to talk about her experience with the process)며 우샤 마단 씨께 귀를 기울여 달라(Please give your attention to Usha Madan)고 요청하고 있으므로 정답은 (D)이다.

> Paraphrasing　담화의 give your attention to Usha Madan
> → 정답의 Listen to a guest speaker

기출 TEST 6

동영상 강의

1 (B)	**2** (A)	**3** (D)	**4** (B)	**5** (C)
6 (A)	**7** (A)	**8** (A)	**9** (A)	**10** (C)
11 (B)	**12** (C)	**13** (A)	**14** (C)	**15** (A)
16 (B)	**17** (B)	**18** (B)	**19** (B)	**20** (C)
21 (A)	**22** (A)	**23** (C)	**24** (A)	**25** (C)
26 (B)	**27** (B)	**28** (A)	**29** (A)	**30** (A)
31 (A)	**32** (A)	**33** (B)	**34** (B)	**35** (B)
36 (D)	**37** (C)	**38** (B)	**39** (A)	**40** (D)
41 (B)	**42** (A)	**43** (C)	**44** (C)	**45** (C)
46 (A)	**47** (C)	**48** (B)	**49** (D)	**50** (B)
51 (A)	**52** (C)	**53** (C)	**54** (A)	**55** (C)
56 (C)	**57** (D)	**58** (B)	**59** (C)	**60** (A)
61 (D)	**62** (A)	**63** (D)	**64** (B)	**65** (A)
66 (D)	**67** (C)	**68** (C)	**69** (B)	**70** (B)
71 (A)	**72** (D)	**73** (C)	**74** (C)	**75** (D)
76 (A)	**77** (B)	**78** (A)	**79** (D)	**80** (C)
81 (D)	**82** (A)	**83** (B)	**84** (D)	**85** (B)
86 (B)	**87** (D)	**88** (A)	**89** (A)	**90** (B)
91 (C)	**92** (B)	**93** (A)	**94** (C)	**95** (D)
96 (C)	**97** (A)	**98** (C)	**99** (B)	**100** (D)

PART 1

1 W-Am

(A) She's shoveling snow from a walkway.
(B) She's using walking sticks.
(C) She's removing her cap.
(D) She's drinking from a water bottle.

(A) 여자가 보도에서 삽으로 눈을 치우고 있다.
(B) 여자가 지팡이를 사용하고 있다.
(C) 여자가 모자를 벗고 있다.
(D) 여자가 물병의 물을 마시고 있다.

어휘 shovel 삽질하다 walkway 보도, 산책로 walking stick 지팡이
　　remove 벗다

해설 1인 등장 사진 – 사람의 동작/상태 묘사
(A) 동사 오답. 여자가 삽으로 눈을 치우고 있는(is shoveling snow) 모습이 아니므로 오답.
(B) 정답. 여자가 지팡이를 사용하고 있는(is using walking sticks) 모습이므로 정답.
(C) 동사 오답. 여자가 모자를 벗고 있는(is removing her cap) 모습이 아니므로 오답.

(D) 동사 오답. 여자가 물병의 물을 마시고 있는(is drinking from a water bottle) 모습이 아니므로 오답.

2 M-Cn

(A) A woman is carrying a tray.
(B) A woman is pushing a food trolley.
(C) Some people are leaving a restaurant.
(D) Some diners are looking out a window.

(A) 여자가 쟁반을 나르고 있다.
(B) 여자가 음식 카트를 밀고 있다.
(C) 사람들이 식당을 나서고 있다.
(D) 식사하는 사람들이 창밖을 바라보고 있다.

어휘 tray 쟁반 trolley 카트, 손수레 diner 식사하는 사람, 손님

해설 2인 이상 등장 사진 – 사람의 동작/상태 묘사
(A) 정답. 여자가 쟁반을 나르고 있는(is carrying a tray) 모습이므로 정답.
(B) 사진에 없는 명사를 이용한 오답. 사진에 음식 카트(a food trolley)의 모습이 보이지 않으므로 오답.
(C) 동사 오답. 사람들(Some people)이 식당을 나서고 있는(are leaving a restaurant) 모습이 아니므로 오답.
(D) 사진에 없는 명사를 이용한 오답. 사진에 창문(a window)의 모습이 보이지 않으므로 오답.

3 W-Br

(A) The man is holding a bucket of water.
(B) The man is replacing a tire.
(C) The man is watering a tree.
(D) The man is scrubbing the front of a car.

(A) 남자가 물 한 양동이를 들고 있다.
(B) 남자가 타이어를 교체하고 있다.
(C) 남자가 나무에 물을 주고 있다.
(D) 남자가 차 앞쪽을 문질러 닦고 있다.

어휘 bucket 양동이 replace 교체하다 water 물을 주다 scrub 문질러 씻다, 청소하다

해설 1인 등장 사진 – 사람의 동작/상태 묘사
(A) 사진에 없는 명사를 이용한 오답. 사진에 물 한 양동이(a bucket of water)의 모습이 보이지 않으므로 오답.
(B) 동사 오답. 남자가 타이어를 교체하고 있는(is replacing a tire) 모습이 아니므로 오답.

(C) 동사 오답. 남자가 나무에 물을 주고 있는(is watering a tree) 모습이 아니므로 오답.

(D) 정답. 남자가 차 앞쪽을 문질러 닦고 있는(is scrubbing the front of a car) 모습이므로 정답.

4 M-Au

▶ 동영상 강의

(A) Some tiles are being installed on a roof.
(B) An outdoor dining area is unoccupied.
(C) Flowers have been placed on tables.
(D) Some chairs have been arranged around a fountain.

(A) 지붕에 타일이 설치되고 있다.
(B) **야외 식사 공간이 비어 있다.**
(C) 꽃이 테이블에 놓여 있다.
(D) 의자들이 분수 주위에 정리되어 있다.

어휘 install 설치하다 outdoor 야외의 unoccupied (사람이 없이) 비어 있는 place 놓다, 두다 arrange 정리하다, 배열하다 fountain 분수

해설 사물/풍경 사진 – 풍경 묘사

(A) 동사 오답. 타일(Some tiles)이 설치되고 있는(are being installed) 모습이 아니므로 오답.

(B) 정답. 야외 식사 공간(An outdoor dining area)이 비어 있는(is unoccupied) 모습이므로 정답.

(C) 사진에 없는 명사를 이용한 오답. 사진에 꽃(Flowers)의 모습이 보이지 않으므로 오답.

(D) 사진에 없는 명사를 이용한 오답. 사진에 분수(a fountain)의 모습이 보이지 않으므로 오답.

5 W-Br

(A) Some people are gathered on top of a building.
(B) Some trees are blocking the entrance to a stairway.
(C) A woman is taking some stairs to a lower level.
(D) A woman is walking across a pedestrian bridge.

(A) 사람들이 건물 꼭대기에 모여 있다.
(B) 나무들이 계단 입구를 막고 있다.
(C) **여자가 아래층으로 가는 계단을 내려가고 있다.**
(D) 여자가 보행자용 다리를 건너고 있다.

어휘 gather 모으다, 모이다 block 막다 entrance 입구 stairway 계단 pedestrian bridge 보행자용 다리

해설 혼합 사진 – 사람/사물/풍경 혼합 묘사

(A) 위치 오답. 사람들이 건물 꼭대기에(on top of a building) 모여 있는 모습이 아니므로 오답.

(B) 동사 오답. 나무들(Some trees)이 계단 입구를 막고 있는(are blocking the entrance) 모습이 아니므로 오답.

(C) 정답. 여자가 아래층으로 가는 계단을 내려가고 있는(is taking some stairs to a lower level) 모습이므로 정답.

(D) 사진에 없는 명사를 이용한 오답. 사진에 보행자용 다리(a pedestrian bridge)의 모습이 보이지 않으므로 오답.

6 M-Cn

(A) Some wooden planter boxes have been set next to each other.
(B) Some wood logs have been piled in a corner.
(C) The outside walls of a house are made of bricks.
(D) Some windows are being installed.

(A) **나무로 만들어진 화분들이 나란히 놓여 있다.**
(B) 통나무들이 구석에 쌓여 있다.
(C) 집 외벽이 벽돌로 만들어져 있다.
(D) 창문들이 설치되고 있다.

어휘 wooden 나무로 만들어진 planter box 화분 next to each other 나란히 log 통나무 pile 쌓다, 포개다 brick 벽돌 install 설치하다

해설 사물/풍경사진 – 사물 묘사

(A) 정답. 나무로 만들어진 화분들(Some wooden planter boxes)이 나란히 놓여 있는(have been set next to each other) 모습이므로 정답.

(B) 사진에 없는 명사를 이용한 오답. 사진에 통나무들(Some wood logs)의 모습이 보이지 않으므로 오답.

(C) 사진에 없는 명사를 이용한 오답. 사진에 벽돌(bricks)의 모습이 보이지 않으므로 오답.

(D) 동사 오답. 창문들(Some windows)이 설치되고 있는(are being installed) 모습이 아니므로 오답.

PART 2

7

M-Cn Who's going to take home the leftover cake?

M-Au (A) Marcel said he would.
(B) A lovely selection of desserts.
(C) No, I thought it started at noon.

남은 케이크는 누가 집으로 가져갈 건가요?

(A) **마르셀이 그러겠다고 했어요.**
(B) 멋진 디저트 모음이네요.
(C) 아니요, 정오에 시작한다고 생각했어요.

어휘 leftover 먹다 남은; 남은 음식 a selection of 다양한, 엄선된

해설 남은 케이크를 가져갈 사람을 묻는 Who 의문문
(A) 정답. 남은 케이크를 가져갈 사람을 묻는 질문에 마르셀이 그러겠다고 했다고 알려 주고 있으므로 정답.
(B) 연상 단어 오답. 질문의 cake에서 연상 가능한 desserts를 이용한 오답.
(C) Yes/No 불가 오답. Who 의문문에는 Yes/No 응답이 불가능하므로 오답.

8

▶ 동영상 강의

W-Br Can you tell me where the security office is?

M-Au (A) Today's my first day here.
(B) A photograph for the badge.
(C) Because it's after lunch.

경비실이 어디 있는지 알려 주실 수 있나요?
(A) 저는 오늘 여기 처음 왔어요.
(B) 신분증 사진이요.
(C) 점심 이후라서요.

어휘 security office 경비실 badge 배지, 신분증

해설 경비실 위치를 묻는 간접 의문문
(A) 정답. 경비실 위치를 묻는 질문에 오늘 여기 처음 와서 위치를 알지 못함을 우회적으로 알려 주고 있으므로 정답.
(B) 연상 단어 오답. 질문의 security office에서 연상 가능한 badge를 이용한 오답.
(C) 질문과 상관없는 오답. Why 의문문에 대한 응답이므로 오답.

9

W-Am What's the best way to contact you?

W-Br (A) On my mobile phone.
(B) No, I have to wear glasses.
(C) This résumé is better.

어떻게 연락 드리는 것이 가장 좋을까요?
(A) 휴대전화로요.
(B) 아니요, 저는 안경을 써야 해요.
(C) 이 이력서가 낫네요.

어휘 contact 연락하다 mobile phone 휴대전화 résumé 이력서

해설 연락 방법을 묻는 What 의문문
(A) 정답. 연락 방법을 묻는 질문에 휴대전화라고 구체적인 방법으로 응답하고 있으므로 정답.
(B) Yes/No 불가 오답. What 의문문에는 Yes/No 응답이 불가능하므로 오답.
(C) 파생어 오답. 질문의 best와 파생어 관계인 better를 이용한 오답.

10

W-Br Who's joining us for the waterfront boat ride?

M-Cn (A) Conference room three.
(B) The admission fee is reasonable.
(C) Everybody on our team is coming.

해안가 보트 타러 가는 데 누가 함께하실 건가요?

(A) 3번 회의실요.
(B) 입장료가 적정해요.
(C) 우리 팀 전원이 가요.

어휘 waterfront 해안가 admission fee 입장료 reasonable 적정한, 너무 비싸지 않은

해설 보트 탑승을 함께할 사람을 묻는 Who 의문문
(A) 질문과 상관없는 오답.
(B) 연상 단어 오답. 질문의 boat ride에서 연상 가능한 admission fee를 이용한 오답.
(C) 정답. 해안가 보트 타러 같이 갈 사람을 묻는 질문에 우리 팀 전원이라고 응답하고 있으므로 정답.

11

W-Am Could you request a technician to repair the packaging machine?

M-Au (A) Three years of technical school.
(B) Sure, I'll do that.
(C) The blue one with gold trim.

포장 기계를 수리할 기술자를 요청해 주실 수 있어요?
(A) 기술 전문학교 3년 과정이요.
(B) 물론이죠, 그럴게요.
(C) 금색 테두리를 두른 파란색이요.

어휘 packaging 포장, 포장재 trim 장식, 테두리

해설 부탁/요청의 의문문
(A) 파생어 오답. 질문의 technician과 파생어 관계인 technical을 이용한 오답.
(B) 정답. 포장 기계를 수리할 기술자를 요청해 달라는 부탁에 물론(Sure)이라고 대답한 뒤, 그러겠다고 하므로 정답.
(C) 질문과 상관없는 오답. Which 의문문에 대한 응답이므로 오답.

12

W-Br How many copies of the proposal should I make?

M-Cn (A) There's blue paper in the cabinet.
(B) Yes, it was my idea.
(C) Fifty should be enough for everyone.

제안서를 몇 부 복사해야 할까요?
(A) 캐비닛 안에 파란색 종이가 있어요.
(B) 네, 그건 제 아이디어였어요.
(C) 50부면 모두가 보기에 충분할 거예요.

어휘 proposal 제안, 제안서

해설 제안서 복사 부수를 묻는 How many 의문문
(A) 연상 단어 오답. 질문의 copies에서 연상 가능한 paper를 이용한 오답.
(B) Yes/No 불가 오답. How many 의문문에는 Yes/No 응답이 불가능하므로 오답.
(C) 정답. 제안서를 몇 부 복사할지 묻는 질문에 50부면 충분할 거라며 구체적인 숫자로 응답하고 있으므로 정답.

13

M-Au Why is Jonathan leaving early?

W-Am (A) To catch the six o'clock train.
(B) On the early morning news.
(C) That's where he lives now.

조나단은 왜 일찍 가요?
(A) 6시 기차를 타려고요.
(B) 새벽 뉴스에서요.
(C) 그가 지금 사는 곳입니다.

어휘 catch the train 기차를 잡아타다

해설 조나단이 일찍 떠나는 이유를 묻는 Why 의문문
(A) 정답. 조나단이 일찍 떠나는 이유를 묻는 질문에 6시 기차를 타기 위해서라고 이유를 제시하고 있으므로 정답.
(B) 단어 반복 오답. 질문의 early를 반복 이용한 오답.
(C) 유사 발음 오답. 질문의 leaving과 부분적으로 발음이 유사한 lives를 이용한 오답.

14

W-Br Where's the company party being held?

M-Au (A) It's a publishing firm.
(B) Party of five at the table in the corner.
(C) At the Chesterville Hotel.

회사 파티는 어디서 열리나요?
(A) 출판사예요.
(B) 구석 테이블 일행 5명요.
(C) 체스터빌 호텔에서요.

어휘 publishing firm 출판사 party of ~명의 일행

해설 회사 파티 장소를 묻는 Where 의문문
(A) 연상 단어 오답. 질문의 company에서 연상 가능한 firm을 이용한 오답.
(B) 단어 반복 오답. 질문의 party를 반복 이용한 오답.
(C) 정답. 회사 파티 장소를 묻는 질문에 체스터빌 호텔이라고 구체적인 장소를 알려 주고 있으므로 정답.

15

W-Am Did you want to sign up for a one-year magazine subscription?

M-Au (A) How much will it cost?
(B) Near the service center.
(C) Akiko works at the front desk.

잡지 1년 구독 신청을 원하셨죠?
(A) 비용이 얼마예요?
(B) 서비스 센터 근처요.
(C) 아키코는 안내 데스크에서 일해요.

어휘 sign up for ~을 신청하다 magazine 잡지 subscription 구독
cost 비용이 들다

해설 잡지 구독 신청 희망 여부를 확인하는 조동사(Did) 의문문
(A) 정답. 잡지 1년 구독 신청을 원했는지 묻는 질문에 비용이 얼마인지를 되물으며, 신청하는 데 필요한 추가 정보를 확인하고 있으므로 정답.
(B) 질문과 상관없는 오답.
(C) 연상 단어 오답. 질문의 sign up에서 연상 가능한 front desk를 이용한 오답.

16

W-Br Does this pasta come with a side salad?

M-Cn (A) We do have a tablecloth.
(B) No, I'm afraid not.
(C) I like it too.

이 파스타는 곁들임 샐러드가 같이 나오나요?
(A) 저희는 테이블보가 있어요.
(B) 아니요, 그렇지 않습니다.
(C) 저도 그거 좋아해요.

어휘 tablecloth 식탁보, 테이블보

해설 곁들임 샐러드가 나오는지 여부를 확인하는 조동사(Does) 의문문
(A) 질문과 상관없는 오답.
(B) 정답. 파스타에 곁들임 샐러드가 같이 나오는지를 묻는 질문에 아니다(No)라고 대답한 뒤, 그렇지 않다고 덧붙이고 있으므로 정답.
(C) 연상 단어 오답. 질문의 pasta와 salad 등에서 연상할 수 있는 음식을 좋아한다는 의미의 like를 이용한 오답.

17

M-Au When can we meet about the invoices?

M-Cn (A) Supplies for the office.
(B) I'm free after two.
(C) Probably on Harold's desk.

청구서 건으로 언제 만날 수 있을까요?
(A) 사무실에서 쓸 용품이요.
(B) 저는 두 시 이후에 시간이 있어요.
(C) 아마 해럴드의 책상에 있을 거예요.

어휘 invoice 청구서, 송장 supplies 물품, 보급품

해설 청구서 건으로 만날 시간을 묻는 When 의문문
(A) 연상 단어 오답. 질문의 invoices에서 연상 가능한 Supplies를 이용한 오답.
(B) 정답. 만날 시간을 묻는 질문에 두 시 이후에 시간이 있다고 응답하고 있으므로 정답.
(C) 질문과 상관없는 오답. Where 의문문에 대한 응답이므로 오답.

18

M-Au Would you like me to help you open a savings account?

W-Am (A) I've already counted them.
(B) That'd be great.
(C) 50 euros each.

예금 계좌 개설하는 것을 도와드릴까요?

(A) 이미 그것들을 셌어요.

(B) 그래 주시면 좋겠어요.

(C) 각 50유로로.

어휘 open a savings account 예금 계좌를 개설하다   count 세다, 계산하다

해설 제안/권유의 의문문

(A) 유사 발음 오답. 질문의 account와 부분적으로 발음이 유사한 counted를 이용한 오답.

(B) 정답. 예금 계좌 개설을 도와주겠다는 제안에 그래 주면 좋겠다는 긍정의 답변을 하고 있으므로 정답.

(C) 연상 단어 오답. 질문의 savings에서 연상 가능한 50 euros를 이용한 오답.

19

W-Am When did you post the job opening?

M-Au (A) On the bulletin board in the hallway.

(B) It's been on the Web site for a month.

(C) Can you close the door?

언제 채용 공고를 게시했어요?

(A) 복도 게시판에요.

(B) 한 달 동안 웹사이트에 있었는데요.

(C) 문을 닫아 주시겠어요?

어휘 post 게시하다   job opening 채용 공고   bulletin board 게시판   hallway 복도

해설 채용 공고를 게시한 시기를 묻는 When 의문문

(A) 질문과 상관없는 오답. Where 의문문에 대한 응답이므로 오답.

(B) 정답. 채용 공고를 게시한 시기를 묻는 질문에 한 달 동안 웹사이트에 있었다고 알려 주고 있으므로 정답.

(C) 연상 단어 오답. 질문의 opening에서 연상 가능한 close를 이용한 오답.

20

W-Am Are you applying for the manager position?

M-Cn (A) About sixteen more employees.

(B) I'll check her schedule again.

(C) Yes... I hope I get it.

관리자 직에 지원하시나요?

(A) 직원 16명쯤 더요.

(B) 그녀의 일정을 다시 확인해 볼게요.

(C) 네… 됐으면 좋겠어요.

어휘 apply for ~에 지원하다

해설 관리자 직에 지원하는지 묻는 Be동사 의문문

(A) 질문과 상관없는 오답. How many 의문문에 대한 응답이므로 오답.

(B) 질문과 상관없는 오답. 질문에 3인칭 대명사 her로 지칭할 인물이 언급된 적이 없으므로 오답.

(C) 정답. 관리자 직책에 지원하는지 묻는 질문에 네(Yes)라고 대답한 뒤, 됐으면 좋겠다고 덧붙이고 있으므로 정답.

21

M-Au Are you traveling in business class or economy?

M-Cn (A) My flight was just canceled.

(B) My focus is history.

(C) London, then New York.

비즈니스 클래스를 타세요, 아니면 이코노미 클래스를 타세요?

(A) 제가 탈 항공편이 막 취소됐어요.

(B) 제 관심사는 역사입니다.

(C) 런던, 그 다음 뉴욕이요.

해설 좌석 등급을 묻는 선택 의문문

(A) 정답. 비즈니스와 이코노미 중 어느 좌석을 이용하는지 묻는 질문에 항공편이 막 취소됐다며 둘 다 해당 없음을 우회적으로 응답하고 있으므로 정답.

(B) 연상 단어 오답. 질문의 economy(경제, 경제학)에서 연상 가능한 history를 이용한 오답.

(C) 연상 단어 오답. 질문의 traveling에서 연상 가능한 London, New York을 이용한 오답.

22

W-Am The number of subscribers for our magazine has decreased recently.

M-Au (A) There's room in the budget for more advertising.

(B) An annual membership fee.

(C) There are six folders on the table.

최근 우리 잡지 구독자 수가 감소했어요.

(A) 예산에 광고를 늘릴 수 있는 여유가 있습니다.

(B) 연회비요.

(C) 탁자에 폴더 여섯 개가 있어요.

어휘 subscriber 구독자   budget 예산   advertising 광고   annual 연례의, 매년의   membership fee 회비

해설 정보 전달의 평서문

(A) 정답. 최근 잡지 구독자 수가 감소했다는 평서문에 예산에 광고를 더 늘릴 수 있는 여유가 있다며 문제에 대한 해결책을 제시하고 있으므로 정답.

(B) 연상 단어 오답. 평서문의 subscribers에서 연상 가능한 membership fee를 이용한 오답.

(C) 연상 단어 오답. 평서문의 number에서 연상할 수 있는 six를 이용한 오답.

23

W-Am How do you clean the solar panels without damaging them?

M-Cn (A) The glass can be any color you want.

(B) No, the sun isn't out today.

(C) I pay a company to do all the maintenance.

태양 전지판을 손상시키지 않고 어떻게 청소하죠?

(A) 유리는 원하는 어떤 색이든 가능해요.

(B) 아니요, 오늘은 밖에 해가 안 떴어요.

(C) 업체에 비용을 지불하고 유지보수 작업을 전부 맡겨요.

어휘 solar panel 태양 전지판 maintenance 유지보수

해설 청소 방법을 묻는 How 의문문
(A) 질문과 상관없는 오답.
(B) Yes/No 불가 오답. How 의문문에는 Yes/No 응답이 불가능하므로 오답.
(C) 정답. 전지판을 손상시키지 않고 청소하는 방법을 묻는 질문에 업체에 비용을 지불하고 유지보수 작업을 전부 맡긴다고 대답한 것은, 전문 업체를 이용하고 있어서 손상시키지 않고 청소가 가능함을 우회적으로 말하는 것이므로 정답.

24

 동영상 강의

W-Br When will I receive my certificate in the mail?

M-Cn (A) I'll have to check with the office.
(B) Turn left at the light.
(C) No, thank you.

증명서를 언제 우편으로 받게 될까요?
(A) 제가 사무실에 확인해 봐야겠네요.
(B) 신호등에서 좌회전하세요.
(C) 아니요, 괜찮아요.

어휘 certificate 증명서, 자격증

해설 우편 수령 시점을 묻는 When 의문문
(A) 정답. 증명서를 우편으로 받을 시점을 묻는 질문에 사무실에 확인해 봐야겠다며 자신도 알지 못함을 우회적으로 말하고 있으므로 정답.
(B) 질문과 상관없는 오답. How 의문문에 대한 응답이므로 오답.
(C) Yes/No 불가 오답. When 의문문에는 Yes/No 응답이 불가능하므로 오답.

25

M-Cn Don't we sell Ramirez lawn mowers?

W-Br (A) The plants need more water.
(B) Sorry, refunds are not allowed.
(C) I work in the home decor area.

우리 라미레즈 잔디깎이 팔지 않나요?
(A) 그 식물은 물이 더 필요해요.
(B) 죄송하지만, 환불은 안 됩니다.
(C) 저는 실내 장식 구역에서 일하는데요.

어휘 lawn mower 잔디 깎는 기계 plant 식물 refund 환불
be allowed 허용되다 home decor 실내 장식

해설 특정 잔디깎이의 판매 여부를 확인하는 부정 의문문
(A) 연상 단어 오답. 질문의 lawn mowers에서 연상 가능한 plants를 이용한 오답.
(B) 연상 단어 오답. 질문의 sell에서 연상 가능한 refunds를 이용한 오답.
(C) 정답. 특정 잔디깎이의 판매 여부를 확인하는 질문에 실내 장식 구역에서 일한다며 자신도 알지 못한다는 것을 우회적으로 알려 주고 있으므로 정답.

26

W-Am Should we meet to discuss our research project?

M-Cn (A) A publishing manual.
(B) Put something on my calendar.
(C) Alphabetical order is fine, I think.

연구 프로젝트에 대해 논의하기 위해 만나야 하나요?
(A) 출판 설명서요.
(B) 제 일정표에 넣어 주세요.
(C) 알파벳 순서가 좋은 것 같아요.

어휘 publishing 출판 manual 설명서 order 순서

해설 제안/권유의 의문문
(A) 질문과 상관없는 오답.
(B) 정답. 연구 프로젝트 논의를 위해 만나야 할지 묻는 질문에 일정표에 넣어 달라며 만나야 한다는 긍정의 답변을 우회적으로 하고 있으므로 정답.
(C) 질문과 상관없는 오답.

27

W-Br When does the cleaning staff leave for the day?

W-Am (A) A supply closet in the hall.
(B) By six o'clock, usually.
(C) The leaves come out in the spring.

청소 직원들은 언제 퇴근합니까?
(A) 현관에 있는 비품 보관함이요.
(B) 보통 6시까지예요.
(C) 봄에는 잎이 나와요.

어휘 leave for the day 퇴근하다 supply closet 비품 보관함

해설 청소 직원들의 퇴근 시간을 묻는 When 의문문
(A) 연상 단어 오답. 질문의 cleaning에서 연상 가능한 supply closet을 이용한 오답.
(B) 정답. 청소 직원들의 퇴근 시간을 묻는 질문에 보통 6시까지라고 구체적인 시간을 알려 주고 있으므로 정답.
(C) 단어 반복 오답. 질문의 leave를 반복 이용한 오답.

28

 동영상 강의

W-Br How would you like to pay for these shoes today?

M-Cn (A) With a store gift card.
(B) I wear a size 38.
(C) A friend recommended them.

오늘 이 신발은 어떻게 계산하실 건가요?
(A) 매장 상품권으로요.
(B) 저는 38사이즈를 신어요.
(C) 친구가 추천했어요.

해설 지불 수단에 대해 묻는 How 의문문
(A) 정답. 신발 값 계산 수단을 묻는 질문에 매장 상품권이라는 구체적인 지불 수단을 알려 주고 있으므로 정답.

(B) 연상 단어 오답. 질문의 shoes에서 연상 가능한 size 38을 이용한 오답.
(C) 질문과 상관없는 오답.

29

M-Au It's an effective advertisement, isn't it?

W-Am (A) I've heard that sales have increased.
(B) The next issue of the magazine.
(C) Isn't the policy in effect already?

효과적인 광고예요, 그렇지 않아요?
(A) 판매량이 증가했다고 들었어요.
(B) 잡지 다음 호요.
(C) 그 정책은 이미 시행 중이지 않나요?

어휘 effective 효과적인 advertisement 광고 issue 호 in effect 발효 중인, 시행 중인

해설 효과적인 광고인지를 확인하는 부가 의문문
(A) 정답. 효과적인 광고인지를 확인하는 질문에 판매량이 증가했다며 긍정의 의사를 우회적으로 표현하고 있으므로 정답.
(B) 연상 단어 오답. 질문의 advertisement에서 연상 가능한 magazine을 이용한 오답.
(C) 파생어 오답. 질문의 effective와 파생어 관계인 effect를 이용한 오답.

30

W-Br Why don't we take a walk after lunch?

M-Au (A) The sales report is due at one o'clock.
(B) No, in parking area B.
(C) I'll have spaghetti, please.

점심 식사 후에 산책하는 게 어때요?
(A) 영업 보고서가 1시까지예요.
(B) 아니요, B 주차 구역에서요.
(C) 저는 스파게티를 먹을게요.

어휘 take a walk 산책하다 due 예정된, ~하기로 되어 있는

해설 제안/권유의 의문문
(A) 정답. 점심 식사 후 산책을 하자는 제안문에 영업 보고서가 1시까지라며 거절하는 의사를 우회적으로 표현하고 있으므로 정답.
(B) 질문과 상관없는 오답.
(C) 연상 단어 오답. 질문의 lunch에서 연상 가능한 spaghetti를 이용한 오답.

31

W-Am I decided to move the seasonal merchandise to the front of the store.

W-Br (A) Did you put some of it in the window display?
(B) For our summer clothing collection.
(C) The moving van is coming tomorrow.

계절 상품을 매장 앞쪽으로 옮기기로 결정했어요.
(A) 그중 일부를 진열창에 놓았나요?
(B) 여름 의류 상품들을 위해서요.
(C) 이삿짐 트럭이 내일 올 거예요.

어휘 merchandise 상품 collection 신상품들 moving van 이삿짐 트럭

해설 정보 전달의 평서문
(A) 정답. 계절 상품을 매장 앞쪽으로 옮기기로 결정했다는 평서문에 그 중 일부를 진열창에 놓았는지 되물으며, 관련된 정보를 확인하고 있으므로 정답.
(B) 연상 단어 오답. 평서문의 seasonal에서 연상 가능한 summer를 이용한 오답.
(C) 파생어 오답. 평서문의 move와 파생어 관계인 moving을 이용한 오답.

PART 3

32-34

M-Cn 32 The renovations we're planning for the theater are long overdue.

W-Br 32 I'm glad we have time between productions so we can get the work done.

M-Cn I agree—and even though 33 it's great that our latest musical production has had such a successful run, we can all use the break.

W-Br Plus, 34 it gives us time to focus on next month's fund-raiser.

M-Cn 34 Hopefully we'll raise enough money at that event to replace the old lighting system too.

남 극장을 위해 계획한 보수 작업이 너무 늦어지고 있어요.
여 작품들 사이에 시간이 있어서 작업을 마칠 수 있으니 다행이네요.
남 맞아요. 최근 뮤지컬 작품이 성황리에 상연되어서 좋기는 하지만, 모두 휴식기를 가질 수 있어요.
여 게다가 다음 달 모금 행사에 집중할 수 있는 시간이 생기죠.
남 그 행사에서 낡은 조명 시스템도 교체할 만큼 충분한 기금이 모였으면 해요.

어휘 renovation 보수, 개조 long overdue 훨씬 전에 했어야 하는, 기한이 많이 지난 production (영화, 연극 등의) 제작 get ~ done ~을 끝내다 latest 최근의 have a run 연속 상연하다, 공연하다 successful 성공적인 break 휴식 focus on ~에 초점을 맞추다 fund-raiser 모금 행사 raise money 자금을 조달하다, 돈을 마련하다 lighting 조명

32

What are the speakers mainly discussing?
(A) Theater renovations
(B) Changes to a performance schedule
(C) Selection of a new lighting director
(D) A promotional gift

화자들은 주로 무엇에 관해 이야기하는가?
(A) 극장 보수
(B) 공연 일정 변경
(C) 새 조명 감독 선발
(D) 사은품

어휘 performance 공연　selection 선택　director 감독
　　　promotional 홍보의

해설 전체 내용 관련 – 대화의 주제
남자가 첫 대사에서 극장 보수 작업이 너무 늦어지고 있다(The renovations we're planning for the theater are long overdue)고 말하자, 여자가 작품들 사이에 시간이 있어서 작업을 마칠 수 있으니 다행(I'm glad we have time between productions so we can get the work done)이라며 극장 보수 작업에 대한 대화를 이어 가고 있으므로 정답은 (A)이다.

> **Paraphrasing** 대화의 The renovations we're planning for the theater → 정답의 Theater renovations

33

What does the man say about a musical production?
(A) It was based on a book.
(B) It has been successful.
(C) It will be performed overseas.
(D) Some casting changes were made.

남자는 뮤지컬 작품에 대해 뭐라고 말하는가?
(A) 책에 기반을 두고 있다.
(B) 성공을 거뒀다.
(C) 해외에서 공연될 것이다.
(D) 캐스팅 일부가 변경됐다.

어휘 be based on ~에 기반을 두다　overseas 해외에　casting
　　　캐스팅, 배역 선정

해설 세부 사항 관련 – 남자가 뮤지컬 작품에 대해 하는 말
남자가 두 번째 대사에서 최근 뮤지컬 작품이 성황리에 상연되어서 좋다(it's great that our latest musical production has had such a successful run)고 하므로 정답은 (B)이다.

34

What event are the speakers planning?
(A) A press conference
(B) A fund-raiser
(C) An audition
(D) An autograph session

화자들은 어떤 행사를 계획하는가?
(A) 기자회견
(B) 모금 행사
(C) 오디션
(D) 사인회

해설 세부 사항 관련 – 화자들이 계획하는 행사
여자가 두 번째 대사에서 다음 달 모금 행사에 집중할 수 있는 시간이 생긴다(it gives us time to focus on next month's fund-raiser)고 하자, 남자가 그 행사에서 충분한 기금이 모였으면 한다(Hopefully we'll raise enough money at that event ~)고 응답하는 것으로 보아 화자들은 모금 행사를 계획하고 있음을 알 수 있다. 따라서 정답은 (B)이다.

35-37

M-Au　Fernanda, **35 I wanted to tell you that the top candidate we chose for the customer-care position just accepted our job offer.** I'll send him a contract later today.

W-Am　Great! But now I think we need a bigger office space for our business. With the new hire, there'll be ten of us in the office.

M-Au　I agree. Our lease expires next month, so we should look at a different space. **36 There's a new office building on Second Street. It has solar panels, so all of its energy comes from renewable sources.**

W-Am　**36 I like that. 37 But I'm worried we may not be able to afford the lease.**

M-Au　We'll see. I'll contact the rental agency today.

남　페르난다, **고객 관리직에 우리가 선택한 최고의 후보자가 일자리 제안을 막 수락했다는 말씀 드리려고요.** 이따가 계약서를 보낼 겁니다.

여　잘됐네요! 하지만 이젠 업무를 위해 더 큰 사무실이 필요할 것 같아요. 신규 채용자까지 사무실에 열 명이 있게 될 테니까요.

남　맞아요. 임대차 계약이 다음 달에 만료되니 다른 공간을 살펴봐야 해요. **2번 가에 새 사무실 건물이 있어요. 태양 전지판이 있어서 에너지 전부를 재생 에너지원에서 얻죠.**

여　**맘에 드네요. 하지만 임대료를 감당하지 못할까 봐 걱정되는데요.**

남　한번 봅시다. 오늘 임대업체에 연락해 볼게요.

어휘 candidate 지원자, 후보자　customer-care 고객 서비스
job offer 일자리 제안　contract 계약, 계약서　lease
임대차 계약　expire 만료되다　solar panel 태양 전지판
renewable 재생 가능한　source 원천　afford ~할
여유가 되다, 형편이 되다　rental agency 임대업체

35

What did the speakers recently do?
(A) They launched a new product.
(B) They chose a job candidate.
(C) They moved to a different city.
(D) They renovated a space.

화자들은 최근 무엇을 했는가?
(A) 신상품을 출시했다.
(B) 입사 지원자를 뽑았다.
(C) 다른 도시로 이전했다.
(D) 공간을 개조했다.

어휘 launch 개시하다, 출시하다   renovate 개조하다, 보수하다

해설 세부 사항 관련 – 화자들이 최근에 한 일
남자가 첫 대사에서 고객 관리직에 우리가 선택한 최고의 후보자가 일자리 제안을 막 수락했다는 말씀을 드리려고 했다(I wanted to tell you that the top candidate we chose for the customer-care position just accepted our job offer)고 말하고 있으므로 화자들은 최근에 고객 관리직 입사 지원자를 뽑았다는 것을 알 수 있다. 따라서 정답은 (B)이다.

36

What do the speakers like about a building?
(A) It provides 24-hour access.
(B) It has an outdoor space.
(C) It is near public transportation.
(D) It uses renewable energy.

화자들은 건물에 대해 어떤 점을 마음에 들어 하는가?
(A) 24시간 출입할 수 있다.
(B) 실외 공간이 있다.
(C) 대중교통과 가깝다.
(D) 재생 에너지를 사용한다.

어휘 access 입장, 접근   public transportation 대중교통

해설 세부 사항 관련 – 화자들이 건물에 대해 마음에 들어 하는 점
남자가 두 번째 대사에서 2번 가에 새 사무실 건물이 있는데 태양 전지 판이 있어서 에너지 전부를 재생 에너지원에서 얻는다(There's a new office building on Second Street. It has solar panels, so all of its energy comes from renewable sources)고 하자, 여자가 맘에 든다(I like that)고 응답하므로 정답은 (D)이다.

> **Paraphrasing** 대화의 all of its energy comes from renewable sources
> → 정답의 It uses renewable energy.

37

What is the woman worried about?
(A) A new competitor
(B) A longer commute
(C) A high price
(D) An upcoming deadline

여자는 무엇에 대해 걱정하는가?
(A) 새로운 경쟁업체
(B) 길어지는 통근 거리
(C) 높은 가격
(D) 다가오는 기한

어휘 competitor 경쟁자   commute 통근 (거리)   upcoming 다가오는, 곧 있을   deadline 기한

해설 세부 사항 관련 – 여자의 우려 사항
여자가 두 번째 대사에서 임대료를 감당하지 못할까 봐 걱정된다(But I'm worried we may not be able to afford the lease)고 말하고 있으므로 정답은 (C)이다.

38-40

M-Au	How can I help you?
W-Br	Hi, ³⁸,³⁹I'd like to order a cake for my son's birthday next week. He really likes dinosaurs.
M-Au	³⁹I have several different dinosaur-shaped pans for you to choose from.
W-Br	Actually, ⁴⁰I was hoping you could make a standing cake instead of a flat one.
M-Au	Oh, I see. ⁴⁰I'm sorry. I do have someone on staff who can make those, but she's all booked up for the next few weeks. Try Carmen's Creations on Pine Street.

남	어떻게 도와드릴까요?
여	안녕하세요. **다음 주 아들 생일에 쓸 케이크를 주문하고 싶은데요.** 아들이 공룡을 무척 좋아해요.
남	**선택하실 수 있는 여러 가지 다양한 공룡 모양 팬이 있어요.**
여	실은 **평평한 케이크 대신 스탠딩 케이크를 만들어 주셨으면 했거든요.**
남	아, 그렇군요. **죄송합니다. 그걸 만들 수 있는 직원이 있는데, 앞으로 몇 주간 예약이 다 찼어요.** 파인 가에 있는 카르멘 크리에이션에 가 보시죠.

어휘	dinosaur 공룡 standing cake 세워 만든 케이크 flat 평평한 be booked up 예약이 다 차다, 선약이 있다

38

What event is the woman planning?
(A) A retirement party
(B) A birthday party
(C) A science fair
(D) A school festival

여자는 어떤 행사를 계획하고 있는가?
(A) 은퇴 기념 파티
(B) 생일 파티
(C) 과학전람회
(D) 학교 축제

해설 세부 사항 관련 – 여자가 계획하는 행사

여자가 첫 대사에서 다음 주 아들 생일에 쓸 케이크를 주문하고 싶다(I'd like to order a cake for my son's birthday next week)고 말하고 있으므로 정답은 (B)이다.

39

Who most likely is the man?

(A) A baker
(B) A musician
(C) A gardener
(D) A teacher

남자는 누구이겠는가?

(A) 제빵사
(B) 음악가
(C) 정원사
(D) 교사

해설 전체 내용 관련 – 남자의 직업

여자가 첫 대사에서 다음 주 아들 생일에 쓸 케이크를 주문하고 싶다(I'd like to order a cake for my son's birthday next week)고 하자, 남자가 선택할 수 있는 여러 가지 다양한 공룡 모양 팬이 있다(I have several different dinosaur-shaped pans for you to choose from)며 케이크 주문에 대해 구체적으로 응답하므로 남자는 제빵사임을 추론할 수 있다. 따라서 정답은 (A)이다.

40

Why does the man apologize?

(A) Some tools cannot be found.
(B) Some invitations were sent late.
(C) A store is closed for a holiday.
(D) A request cannot be fulfilled.

남자는 왜 사과하는가?

(A) 도구 일부를 찾을 수 없다.
(B) 초대장 일부를 늦게 보냈다.
(C) 매장이 휴일에 문을 닫는다.
(D) 요청을 들어줄 수 없다.

어휘 apologize 사과하다 invitation 초대, 초대장 fulfill a request 요청을 이행하다, 부탁을 들어주다

해설 세부 사항 관련 – 남자가 사과하는 이유

여자가 두 번째 대사에서 평평한 케이크 대신 스탠딩 케이크를 만들어 줬으면 했다(I was hoping you could make a standing cake instead of a flat one)고 요청하는 말을 하자, 남자가 죄송하지만 그걸 만들 수 있는 직원이 있는데, 앞으로 몇 주간 예약이 다 찼다(I'm sorry. I do have someone on staff who can make those, but she's all booked up for the next few weeks)고 하므로 여자의 요청을 들어줄 수 없다는 것을 알 수 있다. 따라서 정답은 (D)이다.

41-43

W-Am	Hello, you've reached Quick Phone Repair Service.
M-Cn	Hi, **[41] I went online to schedule a repair for my mobile phone, but all appointments in your store were booked for today.** Have you had any cancellations?
W-Am	No, unfortunately not. What's the problem with your phone?
M-Cn	**[42] The phone only lasts about an hour before it has to be recharged.**
W-Am	It sounds like you need a new battery. **[43] If you come to the store now, we can try to fit you in as a walk-in appointment. You may have to wait around for a bit.**
M-Cn	**[43] I don't mind waiting.**

여	안녕하세요, 퀵 폰 리페어 서비스입니다.
남	안녕하세요. **제 휴대전화 수리 일정을 잡으려고 온라인에 접속했는데요. 오늘 매장 예약이 다 찼더라고요.** 취소된 거 있나요?
여	아니요, 안타깝게도 없네요. 전화기에 어떤 문제가 있나요?
남	**전화기가 한 시간 정도밖에 안 가고 다시 충전해야 해요.**
여	새 배터리가 필요하신 것 같네요. **지금 매장으로 오시면 현장 예약으로 넣어드려 볼게요. 약간 기다리셔야 할 수도 있습니다.**
남	**기다려도 괜찮아요.**

어휘 reach (전화로) 연락하다 appointment 약속 book 예약하다 cancellation 취소 unfortunately 유감스럽게도, 안타깝게도 last 지속되다 recharge 충전하다, 재충전하다 walk-in 사전 예약 없이 오는 손님

41

What did the man try to do online?

(A) Purchase a new phone
(B) Make an appointment
(C) Order a part
(D) Cancel a contract

남자는 온라인으로 무엇을 하려 했는가?

(A) 새 전화기 구입
(B) 예약
(C) 부품 주문
(D) 계약 취소

해설 세부 사항 관련 – 남자가 온라인으로 하려 한 일

남자가 첫 대사에서 휴대전화 수리 일정을 잡으려고 온라인에 접속했다(I went online to schedule a repair for my mobile phone)고 말하고 있으므로 정답은 (B)이다.

42

What does the man say is wrong with his mobile phone?
(A) It has a short battery life.
(B) The screen is damaged.
(C) A cable is missing.
(D) It has limited storage space.

남자는 자신의 휴대전화에 어떤 문제가 있다고 말하는가?
(A) 배터리 수명이 짧다.
(B) 화면이 손상됐다.
(C) 케이블이 없어졌다.
(D) 저장 공간이 많지 않다.

어휘 missing 없어진 limited 제한된, 아주 많지는 않은, 한정된
storage 저장, 보관

해설 세부 사항 관련 – 남자가 언급하는 휴대전화의 문제점
남자가 두 번째 대사에서 전화기가 한 시간 정도밖에 안 가고 다시 충전해야 한다(The phone only lasts about an hour before it has to be recharged)고 말하고 있으므로 정답은 (A)이다.

43

What will the man most likely do next?
(A) Speak with a manager
(B) Call technical support
(C) Visit a store
(D) Restart a device

남자는 다음에 무엇을 하겠는가?
(A) 관리자와 이야기하기
(B) 기술 지원팀에 전화하기
(C) 매장 방문하기
(D) 기기 재시작하기

어휘 technical support 기술 지원 device 기기, 장치

해설 세부 사항 관련 – 남자가 다음에 할 일
여자가 마지막 대사에서 지금 매장으로 오면 현장 예약으로 넣어줄 수 있는데 약간 기다려야 할 수도 있다(If you come to the store now, we can try to fit you in as a walk-in appointment. You may have to wait around for a bit)고 하자, 남자가 기다려도 괜찮다(I don't mind waiting)고 응답하고 있으므로 남자는 매장을 방문할 것이라는 것을 알 수 있다. 따라서 정답은 (C)이다.

44-46

 동영상 강의

M-Au Asako, **44 how far along are you on that news report about the bank merger?** If you want it to be included in tomorrow morning's newspaper, it has to be on my desk by nine P.M.

W-Am Well, **45 I'm still doing research for this article.** I'm having trouble getting all the facts from the people involved. They haven't returned my phone calls.

M-Au Well, we can't print the story without confirming the details. But **46 if you can have it finished by Wednesday night, I can put it in Thursday's paper.**

남 아사코, 은행 합병에 대한 뉴스 보도 건은 어디까지 진행됐나요? 내일 아침 신문에 싣고 싶으면 오후 9시까지 제 책상 위에 올려 놔야 해요.

여 음, 아직 기사를 위한 조사를 하고 있어요. 관련된 사람들로부터 모든 사실을 파악하는 데 어려움이 있습니다. 제 전화에 회신을 안 하고 있어요.

남 음, 세부 사항을 확인하지 않고 기사를 인쇄할 순 없어요. 하지만 수요일 밤까지 마칠 수 있다면, 목요일 신문에 실을 수 있습니다.

어휘 merger 합병 include 포함시키다 have trouble -ing ~하는 데 어려움을 겪다 involved 관련된, 연루된 confirm 확인하다 detail 세부 사항

44

Where do the speakers most likely work?
(A) At a bank
(B) At a research laboratory
(C) At a newspaper company
(D) At a legal firm

화자들은 어디서 일하겠는가?
(A) 은행
(B) 연구소
(C) 신문사
(D) 법률사무소

해설 전체 내용 관련 – 화자들의 근무지
남자가 첫 대사에서 은행 합병에 대한 뉴스 보도 건의 진행 상황(how far along are you on that news report about the bank merger?)을 물은 뒤, 내일 아침 신문에 싣고 싶으면 오후 9시까지 내 책상 위에 올려 두라(If you want it to be included in tomorrow morning's newspaper, it has to be on my desk by nine P.M.)고 말하고 있으므로 화자들은 신문사에서 근무하고 있음을 알 수 있다. 따라서 정답은 (C)이다.

45

Why has the woman been unable to finish a task?
(A) She needs a manager's signature.
(B) She cannot access her files.
(C) She cannot get the necessary information.
(D) Some data are incorrect.

여자는 왜 업무를 마칠 수 없었는가?
(A) 관리자의 서명이 필요하다.
(B) 파일에 접속할 수 없다.
(C) 필요한 정보를 얻을 수 없다.
(D) 일부 자료가 부정확하다.

어휘 unable to ~할 수 없는 signature 서명 access 접근하다, 접속하다 necessary 필요한 incorrect 부정확한, 맞지 않는

해설 세부 사항 관련 – 여자가 업무를 마칠 수 없는 이유
여자가 첫 대사에서 아직 기사를 위한 조사를 하고 있으며 관련된 사람들로부터 모든 사실을 파악하는 데 어려움이 있다(I'm still doing research for this article. I'm having trouble getting all the facts from the people involved)고 말하고 있으므로 정답은 (C)이다.

Paraphrasing	대화의 having trouble getting all the facts → 정답의 cannot get the necessary information

46

What solution does the man propose?
(A) Changing a deadline
(B) Scheduling a meeting
(C) Asking a colleague for help
(D) Reviewing some documents

남자는 어떤 해결책을 제안하는가?
(A) 기한 변경하기
(B) 회의 일정 잡기
(C) 동료에게 도움 요청하기
(D) 서류 검토하기

어휘 solution 해답, 해결책 propose 제안하다 deadline 기한 colleague 동료

해설 세부 사항 관련 – 남자가 제안하는 해결책
남자가 마지막 대사에서 수요일 밤까지 마칠 수 있다면, 목요일 신문에 실을 수 있다(if you can have it finished by Wednesday night, I can put it in Thursday's paper)고 말하고 있으므로 정답은 (A)이다.

47-49

M-Cn ⁴⁷ **We'll have to remove the soil from the garden bed and lay down drainpipes that'll take the water out through holes in the retaining wall.**

W-Am Sounds like a lot of work, but it'll be worth it to be able to grow the garden that I want to.

M-Cn Do you think you'd like bricks or stones for the retaining wall? Many homeowners prefer brick because it creates a nice, uniform look. But ⁴⁸**stones will last longer. They are more expensive, though.**

W-Am I don't want to have to make repairs.

M-Cn You have several different kinds of stones to choose from. ⁴⁹**I have some pictures of projects I've completed in the past you can look at.**

남 우리는 화단의 흙을 제거하고 옹벽의 구멍을 통해 물을 빼낼 배수관을 깔아야 할 겁니다.
여 일이 많겠네요, 하지만 제가 원하는 정원을 가꿀 수 있으니 가치 있는 일일 거예요.
남 옹벽은 벽돌이 좋아요, 아니면 돌이 좋아요? 많은 주택 소유주들은 벽돌을 선호해요. 멋지고 균일한 모습을 만들어 주니까요. 하지만 석조가 더 오래 지속됩니다. 더 비싸긴 하지만요.
여 수리를 해야 하는 건 원치 않아요.
남 고르실 수 있는 돌이 여러 종류 다양하게 있습니다. 과거에 제가 완료한 프로젝트 사진들을 보시면 돼요.

어휘 remove 치우다, 제거하다 soil 토양 lay down 놓다 drainpipe 하수관 retaining wall 옹벽 worth 가치가 있는 brick 벽돌 prefer 선호하다 uniform 균일한, 획일적인, 한결 같은 last 지속되다 expensive 비싼 complete 완료하다, 끝마치다

47

What kind of work does the man do?
(A) Appliance repair
(B) Painting
(C) Landscaping
(D) Roofing

남자는 어떤 종류의 일을 하는가?
(A) 가전 제품 수리
(B) 페인트칠
(C) 조경
(D) 지붕 공사

해설 전체 내용 관련 – 남자의 근무 업종
남자가 첫 대사에서 화단의 흙을 제거하고 배수관을 깔아야 할 것(We'll have to remove the soil from the garden bed and lay down drainpipes)이라고 말하고 있으므로 조경 일을 하고 있다는 것을 알 수 있다. 따라서 정답은 (C)이다.

48

What does the woman imply when she says, "I don't want to have to make repairs"?
(A) She is not qualified for a task.
(B) She prefers durable materials.
(C) She will buy a new appliance.
(D) She is not happy with a cost estimate.

여자가 "수리를 해야 하는 건 원치 않아요"라고 말하는 의도는 무엇인가?
(A) 여자는 일을 할 자격을 갖추지 못했다.
(B) 여자는 내구성 있는 자재를 선호한다.
(C) 여자는 새 가전 제품을 살 것이다.
(D) 여자는 견적서가 마음에 들지 않는다.

어휘 be qualified for ~의 자격을 갖추다, ~에 적격이다   durable
내구성이 있는   material 재료, 자재   cost estimate 견적서

해설 화자의 의도 파악 – 수리를 해야 하는 건 원치 않는다는 말의 의도
남자가 두 번째 대사에서 벽돌과 돌 중 무엇이 좋은지 물은 뒤 석조가 더 오래 지속되지만 비싸다(stones will last longer. They are more expensive, though)고 말하자, 여자가 인용문을 언급한 것으로 보아 내구성 있는 자재를 선호한다는 의미로 볼 수 있다. 따라서 정답은 (B)이다.

49

What will the man show to the woman?
(A) A list of prices
(B) A license
(C) Some references
(D) Some photographs

남자는 여자에게 무엇을 보여줄 것인가?
(A) 가격 목록
(B) 자격증
(C) 참고 문헌
(D) 사진

해설 세부 사항 관련 – 남자가 여자에게 보여줄 것
남자가 마지막 대사에서 과거에 완료한 프로젝트 사진들을 보면 된다(I have some pictures of projects I've completed in the past you can look at)고 말하므로 정답은 (D)이다.

> **Paraphrasing**   대화의 pictures → 정답의 photographs

50-52

W-Br	Good morning. You've reached Accounts Payable.
M-Cn	Hi. I'm calling from the editorial department. **⁵⁰One of our freelance writers has not received payment yet, so I'm calling to inquire about it.** Her contract number is 9356.
W-Br	OK, let me check. Hmm. It looks like she

should have been paid last week. But **⁵¹Adem handles those requests, and he was on vacation.** He's just catching up today.

M-Cn	**⁵²Do you have an estimate of how long it will take to process the request?**
W-Br	**⁵²I'm not sure, but I can speak to Adem.**

여	안녕하세요. 어카운트 페이어블입니다.
남	안녕하세요. 편집부인데요. **저희 프리랜서 작가 중 한 분이 아직 급여를 받지 못해서 문의하려고 전화 드립니다.** 계약 번호는 9356입니다.
여	네, 확인해 볼게요. 지난주에 지급을 받으셨어야 하는 것 같은데요. **아뎀이 해당 요청을 처리하는데, 휴가 중이었네요.** 오늘 밀린 일을 하고 있어요.
남	요청을 처리하는 데 얼마나 걸릴 거라고 추정하시나요?
여	잘 모르겠습니다만, 아뎀한테 얘기해 볼게요.

어휘 reach (전화로) 연락하다   editorial 편집의   payment 지불, 지급   inquire 문의하다   contract 계약   handle 처리하다, 다루다   on vacation 휴가 중인   catch up 밀린 일을 하다, 따라잡다   estimate 추정, 추산   process 처리하다

50

Why is the man calling?
(A) To track a shipment
(B) To ask about a payment
(C) To close an account
(D) To request computer help

남자가 전화한 이유는?
(A) 배송을 추적하려고
(B) 지급에 대해 물어보려고
(C) 계좌를 해지하려고
(D) 컴퓨터 관련 도움을 요청하려고

어휘 track 추적하다   shipment 배송, 수송   close an account
계좌를 해지하다, 신용 거래를 끊다

해설 전체 내용 관련 – 남자가 전화한 이유
남자가 첫 대사에서 프리랜서 작가 중 한 분이 아직 급여를 받지 못해서 문의하려고 전화한다(One of our freelance writers has not received payment yet, so I'm calling to inquire about it)고 하므로 정답은 (B)이다.

> **Paraphrasing**   대화의 inquire → 정답의 ask

51

According to the woman, what caused a delay?
(A) An employee was out of the office.
(B) A software program was updated.
(C) A document was mislabeled.
(D) A new policy was implemented.

여자에 따르면, 무엇 때문에 지연됐는가?

(A) 직원이 자리를 비웠다.
(B) 소프트웨어 프로그램이 업데이트되었다.
(C) 문서에 라벨을 잘못 붙였다.
(D) 새로운 정책이 시행됐다.

어휘 mislabel 라벨을 잘못 붙이다 implement 시행하다

해설 세부 사항 관련 – 지연 이유

여자가 두 번째 대사에서 아뎀이 해당 요청을 처리하는데, 휴가 중이었다
(Adem handles those requests, and he was on vacation)고 말하
고 있으므로 정답은 (A)이다.

Paraphrasing	대화의 he was on vacation → 정답의 An employee was out of the office.

52

What information will the woman most likely provide later?
(A) A cost breakdown
(B) An account number
(C) A time estimate
(D) A phone number

여자는 나중에 어떤 정보를 제공할 것인가?
(A) 가격 명세서
(B) 계좌 번호
(C) 추정 시간
(D) 전화번호

어휘 breakdown 명세, 명세서 account 계좌

해설 세부 사항 관련 – 여자가 제공할 정보

남자가 두 번째 대사에서 요청을 처리하는 데 추정되는 시간(Do you
have an estimate of how long it will take to process the
request?)을 묻자, 여자가 잘 모르지만 아뎀한테 얘기해 보겠다(I'm not
sure, but I can speak to Adem)고 하므로 정답은 (C)이다.

Paraphrasing	대화의 an estimate of how long it will take → 정답의 A time estimate

53-55 3인 대화

M-Au	I'm the general manager ⁵³**here at Rev It Auto Repair,** and this is Mr. Singh, our service manager. We're eager to hear how your product can benefit our shop.
W-Am	Well, ⁵⁴**my product is called Video Room. It's a library of short videos that your business can offer in the waiting room.** These videos will explain common auto repairs and educate your customers on the repair process.
M-Cn	⁵⁵**Can we add our own customized content?** I'd love to include a description of our exclusive lifetime warranty.

M-Au	Yes. And ⁵⁵**can we also add at-home auto-care advice?**
남1	저는 **여기 레브잇 자동차 정비소**의 총괄 관리자이고, 이분은 저희 서비스 관리자 싱 씨입니다. 귀사의 제품이 저희 매장에 어떻게 이익이 되는지 듣고 싶은데요.
여	음, 저희 제품은 비디오 룸이라고 불리는데요. 귀사의 대기실에서 제공할 수 있는 짧은 동영상 라이브러리입니다. 동영상에선 일반적인 자동차 수리에 대해 설명하고, 고객들에게 수리 과정을 가르쳐 줍니다.
남2	**저희만의 맞춤형 내용을 추가할 수 있나요?** 저희가 독점 제공하는 평생 품질 보증에 관한 설명을 포함시키고 싶은데요.
남1	네. **집에서 하는 자동차 관리 조언도 추가할 수 있을까요?**

어휘	general manager 총지배인, 총관리인 be eager to ~을 간절히 바라다, 하고 싶어 하다 benefit 이익을 주다 educate 교육하다, 가르치다 process 과정 customized 개인의 요구에 맞춘 content 내용 include 포함시키다 description 설명, 기술 exclusive 독점적인, 배타적인 lifetime warranty 평생 품질 보증

53

Where does the conversation take place?
(A) At a game arcade
(B) At a grocery store
(C) At an auto repair shop
(D) At a parking garage

대화는 어디서 이루어지는가?
(A) 게임 센터
(B) 식료품점
(C) 자동차 정비소
(D) 주차장

해설 전체 내용 관련 – 대화의 장소

첫 번째 남자가 첫 대사에서 여기 레브잇 자동차 정비소(here at Rev
It Auto Repair)라고 했으므로 대화 장소는 자동차 정비소라는 것을 알 수
있다. 따라서 정답은 (C)이다.

54

What type of product does the woman mention?
(A) Some videos
(B) Some brochures
(C) A price scanner
(D) A mobile phone application

여자는 어떤 종류의 제품을 언급하는가?
(A) 동영상
(B) 안내책자
(C) 가격 스캐너
(D) 휴대전화 앱

여자가 첫 대사에서 비디오 룸이라는 제품이 귀사의 대기실에서 제공할 수 있는 짧은 동영상 라이브러리(my product is called Video Room. It's a library of short videos ~ in the waiting room)라고 말하고 있으므로 정답은 (A)이다.

55

What do the men want to do?
(A) Extend business hours
(B) Enter a local contest
(C) Include customized content
(D) Upgrade some equipment

남자들은 무엇을 하고 싶어 하는가?
(A) 영업시간 연장하기
(B) 지역 대회 참가하기
(C) 맞춤형 내용 포함시키기
(D) 장비 업그레이드하기

어휘 extend 연장하다, 늘리다 business hours 영업시간, 운영 시간 enter a contest 대회에 참가하다 local 지역의 equipment 장비

해설 세부 사항 관련 – 남자들이 하고 싶어 하는 일
두 번째 남자의 대사에서 맞춤형 내용을 추가할 수 있는지(Can we add our own customized content?)를 묻자, 첫 번째 남자가 마지막 대사에서 집에서 하는 자동차 관리 조언도 추가할 수 있는지(can we also add at-home auto-care advice?) 묻고 있으므로 남자들은 맞춤형 내용을 포함시키고 싶어 한다는 것을 알 수 있다. 따라서 정답은 (C)이다.

56-58

M-Au	Hi, Carmen. **56 I've just reviewed the outline you gave me for the nature documentary we're making. I think it'll be a great film,** but I'm a bit concerned. I want it to be less than an hour.
W-Br	**57 I understand. I'll take another look at it and see where I can take out some unnecessary scenes from the storyboard.**
M-Au	Great. In the meantime, **58 I need to follow up with our camera team to make sure they have all the equipment they need to begin filming.**

남	안녕하세요, 카르멘. 제게 주신 우리가 만들 자연 다큐멘터리의 개요를 막 검토했어요. 훌륭한 영화가 될 것 같은데, 조금 우려가 되네요. 한 시간 미만이었으면 해요.
여	알겠습니다. 다시 보면서 스토리보드에서 뺄 수 있는 불필요한 장면들이 어디인지 확인해 보겠습니다.
남	좋아요. 그동안 저는 카메라팀에 연락해서 촬영을 시작하는 데 필요한 모든 장비를 갖추도록 해야겠어요.

어휘 outline 개요 concerned 걱정하는, 관심이 있는 take a look 보다 take out 빼다, 가지고 나가다 unnecessary 불필요한 in the meantime 그동안 follow up with (추가 조치나 확인을 위해) 연락하다 equipment 장비

56

What industry do the speakers most likely work in?
(A) Fashion photography
(B) Information technology
(C) Filmmaking
(D) Marketing

화자들은 어떤 업계에서 일하겠는가?
(A) 패션 촬영
(B) 정보 통신 기술
(C) 영화 제작
(D) 마케팅

해설 전체 내용 관련 – 화자들의 근무 업종
남자가 첫 대사에서 우리가 만들 자연 다큐멘터리(the nature documentary we're making)를 언급하며, 훌륭한 영화가 될 것 같다(I think it'll be a great film)고 말하고 있으므로 화자들은 영화 제작 업종에서 근무하고 있음을 알 수 있다. 따라서 정답은 (C)이다.

57

What does the man imply when he says, "I want it to be less than an hour"?
(A) He is very busy.
(B) He approves an itinerary.
(C) A route has a lot of traffic.
(D) Some revisions are needed.

남자가 "한 시간 미만이었으면 해요"라고 말하는 의도는 무엇인가?
(A) 남자는 매우 바쁘다.
(B) 남자가 일정을 승인한다.
(C) 노선에 교통량이 많다.
(D) 일부 변경이 필요하다.

어휘 approve 승인하다 itinerary 여행 일정표 traffic 교통량 revision 변경, 수정

해설 화자의 의도 파악 – 한 시간 미만이었으면 한다는 말의 의도
남자가 첫 대사에서 인용문을 언급하자 여자가 다시 보면서 스토리보드에서 뺄 수 있는 불필요한 장면들이 어디인지 확인해 보겠다(I'll take another look at it and see where I can take out some unnecessary scenes from the storyboard)고 하는 것을 보아 남자는 변경이 필요하다는 의도로 한 말임을 알 수 있다. 따라서 정답은 (D)이다.

TEST 6

58

Why does the man need to contact a team?
(A) To explain a permit procedure
(B) To confirm equipment availability
(C) To introduce a colleague
(D) To devise a safety plan

남자는 왜 팀에 연락을 해야 하는가?
(A) 허가 절차를 설명하려고
(B) 장비 이용 가능 여부를 확인하려고
(C) 동료를 소개하려고
(D) 안전 계획을 고안하려고

어휘 permit 허가증 procedure 절차 confirm 확인해 주다,
확정하다 availability 이용 가능성 colleague 동료 devise
고안하다 safety 안전

해설 세부 사항 관련 – 남자가 팀에 연락해야 하는 이유
남자가 마지막 대사에서 카메라팀에 연락해서 촬영을 시작하는 데 필요한
모든 장비를 갖추도록 해야겠다(I need to follow up with our camera
team to make sure they have all the equipment they need to
begin filming)고 하므로 정답은 (B)이다.

> Paraphrasing 대화의 follow up with our camera team
> → 질문의 contact a team
>
> 대화의 to make sure they have all the
> equipment
> → 정답의 To confirm equipment availability

59-61 3인 대화

M-Au Kriti and Melissa, **59I reviewed the results
of the soil tests yesterday**, and **60most of
the sports fields we manage have healthy
soil. But unfortunately, the baseball field
on Smith Drive has elevated levels of
potassium.**

W-Am The grass on that field is so brown and
weedy. Now we know why.

W-Br **60We'll need to order some special
fertilizer to put on it.** Do you think we need
approval to do that?

M-Au Yes—since it's an unforeseen expense,
it has to be approved by the acquisitions
department. **61Melissa, do you have time
to prepare a cost estimate?**

W-Br **61Sure. It won't take long. I'll send it by
lunchtime, and I'll cc you both on the
e-mail.**

남 크리티, 멜리사. 어제 토양 검사 결과를 검토했는데요.
우리가 관리하는 운동장 대부분의 토양이 건강합니다.
하지만 안타깝게도, 스미스 길에 있는 야구장의 칼륨 수치가
높아졌어요.

여1 야구장 잔디가 아주 갈색이고 잡초투성이예요. 이제 이유를
알았네요.

여2 **거기에 뿌릴 특수 비료를 주문해야겠어요. 그러려면 승인이
필요할까요?**

남 네, 예측하지 못한 비용이니 매입 부서의 승인을 받아야
해요. 멜리사, 견적서를 준비할 시간이 있나요?

여2 그럼요, 오래 걸리지 않을 겁니다. 점심 시간까지 보낼게요,
그리고 두 분 모두 이메일 참조로 넣을게요.

어휘 soil 토양 manage 관리하다 unfortunately
안타깝게도, 아쉽게도 elevate 높이다, 증가시키다
potassium 칼륨 weedy 잡초투성이의 fertilizer 비료
approval 승인 unforeseen 예측하지 못한, 뜻밖의
expense 비용, 경비 acquisition 습득, 획득, 매입
cost estimate 견적서 cc (= carbon copy) 참조;
참조로 넣다

59

What did the man review yesterday?
(A) A budget
(B) A weather report
(C) Some test results
(D) Some hiring plans

남자는 어제 무엇을 검토했는가?
(A) 예산
(B) 일기 예보
(C) 검사 결과
(D) 고용 계획

해설 세부 사항 관련 – 남자가 어제 검토한 것
남자가 첫 대사에서 어제 토양 검사 결과를 검토했다고(I reviewed the
results of the soil tests yesterday)고 말하고 있으므로 정답은 (C)이
다.

> Paraphrasing 대화의 the results of the soil tests
> → 정답의 Some test results

60

What do the speakers hope to do?
(A) Improve the condition of a sports field
(B) Expand the city's athletic programs
(C) Plan a fund-raising event
(D) Acquire more public land

화자들은 무엇을 하고 싶어 하는가?
(A) 운동장 상태 개선하기
(B) 시의 체육 프로그램 확대하기
(C) 모금 행사 계획하기
(D) 더 많은 공유지 획득하기

어휘 improve 향상시키다, 개선하다 expand 확대하다, 확장하다
athletic 육상의, 체육의 fund-raising 모금 acquire 획득하다
public land 공유지

해설 세부 사항 관련 – 화자들이 하고자 하는 일

남자가 첫 대사에서 우리가 관리하는 운동장 대부분의 토양이 건강하지만(most of the sports fields we manage have healthy soil) 스미스 길에 있는 야구장의 칼륨 수치가 높아졌다(the baseball field on Smith Drive has elevated levels of potassium)고 말하자, 두 번째 여자가 거기에 뿌릴 특수 비료를 주문해야겠다(We'll need to order some special fertilizer to put on it)고 말하는 것을 보아 화자들은 관리하는 운동장 중의 하나인 스미스 길의 야구장의 상태를 개선하려고 한다는 것을 알 수 있다. 따라서 정답은 (A)이다.

61

What will Melissa send by e-mail?
(A) A summary of work tasks
(B) A letter of appreciation
(C) A news article
(D) A cost estimate

멜리사는 이메일로 무엇을 보낼 것인가?
(A) 업무 요약
(B) 감사 편지
(C) 뉴스 기사
(D) 견적서

어휘 summary 요약　appreciation 감사

해설 세부 사항 관련 – 멜리사가 이메일로 보낼 것

남자가 두 번째 대사에서 멜리사에게 견적서를 준비할 시간이 있는지(Melissa, do you have time to prepare a cost estimate?)를 묻자, 두 번째 여자가 수락의 답변과 함께 오래 걸리지 않을 것(Sure. It won't take long)이라고 하며 점심 시간까지 보내고 두 사람을 이메일 참조로 넣겠다(I'll send it by lunchtime, and I'll cc you both on the e-mail)고 말하고 있으므로 정답은 (D)이다.

62-64 대화 + 일정표

W-Am Rodrigo, **62 you wanted to talk to me about the schedule for the bowling leagues at our alley?**

M-Cn Yes. As you know, many of the members in the adult league have young children who participate in the junior league. And **63 they explained to me that it would be really convenient if we moved the junior league to the same night that the adult league plays.** That way they could all come together on the same night.

W-Am **63 That's a great idea.** We have a few available bowling lanes on that day that the junior league can use. **63, 64 I'll e-mail the parents of the junior bowlers and let them know the day will change starting next month.**

여 로드리고, 우리 볼링장의 볼링 리그 일정에 대해 저와 얘기하고 싶어 하셨죠?

남 네. 아시다시피, 많은 성인 리그 회원들에게 주니어 리그에 참가하는 어린 자녀가 있어요. 그래서 저희가 주니어 리그를 성인 리그와 같은 날 밤으로 옮기면 정말 편리하겠다고 하시더라구요. 그렇게 하면 모두 같은 날 밤에 함께 올 수 있잖아요.

여 좋은 생각이네요. 해당 요일에 주니어 리그가 이용할 수 있는 볼링 레인이 몇 개 있어요. 제가 주니어 볼링 선수들의 부모님께 이메일을 보내서 다음 달부터 요일이 바뀐다고 알려 드릴게요.

어휘 bowling alley 볼링장　adult 성인　participate in ~에 참가하다　convenient 편리한　available 이용 가능한

League Schedule	
Junior League (ages 9–12)	
Monday	5:30 P.M.
Teen League (ages 13–17)	
Tuesday	6:00 P.M.
Wednesday	7:00 P.M.
Adult League	
63 Thursday	6:00 P.M.

리그 일정표	
주니어 리그 (9–12세)	
월요일	오후 5시 30분
청소년 리그 (13–17세)	
화요일	오후 6시
수요일	오후 7시
성인 리그	
63 목요일	오후 6시

62

Where do the speakers work?
(A) At a bowling alley
(B) At a swimming pool
(C) At an ice-skating rink
(D) At a baseball field

화자들은 어디서 일하는가?
(A) 볼링장
(B) 수영장
(C) 아이스 스케이트장
(D) 야구장

해설 전체 내용 관련 – 화자들의 근무지

여자가 첫 대사에서 우리 볼링장의 볼링 리그 일정(the schedule for the bowling leagues at our alley)이라고 말하고 있으므로 정답은 (A)이다.

63

Look at the graphic. On which day will the Junior League meet starting next month?
(A) Monday
(B) Tuesday
(C) Wednesday
(D) Thursday

시각 정보에 의하면, 주니어 리그는 다음 달부터 무슨 요일에 만나는가?
(A) 월요일
(B) 화요일
(C) 수요일
(D) 목요일

해설 시각 정보 연계 – 주니어 리그가 다음 달부터 만나는 요일
남자가 첫 대사에서 성인 리그 회원들이 주니어 리그를 성인 리그와 같은 날 밤으로 옮기면 정말 편리하겠다고 한다(they explained to me that it would be really convenient if we moved the junior league to the same night that the adult league plays)고 하자, 여자가 좋은 생각(That's a great idea)이라고 하면서, 주니어 선수들의 부모님께 이메일을 보내서 다음 달부터 요일이 바뀐다고 알리겠다(I'll e-mail the parents of the junior bowlers and let them know the day will change starting next month)고 한 것으로 보아 주니어 리그는 다음 달부터 성인 리그와 같은 요일로 변경된다는 것을 알 수 있다. 리그 일정표에 따르면 성인 리그가 목요일에 있으므로 정답은 (D)이다.

64

What does the woman say she will do?
(A) Hang a poster
(B) Send an e-mail
(C) Deliver a package
(D) Process a payment

여자는 무엇을 할 것이라고 말하는가?
(A) 포스터 걸기
(B) 이메일 보내기
(C) 소포 배달하기
(D) 비용 지불 처리하기

어휘 hang 걸다, 매달다　process 처리하다　payment 지불

해설 세부 사항 관련 – 여자가 할 일
여자가 마지막 대사에서 주니어 선수들의 부모님께 이메일을 보내서 다음 달부터 요일이 바뀐다고 알리겠다(I'll e-mail the parents of the junior bowlers and let them know the day will change starting next month)고 말하고 있으므로 정답은 (B)이다.

Paraphrasing 대화의 e-mail → 정답의 Send an e-mail

65-67 대화 + 달력

M-Cn　Hi. Where can I find a schedule of library events?

W-Br　Oh, I've got it right here. We usually have events almost every day, but ⁶⁵**we're**

closed this Friday. The library is being used for the district elections.

M-Cn　I see. ⁶⁶**Are there any movies showing?**

W-Br　⁶⁶**Yes, there's one on Thursday evening.**

M-Cn　Oh, too bad. ⁶⁶**I'm away for a client meeting on Thursday.**

W-Br　Well, ⁶⁷**if you like Sumit Mehta's books, you might be interested in his book signing.**

M-Cn　I do like his novels! ⁶⁷**Thanks, I'll come back for that.**

남　안녕하세요. 도서관 행사 일정표는 어디서 볼 수 있죠?

여　아, 여기 있습니다. 보통 거의 매일 행사가 있는데, **이번 주 금요일은 휴관입니다.** 도서관이 지역 선거를 위해 사용될 예정이에요.

남　알겠습니다. **상영되는 영화가 있나요?**

여　네, 목요일 저녁에 한 편 있어요.

남　아, 아쉽네요. **목요일에는 고객 회의 때문에 여기 없거든요.**

여　음, 수밋 메타의 책을 좋아하시면 그의 책 사인회에도 관심이 있으실 것 같네요.

남　그의 소설을 정말 좋아해요! **감사합니다. 그때 다시 올게요.**

어휘 district 구역, 지구　election 선거　book signing 책 사인회

Monday	2 P.M.	Children's Story Time
Tuesday	3 P.M.	Computer Class
⁶⁷Wednesday	6 P.M.	Book Signing: Sumit Mehta
Thursday	7 P.M.	Movie: Red Sunrise
Friday	Closed	

월요일	오후 2시	어린이 이야기 시간
화요일	오후 3시	컴퓨터 강좌
⁶⁷수요일	오후 6시	**책 사인회: 수밋 메타**
목요일	오후 7시	영화: 레드 선라이즈
금요일	휴관	

65

According to the woman, why will the library be closed on Friday?
(A) An election will be held there.
(B) Some renovations will take place.
(C) Bad weather is expected.
(D) A national holiday will be observed.

여자에 따르면, 도서관이 금요일에 휴관하는 이유는?
(A) 도서관에서 선거가 열린다.
(B) 보수 작업이 있다.
(C) 기상 악화가 예상된다.
(D) 국경일을 기념한다.

어휘 renovation 개조, 보수　take place 열리다　observe 축하하다, 기념하다

여자가 첫 대사에서 이번 주 금요일은 휴관이고 도서관이 지역 선거를 위해 사용될 예정(we're closed this Friday. The library is being used for the district elections)이라고 하므로 정답은 (A)이다.

| Paraphrasing | 대화의 The library is being used for the district elections.
→ 정답의 An election will be held there. |

66

What schedule conflict does the man mention?
(A) He has a family obligation.
(B) His car will be at a mechanic's shop.
(C) He will be attending a performance.
(D) He has a business meeting.

남자는 어떤 일정이 겹친다고 말하는가?
(A) 꼭 참석해야 하는 가족 행사가 있다.
(B) 차가 정비소에 있을 것이다.
(C) 공연에 갈 것이다.
(D) 업무 회의가 있다.

어휘 schedule conflict 일정이 겹침 family obligation 가족의 의무 mechanic 정비공 performance 공연

해설 세부 사항 관련 – 남자가 겹친다고 말하는 일정
남자가 두 번째 대사에서 상영되는 영화가 있는지(Are there any movies showing?) 물었고, 여자가 목요일 저녁에 한 편 있다(Yes, there's one on Thursday evening)고 답하자, 남자는 아쉽지만 목요일에는 고객 회의 때문에 여기 없다(I'm away for a client meeting on Thursday)고 말하므로 정답은 (D)이다.

| Paraphrasing | 대화의 a client meeting
→ 정답의 a business meeting |

67

Look at the graphic. When will the man most likely attend a library event?
(A) On Monday
(B) On Tuesday
(C) On Wednesday
(D) On Thursday

시각 정보에 의하면, 남자는 언제 도서관 행사에 참석하겠는가?
(A) 월요일
(B) 화요일
(C) 수요일
(D) 목요일

해설 시각 정보 연계 – 남자가 도서관 행사에 참석하는 요일
여자가 세 번째 대사에서 수밋 메타의 책을 좋아하면 그의 책 사인회에도 관심이 있을 것 같다(if you like Sumit Mehta's books, you might be interested in his book signing)고 말하자, 남자가 감사의 인사와 함께 그때 다시 오겠다(Thanks, I'll come back for that)고 말하는 것으로 보아 남자는 수밋 메타의 책 사인회에 참석하고자 한다는 것을 알 수 있다. 달력에 따르면 수밋 메타 책 사인회가 수요일에 열리므로 정답은 (C)이다.

68-70 대화 + 페인트 옵션

W-Br Good news, Tariq. **68 We'll have enough money to make those repairs to the bridge over the fish pond that you mentioned. 69 We've been awarded a grant to make some repairs to the park grounds.**

M-Au That's great! **68 That bridge needs a new coat of paint to protect it from the elements.** I think I sent you a list of paint colors when I first talked to you about the project.

W-Br You did. **70 Because it's such an iconic symbol of the park, and it's in so many photographs, we want it to be as close to the original color as when it was first built, even though that's the most expensive option on the list.**

여 좋은 소식이 있어요, 타릭. **언급하신 양어장 다리를 수리할 충분한 돈이 생길 거예요. 공원 부지를 수리할 보조금을 받았거든요.**

남 잘됐네요! 그 다리는 비바람으로부터 보호하기 위해 페인트를 한 겹 새로 칠해야 해요. 처음 프로젝트에 대해 얘기할 때 페인트 색상 목록을 보내드린 것 같은데요.

여 맞아요. 다리가 워낙 공원의 상징이고 많은 사진에 등장하기 때문에 처음 건설될 때의 원래 색상과 최대한 가까웠으면 합니다. 목록 중 가장 값비싼 선택지이긴 하지만요.

어휘 fish pond 양어장 award a grant 보조금을 주다 grounds 부지, 구내 protect 보호하다 elements 비바람, 폭풍우 iconic 상징적인 symbol 상징 option 선택지

Color	Price
Garden Green	$23
70 Misty Blue	$27
Sunrise Peach	$19
Antique White	$16

색상	가격
가든 그린	23달러
70 미스티 블루	**27달러**
선라이즈 피치	19달러
앤티크 화이트	16달러

68

What is the conversation about?
(A) Extending a fence
(B) Building a storage shed
(C) Repairing a bridge
(D) Updating an entrance area

무엇에 관한 대화인가?
(A) 울타리 연장
(B) 보관 창고 건설
(C) 다리 수리
(D) 입구 개선

어휘 extend 연장하다, 늘리다 storage shed 보관 창고, 저장고
entrance 입구

해설 전체 내용 관련 – 대화의 주제
여자가 첫 대사에서 양어장 다리를 수리할 충분한 돈이 생길 것(We'll
have enough money to make those repairs to the bridge
over the fish pond that you mentioned)이라고 하자, 남자가
비바람으로부터 보호하기 위해 다리에 페인트를 한 겹 새로 칠해야
한다(That bridge needs a new coat of paint to protect it from the
elements)고 대답하며 다리 수리와 관련된 이야기를 이어 가고 있으므로
정답은 (C)이다.

69

According to the woman, how is a project being
funded?
(A) With donations from visitors
(B) With money from a grant
(C) With revenue from ticket sales
(D) With proceeds from a charity auction

여자에 따르면, 프로젝트는 어떻게 기금을 마련하고 있는가?
(A) 방문객 기부금으로
(B) 보조금으로
(C) 표 판매 수익금으로
(D) 자선 경매 수익금으로

어휘 fund 자금을 대다 donation 기부 revenue 수익, 수입
proceeds 수익금 charity 자선 auction 경매

해설 세부 사항 관련 – 프로젝트의 기금 마련 방법
여자가 첫 대사에서 공원 부지를 수리할 보조금을 받았다(We've been
awarded a grant to make some repairs to the park grounds)고
하므로 정답은 (B)이다.

70

Look at the graphic. Which color does the woman
select?
(A) Garden Green
(B) Misty Blue
(C) Sunrise Peach
(D) Antique White

시각 정보에 의하면, 여자는 어떤 색을 선택하는가?
(A) 가든 그린
(B) 미스티 블루
(C) 선라이즈 피치
(D) 앤티크 화이트

해설 시각 정보 연계 – 여자가 선택하는 색상
여자가 마지막 대사에서 처음 건설된 때의 원래 색상과 최대한 가까웠으면

한다면서 목록 중 가장 값비싼 선택지(we want it to be as close to
the original color as when it was first built, even though that's
the most expensive option on the list)라고 말하고 있다. 페인트
옵션에 따르면 미스티 블루가 가장 가격이 비싸므로 정답은 (B)이다.

PART 4

71-73 담화

M-Au Hi, everyone—big news. **71,72Our clinic is
getting a check-in kiosk. 72What this means is
that patients will be able to check themselves in
to their medical appointments by clicking through
some buttons in the kiosk.** You will no longer have
to do it for them. I know all of you have been very
busy answering phones, scheduling appointments,
and checking patients in, so hopefully, this helps to
make your work easier. **73We'll have a very short
training session next Tuesday on how the check-in
kiosk works.**

안녕하세요, 여러분. 중대한 소식이 있습니다. **우리 병원에 체크인 키
오스크가 들어옵니다. 이는 환자들이 키오스크의 버튼 몇 개를 클릭하
면 진료 예약 건에 대해 스스로 수속을 밟을 수 있다는 뜻입니다.** 더 이
상 여러분이 해주지 않아도 되는 거죠. 여러분 모두 전화 받고 예약 잡
고 환자 수속해 주느라 아주 바빴다는 것을 잘 알고 있어요. 그래서 이
것이 여러분의 업무를 더 수월하게 해주는 데 도움이 되었으면 합니다.
**다음 주 화요일에 체크인 키오스크가 어떻게 작동하는지에 대해 아주
짧은 교육 시간을 갖겠습니다.**

어휘 kiosk 키오스크, 단말기 patient 환자 medical
appointment 진료 예약 hopefully 바라건대

71

Where does the talk most likely take place?
(A) At a medical clinic
(B) At an airport
(C) At a fitness center
(D) At a bank

담화는 어디서 이뤄지겠는가?
(A) 병원
(B) 공항
(C) 피트니스 센터
(D) 은행

해설 전체 내용 관련 – 담화의 장소
화자가 초반부에서 우리 병원에 체크인 키오스크가 들어온다(Our clinic
is getting a check-in kiosk)고 말하고 있으므로 정답은 (A)이다.

Paraphrasing 담화의 clinic → 정답의 medical clinic

72

What is mainly being discussed?
(A) A hiring decision
(B) A marketing campaign
(C) A customer satisfaction survey
(D) An electronic check-in system

주로 무엇에 관해 이야기하는가?
(A) 고용 결정
(B) 마케팅 캠페인
(C) 고객 만족 조사
(D) 전자 체크인 시스템

어휘 hiring 고용   satisfaction 만족

해설 전체 내용 관련 – 공지의 주제

화자가 초반부에서 우리 병원에 체크인 키오스크가 들어온다(Our clinic is getting a check-in kiosk)며, 이는 환자들이 키오스크 버튼 몇 개를 클릭하면 진료 예약 건에 대해 스스로 수속을 밟을 수 있다는 뜻(What this means is that patients will be able to check themselves in to their medical appointments by clicking through some buttons in the kiosk)이라고 말하고 있으므로 정답은 (D)이다.

> **Paraphrasing** 담화의 check-in kiosk
> → 정답의 check-in system

73

What will happen next Tuesday?
(A) A new security system will be installed.
(B) A branch location will open.
(C) A training session will take place.
(D) A product will be delivered.

다음 주 화요일에 무슨 일이 있을 것인가?
(A) 새 보안 시스템이 설치된다.
(B) 지점이 문을 연다.
(C) 교육이 진행된다.
(D) 제품이 배송된다.

어휘 security 보안   install 설치하다   branch 지사

해설 세부 사항 관련 – 다음 주 화요일에 일어날 일

화자가 마지막 부분에서 다음 주 화요일에 체크인 키오스크가 어떻게 작동하는지에 대해 아주 짧은 교육 시간을 갖겠다(We'll have a very short training session next Tuesday on how the check-in kiosk works)고 말하고 있으므로 정답은 (C)이다.

> **Paraphrasing** 담화의 We'll have a very short training
> session
> → 정답의 A training session will take place.

74-76 팟캐스트

> W-Br   **74Welcome to a new episode of *Tomorrow's
> Technology*. Today we'll be talking about drones.**
> If you're planning to buy your first drone, here

are a few things you need to know. **75To begin with, if you want to use the device for commercial purposes, such as photography or videography, then you'll need to apply for a license. 76I'll share some resources at the end of this podcast to guide your application process.**

〈투모로우 테크놀로지〉의 새 에피소드입니다. 오늘은 드론에 관해 이야기할 예정입니다. 처음 드론을 살 계획이라면 아셔야 할 것들이 있습니다. 우선 해당 기기를 사진 촬영 또는 동영상 촬영 같은 상업적 용도로 사용하고자 한다면, 면허증을 신청해야 할 것입니다. 이 팟캐스트 마지막에 신청 과정을 안내하는 자료를 공유하겠습니다.

어휘 to begin with 우선, 먼저   device 장치, 기구   commercial 상업적인   apply for ~을 신청하다   license 자격증, 면허증   share 공유하다   resource 자원   application 신청   process 과정

74

Who is the podcast intended for?
(A) Party organizers
(B) Travel agents
(C) Technology enthusiasts
(D) Carpenters

팟캐스트는 누구를 위한 것인가?
(A) 파티 주최자
(B) 여행사 직원
(C) 기술 애호가
(D) 목수

해설 전체 내용 관련 – 팟캐스트의 대상

화자가 도입부에서 〈투모로우 테크놀로지〉의 새 에피소드(Welcome to a new episode of *Tomorrow's Technology*)라고 하면서 오늘은 드론에 대해 이야기하겠다(Today we'll be talking about drones)고 하는 것으로 보아 기술 애호가들을 대상으로 함을 알 수 있다. 따라서 정답은 (C)이다.

75

According to the speaker, what will some listeners need?
(A) An insurance policy
(B) A letter of recommendation
(C) An event venue
(D) A license

화자에 따르면, 일부 청자들은 무엇이 필요할 것인가?
(A) 보험 증서
(B) 추천서
(C) 행사 장소
(D) 면허증

어휘 insurance 보험   venue 장소

화자가 중반부에서 해당 기기를 사진 촬영 또는 동영상 촬영 같은 상업적 용도로 사용하고자 한다면, 면허증을 신청해야 할 것(then you'll need to apply for a license)이라고 하므로 정답은 (D)이다.

76

What information will the speaker share?
(A) Application instructions
(B) Retail locations
(C) Names of instructors
(D) User reviews

화자는 어떤 정보를 공유할 것인가?
(A) 신청 설명
(B) 소매점 위치
(C) 강사 이름
(D) 사용자 후기

어휘 instruction 설명, 지시   instructor 강사

해설 세부 사항 관련 – 화자가 공유할 정보

화자가 마지막 부분에서 이 팟캐스트 마지막에 신청 과정을 안내하는 자료를 공유하겠다(I'll share some resources at the end of this podcast to guide your application process)고 말하고 있으므로 정답은 (A)이다.

> Paraphrasing 담화의 some resources ~ to guide your application process
> → 정답의 Application instructions

77-79 공지

M-Au **77 Attention, exhibitors. Welcome to the Digital Signage Expo, where representatives selling digital billboards and video displays can interact directly with buyers.** The exhibit hall will open in fifteen minutes. **78 To ensure everyone's safety, we request that you clear your exhibit area of boxes and debris and be sure cables and electrical cords are securely taped to the floor. 79 And remember, the exhibit hall will close at five P.M. today so that exhibitors can attend this evening's reception.** That will be held in the building's main lobby.

출품자 여러분께 알립니다. 디지털 사이니지 엑스포에 오신 것을 환영합니다. 이곳에서는 옥외 디지털 광고판과 비디오 디스플레이를 판매하는 판매업자들이 구매자와 직접 교류할 수 있습니다. 전시장은 15분 후에 문을 엽니다. 모두의 안전을 보장하기 위해 여러분의 전시 공간에서 상자와 쓰레기를 치우고 전선과 전기 코드를 바닥에 단단히 붙이실 것을 요청합니다. 또한 기억해주세요. 출품자들께서 저녁 환영 연회에 참석할 수 있도록 전시장은 오늘 오후 5시에 문을 닫습니다. 연회는 건물 중앙 로비에서 열릴 예정입니다.

어휘 attention 알립니다, 주목하세요   exhibitor 출품자   representative 판매 대리인, 대표자   billboard 옥외 광고판   interact 교류하다, 소통하다   directly 직접   ensure 보장하다   safety 안전   debris 쓰레기, 잔해   electrical 전기의   securely 단단히   reception 환영 연회

77

Who are the listeners?
(A) Mechanical engineers
(B) Trade show participants
(C) Government officials
(D) Laboratory assistants

청자들은 누구인가?
(A) 기계 엔지니어
(B) 무역 박람회 참가자
(C) 공무원
(D) 실험실 조수

어휘 mechanical 기계의   trade show 무역 박람회   participant 참가자   laboratory 실험실

해설 전체 내용 관련 – 청자들의 신분

화자가 도입부에서 청자들에게 출품자 여러분(Attention, exhibitors)이라고 부르면서, 옥외 디지털 광고판과 비디오 디스플레이를 판매하는 판매업자들이 구매자와 직접 교류할 수 있는 디지털 사이니지 엑스포에 오신 것을 환영한다(Welcome to the Digital Signage Expo, where representatives selling digital billboards and video displays can interact directly with buyers)고 말하고 있으므로 정답은 (B)이다.

78

What does the speaker request that the listeners do?
(A) Take safety precautions
(B) Sign a registration sheet
(C) Wear name tags
(D) Move their vehicles

화자는 청자들에게 무엇을 하라고 요청하는가?
(A) 안전 예방 조치 취하기
(B) 등록부에 서명하기
(C) 이름표 달기
(D) 차량 이동시키기

어휘 precaution 예방 조치, 예방책   registration 등록   vehicle 차량

해설 세부 사항 관련 – 화자가 청자들에게 요청하는 일

화자가 중반부에서 모두의 안전을 보장하기 위해 전시 공간에서 상자와 쓰레기를 치우고 전선과 전기 코드를 바닥에 단단히 붙일 것을 요청한다(To ensure everyone's safety, we request that you clear your exhibit area of boxes and debris and be sure cables and electrical cords are securely taped to the floor)고 말하고 있으므로 정답은 (A)이다.

79

What will take place in the evening?
(A) A debate
(B) An award ceremony
(C) A film screening
(D) A reception

저녁에 무엇이 열릴 것인가?
(A) 토론
(B) 시상식
(C) 영화 상영
(D) 환영 연회

해설 세부 사항 관련 – 저녁에 일어날 일
화자가 후반부에서 출품자들은 저녁 환영 연회에 참석할 수 있다(exhibitors can attend this evening's reception)고 말하고 있으므로 정답은 (D)이다.

80-82 광고

> M-Cn **80 Welcome to *Money Reveals*, the podcast for smart investors.** This week, I'll be discussing the best tips for amateur investors, if you're just getting started. But first, this episode is brought to you by CodeWord. **81 Don't search online for discount coupons any longer! CodeWord is a software application that scans the Internet for promotional codes and applies them to your online shopping cart.** If CodeWord finds any discounts, an Apply Coupon button will automatically appear at checkout. **82 What's more, the first 100 listeners to use the download link on my Web site will receive free music festival tickets.**

> 현명한 투자자들을 위한 팟캐스트, 〈머니 리빌〉입니다. 이번 주에는 아마추어 투자자들을 위한 최고의 조언에 대해 이야기합니다. 여러분께서 이제 막 시작하셨다면 말이죠. 먼저, 이번 에피소드는 코드워드가 전해 드립니다. 더 이상 할인 쿠폰을 온라인으로 검색하지 마세요! 코드워드는 인터넷에서 프로모션 코드를 검색하여 이를 여러분의 온라인 장바구니에 적용하는 소프트웨어 어플리케이션입니다. 코드워드가 할인을 발견하면 결제 시 '쿠폰 적용' 버튼이 자동으로 나타납니다. 게다가 저희 웹사이트에서 다운로드 링크를 이용하신 선착순 100명의 청취자는 음악 축제 무료 입장권을 받게 됩니다.

> **어휘** investor 투자자 promotional 홍보의, 판촉의 apply 적용하다 automatically 자동으로 appear 나타나다 checkout 계산대 what's more 게다가

80

Who most likely is the speaker?
(A) A customer service representative
(B) A software developer
(C) A podcast host
(D) An event coordinator

화자는 누구이겠는가?
(A) 고객 서비스 담당자
(B) 소프트웨어 개발자
(C) 팟캐스트 진행자
(D) 행사 담당자

어휘 representative 대표, 대리인 developer 개발자 host (TV, 라디오 프로) 진행자 coordinator 진행 담당자, 조정자

해설 전체 내용 관련 – 화자의 직업
화자가 도입부에서 현명한 투자자들을 위한 팟캐스트, 〈머니 리빌〉(Welcome to *Money Reveals*, the podcast for smart investors)이라고 말하고 있으므로 화자는 팟캐스트 진행자임을 알 수 있다. 따라서 정답은 (C)이다.

81

According to the speaker, what can a software application be used for?
(A) Making travel reservations
(B) Uploading documents
(C) Managing subscriptions
(D) Searching for discounts

화자에 따르면, 소프트웨어 어플리케이션은 무엇에 이용할 수 있는가?
(A) 여행 예약
(B) 문서 업로드
(C) 구독 관리
(D) 할인 검색

어휘 subscription 구독

해설 세부 사항 관련 – 소프트웨어 어플리케이션을 이용할 수 있는 곳
화자가 중반부에서 더 이상 할인 쿠폰을 온라인으로 검색하지 말라(Don't search online for discount coupons any longer!)고 말한 뒤, 코드워드는 인터넷에서 프로모션 코드를 검색하여 이를 온라인 장바구니에 적용하는 소프트웨어 어플리케이션(CodeWord is a software application that scans the Internet for promotional codes and applies them to your online shopping cart)이라고 말하는 것으로 보아 CodeWord 어플리케이션은 할인 검색에 이용된다는 것을 알 수 있다. 따라서 정답은 (D)이다.

82

How can the listeners receive some free tickets?
(A) By clicking on a link
(B) By signing up for a newsletter
(C) By buying a product in-store
(D) By writing a review

청자들은 어떻게 무료 입장권을 받을 수 있는가?

(A) 링크 클릭
(B) 소식지 신청
(C) 매장 내 제품 구매
(D) 후기 작성

어휘 sign up for ~을 신청하다   newsletter 소식지   in-store 매장 내의

해설 세부 사항 관련 – 청자들이 무료 입장권을 받을 수 있는 방법
화자가 마지막에 웹사이트에서 다운로드 링크를 이용한 선착순 100명의 청취자는 음악 축제 무료 입장권을 받게 된다(the first 100 listeners to use the download link on my Web site will receive free music festival tickets)고 하므로 정답은 (A)이다.

> **Paraphrasing**   담화의 use the download link
> → 정답의 clicking on a link

83-85 전화 메시지

 동영상 강의

W-Br Hi. ⁸³**This is So-Jin—in Apartment 2A. I just moved into the complex last month.** ⁸³﹐⁸⁴**I'm calling about a problem with my kitchen sink.** ⁸⁴**The drain is completely clogged, so the water won't go down.** ⁸⁵**I've tried a few different drain cleaning products, but they didn't help.** I think I've done all I can do. **I'm at work now, but I'll be home this afternoon.** ⁸⁵**Could you call me back, so we can arrange a time to meet there?** Thanks.

안녕하세요. 2A호에 사는 소진입니다. 지난달에 이 단지로 이사 왔어요. 주방 개수대 문제로 전화했는데요. 배수관이 완전히 막혀서 물이 내려가시 않아요. 몇 가지 다양한 배수관 청소 제품을 써 봤지만 도움이 되지 않았어요. 할 수 있는 건 다 해 본 것 같아요. 지금은 직장에 있지만, 오늘 오후엔 집에 있을 거예요. 저에게 다시 전화 주셔서 만날 시간을 잡을 수 있을까요? 감사합니다.

어휘 complex (건물) 단지   drain 배수관   completely 완전히   clogged 막힌   arrange a time 시간을 정하다

83

Who is the speaker most likely calling?
(A) A store owner
(B) A property manager
(C) A delivery driver
(D) A restaurant supplier

화자는 누구에게 전화하겠는가?
(A) 매장 주인
(B) 건물 관리인
(C) 배달 운전기사
(D) 식당 납품업체

어휘 property 건물, 부동산   supplier 공급자

해설 전체 내용 관련 – 화자가 전화를 건 대상
화자가 도입부에서 2A호에 사는 소진이고 지난달에 이 단지로 이사 왔다(This is So-Jin—in Apartment 2A. I just moved into the complex last month)고 말한 뒤, 주방 개수대 문제로 전화했다(I'm calling about a problem with my kitchen sink)고 하므로 전화 수신인은 건물 관리인임을 추론할 수 있다. 따라서 정답은 (B)이다.

> **Paraphrasing**   담화의 Apartment → 정답의 property

84

What problem does the speaker have?
(A) Some appliances have not arrived.
(B) Some boxes have been damaged.
(C) A water cooler is not working.
(D) A sink is not draining.

화자는 어떤 문제가 있는가?
(A) 가전 제품들이 도착하지 않았다.
(B) 상자들이 훼손됐다.
(C) 냉수기가 작동하지 않는다.
(D) 개수대 물이 빠지지 않는다.

어휘 appliance 가전 제품   drain 물이 빠지다

해설 세부 사항 관련 – 화자가 언급하는 문제
화자가 중반부에서 주방 개수대 문제로 전화했는데 배수관이 완전히 막혀서 물이 내려가지 않는다(I'm calling about a problem with my kitchen sink. The drain is completely clogged, so the water won't go down)고 말하고 있으므로 정답은 (D)이다.

85

Why does the speaker say, "I think I've done all I can do"?
(A) To request that the listener give her a refund
(B) To indicate that she needs the listener's assistance
(C) To explain why she enrolled in a training course
(D) To confirm that a task has been completed

화자가 "할 수 있는 건 다 해 본 것 같아요"라고 말하는 이유는 무엇인가?
(A) 청자에게 환불을 해달라고 요청하려고
(B) 청자의 도움이 필요하다는 것을 나타내려고
(C) 교육 과정에 등록한 이유를 설명하려고
(D) 업무가 완료됐다는 것을 확인하려고

어휘 refund 환불   indicate 나타내다, 내비치다   assistance 도움   enroll 등록하다   confirm 확인해 주다, 확정하다   complete 완료하다

해설 화자의 의도 파악 – 할 수 있는 건 다 해 본 것 같다는 말의 의도
화자가 중반부에서 몇 가지 다양한 배수관 청소 제품을 써 봤지만 도움이 되지 않았다(I've tried a few different drain cleaning products, but they didn't help)고 말한 뒤, 인용문을 언급하고 있으며, 마지막에 만날 시간을 잡을 수 있는지(Could you call me back, so we can arrange a time to meet there?)를 묻고 있으므로 청자의 도움이 필요하다는 의도로 한 말임을 알 수 있다. 따라서 정답은 (B)이다.

M-Cn **86 Next Tuesday the eleventh is our office cleanup**. We'll have bins stationed all around the office for you to put garbage and recycling in. Be sure to shred any documents that have private client information on them. **87 Our office manager Rajeev has rented some extra document shredders for us to use. Thanks for taking care of that, Rajeev.** Now, **88 we've hired two new accountants who are supposed to start in a month, and we need to make space for their desks.** Now that our work is mostly paperless, the south corner of the office has a lot of empty file cabinets.

다음 주 화요일인 11일은 사무실 대청소가 있습니다. 사무실 곳곳에 쓰레기통을 배치해 여러분이 쓰레기와 재활용품을 넣을 수 있도록 할 것입니다. 고객 개인 정보가 있는 문서는 반드시 모두 파쇄하십시오. **사무실 관리자 라지브가 우리가 사용할 수 있도록 여분의 문서 파쇄기를 빌렸어요. 라지브, 수고해 주셔서 감사합니다.** 자, **한 달 뒤 업무를 시작하기로 되어 있는 신입 회계원 두 분을 채용해서, 이들의 책상을 놓을 공간을 만들어야 해요.** 우리 업무가 대부분 컴퓨터로 이뤄지기 때문에 사무실 남쪽 구석에 비어 있는 문서 보관함이 많아요.

어휘 station 배치하다 garbage 쓰레기 recycling 재활용품 shred 자르다, 채를 썰다 take care of ~을 돌보다, 처리하다 accountant 회계원, 회계사 be supposed to ~하기로 되어 있다 paperless (컴퓨터로 이뤄져) 종이를 쓰지 않는 file cabinet 문서 보관함

86

What will the listeners do next Tuesday?
(A) Renew their contracts
(B) Clean their offices
(C) Visit a recycling center
(D) Greet new clients

청자들은 다음 주 화요일에 무엇을 할 것인가?
(A) 계약서 갱신
(B) 사무실 청소
(C) 재활용 센터 방문
(D) 신규 고객 맞이

어휘 renew 갱신하다 contract 계약, 계약서 greet 맞다, 환영하다

해설 세부 사항 관련 – 청자들이 다음 주 화요일에 할 일
화자가 도입부에서 다음 주 화요일인 11일은 사무실 대청소가 있다(Next Tuesday the eleventh is our office cleanup)고 하므로 정답은 (B)이다.

> **Paraphrasing** 담화의 our office cleanup
> → 정답의 Clean their offices

87

What does the speaker thank Rajeev for doing?
(A) Paying for refreshments
(B) Reserving a meeting room
(C) Arranging transportation
(D) Renting some equipment

화자는 라지브가 무엇을 한 것에 대해 감사하는가?
(A) 다과 비용 지불
(B) 회의실 예약
(C) 교통편 마련
(D) 장비 대여

어휘 refreshments 다과 arrange 주선하다, 마련하다 equipment 장비

해설 세부 사항 관련 – 화자가 라지브에게 감사해 하는 일
화자가 중반부에서 사무실 관리자 라지브가 여분의 문서 파쇄기를 빌렸다(Our office manager Rajeev has rented some extra document shredders ~)고 말하면서 라지브에게 수고해 줘서 고맙다(Thanks for taking care of that, Rajeev)고 하므로 정답은 (D)이다.

> **Paraphrasing** 담화의 document shredders
> → 정답의 equipment

88

Why does the speaker say, "the south corner of the office has a lot of empty file cabinets"?
(A) To suggest a location for some desks
(B) To indicate where some files should be stored
(C) To explain that a task has already been completed
(D) To ask for more office supplies to be ordered

화자가 "사무실 남쪽 구석에 비어 있는 문서 보관함이 많아요"라고 말하는 이유는 무엇인가?
(A) 책상 놓을 장소를 제안하려고
(B) 파일 보관 장소를 알려 주려고
(C) 업무가 이미 완료되었음을 설명하려고
(D) 사무용품을 더 주문해 달라고 요청하려고

어휘 indicate 알려 주다, 나타내다 store 보관하다, 저장하다 office supply 사무용품

해설 화자의 의도 파악 – 사무실 남쪽 구석에 비어 있는 문서 보관함이 많다는 말의 의도
화자가 중반부에서 신입 회계원 두 분을 채용했기에 이들의 책상을 놓을 공간을 만들어야 한다(we've hired two new accountants ~, and we need to make space for their desks)고 말한 뒤 인용문을 언급하고 있으므로 화자가 책상 놓을 장소를 제안하려는 의도로 한 말임을 알 수 있다. 따라서 정답은 (A)이다.

89-91 녹음 메시지

M-Au Hello, and **89 thank you for calling Ziegler Incorporated, the area's top supplier of office**

paper. Due to bad weather conditions last week, roads around our warehouse were closed. As a result, ⁹⁰**customers may be experiencing delays in receiving their recent orders.** Now that the roads are clear, we've resumed deliveries. However, we'll need a few days to catch up. To make up for this inconvenience, we're offering customers a twenty percent discount on their next purchase. To claim the discount, enter your invoice number on our Web site. ⁹¹**Once you do, your discount code will arrive in an e-mail.**

안녕하세요. **지역 최고의 사무용지 공급업체 지글러 주식회사에 전화 주셔서 감사합니다.** 지난주 악천후 때문에 저희 창고 인근 도로가 봉쇄됐습니다. 그 결과, **고객들이 최근 주문 물품을 받는 데 지연을 겪고 있습니다.** 도로가 깨끗이 치워져서 배송을 재개했습니다만, 따라잡는 데는 며칠 걸릴 것입니다. 불편을 보상해 드리기 위해 고객들께 다음 구매 시 20퍼센트 할인을 제공해 드립니다. 할인을 받으려면 저희 웹 사이트에 청구서 번호를 입력하세요. **입력하시면 이메일로 할인 코드가 도착할 겁니다.**

어휘 incorporated 주식회사 supplier 공급자 warehouse 창고 experience 경험하다, 겪다 delay 지연 now that ~이므로 resume 재개하다 catch up 따라잡다 make up for 보상하다, 만회하다 inconvenience 불편 invoice 청구서

89

What does Ziegler Incorporated sell?
(A) Office paper
(B) Gardening tools
(C) Computers
(D) Car parts

지글러 주식회사는 무엇을 판매하는가?
(A) 사무용지
(B) 원예 도구
(C) 컴퓨터
(D) 자동차 부품

해설 세부 사항 관련 – 지글러 주식회사가 판매하는 제품
화자가 도입부에서 지역 최고의 사무용지 공급업체 지글러 주식회사에 전화 주셔서 감사하다(thank you for calling Ziegler Incorporated, the area's top supplier of office paper)고 하므로 정답은 (A)이다.

90

According to the speaker, what problem is the company experiencing?
(A) Staffing shortages
(B) Shipping delays
(C) Limited warehouse space
(D) Insufficient inventory

화자에 따르면, 회사는 어떤 문제를 겪고 있는가?
(A) 직원 부족
(B) 배송 지연
(C) 한정된 창고 공간
(D) 불충분한 재고

어휘 staffing 직원 채용 shortage 부족 limited 제한된, 한정된 insufficient 불충분한 inventory 재고, 물품 목록

해설 세부 사항 관련 – 회사가 겪고 있는 문제점
화자가 중반부에서 고객들이 최근 주문 물품을 받는 데 지연을 겪고 있다(customers may be experiencing delays in receiving their recent orders)고 말하고 있으므로 정답은 (B)이다.

> **Paraphrasing** 담화의 delays in receiving their recent orders → 정답의 Shipping delays

91

What will arrive in an e-mail?
(A) Some contact information
(B) An order form
(C) A discount code
(D) A price list

이메일로 무엇이 도착할 것인가?
(A) 연락처
(B) 주문서
(C) 할인 코드
(D) 가격 목록

해설 세부 사항 관련 – 이메일로 도착할 것
화자가 마지막 부분에서 웹 사이트에 청구서 번호를 입력하면 이메일로 할인 코드가 도착할 것(Once you do, your discount code will arrive in an e-mail)이라고 말하고 있으므로 정답은 (C)이다.

92-94 회의 발췌

W-Am As members of the city's Arts Commission, it's our responsibility to manage arts programs and initiatives. ⁹²**The mayor's decision to redevelop the Hoverton District is welcome news across the community.** And for our commission, it's an opportunity to integrate sculptures into public spaces there. ⁹³**We'll need to determine what overall community themes should be addressed and prioritized. So I think it's important that we conduct a survey regarding the residents' preferences.** It's a diverse community with a range of perspectives to consider. ⁹⁴**And, of course, in order for the artwork to be built, we'll need to hire a skilled artist for the task.** I think Alvaro Gomez has won several awards.

시 예술 위원회 회원으로서 예술 프로그램과 계획을 관리하는 것은 우리 책임입니다. **호버튼 지구를 재개발하겠다는 시장의 결정은 지역사회 전체에 반가운 소식입니다.** 그리고 우리 위원회는 조각품들을 그곳 공공장소에 접목시킬 기회입니다. 우리는 지역사회 전체 테마로 어떤 것들을 다루고 어떤 것을 우선시해야 할지 결정해야 합니다. 그래서 저는 주민들의 선호도 조사를 하는 것이 중요하다고 생각합니다. 고려해야 할 폭넓은 관점이 있는 다양한 지역사회입니다. **물론 예술품이 만들어지려면 그 일을 위해 숙련된 예술가를 고용해야 할 것입니다. 알바로 고메즈가 여러 번 상을 받은 것 같습니다.**

어휘 commission 위원회   responsibility 책임   manage 관리하다   initiative 계획   mayor 시장   decision 결정   redevelop 재개발하다   opportunity 기회   integrate 통합하다   sculpture 조각, 조각품   determine 결정하다, 알아내다   overall 전체의   theme 테마, 주제   address 다루다, 고심하다   prioritize 우선적으로 처리하다   conduct 하다   resident 주민, 거주자   preference 선호   diverse 다양한   a range of 다양한, 폭넓은   perspective 관점   skilled 숙련된, 노련한   win an award 상을 받다

92

What has the mayor decided to do?
(A) Run for election again
(B) Redevelop an area of the city
(C) Host an art festival
(D) Provide public art classes

시장은 무엇을 하기로 결정했는가?
(A) 선거 재출마
(B) 시의 한 지역 재개발
(C) 예술제 개최
(D) 대중 대상 미술 강좌 제공

어휘 run for election 선거에 출마하다   host 개최하다

해설 세부 사항 관련 – 시장이 하기로 결정한 일
화자가 초반부에서 호버튼 지구를 재개발하겠다는 시장의 결정은 지역사회 전체에 반가운 소식(The mayor's decision to redevelop the Hoverton District is welcome news across the community)이라고 하므로 정답은 (B)이다.

> **Paraphrasing**   담화의 the Hoverton District
> → 정답의 an area of the city

93

What is the goal of a survey?
(A) To decide on a theme
(B) To raise money for a project
(C) To educate the public about a problem
(D) To recruit some volunteers

설문 조사의 목적은 무엇인가?
(A) 주제 결정
(B) 프로젝트 자금 조달
(C) 문제에 관한 대중 교육
(D) 자원봉사자 모집

어휘 raise money 자금을 조성하다, 돈을 마련하다   educate 교육하다, 가르치다   recruit 모집하다

해설 세부 사항 관련 – 조사의 목적
화자가 중반부에서 지역사회 전체 테마로 어떤 것들을 다루고 어떤 것을 우선시해야 할지 결정해야 할(We'll need to determine what overall community themes should be addressed and prioritized)이라고 말한 뒤, 그래서 주민들의 선호도 조사를 하는 것이 중요하다고 생각한다(So I think it's important that we conduct a survey regarding the residents' preferences)고 하므로 정답은 (A)이다.

> **Paraphrasing**   담화의 to determine what overall
> community themes
> → 정답의 To decide on a theme

94

Why does the speaker say, "I think Alvaro Gomez has won several awards"?
(A) To correct some information
(B) To praise a museum exhibit
(C) To recommend a suitable candidate
(D) To congratulate a colleague

화자가 "알바로 고메즈가 여러 번 상을 받은 것 같습니다"라고 말하는 이유는 무엇인가?
(A) 정보를 바로잡기 위해
(B) 미술관 전시회를 칭찬하기 위해
(C) 적합한 후보자를 추천하기 위해
(D) 동료를 축하하기 위해

어휘 correct 바로잡다   praise 칭찬하다   exhibit 전시회, 전시품   suitable 적합한   candidate 후보자, 지원자   colleague 동료

해설 화자의 의도 파악 – 알바로 고메즈가 여러 번 상을 받은 것 같다는 말의 의도
화자가 후반부에서 예술품이 만들어지려면 그 일을 위해 숙련된 예술가를 고용해야 할 것(in order for the artwork to be built, we'll need to hire a skilled artist for the task)이라고 말한 뒤 인용문을 언급한 것으로 보아, 적합한 사람을 추천하기 위한 의도로 한 말임을 알 수 있다. 따라서 정답은 (C)이다.

W-Br Good afternoon, Mr. Kwon,⁹⁵**this is Olga Popova from the Smith Theater. You're next on the wait list for theater tickets.** On your preference form, you requested four tickets together in either the orchestra or the mid-balcony. Unfortunately, those sections are completely sold out on the date you requested. ⁹⁶**But I do have four tickets together in the lower balcony for that date.** I'll be happy to set aside those tickets if you'd like. I can hold this request for 24 hours. ⁹⁷**Please call our box office as soon as possible to let me know if you're still interested.**

안녕하세요, 권 씨. **스미스 극장의 올가 포포바입니다. 귀하가 극장표 대기자 명단의 다음 차례이신데요.** 선호도 양식에서 오케스트라석이나 중간 발코니석으로 표 4장을 요청하셨는데요. 안타깝게도 해당 구역은 요청하신 날짜에 완전히 매진됐어요. **하지만 해당 날짜에 아래 발코니석에는 함께 붙은 4장의 표가 있습니다.** 원하신다면 해당 표를 확보해 두겠습니다. 해당 요청은 24시간 동안 유지할 수 있어요. **최대한 빨리 저희 매표소로 전화 주셔서 아직 관심이 있으신지 알려 주세요.**

어휘 wait list 대기자 목록　preference 선호　form 양식　section 부문, 구획　be sold out 매진되다　set aside 확보하다, 챙겨두다　hold 유지하다　box office 매표소　interested 관심 있는

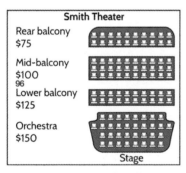

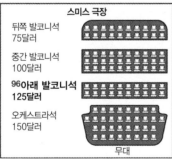

어휘 rear 뒤쪽의　lower 아래쪽의　stage 무대

95

Who most likely is the speaker?
(A) A seating usher
(B) A band director
(C) A stage actor
(D) A sales agent

화자는 누구이겠는가?
(A) 좌석 안내원
(B) 악단 지휘자
(C) 연극 배우
(D) 판매원

해설 전체 내용 관련 – 화자의 직업

화자가 도입부에서 스미스 극장의 올가 포포바(this is Olga Popova from the Smith Theater)라고 자기를 소개하면서 권 씨가 극장표 대기자 명단의 다음 차례(You're next on the wait list for theater tickets)라고 말하고 있으므로 화자는 극장 티켓 판매원임을 알 수 있다. 따라서 정답은 (D)이다.

96

Look at the graphic. How much do tickets in the available section cost?
(A) $75
(B) $100
(C) $125
(D) $150

시각 정보에 의하면, 이용 가능한 구역의 표는 얼마인가?
(A) 75달러
(B) 100달러
(C) 125달러
(D) 150달러

해설 시각 정보 연계 – 이용 가능한 구역의 표 가격

화자가 중반부에서 해당 날짜에 아래 발코니석에는 함께 붙은 4장의 표가 있다(I do have four tickets together in the lower balcony for that date)고 했고, 좌석표에 따르면 아래 발코니석은 125달러이므로 정답은 (C)이다.

97

What does the listener need to do within 24 hours?
(A) Make a phone call
(B) Send in a payment
(C) Pick up an item
(D) Fill out a form

청자는 24시간 이내에 무엇을 해야 하는가?
(A) 전화하기
(B) 지불하기
(C) 물품 가져가기
(D) 서식 기입하기

어휘 send in 발송하다　payment 지불금, 대금

해설 세부 사항 관련 – 청자가 24시간 이내에 해야 할 일

화자가 마지막 부분에서 최대한 빨리 매표소로 전화해서 아직 관심이 있는지 알려 달라(Please call our box office as soon as possible to let me know if you're still interested)고 요청하고 있으므로 정답은 (A)이다.

| Paraphrasing | 담화의 call → 정답의 Make a phone call |

98-100 여행 정보 + 지도

W-Am Welcome to this bus tour of the Kensey Harbor. **98 Unfortunately, one of the stops on our itinerary, the museum, is closed, and we won't be able to visit it. 99 The museum had a water pipe burst overnight. It looks like repair and cleanup work will last this whole week.** I apologize, since I know many of you were looking forward to seeing the museum's exhibit on local fish. **100 To make up for this, we're providing complimentary meal vouchers so you can enjoy a free lunch, on us, when we get to the area around the cannery.**

켄시 하버 버스 투어에 오신 것을 환영합니다. **안타깝게도, 일정표에 있는 목적지 중 하나인 박물관이 문을 닫아서 방문할 수가 없습니다.** 간밤에 박물관에서 배수관이 터졌답니다. 이번 주 내내 수리 및 청소 작업이 지속될 것 같습니다. 많은 분께서 박물관의 현지 물고기 전시를 보고 싶어 하셨다는 걸 알기에 사과의 말씀을 드립니다. **이를 보상하기 위해 무료 식권을 제공해 드리니 통조림 공장 근처 지역에 도착하면 무료 점심 식사를 하실 수 있습니다.**

어휘 itinerary 여행 일정표 museum 박물관, 미술관 water pipe 배수관, 송수관 burst 터지다 last 지속되다 apologize 사과하다 look forward to ~을 고대하다 exhibit 전시품 local 현지의 make up for ~을 보상하다, 만회하다 complimentary 무료의 cannery 통조림 공장

어휘 city hall 시청 harbor 항구

98

Look at the graphic. Which stop has been canceled?
(A) Stop 1
(B) Stop 2
(C) Stop 3
(D) Stop 4

시각 정보에 의하면, 어떤 목적지가 취소됐는가?
(A) 1번 목적지
(B) 2번 목적지
(C) 3번 목적지
(D) 4번 목적지

해설 시각 정보 연계 – 취소된 목적지

화자가 초반부에서 일정표에 있는 목적지 중 하나인 박물관이 문을 닫아서 방문할 수가 없다(one of the stops on our itinerary, the museum, is closed, and we won't be able to visit it)고 말하고 있으며, 지도에 따르면 박물관은 3번 목적지이므로 정답은 (C)이다.

99

Why has a stop been canceled?
(A) A guest speaker is unavailable.
(B) A building is undergoing maintenance.
(C) An area has closed for a festival.
(D) A private event has been scheduled.

목적지가 왜 취소됐는가?
(A) 초청 연사가 시간이 안 된다.
(B) 건물이 유지보수 작업을 하고 있다.
(C) 지역이 축제로 폐쇄됐다.
(D) 개인 행사 일정이 잡혔다.

어휘 guest speaker 초청 연사 unavailable 시간이 안 되는 undergo 겪다 maintenance 유지보수 private 사적인, 개인의

해설 세부 사항 관련 – 목적지가 취소된 이유

화자가 중반부에서 간밤에 박물관에서 배수관이 터졌다(The museum had a water pipe burst overnight)며 이번 주 내내 수리 및 청소 작업이 지속될 것 같다(It looks like repair and cleanup work will last this whole week)고 말하고 있으므로 정답은 (B)이다.

| Paraphrasing | 담화의 repair and cleanup work → 정답의 maintenance |

100

What will the listeners receive?
(A) A refund
(B) A souvenir
(C) A printed map
(D) Meal vouchers

청자들은 무엇을 받을 것인가?
(A) 환불
(B) 기념품
(C) 지도 인쇄물
(D) 식권

해설 세부 사항 관련 – 청자들이 받을 것
화자가 마지막 부분에서 이를 보상하기 위해 무료 식권을 제공하겠다(To make up for this, we're providing complimentary meal vouchers)고 하므로 정답은 (D)이다.

1 (D)	**2** (D)	**3** (A)	**4** (B)	**5** (C)
6 (C)	**7** (A)	**8** (C)	**9** (B)	**10** (C)
11 (A)	**12** (A)	**13** (C)	**14** (B)	**15** (C)
16 (C)	**17** (A)	**18** (A)	**19** (A)	**20** (B)
21 (A)	**22** (A)	**23** (B)	**24** (B)	**25** (C)
26 (A)	**27** (A)	**28** (B)	**29** (B)	**30** (A)
31 (A)	**32** (C)	**33** (D)	**34** (C)	**35** (B)
36 (A)	**37** (C)	**38** (B)	**39** (C)	**40** (D)
41 (B)	**42** (C)	**43** (D)	**44** (A)	**45** (B)
46 (B)	**47** (C)	**48** (D)	**49** (A)	**50** (A)
51 (D)	**52** (C)	**53** (B)	**54** (C)	**55** (C)
56 (D)	**57** (C)	**58** (A)	**59** (A)	**60** (B)
61 (C)	**62** (C)	**63** (C)	**64** (B)	**65** (D)
66 (C)	**67** (C)	**68** (C)	**69** (D)	**70** (C)
71 (D)	**72** (C)	**73** (D)	**74** (C)	**75** (D)
76 (D)	**77** (D)	**78** (B)	**79** (B)	**80** (C)
81 (A)	**82** (D)	**83** (C)	**84** (D)	**85** (B)
86 (D)	**87** (B)	**88** (C)	**89** (A)	**90** (A)
91 (D)	**92** (C)	**93** (A)	**94** (D)	**95** (D)
96 (B)	**97** (C)	**98** (A)	**99** (D)	**100** (B)

PART 1

1 M-Cn

▶ 동영상 강의

(A) He's digging in a garden.
(B) He's stacking wooden pallets.
(C) He's emptying soil from a pot.
(D) He's examining some plants.

(A) 남자가 정원에서 땅을 파고 있다.
(B) 남자가 목재 화물 운반대를 쌓고 있다.
(C) 남자가 화분에서 흙을 비워내고 있다.
(D) 남자가 식물을 살펴보고 있다.

어휘 dig (구멍 등을) 파다 stack 쌓다 pallet 화물 운반대 empty 비우다 examine 살펴보다, 검사하다

해설 1인 등장 사진 – 사람의 동작/상태 묘사
(A) 동사 오답. 남자가 정원에서 땅을 파고 있는(is digging in a garden) 모습이 아니므로 오답.
(B) 동사 오답. 남자가 목재 화물 운반대를 쌓고 있는(is stacking wooden pallets) 모습이 아니므로 오답.
(C) 동사 오답. 남자가 화분에서 흙을 비워내고 있는(is emptying soil from a pot) 모습이 아니므로 오답.

(D) 정답. 남자가 식물을 살펴보고 있는(is examining some plants) 모습이므로 정답.

2 W-Br

(A) One of the women is pushing a cart towards an exit.
(B) One of the women is hanging a coat on a hook.
(C) The women are restocking some store shelves.
(D) The women are purchasing some groceries.

(A) 여자 한 명이 출구 쪽으로 카트를 밀고 있다.
(B) 여자 한 명이 고리에 코트를 걸고 있다.
(C) 여자들이 매장 선반을 다시 채우고 있다.
(D) 여자들이 식료품을 구입하고 있다.

어휘 hang 걸다 restock 다시 채우다 shelf 선반 grocery 식료품

해설 2인 이상 등장 사진 – 사람의 동작/상태 묘사
(A) 동사 오답. 출구 쪽으로 카트를 밀고 있는(is pushing a cart towards an exit) 여자의 모습이 보이지 않으므로 오답.
(B) 동사 오답. 고리에 코트를 걸고 있는(is hanging a coat on a hook) 여자의 모습이 보이지 않으므로 오답.
(C) 동사 오답. 여자들이 매장 선반을 다시 채우고 있는(are restocking some store shelves) 모습이 아니므로 오답.
(D) 정답. 여자들이 식료품을 구입하고 있는(are purchasing some groceries) 모습이므로 정답.

3 M-Au

(A) The man is resting his arm on a counter.
(B) The man is folding his coat.
(C) A cabinet door has been left open.
(D) Some stools are being wiped down.

(A) 남자가 카운터에 팔을 올려놓고 있다.
(B) 남자가 코트를 개고 있다.
(C) 캐비닛 문이 열려 있다.
(D) 의자가 깨끗이 닦이고 있다.

어휘 rest 받치다, 기대다 fold 접다, 개다 stool (등받이와 팔걸이가 없는) 의자 wipe down 깨끗이 닦다

해설 혼합 사진 – 사람/사물/풍경 혼합 묘사

(A) 정답. 남자가 카운터에 팔을 올려놓고 있는(is resting his arm on a counter) 모습이므로 정답.

(B) 동사 오답. 남자가 코트를 개고 있는(is folding his coat) 모습이 아니므로 오답.

(C) 동사 오답. 캐비닛 문(A cabinet door)이 열려 있는(has been left open) 모습이 아니므로 오답.

(D) 동사 오답. 의자(Some stools)가 닦이고 있는(are being wiped down) 모습이 아니므로 오답.

---

4 M-Cn

(A) Some balconies are decorated with banners.
(B) Some signs have been posted in front of a building.
(C) A café has been set up on a street corner.
(D) A tour group is standing outside a building.

(A) 발코니가 현수막으로 장식되어 있다.
(B) 표지판들이 건물 앞에 세워져 있다.
(C) 길모퉁이에 카페가 차려져 있다.
(D) 단체 관광객들이 건물 밖에 서 있다.

어휘 decorate 장식하다 banner 현수막 post 게시하다, 공고하다

해설 혼합 사진 – 사람/사물/풍경 혼합 묘사

(A) 사진에 없는 명사를 이용한 오답. 사진에 현수막(banners)의 모습이 보이지 않으므로 오답.

(B) 정답. 표지판들(Some signs)이 건물 앞에 세워져 있는(have been posted in front of a building) 모습이므로 정답.

(C) 사진에 없는 명사를 이용한 오답. 사진에 카페(A café)의 모습이 보이지 않으므로 오답.

(D) 사진에 없는 명사를 이용한 오답. 사진에 단체 관광객들(A tour group)의 모습이 보이지 않으므로 오답.

---

5 W-Br

(A) Some people are waiting at a bus stop.
(B) Bike racks have been placed near a lawn.
(C) Some cars are parked along a sidewalk.
(D) Some people are gathered in a city square.

(A) 사람들이 버스 정류장에서 기다리고 있다.
(B) 자전거 거치대가 잔디밭 근처에 설치되어 있다.
(C) 차들이 보도를 따라 주차되어 있다.
(D) 사람들이 시 광장에 모여 있다.

어휘 bike rack 자전거 거치대 place 설치하다, 두다 lawn 잔디밭 sidewalk 보도, 인도 gather 모으다, 모이다 square 광장

해설 혼합 사진 – 사람/사물/풍경 혼합 묘사

(A) 사진에 없는 명사를 이용한 오답. 사진에 버스 정류장(a bus stop)의 모습이 보이지 않으므로 오답.

(B) 사진에 없는 명사를 이용한 오답. 사진에 자전거 거치대(Bike racks)와 잔디밭(a lawn)의 모습이 보이지 않으므로 오답.

(C) 정답. 차들(Some cars)이 보도를 따라 주차되어 있는(are parked along a sidewalk) 모습이므로 정답.

(D) 동사 오답. 사람들이 시 광장에 모여 있는(are gathered in a city square) 모습이 아니므로 오답.

---

6 W-Am

(A) The sun is being blocked by some curtains.
(B) There's a large carpet underneath a piano.
(C) There are some windows by a seating area.
(D) Some furniture is being stored in a closet.

(A) 해가 커튼에 의해 가려져 있다.
(B) 피아노 아래 큰 카펫이 있다.
(C) 앉는 자리 옆에 창문들이 있다.
(D) 가구가 벽장에 보관되어 있다.

어휘 block 막다 underneath 아래에 furniture 가구 store 보관하다 closet 벽장

해설 사물/풍경 사진 – 사물 묘사

(A) 동사 오답. 해(The sun)가 커튼으로 가려져 있는(is being blocked by some curtains) 모습이 아니므로 오답.

(B) 사진에 없는 명사를 이용한 오답. 사진에 피아노(a piano)의 모습이 보이지 않으므로 오답.

(C) 정답. 창문들(some windows)이 앉는 자리 옆에(by a seating area) 있는 모습이므로 정답.

(D) 동사 오답. 가구(Some furniture)가 벽장에 보관되어 있는(is being stored in a closet) 모습이 아니므로 오답.

PART 2

7

M-Cn Who's providing the floral arrangements for the party?

M-Au (A) The florist on Main Street.
(B) She's had a long career.
(C) Yes, his flight has been arranged.

파티 꽃 장식은 누가 제공하나요?
(A) 메인 가의 꽃집이요.
(B) 그녀는 경력이 길어요.
(C) 네, 그가 탈 항공편이 마련됐어요.

어휘 floral 꽃의, 꽃을 사용한 arrangement 준비, 배열 florist 꽃집 flight 항공편 arrange 마련하다, 주선하다

해설 파티 꽃 장식 제공처를 묻는 Who 의문문
(A) 정답. 파티 꽃 장식 제공처를 묻는 질문에 메인 가의 꽃집이라고 제공하는 업체를 알려 주고 있으므로 정답.
(B) 질문과 상관없는 오답. 질문에 3인칭 대명사 She로 지칭할 인물이 언급된 적이 없으므로 오답.
(C) Yes/No 불가 오답. Who 의문문에는 Yes/No 응답이 불가능하므로 오답.

8

W-Am Why didn't you finish the budget report?

M-Au (A) At the finish line.
(B) No, it wasn't expensive.
(C) I was meeting with a client.

왜 예산 보고서를 끝내지 못했나요?
(A) 결승선에서요.
(B) 아니요, 그것은 비싸지 않았어요.
(C) 저는 고객과 만나고 있었어요.

어휘 budget 예산 finish line 결승선 expensive 비싼

해설 예산 보고서를 끝내지 못한 이유를 묻는 Why 의문문
(A) 단어 반복 오답. 질문의 finish를 반복 이용한 오답.
(B) Yes/No 불가 오답. Why 의문문에는 Yes/No 응답이 불가능하므로 오답.
(C) 정답. 예산 보고서를 끝내지 못한 이유를 묻는 질문에 고객과 만나고 있었다고 구체적인 이유를 제시하고 있으므로 정답.

9

W-Am What floor are you going to?

M-Cn (A) Can I have a copy of this?
(B) The twenty-fifth.
(C) That painting will look nice there.

몇 층으로 가세요?
(A) 사본을 받을 수 있을까요?
(B) 25층이요.
(C) 그 그림은 거기 두면 멋질 거예요.

어휘 floor 층

해설 목적지의 층수를 묻는 What 의문문
(A) 질문과 상관없는 오답.
(B) 정답. 목적지의 층수를 묻는 질문에 25층이라고 구체적인 층수를 제시하고 있으므로 정답.
(C) 연상 단어 오답. 질문의 going to에서 연상 가능한 there를 이용한 오답.

10

M-Au How do I set up this projector?

W-Am (A) The storage area downstairs.
(B) A new project code.
(C) There's a manual in the drawer.

이 프로젝터는 어떻게 설치하나요?
(A) 아래층 보관 구역이요.
(B) 새 프로젝트 코드요.
(C) 서랍에 설명서가 있어요.

어휘 set up 설치하다 storage 보관 manual 설명서 drawer 서랍

해설 프로젝터 설치 방법을 묻는 How 의문문
(A) 질문과 상관없는 오답.
(B) 파생어 오답. 질문의 projector와 파생어 관계인 project를 이용한 오답.
(C) 정답. 프로젝터 설치 방법을 묻는 질문에 서랍에 설명서가 있다며 설명서를 참고하라고 알려 주고 있으므로 정답.

11

W-Am Who has already received their promotion letter?

M-Cn (A) I did yesterday.
(B) A party invitation.
(C) Polina gave the speech.

누가 승진 통지서를 이미 받았나요?
(A) 제가 어제 받았어요.
(B) 파티 초대장이요.
(C) 폴리나가 연설을 했어요.

어휘 promotion letter 승진 통지서 invitation 초대 give a speech 연설하다

해설 승진 통지서를 받은 사람을 묻는 Who 의문문
(A) 정답. 승진 통지서를 받은 사람을 묻는 질문에 자신이 받았다고 알려 주고 있으므로 정답.
(B) 연상 단어 오답. 질문의 letter에서 연상 가능한 invitation을 이용한 오답.
(C) 연상 단어 오답. 질문의 Who에서 연상 가능한 사람 이름 Polina를 이용한 오답.

12

W-Br Did you read the press release?

W-Am (A) I haven't checked my e-mail all day.
(B) It's not raining here yet.
(C) The switch works fine.

보도 자료를 보셨나요?
(A) 종일 이메일을 확인하지 못했어요.
(B) 여기는 아직 비가 안 와요.
(C) 스위치는 잘 작동해요.

어휘 press release 보도 자료

해설 보도 자료를 봤는지 여부를 묻는 조동사(Did) 의문문
(A) 정답. 보도 자료를 봤는지 여부를 묻는 질문에 이메일을 확인하지 못했다며 부정의 답변을 간접적으로 알려 주고 있으므로 정답.
(B) 질문과 상관없는 오답.
(C) 질문과 상관없는 오답.

13

M-Cn Didn't we renew our newspaper subscription last month?

W-Am (A) That photo's on the front page.
(B) Here's the paper for your newsletter.
(C) Yes, it was renewed for another six months.

우리 지난달에 신문 구독을 갱신하지 않았어요?
(A) 그 사진은 1면에 있어요.
(B) 여기 소식지를 위한 서류가 있어요.
(C) 네, 6개월 더 보는 걸로 갱신됐어요.

어휘 renew 갱신하다 subscription 구독 newsletter 소식지

해설 신문 구독 갱신 여부를 확인하는 부정 의문문
(A) 연상 단어 오답. 질문의 newspaper에서 연상 가능한 front page를 이용한 오답.
(B) 유사 발음 오답. 질문의 newspaper와 부분적으로 발음이 유사한 paper와 newsletter를 이용한 오답.
(C) 정답. 지난달 신문 구독 갱신 여부를 묻는 질문에 네(Yes)라고 대답한 뒤, 6개월 더 보는 걸로 갱신됐다며 긍정 답변과 일관된 내용을 덧붙였으므로 정답.

14

W-Br When will we mention our budgetary needs to the outreach coordinator?

M-Cn (A) I can't quite reach the top shelf.
(B) We're fully funded through the end of the year.
(C) Because our accountant is on vacation.

우리 예산 요구를 봉사 활동 조정자에게 언제 언급할까요?
(A) 저는 맨 위 선반에 닿지가 않네요.
(B) 연말까지 자금을 다 받았어요.
(C) 우리 회계원이 휴가 중이라서요.

어휘 mention 언급하다 budgetary 예산의 need 필요한 것, 요구

outreach 봉사 활동 coordinator 조정자 reach 닿다 fund 자금을 지원하다 accountant 회계원, 회계사

해설 예산 요구를 언급할 시기를 묻는 When 의문문
(A) 유사 발음 오답. 질문의 outreach와 부분적으로 발음이 유사한 reach를 이용한 오답.
(B) 정답. 예산 요구를 봉사 활동 조정자에게 언급할 시기를 묻는 질문에 연말까지 자금을 다 받았다며 언급할 필요가 없음을 우회적으로 알려 주고 있으므로 정답.
(C) 질문과 상관없는 오답. Why 의문문에 대한 응답이므로 오답.

15

W-Am My appointment is with Dr. Hamdy today, right?

W-Br (A) Usually an annual checkup.
(B) No, parking is not free.
(C) Yes, and she'll see you in a minute.

저 오늘 햄디 선생님 예약이죠, 맞죠?
(A) 대개 연례 검진이요.
(B) 아니요, 주차는 무료가 아닙니다.
(C) 네, 잠시 후 선생님과 만나실 겁니다.

어휘 appointment 약속 annual 연례의, 매년의 checkup 검진

해설 햄디 선생님 예약을 확인하는 부가 의문문
(A) 연상 단어 오답. 질문의 appointment와 Dr.에서 연상 가능한 annual checkup을 이용한 오답.
(B) 질문과 상관없는 오답.
(C) 정답. 햄디 선생님과의 예약을 확인하는 질문에 네(Yes)라고 대답한 뒤, 잠시 후 선생님과 만날 거라며 긍정 답변과 일관된 내용을 덧붙였으므로 정답.

16

W-Br Where should I store this shipment of paper?

M-Cn (A) The store closes at four.
(B) By express delivery.
(C) Well, the supply room is full.

이 종이 배송품은 어디에 보관해야 할까요?
(A) 가게는 네 시에 문을 닫아요.
(B) 속달 우편으로요.
(C) 음, 비품실이 꽉 찼어요.

어휘 store 보관하다 shipment 수송, 수송품 express delivery 속달 우편 supply room 비품실

해설 종이 배송품의 보관 장소를 묻는 Where 의문문
(A) 단어 반복 오답. 질문의 store를 반복 이용한 오답.
(B) 연상 단어 오답. 질문의 shipment에서 연상 가능한 express delivery를 이용한 오답.
(C) 정답. 종이 배송품을 보관할 장소를 묻는 질문에 비품실이 꽉 찼다며, 비품실에는 보관할 수 없음을 우회적으로 알려 주고 있으므로 정답.

17

M-Au Would you be able to reschedule my haircut for Monday?

W-Am (A) No, we're fully booked that day.
(B) I'll open a window to let in some fresh air.
(C) The grass needs cutting.

제 헤어컷 일정을 월요일로 변경해 주실 수 있나요?
(A) 아니요, 그날은 예약이 다 찼어요.
(B) 신선한 공기가 들어오도록 창문을 열게요.
(C) 잔디를 깎아야 해요.

어휘 reschedule 일정을 변경하다   fully booked 예약이 다 찬

해설 부탁/요청의 의문문
(A) 정답. 헤어컷 일정을 월요일로 변경해 달라는 요청에 아니요(No)라고 대답한 뒤, 그날은 예약이 다 찼다며 부정 답변과 일관된 내용을 덧붙이고 있으므로 정답.
(B) 유사 발음 오답. 질문의 haircut과 부분적으로 발음이 유사한 air를 이용한 오답.
(C) 유사 발음 오답. 질문의 haircut과 부분적으로 발음이 유사한 cutting을 이용한 오답.

18

M-Au Should I take the train or the bus to the airport?

M-Cn (A) The bus stop is five kilometers away.
(B) There are enough for all of us.
(C) No, I went to a training session.

공항까지 기차를 타야 할까요, 아니면 버스를 타야 할까요?
(A) 버스 정류장은 5km 거리예요.
(B) 우리 모두를 위해 충분히 있어요.
(C) 아니요, 저는 교육에 갔는데요.

해설 더 나은 교통수단을 묻는 선택 의문문
(A) 정답. 기차와 버스 중 더 나은 교통수단을 묻는 질문에 버스 정류장은 5km 거리라며 버스 정류장이 멀리 있으므로 기차가 낫다는 것을 우회적으로 알려 주고 있으므로 정답.
(B) 질문과 상관없는 오답.
(C) Yes/No 불가 오답. 문장과 문장을 연결하는 경우를 제외하고는 선택 의문문에는 Yes/No 응답이 불가능하므로 오답.

19

W-Br How long will the online course take?

M-Cn (A) You can finish it in a few hours.
(B) Forty dollars a month.
(C) I'll take the blue jacket.

온라인 강좌는 얼마나 걸릴까요?
(A) 몇 시간만에 끝낼 수 있어요.
(B) 한 달에 40달러입니다.
(C) 파란색 재킷으로 할게요.

해설 온라인 강좌를 마치는 데 걸리는 시간을 묻는 How long 의문문
(A) 정답. 온라인 강좌를 마치는 데 걸리는 시간을 묻는 질문에 몇 시간만에 끝낼 수 있다고 알려 주고 있으므로 정답.

(B) 질문과 상관없는 오답. How much 의문문에 대한 응답이므로 오답.
(C) 단어 반복 오답. 질문의 take를 반복 이용한 오답.

20

W-Am Will this month's company gathering be held in Benson Park?

M-Au (A) I usually park by the fountain.
(B) It's still cold outside most days.
(C) Those should be printed in color.

이번 달 회사 모임은 벤슨 공원에서 열릴 예정인가요?
(A) 저는 보통 분수 옆에 주차해요.
(B) 바깥은 아직도 거의 매일 추워요.
(C) 그것들은 컬러로 출력해야 해요.

어휘 gathering 모임   be held 열리다   usually 대개, 보통
fountain 분수

해설 회사 모임 장소를 확인하는 조동사(Will) 의문문
(A) 단어 반복 오답. 질문의 park를 반복 이용한 오답.
(B) 정답. 이번 달 회사 모임은 벤슨 공원에서 열리는지 여부를 묻는 질문에 바깥은 아직도 춥다며 벤슨 공원에서 열릴 수 없음을 우회적으로 알려 주고 있으므로 정답.
(C) 질문과 상관없는 오답.

21

M-Cn When will the tickets for the performance be ready to pick up?

W-Br (A) We should get them by the end of the week.
(B) A famous director.
(C) Twenty-five euros.

공연 입장권은 언제 수령할 수 있을까요?
(A) 주말쯤에는 받을 수 있을 거예요.
(B) 유명 감독이요.
(C) 25유로요.

어휘 performance 공연   director 감독, 연출자, 책임자

해설 공연 입장권의 수령 가능 시점을 묻는 When 의문문
(A) 정답. 공연 입장권의 수령 가능 시점을 묻는 질문에 주말쯤에는 받을 수 있을 것이라고 알려 주고 있으므로 정답.
(B) 연상 단어 오답. 질문의 performance에서 연상 가능한 famous director를 이용한 오답.
(C) 질문과 상관없는 오답. How much 의문문에 대한 응답이므로 오답.

22

W-Br I don't know if the packaging materials were ordered already.

M-Au (A) I saw some boxes on the loading dock.
(B) She's wearing a red hat.
(C) A lunch appointment at twelve thirty.

포장 재료가 이미 주문됐는지 잘 모르겠네요.

(A) 짐 싣는 곳에서 상자들을 봤어요.

(B) 그녀는 빨간 모자를 쓰고 있어요.

(C) 12시 30분 점심 약속이요.

어휘 packaging 포장　material 재료　loading dock (건물의) 짐 싣는 곳　appointment 약속

해설 의견 전달의 평서문

(A) 정답. 포장 재료가 이미 주문됐는지 잘 모르겠다는 평서문에 짐 싣는 곳에서 상자들을 봤다며 이미 주문됐음을 간접적으로 알려 주고 있으므로 정답.

(B) 평서문과 상관없는 오답. 평서문에 3인칭 대명사 She로 지칭할 인물이 언급된 적이 없으므로 오답.

(C) 평서문과 상관없는 오답.

23

W-Am　Could you please send me the sales report?

M-Cn　(A) Fifty percent off last season's merchandise.

(B) Of course—I'll do it now.

(C) Did you check the weather report?

영업 보고서를 저에게 보내주실 수 있나요?

(A) 지난 시즌 상품은 50퍼센트 할인입니다.

(B) 그럼요, 지금 그렇게 할게요.

(C) 일기 예보를 확인하셨나요?

어휘 merchandise 상품　weather report 일기 예보

해설 부탁/요청의 의문문

(A) 연상 단어 오답. 질문의 sales에서 연상 가능한 Fifty percent off를 이용한 오답.

(B) 정답. 영업 보고서를 보내 달라는 요청에 그럼요(Of course)라고 수락한 뒤, 지금 그렇게 하겠다며 긍정 답변과 일관된 내용을 덧붙이고 있으므로 정답.

(C) 단어 반복 오답. 질문의 report를 반복 이용한 오답.

24

M-Cn　What type of view will your apartment have?

W-Br　(A) The kitchen lighting looks great.

(B) I haven't signed a lease yet.

(C) We're in complete agreement on that.

당신의 아파트는 조망이 어떤가요?

(A) 주방 조명이 멋져요.

(B) 아직 임대차 계약서에 서명하지 않았어요.

(C) 우리는 거기에 완전히 동의해요.

어휘 lighting 조명　lease 임대차 계약　complete 완전한 agreement 동의

해설 아파트의 조망을 묻는 What 의문문

(A) 연상 단어 오답. 질문의 apartment에서 연상 가능한 kitchen lighting을 이용한 오답.

(B) 정답. 아파트의 조망을 묻는 질문에 아직 임대차 계약서에 서명하지 않았다며 아직 그 아파트에 입주하지 않아 모른다는 사실을 우회적으로 알려 주고 있으므로 정답.

(C) 유사 발음 오답. 질문의 apartment와 부분적으로 발음이 유사한 agreement를 이용한 오답.

25

M-Au　How much oil does your heater use in the winter?

W-Am　(A) We may need to stop for gas on our trip.

(B) That recipe calls for butter.

(C) We only use electric appliances.

당신의 히터는 겨울철에 기름을 얼마나 쓰죠?

(A) 우리는 여행하면서 주유를 위해 정차해야 할지도 몰라요.

(B) 그 조리법은 버터가 필요해요.

(C) 우리는 전기 제품만 사용해요.

어휘 recipe 조리법　call for ~을 필요로 하다　electric 전기의 appliance 기기, 가전 제품

해설 겨울철 히터에 쓰이는 기름 양을 묻는 How much 의문문

(A) 연상 단어 오답. 질문의 heater에서 연상 가능한 gas를 이용한 오답.

(B) 연상 단어 오답. 질문의 oil에서 연상 가능한 butter를 이용한 오답.

(C) 정답. 겨울철 히터에 쓰이는 기름 양을 묻는 질문에 전기 제품만 사용한다며 기름을 사용하지 않음을 간접적으로 알려 주고 있으므로 정답.

26

W-Am　Where can I find the vitamins?

M-Cn　(A) In aisle six.

(B) That's a really healthy recipe.

(C) The library is closed on Sundays.

비타민은 어디 있어요?

(A) 6번 통로예요.

(B) 정말 건강에 좋은 조리법이네요.

(C) 도서관은 일요일마다 닫아요.

어휘 aisle 통로　healthy 건강에 좋은　library 도서관

해설 비타민이 비치된 위치를 묻는 Where 의문문

(A) 정답. 비타민이 비치된 위치를 묻는 질문에 6번 통로라고 구체적인 위치로 알려 주고 있으므로 정답.

(B) 연상 단어 오답. 질문의 vitamins에서 연상 가능한 healthy를 이용한 오답.

(C) 질문과 상관없는 오답.

27

W-Br　Thank you for helping me create a survey.

M-Au　(A) The software did most of the work.

(B) Our loyal customers.

(C) The crates are still in the warehouse.

설문 제작을 도와주셔서 감사합니다.
(A) 작업 대부분을 소프트웨어가 했어요.
(B) 우리 단골 고객들이요.
(C) 상자들은 아직 창고에 있어요.

어휘 survey 설문 loyal customer 충성 고객, 단골 고객 crate 상자 warehouse 창고

해설 의사 전달의 평서문
(A) 정답. 설문 제작을 도와줘서 감사하다는 평서문에 작업 대부분을 소프트웨어가 했다며 자신이 직접 한 일은 적다는 내용을 간접적으로 알려 주고 있으므로 정답.
(B) 연상 단어 오답. 평서문의 survey에서 연상 가능한 loyal customers를 이용한 오답.
(C) 유사 발음 오답. 평서문의 create와 부분적으로 발음이 유사한 crates를 이용한 오답.

28
W-Am When will you be done testing the new mobile app?
M-Cn (A) No, just an older laptop model.
(B) I'm almost finished.
(C) It's about a two-hour drive from here.

새 모바일 앱 시험은 언제 완료하실 건가요?
(A) 아니요, 더 오래된 노트북 모델이요.
(B) 거의 끝났어요.
(C) 여기서 차로 2시간쯤이요.

해설 새 모바일 앱 시험의 완료 시점을 묻는 When 의문문
(A) Yes/No 불가 오답. When 의문문에는 Yes/No 응답이 불가능하므로 오답.
(B) 정답. 새 모바일 앱 시험의 완료 시점을 묻는 질문에 거의 끝났다며 완료 시점이 임박했음을 우회적으로 알려 주고 있으므로 정답.
(C) 연상 단어 오답. 질문의 testing에서 연상 가능한 drive를 이용한 오답.

29
W-Br Don't forget to turn off the projector after your presentation.
M-Au (A) I don't have a summary.
(B) Should I return it to the supply closet?
(C) Please distribute these handouts.

발표 후 잊지 말고 프로젝터를 끄세요.
(A) 저는 요약본이 없어요.
(B) 비품 창고에 다시 가져다 놔야 하나요?
(C) 이 인쇄물을 나눠주세요.

어휘 presentation 발표 summary 요약 supply 물품 distribute 배포하다, 나눠주다 handout 유인물, 인쇄물

해설 제안/권유의 평서문
(A) 연상 단어 오답. 평서문의 presentation에서 연상 가능한 summary를 이용한 오답.
(B) 정답. 발표 후 잊지 말고 프로젝터를 끄라는 권유에 대해 비품 창고에 다시 가져다 놔야 하는지 관련된 내용을 묻고 있으므로 정답.

(C) 연상 단어 오답. 평서문의 presentation에서 연상 가능한 handouts를 이용한 오답.

30

W-Br Didn't there use to be a parking garage on this street?
M-Cn (A) Yes, but it's been torn down.
(B) You can hang your keys on this hook.
(C) My car has a flat tire.

이 거리에 주차장이 있지 않았나요?
(A) 네, 그런데 허물었어요.
(B) 이 고리에 열쇠를 거시면 됩니다.
(C) 제 차 타이어가 펑크 났어요.

어휘 parking garage 주차장 tear down (건물을) 허물다, 철거하다 hang 걸다 have a flat tire 타이어에 펑크가 나다

해설 거리에 주차장이 있었는지 확인하는 부정 의문문
(A) 정답. 거리에 주차장이 있었는지 여부를 확인하는 질문에 네(Yes)라고 대답한 뒤, 그런데 허물었다며 부연 설명을 덧붙이고 있으므로 정답.
(B) 질문과 상관없는 오답.
(C) 연상 단어 오답. 질문의 parking에서 연상 가능한 car를 이용한 오답.

31

W-Am Will you be available to work on Thursday or Friday?
M-Au (A) There's mandatory training on Friday.
(B) Yes, it was a good show.
(C) A daily schedule.

목요일에 일할 시간이 되세요, 아니면 금요일에 되세요?
(A) 금요일에는 의무 교육이 있어요.
(B) 네, 멋진 공연이었어요.
(C) 일과 시간표요.

어휘 available 시간이 되는 mandatory 의무의

해설 근무 가능한 날을 묻는 선택 의문문
(A) 정답. 목요일과 금요일 중 근무 가능한 날을 묻는 질문에 금요일에는 의무 교육이 있다고 두 선택지 중 하나인 목요일을 우회적으로 선택하고 있으므로 정답.
(B) Yes/No 불가 오답. 문장과 문장을 연결하는 경우를 제외하고는 선택 의문문에는 Yes/No 응답이 불가능하므로 오답.
(C) 연상 단어 오답. 질문의 Thursday와 Friday에서 연상 가능한 daily schedule을 이용한 오답.

PART 3

32-34

> W-Am Hi. I'm Gabriela Alvarez of Organic Easy Meals. ³²**I'm scheduled to offer some samples of our new vegetable chips to your customers from three to five** P.M.
>
> M-Cn Oh yes. Hello, Ms. Alvarez. I'm Ryan Hughes, the manager. ³³**We have a table set up for you at the end of aisle eight. That's our snacks aisle.**
>
> W-Am Thanks. I'll start bringing in food and some equipment from my truck. But first I'd like to take a look at the table I'll be using.
>
> M-Cn Sounds good. ³⁴**If you'd like any help bringing in your stuff, just let me know.**

> 여 안녕하세요. 오가닉 이지밀의 가브리엘라 알바레즈입니다. **오후 3시부터 5시까지 저희 새 채소칩 견본을 귀사 고객들께 제공할 예정인데요.**
>
> 남 아, 네. 안녕하세요, 알바레즈 씨. 저는 관리자인 라이언 휴즈입니다. **8번 통로 끝에 테이블을 설치해 두었어요. 스낵 통로입니다.**
>
> 여 감사합니다. 트럭에서 음식과 장비를 들여오기 시작할게요. 그런데 먼저 제가 사용할 테이블을 좀 보고 싶어요.
>
> 남 좋아요. **물건을 들여오는 데 도움이 필요하시면 알려 주세요.**

> 어휘 be scheduled to ~할 예정이다 vegetable 채소 aisle 통로 equipment 장비 stuff 물건

32

What is the woman preparing to do?
(A) Conduct an inspection
(B) Film a cooking demonstration
(C) Offer some product samples
(D) Make a purchase

여자는 무엇을 하려고 준비하고 있는가?
(A) 점검 시행
(B) 요리 시연 촬영
(C) 제품 견본 제공
(D) 구매

어휘 conduct 하다 inspection 점검 demonstration 설명, 시연

해설 세부 사항 관련 – 여자가 준비하고 있는 것
여자가 첫 대사에서 오후 3시부터 5시까지 새 채소칩 견본을 고객들께 제공할 예정(I'm scheduled to offer some samples of our new vegetable chips to your customers from three to five P.M.)이라고 말하고 있으므로 정답은 (C)이다.

Paraphrasing 대화의 some samples of our new vegetable chips → 정답의 some product samples

33

Where is the conversation most likely taking place?
(A) At a restaurant
(B) At a factory
(C) At an organic farm
(D) At a grocery store

대화는 어디서 이루어지겠는가?
(A) 음식점
(B) 공장
(C) 유기농 농장
(D) 식료품점

어휘 organic 유기농의 grocery 식료품

해설 전체 내용 관련 – 대화의 장소
남자가 첫 대사에서 8번 통로 끝에 테이블을 설치해 두었다(We have a table set up for you at the end of aisle eight)면서 스낵 통로(That's our snacks aisle)라고 말하고 있으므로 화자들이 식료품점에서 대화하고 있다는 것을 알 수 있다. 따라서 정답은 (D)이다.

Paraphrasing 대화의 snacks → 정답의 grocery

34

What does the man offer to help with?
(A) Scheduling an interview
(B) Mixing some ingredients
(C) Carrying some supplies
(D) Assembling some equipment

남자는 무엇을 돕겠다고 제안하는가?
(A) 면접 일정 잡기
(B) 재료 혼합하기
(C) 물품 운반하기
(D) 장비 조립하기

어휘 ingredient 성분, 재료 supply 물품 assemble 조립하다

해설 세부 사항 관련 – 남자가 돕겠다고 제안하는 것
남자가 마지막 대사에서 물건을 들여오는 데 도움이 필요하면 알려 달라(If you'd like any help bringing in your stuff, just let me know)고 제안하고 있으므로 정답은 (C)이다.

Paraphrasing 대화의 bringing in your stuff → 정답의 Carrying some supplies

35-37

W-Br	Hello. ³⁵**I received a notice in the mail about a fee I need to pay because I returned some books late.** My name is Ling Gao.
M-Cn	Hmm. ³⁵**Yes, it says here in the system that you owe ten dollars for overdue materials.** Would you like to pay that now?
W-Br	³⁶**Do you take credit cards?**
M-Cn	We usually accept either cash or credit, ³⁷**but our card reader has been malfunctioning. Let me see if it's working again.**

여	안녕하세요. **책을 늦게 반납해서 내야 할 연체료가 있다는 우편 통지를 받았어요.** 저는 링 가오라고 해요.
남	음… 네, 시스템에는 자료 제출 기한이 지나서 10달러를 내야 한다고 되어 있네요. 지금 내시겠어요?
여	**신용카드 받나요?**
남	보통 현금이나 신용카드를 받는데, 카드 리더기가 오작동하고 있어요. 작동이 다시 되는지 한번 보죠.

어휘	fee 요금, 수수료 return 돌려주다 owe 빚지고 있다 overdue 기한이 지난 material 자료 accept 수락하다 malfunction 오작동하다, 제대로 작동하지 않다

35

Who most likely is the man?
(A) A bank teller
(B) A librarian
(C) A mail carrier
(D) A truck driver

남자는 누구이겠는가?
(A) 은행 출납원
(B) 사서
(C) 우체부
(D) 트럭 운전기사

해설 전체 내용 관련 – 남자의 직업

여자가 첫 대사에서 책을 늦게 반납해서 내야 할 연체료가 있다는 우편 통지를 받았다(I received a notice in the mail about a fee I need to pay because I returned some books late)고 말하자 남자가 네(Yes)라고 대답한 뒤 시스템에는 자료 제출 기한이 지나서 10달러를 내야 한다고 되어 있다(it says here in the system that you owe ten dollars for overdue materials)고 말하는 것으로 보아 남자는 도서관에서 근무하는 사서임을 알 수 있다. 따라서 정답은 (B)이다.

36

What does the woman ask about?
(A) A method of payment
(B) A type of delivery service
(C) A way to fill out a form
(D) A schedule change

여자는 무엇에 대해 물어보는가?
(A) 결제 방법
(B) 배송 서비스 유형
(C) 서식 작성 방법
(D) 일정 변경

어휘 method 방법 payment 지불, 결제 fill out 작성하다

해설 세부 사항 관련 – 여자의 문의 사항

여자가 두 번째 대사에서 신용카드 받는지(Do you take credit cards?)를 묻고 있으므로 정답은 (A)이다.

37

What does the man say he will do?
(A) Look up some information
(B) Print a document
(C) Check on a machine
(D) Update an account

남자는 무엇을 하겠다고 말하는가?
(A) 정보 찾기
(B) 서류 출력하기
(C) 기계 확인하기
(D) 계정 업데이트하기

어휘 account 계정, 계좌

해설 세부 사항 관련 – 남자가 할 일

남자가 마지막 대사에서 카드 리더기가 오작동하고 있다(our card reader has been malfunctioning)며 작동이 다시 되는지 한번 보겠다(Let me see if it's working again)고 말하고 있으므로 정답은 (C)이다.

> **Paraphrasing** 대화의 see → 정답의 Check on
> 대화의 card reader → 정답의 a machine

38-40 3인 대화

M-Cn	Hi, everybody. Are we ready for the sales meeting this morning?
W-Br	Yes, ³⁸**I've finished putting together my presentation.**
M-Au	³⁹**The meeting's in the conference room, right?**
M-Cn	³⁹**No—there's been a last-minute change. The conference room is being used by the IT department all day to interview job candidates.**

W-Br	Oh no! **⁴⁰My presentation requires the use of a television.**
M-Cn	**⁴⁰Don't worry.** We're meeting in the boardroom. There's a smart TV there.
M-Au	Is that room large enough for our team?
M-Cn	Yes, we won't have a problem.

남1	안녕하세요, 여러분. 오늘 오전 영업회의 준비가 되셨나요?
여	네. 저는 발표 준비를 마쳤습니다.
남2	회의는 회의실에서 하는 거죠, 맞나요?
남1	아니요, 막바지에 변경됐어요. IT 부서가 지원자들을 면접하느라 하루 종일 회의실을 쓰고 있어요.
여	저런! 제 발표는 TV를 이용해야 하는데요.
남1	걱정 마세요. 중역 회의실에서 회의를 해요. 거기 스마트 TV가 있습니다.
남2	저희 팀이 다 들어갈 만큼 충분히 클까요?
남1	네, 문제없을 겁니다.

어휘	put together 만들다, 준비하다 presentation 발표 conference room 회의실 last-minute 막판의, 막바지의 department 부서 job candidate 구직자, 지원자 boardroom 중역 회의실

38

What does the woman say she has finished doing?
(A) Organizing a luncheon
(B) Preparing some materials
(C) Submitting a purchase order
(D) Reviewing some résumés

여자는 무엇을 끝마쳤다고 말하는가?
(A) 오찬 준비
(B) 자료 준비
(C) 구매 주문서 제출
(D) 이력서 검토

어휘 organize 조직하다, 준비하다 luncheon 오찬 material 자료 purchase order 구매 주문서 résumé 이력서

해설 세부 사항 관련 – 여자가 끝마친 일
여자가 첫 대사에서 발표 준비를 마쳤다(I've finished putting together my presentation)고 말하고 있으므로 정답은 (B)이다.

> Paraphrasing 대화의 putting together my presentation
> → 정답의 Preparing some materials

39

Why was a change made at the last minute?
(A) An area is too noisy.
(B) Some participants are delayed.
(C) A room was already taken.
(D) Some revisions were requested.

왜 막바지에 변경이 이뤄졌는가?
(A) 구역이 너무 시끄럽다.
(B) 일부 참가자가 늦어졌다.
(C) 회의실이 이미 사용 중이다.
(D) 수정 요청을 받았다.

어휘 participant 참가자 delay 지연시키다, 늦추다 revision 수정

해설 세부 사항 관련 – 막바지에 변경이 이뤄진 이유
두 번째 남자가 첫 대사에서 회의는 회의실에서 하는 거 맞는지(The meeting's in the conference room, right?)를 묻자 첫 번째 남자가 아니요(No)라고 답한 뒤, 막바지에 변경됐다(there's been a last-minute change)며 IT 부서가 하루 종일 회의실을 쓰고 있다(The conference room is being used by the IT department all day ~)고 변경된 이유를 덧붙이고 있으므로 정답은 (C)이다.

> Paraphrasing 대화의 The conference room is being used by the IT department all day
> → 정답의 A room was already taken.

40

What is the woman concerned about?
(A) The security of an Internet connection
(B) The amount of approved funding
(C) The feedback from some colleagues
(D) The availability of some equipment

여자는 무엇에 대해 우려하는가?
(A) 인터넷 연결의 보안
(B) 승인된 자금 규모
(C) 동료의 피드백
(D) 장비 이용 가능 여부

어휘 security 보안 connection 연결 approve 승인하다 funding 자금 colleague 동료 availability 이용 가능성 equipment 장비

해설 세부 사항 관련 – 여자의 우려 사항
여자가 마지막 대사에서 TV를 이용해야 한다(My presentation requires the use of a television)고 말하자, 첫 번째 남자가 세 번째 대사에서 걱정 말라(Don't worry)고 말하는 것으로 보아, 여자는 TV 사용에 대해 걱정하고 있음을 알 수 있다. 따라서 정답은 (D)이다.

> Paraphrasing 대화의 the use of a television
> → 정답의 The availability of some equipment

41-43

M-Cn	**⁴¹Did you see the road construction sign at the corner? All traffic is being directed away from our street**—no one can come this way!
W-Am	**⁴¹I know!** **⁴²How will customers visit our store to make copies and pick up photo prints?**

M-Cn	**42 I'm afraid they'll have to park on another street**. They can still access the store on foot.
W-Am	OK. **43 I'll update our social media page to direct our customers**.
남	모퉁이에서 도로 공사 표지판 봤어요? 모든 차량들이 우리 거리를 피해 안내되고 있어요. 아무도 이쪽으로 올 수 없어요!
여	알아요! 손님들이 복사하고 출력된 사진을 찾으러 우리 가게에 어떻게 오죠?
남	다른 거리에 주차해야 할 것 같아요. 여전히 걸어서는 가게로 올 수 있어요.
여	알겠어요. 소셜미디어 페이지에 고객들에게 길을 안내하는 내용을 새로 올릴게요.
어휘	construction 공사, 건설 direct 안내하다 access 접근하다, 이용하다 on foot 걸어서

41

What problem do the speakers discuss?
(A) A parking garage is full.
(B) A street is closed.
(C) Some equipment is broken.
(D) Some items are damaged.

화자들은 어떤 문제에 대해 이야기하는가?
(A) 주차장이 다 찼다.
(B) 도로가 폐쇄됐다.
(C) 장비가 고장 났다.
(D) 물품이 훼손됐다.

어휘 equipment 장비 damage 손상시키다, 훼손하다

해설 세부 사항 관련 – 화자들이 언급하는 문제점
남자가 첫 대사에서 모퉁이에서 도로 공사 표지판 봤는지(Did you see the road construction sign at the corner?)를 물으며 모든 차량들이 우리 거리를 피해 안내되고 있다(All traffic is being directed away from our street)고 하자, 여자가 안다(I know!)고 말하고 있으므로 화자들은 도로 공사로 인한 도로 폐쇄에 대해 이야기하는 것을 알 수 있다. 따라서 정답은 (B)이다.

42

What does the man say customers will have to do?
(A) Visit an online store
(B) Present a receipt
(C) Park in a different area
(D) Schedule a delivery

남자는 고객들이 무엇을 해야 한다고 말하는가?
(A) 온라인 매장 방문하기
(B) 영수증 제시하기
(C) 다른 곳에 주차하기
(D) 배송 일정 잡기

어휘 present 제시하다 receipt 영수증

해설 세부 사항 관련 – 남자가 고객들이 해야 한다고 말하는 것
여자가 첫 대사에서 손님들이 우리 가게에 어떻게 오는지(How will customers visit our store ~?)를 묻자 남자가 다른 거리에 주차해야 할 것 같다(I'm afraid they'll have to park on another street)고 말하고 있으므로 정답은 (C)이다.

Paraphrasing 대화의 park on another street
→ 정답의 Park in a different area

43

What will the woman do next?
(A) Cancel her plans for the weekend
(B) Close the shop early
(C) Drive slowly
(D) Post an update on social media

여자는 다음으로 무엇을 할 것인가?
(A) 주말 계획 취소하기
(B) 매장 일찍 닫기
(C) 천천히 운전하기
(D) 소셜미디어에 새 게시물 올리기

어휘 post 게시하다

해설 세부 사항 관련 – 여자가 다음에 할 일
여자가 마지막 대사에서 소셜미디어 페이지에 고객들에게 길을 안내하는 내용을 새로 올리겠다(I'll update our social media page to direct our customers)고 말하고 있으므로 정답은 (D)이다.

Paraphrasing 대화의 update our social media page
→ 정답의 Post an update on social media

44-46

M-Au	**44 It's your first day working here**, so we'll spend the morning surveying the walking trails so you can get a sense of the area. **44 While we're at it, we'll also collect soil samples from different areas of the park.**
W-Br	**44,45 We need to test the soil samples to monitor the health of the preserve, right?**
M-Au	Yes. **45 We don't have a laboratory, so we send them out for testing every month.** And **46 since it's a sunny day today, it's a good time to take photographs for our social media page.**
W-Br	**46 I can do that. I brought my camera.**
남	이곳에서 일하시는 첫날이네요. 그래서 이 지역에 대해 감을 잡으실 수 있도록 산책로를 살펴보며 오전 시간을 보내려고 합니다. 그렇게 하는 동안 공원의 다양한 구역에서 토양 견본을 모으기도 할 겁니다.

여	보호 구역의 상태를 추적 관찰하기 위해 토양 견본을 검사해야 하는 거죠, 그렇죠?
남	네. 실험실이 없어서 검사를 위해 매달 외부로 내보냅니다. 오늘은 화창하니까 소셜미디어 페이지에 올릴 사진을 찍기에 좋은 때네요.
여	제가 할 수 있습니다. 카메라를 가져왔어요.

어휘	survey 살피다, 조사하다 walking trail 산책로 get a sense of ~을 감지하다, 짐작하다 collect 모으다, 수집하다 monitor 감시하다, 추적 관찰하다 preserve 보호 구역 laboratory 실험실

44

Where do the speakers most likely work?
(A) At a nature preserve
(B) At a vegetable farm
(C) At a garden supply store
(D) At a construction site

화자들은 어디서 일하겠는가?
(A) 자연 보호 구역
(B) 채소 농장
(C) 정원용품 매장
(D) 공사 현장

어휘 supply 물품, 용품   construction 건설, 공사

해설 전체 내용 관련 – 화자들의 근무지

남자가 첫 대사에서 이곳에서 일하는 첫날(It's your first day working here)이라며 공원의 다양한 구역에서 토양 견본을 모으기도 할 것(we'll also collect soil samples from different areas of the park)이라고 했고, 여자가 보호 구역의 상태를 추적 관찰하기 위해 토양 견본을 검사해야 하는 건지(We need to test the soil samples to monitor the health of the preserve, right?)를 묻고 있는 것으로 보아 화자들은 공원 자연 보호 구역에서 근무 중임을 알 수 있다. 따라서 정답은 (A)이다.

45

What will the speakers do with some samples?
(A) Display them in a window
(B) Send them to a laboratory
(C) Distribute them to customers
(D) Donate them to a university

화자들은 견본으로 무엇을 할 것인가?
(A) 창문에 진열하기
(B) 실험실로 보내기
(C) 고객들에게 나눠주기
(D) 대학교에 기부하기

어휘 distribute 나눠주다, 배포하다   donate 기부하다

해설 세부 사항 관련 – 화자들이 견본으로 할 일

여자가 첫 대사에서 보호 구역의 상태를 추적 관찰하기 위해 토양 견본을 검사해야 하는지(We need to test the soil samples to monitor the health of the preserve, right?)를 묻자 남자가 실험실이 없어서

검사를 위해 매달 외부로 내보낸다(We don't have a laboratory, so we send them out for testing every month)고 말하고 있는 것으로 보아 정답은 (B)이다.

46

What does the woman volunteer to do?
(A) Lead a training session
(B) Take some photographs
(C) Order some supplies
(D) Organize a tour

여자는 무엇을 하겠다고 자원하는가?
(A) 교육 시간 진행하기
(B) 사진 찍기
(C) 용품 주문하기
(D) 투어 준비하기

어휘 volunteer 자원하다   lead 이끌다   organize 조직하다, 준비하다

해설 세부 사항 관련 – 여자가 자원하는 일

남자가 마지막 대사에서 오늘은 화창하니까 소셜미디어 페이지에 올릴 사진을 찍기에 좋은 때(since it's a sunny day today, it's a good time to take photographs for our social media page)라고 하자 여자가 자신이 할 수 있다(I can do that)며 카메라를 가져왔다(I brought my camera)고 말하고 있으므로 정답은 (B)이다.

47-49

W-Br	Good morning, Ivan. **⁴⁸Everyone's talking about the flyer that was posted on our bulletin board yesterday.** Have you seen it?
M-Cn	I was out of the office yesterday, but I've heard. Big changes are coming for all mail carriers in the city.
W-Br	That's right. **⁴⁷,⁴⁸Our entire postal delivery fleet is being replaced with electric vehicles.**
M-Cn	I just hope that we don't have to charge them every few hours. **⁴⁹I'm concerned that the battery won't last through my entire route.**

여	안녕하세요, 이반. **모두들 어제 게시판에 붙은 전단에 대해 얘기하고 있어요.** 보셨나요?
남	어제 사무실에 없었지만 들었어요. 시의 모든 우체부들에게 큰 변화가 생길 거예요.
여	맞아요. **우편 배달 차량 전체가 전기차로 교체되고 있어요.**
남	몇 시간마다 충전해야 하는 건 아니길 바라요. **노선을 전부 돌 때까지 배터리가 버티지 못할까 봐 걱정되네요.**

47

Who are the speakers?
(A) Executive assistants
(B) Maintenance supervisors
(C) Postal workers
(D) Food delivery drivers

화자들은 누구인가?
(A) 비서
(B) 유지보수 관리자
(C) 우편 배달원
(D) 음식 배달 기사

해설 전체 내용 관련 – 화자들의 직업
여자가 두 번째 대사에서 우리의 우편 배달 차량 전체(Our entire postal
delivery fleet)라고 말하고 있으므로 정답은 (C)이다.

48

What was announced in a flyer?
(A) Some computer software will be replaced.
(B) A building will be sold.
(C) A route will be added.
(D) Some vehicles will be replaced.

전단에서 무엇이 발표됐는가?
(A) 컴퓨터 소프트웨어가 교체될 것이다.
(B) 건물이 팔릴 것이다.
(C) 노선이 추가될 것이다.
(D) 차량이 교체될 것이다.

어휘 replace 교체하다

해설 세부 사항 관련 – 전단에서 발표된 것
여자가 첫 대사에서 모두들 게시판에 붙은 전단에 대해 얘기하고 있
다(Everyone's talking about the flyer that was posted on our
bulletin board yesterday)고 했고 두 번째 대사에서 우편 배달 차량
전체가 전기차로 교체되고 있다(Our entire postal delivery fleet is
being replaced with electric vehicles)고 전단의 내용을 덧붙이고 있
으므로 정답은 (D)이다.

> Paraphrasing 대화의 postal delivery fleet
> → 정답의 Some vehicles

49

What is the man concerned about?
(A) How long a battery will last
(B) How expensive a purchase will be
(C) How accurate a weather forecast is
(D) How current a training program is

남자는 무엇을 우려하는가?
(A) 배터리가 얼마나 지속될지
(B) 구매 물품이 얼마나 비쌀지
(C) 일기 예보가 얼마나 정확한지
(D) 교육 프로그램이 현재를 얼마나 반영하는지

어휘 accurate 정확한 current 현재의, 현행의

해설 세부 사항 관련 – 남자의 우려 사항
남자가 마지막 대사에서 노선을 전부 돌 때까지 배터리가 버티지 못할까
봐 걱정된다(I'm concerned that the battery won't last through my
entire route)고 말하고 있으므로 정답은 (A)이다.

50-52 3인 대화

W-Am Kota, I want you to meet Claudia. **50 Claudia
is starting work today. Could you show
her around and explain some of our
processes?**

M-Au **50 Of course, Ms. Park.** Welcome to the
team, Claudia!

W-Br Thank you. **51 I'm coming from the Silver
Ridge Inn, where I also worked at the front
desk.**

M-Au So you already have experience with
taking reservations and checking in
guests?

W-Br Yes, but **51, 52 we used a different software
system than the one I see you have here.**

M-Au It's easy to use. **52 Let me show you how.**

여1 코타, 클라우디아를 만나봐 줬으면 좋겠어요. **클라우디아가
오늘 일을 시작하거든요. 안내를 좀 해 주고 우리 절차를
설명해 주실 수 있나요?**
남 **물론이죠, 박 씨.** 팀에 들어온 것을 환영해요, 클라우디아!
여2 감사합니다. **실버 리지 인에서 왔어요. 거기서도 안내
데스크에서 일했어요.**
남 예약을 받고 손님 체크인을 해 본 경험이 이미 있으시군요?
여2 네, 하지만 **여기서 사용하는 소프트웨어 시스템과 다른 걸
사용했어요.**
남 사용하기 쉬워요. **어떻게 하는지 알려 드릴게요.**

어휘 show ~ around … ~에게 …을 안내하다, 구경시켜 주다
process 절차, 과정 inn 호텔, 여관 experience
경험, 경력 take a reservation 예약을 받다

50

What does Ms. Park ask the man to do?
(A) Assist a new employee
(B) Book an event
(C) Meet with a vendor
(D) Prepare a presentation

박 씨는 남자에게 무엇을 해 달라고 요청하는가?

(A) 신입사원 도와주기
(B) 행사 예약하기
(C) 판매자와 만나기
(D) 발표 준비하기

어휘 assist 돕다　book 예약하다　vendor 판매자

해설 세부 사항 관련 – 박 씨가 남자에게 요청하는 일

첫 번째 여자가 남자에게 클라우디아가 오늘 일을 시작한다(Claudia is starting work today)면서 안내를 좀 해 주고 우리 절차를 설명해 줄 수 있는지(Could you show her around and explain some of our processes?)를 묻자 남자가 물론이죠, 박 씨(Of course, Ms. Park)라고 답하는 것으로 보아 박 씨는 남자에게 신입사원 클라우디아를 도와달라고 요청하고 있음을 알 수 있다. 따라서 정답은 (A)이다.

51

Where does the conversation most likely take place?
(A) At a museum
(B) At a technology firm
(C) At an airport
(D) At a hotel

대화는 어디서 이루어지겠는가?
(A) 박물관
(B) 기술업체
(C) 공항
(D) 호텔

해설 전체 내용 관련 – 대화의 장소

두 번째 여자가 첫 대사에서 실버 리지 인에서 왔고 거기서도 안내 데스크에서 일했다(I'm coming from the Silver Ridge Inn, where I also worked at the front desk)고 했고, 마지막 대사에서 여기서 사용하는 소프트웨어 시스템과 다른 걸 사용했다(we used a different software system than the one I see you have here)고 덧붙이고 있으므로 대화 장소는 호텔임을 알 수 있다. 따라서 정답은 (D)이다.

52

What will the man do next?
(A) Provide some feedback
(B) Check a calendar
(C) Demonstrate a computer program
(D) Help a coworker find some supplies

남자는 다음으로 무엇을 할 것인가?
(A) 피드백 제공하기
(B) 달력 확인하기
(C) 컴퓨터 프로그램 설명하기
(D) 동료가 용품을 찾도록 돕기

어휘 demonstrate (사용법을) 보여주다, 설명하다　coworker 동료

해설 세부 사항 관련 – 남자가 다음에 할 일

두 번째 여자가 마지막 대사에서 여기서 사용하는 소프트웨어 시스템과 다른 걸 사용했다(we used a different software system than the one

I see you have here)고 하자, 남자가 어떻게 하는지 알려 주겠다(Let me show you how)고 말하고 있으므로 정답은 (C)이다.

> **Paraphrasing** 대화의 show → 정답의 Demonstrate
> 대화의 a different software system
> → 정답의 a computer program

53-55

W-Br　Wow. ⁵³I didn't expect this restaurant to be so popular—look at all the people waiting to be seated.

W-Am　⁵³I know. It's brand-new—I didn't think anyone knew about it yet. Looks like we won't be able to get a table for a while.

W-Br　Well, ⁵⁴we don't have much time. We need to drive back to the office to train our interns at one o'clock. Should we go somewhere else?

W-Am　Let's see if they offer takeout—⁵⁵we can just order something to go.

W-Br　⁵⁵Good idea. I'm looking forward to trying the spicy noodles!

여1　우와! **이 식당이 이렇게 인기 있을지 예상 못했어요.** 자리를 기다리는 이 사람들을 좀 보세요.

여2　**맞아요.** 아주 최근에 생겼어요. 누가 벌써 알 거라고 생각하지 못했어요. 얼마 동안은 자리를 못 잡을 것 같네요.

여1　음, **우린 시간이 많지 않아요. 사무실로 다시 차를 타고 가서 1시에 인턴 교육을 해야 하잖아요.** 다른 곳으로 가야 할까요?

여2　포장도 해 주는지 보죠. **가져갈 걸 주문하면 돼요.**

여1　**좋은 생각이네요.** 매운 면 요리를 정말 먹어보고 싶어요!

어휘 be seated 자리에 앉다　brand-new 완전히 새로운 for a while 얼마 동안은, 잠깐　takeout 사 가지고 가는 음식　look forward to ~을 고대하다

53

What do the speakers find surprising about a restaurant?
(A) Its prices
(B) Its popularity
(C) Its menu options
(D) Its decor

화자들은 식당의 어떤 점을 놀라워하는가?
(A) 가격
(B) 인기
(C) 메뉴
(D) 장식

해설 세부 사항 관련 – 화자들이 식당에 놀라는 점

첫 번째 여자가 첫 대사에서 이 식당이 이렇게 인기 있을지 예상 못했다(I

didn't expect this restaurant to be so popular)고 하자, 두 번째 여자가 맞다(I know)고 대답하고 있으므로 정답은 (B)이다.

54

Why are the speakers in a hurry?
(A) They need to catch a train.
(B) They will be conducting an interview.
(C) They will be leading a training session.
(D) A business is about to close.

화자들은 왜 서두르는가?
(A) 기차를 타야 한다.
(B) 면접을 진행할 것이다.
(C) 교육을 진행할 것이다.
(D) 영업을 종료할 때가 됐다.

어휘 conduct 하다 lead 진행하다 be about to 막 ~하려고 하다

해설 세부 사항 관련 – 화자들이 서두르는 이유
첫 번째 여자가 두 번째 대사에서 시간이 많지 않다(we don't have much time)면서 사무실로 다시 차를 타고 가서 1시에 인턴 교육을 해야 한다(We need to drive back to the office to train our interns at one o'clock)고 말하고 있으므로 정답은 (C)이다.

> **Paraphrasing** 대화의 train our interns
> → 정답의 leading a training session

55

What will the speakers most likely do next?
(A) Go to another restaurant
(B) Try a free sample
(C) Order food to go
(D) Pay a bill

화자들은 다음으로 무엇을 할 것인가?
(A) 다른 식당으로 가기
(B) 무료 견본 시식하기
(C) 포장할 음식 주문하기
(D) 지불하기

해설 세부 사항 관련 – 화자들이 다음에 할 일
두 번째 여자가 마지막 대사에서 가져갈 걸 주문하면 된다(we can just order something to go)고 하자 첫 번째 여자가 좋은 생각(Good idea)이라고 말하고 있으므로 정답은 (C)이다.

56-58

W-Am	Hi, Ahmed. Did you see the e-mail from management?
M-Au	56 I just got here to teach my aerobics class.
W-Am	56,57 It looks like the gym is opening

another facility just a few miles from here. 57 I'm surprised they want to open another location so close by.

M-Au	Well, this is a densely populated area.
W-Am	True. 58 I guess they'll have to hire more employees. There's just not enough of us to staff both locations.

여	안녕하세요, 아메드. 경영진에게서 온 이메일 봤어요?
남	에어로빅 수업을 하러 방금 왔는데요.
여	체육관이 여기서 몇 마일 떨어진 곳에 또 하나의 시설을 여는 것 같아요. 그렇게 가까운 곳에 또 다른 지점을 열고 싶어 하다니 놀라운데요.
남	음, 인구가 밀집되어 있는 지역이잖아요.
여	맞아요. 직원을 더 고용해야 할 것 같아요. 두 곳 모두에 직원을 배치하기에는 인원이 충분하지 않아요.

어휘 management 경영진, 운영진 facility 시설 location 장소, 위치 close by 인근에, 가까운 곳에 densely populated 인구가 밀집한 staff 직원을 제공하다, 직원으로 일하다

56

Where do the speakers most likely work?
(A) At a sporting goods store
(B) At a campground
(C) At a footwear factory
(D) At a fitness center

화자들은 어디서 일하겠는가?
(A) 스포츠용품점
(B) 캠핑장
(C) 신발 공장
(D) 피트니스 센터

해설 전체 내용 관련 – 화자들의 근무지
남자가 첫 대사에서 에어로빅 수업을 하러 방금 왔다(I just got here to teach my aerobics class)고 하자 여자가 체육관이 여기서 몇 마일 떨어진 곳에 또 하나의 시설을 여는 것 같다(It looks like the gym is opening another facility just a few miles from here)고 말하고 있는 것으로 보아 화자들은 체육관에서 근무하는 강사임을 알 수 있다. 따라서 정답은 (D)이다.

> **Paraphrasing** 대화의 the gym → 정답의 a fitness center

57

Why does the man say, "this is a densely populated area"?
(A) To complain that traffic is heavy
(B) To suggest changes in regulations
(C) To explain a decision
(D) To request a review of property values

남자가 "인구가 밀집되어 있는 지역이잖아요"라고 말하는 이유는?
(A) 교통이 혼잡한 것을 불평하려고
(B) 규정 변경을 제안하려고
(C) 결정에 대해 설명하려고
(D) 부동산 가치 검토를 요청하려고

어휘 complain 불평하다　regulation 규정　decision 결정, 결심
　　property 재산, 부동산　value 가치

해설 화자의 의도 파악 – 인구가 밀집되어 있는 지역이라는 말의 의도
앞에서 여자가 체육관이 여기서 몇 마일 떨어진 곳에 또 하나의 시설을
여는 것 같다(It looks like the gym is opening another facility just
a few miles from here)며 그렇게 가까운 곳에 다른 지점을 열고 싶어
하다니 놀랍다(I'm surprised they want to open another location
so close by)고 말한 뒤 남자가 인용문을 언급한 것으로 보아, 새로운
시설을 여는 것에 대한 경영진의 결정에 대해 합리적인 이유가 있음을
설명하려는 의도로 한 말임을 알 수 있다. 따라서 정답은 (C)이다.

58

What does the woman think a business should do?
(A) Hire more employees
(B) Place a large order
(C) Revise an employee handbook
(D) Advertise on social media

여자는 업체가 무엇을 해야 한다고 생각하는가?
(A) 직원을 더 채용하기
(B) 대량 주문하기
(C) 직원 안내서 개정하기
(D) 소셜미디어에 광고하기

어휘 revise 개정하다, 수정하다　employee handbook 직원 안내서
　　advertise 광고하다

해설 세부 사항 관련 – 여자가 업체가 해야 할 일이라고 생각하는 것
여자가 마지막 대사에서 직원을 더 고용해야 할 것 같다(I guess they'll
have to hire more employees)고 말하고 있으므로 정답은 (A)이다.

59-61

 동영상 강의

W-Br	Marcel, [59] **I'd like to plan a team-building event with our graphic design group.**
M-Au	[59] **Sure. We could reserve the conference room upstairs.**
W-Br	But the event wouldn't be just for on-site graphic designers. Nearly a third of our staff will be participating remotely.
M-Au	Oh, [60] **you're right. Everyone needs to feel equally included. Let's have our on-site staff join the event from their desks.**
W-Br	OK. [61] **I'll do a search for effective team-building activities that we can do online.**

여	마르셀, 우리 그래픽 디자인 그룹과 함께 팀워크 행사를 계획하고 싶은데요.
남	그래요. 위층 회의실을 예약할 수 있어요.
여	그런데 행사는 사내 근무 그래픽 디자이너들만을 위한 것이 아닙니다. 직원의 거의 3분의 1이 원격으로 참석할 거예요.
남	아, 맞아요. 모두가 똑같이 소속감을 느껴야 해요. 사내 근무 직원들이 자신의 자리에서 행사에 참여할 수 있도록 하죠.
여	좋아요. 온라인으로 할 수 있는 효과적인 팀워크 활동에 대해 찾아볼게요.

어휘　reserve 예약하다　conference room 회의실
　on-site 현장의　nearly 거의　participate 참여하다
　remotely 멀리서, 원격으로　feel included 소속감을
　느끼다　equally 똑같이, 동등하게　do a search
　검색하다, 찾아보다　effective 효과적인　activity 활동

59

What is the conversation about?
(A) Organizing an event
(B) Preparing for a renovation
(C) Updating some software
(D) Selecting a caterer

무엇에 관한 대화인가?
(A) 행사 준비
(B) 보수 공사 준비
(C) 소프트웨어 업데이트
(D) 케이터링 업체 선정

어휘 organize 준비하다　renovation 개조, 보수　select 선택하다

해설 전체 내용 관련 – 대화의 주제
여자가 첫 대사에서 우리 그래픽 디자인 그룹과 함께 팀워크 행사를
계획하고 싶다(I'd like to plan a team-building event with our
graphic design group)고 하자, 남자가 그래요(Sure)라고 긍정
답변을 한 뒤 위층 회의실을 예약할 수 있다(We could reserve the
conference room upstairs)고 팀워크 행사 준비에 대한 대화를 이어
가고 있으므로 정답은 (A)이다.

60

What does the woman imply when she says, "Nearly a third of our staff will be participating remotely"?
(A) Travel expenses should be refunded.
(B) Some workers may feel excluded.
(C) A venue is not the correct size.
(D) A workshop should be postponed.

여자가 "직원의 거의 3분의 1이 원격으로 참석할 거예요"라고 말하는 의도
는 무엇인가?
(A) 출장비가 환급될 것이다.
(B) 일부 직원들은 소외감을 느낄 수도 있다.
(C) 장소 크기가 알맞지 않다.
(D) 워크숍이 연기되어야 한다.

어휘 travel expense 출장비 refund 환불해 주다 feel excluded 소외감을 느끼다 venue 장소 correct 알맞은, 적절한 postpone 연기하다

해설 화자의 의도 파악 – 직원의 거의 3분의 1이 원격으로 참석한다는 말의 의도

인용문을 언급한 뒤 남자가 맞아요(you're right)라고 말한 뒤 모두가 똑같이 소속감을 느껴야 한다(Everyone needs to feel equally included)며 사내 근무 직원들이 자신의 자리에서 행사에 참여할 수 있도록 하자(Let's have our on-site staff join the event from their desks)고 제안하는 것으로 보아 일부 직원은 참석하지 못하여 소외감을 느낄 수도 있다는 의도로 한 말임을 알 수 있다. 따라서 정답은 (B)이다.

61

What will the woman do next?
(A) Review an agenda
(B) Reserve an event space
(C) Research some online activities
(D) Check a budget

여자는 다음으로 무엇을 할 것인가?
(A) 안건 검토하기
(B) 행사 공간 예약하기
(C) 온라인 활동 조사하기
(D) 예산 확인하기

어휘 review 검토하다 agenda 의제, 안건 research 조사하다, 연구하다 budget 예산

해설 세부 사항 관련 – 여자가 다음에 할 일

여자가 마지막 대사에서 온라인으로 할 수 있는 효과적인 팀워크 활동에 대해 찾아보겠다(I'll do a search for effective team-building activities that we can do online)고 말하고 있으므로 정답은 (C)이다.

Paraphrasing 대화의 do a search → 정답의 Research

62-64 대화 + 백화점 안내판   ▶ 동영상 강의

M-Au Hi. 63 I'm calling because I saw some coffee tables on your department store's Web site. I'd like to see them in person. 62,63 Can you tell me if you have the same furniture selection in your store?

W-Br 62 Yes, we do. We're fully stocked at the moment, so you'll be able to see everything that's on our online catalog.

M-Au OK. One more thing. 64 I use a wheelchair, and I'm concerned about navigating your store.

W-Br Oh, 64 that's not a problem. We have large elevators that can easily accommodate a wheelchair.

M-Au Great. Thanks for the information. I'll stop by later this afternoon.

남 안녕하세요. **귀사의 백화점 웹사이트에서 커피 탁자를 보고 전화했어요. 직접 보고 싶은데요. 매장에 같은 가구 제품들이 있는지 알려 주실 수 있나요?**

여 **네, 있습니다.** 현재 모든 물건이 갖춰져 있으니 온라인 카탈로그에 있는 모든 제품을 보실 수 있습니다.

남 네. 하나 더요. **제가 휠체어를 이용하고 있어서 매장을 가는 게 걱정되네요.**

여 아, **괜찮습니다. 휠체어를 거뜬히 수용할 수 있는 대형 엘리베이터가 있어요.**

남 좋아요. 정보를 주셔서 감사합니다. 이따가 오후에 들를게요.

어휘 department store 백화점 in person 직접 selection 선택, 선택한 것들의 집합 stock (판매할 상품을) 갖춰 두다 concerned 걱정하는, 염려하는 navigate 길을 찾다, 항해하다 accommodate 수용하다 stop by 잠깐 들르다

Woodlands Store	
Floor	**Department**
1	Customer Service
2	Jewelry
62 3	Furniture
4	Appliances
5	Clothing

우드랜즈 매장	
층	**부서**
1	고객 서비스
2	장신구
62 3	**가구**
4	가전제품
5	의류

62

Look at the graphic. Which floor will the man visit?
(A) Floor 1
(B) Floor 2
(C) Floor 3
(D) Floor 4

시각 정보에 의하면, 남자는 어떤 층을 방문할 것인가?
(A) 1층
(B) 2층
(C) 3층
(D) 4층

해설 시각 정보 연계 – 남자가 방문할 층

남자가 첫 대사에서 웹사이트에 있는 가구들이 매장에도 있는지(Can you tell me if you have the same furniture selection in your store?) 물었고, 여자가 있다(Yes, we do)고 답변했다. 백화점 안내판을 보면 가구 매장이 3층이므로 정답은 (C)이다.

63

Why is the man calling the store?
(A) To complain about receiving a faulty product
(B) To point out an error in an invoice
(C) To ask about seeing some merchandise
(D) To request delivery of a catalog

남자가 매장에 전화를 건 이유는?
(A) 결함 있는 제품을 받아서 항의하려고
(B) 청구서에 있는 오류를 지적하려고
(C) 상품을 보는 것에 대해 문의하려고
(D) 카탈로그 배송을 요청하려고

어휘 complain 불평하다, 항의하다 faulty 결함이 있는 point out 지적하다 invoice 송장, 청구서 merchandise 상품

해설 전체 내용 관련 – 남자가 매장에 전화한 이유
남자가 첫 대사에서 백화점 웹사이트에서 커피 탁자를 보고 전화했다(I'm calling because I saw some coffee tables on your department store's Web site)면서 직접 보고 싶다(I'd like to see them in person)고 말한 뒤 매장에 같은 가구 제품들이 있는지 알려줄 수 있는지(Can you tell me if you have the same furniture selection in your store?)를 묻고 있으므로 정답은 (C)이다.

> Paraphrasing 대화의 some coffee tables
> → 정답의 some merchandise

64

What does the woman assure the man about?
(A) An online payment system is secure.
(B) A building is wheelchair accessible.
(C) A product is eligible for a refund.
(D) A food court is open daily.

여자는 남자에게 무엇에 대해 확답을 주는가?
(A) 온라인 결제 시스템이 안전하다.
(B) 건물은 휠체어를 이용할 수 있다.
(C) 제품은 환불을 받을 수 있다.
(D) 푸드코트는 매일 문을 연다.

어휘 assure 장담하다, 보장하다 payment 결제, 지불 secure 안전한, 확실한 accessible 접근 가능한, 이용할 수 있는 be eligible for ~할 자격이 있다 refund 환불

해설 세부 사항 관련 – 여자가 남자에게 확답을 주는 것
남자가 마지막 대사에서 자신이 휠체어를 이용하고 있어서 매장을 가는 게 걱정된다(I use a wheelchair, and I'm concerned about navigating your store)고 하자, 여자가 괜찮다(that's not a problem)면서 휠체어를 거뜬히 수용할 수 있는 대형 엘리베이터가 있다(We have large elevators that can easily accommodate a wheelchair)고 말하고 있으므로 정답은 (B)이다.

65-67 대화 + 출발 안내판

W-Br　Adam, **65 our Kyoto office just called. Our investors want me to present a project update there as soon as possible.** Can you get me on the first flight to Kyoto tomorrow morning?

M-Cn　Let me check. **66 Per company policy, we can only use Blue Jet airlines for international travel**—and unfortunately, that flight's not the first one out tomorrow.

W-Br　That will have to do, thanks. And I'll need a ride to the airport too. Can you arrange that?

M-Cn　Sure thing. **67 I'll finalize the reservations and e-mail you the details.**

여　아담, **우리 교토 사무실에서 방금 전화가 왔는데요. 투자자들이 최대한 빨리 제가 그곳에서 프로젝트 최신 사항을 발표해 줬으면 한대요.** 내일 아침 교토로 가는 첫 항공편을 구해주실 수 있나요?

남　확인해 보죠. **회사 방침에 따라 해외 출장은 블루젯 항공만 이용할 수 있는데요.** 안타깝게도 그 항공편이 내일 첫 비행기가 아니네요.

여　그렇게라도 해야 할 거예요. 감사합니다. 공항으로 갈 교통편도 필요해요. 마련해 주실 수 있나요?

남　그럼요, **예약을 마무리하고 이메일로 세부 사항을 보내드릴게요.**

어휘 investor 투자자 present 발표하다 as soon as possible 최대한 빨리 per company policy 회사 방침에 따라 unfortunately 안타깝게도, 아쉽게도 arrange 마련하다, 주선하다 finalize 마무리하다 reservation 예약 detail 세부 사항

Flights to Kyoto		
From	**Airline**	**Departure Time**
Newark	Sky Air	6:02 A.M.
New York	Alpha Star	8:15 A.M.
New York	**66 Blue Jet**	9:07 A.M.
Newark	High Wings	10:20 A.M.

교토행 항공편		
출발	**항공사**	**출발 시간**
뉴어크	스카이 에어	오전 6시 2분
뉴욕	알파 스타	오전 8시 15분
뉴욕	**66 블루젯**	오전 9시 7분
뉴어크	하이 윙즈	오전 10시 20분

어휘 departure 출발

65

Why does the woman need to go to Kyoto?
(A) To attend a conference
(B) To sign a contract
(C) To find investors
(D) To report on a project

여자는 왜 교토에 가야 하는가?
(A) 회의에 참석하려고
(B) 계약을 체결하려고
(C) 투자자를 찾으려고
(D) 프로젝트에 대해 보고하려고

어휘 sign a contract 계약을 맺다, 계약서에 서명하다

해설 세부 사항 관련 – 여자가 교토에 가는 이유

여자가 첫 대사에서 교토 사무실에서 방금 전화가 왔는데(our Kyoto office just called) 투자자들이 최대한 빨리 제가 그곳에서 프로젝트 최신 사항을 발표해 줬으면 한다(Our investors want me to present a project update there as soon as possible)고 말하고 있으므로 정답은 (D)이다.

> **Paraphrasing** 대화의 present a project update
> → 정답의 report on a project

66

Look at the graphic. What time will the woman depart for Kyoto?
(A) At 6:02 A.M.
(B) At 8:15 A.M.
(C) At 9:07 A.M.
(D) At 10:20 A.M.

시각 정보에 의하면, 여자는 몇 시에 교토로 출발할 것인가?
(A) 오전 6시 2분
(B) 오전 8시 15분
(C) 오전 9시 7분
(D) 오전 10시 20분

해설 시각 정보 연계 – 여자가 교토로 출발하는 시간

남자가 첫 대사에서 회사 방침에 따라 해외 출장은 블루젯 항공만 이용할 수 있다(Per company policy, we can only use Blue Jet airlines for international travel)고 말하고 있고, 출발 안내판에 따르면 블루젯 항공은 오전 9시 7분에 출발하므로 정답은 (C)이다.

67

What does the man say he will do?
(A) Drive the woman to the airport
(B) Reserve a hotel
(C) E-mail some information
(D) Print out a boarding pass

남자는 무엇을 할 것이라고 말하는가?
(A) 여자를 공항으로 태워다 주기
(B) 호텔 예약하기
(C) 정보를 이메일로 보내기
(D) 탑승권 출력하기

어휘 print out 출력하다   boarding pass 탑승권

해설 세부 사항 관련 – 남자가 할 일

남자가 마지막 대사에서 예약을 마무리하고 이메일로 세부 사항을 보내주겠다(I'll finalize the reservations and e-mail you the details)고 말하고 있으므로 정답은 (C)이다.

> **Paraphrasing** 대화의 e-mail you the details
> → 정답의 E-mail some information

68-70 대화 + 지도

M-Au Hi, Astrid. **68 For tonight's six o'clock news broadcast, the lead story is going to be on the rumor that the Beavers' football team is going to build a stadium.** Have you heard about the project?

W-Br My sources have confirmed the story, actually. **69 I've just gained exclusive access to some bidding proposals.** Four cities are competing for the project.

M-Au **68 It's great you were able to confirm this before we went on the air. 70 Do you know where the new stadium might be built?**

W-Br Well, **70 one document suggests that Columbia City's proposal is the favorite.** However, the team does have three other bids to consider.

남 안녕하세요, 아스트리드. **오늘 저녁 6시 뉴스의 헤드라인은 비버 축구팀이 경기장을 짓는다는 소문이 될 거예요.** 그 프로젝트에 대해 들어봤나요?

여 사실 제 소식통이 그 얘기를 확인해 줬어요. **방금 몇 가지 입찰 제안서에 대한 독점 접근권을 얻었는데요.** 도시 네 곳이 프로젝트를 놓고 경쟁하고 있어요.

남 **방송 전에 이걸 확인할 수 있었다니 대단해요. 새 경기장을 어디에 지을지 아세요?**

여 음, **한 문서에 따르면 콜롬비아 시티의 제안이 가장 유력하다고 해요.** 그런데 팀에서는 고려할 다른 제안도 세 개 더 있으니까요.

어휘 broadcast 방송   lead story 헤드라인, 톱뉴스   source 정보원, 소식통   confirm 확인해 주다, 확정하다   actually 실은   gain 얻다   exclusive 독점적인, 배타적인   access 접근, 이용   bidding 응찰, 입찰   proposal 제안, 제안서   compete 경쟁하다   go on the air 방송하다   suggest 암시하다, 제안하다   consider 고려하다

TEST 7

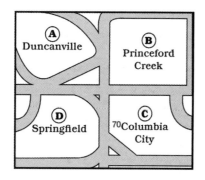

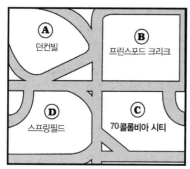

68

Who most likely are the speakers?
(A) Architects
(B) Government officials
(C) News reporters
(D) Contractors

화자들은 누구이겠는가?
(A) 건축가
(B) 공무원
(C) 기자
(D) 도급업자

해설 전체 내용 관련 – 화자들의 직업
남자가 첫 대사에서 오늘 저녁 6시 뉴스의 헤드라인(For tonight's six o'clock news broadcast, the lead story is ~)에 대해 말하고 있고, 두 번째 대사에서 우리가 방송 전에 이걸 확인할 수 있었다니 대단하다(It's great you were able to confirm this before we went on the air)고 말하는 것으로 보아 화자들은 기자임을 알 수 있다. 따라서 정답은 (C)이다.

69

What does the woman say she had access to?
(A) Uniform designs
(B) Sporting event tickets
(C) A company vehicle
(D) Bid proposals

여자는 무엇을 볼 수 있었다고 말하는가?
(A) 유니폼 디자인
(B) 스포츠 행사 입장권
(C) 회사 차량
(D) 입찰 제안서

어휘 vehicle 차량

해설 세부 사항 관련 – 여자가 볼 수 있었다고 말하는 것
여자가 첫 대사에서 입찰 제안서에 대한 독점 접근권을 얻었다(I've just gained exclusive access to some bidding proposals)고 말하고 있으므로 정답은 (D)이다.

70

Look at the graphic. According to the woman, where will a stadium most likely be located?
(A) At site A
(B) At site B
(C) At site C
(D) At site D

시각 정보에 의하면, 여자는 경기장이 어디에 위치할 것 같다고 말하는가?
(A) A 부지
(B) B 부지
(C) C 부지
(D) D 부지

어휘 be located 위치해 있다

해설 시각 정보 연계 – 여자가 말하는 경기장의 위치
남자가 두 번째 대사에서 새 경기장을 어디에 지을지 아는지(Do you know where the new stadium might be built?)를 묻자 여자는 한 문서에 따르면 콜롬비아 시티의 제안이 가장 유력하다고 한다(one document suggests that Columbia City's proposal is the favorite)고 말하고 있으며, 지도에 따르면 콜롬비아 시티는 C 부지이므로 정답은 (C)이다.

PART 4

71-73 광고

W-Am **71 Are you interested in learning how to start your own business? Winston Community College is the place for you! 72Last month, we opened a new campus in Cedarview** that offers lots of business courses to equip aspiring entrepreneurs with the tools to launch a new career. We offer flexible schedules so you can take courses in the evenings or on weekends. **73Visit us at our new campus or online to submit your application.**

자신의 사업을 시작하는 방법을 배우고 싶으신가요? 윈스턴 커뮤니티 칼리지가 바로 여러분을 위한 곳입니다! 지난달 시더뷰에 새 캠퍼스를 열고, 예비 창업가들에게 새로운 일을 시작할 수 있는 도구를 갖출 수 있게 해주는 다양한 비즈니스 과정을 제공하고 있습니다. 유연한 일정을 제공하니 저녁이나 주말에 강의를 들을 수 있습니다. 저희 새 캠퍼스나 온라인 방문을 통해 지원서를 제출하세요.

71

What is being advertised?
(A) An accounting firm
(B) A real estate office
(C) A trucking company
(D) A community college

무엇을 광고하고 있는가?
(A) 회계 사무소
(B) 부동산 사무소
(C) 화물 운송업체
(D) 커뮤니티 칼리지

어휘 advertise 광고하다

해설 전체 내용 관련 – 광고되고 있는 것

화자가 도입부에 사업을 시작하는 방법을 배우고 싶은지(Are you interested in learning how to start your own business?) 물으며 윈스턴 커뮤니티 칼리지가 바로 여러분을 위한 곳(Winston Community College is the place for you!)이라며 윈스턴 커뮤니티 칼리지를 홍보하고 있으므로 정답은 (D)이다.

72

What happened last month?
(A) A Web site was launched.
(B) A company merger was finalized.
(C) A new location was opened.
(D) A new director was hired.

지난달에 무슨 일이 있었는가?
(A) 웹사이트를 열었다.
(B) 회사 합병이 마무리됐다.
(C) 새로운 장소가 문을 열었다.
(D) 새 관리자가 고용됐다.

어휘 merger 합병 finalize 마무리하다 director 관리자, 책임자

해설 세부 사항 관련 – 지난달 있었던 일

화자가 중반부에 지난달 시더뷰에 새 캠퍼스를 열었다(Last month, we opened a new campus in Cedarview ~)고 말하고 있으므로 정답은 (C)이다.

> Paraphrasing 담화의 we opened a new campus in Cedarview
> → 정답의 A new location was opened.

73

What are the listeners invited to do?
(A) Join an online group
(B) Participate in a study
(C) Attend a workshop
(D) Submit an application

청자들이 권유받는 것은 무엇인가?
(A) 온라인 그룹에 가입하기
(B) 스터디 참여하기
(C) 워크숍 참석하기
(D) 지원서 제출하기

어휘 participate 참여하다

해설 세부 사항 관련 – 청자들이 권유받은 일

화자가 마지막에 새 캠퍼스나 온라인 방문을 통해 지원서를 제출하라(Visit us at our new campus or online to submit your application)고 권하고 있으므로 정답은 (D)이다.

74-76 회의 발췌

M-Cn **74Please be sure to mark your calendars for a get-together on April sixteenth.** We all work on different biochemistry research projects, and **74it's nice to share and celebrate our progress.** **75Sung-Hee has reserved us rooms at a conference center off-site where we'll be able to relax outdoors after our sessions.** Thanks for taking care of that, Sung-Hee. **76A few of you have asked whether we can hold other social events throughout the year.** We don't have the budget to do anything big, but I'd like to hear your ideas. Everyone has my e-mail address.

일정표에 4월 16일 모임을 꼭 표시해 두세요. 모두 서로 다른 생화학 업무 프로젝트를 수행하고 있으니 진행 상황을 공유하고 축하하면 좋겠습니다. 성희 씨가 컨퍼런스 센터 야외 공간을 예약했어요. 세션이 끝나고 그곳 야외에서 휴식을 취할 수 있습니다. 성희 씨, 처리해 주셔서 감사합니다. 몇몇 분들께서 일년 내내 친목 행사를 개최할 수 있는지 여부를 문의하셨어요. 큰 행사를 치를 예산은 없지만 여러분의 의견을 듣고 싶군요. 모두 제 이메일 주소를 알고 있죠.

어휘 get-together 모임 biochemistry 생화학 share 나누다, 공유하다 celebrate 기념하다, 축하하다 progress 진행, 진척 reserve 예약하다 off-site 부지 밖의, 실외의 throughout the year 일년 내내 budget 예산

74

What is scheduled for April 16?
(A) An awards banquet
(B) A software demonstration
(C) A company celebration
(D) A national holiday

4월 16일에 무엇이 예정되어 있는가?
(A) 시상식 연회
(B) 소프트웨어 시연
(C) 회사 축하 행사
(D) 국경일

어휘 demonstration 시연, 시범 설명

해설 세부 사항 관련 – 4월 16일에 예정되어 있는 일
화자가 도입부에 일정표에 4월 16일 모임을 꼭 표시해 두라(Please be sure to mark your calendars for a get-together on April sixteenth)고 권하면서 진행 상황을 공유하고 축하하면 좋겠다(it's nice to share and celebrate our progress)고 말하고 있는 것으로 보아 4월 16일에 회사 축하 행사가 예정되어 있음을 알 수 있다. 따라서 정답은 (C)이다.

75

What does the speaker thank Sung-Hee for doing?
(A) Presenting her research
(B) Approving a budget
(C) E-mailing an agenda
(D) Reserving some space

화자는 성희에게 무엇에 대해 감사하는가?
(A) 연구 발표
(B) 예산 승인
(C) 안건 이메일 송부
(D) 장소 예약

어휘 approve 승인하다 agenda 의제, 안건

해설 세부 사항 관련 – 화자가 성희에게 감사하는 것
화자가 중반부에 성희 씨가 컨퍼런스 센터 야외 공간을 예약했다(Sung-Hee has reserved us rooms at a conference center off-site ~)면서 성희 씨에게 처리해 줘서 감사하다(Thanks for taking care of that, Sung-Hee)고 했으므로 정답은 (D)이다.

> **Paraphrasing** 담화의 reserved us rooms
> → 정답의 Reserving some space

76

Why does the speaker say, "Everyone has my e-mail address"?
(A) To discourage the listeners from calling his phone
(B) To complain that he receives too many e-mails
(C) To explain how he learned about an opportunity
(D) To encourage the listeners to make suggestions

화자가 "모두 제 이메일 주소를 알고 있죠"라고 말하는 의도는 무엇인가?
(A) 청자들이 그에게 전화하지 못하게 하려고
(B) 너무 많은 이메일을 받고 있다고 불평하려고
(C) 기회에 대해 어떻게 알았는지 설명하려고
(D) 청자들에게 제안하는 것을 장려하려고

어휘 discourage ~ from … ~가 …하지 못하도록 막다 opportunity 기회 encourage 장려하나, 권장하다 make a suggestion 제안하다

해설 화자의 의도 파악 – 모두 이메일 주소를 알고 있다는 말의 의도
앞에서 몇몇 사람들이 일년 내내 친목 행사를 개최할 수 있는지 여부를 문의했다(A few of you have asked whether we can hold other social events throughout the year)면서 여러분의 의견을 듣고 싶다(~ I'd like to hear your ideas)고 말한 뒤 인용문을 언급하고 있으므로, 청자들이 이메일로 의견을 보내줄 것을 장려하는 의도로 한 말임을 알 수 있다. 따라서 정답은 (D)이다.

77-79 전화 메시지

M-Au My name is Raul Phillips. I know it's short notice, but **77 I'm a patient at your clinic, and I'd like to see a doctor today. 78 I ran in a local half-marathon yesterday,** and, well, I didn't feel pain at the time, but I think I sprained my ankle during the race. It's been sore since after the race, and I might need an x-ray. Could you call me back? **79 I'll be conducting some job interviews this morning,** so I may not be able to answer my phone, but please leave a message. My number is 555-0167. Thanks!

저는 라울 필립스입니다. 촉박한 통보라는 건 아는데요. **제가 그 병원 환자인데 오늘 진료를 받고 싶어요. 어제 지역 하프 마라톤에서 달리기를 했는데요.** 음, 당시엔 통증을 느끼지 않았는데 경기 중 발목을 삐끗한 것 같아요. 경기 이후로 아파서 엑스레이를 찍어야 할 것 같습니다. 저에게 전화해 주시겠어요? **오늘 오전에 면접을 진행할 예정이라서** 전화를 받지 못할 수도 있지만 메시지를 남겨 주세요. 제 번호는 555-0167입니다. 감사합니다!

어휘 short notice 촉박한 통보 local 지역의 feel pain 통증을 느끼다 sprain 삐다 ankle 발목 sore 아픈 conduct 하다 job interview 면접

77

Why is the speaker calling?
(A) To obtain a copy of his medical records
(B) To express interest in a job
(C) To complain about a service
(D) To request an appointment

화자가 전화한 이유는?
(A) 진료 기록 사본을 받으려고
(B) 일자리에 대한 관심을 표하려고
(C) 서비스에 대해 항의하려고
(D) 예약을 요청하려고

어휘 obtain 얻다, 구하다   medical record 진료 기록   express 나타내다, 표현하다   request 요청하다   appointment 약속

해설 전체 내용 관련 – 전화한 이유
화자가 초반부에 자신이 그 병원 환자인데 오늘 진료를 받고 싶다(~ I'm a patient at your clinic, and I'd like to see a doctor today)고 말하는 것으로 보아, 병원 진료 예약을 요청하려고 전화했음을 알 수 있다. 따라서 정답은 (D)이다.

> **Paraphrasing**   담화의 to see a doctor
> → 정답의 To request an appointment

78

What event did the speaker recently participate in?
(A) An art festival
(B) An athletic competition
(C) A career fair
(D) A walking tour

화자는 최근 어떤 행사에 참가했는가?
(A) 예술 축제
(B) 운동 경기
(C) 취업 박람회
(D) 도보 투어

해설 세부 사항 관련 – 화자가 최근에 참가한 행사
화자가 초반부에 어제 지역 하프 마라톤에서 달리기를 했다(I ran in a local half-marathon yesterday, ~)고 말하고 있으므로 정답은 (B)이다.

> **Paraphrasing**   담화의 half-marathon
> → 정답의 An athletic competition

79

What does the speaker say he will be doing this morning?
(A) Picking up supplies
(B) Holding interviews
(C) Giving a demonstration
(D) Touring a facility

화자는 오늘 오전에 무엇을 할 것이라고 말하는가?
(A) 물품 찾으러 가기
(B) 면접 진행하기
(C) 시연하기
(D) 시설 견학하기

어휘 supply 용품, 물품   demonstration 시연   facility 시설

해설 세부 사항 관련 – 화자가 오늘 오전에 할 것
화자가 후반부에 오늘 오전에 면접을 진행할 예정(I'll be conducting some job interviews this morning, ~)이라고 말하고 있으므로 정답은 (B)이다.

> **Paraphrasing**   담화의 conducting some job interviews
> → 정답의 Holding interviews

80-82 전화 메시지

M-Cn This is Giovanni calling from Salazar Market. **80 We're excited about selling your breakfast cereal in our store.** Our customers have been asking for your brand for several months now. **81 I'll be e-mailing you a contract later today.** You can sign it and send it back to me at your convenience. It states that we'll be displaying your cereals at the end of an aisle, on the endcap, as you requested. **82 You'll want to make sure we have enough boxes in the store to create a nice display and keep the shelves well stocked for you.**

살라자르 마켓의 지오반니입니다. **저희 매장에서 귀사의 아침 식사용 시리얼을 판매하게 되어 기쁩니다.** 저희 고객들이 몇 달째 귀사 상품을 요청했거든요. **오늘 오후 계약서를 이메일로 보내 드리겠습니다.** 편하실 때 서명하셔서 다시 보내주시면 됩니다. 요청하신 대로, 통로 끝에 있는 진열대에 시리얼을 진열하는 것으로 명시하고 있어요. **매장에 상자를 충분히 두어 진열을 멋지게 하고 선반에 물건을 잘 갖춰 두면 좋을 것 같습니다.**

어휘 contract 계약서   at one's convenience 편리한 때에, 형편이 되는 대로   state 명시하다   endcap 통로 끝 진열대   display 진열, 전시   stock (판매할 물건을) 갖춰 두다

80

What does the listener produce?
(A) Furniture
(B) Electronics
(C) Food
(D) Vehicles

청자는 무엇을 생산하는가?
(A) 가구
(B) 전자 제품
(C) 음식
(D) 차량

해설 세부 사항 관련 – 청자가 생산하는 것
화자가 초반부에 저희 매장에서 귀사의 아침 식사용 시리얼을 판매하게 되어 기쁘다(We're excited about selling your breakfast cereal in our store)고 했으므로 청자는 시리얼을 생산한다는 것을 알 수 있다. 따라서 정답은 (C)이다.

> **Paraphrasing**   담화의 breakfast cereal → 정답의 Food

81

What does the speaker say he will send the listener?
(A) A contract
(B) A delivery schedule
(C) Some display ideas
(D) Some coupons

화자는 청자에게 무엇을 보낼 것이라고 말하는가?
(A) 계약서
(B) 배송 일정
(C) 진열 아이디어
(D) 쿠폰

해설 세부 사항 관련 – 화자가 청자에게 보낼 것
화자가 중반부에 오후에 계약서를 이메일로 보내겠다(I'll be e-mailing you a contract later today)고 했으므로 정답은 (A)이다.

82

What does the speaker recommend doing?
(A) Lowering a price
(B) Advertising in a newspaper
(C) Developing new flavors
(D) Sending plenty of inventory

화자는 무엇을 하라고 권하는가?
(A) 가격 인하하기
(B) 신문에 광고 내기
(C) 새로운 맛 개발하기
(D) 재고 많이 보내기

어휘 lower 낮추다　develop 개발하다　plenty of 많은

해설 세부 사항 관련 – 화자의 추천 사항
화자가 마지막에 매장에 상자를 충분히 두어 진열을 멋지게 하고 선반에 물건을 잘 갖춰 두면 좋을 것 같다(You'll want to make sure we have enough boxes in the store to create a nice display and keep the shelves well stocked for you)며 제품을 많이 보내 달라고 권하고 있으므로 정답은 (D)이다.

83-85 회의 발췌

W-Am ⁸³**Team, let's debrief on the trial run of the DQY-5, our satellite Internet system. As you know, the DQY-5 is a small satellite dish that can be used to access the Internet in remote locations.** Test users have said that it generally works very well. ⁸⁴**However, they all report service interruptions when winter storms cover the satellite dish in snow.** That means we need to focus on designing an internal system that can heat up the satellite receiver and melt the snow to ensure that the connection is not disrupted. ⁸⁵**Let's break into groups of three and start brainstorming technical solutions.**

팀 여러분, 우리 위성 인터넷 시스템인 DQY-5의 시험 가동에 대한 보고를 듣도록 하죠. 아시다시피 DQY-5는 외딴 지역에서 인터넷에 접속할 때 사용할 수 있는 소형 위성 방송 수신 안테나입니다. 시험 사용자들은 대체로 잘 작동한다고 말했습니다. 그런데 모두들 겨울철 폭풍우로 안테나가 눈에 덮일 때 서비스 중단이 일어난다고 보고했어요. 위성 수신기를 덥혀 눈을 녹여서 연결이 중단되지 않도록 하는 내부 시스템을 설계하는 데 초점을 맞춰야 한다는 뜻입니다. 세 명씩 그룹을 나눠서 기술적인 해결책에 대해 아이디어를 내 보죠.

어휘 debrief 보고를 듣다　satellite 위성　satellite dish 위성 방송 수신 안테나　access 접속하다　remote 외딴, 먼　generally 대체로　interruption 중단　receiver 수신기　melt 녹이다　connection 연결　disrupt 방해하다, 지장을 주다　brainstorm 아이디어를 짜내다　technical 기술적인　solution 해결책

83

What type of product has the team developed?
(A) A robot for household tasks
(B) A mobile application for weather updates
(C) A satellite dish for Internet access
(D) A smartwatch for fitness tracking

팀은 어떤 종류의 제품을 개발했는가?
(A) 가사일을 위한 로봇
(B) 날씨 업데이트를 위한 모바일 앱
(C) 인터넷 접속을 위한 위성 방송 수신 안테나
(D) 피트니스 추적을 위한 스마트 워치

어휘 household task 가사일　tracking 추적

해설 세부 사항 관련 – 팀이 개발한 제품의 종류
화자가 초반부에 팀에게 위성 인터넷 시스템인 DQY-5의 시험 가동에 대한 보고를 듣도록 하자(Team, let's debrief on the trial run of the DQY-5, our satellite Internet system)면서 DQY-5는 외딴 지역에서 인터넷에 접속할 때 사용할 수 있는 소형 위성 방송 수신 안테나(the DQY-5 is a small satellite dish that can be used to access the Internet in remote locations)라고 설명하고 있으므로 정답은 (C)이다.

> **Paraphrasing** 담화의 a small satellite dish that can be used to access the Internet
> → 정답의 A satellite dish for Internet access

84

What has caused a problem for some users?
(A) Limited screen options
(B) A short battery life
(C) Unclear instructions
(D) Poor weather conditions

무엇이 일부 사용자들에게 문제를 일으켰는가?
(A) 한정된 스크린 선택지
(B) 짧은 배터리 수명
(C) 명확하지 않은 설명
(D) 좋지 않은 기상 조건

어휘 limited 제한된, 한정된 option 선택 instruction 설명, 지시
weather condition 기상 조건

해설 세부 사항 관련 – 일부 사용자들에게 일어난 문제의 원인

화자가 중반부에 모두들 겨울철 폭풍우로 안테나가 눈에 덮일 때 서비스 중단이 일어난다고 보고했다(they all report service interruptions when winter storms cover the satellite dish in snow)고 했으므로 정답은 (D)이다.

> **Paraphrasing** 담화의 winter storms
> → 정답의 Poor weather conditions

85

What will the listeners most likely do next?
(A) Take a break
(B) Work in small groups
(C) Visit a production facility
(D) Take some measurements

청자들은 다음으로 무엇을 하겠는가?
(A) 휴식 취하기
(B) 소그룹으로 작업하기
(C) 생산 시설 방문하기
(D) 치수 재기

어휘 take a break 휴식을 취하다 production facility 생산 시설
take measurements 치수를 재다

해설 세부 사항 관련 – 청자들이 다음에 할 일

화자가 마지막에 세 명씩 그룹을 나눠서 기술적인 해결책에 대해 아이디어를 내 보자(Let's break into groups of three and start brainstorming technical solutions)고 말하는 것으로 보아 청자들은 소그룹으로 작업할 예정임을 알 수 있다. 따라서 정답은 (B)이다.

> **Paraphrasing** 담화의 break into groups of three and
> start brainstorming technical solutions
> → 정답의 Work in small groups

86-88 공지　　　　　　　　 동영상 강의

> M-Au Thanks for joining us for this evening's community orchestra performance. **86The concert was scheduled to begin at eight P.M. Unfortunately, some of the microphones aren't working.** **86So while our sound engineers are correcting the issue,** I'd like to tell you about an opportunity to help the theater. **87You may notice that all our ushers are volunteers, and we're always looking for more.** Ushers take tickets, help patrons find their seats, and then, of course, get to enjoy the concert for free. **88If you're interested, be sure to check page four of your program booklet for more details.**

> 오늘 저녁 지역 오케스트라 공연에 와 주셔서 감사합니다. **음악회는 오후 8시에 시작될 예정이었는데요.** **안타깝게도 마이크 일부가 작동하지 않고 있습니다.** 그래서 저희 음향 기술자들이 문제를 바로잡는 동안 여러분께 극장을 도울 수 있는 기회에 대해 말씀드리고자 합니다. **저희 좌석 안내원 전원이 자원봉사자라는 것을 아셨을 텐데요. 항상 더 많은 분들을 찾고 있습니다.** 안내원은 표를 받고 고객이 좌석을 찾도록 도와드리는 일을 합니다. 그리고 물론 음악회를 무료로 즐길 수 있지요. **관심이 있으시면 저희 프로그램 소책자 4페이지에서 세부 사항을 확인해 주세요.**

어휘 performance 공연 be scheduled to ~할 예정이다
engineer 기사, 기술자 correct 바로잡다, 고치다 issue 문제
opportunity 기회 notice (보거나 듣고) 알다 usher 좌석
안내원 volunteer 자원봉사자 patron 후원자, 고객 booklet
소책자

86

Why does the speaker say, "Unfortunately, some of the microphones aren't working"?
(A) To suggest purchasing new equipment
(B) To recommend changing a venue
(C) To ask the listeners to remain silent
(D) To apologize for a delay

화자가 "안타깝게도 마이크 일부가 작동하지 않고 있습니다"라고 말하는 이유는?
(A) 새 장비 구입을 제안하려고
(B) 장소 변경을 권하려고
(C) 청자들에게 정숙을 유지해 달라고 요청하려고
(D) 지연에 대해 사과하려고

어휘 equipment 장비 venue 장소 apologize 사과하다 delay
지연

해설 화자의 의도 파악 – 안타깝게도 마이크 일부가 작동하지 않고 있다는 말의 의도

앞에서 화자가 음악회는 오후 8시에 시작될 예정이었다(The concert was scheduled to begin at eight P.M.)고 말한 뒤 인용문을 언급했고, 뒤이어 음향 기술자들이 문제를 바로잡고 있다(while our sound engineers are correcting the issue ~)고 알렸으므로 청자들에게 지연에 대해 사과하려는 의도로 한 말임을 알 수 있다. 따라서 정답은 (D)이다.

87

What are the listeners invited to do?
(A) Upgrade their tickets
(B) Become volunteers
(C) Participate in a contest
(D) Ask the performers some questions

청자들이 권유받는 것은 무엇인가?
(A) 표 업그레이드하기
(B) 자원봉사하기

(C) 대회 참가하기
(D) 연주자들에게 질문하기

어휘 participate 참가하다   performer 연주자, 연기자

해설 세부 사항 관련 – 청자들이 권유받은 일

화자가 중반부에 좌석 안내원 전원이 자원봉사자인데 더 많은 분들을 찾고 있나(You may notice that all our ushers are volunteers, and we're always looking for more)며 자원봉사를 권하고 있으므로 정답은 (B)이다.

88

Where does the speaker say some information can be found?

(A) On a posted sign
(B) At the box office
(C) In a program booklet
(D) On a Web site

화자는 어디서 정보를 찾을 수 있다고 말하는가?

(A) 게시된 표지판
(B) 매표소
(C) 프로그램 소책자
(D) 웹사이트

어휘 post 게시하다   box office 매표소

해설 세부 사항 관련 – 정보를 찾을 수 있는 곳

화자가 마지막에 관심이 있으면 프로그램 소책자 4페이지에서 세부 사항을 확인하라(If you're interested, be sure to check page four of your program booklet for more details)고 말하고 있으므로 정답은 (C)이다.

89-91 연설

 동영상 강의

> W-Br I'm Natalie from Akroy Technologies, and **⁸⁹I'm here to train everyone on using System Ace, your new project management software. ⁹⁰Since you organize and provide a venue for professional conferences and trade shows,** System Ace will allow you to create separate project folders for each event. This means that event-related to-do lists, schedules, and other documents for each folder will all be in one place. Now—the best way to learn a new program is by using it. ⁹¹**So please, get out your tablet or laptop.** We're going to try a few things together.

아크로이 테크놀로지의 나탈리입니다. **새 프로젝트 관리 소프트웨어인 시스템 에이스 사용에 대해 여러분을 교육해 드리러 왔습니다. 여러분은 전문가 회의와 무역 박람회 장소를 준비하고 제공하시니,** 시스템 에이스가 행사별로 별도의 프로젝트 폴더를 만드실 수 있도록 해 드릴 겁

니다. 이벤트 관련하여 각 폴더의 해야 할 일 목록, 일정, 기타 문서가 한곳에 있게 된다는 뜻입니다. 자, 새 프로그램을 배우는 가장 좋은 방법은 사용해 보는 것이죠. **여러분의 태블릿이나 노트북 컴퓨터를 꺼내 주세요.** 다같이 몇 가지 해 볼게요.

어휘 management 관리   organize 준비하다, 조직하다
venue 장소   professional 전문가의   trade show 무역 박람회
separate 별개의, 분리된   -related ~에 관련된

89

What is the focus of the training?

(A) Using some software
(B) Processing customer complaints
(C) Securing sensitive documents
(D) Creating advertisements

교육은 무엇에 중점을 두는가?

(A) 소프트웨어 사용
(B) 고객 불만 처리
(C) 민감한 문서 보호
(D) 광고 제작

어휘 process 처리하다   complaint 불평, 불만   secure 보호하다
sensitive 민감한, 예민한   advertisement 광고

해설 전체 내용 관련 – 교육의 주제

화자가 도입부에 새 프로젝트 관리 소프트웨어인 시스템 에이스 사용에 대한 교육을 하러 왔다(I'm here to train everyone on using System Ace, your new project management software)고 말하고 있으므로 정답은 (A)이다.

90

Where do the listeners most likely work?

(A) At a conference center
(B) At a factory
(C) At a warehouse
(D) At a department store

청자들은 어디서 일하겠는가?

(A) 컨퍼런스 센터
(B) 공장
(C) 창고
(D) 백화점

해설 전체 내용 관련 – 청자들의 근무지

화자가 중반부에 여러분은 전문가 회의와 무역 박람회 장소를 준비하고 제공한다(Since you organize and provide a venue for professional conferences and trade shows ~)고 말하고 있는 것으로 보아 청자들은 컨퍼런스 센터에서 근무하는 사람들임을 알 수 있다. 따라서 정답은 (A)이다.

91

What does the speaker ask the listeners to do?
(A) Create an account
(B) Open a manual
(C) Fill out a form
(D) Take out an electronic device

화자는 청자들에게 무엇을 하라고 요청하는가?
(A) 계정 만들기
(B) 설명서 펴기
(C) 서식 작성하기
(D) 전자 기기 꺼내기

어휘 account 계정, 계좌   manual 설명서   fill out a form 서식을 작성하다, 양식을 기입하다   electronic device 전자 기기

해설 세부 사항 관련 – 화자의 요청 사항
화자가 마지막에 청자들에게 태블릿이나 노트북 컴퓨터를 꺼낼 것(So please, get out your tablet or laptop)을 요청하고 있으므로 정답은 (D)이다.

Paraphrasing   담화의 get out your tablet or laptop
→ 정답의 Take out an electronic device

92-94 담화

M-Au ⁹²In this online session, I'd like to discuss how small businesses like those represented here today can be more energy efficient. For example, some companies install solar panels to reduce their electricity costs. Now, we all have different ideas about how to conserve energy. ⁹³What does your company do to reduce its carbon footprint? There's a lot of combined knowledge at this meeting. Let's take advantage of that. Please submit your questions and comments in the chat. ⁹⁴By the way, this session is being recorded so that it's available to all participants after the session.

이번 온라인 시간에는 오늘 여기서 제시한 소기업들이 어떻게 에너지 **효율성을 높일 수 있는지에 대해 이야기하고 싶습니다.** 예를 들어 일부 회사는 전기 요금을 줄이기 위해 태양 전지판을 설치합니다. 자, 우리 모두는 에너지 보존 방법에 대해 서로 다른 생각을 갖고 있죠. **여러분의 회사는 탄소 발자국을 줄이기 위해 무엇을 하고 있나요?** 이 회의에는 많은 지식이 모여 있습니다. 이걸 이용해 보죠. 여러분의 질문과 의견을 채팅으로 말해 주세요. **그런데 이번 시간은 세션이 끝난 후 모든 참가자들이 이용할 수 있도록 녹화되고 있습니다.**

어휘 represent 제시하다   energy efficient 에너지 효율성이 있는   install 설치하다   solar panel 태양 전지판   reduce 줄이다, 감소시키다   electricity cost 전기 요금   conserve 보존하다   carbon footprint 탄소 발자국   combined 결합된, 결부된   knowledge 지식   take advantage of ~을 이용하다   available 이용 가능한, 구할 수 있는   participant 참가자

92

What is the topic of the talk?
(A) Customer satisfaction
(B) Career development
(C) Energy efficiency
(D) Time management

담화의 주제는 무엇인가?
(A) 고객 만족
(B) 경력 개발
(C) 에너지 효율성
(D) 시간 관리

어휘 satisfaction 만족

해설 전체 내용 관련 – 담화의 주제
화자가 도입부에 이번 온라인 시간에는 오늘 여기서 제시한 소기업들이 어떻게 에너지 효율성을 높일 수 있는지에 대해 이야기하고 싶다(In this online session, I'd like to discuss how small businesses like those represented here today can be more energy efficient)고 했으므로 정답은 (C)이다.

93

Why does the speaker say, "There's a lot of combined knowledge at this meeting"?
(A) To encourage participation
(B) To indicate an agenda change
(C) To stress the importance of leadership
(D) To correct a misconception

화자가 "이 회의에는 많은 지식이 모여 있습니다"라고 말하는 이유는?
(A) 참여를 장려하려고
(B) 안건 변경을 시사하려고
(C) 리더십의 중요성을 강조하려고
(D) 오해를 바로잡으려고

어휘 encourage 장려하다, 권장하다   indicate 나타내다, 시사하다   agenda 안건, 의제   stress 강조하다   correct 바로잡다   misconception 오해

해설 화자의 의도 파악 – 회의에 많은 지식이 모여 있다는 말의 의도
앞에서 여러분의 회사는 탄소 발자국을 줄이기 위해 무엇을 하고 있는지(What does your company do to reduce its carbon footprint?)를 물은 뒤 인용문을 언급하는 것으로 보아, 청자들의 참여를 독려하기 위한 의도로 한 말임을 알 수 있다. 따라서 정답은 (A)이다.

94

What does the speaker say will happen after the talk?
(A) Refreshments will be served.
(B) Payment will be collected.
(C) A group photograph will be taken.
(D) A recording will be shared.

화자는 담화 후 무슨 일이 있을 것이라고 말하는가?
(A) 다과가 제공된다.
(B) 지불할 돈을 걷는다.
(C) 단체 사진을 찍는다.
(D) 녹화본을 공유한다.

어휘 refreshments 다과   payment 지불, 결제   collect 모으다

해설 세부 사항 관련 – 담화 후에 있을 일

화자가 마지막에 이번 시간은 세션이 끝난 후 모든 참가자들이 이용할 수 있도록 녹화된다(this session is being recorded so that it's available to all participants after the session)고 말하고 있으므로 정답은 (D)이다.

95-97 회의 발췌 + 표

M-Cn Thanks for coming to this weekly briefing. As you know, **95 Joe's Trucking Company takes safety very seriously, and I'm glad all our drivers are able to attend today.** So we have five loads to deliver, including two loads of steel beams. **96 Yasushi, you've been assigned to the car carrier, so please be sure to follow the safety checklist,** especially the part about securely fastening all restraints. Junko, **97 I'm concerned the lumber you're carrying will be considered oversize.** I think the company will need to obtain a permit for you— we'll talk after the meeting.

이번 주간 브리핑에 와 주셔서 감사합니다. 아시다시피 조 화물 운송업체는 안전을 매우 중요하게 여기며 운전기사 전원이 오늘 참석하실 수 있게 되어 기쁩니다. 강철 빔 두 개를 포함해 배송할 화물이 다섯 개 있습니다. 야스시 씨, 자동차 운반차로 배정되었으니 안전 점검 목록을 잘 따라 주세요. 특히 모든 안전 장치를 단단히 죄는 것에 대한 부분이요. 준코 씨, 운반하실 목재가 너무 크다고 여겨질까 우려됩니다. 회사에서 허가증을 받아야 할 거예요. 회의 이후 얘기할 겁니다.

어휘 safety 안전   seriously 진지하게, 심각하게   load 짐, 화물   assign 배정하다   car carrier 자동차 운반차   especially 특히   securely 확실하게, 단단하게   fasten 조이다, 매다   restraint (움직임을 제한하는) 안전 장치   concerned 걱정하는, 염려하는   lumber 목재   obtain 얻다, 구하다   permit 허가증

Load Description	Load Length
Propane	10 meters
Automobiles	13 meters
97 Lumber	**20 meters**
Steel beams	25 meters

화물 설명	화물 길이
프로판	10미터
자동차	13미터
97 목재	**20미터**
강철 빔	25미터

어휘 description 설명   length 길이

95

Who most likely are the listeners?
(A) Warehouse supervisors
(B) Construction workers
(C) Safety inspectors
(D) Truck drivers

청자들은 누구이겠는가?
(A) 창고 관리자
(B) 건설 근로자
(C) 안전 감독관
(D) 트럭 기사

어휘 warehouse 창고   supervisor 감독관, 관리자   construction 공사, 건설   inspector 감독관

해설 전체 내용 관련 – 청자들의 직업

화자가 초반부에 조 화물 운송업체는 안전을 매우 중요하게 여기며 운전기사 전원이 오늘 참석할 수 있게 되어 기쁘다(Joe's Trucking Company takes safety very seriously, and I'm glad all our drivers are able to attend today)고 말하고 있으므로 청자들은 트럭 기사임을 알 수 있다. 따라서 정답은 (D)이다.

96

What does the speaker remind Yasushi to do?
(A) Park in a different location
(B) Follow a checklist
(C) Contact a customer
(D) Check a schedule

화자는 야스시에게 무엇을 하라고 상기시키는가?
(A) 다른 장소에 주차하기
(B) 점검 목록 따르기
(C) 고객에게 연락하기
(D) 일정 확인하기

어휘 contact 연락하다

해설 세부 사항 관련 – 화자가 야스시에게 상기시키는 것

화자가 중반부에 야스시 씨에게 자동차 운반차로 배정되었으니 안전 점검 목록을 잘 따르라(Yasushi, you've been assigned to the car carrier, so please be sure to follow the safety checklist)고 말하고 있으므로 정답은 (B)이다.

97

Look at the graphic. Which load length is the speaker concerned about?

(A) 10 meters
(B) 13 meters
(C) 20 meters
(D) 25 meters

시각 정보에 의하면, 화자는 어떤 화물 길이에 대해 염려하는가?

(A) 10미터
(B) 13미터
(C) 20미터
(D) 25미터

해설 시각 정보 연계 – 화자가 염려하는 화물 길이

화자가 후반부에 운반할 목재가 너무 크다고 여겨질까 우려된다(I'm concerned the lumber you're carrying will be considered oversize)고 말하고 있고, 표에 따르면 목재의 화물 길이는 20미터이므로 정답은 (C)이다.

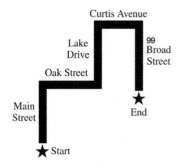

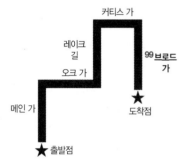

98-100 방송 + 지도

W-Br Welcome to the evening news program on WXNL Radio. In local news, **98the much-anticipated holiday parade will be held downtown this Saturday, beginning promptly at ten A.M.** on Main Street. However, according to the city government's Web site, there's been one important change. The parade was supposed to follow a route along five city roads, **99but because of traffic concerns, the parade will now stop at the end of Curtis Avenue instead of continuing to the originally planned end point.** Now, in case you're wondering whether we'll have sunny skies or clouds on the day of the parade, **100stay tuned after the commercial break for our weekend forecast.**

WXNL 라디오 저녁 뉴스 프로그램에 오신 것을 환영합니다. 지역 소식으로, 학수고대하던 휴일 퍼레이드가 이번 주 토요일 오전 10시 정각부터 시내 메인 가에서 열립니다. 그런데 시 정부 웹사이트에 따르면 한 가지 중요한 변경 사항이 있는데요. 퍼레이드는 5개의 시 도로 노선을 따라가기로 되어 있었는데, 교통에 대한 우려 때문에 원래 계획한 도착점까지 계속 가는 대신 커티스 가 끝에서 끝날 예정입니다. 자, 퍼레이드 당일 화창할지 흐릴지 궁금하시다면 광고 후 주말 일기 예보를 전해 드릴 테니 주파수를 고정해 주세요.

어휘 local 지역의 much-anticipated 몹시 기다리던 parade 퍼레이드, 가두 행진 promptly 정확히 제시간에 according to ~에 따르면 government 정부 be supposed to ~하기로 되어 있다 concern 우려 instead of ~ 대신에 originally 원래 in case ~할 경우에 stay tuned 주파수를 고정하다 commercial break 광고 방송 시간 forecast 예보, 예측

98

What will begin at 10 A.M. on Saturday?

(A) A holiday parade
(B) A bicycle race
(C) A new bus route
(D) Some road construction

토요일 오전 10시에 무엇이 시작될 것인가?

(A) 휴일 퍼레이드
(B) 자전거 경주
(C) 새 버스 노선
(D) 도로 공사

어휘 construction 공사, 건설

해설 세부 사항 관련 – 토요일 오전 10시에 시작되는 것

화자가 초반부에 학수고대하던 휴일 퍼레이드가 이번 주 토요일 오전 10시 정각부터 시내 메인 가에서 열린다(the much-anticipated holiday parade will be held downtown this Saturday, beginning promptly at ten A.M.)고 안내하고 있으므로 정답은 (A)이다.

99

Look at the graphic. Which road will be excluded?

(A) Oak Street
(B) Lake Drive
(C) Curtis Avenue
(D) Broad Street

시각 정보에 의하면, 어떤 길이 제외될 것인가?

(A) 오크 가
(B) 레이크 길
(C) 커티스 가
(D) 브로드 가

해설 시각 정보 연계 – 제외될 길

화자가 중반부에 교통에 대한 우려 때문에 원래 계획한 도착점까지 계속 가는 대신 커티스 가 끝에서 끝날 예정(because of traffic concerns, the parade will now stop at the end of Curtis Avenue instead of continuing to the originally planned end point)이라고 말하고 있고, 지도에 따르면 커티스 가 다음 길이 브로드 가이므로 브로드 가가 제외된다는 것을 알 수 있다. 따라서 정답은 (D)이다.

100

What will the listeners hear after a commercial break?
(A) A financial report
(B) A weather forecast
(C) An interview with a government official
(D) A live musical performance

청자들은 광고 후 무엇을 들을 것인가?
(A) 금융 정보
(B) 일기 예보
(C) 공무원과의 인터뷰
(D) 음악 공연 생방송

어휘 financial 금융의, 재무의   government official 공무원
performance 공연

해설 세부 사항 관련 – 청자들이 광고 시간 이후 들을 내용

화자가 마지막에 광고 후 주말 일기 예보가 있으니 주파수를 고정하라(stay tuned after the commercial break for our weekend forecast)고 말하고 있으므로 정답은 (B)이다.

Paraphrasing	담화의 weekend forecast
	→ 정답의 A weather forecast

1 (D)	2 (B)	3 (D)	4 (C)	5 (B)
6 (A)	7 (B)	8 (A)	9 (B)	10 (B)
11 (C)	12 (B)	13 (B)	14 (B)	15 (A)
16 (C)	17 (A)	18 (B)	19 (C)	20 (A)
21 (B)	22 (C)	23 (B)	24 (B)	25 (A)
26 (A)	27 (C)	28 (A)	29 (C)	30 (C)
31 (B)	32 (A)	33 (C)	34 (B)	35 (B)
36 (A)	37 (D)	38 (D)	39 (C)	40 (A)
41 (B)	42 (C)	43 (B)	44 (D)	45 (A)
46 (A)	47 (B)	48 (C)	49 (D)	50 (D)
51 (A)	52 (D)	53 (B)	54 (A)	55 (D)
56 (C)	57 (A)	58 (D)	59 (D)	60 (B)
61 (A)	62 (B)	63 (A)	64 (D)	65 (B)
66 (C)	67 (B)	68 (A)	69 (D)	70 (D)
71 (B)	72 (A)	73 (C)	74 (A)	75 (B)
76 (C)	77 (C)	78 (A)	79 (D)	80 (D)
81 (B)	82 (A)	83 (B)	84 (C)	85 (D)
86 (C)	87 (B)	88 (C)	89 (A)	90 (A)
91 (B)	92 (B)	93 (D)	94 (A)	95 (A)
96 (C)	97 (B)	98 (B)	99 (D)	100 (C)

PART 1

1 W-Am

(A) She's taking off her badge.
(B) She's leaning over a desk.
(C) She's locking a door.
(D) She's lifting a bin.

(A) 여자가 명찰을 떼고 있다.
(B) 여자가 책상 위로 몸을 구부리고 있다.
(C) 여자가 문을 잠그고 있다.
(D) 여자가 쓰레기통을 들어올리고 있다.

어휘 lean over ~ 너머로 몸을 구부리다 lock 잠그다 lift 들어올리다

해설 1인 등장 사진 – 사람의 동작/상태 묘사
(A) 동사 오답. 여자가 명찰을 떼고 있는(is taking off her badge) 모습이 아니므로 오답.
(B) 사진에 없는 명사를 이용한 오답. 사진에 책상(a desk)의 모습이 보이지 않으므로 오답.

(C) 동사 오답. 여자가 문을 잠그고 있는(is locking a door) 모습이 아니므로 오답.
(D) 정답. 여자가 쓰레기통을 들어올리고 있는(is lifting a bin) 모습이므로 정답.

2 M-Au

(A) A man is repairing a railing.
(B) A man is climbing some stairs.
(C) A man is carrying a ladder.
(D) A man is looking up at a roof.

(A) 남자가 난간을 수리하고 있다.
(B) 남자가 계단을 오르고 있다.
(C) 남자가 사다리를 나르고 있다.
(D) 남자가 지붕을 쳐다보고 있다.

어휘 repair 수리하다 railing 난간 climb 오르다 ladder 사다리
look up at (시선을 들어) ~을 쳐다보다

해설 1인 등장 사진 – 사람의 동작/상태 묘사
(A) 동사 오답. 남자가 난간을 수리하고 있는(is repairing a railing) 모습이 아니므로 오답.
(B) 정답. 남자가 계단을 오르고 있는(is climbing some stairs) 모습이므로 정답.
(C) 사진에 없는 명사를 이용한 오답. 사진에 사다리(a ladder)의 모습이 보이지 않으므로 오답.
(D) 동사 오답. 남자가 지붕을 쳐다보고 있는(is looking up at a roof) 모습이 아니므로 오답.

3 W-Br

(A) A person is swimming in a lake.
(B) A sign is posted on a building.
(C) A bird is resting on a pole.
(D) A person is rowing a boat.

(A) 한 사람이 호수에서 수영하고 있다.
(B) 건물에 표지판이 붙어 있다.
(C) 새가 장대에서 쉬고 있다.
(D) 한 사람이 배를 젓고 있다.

어휘 post 게시하다 rest 쉬다 pole 기둥, 장대 row 노를 젓다

해설 혼합 사진 – 사람/사물/풍경 혼합 묘사

(A) 동사 오답. 호수에서 수영하고 있는(is swimming in a lake) 사람의 모습이 보이지 않으므로 오답.
(B) 사진에 없는 명사를 이용한 오답. 사진에 표지판(A sign)의 모습이 보이지 않으므로 오답.
(C) 사진에 없는 명사를 이용한 오답. 사진에 새(A bird)의 모습이 보이지 않으므로 오답.
(D) 정답. 배를 젓고 있는(is rowing a boat) 사람의 모습이 보이므로 정답.

---

4 M-Au

(A) One of the workers is opening a display case.
(B) One of the workers is tying a necktie.
(C) The workers are behind a counter.
(D) The workers are greeting some customers.

(A) 직원들 중 한 명이 진열장을 열고 있다.
(B) 직원들 중 한 명이 넥타이를 매고 있다.
(C) 직원들이 카운터 뒤편에 있다.
(D) 직원들이 손님들을 맞이하고 있다.

어휘 display 전시, 진열   tie 묶다, 매다   greet 맞다, 환영하다

해설 2인 이상 등장 사진 – 사람의 동작/상태 묘사

(A) 동사 오답. 진열장을 열고 있는(is opening a display case) 직원의 모습이 보이지 않으므로 오답.
(B) 동사 오답. 넥타이를 매고 있는(is tying a necktie) 직원의 모습이 보이지 않으므로 오답.
(C) 정답. 직원들이 카운터 뒤편에 있는(are behind a counter) 모습이므로 정답.
(D) 동사 오답. 직원들이 손님들을 맞이하고 있는(are greeting some customers) 모습이 아니므로 오답.

---

5 M-Cn

▶ 동영상 강의

(A) Some rocks are piled in a wheelbarrow.
(B) Some telephone wires are suspended over a road.
(C) Some benches are occupied.
(D) Some trees are shading a picnic table.

(A) 손수레에 돌이 쌓여 있다.
(B) 길 위에 전화선이 걸려 있다.
(C) 벤치들이 사용되고 있다.
(D) 나무들이 피크닉 테이블에 그늘을 드리우고 있다.

어휘 pile 쌓다   wheelbarrow 외바퀴 손수레   suspend 매달다, 걸다
occupied 사용 중인, 점령된   shade 그늘지게 하다

해설 사물/풍경 사진 – 풍경 묘사

(A) 사진에 없는 명사를 이용한 오답. 사진에 손수레(a wheelbarrow)의 모습이 보이지 않으므로 오답.
(B) 정답. 전화선(Some telephone wires)이 길 위에 걸려 있는(are suspended over a road) 모습이므로 정답.
(C) 상태 오답. 벤치들(Some benches)이 사용되고 있는(are occupied) 상태가 아니므로 오답.
(D) 동사 오답. 나무들(Some trees)이 피크닉 테이블에 그늘을 드리우고 있는(are shading a picnic table) 모습이 아니므로 오답.

---

6 W-Am

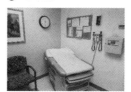

(A) Some papers have been pinned to a bulletin board.
(B) A clock has been set on a bedside table.
(C) A painting has been propped against a chair.
(D) Some medical equipment has been placed on a shelf.

(A) 게시판에 종이들이 핀으로 꽂혀 있다.
(B) 시계가 침대 옆 탁자 위에 놓여 있다.
(C) 그림이 의자에 받쳐져 있다.
(D) 의료 장비가 선반에 놓여 있다.

어휘 pin (핀 등으로) 고정시키다   bulletin board 게시판
prop against ~에 받쳐 놓다, 괴어 두다   medical equipment
의료 장비   place 놓다, 두다

해설 사물/풍경 사진 – 사물 묘사

(A) 정답. 종이들(Some papers)이 게시판에 핀으로 꽂혀 있는(have been pinned to a bulletin board) 모습이므로 정답.
(B) 사진에 없는 명사를 이용한 오답. 사진에 침대 옆 탁자(a bedside table)의 모습이 보이지 않으므로 오답.
(C) 동사 오답. 그림(A painting)이 의자에 받쳐져 있는(has been propped against a chair) 모습이 아니므로 오답.
(D) 사진에 없는 명사를 이용한 오답. 사진에 선반(a shelf)의 모습이 보이지 않으므로 오답.

PART 2

7

W-Br Who's picking up the newspaper?

M-Au (A) Some paper napkins.
　　　(B) Camille said she will.
　　　(C) He took out the trash.

누가 신문을 가져올 건가요?

(A) 종이 냅킨이요.

(B) 카밀이 자기가 할 거라고 했어요.

(C) 그가 쓰레기를 꺼냈어요.

어휘 take out 꺼내다   trash 쓰레기

해설 신문을 가져올 사람을 묻는 Who 의문문

(A) 유사 발음 오답. 질문의 newspaper와 부분적으로 발음이 유사한 paper를 이용한 오답.

(B) 정답. 신문을 가져올 사람이 누구인지 묻는 질문에 카밀이 하겠다고 했다고 구체적으로 알려 주고 있으므로 정답.

(C) 질문과 상관없는 오답. 질문에 3인칭 대명사 He로 지칭할 인물이 언급된 적이 없으므로 오답.

8

W-Br   When is your doctor's appointment?

M-Cn   (A) This afternoon.

(B) That's a good point.

(C) At a medical clinic.

진료 예약이 언제죠?

(A) 오늘 오후요.

(B) 좋은 지적이네요.

(C) 병원에서요.

어휘 appointment 약속   medical clinic 병원

해설 진료 예약 시간을 묻는 When 의문문

(A) 정답. 진료 예약 시간을 묻는 질문에 오늘 오후라고 응답하고 있으므로 정답.

(B) 유사 발음 오답. 질문의 appointment와 부분적으로 발음이 유사한 point를 이용한 오답.

(C) 연상 단어 오답. 질문의 doctor에서 연상 가능한 a medical clinic을 이용한 오답.

9

M-Cn   Why don't we have a company picnic?

W-Am   (A) Potato salad and green beans.

(B) Because it costs a lot of money.

(C) I already have that one.

우리는 회사 야유회를 왜 안 가죠?

(A) 감자 샐러드와 그린빈이요.

(B) 비용이 많이 들어서요.

(C) 그건 이미 갖고 있어요.

어휘 cost 비용이 들다

해설 회사 야유회를 가지 않는 이유를 묻는 Why 의문문

(A) 연상 단어 오답. 질문의 picnic에서 연상 가능한 salad를 이용한 오답.

(B) 정답. 회사 야유회를 가지 않는 이유를 묻는 질문에 비용이 많이 들기 때문이라고 구체적인 이유를 제시하고 있으므로 정답.

(C) 단어 반복 오답. 질문의 have를 반복 이용한 오답.

10

W-Br   What do you think I should take to the conference?

M-Au   (A) In the lobby.

(B) Just your laptop.

(C) A three o'clock shift.

제가 회의에 뭘 가져가야 할 것 같아요?

(A) 로비에서요.

(B) 노트북 컴퓨터만요.

(C) 3시 교대 근무예요.

어휘 conference 회의   shift 교대 근무 시간

해설 회의에 가져가야 할 것에 대해 묻는 What 의문문

(A) 질문과 상관없는 오답. Where 의문문에 대한 응답이므로 오답.

(B) 정답. 회의에 가져가야 할 것에 대해 묻는 질문에 노트북 컴퓨터라고 구체적으로 제시하고 있으므로 정답.

(C) 질문과 상관없는 오답.

11

M-Au   Where's the festival being held?

W-Br   (A) A music concert.

(B) Probably sometime in December.

(C) In the town center.

축제는 어디서 열릴 예정이죠?

(A) 음악회요.

(B) 아마 12월 중으로요.

(C) 도심에서요.

해설 축제가 열릴 장소를 묻는 Where 의문문

(A) 연상 단어 오답. 질문의 festival에서 연상 가능한 A music concert를 이용한 오답.

(B) 질문과 상관없는 오답. When 의문문에 대한 응답이므로 오답.

(C) 정답. 축제가 열릴 장소를 묻는 질문에 도심에서라고 알려 주고 있으므로 정답.

12

M-Au   Who do I present my proposal to?

W-Am   (A) A hotel reservation.

(B) The acquisitions committee.

(C) At noon today.

제 제안서를 누구에게 보여주죠?

(A) 호텔 예약이요.

(B) 인수 위원회요.

(C) 오늘 정오예요.

어휘 present 보여주다   proposal 제안(서)   reservation 예약   acquisition 인수, 습득   committee 위원회

해설 제안서를 보여줄 대상을 묻는 Who 의문문

(A) 질문과 상관없는 오답.

(B) 정답. 제안서를 보여줄 대상을 묻는 질문에 인수 위원회라고 알려 주고 있으므로 정답.

(C) 질문과 상관없는 오답. When 의문문에 대한 응답이므로 오답.

13

M-Cn Could you please look up the location on your phone?

W-Am (A) Here's my phone number.
(B) OK, one moment.
(C) The weather is nice right now.

핸드폰으로 그 장소를 찾아봐 주실 수 있나요?
(A) 제 전화번호입니다.
(B) 네, 잠시만요.
(C) 지금은 날씨가 좋아요.

어휘 look up 찾아보다   location 장소, 위치   weather 날씨

해설 부탁/요청의 의문문
(A) 단어 반복 오답. 질문의 phone을 반복 이용한 오답.
(B) 정답. 핸드폰으로 장소를 찾아달라는 요청에 네(OK)라고 수락한 뒤, 잠시만이라며 긍정 답변과 일관된 내용을 덧붙이고 있으므로 정답.
(C) 질문과 상관없는 오답.

14

W-Am Isn't the accounting seminar tomorrow?

M-Au (A) I'd like to open an account, please.
(B) Actually, it's on Friday.
(C) Time management.

회계 세미나는 내일 아닌가요?
(A) 계좌를 개설해 주세요.
(B) 실은 금요일이에요.
(C) 시간 관리요.

어휘 accounting 회계   open an account 계좌를 개설하다   management 관리

해설 회계 세미나가 내일인지 여부를 확인하는 부정 의문문
(A) 파생어 오답. 질문의 accounting과 파생어 관계인 account를 이용한 오답.
(B) 정답. 회계 세미나가 내일인지 여부를 묻는 질문에 실은 금요일이라고 회계 세미나가 내일이 아님을 알려 주고 있으므로 정답.
(C) 연상 단어 오답. 질문의 seminar에서 연상 가능한 time management를 이용한 오답.

15

M-Cn When's the dishwasher being repaired?

W-Br (A) The technician came this morning.
(B) I store the knives in a separate drawer.
(C) The bread is in the pantry.

식기세척기는 언제 수리되나요?
(A) 오늘 아침에 기술자가 왔어요.
(B) 칼은 별도의 서랍에 보관해요.
(C) 빵은 식료품 저장실에 있어요.

어휘 dishwasher 식기세척기   store 보관하다, 저장하다   separate 별개의, 서로 다른   drawer 서랍   pantry 식료품 저장실

해설 식기세척기 수리 시점을 묻는 When 의문문
(A) 정답. 식기세척기 수리 시점을 묻는 질문에 오늘 아침에 기술자가 왔다며 이미 수리가 완료되었음을 간접적으로 알려 주고 있으므로 정답.
(B) 연상 단어 오답. 질문의 dishwasher에서 연상 가능한 knives를 이용한 오답.
(C) 질문과 상관없는 오답.

16

W-Br Should we move the employee lounge to the basement?

M-Cn (A) He attended the talk.
(B) The reservation is for two people.
(C) No, it's too dark down there.

직원 라운지를 지하로 옮겨야 하나요?
(A) 그는 논의에 참석했어요.
(B) 두 명 예약이에요.
(C) 아니요, 거기는 너무 어두워요.

어휘 basement 지하층   reservation 예약

해설 제안/권유의 의문문
(A) 질문과 상관없는 오답. 질문에 3인칭 대명사 He로 지칭할 인물이 언급된 적이 없으므로 오답.
(B) 연상 단어 오답. 질문의 employee에서 연상 가능한 people을 이용한 오답.
(C) 정답. 직원 라운지를 지하로 옮겨야 할지 묻는 질문에 아니요(No)라고 대답한 뒤, 거기는 너무 어둡다며 부정 답변과 일관된 내용을 덧붙이고 있으므로 정답.

17

M-Au You changed the color printer cartridge recently, didn't you?

W-Am (A) Right, just a few days ago.
(B) They're painting the walls blue.
(C) A different password.

최근에 컬러 프린터 카트리지를 바꾸셨죠, 그렇죠?
(A) 맞아요, 며칠 전에요.
(B) 그들은 벽을 파란색으로 칠하고 있어요.
(C) 다른 비밀번호요.

해설 컬러 프린터 카트리지 교체 여부를 확인하는 부가 의문문
(A) 정답. 컬러 프린터 카트리지 교체 여부를 확인하는 질문에 맞아요(Right)라고 대답한 뒤, 며칠 전이라며 긍정 답변과 일관된 내용을 덧붙였으므로 정답.
(B) 연상 단어 오답. 질문의 color에서 연상 가능한 blue를 이용한 오답.
(C) 연상 단어 오답. 질문의 changed에서 연상 가능한 different를 이용한 오답.

18

W-Br We're not going to be able to fit everyone in this space.

M-Au (A) A professional-development workshop.
(B) There's a larger room down the hallway.
(C) These shoes are exactly the right size.

이 공간에 모두를 들어가게 할 수는 없을 거예요.
(A) 전문성 개발 워크숍이요.
(B) 복도 끝에 더 큰 방이 있어요.
(C) 이 신발이 사이즈가 정확히 딱 맞아요.

어휘 professional 전문적인, 직업의 development 개발, 성장 hallway 복도 exactly 정확히

해설 정보 전달의 평서문
(A) 평서문과 상관없는 오답.
(B) 정답. 이 공간에 모두를 들어가게 할 수는 없을 것이라는 평서문에 복도 끝에 더 큰 방이 있다며 문제에 대한 해결책을 제시하고 있으므로 정답.
(C) 연상 단어 오답. 평서문의 fit에서 연상 가능한 right size를 이용한 오답.

19

M-Cn Is it easiest for me to take a bus to the city center?

W-Am (A) A new department store.
(B) When did you buy it?
(C) I usually do.

도심으로 버스를 타고 가는 것이 가장 편한가요?
(A) 새 백화점이요.
(B) 언제 사셨어요?
(C) 저는 보통 그래요.

어휘 department store 백화점

해설 버스를 타고 가는 것이 가장 편한지 여부를 묻는 Be동사 의문문
(A) 연상 단어 오답. 질문의 city center에서 연상 가능한 department store를 이용한 오답.
(B) 질문과 상관없는 오답.
(C) 정답. 버스를 타고 가는 것이 가장 편한지 묻는 질문에 자신은 보통 그런다며 긍정의 대답을 우회적으로 표현하고 있으므로 정답.

20

W-Br Are you able to make a prototype soon?

W-Am (A) Yes, my team is working on it.
(B) I thought it was very innovative.
(C) He's a good typist.

시제품을 곧 만드실 수 있나요?
(A) 네, 저희 팀이 작업 중입니다.
(B) 굉장히 획기적이라고 생각했어요.
(C) 그는 타이핑을 잘해요.

어휘 prototype 원형, 시제품 innovative 획기적인, 혁신적인

해설 시제품을 곧 만들 수 있는지 여부를 묻는 Be동사 의문문
(A) 정답. 시제품을 곧 만들 수 있는지 여부를 묻는 질문에 네(Yes)라고 대답한 뒤, 팀이 작업 중이라며 긍정 답변과 일관된 내용을 덧붙였으므로 정답.
(B) 연상 단어 오답. 질문의 prototype에서 연상 가능한 innovative를 이용한 오답.
(C) 질문과 상관없는 오답. 질문에 3인칭 대명사 He로 지칭할 인물이 언급된 적이 없으므로 오답.

21

M-Cn Where can I buy a lamp like that?

M-Au (A) On my desk.
(B) I got this one as a gift.
(C) After my client meeting.

그런 램프를 어디서 살 수 있어요?
(A) 제 책상 위에요.
(B) 저는 이걸 선물로 받았어요.
(C) 고객 회의 후에요.

해설 램프 구매 장소를 묻는 Where 의문문
(A) 연상 단어 오답. 질문의 Where에서 연상 가능한 on my desk를 이용한 오답.
(B) 정답. 램프를 구매할 수 있는 장소를 묻는 질문에 선물로 받았다며 구매한 것이 아님을 알려 주고 있으므로 정답.
(C) 질문과 상관없는 오답. When 의문문에 대한 응답이므로 오답.

22

M-Cn How often do you have to install updates?

W-Am (A) This letter needs more postage.
(B) An incorrect serial code.
(C) Waseem is the software administrator.

업데이트를 얼마나 자주 설치해야 해요?
(A) 이 편지는 우편 요금을 더 내야 해요.
(B) 잘못된 일련번호입니다.
(C) 와심이 소프트웨어 관리자예요.

어휘 install 설치하다 postage 우편 요금 incorrect 부정확한, 맞지 않는 administrator 관리자

해설 업데이트 설치 빈도를 묻는 How often 의문문
(A) 질문과 상관없는 오답.
(B) 연상 단어 오답. 질문의 updates에서 연상 가능한 소프트웨어의 serial code를 이용한 오답.
(C) 정답. 업데이트를 얼마나 자주 설치해야 하는지 묻는 질문에 와심이 소프트웨어 관리자라며 대신 문의할 사람을 알려 주고 자신은 답변해 줄 수 없다는 것을 우회적으로 표현하고 있으므로 정답.

23

W-Br Let's talk about your project after lunch.

M-Cn (A) Because her microphone is broken.
(B) I'm leaving work early today.
(C) I have two pairs of shoes.

점심 식사 후 당신의 프로젝트에 관해 얘기해 봅시다.
(A) 그녀의 마이크가 고장 나서요.
(B) 오늘 일찍 퇴근하는데요.
(C) 저는 신발 두 켤레가 있어요.

어휘 broken 고장 난 leave work 퇴근하다

해설 제안/권유의 평서문
(A) 평서문과 상관없는 오답. Why 의문문에 대한 응답이므로 오답.
(B) 정답. 점심 식사 후 프로젝트에 관해 얘기해 보자는 제안에 대해 오늘 일찍 퇴근한다며 제안대로 프로젝트에 관해 얘기하는 것이 불가능하다는 것을 우회적으로 알리고 있으므로 정답.
(C) 평서문과 상관없는 오답.

24

M-Cn Is there a list of guests who have been invited?

W-Am (A) Room 305 is being prepared for you.
(B) The caterer has all the necessary information.
(C) A banquet hall on Main Street.

초대된 손님 명단이 있나요?
(A) 305호실이 준비되어 있습니다.
(B) 케이터링 업체가 필요한 모든 정보를 갖고 있어요.
(C) 메인 가에 있는 연회장이요.

어휘 invite 초대하다 prepare 준비하다 necessary 필요한 banquet 연회

해설 초대된 손님 명단 여부를 묻는 Be동사 의문문
(A) 연상 단어 오답. 질문의 guests에서 연상 가능한 Room 305를 이용한 오답.
(B) 정답. 초대된 손님 명단이 있는지 묻는 질문에 케이터링 업체가 필요한 모든 정보를 갖고 있다며 자신은 답변해 줄 수 없다는 것을 우회적으로 표현하고 있으므로 정답.
(C) 연상 단어 오답. 질문의 invited에서 연상 가능한 a banquet hall을 이용한 오답.

25

M-Au Would it be cheaper to ship by express mail or overnight delivery?

W-Br (A) Express mail is less expensive.
(B) I'd like a large.
(C) It's in the next shipment.

속달 우편으로 운송하는 게 더 싸요, 아니면 익일 배송이 더 싸요?
(A) 속달 우편이 덜 비싸요.
(B) 저는 라지로 할게요.
(C) 다음 수송품에 있어요.

어휘 express mail 속달 우편 overnight 야간의 expensive 비싼 shipment 수송, 수송품

해설 더 저렴한 운송 방법을 묻는 선택 의문문
(A) 정답. 더 저렴한 운송 방법을 묻는 질문에 속달 우편이 덜 비싸다며 둘 중 하나를 선택해 응답하고 있으므로 정답.
(B) 질문과 상관없는 오답.
(C) 파생어 오답. 질문의 ship과 파생어 관계인 shipment를 이용한 오답.

---

26 ▶ 동영상 강의

W-Br How do I turn on the air conditioner in this office?

M-Cn (A) The temperature is controlled automatically.
(B) Turn left after the post office.
(C) No, I shut off all the lights.

사무실 에어컨을 어떻게 켜죠?
(A) 온도는 자동으로 조절돼요.
(B) 우체국을 지나서 좌회전하세요.
(C) 아니요, 제가 불을 다 껐어요.

어휘 turn on 켜다 temperature 온도 automatically 자동으로 shut off 차단하다

해설 사무실 에어컨 작동 방법을 묻는 How 의문문
(A) 정답. 사무실 에어컨을 켜는 방법을 묻는 질문에 온도는 자동으로 조절된다며 직접 켤 필요가 없음을 간접적으로 알려 주고 있으므로 정답.
(B) 단어 반복 오답. 질문의 turn과 office를 반복 이용한 오답.
(C) Yes/No 불가 오답. How 의문문에는 Yes/No 응답이 불가능하므로 오답.

27

W-Am Have you trained Hikaru to use the new microscope?

W-Br (A) I have my own car.
(B) That's enough, thanks.
(C) I misplaced the instruction manual.

히카루에게 새 현미경 사용법을 교육하셨나요?
(A) 제 차가 있어요.
(B) 충분해요. 감사합니다.
(C) 설명서를 어디에 뒀는지 모르겠어요.

어휘 train 교육하다 microscope 현미경 misplace 제자리에 두지 않아 찾지 못하다 instruction manual 설명서

해설 현미경 사용법을 교육했는지 여부를 묻는 조동사(Have) 의문문
(A) 연상 단어 오답. 질문의 trained를 기차 train으로 잘못 들었을 경우 연상 가능한 car를 이용한 오답.
(B) 질문과 상관없는 오답.
(C) 정답. 히카루에게 새 현미경 사용법을 교육했는지 여부를 묻는 질문에 설명서를 어디에 뒀는지 모르겠다며 교육하지 못했음을 우회적으로 표현하고 있으므로 정답.

28

▶ 동영상 강의

W-Am We're meeting this week to discuss the upcoming merger.

M-Au (A) I have it on my calendar.
(B) Please merge onto the highway.
(C) A law firm in Glenview.

다가올 합병에 대해 논의하러 이번 주에 만납니다.
(A) 일정표에 적혀 있어요.
(B) 고속도로로 합류하세요.
(C) 글렌뷰에 있는 법률사무소요.

어휘 upcoming 다가오는, 곧 있을 merger 합병 merge 합병하다, 합치다 law firm 법률사무소

해설 정보 전달의 평서문
(A) 정답. 다가올 합병에 대해 논의하러 이번 주에 만나자는 평서문에 일정표에 적혀 있다며 이미 알고 있음을 우회적으로 알려 주고 있으므로 정답.
(B) 파생어 오답. 평서문의 merger와 파생어 관계인 merge를 이용한 오답.
(C) 평서문과 상관없는 오답.

29

▶ 동영상 강의

M-Au How long will we have to wait for a taxi to arrive?

W-Br (A) About twelve kilometers.
(B) No, I don't think so.
(C) Would you prefer to walk?

얼마나 오래 택시가 도착하기를 기다려야 할까요?
(A) 12킬로미터 정도요.
(B) 아니요, 제 생각은 그렇지 않아요.
(C) 걷는 게 좋겠어요?

해설 택시 도착 시간을 묻는 How long 의문문
(A) 연상 단어 오답. 질문의 How long을 거리를 묻는 의문문으로 착각한 경우 연상 가능한 kilometers를 이용한 오답.
(B) Yes/No 불가 오답. How long 의문문에는 Yes/No 응답이 불가능하므로 오답.
(C) 정답. 택시 도착 시간을 묻는 질문에 걸어가기를 바라냐며 택시를 기다리지 않는 다른 방법에 대한 의견을 묻고 있으므로 정답.

30

W-Br Did the deal to lease the equipment go through?

M-Cn (A) A one-bedroom apartment.
(B) The supply catalog is in the filing cabinet.
(C) Not yet—but we hope to have it finalized this quarter.

장비 대여 거래가 성사됐나요?
(A) 침실 하나짜리 아파트요.
(B) 물품 카탈로그가 문서 보관함에 있어요.
(C) 아직이요. 하지만 이번 분기에 마무리되길 바라요.

어휘 deal 거래, 합의 lease 대여하다, 임대하다 equipment 장비 go through 성사되다, 통과되다 supply 물품, 보급품 filing cabinet 문서 보관함 finalize 마무리하다 quarter 분기

해설 장비 대여 거래 성사 여부를 묻는 조동사(Did) 의문문
(A) 연상 단어 오답. 질문의 lease에서 연상 가능한 apartment를 이용한 오답.
(B) 연상 단어 오답. 질문의 equipment에서 연상 가능한 filing cabinet을 이용한 오답.
(C) 정답. 장비 대여 거래 성사 여부를 묻는 질문에 아직(Not yet)이라고 답한 뒤 이번 분기에 마무리되길 바란다며 부정 답변과 일관된 내용을 덧붙였으므로 정답.

31

W-Am Would you like to take this vehicle for a test drive?

M-Cn (A) Because there's no parking available.
(B) I heard a new model is coming out in March.
(C) Only two doors.

이 차를 시승해 보시겠어요?
(A) 주차할 곳이 없어서요.
(B) 새 모델이 3월에 나온다고 들었어요.
(C) 문 두 개만요.

어휘 vehicle 차량 available 이용 가능한, 구할 수 있는

해설 제안/권유의 의문문
(A) 연상 단어 오답. 질문의 vehicle과 drive에서 연상 가능한 parking을 이용한 오답.
(B) 정답. 차를 시승해 보겠냐는 제안에 새 모델이 3월에 나온다고 들었다며 거부의 의사를 간접적으로 표현하고 있으므로 정답.
(C) 연상 단어 오답. 질문의 vehicle에서 연상 가능한 two doors를 이용한 오답.

PART 3

32-34

W-Am Matteo, do you have time to help me organize the storage room? **[32] The construction crew's going to be starting renovations on the lobby next week. [33] We need to make space to store the lobby furniture.**

M-Cn Actually, I know the plan is to replace those tables and chairs. **[33] Maybe we should just donate them now rather than putting them in storage.**

W-Am Good idea! **[34] I'll do some research to see which organizations accept donations of furniture.** I'm sure there are several in the area.

TEST 8

여	마테오, 시간 있으면 창고 정리 좀 도와주실래요? **공사 인부들이 다음 주 로비 보수를 시작할 건데요.** 로비 가구를 보관할 공간을 마련해야 해서요.
남	실은 탁자와 의자를 교체할 계획으로 알고 있어요. **창고에 보관하지 말고 지금 바로 기부하는 것이 좋을 것 같습니다.**
여	좋은 생각이네요! **어떤 단체가 가구 기부를 받는지 조사해 볼게요.** 분명 지역 내에 여러 곳이 있을 겁니다.

어휘	organize 준비하다, 정리하다 storage 보관, 저장 construction 공사, 건설 renovation 개조, 보수 replace 교체하다 donate 기부하다 rather than ~보다는 organization 기관, 단체 accept 수락하다

32

According to the woman, what will happen next week?
(A) A renovation project will begin.
(B) A company will move to a new location.
(C) Some technology will be updated.
(D) Some new employees will be trained.

여자에 따르면, 다음 주에 어떤 일이 있을 것인가?
(A) 보수 프로젝트가 시작될 것이다.
(B) 회사가 새로운 장소로 이전할 것이다.
(C) 기술이 업데이트될 것이다.
(D) 신입사원들이 교육을 받을 것이다.

어휘 location 위치, 장소

해설 세부 사항 관련 – 다음 주에 있을 일

여자가 첫 대사에서 공사 인부들이 다음 주 로비 보수를 시작할 것(The construction crew's going to be starting renovations on the lobby next week)이라고 말하고 있으므로 정답은 (A)이다.

Paraphrasing	대화의 The construction crew's going to be starting renovations → 정답의 A renovation project will begin.

33

What does the man recommend?
(A) Ordering some equipment
(B) Printing some instructions
(C) Donating some furniture
(D) Arranging a catered meal

남자는 무엇을 권장하는가?
(A) 장비 주문하기
(B) 설명서 출력하기
(C) 가구 기부하기
(D) 케이터링 음식 마련하기

어휘 equipment 장비 instruction 설명(서) arrange 마련하다

해설 세부 사항 관련 – 남자의 권유 사항

여자가 첫 대사에서 로비 가구를 보관할 공간을 마련해야 한다(We need to make space to store the lobby furniture)고 하자 남자가 창고에 보관하지 말고 기부하는 것이 좋을 것 같다(Maybe we should just

donate them now rather than putting them in storage)고 말하고 있으므로 정답은 (C)이다.

34

What does the woman say she will do?
(A) Meet a client
(B) Research some options
(C) Make a presentation
(D) Sign a contract

여자는 무엇을 하겠다고 말하는가?
(A) 고객 만나기
(B) 선택 사항 조사하기
(C) 발표하기
(D) 계약서에 서명하기

어휘 option 선택 사항 contract 계약, 계약서

해설 세부 사항 관련 – 여자가 할 일

여자가 마지막 대사에서 어떤 단체가 가구 기부를 받는지 조사해 보겠다(I'll do some research to see which organizations accept donations of furniture)고 말하고 있으므로 정답은 (B)이다.

35-37 3인 대화

W-Am	Hi, Liam. We're really glad to have you join our team. **35 The harvest season is our busiest!**
M-Au	I'm excited to get started.
W-Am	Let me introduce you to Brian. **35 He will take you out to the berry fields for your training.**
M-Cn	Hi, **36 Liam. Here's a pair of gloves for you to use.**
M-Au	Thanks!
M-Cn	The berry picking is really straightforward. But **37 it's important that you get plenty of water and stay hydrated in this heat.**
M-Au	I brought a big bottle of it with me, so I should be fine.

여	안녕하세요, 리암. 저희 팀에 들어오셔서 정말 좋아요. **수확기가 가장 바쁘거든요!**
남1	일을 시작하게 되어 기뻐요.
여	브라이언에게 소개해 드릴게요. **딸기밭으로 데리고 나가서 교육을 해 드릴 겁니다.**
남2	안녕하세요, **리암. 쓰실 장갑이 여기 있어요.**
남1	감사합니다!
남2	딸기 따기는 무척 간단해요. 하지만 **이 더위엔 물을 많이 마시고 수분을 유지하는 것이 중요하죠.**
남1	큰 병을 가져왔으니까 괜찮을 거예요.

어휘 straightforward 간단한, 쉬운 plenty of 많은
stay hydrated 수분을 유지하다

35

Where do the speakers most likely work?
(A) At a restaurant
(B) At a farm
(C) On a fishing boat
(D) At a public park

화자들은 어디서 일하겠는가?
(A) 음식점
(B) 농장
(C) 어선
(D) 공원

해설 전체 내용 관련 – 화자들의 근무지

여자가 첫 대사에서 수확기가 가장 바쁘다(The harvest season is our busiest!)고 했고, 두 번째 대사에서 첫 번째 남자를 브라이언에게 소개하며, 그가 딸기밭으로 데리고 나가서 교육을 해 줄 것(He will take you out to the berry fields for your training)이라고 말하는 것으로 보아 화자들은 딸기 농장에서 근무한다는 것을 알 수 있다. 따라서 정답은 (B)이다.

36

What does Brian give to Liam?
(A) Some gloves
(B) Some bags
(C) A plastic bucket
(D) A clipboard

브라이언은 리암에게 무엇을 주는가?
(A) 장갑
(B) 가방
(C) 플라스틱 바구니
(D) 서류철

해설 세부 사항 관련 – 브라이언이 리암에게 주는 것

두 번째 남자가 첫 대사에서 리암에게 장갑이 여기 있다(Liam. Here's a pair of gloves for you to use)고 말하고 있으므로 정답은 (A)이다.

37

According to Brian, what is important?
(A) Using sunscreen lotion
(B) Labeling some items
(C) Following a schedule
(D) Drinking water

브라이언에 따르면, 중요한 것은 무엇인가?
(A) 자외선 차단 로션 사용하기
(B) 물품에 라벨 붙이기
(C) 일정 따르기
(D) 물 마시기

어휘 sunscreen 자외선 차단제 label 표[라벨]를 붙이다 follow 따르다

해설 세부 사항 관련 – 브라이언이 중요하다고 말하는 것

두 번째 남자가 마지막 대사에서 이 더위엔 물을 많이 마시고 수분을 유지하는 것이 중요하다(it's important that you get plenty of water and stay hydrated in this heat)고 말하고 있으므로 정답은 (D)이다.

> Paraphrasing 대화의 get plenty of water
> → 정답의 Drinking water

38-40

M-Cn	38 **Welcome to my gardening podcast.** I'm Rajesh Varma, and today I'm here with So-Jin Lee, a botanist from Denton University who recently developed a new hybrid flower. Could you tell us more, Professor Lee?
W-Br	Certainly. 39 **I developed a new type of rose—it's special because it blooms longer than any other rose.**
M-Cn	That's interesting. Is it difficult to grow?
W-Br	Not if it's planted under the right conditions. 40 **Next month, the rose will be featured at the botanical show downtown.** I hope your listeners will come to see it.

남	**정원 가꾸기 팟캐스트입니다.** 저는 라제쉬 바르마이고요. 오늘은 최근 새로운 교배종 꽃을 개발한 덴튼 대학교의 식물학자 이소진 씨와 함께합니다. 이 교수님, 더 얘기해 주시겠어요?
여	네. **저는 새로운 종류의 장미를 개발했는데요. 다른 장미보다 오래 꽃을 피운다는 점이 특별하죠.**
남	흥미롭네요. 기르기가 어렵나요?
여	알맞은 조건에서 키운다면 어렵지 않아요. **다음 달에 시내에서 열리는 식물 박람회에 이 장미가 나올 겁니다.** 청취자들이 와서 보시면 좋겠어요.

어휘 botanist 식물학자 hybrid (동·식물의) 교배종, 잡종
bloom 꽃을 피우다 plant 심다, 가꾸다 condition 조건
feature 특별히 포함하다 botanical 식물의

38

Who most likely is the man?
(A) An event coordinator
(B) A book publisher
(C) A city official
(D) A podcast host

TEST 8

남자는 누구이겠는가?

(A) 행사 조직자
(B) 도서 출판업자
(C) 시 공무원
(D) **팟캐스트 진행자**

어휘 coordinator 조정자, 조직자   publisher 출판업자   official
   공무원   host 진행자

해설 전체 내용 관련 – 남자의 직업

남자가 첫 대사에서 정원 가꾸기 팟캐스트(Welcome to my gardening podcast)라고 소개하고 있으므로 정답은 (D)이다.

39

What does the woman say is special about a flower?

(A) It is resistant to insects.
(B) It has an unusual color.
(C) It can bloom for a long time.
(D) It has a unique smell.

여자는 꽃의 어떤 점이 특별하다고 말하는가?

(A) 곤충에 강하다.
(B) 색깔이 특이하다.
(C) **오랫동안 꽃을 피울 수 있다.**
(D) 향기가 독특하다.

어휘 resistant 저항력 있는   insect 곤충   unusual 특이한, 색다른

해설 세부 사항 관련 – 여자가 꽃에 대해 특별하다고 말하는 것

여자가 첫 대사에서 새로운 종류의 장미를 개발했는데 다른 장미보다 오래 꽃을 피운다는 점이 특별하다(I developed a new type of rose—it's special because it blooms longer than any other rose)고 말하고 있으므로 정답은 (C)이다.

> **Paraphrasing** 대화의 it blooms longer than any other rose → 정답의 It can bloom for a long time.

40

What will happen next month?

(A) A botanical show will be held.
(B) A public garden will open.
(C) An experiment will be conducted.
(D) A gardening class will be offered.

다음 달에 무슨 일이 있을 것인가?

(A) **식물 박람회가 열릴 것이다.**
(B) 공원이 문을 열 것이다.
(C) 실험이 시행될 것이다.
(D) 정원 가꾸기 강좌가 제공될 것이다.

어휘 be held 열리다   experiment 실험   conduct 하다

해설 세부 사항 관련 – 다음 달에 일어날 일

여자가 마지막 대사에서 다음 달에 시내에서 열리는 식물 박람회에 이 장미가 나올 것(Next month, the rose will be featured at the botanical show downtown)이라고 말하고 있으므로 정답은 (A)이다.

41-43

W-Am	So, Vivek, I think our employees could benefit from some more training. **41 How about using this software application that I found? The app provides a platform for uploading our own training videos.** And employees could view them on their phones at any time.
M-Au	You know, I've heard that those online programs help employees retain knowledge. But **42 aren't those apps expensive?**
W-Am	Actually, the cost is reasonable. And **43 the Web site has some interesting reviews from other businesses that have used the app and found it helpful.**

여	자, 비벡, 우리 직원들이 더 많은 교육으로 혜택을 받을 수 있을 것 같아요. **제가 찾은 이 소프트웨어 앱을 사용하면 어때요? 그 앱은 우리의 교육 동영상을 업로드할 플랫폼을 제공하거든요.** 그리고 직원들은 언제든 핸드폰으로 동영상을 볼 수 있고요.
남	그런 온라인 프로그램은 직원들이 지식을 보유할 수 있도록 도와준다고 들었어요. 그런데 **그런 앱은 비싸지 않나요?**
여	사실 비용이 적정해요. **그 앱을 쓰고 유용하다고 생각한 업체들의 흥미로운 후기가 웹사이트에 있어요.**

어휘 benefit 혜택을 입다, 득을 보다   retain 보유하다
   knowledge 지식   expensive 비싼   reasonable (가격이)
   적정한, 합리적인

41

What does the woman propose doing?

(A) Hiring a computer technician
(B) Using a training application
(C) Replacing some printers
(D) Changing business hours

여자는 무엇을 하자고 제안하는가?

(A) 컴퓨터 기사 고용하기
(B) **교육 앱 사용하기**
(C) 프린터 교체하기
(D) 운영시간 변경하기

어휘 propose 제안하다   technician 기사, 기술자   replace 교체하다
   business hours 영업시간, 운영시간

해설 세부 사항 관련 – 여자가 제안하는 일

여자가 첫 대사에서 소프트웨어 앱을 사용할 것(How about using this software application ~?)을 제안하면서 그 앱은 교육 동영상을 업로드할 플랫폼을 제공한다(The app provides a platform for uploading our own training videos)고 말하고 있으므로 정답은 (B)이다.

42

What is the man concerned about?
(A) Scheduling delays
(B) Employee satisfaction
(C) The cost of a product
(D) The quality of a product

남자는 무엇에 대해 염려하는가?
(A) 일정 지연
(B) 직원 만족
(C) 제품 가격
(D) 제품 품질

어휘 delay 지연 satisfaction 만족 quality 품질

해설 세부 사항 관련 – 남자의 우려 사항

남자가 첫 대사에서 그런 앱은 비싸지 않은지(aren't those apps expensive?) 묻고 있으므로 정답은 (C)이다.

43

According to the woman, what can be found on a Web site?
(A) A company address
(B) Customer reviews
(C) A chat feature
(D) Discount coupons

여자에 따르면, 웹사이트에서 무엇을 찾을 수 있는가?
(A) 업체 주소
(B) 고객 후기
(C) 채팅 기능
(D) 할인 쿠폰

어휘 feature 기능, 특징

해설 세부 사항 관련 – 여자가 웹사이트에서 찾을 수 있다고 말하는 것

여자가 마지막 대사에서 그 앱을 쓰고 유용하다고 생각한 업체들의 흥미로운 후기가 웹사이트에 있다(the Web site has some interesting reviews from other businesses that have used the app and found it helpful)고 말하고 있으므로 정답은 (B)이다.

44-46

M-Cn Hi, Christina. **⁴⁴Did you have a chance to look over the applications from our sales representatives who are interested in the new team leader role?** We'll need to decide on a team leader soon.

W-Br ⁴⁴**I did.** ⁴⁵**I really liked Amanda Diop's application. She's the one who signed that deal with Wallerston Corporation.**

M-Cn I agree. That was an impressive deal. Wallerston is one of our biggest clients now. I think Amanda would be a great choice.

W-Br OK. I'm glad we're on the same page. ⁴⁶**I'll complete the paperwork and send it to the human resources department later today.**

남 안녕하세요, 크리스티나. **신임 팀장 역할에 관심 있는 영업 사원들의 지원서를 살펴볼 기회가 있었나요?** 곧 팀장을 결정해야 해요.

여 **봤어요. 저는 아만다 디오프의 지원서가 무척 맘에 들었어요. 월러스톤 코퍼레이션과의 계약을 체결했잖아요.**

남 동의해요. 인상적인 계약이었죠. 월러스톤은 지금 가장 중요한 고객 중 하나고요. 아만다가 좋을 것 같네요.

여 네. 의견이 같아서 좋습니다. **서류 작업을 완료해서 이따가 인사부로 보낼게요.**

어휘 look over ~을 살펴보다 application 지원, 지원서 sales representative 판매원, 영업 사원 be interested in ~에 관심이 있다 role 역할 deal 계약, 거래 impressive 인상적인 on the same page 합심한, 의견이 같은 complete 완료하다 paperwork 서류 작업 human resources department 인사부

44

What are the speakers mainly discussing?
(A) A presenter at an event
(B) End-of-year bonuses
(C) Vacation requests
(D) An applicant for a new role

화자들은 주로 무엇에 대해 이야기하는가?
(A) 행사 진행자
(B) 연말 보너스
(C) 휴가 요청
(D) 새로운 역할 지원자

어휘 presenter 진행자, 발표자 vacation 휴가 applicant 지원자

해설 전체 내용 관련 – 대화의 주제

남자가 첫 대사에서 신임 팀장 역할에 관심 있는 영업 사원들의 지원서를 살펴볼 기회가 있었는지(Did you have a chance to look over the applications from our sales representatives who are interested in the new team leader role?)를 묻자 여자가 봤다(I did)고 답하면서 팀장 역할 지원자에 대한 내용을 언급하고 있으므로 정답은 (D)이다.

45

According to the speakers, what has Amanda Diop accomplished?
(A) She secured a business deal.
(B) She completed a professional certification.
(C) She won an industry award.
(D) She reduced production costs.

화자들에 따르면, 아만다 디오프는 무엇을 해냈는가?
(A) 사업 계약을 따냈다.
(B) 전문 자격증을 땄다.
(C) 업계 상을 받았다.
(D) 생산 비용을 줄였다.

어휘 secure a deal 계약을 따내다 professional certification
전문 자격증 win an award 상을 받다 reduce 줄이다
production cost 생산 비용

해설 세부 사항 관련 – 화자들이 아만다 디오프가 해냈다고 말하는 것
여자가 첫 대사에서 아만다 디오프의 지원서가 무척 맘에 들었다(I really
liked Amanda Diop's application)며 아만다 디오프가 월러스톤 코
퍼레이션과의 계약을 체결했다(She's the one who signed that deal
with Wallerston Corporation)고 말하고 있으므로 정답은 (A)이다.

> **Paraphrasing** 대화의 signed that deal with Wallerston
> Corporation
> → 정답의 secured a business deal

46

What does the woman say she will do?
(A) Submit some documents
(B) Reserve a venue
(C) Calculate a budget
(D) Check some references

여자는 무엇을 할 것이라고 말하는가?
(A) 문서 제출하기
(B) 장소 예약하기
(C) 예산 계산하기
(D) 추천서 확인하기

어휘 reserve 예약하다 venue 장소 calculate 계산하다 budget
예산 reference 추천서, 참조

해설 세부 사항 관련 – 여자가 할 일
여자가 마지막 대사에서 서류 작업을 완료해서 이따가 인사부로
보내겠다(I'll complete the paperwork and send it to the human
resources department later today)고 말하고 있으므로 정답은
(A)이다.

47-49 3인 대화

W-Br	Thanks for agreeing to this interview for our upcoming article in the *Thomasville Gazette*, Ms. Haddad.
W-Am	Of course. As you know, ⁴⁷**the city council is proposing the implementation of a road tax. And I want to make sure the public is informed about it.**
M-Cn	Well, we like to keep our readers in the know, so we have a long list of questions for you.

W-Br	I'll start. What does the city plan to do with this tax revenue, Ms. Haddad?
W-Am	⁴⁸**The money will be used to add bicycle lanes citywide, which I'm excited about.** Bicycle lanes should reduce traffic and promote health.
M-Cn	⁴⁹**Some business owners are concerned about losing street parking.** Are you worried about that?

여1	〈토마스빌 가제트〉에 나오게 될 저희 기사 인터뷰에 응해 주셔서 감사합니다, 하다드 씨.
여2	당연한 일이죠. 아시다시피, **시 의회는 도로세 시행을 발의하고 있는데요. 이에 대해 대중에게 알리고 싶습니다.**
남	자, 독자들이 잘 알 수 있도록 많은 질문을 준비했습니다.
여1	제가 시작할게요. 시는 이 세수입을 어떻게 활용할 계획인가요, 하다드 씨?
여2	자금은 도시 전역에 자전거 전용 도로를 추가하는 데 사용될 텐데요. 아주 기대가 됩니다. 자전거 도로는 교통량을 줄이고 건강을 증진시킬 겁니다.
남	**사업주들은 노상 주차 공간이 없어질까 봐 걱정하고 있습니다.** 이 부분을 염려하시나요?

| 어휘 | upcoming 다가오는, 곧 있을 city council 시 의회 propose 발의하다 implementation 시행 in the know 잘 알고 있는 tax revenue 세수입 citywide 전 도시에 reduce 줄이다, 감소시키다 promote 촉진하다 be concerned 우려하다 worried 걱정하는 |

47

What is the topic of the conversation?
(A) A hiring initiative
(B) A tax proposal
(C) A volunteer opportunity
(D) A community festival

대화의 주제는?
(A) 고용 계획
(B) 세제안 발의
(C) 자원봉사 기회
(D) 지역사회 축제

어휘 initiative 계획 proposal 제안 volunteer 자원봉사(자)
opportunity 기회

해설 전체 내용 관련 – 대화의 주제
두 번째 여자가 첫 대사에서 시 의회는 도로세 시행을 발의하고 있는데
이에 대해 대중에게 알리고 싶다(the city council is proposing the
implementation of a road tax. And I want to make sure the
public is informed about it)고 한 후, 도로세 시행 제안에 대한 대화를
이어 나가고 있으므로 정답은 (B)이다.

48

What is Ms. Haddad excited about?
(A) Attracting international visitors
(B) Increasing employment opportunities
(C) Installing bicycle lanes
(D) Improving a health-care facility

하다드 씨가 기대하는 것은?
(A) 해외 방문객 유치
(B) 고용 기회 증가
(C) 자전거 도로 설치
(D) 의료 시설 개선

어휘 attract 유치하다, 끌어모으다 increase 증가시키다
employment 고용 opportunity 기회 install 설치하다
improve 개선하다, 향상시키다 facility 시설

해설 세부 사항 관련 – 하다드 씨가 기대하는 것
첫 번째 여자가 두 번째 대사에서 하다드 씨에게 시의 세수입을 어떻게 활용할 계획인지 묻자 하다드 씨가 지금은 도시 전역에 자전거 전용 도로를 추가하는 데 사용될 텐데 아주 기대가 된다(The money will be used to add bicycle lanes citywide, which I'm excited about)고 대답하고 있으므로 정답은 (C)이다.

Paraphrasing	대화의 add bicycle lanes → 정답의 Installing bicycle lanes

49

What concern does the man point out?
(A) Some equipment is missing.
(B) A project may be understaffed.
(C) Some safety guidelines are unclear.
(D) Some parking spaces may be lost.

남자는 어떤 우려 사항을 지적하는가?
(A) 일부 장비가 없다.
(B) 프로젝트에 인원이 부족할 수도 있다.
(C) 안전 지침이 명확하지 않다.
(D) 주차 공간이 없어질 수도 있다.

어휘 equipment 장비 understaffed 인원이 부족한 safety 안전
guideline 지침

해설 세부 사항 관련 – 남자가 지적하는 우려 사항
남자가 마지막 대사에서 사업주들은 노상 주차 공간이 없어질까 봐 걱정하고 있다(Some business owners are concerned about losing street parking)고 말하고 있으므로 정답은 (D)이다.

Paraphrasing	대화의 losing street parking → 정답의 Some parking spaces may be lost.

50-52

M-Au Good morning, Ms. Gomez. ⁵⁰**I wanted to update you on the travel plans for your meeting with Scarney Department Store.**

W-Am Thanks for taking care of that. ⁵⁰**They're prospective clients**, and I've been so busy sending them samples and preparing my presentation that I haven't given a thought to my reservations.

M-Au Happy to help. I've confirmed your plane reservation. ⁵¹**Just remember, Vela Air only allows one free piece of carry-on luggage.** Otherwise, there'll be an extra charge.

W-Am OK. ⁵²**Can you forward the plane ticket confirmation, please?**

M-Au ⁵²**I'll e-mail you right now.**

남 안녕하세요, 고메즈 씨. **스카니 백화점과의 회의를 위한 출장 계획 최신 사항을 알려드리려고요.**

여 처리해 주셔서 고마워요. **가능성 높은 고객이라** 그들에게 견본을 보내고 발표 준비를 하느라 너무 바빠서 예약은 생각도 못했어요.

남 도와드릴 수 있어서 기쁩니다. 항공권 예약을 확정했는데요. **벨라 항공은 기내 휴대용 수하물을 한 개만 무료로 허용하니 이 점만 명심하세요.** 그렇지 않으면 추가 요금이 있을 겁니다.

여 알겠어요. **항공권 확인서를 보내주실 수 있나요?**

남 **지금 이메일로 보내겠습니다.**

어휘 take care of ~을 돌보다, 처리하다 prospective 유망한, 가능성 있는 presentation 발표 give a thought to ~을 염두에 두다, 생각하다 reservation 예약 confirm 확인해 주다, 확정하다 allow 허락하다 carry-on luggage 기내 휴대용 수하물 otherwise 그렇지 않으면 charge 요금 forward 보내다

50

Who is the woman scheduled to meet with?
(A) A company lawyer
(B) A senior partner
(C) A prospective employee
(D) A potential customer

여자는 누구를 만날 예정인가?
(A) 회사 변호사
(B) 사장
(C) 유망한 직원
(D) 잠재 고객

어휘 lawyer 법률가, 변호사 senior partner 사장, 간부 사원
potential 잠재적인, 가능성 있는

해설 세부 사항 관련 – 여자가 만날 예정인 사람
남자가 첫 대사에서 여자의 스카니 백화점과의 회의를 위한 출장 계획과 관련해서 현재 상황을 알려 주려고 한다(I wanted to update you on the travel plans for your meeting with Scarney Department

Store)고 했고 여자가 그들은 가능성 높은 고객(They're prospective clients)이라고 말하고 있으므로 여자는 잠재 고객을 만날 예정임을 알 수 있다. 따라서 정답은 (D)이다.

> **Paraphrasing** 대화의 prospective clients
> → 정답의 A potential customer

51

What does the man remind the woman about?
(A) A luggage restriction
(B) A required signature
(C) An online guidebook
(D) A refund policy

남자는 여자에게 무엇에 대해 상기시키는가?
(A) 수하물 제한
(B) 필수 서명
(C) 온라인 안내서
(D) 환불 정책

어휘 restriction 제한 required 필수의 guidebook 안내서

해설 세부 사항 관련 – 남자가 여자에게 상기시키는 것
남자가 두 번째 대사에서 벨라 항공은 기내 휴대용 수하물을 한 개만 무료로 허용하니 명심하라(Just remember, Vela Air only allows one free piece of carry-on luggage)고 말하고 있으므로 정답은 (A)이다.

> **Paraphrasing** 대화의 only allows one free piece of carry-on luggage → 정답의 A luggage restriction

52

What does the man agree to do?
(A) Look up a phone number
(B) Arrange for a car rental
(C) File an expense report
(D) Forward an e-mail

남자는 무엇을 하는 데 동의하는가?
(A) 전화번호 찾아보기
(B) 차량 대여 준비하기
(C) 지출 품의서 제출하기
(D) 이메일 보내기

어휘 look up 찾아보다 arrange 준비하다, 마련하다 file 문서를 제출하다 expense report 지출 품의서

해설 세부 사항 관련 – 남자가 동의한 일
여자가 마지막 대사에서 항공권 확인서를 보내줄 수 있는지(Can you forward the plane ticket confirmation, please?) 요청하자 남자가 지금 이메일로 보내겠다(I'll e-mail you right now)고 말하고 있으므로 정답은 (D)이다.

53-55

M-Cn	Hi. I'm Marcel from Novik Solutions. **53Glad you could stop by my trade show booth today.**
W-Br	Nice to meet you. I'm Silvia from Media Futurescapes. So what type of product does your company provide?
M-Cn	**54We create accounting software so that companies can do their own accounting. Currently, I'm showcasing a new version for companies with under 50 employees.**
W-Br	Well, we have about 200 employees.
M-Cn	I understand. **55Here's a chart that provides an overview of our complete range of products.**

남	안녕하세요. 노빅 솔루션즈의 마셀이라고 합니다. **오늘 무역 박람회의 저희 부스에 들러 주셔서 반갑습니다.**
여	반갑습니다. 미디어 퓨처스케이프에서 온 실비아입니다. 귀사는 어떤 종류의 제품을 제공하나요?
남	**저희는 회계 소프트웨어를 만들어서 회사들이 회계 업무를 직접 할 수 있도록 합니다. 현재 직원이 50명 이하인 회사들을 위한 신규 버전을 선보이고 있어요.**
여	음, 저희는 직원이 200명 정도인데요.
남	알겠습니다. **저희 전 제품의 개요를 제공하는 차트가 여기 있습니다.**

어휘	stop by 들르다 trade show 무역 박람회 accounting 회계 currently 현재 showcase 선보이다, 공개하다 overview 개요 complete 완전한 range 범위

53

Where are the speakers?
(A) At an electronics store
(B) At a trade show
(C) At a seminar
(D) At an award ceremony

화자들은 어디에 있는가?
(A) 전자 제품 매장
(B) 무역 박람회
(C) 세미나
(D) 시상식

해설 전체 내용 관련 – 대화의 장소
남자가 첫 대사에서 무역 박람회 부스에 들러 줘서 고맙다(Glad you could stop by my trade show booth today)고 말하고 있으므로 정답은 (B)이다.

54

What does the woman mean when she says, "we have about 200 employees"?
(A) A product would not be useful for her company.
(B) She is looking to hire a manager.
(C) Her business has recently become successful.
(D) Employees will need to be trained.

여자가 "저희는 직원이 200명 정도인데요"라고 말하는 의도는 무엇인가?
(A) 제품이 자신의 회사에 유용하지 않을 수도 있다.
(B) 관리자를 고용하려고 생각한다.
(C) 자신의 업체가 최근 성공을 거두고 있다.
(D) 직원들이 교육을 받아야 할 것이다.

해설 화자의 의도 파악 – 직원이 200명 정도라는 말의 의도
앞에서 남자가 회계 소프트웨어를 만들어서 회사들이 회계 업무를 직접 할 수 있도록 한다(We create accounting software so that companies can do their own accounting)고 말한 뒤, 현재 직원이 50명 이하인 회사들을 위한 신규 버전을 선보이고 있다(Currently, I'm showcasing a new version for companies with under 50 employees)고 덧붙여 말한 것에 대해 여자가 인용문을 언급하고 있는 것으로 보아, 남자가 언급한 회계 소프트웨어는 여자의 회사에 적합하지 않다는 의도로 한 말임을 알 수 있다. 따라서 정답은 (A)이다.

55

What does the man give to the woman?
(A) A regional map
(B) A name tag
(C) A résumé
(D) A chart

남자는 여자에게 무엇을 주는가?
(A) 지역 지도
(B) 이름표
(C) 이력서
(D) 차트

어휘 regional 지역의

해설 세부 사항 관련 – 남자가 여자에게 주는 것
남자가 마지막 대사에서 전 제품의 개요를 제공하는 차트가 여기 있다(Here's a chart that provides an overview of our complete range of products)고 말하고 있으므로 정답은 (D)이다.

56-58

> **W-Am** Rodrigo, [56] **aren't we scheduled to start the seal-coating job for the street parking around Bevelton Shopping Center next week?**

> **M-Au** [57] **We were going to start those repairs on Monday, but I've been looking at the weather; it's going to rain all weekend. I think we should reschedule.**

> **W-Am** Right. We can't add a protective layer to the asphalt when it's wet. I'll contact the property manager at the shopping center to discuss alternative dates.

> **M-Au** OK. Just so you know, [58] **we've received a few new requests for consultations on our road repair services. I'll try to slot those in for Monday instead.**

여	로드리고, 베벨턴 쇼핑센터 주변 도로 주차를 위한 실 코팅 작업이 다음 주부터 시작되는 것 아닌가요?
남	월요일에 해당 보수를 시작하려고 했는데 날씨를 보고 있어요. 주말 내내 비가 온다네요. 일정을 변경해야 할 것 같네요.
여	그래요. 아스팔트가 젖어 있을 때 보호막을 덧씌울 수는 없으니까요. 제가 쇼핑센터 건물 관리자에게 연락해서 대체 가능한 날짜를 논의해 볼게요.
남	좋아요. 그리고 아시다시피 도로 보수 서비스 상담 신규 요청을 몇 건 받았어요. 월요일에 대신 이 건들을 넣어 볼게요.

어휘 be scheduled to ~할 예정이다 reschedule 일정을 변경하다 protective 보호의, 보호하는 layer 겹, 막, 층 property 건물, 부동산 alternative 대안이 되는, 대체 가능한 consultation 상담

56

Who most likely are the speakers?
(A) Plumbers
(B) Commercial architects
(C) Road repair contractors
(D) Landscapers

화자들은 누구이겠는가?
(A) 배관공
(B) 상업용 건물 건축가
(C) 도로 보수 도급업자
(D) 조경사

어휘 commercial 상업의, 상업적인 architect 건축가 contractor 도급업자

해설 전체 내용 관련 – 화자들의 직업
여자가 첫 대사에서 베벨턴 쇼핑센터 주변 도로 주차를 위한 실 코팅 작업이 다음 주에 시작되는 것이 아닌지(aren't we scheduled to start the seal-coating job for the street parking around Bevelton Shopping Center next week?) 도로 보수 작업에 대해 묻고 있으므로 정답은 (C)이다.

TEST 8

57

Why will a project be rescheduled?
(A) Rainy weather is expected.
(B) A design requires revisions.
(C) Some supplies have not arrived.
(D) A crew member is not available.

프로젝트 일정은 왜 변경되는가?
(A) 비가 예상된다.
(B) 디자인 수정이 필요하다.
(C) 일부 물품이 도착하지 않았다.
(D) 인부를 구할 수 없다.

어휘 revision 수정, 변경 supply 용품, 비품 available 구할 수 있는, 이용 가능한

해설 세부 사항 관련 – 일정이 변경되는 이유
남자가 첫 대사에서 월요일에 해당 보수를 시작하려고 했는데 날씨를 보고 있다(We were going to start those repairs on Monday, but I've been looking at the weather)며 주말 내내 비가 올 거라면서 일정을 변경해야 할 것 같다(it's going to rain all weekend. I think we should reschedule)고 말하고 있으므로 정답은 (A)이다.

> **Paraphrasing**   대화의 it's going to rain
> → 정답의 Rainy weather is expected.

58

What will the speakers most likely do on Monday?
(A) Finalize a contract
(B) Train some employees
(C) Move some vehicles
(D) Provide some consultations

화자들은 월요일에 무엇을 하겠는가?
(A) 계약 마무리
(B) 직원 교육
(C) 차량 이동
(D) 상담 제공

어휘 finalize 마무리하다, 완결하다 vehicle 차량

해설 세부 사항 관련 – 화자들이 월요일에 할 일
남자가 마지막 대사에서 도로 보수 서비스 상담 신규 요청을 몇 건 받았다(we've received a few new requests for consultations on our road repair services)며 월요일에 대신 이 건들을 넣어 보겠다(I'll try to slot those in for Monday instead)고 말하고 있으므로 정답은 (D)이다.

59-61

 동영상 강의

M-Au Tasnim, ⁵⁹ **I've been looking at the production process for soaps in our facility,** and I think there's room for improvement.

W-Br ⁶⁰ **Improvements that could decrease our production time?**

M-Au Yes. Consider this: once the soap mixtures are poured into the molds, employees have to carry the batches across the room.

W-Br I see what you mean. If we reinstalled the drying racks closer to the mixing station, they wouldn't have to walk as far.

M-Au Exactly. A small change like that can have a big effect on total output.

W-Br But wouldn't that be expensive?

M-Au ⁶¹ **Let me show you the cost projection.**

남 태즈님, **우리 시설에서 비누 제작 과정을 봤는데** 개선의 여지가 있는 것 같아요.
여 **생산 시간을 줄일 수 있는 개선이요?**
남 네. 이걸 한번 고려해 보세요. 비누 혼합물을 몰드에 부으면 직원들이 방을 가로질러 묶음을 날라야 하잖아요.
여 무슨 말인지 알겠어요. 건조대를 혼합대 가까이 재설치하면 그렇게 멀리 걸어갈 필요가 없겠네요.
남 그거예요. 그런 작은 변화가 전체 생산량에 큰 영향을 미칠 수 있어요.
여 하지만 비용이 많이 들지 않겠어요?
남 **예상 비용을 보여 드릴게요.**

어휘 production 생산 process 과정, 절차 facility 시설 room 여지 improvement 개선, 향상 decrease 줄이다, 감소시키다 mixture 혼합, 혼합물 batch 한 묶음 reinstall 재설치하다 rack 선반 have an effect on ~에 영향을 미치다 output 산출량, 생산량 projection 예상, 추정

59

Where do the speakers most likely work?
(A) At a bookstore
(B) At a dry cleaning business
(C) At a bakery
(D) At a factory

화자들은 어디서 일하겠는가?
(A) 서점
(B) 드라이클리닝 업체
(C) 제과점
(D) 공장

해설 전체 내용 관련 – 화자들의 근무지
남자가 첫 대사에서 우리 시설에서 비누 제작 과정을 봤다(I've been looking at the production process for soaps in our facility)고 말하고 있으므로 화자들은 비누 공장에서 근무하고 있음을 알 수 있다. 따라서 정답은 (D)이다.

60

What does the man imply when he says, "employees have to carry the batches across the room"?

(A) A machine is malfunctioning.
(B) A process is time-consuming.
(C) Salaries should be increased.
(D) More workers should be hired.

남자가 "직원들은 방을 가로질러 묶음을 날라야 하잖아요"라고 말하는 의도는 무엇인가?

(A) 기계가 제대로 작동하지 않는다.
(B) 절차에 시간이 많이 든다.
(C) 임금이 인상되어야 한다.
(D) 더 많은 근로자를 고용해야 한다.

어휘 malfunction 제대로 작동하지 않다 time-consuming 시간이 많이 걸리는 increase 올리다, 증가시키다

해설 화자의 의도 파악 – 직원들은 방을 가로질러 묶음을 날라야 한다는 말의 의도

앞에서 여자가 생산 시간을 줄일 수 있는 개선인지(Improvements that could decrease our production time?)를 묻자 남자가 인용문을 언급한 것으로 보아, 작업에 시간이 많이 걸린다는 것을 말하려는 의도임을 알 수 있다. 따라서 정답은 (B)이다.

61

What will the man show the woman?

(A) A cost estimate
(B) A floor plan
(C) A schedule
(D) A catalog

남자는 여자에게 무엇을 보여줄 것인가?

(A) 견적서
(B) 평면도
(C) 일정표
(D) 카탈로그

해설 세부 사항 관련 – 남자가 여자에게 보여줄 것

남자가 마지막 대사에서 예상 비용을 보여 주겠다(Let me show you the cost projection)고 말하고 있으므로 정답은 (A)이다.

Paraphrasing	대화의 the cost projection → 정답의 A cost estimate

62-64 대화 + 물품 주문서

M-Au ⁶²I was just looking at the supply request form you submitted for our engineering department.

W-Am Yes?

M-Au I think you might've made a mistake. ⁶³Do we really need that many computer mouses?

W-Am Oh, ⁶³that is a mistake! I meant to request two.

M-Au OK, great. I did think that was strange, given that there are only fifteen of us in our department!

W-Am Thanks for catching that. ⁶⁴Do you know when the supplies will get here?

M-Au I'll place the order this afternoon, so they'll probably arrive next week.

남	당신이 제출하신 우리 엔지니어링 부서의 물품 요청서를 보고 있었어요.
여	그런데요?
남	실수를 하신 것 같네요. **컴퓨터 마우스가 정말 그렇게 많이 필요해요?**
여	아, 실수예요! 두 개를 요청하려고 했어요.
남	아, 네. 부서에 15명밖에 없는데 이상하다고 생각했어요.
여	잡아내 주셔서 고마워요. **물품이 언제 도착할지 아세요?**
남	오늘 오후에 주문을 넣을 겁니다. 그러니 아마 다음 주에 도착할 거예요.

어휘 submit 제출하다 strange 이상한 supply 물품 given that ~을 고려하면

Product Code	Item	Quantity
XPFN	⁶³Computer mouse	20
KDQV	Ballpoint pen	35
LMTS	Microfiber cloth	15
ZUEH	Webcam	10

제품 코드	물품	수량
XPFN	⁶³컴퓨터 마우스	20
KDQV	볼펜	35
LMTS	극세사 천	15
ZUEH	웹캠	10

어휘 quantity 수량, 양 microfiber 초극세사

62

What department do the speakers work in?

(A) Legal
(B) Engineering
(C) Human Resources
(D) Information Technology

화자들은 어떤 부서에서 일하는가?

(A) 법률
(B) 엔지니어링
(C) 인사
(D) 정보 기술

해설 전체 내용 관련 – 화자들의 근무지
남자가 첫 대사에서 우리 엔지니어링 부서(I was just looking at ~ our engineering department) 요청서를 보고 있었다고 말하고 있으므로 정답은 (B)이다.

63

Look at the graphic. Which quantity needs to be changed?

(A) 20
(B) 35
(C) 15
(D) 10

시각 정보에 의하면, 어떤 수량을 변경해야 하는가?

(A) 20
(B) 35
(C) 15
(D) 10

해설 시각 정보 연계 – 변경해야 할 수량
남자가 두 번째 대사에서 컴퓨터 마우스가 정말 그렇게 많이 필요한지(Do we really need that many computer mouses?) 묻자, 여자가 실수(that is a mistake!)라고 하면서 두 개를 요청하려고 했다(I meant to request two)고 덧붙이고 있고, 물품 주문서에 따르면 컴퓨터 마우스는 수량이 20이므로 정답은 (A)이다.

64

What does the woman ask about?

(A) A refund
(B) A signature
(C) A meeting location
(D) A delivery date

여자는 무엇에 대해 물어보는가?

(A) 환불
(B) 서명
(C) 회의 장소
(D) 배송 일자

해설 세부 사항 관련 – 여자가 물어보는 것
여자가 마지막 대사에서 물품이 언제 도착하는지(Do you know when the supplies will get here?) 묻고 있으므로 정답은 (D)이다.

> **Paraphrasing** 대화의 when the supplies will get here
> → 정답의 A delivery date

65-67 대화 + 가격표

W-Am Welcome to Halcyon Florals. How can I help you?

M-Cn Hi. **65 I'm planning the Lambert-Evans wedding that's taking place this weekend.** I received an e-mail this morning that there's a problem with the flowers I ordered for the floral arrangements.

W-Am Yes, **66 unfortunately, my supplier notified me that they're out of stock because of a shortage.** I'm sorry, but **67 you'll have to choose a replacement for the lilies.**

M-Cn I know my client likes orchids, but I'm guessing those are too expensive. **67 We'll still need a flower that's under five dollars per stem.**

W-Am Well, what about these? They fit within your budget.

M-Cn Those will be perfect.

여 핼시언 플로럴입니다. 무엇을 도와드릴까요?

남 안녕하세요. **이번 주말에 열릴 램버트 에반스 결혼식을 계획하고 있어요.** 오늘 오전 이메일을 받았는데 제가 주문한 꽃꽂이 꽃에 문제가 있다고 해서요.

여 네, **유감스럽게도 저희 공급업체에서 물품 부족으로 재고가 없다고 알려왔어요.** 죄송하지만 **백합 대체품을 선택하셔야 해요.**

남 저희 고객이 난초를 좋아하는 걸로 아는데, 그건 너무 비쌀 것 같아요. **여전히 줄기당 5달러 미만인 꽃이 필요해요.**

여 음, 이건 어떠세요? 예산에 맞네요.

남 아주 좋아요.

어휘 floral arrangement 꽃꽂이 out of stock 재고가 떨어진, 품절된 shortage 부족 replacement 대체(품) lily 백합 orchid 난초 expensive 비싼 stem 줄기 fit 적합하다 budget 예산

Flowers	
Flower Type	**Price per Stem**
Lilies	$4.50
65 Tulips	$4.75
Roses	$6.25
Orchids	$8.00

꽃 종류	줄기당 가격
백합	4.50달러
⁶⁵튤립	**4.75달러**
장미	6.25달러
난초	8.00달러

65

What type of event are the speakers discussing?
(A) A retirement party
(B) A wedding
(C) A garden show
(D) A grand opening

화자들은 어떤 종류의 행사에 대해 이야기하는가?
(A) 은퇴 기념 파티
(B) 결혼식
(C) 정원 박람회
(D) 개업식

해설 전체 내용 관련 – 화자들이 논의 중인 행사
남자가 첫 대사에서 이번 주말에 열릴 램버트 에반스 결혼식을 계획하고 있다(I'm planning the Lambert-Evans wedding that's taking place this weekend)고 말하고 있으므로 정답은 (B)이다.

66

According to the woman, what has caused a problem?
(A) An invoice error
(B) A rainstorm
(C) A supply shortage
(D) A reservation cancellation

여자에 따르면, 무엇 때문에 문제가 발생했는가?
(A) 청구서 오류
(B) 폭풍우
(C) 공급 부족
(D) 예약 취소

어휘 invoice 청구서, 송장 reservation 예약 cancellation 취소

해설 세부 사항 관련 – 여자가 문제 발생의 원인이라고 말하는 것
여자가 두 번째 대사에서 유감스럽게도 공급업체에서 물품 부족으로 재고가 없다고 알려왔다(unfortunately, my supplier notified me that they're out of stock because of a shortage)고 말하고 있으므로 정답은 (C)이다.

67

Look at the graphic. Which flowers will be used in the arrangements?
(A) Lilies
(B) Tulips
(C) Roses
(D) Orchids

시각 정보에 의하면, 꽃꽂이에 어떤 꽃이 사용될 것인가?
(A) 백합
(B) 튤립
(C) 장미
(D) 난초

해설 시각 정보 연계 – 꽃꽂이에 사용될 꽃
여자가 두 번째 대사에서 백합 대체품을 선택해야 한다(you'll have to choose a replacement for the lilies)고 했고, 남자가 여전히 줄기당 5달러 미만인 꽃이 필요하다(We'll still need a flower that's under five dollars per stem)고 말하고 있으며, 가격표에 따르면 5달러 미만인 꽃은 백합과 튤립뿐이므로 정답은 (B)이다.

68-70 대화 + 매장 앞 공간　

W-Br	⁶⁸**I think I've inspected enough to determine a fair market value for your store.**
M-Cn	OK. ⁶⁸**You have the paperwork verifying that I replaced my roof last year, right? Buyers look for properties that don't need major repairs.**
W-Br	I do have that. And you're right—recent repairs are a factor that add to the value of a property.
M-Cn	⁶⁹**The historic windows will be a selling point,** I think. They're made of handblown glass. All the storefronts in this row of shops have them.
W-Br	They do add character. Now, ⁷⁰**I need to walk around with my camera to take some photos to file with my paperwork.**

여	**고객님 매장의 공정 시장 가치를 결정하기에 충분히 검토를 한 것 같아요.**
남	네. **작년에 지붕을 교체했다는 것을 증명하는 문서를 갖고 계시죠, 그렇죠? 매수자들은 큰 수리가 필요 없는 건물을 찾거든요.**
여	갖고 있어요. 그리고 맞습니다. 최근 보수 공사가 건물 가치를 더하는 요인입니다.
남	**유서 깊은 창문도 판매에 유리한 점 같아요.** 직접 입으로 불어서 만든 유리로 되어 있거든요. 이쪽 라인에 있는 모든 매장의 앞부분이 그 유리로 되어 있어요.

TEST 8

여　개성을 더하네요. 자, **카메라를 갖고 걸어 다니며 문서에 철할 사진을 좀 찍어야겠어요.**

어휘　inspect 점검하다, 시찰하다　determine 결정하다　fair market value 공정 시장 가치　paperwork 문서 작업　verify 확인하다　replace 교체하다　property 재산, 부동산, 건물　factor 요인　historic 역사적인　selling point 판매에 유리한 점　handblown (유리를) 손에 잡고 불어서 만든　storefront 매장 정면　character 개성

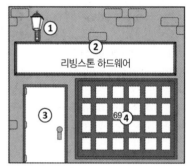

68

What is the man most likely planning to do?
(A) Sell a shop
(B) Expand warehouse space
(C) Replace a sign
(D) Install air-conditioning

남자는 무엇을 하려고 계획하겠는가?
(A) 매장 판매
(B) 창고 공간 확장
(C) 간판 교체
(D) 에어컨 설치

해설 세부 사항 관련 – 남자가 계획하는 일

여자가 첫 대사에서 고객의 매장을 위한 공정 시장 가치를 결정하기에 충분히 검토를 한 것 같다(I think I've inspected enough ~ your store)고 하자 남자가 작년에 지붕을 교체했다는 것을 증명하는 문서를 갖고 있는지(You have the paperwork verifying that I replaced my roof last year, right?) 물으면서 매수자들은 큰 수리가 필요 없는 건물을 찾는다(Buyers look for properties that don't need major repairs)고 말하고 있으므로 남자는 매장을 매도하려는 것을 알 수 있다. 따라서 정답은 (A)이다.

69

Look at the graphic. Which part of the storefront does the man say is historic?
(A) Part 1
(B) Part 2
(C) Part 3
(D) Part 4

시각 정보에 의하면, 남자는 매장 앞부분의 어떤 부분이 유서 깊다고 말하는가?
(A) 1
(B) 2
(C) 3
(D) 4

해설 시각 정보 연계 – 남자가 유서 깊다고 말하는 매장 앞 공간

남자가 두 번째 대사에서 유서 깊은 창문도 판매에 유리한 점 같다(The historic windows will be a selling point)고 말하고 있고, 매장 정면을 보면 창문은 4번이므로 정답은 (D)이다.

70

What will the woman do next?
(A) Recommend a paint color
(B) Inspect some lighting
(C) Measure a wall
(D) Take some photographs

여자는 다음으로 무엇을 할 것인가?
(A) 페인트 색상 추천
(B) 조명 점검
(C) 벽 치수 측정
(D) 사진 촬영

어휘　lighting 조명　measure 측정하다, 재다

해설 세부 사항 관련 – 여자가 다음에 할 일

여자가 마지막 대사에서 카메라를 갖고 걸어 다니며 문서에 철할 사진을 좀 찍어야겠다(I need to walk around with my camera to take some photos to file with my paperwork)고 말하고 있으므로 정답은 (D)이다.

> **Paraphrasing**　대화의 take some photos
> → 정답의 Take some photographs

PART 4

71-73 광고

W-Br　Are you furnishing a small apartment? **71 Go to Jillsbedstore.com and check out Jill's Cabinet Bed. 72 This unique bed fits into a hardwood cabinet, becoming compact and saving you space.** When you need to use it, just open the cabinet and unfold it to set it up. And this month only, we're offering listeners a special deal: **⁷³if you use the code 623Z to order on our Web site, we'll throw in two free pillows with your purchase.** So visit Jillsbedstore.com to start enjoying a more spacious apartment!

소형 아파트에 가구를 비치하고 계십니까? Jillsbedstore.com을 방문하셔서 질의 캐비닛 침대를 확인해 보세요. 이 특별한 침대는 단단한 목재 캐비닛 안으로 쏙 들어가서 크기가 작아지고 공간을 아껴줍니다. 사용해야 할 때는 그저 캐비닛을 열어 펴서 세우시면 됩니다. 이번 달만 청취자들에게 특별 할인을 제공하고 있습니다. **저희 웹사이트에서 주문 시 623Z 코드를 사용하시면 구매품에 베개 2개를 덤으로 드립니다.** Jillsbedstore.com을 방문해 아파트를 더욱 널찍하게 쓰기 시작하세요!

어휘 furnish 가구를 비치하다 unique 특별한, 독특한 fit into 꼭 들어맞다 hardwood 단단한 목재, 경재 compact 소형의 unfold 펴다, 펼치다 special deal 특별 할인 throw in 덤으로 주다 spacious 널찍한

71

What product is being advertised?
(A) A desk
(B) A bed
(C) A bookcase
(D) A chair

어떤 제품을 광고하는가?
(A) 책상
(B) 침대
(C) 책장
(D) 의자

어휘 advertise 광고하다

해설 전체 내용 관련 – 광고되고 있는 제품
화자가 초반부에 Jillsbedstore.com을 방문하여 질의 캐비닛 침대를 확인해 보라(Go to Jillsbedstore.com and check out Jill's Cabinet Bed)고 말하고 있으므로 광고되고 있는 제품은 침대라는 것을 알 수 있다. 따라서 정답은 (B)이다.

72

What advantage of the product does the speaker mention?
(A) It helps save space.
(B) It is guaranteed to last.
(C) It comes in multiple sizes.
(D) It is environmentally friendly.

화자는 제품의 어떤 장점을 언급하는가?
(A) 공간을 아끼는 데 도움이 된다.
(B) 확실히 오래간다.
(C) 다양한 크기로 나온다.
(D) 환경 친화적이다.

어휘 guarantee 보증하다, 확약하다 last 오래가다, 지속되다 multiple 다수의, 다양한 environmentally friendly 환경 친화적인

해설 세부 사항 관련 – 화자가 언급하는 제품의 장점
화자가 중반부에 이 특별한 침대는 단단한 목재 캐비닛 안으로 쏙 들어가서 크기가 작아지고 공간을 아껴준다(This unique bed fits into a hardwood cabinet, becoming compact and saving you space)고 말하고 있으므로 정답은 (A)이다.

73

How can the listeners receive a gift?
(A) By filling out a survey
(B) By going into a store
(C) By entering a code on a Web site
(D) By subscribing to a newsletter

청자들은 어떻게 선물을 받을 수 있는가?
(A) 설문을 작성해서
(B) 매장으로 가서
(C) 웹사이트에 코드를 입력해서
(D) 소식지를 구독해서

어휘 fill out a survey 설문을 작성하다 enter 입력하다 subscribe to ~을 구독하다 newsletter 소식지

해설 세부 사항 관련 – 청자들이 선물을 받을 수 있는 방법
화자가 후반부에 웹사이트에서 주문 시 623Z 코드를 사용하면 구매품에 베개 2개를 덤으로 준다(if you use the code 623Z to order on our Web site, we'll throw in two free pillows with your purchase)고 말하고 있으므로 정답은 (C)이다.

74-76 방송

W-Am **⁷⁴For the rest of today, it is expected to remain dry and cloudy in the Jonesdale area. But beginning tomorrow, we'll see colder temperatures and moderate snowfall. ⁷⁵So please remember to put on a heavy coat if you plan on doing anything outdoors.** As we head into next week, it'll finally start to feel like spring. OK, **⁷⁶next up, we'll be covering our local sports teams' recent events, including a big victory last night.**

오늘 남은 시간 내내 존스데일 지역은 건조하고 구름이 낀 상태가 계속될 것으로 보입니다. 하지만 내일부터 기온이 더 떨어지고 적당한 강설량을 보이겠습니다. 실외에서 무언가를 하실 계획이라면 두꺼운 코트를 입으시기 바랍니다. 다음 주로 향하면서 드디어 봄 기운이 느껴지기 시작할 겁니다. 네, 다음으로 어젯밤 큰 승리 소식을 비롯해 지역 스포츠 팀의 최근 소식을 보도합니다.

TEST 8

74

What is the broadcast mainly about?
(A) The weather
(B) Traffic updates
(C) An outdoor festival
(D) A city cleanup initiative

방송은 주로 무엇에 관한 것인가?
(A) 날씨
(B) 교통 소식
(C) 야외 축제
(D) 도시 정화 계획

어휘 traffic 교통 outdoor 야외의 cleanup 정화 initiative 계획

해설 전체 내용 관련 – 방송의 주제
화자가 도입부에 오늘 남은 시간 내내 존스데일 지역은 건조하고 구름이 낀 상태가 계속될 것으로 보인다(For the rest of today, it is expected to remain dry and cloudy in the Jonesdale area)라고 하면서 내일부터 기온이 더 떨어지고 적당한 강설량을 보이겠다(~ we'll see colder temperatures and moderate snowfall)고 날씨에 대해 언급하고 있으므로 정답은 (A)이다.

75

What does the speaker recommend?
(A) Filling out a form
(B) Wearing appropriate clothing
(C) Checking a map
(D) Using public transportation

화자는 무엇을 권하는가?
(A) 서식 작성하기
(B) 적절한 옷 입기
(C) 지도 확인하기
(D) 대중교통 이용하기

어휘 fill out a form 서식을 작성하다, 양식에 기입하다 appropriate 적절한 public transportation 대중교통

해설 세부 사항 관련 – 화자의 권고 사항
화자가 중반부에 실외에서 무언가를 할 계획이라면 두꺼운 코트를 입길 바란다(So please remember to put on a heavy coat ~)고 말하고 있으므로 정답은 (B)이다.

> Paraphrasing 담화의 put on a heavy coat
> → 정답의 Wearing appropriate clothing

76

What will the listeners hear next?
(A) An interview
(B) An advertisement
(C) Some sports updates
(D) Some newly released songs

청자들은 다음으로 무엇을 들을 것인가?
(A) 인터뷰
(B) 광고
(C) 스포츠 소식
(D) 새로 발매된 노래

어휘 release 발표하다, 공개하다

해설 세부 사항 관련 – 청자들이 다음에 청취할 것
화자가 마지막에 다음으로 지역 스포츠팀의 최근 소식을 보도한다(next up, we'll be covering our local sports teams' recent events, ~)고 말하고 있으므로 정답은 (C)이다.

> Paraphrasing 담화의 sports teams' recent events
> → 정답의 Some sports updates

77-79 전화 메시지

M-Au **77 This is Brilliant Watch Repair calling about the antique wristwatch that you dropped off yesterday. As you mentioned, one of the watch hands was frequently skipping ahead, so we replaced the battery.** That seemed to fix the issue. However, because the watch is quite old, we also took it apart to give it a good cleaning. In the future, **78 we suggest bringing it in for basic maintenance once every three years to keep it in good condition.** The watch is ready for you at any time. **79 Just be aware that tomorrow is a national holiday and we'll be closed.** Thanks!

브릴리언트 시계 수리점입니다. 어제 맡기신 골동품 손목시계 관련해서 전화 드려요. 언급하신 대로 시계 바늘 중 하나가 자주 건너뛰어서 배터리를 교체했습니다. 문제가 해결된 걸로 보여요. 그런데 시계가 꽤 오래됐기 때문에 분해해서 싹 청소했어요. 앞으로는 **좋은 상태를 유지하려면 3년마다 한 번씩 가져와서 기본 정비를 받으셨으면 좋겠습니다.** 시계가 준비되었으니 언제든 가져가세요. **내일은 국경일이라 문을 닫습니다.** 감사합니다!

어휘 antique 골동품의 wristwatch 손목시계 drop off 맡기다 mention 언급하다 frequently 자주 skip ahead 건너뛰다 replace 교체하다 fix 고치다, 수리하다 take apart 분해하다 maintenance 유지, 정비 keep ~ in good condition ~을 좋은 상태로 유지하다 be aware 알다

77

Why is the speaker calling?
(A) To provide a cost estimate
(B) To confirm some warranty information
(C) To report that a service has been completed
(D) To recommend that another business be contacted

화자가 전화한 이유는?
(A) 견적서를 제공하려고
(B) 품질 보증 관련 정보를 확인하려고
(C) 서비스가 완료됐음을 알려 주려고
(D) 다른 업체에 연락하라고 권하려고

어휘 cost estimate 견적서 confirm 확인하다 warranty 품질
보증서 complete 완료하다

해설 전체 내용 관련 – 전화의 이유

화자가 초반에 브릴리언트 시계 수리점인데 어제 맡긴 골동품 손목시계 관련해서 전화했다(This is Brilliant Watch Repair calling about the antique wristwatch that you dropped off yesterday)고 하면서 배터리를 교체했다(~ we replaced the battery)고 말하는 것으로 보아 시계 수리가 완료되어 전화했음을 알 수 있다. 따라서 정답은 (C)이다.

78

What does the speaker suggest the listener do?
(A) Schedule regular maintenance
(B) Wait for a sale price
(C) Call the manufacturer
(D) Ask for a second opinion

화자는 청자에게 무엇을 하라고 제안하는가?
(A) 정기 보수 일정 잡기
(B) 할인 가격 기다리기
(C) 제조업체에 전화하기
(D) 다른 사람의 의견 물어보기

어휘 regular 정기적인 manufacturer 제조업자 opinion 의견

해설 세부 사항 관련 – 화자의 제안 사항

화자가 중반부에 3년마다 한 번씩 정비를 받는 것이 좋겠다(we suggest bringing it in for basic maintenance once every three years ~) 고 말하고 있으므로 정답은 (A)이다.

Paraphrasing 담화의 basic maintenance once every three years → 정답의 regular maintenance

79

Why will a business be closed tomorrow?
(A) Some renovations will be done.
(B) The owner will be on vacation.
(C) An inspection will be conducted.
(D) It will be a national holiday.

업체가 내일 문을 닫는 이유는?
(A) 보수 작업이 진행될 것이다.
(B) 업주가 휴가를 갈 것이다.
(C) 점검이 시행될 것이다.
(D) 국경일이다.

어휘 renovation 개조, 보수 on vacation 휴가 중인 inspection
점검, 검사 conduct 하다

해설 세부 사항 관련 – 업체가 내일 문을 닫는 이유

화자가 마지막에 내일은 국경일이라 문을 닫는다(Just be aware that tomorrow is a national holiday and we'll be closed)고 말하고 있으므로 정답은 (D)이다.

80-82 연설

M-Cn **80 We're here tonight to celebrate Fritz Schneider's outstanding service to the company on the eve of his retirement.** Fritz has been with Elta Footwear since its inception, and without him, we wouldn't be where we are today. With unfailing optimism, he has provided consistent leadership to help us grow as a company. Thanks largely to his efforts, **81 today we produce more than 25 lines of athletic footwear.** We'll miss him, but we wish him well! And now, **82 I'd like to share a short video with some highlights of Fritz's many years with Elta.**

프리츠 슈나이더의 은퇴 전날, 회사에 기여한 뛰어난 업적을 기념하고 자 오늘 밤 이 자리에 모였습니다. 프리츠는 엘타 풋웨어 창립 이래로 계속 함께했으며, 프리츠가 없었다면 오늘날 여기까지 오지 못했을 겁니다. 한결같은 낙관주의로 일관된 리더십을 제공해 회사가 성장하도 록 도왔습니다. 그의 노력에 크게 힘입어 **오늘날 25종 이상의 운동화 를 생산하고 있습니다.** 그를 그리워하겠지만 만사형통하시길 바랍니 다! 이제 프리츠가 엘타와 함께한 세월을 간추린 짧은 동영상을 함께 보 려고 합니다.

어휘 celebrate 기념하다, 축하하다 outstanding 뛰어난,
중요한 service (오랜 기간 동안의) 근무 retirement 은퇴, 퇴직
inception 시작, 개시 unfailing 한결 같은 optimism 낙관주의,
낙천주의 consistent 일관성 있는, 일관된 largely 크게, 주로
effort 노력 produce 생산하다 athletic footwear 운동화

80

What is the purpose of the speech?
(A) To present an award
(B) To announce a job promotion
(C) To introduce a new product
(D) To celebrate a retirement

연설의 목적은?
(A) 상을 주려고
(B) 승진을 알리려고
(C) 신제품을 소개하려고
(D) 은퇴를 기념하려고

어휘 present an award 상을 주다   promotion 승진   introduce 소개하다

해설 전체 내용 관련 – 연설의 목적

화자가 초반부에 프리츠 슈나이더의 은퇴 전날, 회사에 기여한 뛰어난 업적을 기념하고자 오늘 밤 이 자리에 모였다(We're here tonight to celebrate Fritz Schneider's outstanding service to the company on the eve of his retirement)고 말하고 있으므로 정답은 (D)이다.

81

What does the company produce?
(A) Cookware
(B) Shoes
(C) Cameras
(D) Light fixtures

회사는 무엇을 생산하는가?
(A) 조리도구
(B) 신발
(C) 카메라
(D) 조명 기구

해설 세부 사항 관련 – 회사가 생산하는 것

화자가 중반부에 오늘날 우리는 25종 이상의 운동화를 생산하고 있다(today we produce more than 25 lines of athletic footwear)고 말하고 있으므로 정답은 (B)이다.

> **Paraphrasing**   담화의 **athletic footwear** → 정답의 **Shoes**

82

What will the listeners most likely do next?
(A) Watch a video
(B) Ask questions
(C) Eat a meal
(D) Take a group photograph

청자들은 다음으로 무엇을 하겠는가?
(A) 동영상 시청
(B) 질문
(C) 식사
(D) 단체 사진 촬영

해설 세부 사항 관련 – 청자들이 다음에 할 일

화자가 마지막에 짧은 동영상을 함께 보려고 한다(I'd like to share a short video ~)고 말하고 있으므로 정답은 (A)이다.

> **Paraphrasing**   담화의 **share a short video**
> → 정답의 **Watch a video**

83-85 전화 메시지

> **W-Br** This is Yuliya, the building manager. [83]I'm calling to let you know that workers are coming tomorrow morning to replace a defective water pipe under the pavement in front of your apartment. [84]It should only take a few hours to complete, but I know you sometimes work from home, and they'll be using loud machinery. Sorry this is such short notice—part of the pipe runs next to a telephone pole, so [85]I was required to apply for a permit to have the work done safely. I thought approval would take at least a week, but it was issued yesterday.

> 건물 관리인 율리야입니다. 귀하의 아파트 앞 인도 밑 결함이 있는 배수관을 교체하기 위해 내일 아침 작업자들이 옵니다. 몇 시간이면 완료되지만 가끔 재택 근무를 하시는 것으로 아는데, 작업자들이 시끄러운 기계를 사용할 겁니다. 급하게 알려드려 죄송합니다만 배수관 일부가 전신주 옆으로 지나가거든요. 그래서 작업을 무사히 마치도록 허가증을 신청해야 했어요. 승인이 최소 1주일은 걸릴 거라고 생각했는데 어제 허가증이 발급됐어요.

> **어휘** defective 결함이 있는   pavement 인도, 보도   work from home 재택 근무하다   machinery 기계   telephone pole 전신주   be required to ~해야 하다   apply for ~을 신청하다, 지원하다   permit 허가증   approval 승인   at least 최소한   issue 발급하다

83

What does the speaker say will happen tomorrow?
(A) A roof will be repaired.
(B) A pipe will be replaced.
(C) A payment will be processed.
(D) An application will be submitted.

화자는 내일 무슨 일이 있을 것이라고 말하는가?
(A) 지붕이 수리될 것이다.
(B) 관이 교체될 것이다.
(C) 지급이 처리될 것이다.
(D) 지원서가 제출될 것이다.

어휘 payment 지불, 결제   application 지원서

해설 세부 사항 관련 – 내일 있을 일

화자가 초반부에 아파트 앞 인도 밑 결함이 있는 배수관을 교체하기 위해 내일 아침 작업자들이 온다(~ workers are coming tomorrow morning to replace a defective water pipe under the pavement in front of your apartment)고 말하고 있으므로 내일 배수관을 교체할 예정이라는 것을 알 수 있다. 따라서 정답은 (B)이다.

> **Paraphrasing**   담화의 **replace a defective water pipe**
> → 정답의 **A pipe will be replaced.**

84

Why does the speaker say, "they'll be using loud machinery"?
(A) To reject a proposal
(B) To explain a delay
(C) To provide a warning
(D) To make a complaint

화자가 "인부들이 시끄러운 기계를 사용할 겁니다"라고 말하는 이유는?
(A) 제안을 거절하려고
(B) 지연에 대해 설명하려고
(C) 주의를 주려고
(D) 항의하려고

어휘 reject 거절하다 proposal 제안 delay 지연 warning 경고, 주의 complaint 항의, 불평

해설 화자의 의도 파악 – 작업자들이 시끄러운 기계를 사용할 거라는 말의 의도
앞에서 화자가 몇 시간이면 완료되지만 가끔 재택 근무를 하는 것으로 안다(It should only take a few hours to complete, but I know you sometimes work from home)고 말한 뒤 인용문을 언급하고 있으므로, 기계 소리가 재택 근무에 영향을 줄 수 있다는 것을 미리 알리기 위한 의도임을 알 수 있다. 따라서 정답은 (C)이다.

85

What does the speaker say about a permit?
(A) It has been mailed to the listener.
(B) It has been denied.
(C) It cost a lot of money.
(D) It was granted sooner than expected.

화자는 허가증에 대해 뭐라고 말하는가?
(A) 청자에게 우편으로 발송됐다.
(B) 거부됐다.
(C) 비용이 많이 든다.
(D) 예상보다 빨리 승인됐다.

어휘 deny 부인하다, 인정하지 않다 grant 승인하다 sooner than expected 예상보다 빨리

해설 세부 사항 관련 – 화자가 허가증에 대해 언급하는 것
화자가 후반부에 작업을 무사히 마치도록 허가증을 신청해야 했다(I was required to apply for a permit to have the work done safely)고 하면서 승인이 최소 1주일은 걸릴 거라고 생각했는데 어제 허가증이 발급됐다(I thought approval would take at least a week, but it was issued yesterday)고 말하고 있으므로 정답은 (D)이다.

86-88 회의 발췌

> **M-Au** **86I called this quick meeting for hospital staff. 87Our wireless Internet has gone down, and we are in the process of getting it restored.** But don't worry—hardwired access is still available,

so all doctors, nurses, and essential staff will still be able to use the desktop computers at each workstation. However, **88our patients will be wondering why they can't connect to the Wi-Fi. So please remember to let them know what's going on.**

병원 직원들을 위해 짧은 회의를 소집했습니다. 우리 무선 인터넷이 다운돼서 복구 작업이 진행 중입니다. 하지만 염려 마세요. 유선 접속은 여전히 가능하니 의사, 간호사, 필수 직원 여러분은 각자 업무 장소에서 데스크탑 컴퓨터를 쓰실 수 있습니다. 그러나 환자들은 왜 와이파이 연결이 안 되는지 의아해할 겁니다. 잊지 말고 무슨 상황인지 알려 주세요.

어휘 wireless 무선의 process 절차, 과정 restore 복구하다, 복원하다 hardwired 배선으로 연결된, 유선의 available 이용 가능한, 구할 수 있는 essential 필수적인 connect 연결하다, 접속하다

86

Where is the meeting taking place?
(A) At an office building
(B) At a museum
(C) At a hospital
(D) At a hotel

회의는 어디서 이루어지는가?
(A) 사무실 건물
(B) 박물관
(C) 병원
(D) 호텔

해설 전체 내용 관련 – 회의의 장소
화자가 도입부에 병원 직원들을 위해 짧은 회의를 소집했다(I called this quick meeting for hospital staff)고 말하고 있으므로 회의 장소는 병원임을 알 수 있다. 따라서 정답은 (C)이다.

87

What problem does the speaker mention?
(A) A door to a room is locked.
(B) There is a staff shortage.
(C) A delivery has been delayed.
(D) Wireless Internet is not available.

화자는 어떤 문제점을 언급하는가?
(A) 방문이 잠겨 있다.
(B) 인력이 부족하다.
(C) 배송이 지연됐다.
(D) 무선 인터넷을 이용할 수 없다.

어휘 locked 잠겨 있는 shortage 부족 delay 지연시키다

해설 세부 사항 관련 – 화자가 언급하는 문제
화자가 초반부에 무선 인터넷이 다운돼서 복구 작업이 진행 중(Our

wireless Internet has gone down, and we are in the process of getting it restored)이라고 말하고 있으므로 정답은 (D)이다.

> **Paraphrasing** 담화의 wireless Internet has gone down
> → 정답의 Wireless Internet is not available.

88

What does the speaker remind the listeners to do?
(A) Submit their time sheets
(B) Limit their mobile phone usage
(C) Share some information
(D) Use an alternate product

화자는 청자들에게 무엇을 하라고 알려 주는가?
(A) 근무 시간 기록표 제출
(B) 휴대전화 사용 제한
(C) 정보 공유
(D) 대체 제품 이용

어휘 time sheet 근무 시간 기록표 limit 제한하다 share 공유하다
       alternate product 대체품

해설 세부 사항 관련 – 화자가 청자들에게 하라고 알려 주는 것
화자가 마지막에 환자들은 왜 와이파이 연결이 안 되는지 의아해할 것(our patients will be wondering why they can't connect to the Wi-Fi)이라면서 잊지 말고 무슨 상황인지 알려 주라(So please remember to let them know what's going on)고 말하고 있으므로 정답은 (C)이다.

> **Paraphrasing** 담화의 let them know what's going on
> → 정답의 Share some information

89-91 담화
▶ 동영상 강의

> W-Br **89 As a consulting nutritionist, I'll work with your company cafeteria to review the items that are currently sold and suggest updates.** Consuming less meat is not only better for our health but is also better for the environment. And consider this interesting fact: **90 a recent study of thousands of cafeteria meals shows that when additional vegetarian options are offered, there is a significant increase in the number of vegetarian meals consumed. 91 Some of you have expressed concern that I might ask you to completely overhaul the entire menu.** Well, small changes can have surprising results!

> 저는 자문 영양사로서 이 회사 구내식당과 협업하여 현재 판매되는 물품을 검토하고 새로운 사항을 제안할 것입니다. 고기를 덜 먹는 것은 건강에 좋을 뿐 아니라 환경에도 역시 좋습니다. 이 흥미로운 사실을 고려해 보세요. 최근 수천 개의 구내식당 식사를 대상으로 한 연구에서는

채식 메뉴가 추가로 제공될 때 소비되는 채식 식단 수가 크게 증가하는 것을 볼 수 있습니다. 제가 전체 메뉴를 전면 개편하라고 요청할까 봐 걱정하는 분들이 계신데요. 음, 작은 변화가 놀라운 결과를 가져올 수 있습니다!

> 어휘 consulting 상담의, 자문의 nutritionist 영양사 currently 현재 consume 소비하다 environment 환경 recent 최근의 additional 추가의 vegetarian 채식주의자 significant 중요한, 커다란 increase 증가 express concern 우려를 표하다 completely 완전히, 전적으로 overhaul 개편하다, 개선하다 surprising 놀라운

89

What is the speaker mainly discussing?
(A) Updating a menu
(B) Organizing a health fair
(C) Planting a vegetable garden
(D) Reviewing some survey results

화자는 주로 무엇에 대해 이야기하는가?
(A) 메뉴 업데이트
(B) 건강 박람회 개최
(C) 텃밭 가꾸기
(D) 조사 결과 검토

어휘 organize 조직하다, 준비하다 fair 박람회, 전시회 survey 조사

해설 전체 내용 관련 – 담화의 주제
화자가 초반부에 자문 영양사로서 이 회사 구내식당과 협업하여 현재 판매되는 물품을 검토하고 새로운 사항을 제안할 것(As a consulting nutritionist, I'll work with your company cafeteria to review the items that are currently sold and suggest updates)이라고 말하는 것으로 보아 구내식당의 메뉴 업데이트에 대해 언급하고 있음을 알 수 있다. 따라서 정답은 (A)이다.

90

Why does the speaker mention a recent study?
(A) To support her opinion
(B) To suggest a process
(C) To request a guest speaker
(D) To publicize an event

화자가 최근 연구를 언급한 이유는?
(A) 자신의 의견을 뒷받침하려고
(B) 절차를 제안하려고
(C) 객원 연설자를 요청하려고
(D) 행사를 홍보하려고

어휘 support 지지하다 process 절차, 과정 publicize 알리다, 홍보하다

해설 세부 사항 관련 – 최근 연구를 언급한 이유
화자가 중반부에 최근 수천 개의 구내식당 식사를 대상으로 한 연구에서는 채식 메뉴가 추가로 제공될 때 소비되는 채식 식단 수가 크게 증가한 것을 볼 수 있다(a recent study of thousands of cafeteria meals shows that when additional vegetarian options are offered,

there is a significant increase in the number of vegetarian meals consumed)고 하면서 최근 연구를 언급한 것은 메뉴 업데이트가 필요하다는 화자의 의견을 뒷받침하기 위해서라는 것을 알 수 있다. 따라서 정답은 (A)이다.

91

Why does the speaker say, "small changes can have surprising results"?
(A) To agree with a decision
(B) To reassure the listeners
(C) To congratulate the listeners
(D) To request some assistance

화자가 "작은 변화가 놀라운 결과를 가져올 수 있습니다"라고 말하는 이유는?
(A) 결정에 동의하려고
(B) 청자들을 안심시키려고
(C) 청자들을 축하해 주려고
(D) 도움을 요청하려고

어휘 decision 결정, 결심   reassure 안심시키다   congratulate 축하하다   assistance 도움

해설 화자의 의도 파악 – 작은 변화가 놀라운 결과를 가져올 수 있다는 말의 의도

화자가 앞에서 전체 메뉴를 전면 개편하라고 요청할까 봐 걱정하는 사람들이 있다(Some of you have expressed concern that I might ask you to completely overhaul the entire menu)고 한 뒤 인용문을 언급한 것으로 보아, 변화가 그렇게 크지 않을 것이라고 청자들을 안심시키려 한 말임을 알 수 있다. 따라서 정답은 (B)이다.

92-94 회의 발췌

M-Au We've received feedback from one of our major clients. **92 The most recent advertisements we created for social media increased traffic to our client's Web site by 20 percent,** which is great. In other news, we're on track to exceed our annual goal in terms of revenue. Having said that, 40 percent of our business comes from two clients. And either could back out at any time. **93 We plan to ask existing clients to recommend our ad services to their business contacts. 94 As an incentive, we'll offer a discount to those whose referrals result in new business for us.**

주요 고객 중 한 곳에서 피드백을 받았는데요. **우리가 소셜미디어용으로 만든 최근 광고가 고객사의 웹사이트 트래픽을 20퍼센트 증가시켰다고 해요.** 훌륭합니다. 다른 소식으로 수익 관련해서 연간 목표 초과 달성을 착착 이루고 있어요. 그렇긴 해도 우리 일의 40퍼센트가 고객사 두 곳에서 나옵니다. 둘 중 하나라도 언제든 빠져나갈 수 있거든요. 기존 고객들에게 우리 광고 서비스를 업계 인맥에게 추천해 달라고 요청할 계획입니다. 장려책으로, 소개한 곳이 우리에게 새로운 거래로 이어지면 할인 혜택을 제공할 것입니다.

어휘 recent 최근의   advertisement 광고   increase 올리다, 증가시키다   be on track 착착 진행 중이다   exceed 초과하다   annual 연례의, 매년의   in terms of ~에 관해   revenue 수익, 수입   having said that 그렇긴 해도   back out 빠지다   existing 기존의   incentive 장려책   referral 소개

92

What type of service does the speaker's company provide?
(A) Travel planning
(B) Online advertising
(C) Staff recruitment
(D) Inventory management

화자의 회사는 어떤 종류의 서비스를 제공하는가?
(A) 여행 기획
(B) 온라인 광고
(C) 직원 모집
(D) 재고 관리

어휘 recruitment 모집   inventory 재고   management 관리

해설 전체 내용 관련 – 화자의 회사가 제공하는 서비스

화자가 초반부에 우리가 소셜미디어용으로 만든 최근 광고(The most recent advertisements we created for social media)라고 말하는 것으로 보아 화자의 회사는 온라인 광고 서비스를 제공하고 있음을 알 수 있다. 따라서 정답은 (B)이다.

Paraphrasing   담화의 social media → 정답의 Online

93

What does the speaker mean when he says, "40 percent of our business comes from two clients"?
(A) His team should be rewarded.
(B) He has time to develop more projects.
(C) The clients are major corporations.
(D) The company needs more clients.

화자가 "우리 일의 40퍼센트가 고객사 두 곳에서 나옵니다"라고 말하는 의도는 무엇인가?
(A) 팀이 보상을 받아야 한다.
(B) 더 많은 프로젝트를 개발할 시간이 있다.
(C) 그 고객들은 주요 기업이다.
(D) 회사에 고객이 더 필요하다.

어휘 reward 보상하다, 사례하다   corporation 기업

해설 화자의 의도 파악 – 일의 40퍼센트가 고객사 두 곳에서 나온다는 말의 의도

화자가 인용문을 언급한 뒤 기존 고객들에게 우리 광고 서비스를 업계 인맥에게 추천해 달라고 요청할 계획(We plan to ask existing clients to recommend our ad services to their business contacts)이라고 말하는 것으로 보아 화자는 고객을 더 확보할 필요가 있어서 한 말임을 알 수 있다. 따라서 정답은 (D)이다.

94

What incentive does the company plan to offer?
(A) A discount for referrals
(B) A subscription to an online magazine
(C) A satisfaction guarantee
(D) A certification course

회사는 어떤 장려책을 제공할 계획인가?
(A) 소개에 대한 할인
(B) 온라인 잡지 구독권
(C) 만족 보장
(D) 자격증 취득 강좌

어휘 subscription 구독   satisfaction 만족   guarantee 보증, 보장
certification 증명서 교부, 자격증 취득

해설 세부 사항 관련 – 회사가 제공할 계획인 장려책
화자가 마지막에 장려책으로, 소개한 곳이 우리에게 새로운 거래로 이어지면 할인 혜택을 제공할 것(As an incentive, we'll offer a discount to those whose referrals result in new business for us)이라고 말하고 있으므로 정답은 (A)이다.

95-97 공지 + 지도   ▶ 동영상 강의

W-Am Welcome to the annual Chesterfield Community Festival. I have a few quick announcements. First, 95**thank you to all of our vendors. They were selected because they use sustainable, environmentally friendly practices to produce their goods.** We know protecting the environment is important to our community. Second, there are still a few tickets available for tonight's jazz concert. 96**You can stop by Marta's Treats next to Wei Family Farms to buy a ticket.** Finally, remember that we are no longer handing out paper programs. 97**You can download the event program from our Web site at www. chesterfieldcommunityfestival.com.**

체스터필드 커뮤니티 연례 축제에 오신 것을 환영합니다. 몇 가지 간단한 공지 사항이 있습니다. **먼저 모든 판매업체에 감사드립니다. 지속 가능하고 환경 친화적인 방식으로 제품을 생산하기 때문에 선정되셨습니다.** 환경을 보호하는 것이 우리 지역사회에 중요하다는 것을 알고 있으니까요. 둘째, 오늘 밤 재즈 콘서트 표가 아직 남아 있습니다. **웨이**

패밀리 팜스 옆에 있는 마타 트리츠에 들러 표를 구매하실 수 있습니다. 마지막으로 저희는 더 이상 종이 프로그램을 나눠드리지 않습니다. 저희 웹사이트 www.chesterfieldcommunityfestival.com에서 행사 프로그램을 다운로드하실 수 있습니다.

어휘 annual 연례의, 매년의   announcement 공지, 발표
vendor 판매인, 노점상   sustainable 지속 가능한
environmentally friendly 환경 친화적인   practice 방식, 관행
protect 보호하다   available 이용 가능한, 구할 수 있는
no longer 더 이상 ~ 아닌   hand out 나눠주다

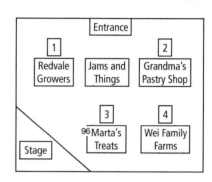

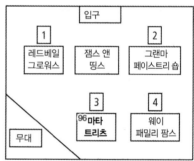

어휘 entrance 입구   stage 무대

95

What does the speaker say about the vendors?
(A) They use sustainable practices.
(B) They are offering free samples.
(C) Their goods are homemade.
(D) Their prices are reasonable.

화자는 판매업체들에 대해 뭐라고 말하는가?
(A) 지속 가능한 방식을 이용한다.
(B) 무료 견본을 제공한다.
(C) 제품을 손수 만든다.
(D) 가격이 적정하다.

어휘 reasonable (가격이) 적정한, 합리적인

해설 세부 사항 관련 – 화자가 판매업체들에 대해 말하는 것
화자가 초반부에 모든 판매업체에 감사드린다(thank you to all of our vendors)며 지속 가능하고 환경 친화적인 방식으로 제품을 생산한다(~ they use sustainable, environmentally friendly practices to produce their goods)고 말하고 있으므로 정답은 (A)이다.

96

Look at the graphic. Where can the listeners purchase concert tickets?

(A) At location 1
(B) At location 2
(C) At location 3
(D) At location 4

시각 정보에 의하면, 청자들은 음악회 표를 어디서 살 수 있는가?

(A) 1번 장소
(B) 2번 장소
(C) 3번 장소
(D) 4번 장소

해설 시각 정보 연계 – 음악회 표를 살 수 있는 장소
화자가 중반부에 웨이 패밀리 팜스 옆에 있는 마타 트리츠에 들러 표를 구매할 수 있다(You can stop by Marta's Treats next to Wei Family Farms to buy a ticket)고 말하고 있고, 지도에 따르면 웨이 패밀리 팜스 옆에 있는 마타 트리츠는 3번 장소이므로 정답은 (C)이다.

97

According to the speaker, what can be found on the festival Web site?

(A) A job listing
(B) An event program
(C) Safety regulations
(D) Names of sponsors

화자에 따르면, 축제 웹사이트에서 무엇을 찾을 수 있는가?

(A) 일자리 목록
(B) 행사 프로그램
(C) 안전 규정
(D) 후원자명

어휘 safety 안전 regulation 규정, 규제 sponsor 후원자

해설 세부 사항 관련 – 축제 웹사이트에서 찾을 수 있는 것
화자가 마지막에 웹사이트에서 행사 프로그램을 다운로드할 수 있다(You can download the event program from our Web site ~)고 말하고 있으므로 정답은 (B)이다.

98-100 담화 + 일정 게시판

M-Cn I hope you enjoyed the conference's keynote speaker, Ms. Olabisi Adewale. What a phenomenal speech. **98If you're interested in more of what she has to say about running a business, her latest book is for sale in the lobby.** It's definitely an engaging read! The rest of the conference is ahead of you now. **99We're excited that this year because of popular demand and all the feedback we received, we've added an additional day to the conference offerings.** And before you head off to your sessions, **100I wanted to announce a change of location for the twelve-thirty session today.** It's been moved, and the schedule board has been updated.

학회 기조 연설자인 올라비시 아드웨일 씨의 연설을 잘 들으셨기를 바랍니다. 정말 감탄이 나오는 연설이었죠. **업체 운영에 대해 더 많은 이야기를 듣고 싶으시다면 그녀의 최신 저서를 로비에서 판매하고 있습니다.** 단연코 멋진 책입니다! 학회 나머지 일정이 여러분을 기다리고 있습니다. 올해는 많은 분들의 요청과 피드백을 반영하여 학회 일정을 하루 더 추가하게 되어 매우 기쁘게 생각합니다. 세션으로 들어가기에 앞서, **오늘 12시 30분 세션의 장소가 변경됐음을 알려드립니다.** 장소가 옮겨졌으며 일정 게시판이 업데이트되었습니다.

어휘 conference 회의, 학회 keynote speaker 기조 연설자 phenomenal 경탄스러운, 경이로운 latest 최신의, 최근의 definitely 분명히, 확실히 engaging 매력적인 demand 수요 additional 추가의 offering 제공하는 것

SESSION	TIME	PLACE
Remote Workforces	9:00–10:00	Sky Room
Team Collaboration	10:00–11:00	Landmark Room
Lunch	11:00–12:15	Cafeteria
100Innovation Tools	12:30–1:30	Orion Room
Problem-Solving	1:30–2:30	Vista Room

세션	시간	장소
원격 인력	9:00-10:00	스카이룸
팀 협력	10:00-11:00	랜드마크룸
점심 식사	11:00-12:15	구내식당
100혁신 도구	12:30-1:30	오리온룸
문제 해결	1:30-2:30	비스타룸

어휘 remote 먼, 원격의 workforce 노동력, 노동 인구 collaboration 협력 innovation 혁신 tool 도구 problem-solving 문제 해결

98

What does the speaker encourage the listeners to do?

(A) Pick up refreshments
(B) Purchase a book
(C) Exchange contact details
(D) Volunteer for an activity

화자는 청자들에게 무엇을 하라고 권하는가?

(A) 다과 가져오기
(B) 책 구매하기
(C) 연락처 교환하기
(D) 활동에 자원하기

어휘 refreshments 다과 exchange 교환하다 volunteer 자원하다

화자가 초반부에 업체 운영에 대해 더 많은 이야기를 듣고 싶다면 그녀의 최신 저서를 로비에서 판매하고 있다(If you're interested in more of what she has to say about running a business, her latest book is for sale in the lobby)며 도서 구매를 권하고 있으므로 정답은 (B)이다.

99

What does the speaker say happened as a result of attendee feedback?
(A) Registration was conducted online.
(B) A more diverse range of speakers were invited.
(C) Extra charging stations were provided.
(D) Another conference day was added.

화자는 참석자 피드백의 결과로 어떤 일이 일어났다고 말하는가?
(A) 등록이 온라인으로 이뤄졌다.
(B) 더욱 다양한 연설자들이 초청됐다.
(C) 추가 충전대가 제공됐다.
(D) 학회 날짜가 추가됐다.

어휘 registration 등록   conduct 하다   diverse 다양한   range 범위   charging 충전

해설 세부 사항 관련 – 참석자 피드백의 결과로 있어난 일
화자가 중반부에 많은 사람들의 요청과 피드백을 반영하여 학회 일정을 하루 더 추가하게 되었다(~ because of popular demand and all the feedback we received, we've added an additional day to the conference offerings)고 말하고 있으므로 정답은 (D)이다.

100

Look at the graphic. Which session's location has changed?
(A) Remote Workforces
(B) Team Collaboration
(C) Innovation Tools
(D) Problem-Solving

시각 정보에 의하면, 어떤 세션의 장소가 변경됐는가?
(A) 원격 인력
(B) 팀 협력
(C) 혁신 도구
(D) 문제 해결

해설 시각 정보 연계 – 장소가 변경된 세션
화자가 후반부에 12시 30분 세션 장소가 변경됐다(I wanted to announce a change of location for the twelve-thirty session today)고 말하고 있고, 일정 게시판에 따르면 12:30-1:30은 혁신 도구 세션이므로 정답은 (C)이다.

1 (C)	2 (D)	3 (C)	4 (B)	5 (A)
6 (C)	7 (C)	8 (A)	9 (B)	10 (A)
11 (A)	12 (C)	13 (A)	14 (A)	15 (B)
16 (B)	17 (A)	18 (C)	19 (B)	20 (A)
21 (C)	22 (B)	23 (A)	24 (A)	25 (C)
26 (B)	27 (A)	28 (A)	29 (A)	30 (C)
31 (C)	32 (B)	33 (A)	34 (D)	35 (D)
36 (C)	37 (B)	38 (C)	39 (B)	40 (A)
41 (C)	42 (C)	43 (A)	44 (D)	45 (A)
46 (C)	47 (B)	48 (A)	49 (D)	50 (C)
51 (B)	52 (A)	53 (C)	54 (B)	55 (C)
56 (A)	57 (C)	58 (C)	59 (C)	60 (D)
61 (A)	62 (A)	63 (D)	64 (D)	65 (C)
66 (A)	67 (B)	68 (D)	69 (C)	70 (D)
71 (B)	72 (A)	73 (D)	74 (C)	75 (B)
76 (A)	77 (B)	78 (C)	79 (A)	80 (D)
81 (A)	82 (B)	83 (A)	84 (A)	85 (C)
86 (A)	87 (C)	88 (B)	89 (C)	90 (C)
91 (A)	92 (D)	93 (B)	94 (D)	95 (C)
96 (A)	97 (D)	98 (D)	99 (C)	100 (D)

PART 1

1 W-Am

(A) He's standing on a rug.
(B) He's turning a doorknob.
(C) He's climbing a ladder.
(D) He's painting a wall.

(A) 남자가 깔개 위에 서 있다.
(B) 남자가 문손잡이를 돌리고 있다.
(C) 남자가 사다리를 오르고 있다.
(D) 남자가 벽을 칠하고 있다.

어휘 doorknob 문손잡이 ladder 사다리

해설 1인 등장 사진 – 사람의 동작/상태 묘사
(A) 위치 오답. 남자가 깔개 위에 서 있는(is standing on a rug) 모습이 아니므로 오답.
(B) 동사 오답. 남자가 문손잡이를 돌리고 있는(is turning a doorknob) 모습이 아니므로 오답.

(C) 정답. 남자가 사다리를 오르고 있는(is climbing a ladder) 모습이므로 정답.
(D) 동사 오답. 남자가 벽을 칠하고 있는(is painting a wall) 모습이 아니므로 오답.

2 M-Au

(A) Some shirts have been hung on a clothing rack.
(B) A light fixture is attached to a column.
(C) Some boxes of clothing have been set on the floor.
(D) Some merchandise is on display in a store.

(A) 셔츠들이 의류 선반에 걸려 있다.
(B) 조명 기구가 기둥에 붙어 있다.
(C) 의류 상자들이 바닥에 놓여 있다.
(D) 상품이 매장에 진열되어 있다.

어휘 rack 받침대, 선반 light fixture 조명 기구 attach 부착하다, 붙이다 column 기둥 merchandise 상품, 물품 on display 진열된, 전시된

해설 사물/풍경 사진 – 사물 묘사
(A) 동사 오답. 셔츠들(Some shirts)이 의류 선반에 걸려 있는(have been hung on a clothing rack) 모습이 아니므로 오답.
(B) 동사 오답. 조명 기구(A light fixture)가 기둥에 붙어 있는(is attached to a column) 모습이 아니므로 오답.
(C) 사진에 없는 명사를 이용한 오답. 사진에 의류 상자들(Some boxes of clothing)의 모습이 보이지 않으므로 오답.
(D) 정답. 상품(Some merchandise)이 매장에 진열되어 있는(is on display in a store) 모습이므로 정답.

3 W-Br

(A) The woman is putting some papers into a file folder.
(B) The woman is typing on a keyboard.
(C) The woman is seated in front of a computer.
(D) The woman is holding a cup.

TEST **9**

(A) 여자가 서류를 파일 폴더에 집어넣고 있다.
(B) 여자가 자판으로 타자를 치고 있다.
(C) 여자가 컴퓨터 앞에 앉아 있다.
(D) 여자가 컵을 잡고 있다.

해설 1인 등장 사진 – 사람의 동작/상태 묘사
(A) 사진에 없는 명사를 이용한 오답. 사진에 파일 폴더(a file folder)의 모습이 보이지 않으므로 오답.
(B) 동사 오답. 여자가 자판으로 타자를 치고 있는(is typing on a keyboard) 모습이 아니므로 오답.
(C) 정답. 여자가 컴퓨터 앞에 앉아 있는(is seated in front of a computer) 모습이므로 정답.
(D) 동사 오답. 여자가 컵을 잡고 있는(is holding a cup) 모습이 아니므로 오답.

---

4 M-Cn

(A) Some employees are washing some windows.
(B) A shopper is carrying a package.
(C) Some shopping carts have been lined up in a row.
(D) Some products have fallen on the ground.

(A) 직원들이 창문을 닦고 있다.
(B) 쇼핑객이 상자를 들고 있다.
(C) 쇼핑 카트가 일렬로 늘어서 있다.
(D) 제품들이 바닥에 떨어져 있다.

어휘 package 상자, 포장물   in a row 일렬로

해설 혼합 사진 – 사람/사물/풍경 혼합 묘사
(A) 사진에 없는 명사를 이용한 오답. 사진에 창문을 닦고 있는 직원(Some employees)의 모습이 보이지 않으므로 오답.
(B) 정답. 쇼핑객(A shopper)이 상자를 들고 있는(is carrying a package) 모습이므로 정답.
(C) 동사 오답. 쇼핑 카트(Some shopping carts)가 일렬로 늘어서 있는(have been lined up in a row) 모습이 아니므로 오답.
(D) 동사 오답. 제품들(Some products)이 바닥에 떨어져 있는(have fallen on the ground) 모습이 아니므로 오답.

---

5 W-Am

(A) Snow is being cleared away.
(B) Bricks are being arranged on a walkway.
(C) Tree branches are being trimmed.
(D) A shovel is leaning against a flowerpot.

(A) 눈이 치워지고 있다.
(B) 벽돌이 보도에 배치되고 있다.
(C) 나뭇가지가 다듬어지고 있다.
(D) 삽이 화분에 기대어져 있다.

어휘 brick 벽돌   arrange 배치하다, 정리하다   walkway 통로
branch 가지   trim 다듬다   lean against ~에 기대다

해설 혼합 사진 – 사람/사물/풍경 혼합 묘사
(A) 정답. 눈(Snow)이 치워지고 있는(is being cleared away) 모습이므로 정답.
(B) 동사 오답. 벽돌(Bricks)이 보도에 배치되고 있는(are being arranged on a walkway) 모습이 아니므로 오답.
(C) 동사 오답. 나뭇가지(Tree branches)가 다듬어지고 있는(are being trimmed) 모습이 아니므로 오답.
(D) 동사 오답. 삽(A shovel)이 화분에 기대어져 있는(is leaning against a flowerpot) 모습이 아니므로 오답.

---

6 W-Br

▶ 동영상 강의

(A) A potted plant is hanging above a window.
(B) There is a lamppost in front of a building.
(C) Some chairs have been arranged in a line.
(D) Some bricks have been piled on a patio.

(A) 화분에 심은 식물이 창문 위에 걸려 있다.
(B) 건물 앞에 가로등 기둥이 있다.
(C) 의자가 일렬로 배치되어 있다.
(D) 벽돌이 테라스에 쌓여 있다.

어휘 hang 매달다, 매달리다   lamppost 가로등 기둥   pile 쌓다

해설 사물/풍경 사진 – 사물 묘사
(A) 사진에 없는 명사를 이용한 오답. 사진에 화분에 심은 식물(A potted plant)의 모습이 보이지 않으므로 오답.
(B) 사진에 없는 명사를 이용한 오답. 사진에 가로등 기둥(a lamppost)의 모습이 보이지 않으므로 오답.
(C) 정답. 의자(Some chairs)가 일렬로 배치되어 있는(have been arranged in a line) 모습이므로 정답.
(D) 동사 오답. 벽돌(Some bricks)이 테라스에 쌓여 있는(have been piled on a patio) 모습이 아니므로 오답.

PART 2

7

M-Au   Who's covering for Ms. Hamada?

W-Am   (A) Yes, it may rain later.
　　　 (B) No, I have enough.
　　　 (C) Her assistant.

하마다 씨를 누가 대신하나요?
(A) 네, 이따가 비가 올지도 몰라요.
(B) 아니요, 충분해요.
(C) 그녀의 비서가요.

어휘 cover (자리를 비운 사람의 일을) 대신하다 assistant 조수, 비서

해설 하마다 씨를 대신할 사람을 묻는 Who 의문문
(A) Yes/No 불가 오답. Who 의문문에는 Yes/No 응답이 불가능하므로 오답.
(B) Yes/No 불가 오답. Who 의문문에는 Yes/No 응답이 불가능하므로 오답.
(C) 정답. 하마다 씨를 대신할 사람이 누구인지 묻는 질문에 그녀의 비서라고 알려 주고 있으므로 정답.

8

M-Cn Where is the fashion seminar?

W-Br (A) It's in room 235.
(B) No, the black one.
(C) Just some blouses.

패션 세미나는 어디서 있죠?
(A) 235호에서요.
(B) 아니요, 검은색이요.
(C) 블라우스만요.

해설 패션 세미나 장소를 묻는 Where 의문문
(A) 정답. 패션 세미나 장소를 묻는 질문에 235호라고 구체적인 장소로 응답하고 있으므로 정답.
(B) Yes/No 불가 오답. Where 의문문에는 Yes/No 응답이 불가능하므로 오답.
(C) 연상 단어 오답. 질문의 fashion에서 연상 가능한 blouses를 이용한 오답.

9

M-Au Why do we have to put on safety goggles?

W-Am (A) No, the door on your left.
(B) Because of safety regulations.
(C) A hat and a scarf.

보호 안경을 왜 써야 하나요?
(A) 아니요, 왼쪽에 있는 문이요.
(B) 안전 규정 때문에요.
(C) 모자와 목도리요.

어휘 safety 안전 regulation 규정, 규제

해설 보호 안경을 써야 하는 이유를 묻는 Why 의문문
(A) Yes/No 불가 오답. Why 의문문에는 Yes/No 응답이 불가능하므로 오답.
(B) 정답. 보호 안경을 써야 하는 이유를 묻는 질문에 안전 규정 때문이라고 이유를 제시하고 있으므로 정답.
(C) 연상 단어 오답. 질문의 put on에서 연상 가능한 A hat과 a scarf를 이용한 오답.

10

W-Br What did you do for Mr. Sugiyama's retirement party?

M-Au (A) I helped decorate the room.
(B) He's not tired.
(C) Try the file cabinet.

수기야마 씨의 은퇴 기념 파티를 위해 뭘 하셨어요?
(A) 방을 꾸미는 걸 도왔어요.
(B) 그는 피곤하지 않아요.
(C) 문서 보관함을 보세요.

어휘 retirement 은퇴, 퇴직 decorate 장식하다, 꾸미다

해설 수기야마 씨의 은퇴 기념 파티를 위해 한 일을 묻는 What 의문문
(A) 정답. 수기야마 씨의 은퇴 기념 파티를 위해 한 일을 묻는 질문에 방을 꾸미는 걸 도왔다고 한 일을 알려 주고 있으므로 정답.
(B) 유사 발음 오답. 질문의 retirement와 부분적으로 발음이 유사한 tired를 이용한 오답.
(C) 질문과 상관없는 오답.

11

M-Au Can I take another bottle of water?

W-Am (A) If there are any left.
(B) An old refrigerator.
(C) No, the clock is fast.

물을 한 병 더 가져가도 되나요?
(A) 남은 물이 있다면요.
(B) 낡은 냉장고요.
(C) 아니요, 그 시계가 빨라요.

어휘 left 남은 refrigerator 냉장고

해설 부탁/요청의 의문문
(A) 정답. 물 한 병 추가 요청에 남은 물이 있다면 줄 수 있다고 답변하고 있으므로 정답.
(B) 연상 단어 오답. 질문의 water에서 연상 가능한 refrigerator를 이용한 오답.
(C) 질문과 상관없는 오답.

12

M-Au Isn't this the last train out?

W-Br (A) A round-trip ticket to New York.
(B) The office next door.
(C) No, there's one more.

이 열차가 막차 아닌가요?
(A) 뉴욕행 왕복 표예요.
(B) 옆 사무실이요.
(C) 아니요, 한 대 더 있어요.

어휘 round-trip 왕복 next door 옆 건물에, 옆집에

해설 열차가 막차인지를 확인하는 부정 의문문
(A) 연상 단어 오답. 질문의 train에서 연상 가능한 A round-trip ticket을 이용한 오답.

(B) 질문과 상관없는 오답.

(C) 정답. 열차가 막차인지를 확인하는 질문에 아니요(No)라고 대답한 뒤, 한 대 더 있다며 부정 답변과 일관된 내용을 덧붙이고 있으므로 정답.

13

W-Br What was the highlight of your visit to the city this weekend?

M-Cn (A) Definitely the art museum!
(B) Sorry, I already have plans.
(C) Yes, the guidebook was helpful.

이번 주말에 그 도시를 방문해서 무엇이 가장 좋았어요?
(A) 물론 미술관이죠!
(B) 미안하지만, 이미 약속이 있어요.
(C) 네, 안내서가 유용했어요.

어휘 highlight 가장 좋은 부분 definitely 분명히, 확실히
art museum 미술관 guidebook 안내서

해설 도시 방문 중 가장 좋았던 점을 묻는 What 의문문

(A) 정답. 도시 방문 중 가장 좋았던 점을 묻는 질문에 물론 미술관이라며 구체적으로 응답하고 있으므로 정답.

(B) 연상 단어 오답. 질문의 this weekend에서 연상 가능한 plans를 이용한 오답.

(C) Yes/No 불가 오답. What 의문문에는 Yes/No 응답이 불가능하므로 오답.

14

W-Am When was that news story about the merger published?

M-Cn (A) A few weeks ago.
(B) A reporter from the *Springfield News*.
(C) No, I think that's the right address.

합병에 관한 그 뉴스가 언제 발표됐나요?
(A) 몇 주 전이에요.
(B) 〈스프링필드 뉴스〉 기자요.
(C) 아니요, 그 주소가 맞는 것 같아요.

어휘 merger 합병 publish 발표하다

해설 합병 뉴스가 발표된 시점을 묻는 When 의문문

(A) 정답. 합병에 관한 뉴스의 발표 시점을 묻는 질문에 몇 주 전이라고 알려 주고 있으므로 정답.

(B) 단어 반복 오답. 질문의 news를 반복 이용한 오답.

(C) Yes/No 불가 오답. When 의문문에는 Yes/No 응답이 불가능하므로 오답.

15

W-Br We need to install a security system at the office.

M-Cn (A) It's a new ID badge.
(B) Yes, I think that's a good idea.
(C) I bought some lightbulbs.

우리 사무실에 보안 시스템을 설치해야 해요.
(A) 그것은 새 신분증입니다.
(B) 네, 좋은 생각인 것 같아요.
(C) 제가 전구를 좀 샀어요.

어휘 install 설치하다 security 보안 lightbulb 전구

해설 의사 전달의 평서문

(A) 연상 단어 오답. 평서문의 security에서 연상 가능한 ID badge를 이용한 오답.

(B) 정답. 사무실에 보안 시스템을 설치해야 한다는 평서문에 좋은 생각이라며 호응하고 있으므로 정답.

(C) 연상 단어 오답. 평서문의 install에서 연상 가능한 lightbulbs를 이용한 오답.

16

W-Am Where are the job fairs being held?

M-Cn (A) I'll take seven of them.
(B) There's a list in the folder.
(C) OK, I can drive.

취업 박람회는 어디서 열리나요?
(A) 제가 일곱 개 가져갈게요.
(B) 폴더에 목록이 있어요.
(C) 좋아요, 제가 운전할 수 있어요.

어휘 job fair 취업 박람회

해설 취업 박람회 개최 장소를 묻는 Where 의문문

(A) 질문과 상관없는 오답. How many 의문문에 대한 응답이므로 오답.

(B) 정답. 취업 박람회 개최 장소를 묻는 질문에 폴더에 목록이 있다며 알 수 있는 장소를 간접적으로 알려 주고 있으므로 정답.

(C) Yes/No 불가 오답. Where 의문문에는 Yes/No 응답이 불가능한데, OK도 일종의 Yes 응답이라고 볼 수 있으므로 오답.

17

M-Cn When can we use the new color printer?

W-Br (A) This afternoon.
(B) OK, that's good to hear.
(C) Sure, I can take a photograph.

새 컬러 프린터는 언제 사용할 수 있죠?
(A) 오늘 오후요.
(B) 알았어요, 좋은 소식이군요.
(C) 물론이죠, 제가 사진을 찍을 수 있어요.

어휘 take a photograph 사진을 찍다

해설 새 컬러 프린터를 사용할 수 있는 시점을 묻는 When 의문문

(A) 정답. 새 컬러 프린터를 사용할 수 있는 시점을 묻는 질문에 오늘 오후라고 알려 주고 있으므로 정답.

(B) Yes/No 불가 오답. When 의문문에는 Yes/No 응답이 불가능한데, OK도 일종의 Yes 응답이라고 볼 수 있으므로 오답.

(C) Yes/No 불가 오답. When 의문문에는 Yes/No 응답이 불가능한데, Sure도 일종의 Yes 응답이라고 볼 수 있으므로 오답.

18

M-Au Could you order some more paper plates?

W-Am (A) Thanks for the invitation.
(B) He got a job at the restaurant.
(C) We have enough for three months.

종이 접시를 좀 더 주문해 주실 수 있나요?
(A) 초대해 주셔서 감사합니다.
(B) 그는 식당에 일자리를 구했어요.
(C) 3개월 분량으로는 충분해요.

어휘 plate 접시 invitation 초대

해설 부탁/요청의 의문문
(A) 질문과 상관없는 오답.
(B) 인칭 오류·연상 단어 오답. 질문에 3인칭 대명사 He로 지칭할 인물이 언급되지 않았고, 질문의 plates에서 연상 가능한 restaurant를 이용한 오답.
(C) 정답. 종이 접시 추가 주문을 요청하는 질문에 3개월 분량으로는 충분하다며 추가 주문할 필요가 없음을 간접적으로 알려 주고 있으므로 정답.

19

M-Cn Should I pick up the food order for Ms. Santos?

W-Br (A) Let's meet next week.
(B) Yes, if you have the time.
(C) I don't cook with vegetable oil.

산토스 씨를 대신해서 제가 주문한 음식을 가지러 가야 하나요?
(A) 다음 주에 만납시다.
(B) 네, 시간이 있으시면요.
(C) 저는 식물성 기름으로 요리하지 않아요.

어휘 vegetable 채소

해설 부탁/요청의 의문문
(A) 질문과 상관없는 오답.
(B) 정답. 산토스 씨를 대신하여 주문한 음식을 가지러 가야 하는지 묻는 질문에 네(Yes)라고 대답한 뒤, 시간이 있다면이라고 긍정 답변과 일관된 내용을 덧붙였으므로 정답.
(C) 연상 단어 오답. 질문의 food에서 연상 가능한 cook과 vegetable oil을 이용한 오답.

20

W-Am Why don't you distribute this flyer around the office?

M-Cn (A) Sure—that's a great idea.
(B) Our flight's been canceled.
(C) I'll take the elevator.

이 전단을 사무실 근처에서 나눠주지 그래요?
(A) 그래요, 좋은 생각이네요.
(B) 저희가 탈 항공편이 취소됐어요.
(C) 저는 엘리베이터를 탈게요.

어휘 distribute 배포하다, 나눠주다 flyer (광고용) 전단

해설 제안/권유의 의문문
(A) 정답. 전단을 사무실 근처에서 나눠줄 것을 제안하는 질문에 좋다(Sure)고 수락한 뒤, 좋은 생각이라며 긍정 답변과 일관된 내용을 덧붙였으므로 정답.
(B) 연상 단어 오답. 질문의 flyer를 fly로 잘못 이해했을 경우 연상 가능한 flight를 이용한 오답.
(C) 연상 단어 오답. 질문의 office에서 연상 가능한 elevator를 이용한 오답.

21

M-Cn How often do you go to concerts?

W-Br (A) I ride my bicycle to work every day.
(B) No, he's not a professional musician.
(C) I don't have a lot of free time.

음악회는 얼마나 자주 가세요?
(A) 저는 매일 자전거를 타고 출근해요.
(B) 아니요, 그는 전문 음악가가 아닙니다.
(C) 저는 여가 시간이 많지 않아요.

어휘 professional 전문적인, 직업의

해설 음악회 관람 빈도를 묻는 How often 의문문
(A) 연상 단어 오답. 질문의 How often에서 연상 가능한 every day를 이용한 오답.
(B) Yes/No 불가 오답. How often 의문문에는 Yes/No 응답이 불가능하므로 오답.
(C) 정답. 음악회에 얼마나 자주 가는지 묻는 질문에 여가 시간이 많지 않다며 자주 가지 못함을 간접적으로 표현하고 있으므로 정답.

22

W-Am Do you want me to fix the printer in your office?

M-Cn (A) An official document.
(B) Yes, that would be helpful.
(C) I printed it on both sides.

사무실에 있는 프린터를 고쳐드릴까요?
(A) 공식 문서예요.
(B) 네, 도움이 될 것 같아요.
(C) 저는 양면 출력했어요.

어휘 official 공식적인

해설 제안/권유의 의문문
(A) 파생어 오답. 질문의 office와 파생어 관계인 official을 이용한 오답.
(B) 정답. 사무실 프린터 수리 제안에 네(Yes)라고 응답한 뒤, 도움이 될 것 같다고 수락하고 있으므로 정답.
(C) 파생어 오답. 질문의 printer와 파생어 관계인 printed를 이용한 오답.

23

M-Au Will the company's warehouse be built in the city or farther out?

W-Am (A) It'll be in the city.
(B) Yes, he's wearing a red sweater.
(C) Two square kilometers.

회사 물류창고는 도시에 지어질 건가요, 아니면 더 멀리 떨어져서 지어질 건가요?
(A) 도시에 지어질 겁니다.
(B) 네, 그는 빨간 스웨터를 입고 있어요.
(C) 2제곱킬로미터요.

어휘 warehouse 창고 farther 더 멀리

해설 회사 물류창고를 지을 장소를 묻는 선택 의문문
(A) 정답. 회사 물류창고를 지을 장소를 묻는 선택 의문문에 도시라며 둘 중 하나를 선택해 응답하고 있으므로 정답.
(B) Yes/No 불가 오답. 문장과 문장을 연결하는 경우를 제외하고는 선택 의문문에는 Yes/No 응답이 불가능하므로 오답.
(C) 연상 단어 오답. 질문의 farther에서 연상 가능한 kilometers를 이용한 오답.

24

▶ 동영상 강의

M-Cn The taxi has finally arrived.

W-Am (A) Oh, did it get stuck in traffic?
(B) Thanks, but I already have some.
(C) It's their final offer.

드디어 택시가 도착했어요.
(A) 아, 교통 체증에 갇혔었나요?
(B) 고맙지만, 이미 좀 있어요.
(C) 그들의 최종 제안이에요.

어휘 stuck in traffic 교통이 정체된, 막힌 final offer 최종 제안

해설 사실/정보 전달의 평서문
(A) 정답. 드디어 택시가 도착했다는 평서문에 교통 체증에 갇혔었는지 늦은 이유에 대해 묻고 있으므로 정답.
(B) 평서문과 상관없는 오답.
(C) 파생어 오답. 평서문의 finally와 파생어 관계인 final을 이용한 오답.

25

M-Au How can we train all the new team members?

W-Br (A) Yes, I worked on those.
(B) It wasn't as long as we thought.
(C) People like watching videos.

신입 팀원들을 전부 어떻게 교육하죠?
(A) 네, 제가 작업했어요.
(B) 우리가 생각했던 것만큼 길지는 않았어요.
(C) 사람들은 동영상 시청을 좋아해요.

어휘 train 교육하다, 훈련하다

해설 신입 팀원들 교육 방법을 묻는 How 의문문
(A) Yes/No 불가 오답. How 의문문에는 Yes/No 응답이 불가능하므로 오답.
(B) 질문과 상관없는 오답.
(C) 정답. 신입 팀원들 교육 방법을 묻는 질문에 사람들은 동영상 시청을 좋아한다며 동영상을 제안하고 있으므로 정답.

26

M-Au The party is supposed to start at six P.M., right?

W-Am (A) I added her name to the guest list.
(B) No, the invitation said seven.
(C) Because the party decorations were expensive.

파티가 오후 6시에 시작하기로 되어 있죠, 그렇죠?
(A) 제가 그녀의 이름을 방문객 명단에 추가했어요.
(B) 아니요, 초대장에는 7시로 되어 있어요.
(C) 파티 장식이 비쌌기 때문이에요.

어휘 be supposed to ~하기로 되어 있다 add 추가하다 invitation 초대, 초대장 decoration 장식

해설 파티 시작 시간을 확인하는 부가 의문문
(A) 연상 단어 오답. 질문의 party에서 연상 가능한 guest list를 이용한 오답.
(B) 정답. 파티가 오후 6시에 시작하는지 여부를 확인하는 질문에 아니(No)라고 대답한 뒤, 초대장에는 7시로 되어 있다며 부정 답변과 일관된 내용을 덧붙였으므로 정답.
(C) 단어 반복 오답. 질문의 party를 반복 이용한 오답.

27

M-Cn Does the manager want us to pick up the supplies or have them delivered?

W-Br (A) She'll be here soon.
(B) You dropped your pen.
(C) You're right about that.

관리자는 우리가 물품을 가지러 가길 바라나요, 아니면 배송시키기를 바라나요?
(A) 그녀가 곧 올 거예요.
(B) 펜을 떨어뜨리셨어요.
(C) 당신 말이 맞아요.

어휘 supply 용품

해설 관리자가 원하는 물품 배송 방식을 묻는 선택 의문문
(A) 정답. 물품 픽업과 배송 중 관리자가 원하는 방식을 묻는 질문에 그녀가 곧 올 거라며 관리자가 오면 어떻게 할지 알게 될 것이라는 제3의 답변을 한 정답.
(B) 연상 단어 오답. 질문의 supplies에서 연상 가능한 pen을 이용한 오답.
(C) 질문과 상관없는 오답.

28

▶ 동영상 강의

W-Am Has Jacob come into the office today?

M-Au (A) His briefcase is on his desk.
(B) Yes, it is a nice office.
(C) I can come in for just a minute.

제이콥은 오늘 사무실에 왔나요?
(A) 그의 서류 가방이 책상 위에 있어요.
(B) 네, 멋진 사무실이에요.
(C) 저는 잠깐만 들어갈 수 있어요.

어휘 briefcase 서류 가방

해설 제이콥이 오늘 사무실에 왔는지를 묻는 조동사(Has) 의문문
(A) 정답. 제이콥이 오늘 사무실에 왔는지를 묻는 질문에 그의 서류 가방이 책상 위에 있다며 사무실에 왔음을 우회적으로 표현하고 있으므로 정답.
(B) 단어 반복 오답. 질문의 office를 반복 이용한 오답.
(C) 단어 반복 오답. 질문의 come을 반복 이용한 오답.

29

▶ 동영상 강의

W-Am Are you joining the team for today's briefing?

M-Cn (A) My top client is in town.
(B) Vittorio's Pizzeria.
(C) I enjoyed that film.

오늘 브리핑 때 팀에 합류하시나요?
(A) 제 최고 고객이 와 있어요.
(B) 비토리오 피자 전문점이요.
(C) 저는 그 영화를 재미있게 봤어요.

어휘 briefing 간단한 보고, 상황 보고

해설 오늘 브리핑 때 팀에 합류하는지를 묻는 Be동사 의문문
(A) 정답. 오늘 브리핑 때 팀에 합류하는지를 묻는 질문에 최고 고객이 와 있다며 갈 수 없는 이유(고객을 만나야 함)를 우회적으로 표현하고 있으므로 정답.
(B) 질문과 상관없는 오답.
(C) 질문과 상관없는 오답. How 의문문에 대한 응답이므로 오답.

30

W-Br I'm organizing a healthy eating program at the office.

M-Au (A) She studied at that theater program.
(B) Right beside the new projector.
(C) Do you need any help with it?

저는 사무실에서 건강한 식사 프로그램을 준비하고 있어요.
(A) 그녀는 그 극장 프로그램을 살펴봤어요.
(B) 새 프로젝터 바로 옆이요.
(C) 도움이 필요하세요?

어휘 organize 조직하다, 준비하다   healthy 건강에 좋은, 건강한

해설 사실/정보 전달의 평서문
(A) 평서문과 상관없는 오답. 평서문에 3인칭 대명사 She로 지칭할 인물이 언급되지 않았으므로 오답.

(B) 평서문과 상관없는 오답. Where 의문문에 대한 응답이므로 오답.
(C) 정답. 건강한 식사 프로그램을 준비하고 있다는 정보를 전달하는 평서문에 도움이 필요한지를 되묻는 응답이므로 정답.

31

W-Am Is your car expensive to repair?

M-Cn (A) The largest model available.
(B) Only a few more times.
(C) It's been running perfectly since I bought it.

당신의 차는 수리 비용이 비싼가요?
(A) 이용 가능한 가장 큰 모델이에요.
(B) 몇 번만 더요.
(C) 구입했을 때부터 완벽하게 작동하고 있어요.

어휘 available 이용 가능한   perfectly 완벽하게

해설 차 수리 비용이 비싼지를 묻는 Be동사 의문문
(A) 연상 단어 오답. 질문의 car에서 연상 가능한 The largest model을 이용한 오답.
(B) 질문과 상관없는 오답.
(C) 정답. 차 수리 비용이 비싼지 묻는 질문에 구입했을 때부터 완벽하게 작동하고 있다며 차를 아직 수리한 적 없어서 알지 못함을 간접적으로 표현하고 있으므로 정답.

PART 3

32-34

W-Am Mr. Hughes? My name is Ms. Ayhan. [32] **I'll be interviewing you today for the open position of patient transporter.** I see on your application that you've worked in health care before.

M-Cn That's right. [33] **I worked at the main reception desk at the Southeast Regional Hospital for a while.** But I'd like to try a different role.

W-Am You'd be responsible for moving patients to various locations throughout the hospital. [34] **It'll involve about six miles of walking every shift.** Are you OK with that?

M-Cn I actually do a lot of hiking and rock climbing in my free time. So I'm looking forward to having a job that'll have me on my feet more.

여   휴스 씨? 저는 아이한이라고 해요. **오늘 환자 운반요원 공석 채용을 위해 제가 휴스 씨 면접을 진행할 겁니다.** 의료 분야에서 일한 적이 있다고 지원서에서 봤는데요.

남   맞습니다. **얼마 동안 사우스이스트 지역 병원 메인 안내데스크에서 일했습니다.** 하지만 다른 역할을 맡아 보고 싶었어요.

여	환자들을 병원의 여러 장소로 이동시킬 책임이 주어질 텐데요. 매 교대 근무마다 6마일 정도 걷게 될 거예요. 괜찮으신가요?
남	실은 여가 시간에 하이킹과 암벽 등반을 많이 합니다. 그래서 발로 더 많이 뛰는 직업을 무척 바라고 있어요.

어휘	open position 공석 patient 환자 transporter 수송자, 운반하는 사람 application 지원, 지원서 health care 의료 for a while 얼마 동안 role 역할 responsible 책임이 있는 various 다양한 involve 수반하다, 포함하다 look forward to ~을 고대하다

32

Where is the conversation taking place?
(A) At an athletic club
(B) At a hospital
(C) At a shipping company
(D) At an accounting firm

대화는 어디서 이루어지는가?
(A) 운동부
(B) 병원
(C) 운송회사
(D) 회계사무소

해설 전체 내용 관련 – 대화의 장소
여자가 첫 대사에서 오늘 환자 운반요원 공석 채용을 위해 본인이 휴스 씨 면접을 진행할 것(I'll be interviewing you today for the open position of patient transporter)이라고 하는 것으로 보아 병원에서 말하고 있음을 알 수 있다. 따라서 정답은 (B)이다.

33

What was the man's previous job?
(A) Receptionist
(B) Custodian
(C) Tour guide
(D) Bus driver

남자의 이전 직업은 무엇인가?
(A) 안내데스크 직원
(B) 관리인
(C) 관광가이드
(D) 버스 운전기사

어휘 previous 이전의

해설 세부 사항 관련 – 남자의 이전 직업
남자가 첫 대사에서 사우스이스트 지역 병원 메인 안내데스크에서 일했다(I worked at the main reception desk at the Southeast Regional Hospital for a while)고 말하고 있으므로 정답은 (A)이다.

Paraphrasing	대화의 I worked at the main reception desk → 정답의 Receptionist

34

What does the woman emphasize about the job being offered?
(A) It demands long hours.
(B) It requires a lot of experience.
(C) It offers a competitive salary.
(D) It involves a lot of walking.

여자는 제공되는 일자리에 대해 무엇을 강조하는가?
(A) 근무 시간이 길다.
(B) 많은 경력이 필요하다.
(C) 높은 급여를 제공한다.
(D) 많이 걷는 것이 포함된다.

어휘 demand 요구하다 experience 경험, 경력 competitive 경쟁력 있는

해설 세부 사항 관련 – 여자가 일자리에 대해 강조하는 것
여자가 두 번째 대사에서 매 교대 근무마다 6마일 정도 걷게 될 것(It'll involve about six miles of walking every shift)이라고 말하고 있으므로 정답은 (D)이다.

Paraphrasing	대화의 six miles of walking → 정답의 a lot of walking

35-37 3인 대화

W-Br	Hello. 35 I'm calling to discuss the men's suit and coat store that you want to open.
M-Cn	Thanks for returning our call. My cousin and I are both on the line.
M-Au	Yes-thanks. At first, we were just going to open the business without any advertising.
M-Cn	Right. 36 But then we consulted a friend in the retail industry. He said a strong advertising campaign makes a difference and referred us to you.
W-Br	He's right. You need to advertise your store before it opens.
M-Au	Have you looked at the information we sent?
W-Br	Yes, and here's what I think: 37 first, you should emphasize the fact that this will be a family-run business. Local customers will appreciate that.

여	안녕하세요. 귀하께서 개업하고 싶어 하시는 남성 정장 및 코트 매장에 대해 상의 드리려고 전화했습니다.
남1	전화 주셔서 감사합니다. 제 사촌과 저 둘 다 듣고 있어요.
남2	네, 감사합니다. 처음에는 저희가 광고 없이 개업하려고 했어요.
남1	맞아요. 그런데 소매업계에 있는 친구에게 상담을 했는데요. 강력한 광고 캠페인이 차이를 만든다고 하면서 저희에게

여기를 소개해주었습니다.

여 그분 말씀이 맞습니다. 개업하기 전에 매장을 광고하셔야 해요.

남2 저희가 보낸 정보는 보셨나요?

여 네, 제 생각을 말씀드릴게요. **우선 가족이 운영하는 업체라는 사실을 강조하셔야 합니다.** 지역 소비자들은 그 점을 높이 평가하거든요.

어휘 suit 정장 advertising 광고 consult 상담하다, 상의하다 retail 소매 make a difference 차이를 낳다 refer 추천[소개]하다 emphasize 강조하다 family-run business 가족이 운영하는 업체 local 지역의 appreciate 인정하다, 진가를 알아보다

35

What kind of business will the men open?
(A) An electronics repair shop
(B) A car dealership
(C) A restaurant
(D) A clothing store

남자들은 어떤 종류의 업체를 열 것인가?
(A) 전자 제품 수리점
(B) 자동차 대리점
(C) 음식점
(D) 의류 매장

해설 세부 사항 관련 – 남자들이 개업하고 싶어 하는 업체
여자가 첫 대사에서 남자들이 개업하고 싶어 하는 남성 정장 및 코트 매장에 대해 상의하려고 전화했다(I'm calling to discuss the men's suit and coat store that you want to open)고 말하고 있는 것으로 보아 남자들은 의류 매장을 열고 싶어 한다는 것을 알 수 있다. 따라서 정답은 (D)이다.

Paraphrasing 대화의 the men's suit and coat store
→ 정답의 A clothing store

36

How did the men learn about the woman's consulting service?
(A) From a local business owner
(B) From a marketing course
(C) From a friend who works in retail
(D) From a newspaper advertisement

남자들은 여자의 자문 서비스에 대해 어떻게 알았는가?
(A) 지역 내 사업주로부터 들어서
(B) 마케팅 강좌에서 들어서
(C) 소매업계에 종사하는 친구에게 들어서
(D) 신문 광고를 통해서

해설 세부 사항 관련 – 남자들이 여자의 자문 서비스를 알게 된 경로
첫 번째 남자가 두 번째 대사에서 소매업계에 있는 친구에게 상담을 했다(we consulted a friend in the retail industry)면서 친구가 여길 소개해줬다(He said ~ and referred us to you)고 말하고 있으므로 정답은 (C)이다.

37

What does the woman say should be emphasized about a business?
(A) That it will provide many jobs
(B) That it will be run by family members
(C) That its owners have a lot of experience
(D) That its owners live in the neighborhood

여자는 업체에 대해 무엇을 강조해야 한다고 말하는가?
(A) 많은 일자리를 제공할 것이라는 점
(B) 가족이 운영할 것이라는 점
(C) 주인이 경력이 많다는 점
(D) 주인이 인근에 거주한다는 점

어휘 neighborhood 인근, 근처

해설 세부 사항 관련 – 여자가 업체에 대해 강조해야 한다고 말하는 것
여자가 마지막 대사에서 우선 가족이 운영하는 업체라는 사실을 강조해야 한다(first, you should emphasize the fact that this will be a family-run business)고 말하고 있으므로 정답은 (B)이다.

Paraphrasing 대화의 be a family-run business
→ 정답의 be run by family members

38-40

M-Au **38 Look what just arrived—they're the new handheld scanners we've been waiting for!**

W-Br **38 That's exciting! 39 It's going to be so much easier to scan the groceries with these.** Do you know when they'll be installed at each of the checkout stations?

M-Au Our manager is hoping to set them up tomorrow night after the store closes. She asked if I could help, but I'm not available.

W-Br Oh, **40 I can stay late tomorrow night. I'll go let her know.**

남 방금 도착한 것 좀 보세요. 우리가 기다리던 신제품 소형 스캐너예요!

여 신나네요! 이걸로 식료품을 스캔하면 훨씬 수월해질 거예요. 각 계산대에 언제 설치될지 아세요?

남 관리자는 내일 밤 매장을 닫은 후 설치했으면 해요. 도와줄 수 있는지 물었는데 제가 시간이 안 되네요.

여 아, 제가 내일 밤 늦게까지 남아 있을 수 있어요. 제가 가서 관리자에게 말할게요.

어휘 handheld 손에 들고 쓰는; 소형 기기 grocery 식료품 install 설치하다 checkout station 계산대 set up 설치하다 available 시간이 되는

38

What are the speakers excited about?
(A) An upcoming holiday
(B) A staff training session
(C) Some new equipment
(D) Some staff discounts

화자들은 무엇에 대해 기뻐하는가?
(A) 다가오는 휴일
(B) 직원 교육
(C) 새 장비
(D) 직원 할인

어휘 upcoming 다가오는, 곧 있을   equipment 장비

해설 세부 사항 관련 – 화자들이 기뻐하는 것
남자가 첫 대사에서 우리가 기다리던 신제품 소형 스캐너가 방금 도착한 것 좀 보라(Look what just arrived—they're the new handheld scanners we've been waiting for!)고 하자, 여자가 신난다(That's exciting!)고 말하고 있으므로 정답은 (C)이다.

> **Paraphrasing**   대화의 the new handheld scanners
> → 정답의 Some new equipment

39

Where most likely do the speakers work?
(A) At a train station
(B) At a grocery store
(C) At an electronics store
(D) At a medical center

화자들은 어디서 일하겠는가?
(A) 기차역
(B) 식료품점
(C) 전자 제품 매장
(D) 병원

어휘 medical 의료의

해설 전체 내용 관련 – 화자들의 근무 장소
여자가 첫 대사에서 이걸로 식료품을 스캔하면 훨씬 수월해질 것(It's going to be so much easier to scan the groceries with these)이라고 말하는 것으로 보아 화자들은 식료품점에서 근무하고 있다는 것을 알 수 있다. 따라서 정답은 (B)이다.

40

What will the woman tell her manager?
(A) She can work extra hours.
(B) She needs more supplies.
(C) She stocked some shelves.
(D) She completed a project.

여자는 관리자에게 뭐라고 말할 것인가?
(A) 초과 근무를 할 수 있다.
(B) 물품이 더 필요하다.
(C) 선반에 물건을 채웠다.
(D) 프로젝트를 완료했다.

어휘 work extra hours 초과 근무하다   supply 용품   stock 판매할 상품을 갖춰 두다, 채우다

해설 세부 사항 관련 – 여자가 관리자에게 할 말
여자가 마지막 대사에서 본인이 내일 밤 늦게까지 남아 있을 수 있다(I can stay late tomorrow night)면서 가서 관리자에게 말하겠다(I'll go let her know)고 하므로 정답은 (A)이다.

> **Paraphrasing**   대화의 stay late → 정답의 work extra hours

41-43 3인 대화

W-Am **41 I'm Mona Pahlavi, from Pahlavi Construction, and this is Ms. Taylor, our interior designer.** We're looking for a source for reclaimed lumber. Many customers are asking to incorporate old wood into their construction projects.

M-Au You've come to the right place. We carry wood rescued from barns, factories, and other structures that have been torn down.

W-Br **42 People think using reclaimed lumber is cost-effective. Is that true?**

M-Au **42 Surprisingly, no. It's actually more expensive because we have to go through a lengthy process to make the wood reusable.**

W-Am Hmm. What do you think about that, Ms. Taylor?

W-Br Customers will pay more for the old wood look, but **43 I'm sure they'd like to see some samples before deciding.**

여1 저는 팔라비 건설의 모나 팔라비입니다. 이쪽은 저희 실내 디자이너 테일러 씨이고요. 저희는 재생 목재 공급자를 찾고 있어요. 많은 고객이 공사 프로젝트에 고목재를 포함해 달라고 요청하고 있어서요.

남 잘 찾아오셨습니다. 저희는 헛간과 공장, 허물어진 구조물에서 건진 목재를 취급합니다.

여2 사람들은 재생 목재가 가성비 높다고 생각하던데요. 사실인가요?

남 놀랍게도 사실이 아닙니다. 목재를 재사용할 수 있도록 만드는 긴 과정을 거쳐야 하기 때문에 사실 더 비싸거든요.

여1 음. 어떻게 생각하세요, 테일러 씨?

여2 고객들은 고목재 외관에 돈을 더 지불할 겁니다. 하지만 **결정하기 전에 분명 견본을 보고 싶어 할 거예요.**

어휘 reclaimed 재생된 lumber 목재 incorporate 포함하다 construction 건설, 공사 rescue 구조하다 barn 헛간 structure 구조물 torn down 허물어진 cost-effective 비용 효율적인 surprisingly 놀랍게도 lengthy 너무 긴, 지루한 process 과정, 절차 reusable 재사용할 수 있는

41

What type of business do the women work at?

(A) A furniture store
(B) A hardware store
(C) A construction company
(D) A landscaping service

여자들은 어떤 종류의 업체에서 일하는가?

(A) 가구점
(B) 철물점
(C) 건설 회사
(D) 조경 서비스 업체

해설 전체 내용 관련 – 여자들의 근무 업종

첫 번째 여자가 첫 대사에서 저는 팔라비 건설의 모나 팔라비이고 이쪽은 저희 실내 디자이너 테일러 씨(I'm Mona Pahlavi, from Pahlavi Construction, and this is Ms. Taylor, our interior designer)라고 소개하고 있으므로 여자들은 건설 회사에서 근무하고 있다는 것을 알 수 있다. 따라서 정답은 (C)이다.

42

According to the man, what may be surprising about a product?

(A) Its weight
(B) Its durability
(C) Its cost
(D) Its color

남자에 따르면, 제품의 어떤 점이 놀라운가?

(A) 무게
(B) 내구성
(C) 비용
(D) 색상

해설 세부 사항 관련 – 제품의 놀라운 점

두 번째 여자가 첫 대사에서 사람들은 재생 목재가 가성비 높다고 생각하는데 사실인지(People think using reclaimed lumber is cost-effective. Is that true?)를 묻자 남자가 놀랍게도 사실이 아니(Surprisingly, no)라면서 목재를 재사용할 수 있도록 만드는 긴 과정을 거쳐야 하기 때문에 사실 더 비싸다(It's actually more expensive because we have to go through a lengthy process to make the wood reusable)고 비용에 대해 말하고 있으므로 정답은 (C)이다.

43

What will Ms. Taylor most likely ask the man for?

(A) Some samples
(B) A software demonstration
(C) Some equipment
(D) Free delivery

테일러 씨는 남자에게 무엇을 요청하겠는가?

(A) 견본
(B) 소프트웨어 시연
(C) 장비
(D) 무료 배송

어휘 demonstration 시연, 입증

해설 세부 사항 관련 – 테일러 씨가 남자에게 요청하는 것

두 번째 여자가 마지막 대사에서 고객들은 결정하기 전에 분명 견본을 보고 싶어 할 것(I'm sure they'd like to see some samples before deciding)이라고 말하고 있으므로 정답은 (A)이다.

44-46

동영상 강의

M-Au	Thanks for agreeing to give me a tour of your company, Ms. Varma. **44It'll provide plenty of information to use in my article for the newspaper.**
W-Am	No problem. Did you say you write a series about local businesses?
M-Au	Yes. I do a weekly column spotlighting the histories of unique companies in our region. Now, **45I read that your father founded the company.**
W-Am	That's right. He started it with only ten employees.
M-Au	**46It seems like it's expanded a lot since then, right?**
W-Am	We export to fifty-nine countries around the world.
M-Au	Impressive!
W-Am	Let me show you the shipping area.

남	제가 귀사 견학을 할 수 있도록 동의해 주셔서 감사합니다, 바르마 씨. **제 신문 기사에 활용할 정보를 많이 제공해주는 기회가 될 것입니다.**
여	별말씀요. 지역 업체에 대한 연재 기사를 쓴다고 하셨나요?
남	네. 우리 지역 내 독특한 업체의 역사를 집중 조명하는 주간 칼럼을 씁니다. 자, **아버님께서 회사를 설립하셨다는 글을 읽었는데요.**
여	맞습니다. 직원 단 열 명으로 시작하셨어요.
남	**그 이후로 많이 확장된 것 같네요, 그렇죠?**
여	저희는 전 세계 59개국에 수출하고 있어요.
남	대단하네요!
여	선적 구역을 보여드릴게요.

어휘	plenty of 많은 article 기사 local 지역의 spotlight 집중 조명하다 region 지역 found 설립하다, 세우다 expand 확장하다, 확대되다 export 수출하다 impressive 인상적인, 감명 깊은 shipping 선적, 수송

TEST 9

44

Who most likely is the man?
(A) A history professor
(B) A mechanic
(C) A lawyer
(D) A journalist

남자는 누구이겠는가?
(A) 역사학 교수
(B) 기계공
(C) 변호사
(D) 기자

해설 전체 내용 관련 – 남자의 직업
남자가 첫 대사에서 자신의 신문 기사에 활용할 정보를 많이 제공해주는 기회가 될 것(It'll provide plenty of information to use in my article for the newspaper)이라고 말한 것으로 보아 남자는 신문사 기자임을 알 수 있다. 따라서 정답은 (D)이다.

45

What does the man say he read about the company?
(A) It was started by the woman's father.
(B) It manufactures automobile parts.
(C) It was recently purchased by a competitor.
(D) It is the area's largest employer.

남자는 회사에 관한 어떤 내용을 읽었다고 말하는가?
(A) 여자의 아버지가 개업했다.
(B) 자동차 부품을 제조한다.
(C) 최근 경쟁업체가 이 회사를 매입했다.
(D) 지역 최대의 고용주이다.

어휘 manufacture 제조하다   competitor 경쟁자

해설 세부 사항 관련 – 남자가 회사에 관해 읽었다는 글의 내용
남자가 두 번째 대사에서 여자의 아버지가 회사를 설립했다는 글을 읽었다(I read that your father founded the company)고 말하고 있으므로 정답은 (A)이다.

46

Why does the woman say, "We export to fifty-nine countries around the world"?
(A) To correct an error
(B) To justify a decision
(C) To confirm an assumption
(D) To explain a delay

여자가 "저희는 전 세계 59개국에 수출하고 있어요"라고 말하는 이유는?
(A) 오류를 바로잡으려고
(B) 결정에 대해 해명하려고
(C) 추정을 확인해 주려고
(D) 지연에 대해 설명하려고

어휘 correct 바로잡다   justify 정당화하다, 해명하다   decision 결정, 결심   confirm 확인해 주다   assumption 추정   delay 지연

해설 화자의 의도 파악 – 전 세계 59개국에 수출하고 있다는 말의 의도
이 문장 앞에서 남자가 그 이후로 회사가 많이 확장된 것 같다(It seems like it's expanded a lot since then, right?)고 묻자, 여자가 인용문을 언급했으므로 남자의 짐작이 옳음을 확인시켜 주려는 의도로 한 말이라는 것을 알 수 있다. 따라서 정답은 (C)이다.

47-49

W-Br	Hi, Sergey. **47 Have you been able to finish the updates for the new bridge we're designing?** I'd like to include them in the agenda for our client meeting next week.
M-Au	Yes. **47 I've reinforced some structural features and added the pedestrian walkway they asked for.**
W-Br	Oh, perfect! **48 Could you take over that part of the meeting to explain the changes to the clients?**
M-Au	Sure, I can do that. But first, **49 I'll send you the updated calculations on the bridge's weight capacity.** Some of the numbers have changed significantly because of the structural changes we've made.
W-Br	OK. I'll take a look tomorrow and get back to you.

여	안녕하세요, 세르게이. **우리가 설계하고 있는 새 교량에 관한 업데이트를 마칠 수 있었나요?** 다음 주에 있을 고객 회의 안건으로 그 내용을 포함하고 싶어서요.
남	네. **구조적 기능을 보강하고 그들이 요청한 보행자용 통로를 추가했어요.**
여	아, 완벽해요! **회의 중에 해당 부분을 넘겨받아서 고객에게 변동사항을 설명할 수 있겠어요?**
남	그럼요, 할 수 있습니다. 하지만 먼저 **교량 하중 용량에 대한 최신 계산 결과를 보내드릴게요.** 저희가 한 구조적 변경 때문에 일부 수치가 상당히 바뀌었어요.
여	알겠어요. 내일 한번 보고 다시 얘기해요.

어휘 include 포함시키다   agenda 안건   reinforce 강화하다, 보강하다   structural 구조상의, 구조적인   feature 기능, 특징   pedestrian 보행자(용)   walkway 통로   calculation 계산, 계산 결과   weight 무게, 하중   capacity 용량, 수용력   significantly 상당히

47

Who most likely are the speakers?
(A) Artists
(B) Engineers
(C) Accountants
(D) Lawyers

화자들은 누구이겠는가?
(A) 화가
(B) 엔지니어
(C) 회계사
(D) 변호사

해설 전체 내용 관련 – 화자들의 직업
여자가 첫 대사에서 우리가 설계하고 있는 새 교량에 관한 업데이트를 마칠 수 있었는지(Have you been able to finish the updates for the new bridge we're designing?)를 묻자 남자가 구조적 기능을 보강하고 고객이 요청한 보행자용 통로를 추가했다(I've reinforced some structural features and added the pedestrian walkway they asked for)고 말한 것으로 보아 화자들은 엔지니어임을 알 수 있다. 따라서 정답은 (B)이다.

48

What does the woman ask the man to do?
(A) Lead part of a meeting
(B) Revise a cost estimate
(C) Contact a client
(D) Perform an inspection

여자는 남자에게 무엇을 해 달라고 요청하는가?
(A) 회의 일부 진행
(B) 견적서 수정
(C) 고객 연락
(D) 검사 시행

어휘 revise 수정하다, 변경하다 cost estimate 견적 perform 수행하다, 실시하다 inspection 점검, 검사

해설 세부 사항 관련 – 여자의 요청 사항
여자가 두 번째 대사에서 회의 중에 해당 부분을 넘겨받아서 고객에게 변동사항을 설명할 수 있는지(Could you take over that part of the meeting to explain the changes to the clients?)를 묻고 있으므로 정답은 (A)이다.

> **Paraphrasing** 대화의 take over that part of the meeting
> → 정답의 Lead part of a meeting

49

What will the man send the woman?
(A) An itinerary
(B) A contract
(C) Some driving directions
(D) Some calculations

남자는 여자에게 무엇을 보낼 것인가?
(A) 여행 일정표
(B) 계약서
(C) 주행 길 안내
(D) 계산 결과

어휘 directions 길 안내

해설 세부 사항 관련 – 남자가 여자에게 보낼 것
남자가 마지막 대사에서 교량 하중 용량에 대한 최신 계산 결과를 보내주겠다(I'll send you the updated calculations on the bridge's weight capacity)고 말하고 있으므로 정답은 (D)이다.

50-52

W-Br	Ketan, what do you think about this month's marketing report? **50 It looks like our computer keyboard sales are decreasing.**
M-Cn	Yes, I saw that. I think it may be connected to our existing marketing strategies. **50, 51 The keyboards are advertised mostly on our Web site.** I think we need to look into expanding our advertising campaign to other types of media.
W-Br	That's a good idea. **52 Perhaps we need to advocate for a larger marketing budget.** That would provide us with more options. **52 Let's bring this up at our next marketing meeting.**

여	케탄, 이번 달 마케팅 보고서에 대해 어떻게 생각하세요? **우리 컴퓨터 키보드 판매가 감소하는 것 같은데요.**
남	네, 봤습니다. 저희 기존 마케팅 전략과 연관이 있는 것 같아요. **키보드는 주로 웹사이트에서 광고하고 있는데요.** 광고 캠페인을 다른 유형의 미디어로 확장하는 걸 고려해 봐야 할 것 같습니다.
여	좋은 의견이네요. **아마 마케팅 예산을 늘려 달라고 설득해야 할 것 같아요.** 선택지가 더 많아질 테니까요. **다음 마케팅 회의에서 이 점을 거론합시다.**

어휘	decrease 감소하다 be connected to ~에 연결되다 existing 기존의 strategy 전략 advertise 광고하다 expand 확장하다 advocate 옹호하다, 지지하다 budget 예산 option 선택

50

What products are the speakers discussing?
(A) Software programs
(B) Screen protectors
(C) Computer keyboards
(D) Wireless printers

화자들은 어떤 제품에 대해 이야기하는가?
(A) 소프트웨어 프로그램
(B) 스크린 보호기
(C) 컴퓨터 키보드
(D) 무선 프린터

어휘 protector 보호기 wireless 무선의

해설 전체 내용 관련 – 화자들이 논의 중인 제품

여자가 첫 대사에서 우리 컴퓨터 키보드 판매가 감소하는 것 같다(It looks like our computer keyboard sales are decreasing)고 하자 남자가 키보드는 주로 웹사이트에서 광고하고 있다(The keyboards are advertised mostly on our Web site)고 하면서 컴퓨터 키보드를 반복해 언급하고 있으므로 정답은 (C)이다.

51

According to the man, how are the products currently being advertised?
(A) On television
(B) On a Web site
(C) In magazines
(D) By direct mail

남자에 따르면, 제품은 현재 어떻게 광고하고 있는가?
(A) TV에서
(B) 웹사이트에서
(C) 잡지에서
(D) 우편 광고로

어휘 direct mail 가정에 우편으로 보내는 광고

해설 세부 사항 관련 – 제품이 현재 광고되고 있는 방식

남자가 첫 대사에서 키보드는 주로 웹사이트에서 광고하고 있다(The keyboards are advertised mostly on our Web site)고 말하고 있으므로 정답은 (B)이다.

52

What topic will the speakers discuss at a meeting?
(A) Budget changes
(B) Design modifications
(C) Production delays
(D) Open job positions

화자들은 회의에서 어떤 주제를 논의할 것인가?
(A) 예산 변경
(B) 디자인 변경
(C) 생산 지연
(D) 공석

어휘 modification 수정, 변경 production 생산

해설 세부 사항 관련 – 화자들이 회의에서 논의할 주제

여자가 마지막 대사에서 아마 마케팅 예산을 늘려 달라고 설득해야 할 것 같다(Perhaps we need to advocate for a larger marketing budget)면서 다음 마케팅 회의에서 이 점을 거론하자(Let's bring this up at our next marketing meeting)고 추가 예산에 대해 말하고 있으므로 정답은 (A)이다.

> **Paraphrasing** 대화의 a larger marketing budget
> → 정답의 Budget changes

53-55

 동영상 강의

W-Am Hi, Raul. ⁵³**I wanted to let you know that we received all of the bids we were waiting on for the Meyerville Bridge replacement project.**

M-Cn Thanks. Are there any acceptable bids? ⁵⁴**I'm worried that with costs rising nowadays we may exceed our budget for city infrastructure projects.**

W-Am Well, steel costs per ton are in the thousands for every bid.

M-Cn I see. We've already reached out to all of the contractors we can, so we'll just need to seek additional funding, then. ⁵⁵**Let's put together a spreadsheet comparing the bids this afternoon.** We'll use that for reference at our next transportation department meeting.

여 안녕하세요, 라울. **우리가 기다리던 메이어빌 교량 교체 프로젝트를 위한 입찰을 모두 받았다고 알려 드리고 싶었어요.**

남 고맙습니다. 받아들일 만한 입찰이 있나요? **요즘 비용이 올라 시 기반시설 프로젝트 예산이 초과될 수도 있어서 걱정스러워요.**

여 음, 1톤당 강철 가격은 입찰마다 수천 단위예요.

남 알겠어요. 이미 가능한 모든 도급업체에 연락을 취했으니 추가 자금만 구하면 돼요. **오늘 오후에 입찰을 비교한 스프레드시트를 만들어 봅시다.** 다음 교통부 회의에서 쓸 참고 자료로 활용할 겁니다.

어휘 bid 입찰, 가격 제시 replacement 교체 acceptable 받아들일 수 있는 nowadays 요즘 exceed 초과하다 budget 예산 infrastructure 기반시설 reach out 연락을 취하려 하다 contractor 도급업자 seek 찾다, 구하다 additional 추가의 funding 자금 put together (이것저것을 모아) 만들다 compare 비교하다 reference 참고, 참조 department 부서

53

What project are the speakers mainly discussing?
(A) The demolition of a shopping center
(B) The construction of a skyscraper
(C) The replacement of a bridge
(D) The redesign of a train station

화자들은 주로 어떤 프로젝트에 대해 이야기하는가?
(A) 쇼핑센터 철거
(B) 마천루 건설
(C) 교량 교체
(D) 기차역 재설계

어휘 demolition 철거 construction 건설 skyscraper 마천루

해설 전체 내용 관련 – 화자들이 논의 중인 프로젝트

여자가 첫 대사에서 기다리던 메이어빌 교량 교체 프로젝트를 위한 입찰을 모두 받았다고 알려 주고 싶었다(I wanted to let you know that we received all of the bids we were waiting on for the Meyerville Bridge replacement project)며 교량 교체 프로젝트에 대해 말하고 있으므로 정답은 (C)이다.

54

What does the woman imply when she says, "steel costs per ton are in the thousands for every bid"?
(A) A coworker's calculations are incorrect.
(B) The man's concern is justified.
(C) A contractor should be replaced.
(D) A new construction method will be used.

여자가 "1톤당 강철 가격은 입찰마다 수천 단위예요"라고 말하는 의도는 무엇인가?
(A) 동료의 계산이 틀렸다.
(B) 남자의 우려가 그럴 만하다.
(C) 도급업체를 교체해야 한다.
(D) 새로운 공사 방법이 사용될 것이다.

어휘 coworker 동료 incorrect 틀린, 잘못된 concern 우려
justified 그럴 만한 이유가 있는, 정당한 method 방법

해설 화자의 의도 파악 – 톤당 강철 가격은 입찰마다 수천 단위라는 말의 의도

앞에서 남자가 요즘 비용이 올라 시 기반시설 프로젝트 예산이 초과될 수도 있어서 걱정스럽다(I'm worried that with costs rising nowadays we may exceed our budget for city infrastructure projects)고 하자 여자가 인용문을 언급한 것으로 보아, 시 기반시설 프로젝트 비용에 대한 남자의 우려가 합당하다는 의미로 한 말임을 알 수 있다. 따라서 정답은 (B)이다.

55

What will the speakers do this afternoon?
(A) Take some photographs
(B) Organize a site visit
(C) Create a spreadsheet
(D) Speak to an accountant

화자들은 오늘 오후에 무엇을 할 것인가?
(A) 사진 촬영
(B) 현장 방문 준비
(C) 스프레드시트 작성
(D) 회계사와 대화

어휘 organize 준비하다 site visit 현장 방문 accountant 회계사

해설 세부 사항 관련 – 화자들이 오늘 오후에 할 일

남자가 마지막 대사에서 오늘 오후에 입찰을 비교한 스프레드시트를 만들어 보자(Let's put together a spreadsheet comparing the bids this afternoon)고 말하고 있으므로 정답은 (C)이다.

Paraphrasing 대화의 put together a spreadsheet
→ 정답의 Create a spreadsheet

56-58

M-Au Hi, Amy. **56 I just got back from that industry trade show in Vancouver:** Thanks for recommending the Arch Coast Hotel.

W-Am I thought you'd like it. I know how important conservation is to you. **57 Did you know that it was the first environmentally sustainable hotel in Canada?**

M-Au Yes, I spoke with the owner: He described the hotel's history and told me about their plans. **58 They'll be closed next month while they work on an addition to the main building.**

남 안녕하세요, 에이미. **저는 밴쿠버에서 열린 산업 무역 박람회에서 이제 막 돌아왔어요.** 아치 코스트 호텔을 추천해 주셔서 고마워요.

여 마음에 들 줄 알았어요. 자연 보존이 당신에게 얼마나 중요한지 잘 알거든요. **그곳이 캐나다 최초의 환경적으로 지속 가능한 호텔이라는 걸 알고 계셨나요?**

남 네, 사장과 얘기를 나눴어요. 호텔 역사에 대해 이야기하면서 자신들의 계획을 알려줬어요. **다음 달에 문을 닫고 본관에 추가 공사를 한대요.**

어휘 industry 산업 trade show 무역 박람회
conservation (자연 환경) 보호 environmentally 환경적으로 sustainable 지속 가능한 describe 묘사하다, 말하다 addition 추가

56

Why was the man in Vancouver?
(A) To attend a trade show
(B) To meet with a client
(C) To take a vacation
(D) To facilitate a workshop

남자는 왜 밴쿠버에 갔는가?
(A) 무역 박람회에 참석하려고
(B) 고객을 만나려고
(C) 휴가를 가려고
(D) 워크숍을 추진하려고

어휘 facilitate 가능하게 하다, 용이하게 하다

해설 세부 사항 관련 – 남자가 밴쿠버에 간 이유

남자가 첫 대사에서 밴쿠버에서 열린 산업 무역 박람회에서 이제 막 돌아왔다(I just got back from that industry trade show in Vancouver)고 말하고 있으므로 정답은 (A)이다.

57

What does the woman say about a hotel?
(A) It was a suitable venue for an event.
(B) It was reserved by a professional organization.
(C) It is environmentally friendly.
(D) It is convenient to public transportation.

여자는 호텔에 대해 뭐라고 말하는가?
(A) 행사를 치르기에 적합한 장소이다.
(B) 전문 기관에서 예약했다.
(C) 환경 친화적이다.
(D) 대중교통을 이용하기에 편리하다.

어휘 suitable 적합한   venue 장소   reserve 예약하다
environmentally friendly 환경 친화적인
public transportation 대중교통

해설 세부 사항 관련 – 여자가 호텔에 대해 말하는 것
여자가 그곳이 캐나다 최초의 환경적으로 지속 가능한 호텔이라는 걸 알고 있었는지(Did you know that it was the first environmentally sustainable hotel in Canada?)를 묻고 있으므로 정답은 (C)이다.

> **Paraphrasing**   대화의 environmentally sustainable
> → 정답의 environmentally friendly

58

Why will the hotel close temporarily?
(A) To allow staff to conduct a training session
(B) To be subject to an inspection
(C) To accommodate an expansion
(D) To ensure movers have access to the rooms

호텔은 왜 임시로 문을 닫는가?
(A) 직원들이 교육을 시행할 수 있도록 하려고
(B) 점검 대상이어서
(C) 확장 공사를 위해
(D) 물건을 옮기는 사람들이 객실에 들어갈 수 있게 하려고

어휘 temporarily 임시로, 일시적으로   conduct 하다   be subject to
~의 대상이다   accommodate 수용하다   expansion 확장, 확대
ensure 보장하다   have access to ~에 접근할 수 있다

해설 세부 사항 관련 – 호텔이 임시로 문을 닫는 이유
남자가 마지막 대사에서 다음 달에 문을 닫고 본관에 추가 공사를 한다(They'll be closed next month while they work on an addition to the main building)고 말하고 있으므로 정답은 (C)이다.

> **Paraphrasing**   대화의 an addition → 정답의 an expansion

59-61

M-Cn   Francesca, welcome! [59] I hope you didn't have too much trouble finding our banking office. Please, take a seat. [59] I've read your application, and it looks like we'll be able to finance your business project.

W-Br   Oh, that's wonderful news! Opening a flower shop has been my dream for so long.

M-Cn   Absolutely. [60] I just have one detail to confirm. Do you still live at 21 Anderson Avenue?

W-Br   Actually, I've recently moved. Here's a card with my new address.

M-Cn   Thanks! I'll be right back. [61] I need to go over to the printer to pick up some documents that I need you to sign.

남   프란체스카, 어서 오세요! 저희 은행을 찾기가 너무 힘들지 않으셨기를 바라요. 어서 앉으세요. 신청서를 봤는데요. 저희가 사업 프로젝트에 자금을 댈 수 있을 것 같습니다.

여   아, 정말 좋은 소식이네요! 꽃집 개업이 제 오랜 꿈이었거든요.

남   그렇죠. 다만 한 가지 확인해야 할 세부 사항이 있어요. 아직 앤더슨 가 21번지에 거주하세요?

여   사실은 최근에 이사했어요. 제 새 주소가 적힌 카드가 여기 있어요.

남   감사합니다! 금방 돌아올게요. 프린터로 가서 서명하실 문서를 가져와야 해요.

어휘 application 신청서, 지원서   finance 자금을 대다
absolutely 전적으로, 틀림없이   confirm 확인하다

59

What did the woman apply for?
(A) A professional license
(B) A job at a bank
(C) A business loan
(D) A credit card

여자는 무엇을 신청했는가?
(A) 전문 면허
(B) 은행 일자리
(C) 사업자 대출
(D) 신용카드

어휘 professional 전문적인   license 자격증, 면허   loan 대출

해설 세부 사항 관련 – 여자가 신청한 것
남자가 첫 대사에서 저희 은행을 찾기가 너무 힘들지 않으셨기를 바란다(I hope you didn't have too much trouble finding our banking office)고 하면서 신청서를 봤는데 사업 프로젝트에 자금을 댈 수 있을 것 같다(I've read your application, and it looks like we'll be able to finance your business project)고 말하고 있으므로 정답은 (C)이다.

60

What information does the man ask the woman to verify?

(A) Her income
(B) Her account number
(C) Her phone number
(D) Her address

남자는 여자에게 어떤 정보를 확인해 달라고 요청하는가?

(A) 소득
(B) 계좌 번호
(C) 전화번호
(D) 주소

어휘 verify 확인하다, 입증하다   income 소득, 수입
account number 계좌 번호

해설 세부 사항 관련 – 남자가 여자에게 확인해 달라고 요청하는 정보
남자가 두 번째 대사에서 다만 한 가지 확인해야 할 세부 사항이 있다(I just have one detail to confirm)면서 아직 앤더슨 가 21번지에 거주하는지(Do you still live at 21 Anderson Avenue?) 주소를 확인하고 있으므로 정답은 (D)이다.

> **Paraphrasing**   대화의 confirm → 질문의 verify

61

What will the woman most likely do next?

(A) Sign some documents
(B) Download some software
(C) Speak with a friend
(D) Make an appointment

여자는 다음으로 무엇을 하겠는가?

(A) 문서에 서명하기
(B) 소프트웨어 다운로드하기
(C) 친구와 대화하기
(D) 약속 잡기

해설 세부 사항 관련 – 여자가 다음에 할 일
남자가 마지막 대사에서 프린터로 가서 여자가 서명할 문서를 가져와야 한다(I need to go over to the printer to pick up some documents that I need you to sign)고 말하고 있으므로 정답은 (A)이다.

62-64 대화 + 차트

W-Am Goodland Nature Preserve and Resort. How may I help you?

M-Cn I have a two-person cabin booked for next Monday night, but I'm hoping to change my reservation.

W-Am OK—to a different day?

M-Cn No, [62]**we still want to stay on Monday night, but we'd like a bigger cabin.**

W-Am What size do you need?

M-Cn One that accommodates three or more people.

W-Am Well, [63]**there's only one larger cabin available. It costs 150 dollars.**

M-Cn [63]**That's fine—we'll take it!** Also, [64]**do you offer private tours of the nature preserve?**

W-Am [64]**We do! It's complimentary with your cabin booking. Just let me know when you'd like to do it, and I'll make arrangements with our guide.**

여 굿랜드 자연보호구역 리조트입니다. 어떻게 도와드릴까요?

남 다음 주 월요일 밤에 2인실이 예약되어 있는데요. 예약을 변경하고 싶어요.

여 네, 다른 날짜로요?

남 아니요, **여전히 월요일 밤에 투숙하고 싶은데 더 큰 객실을 원해요.**

여 어떤 크기가 필요하세요?

남 3인 이상 수용할 수 있는 객실이요.

여 음, 더 큰 객실이 딱 하나 있네요. 150달러입니다.

남 **좋습니다. 그걸로 할게요!** 그리고 자연보호구역 개인 투어를 제공하시나요?

여 제공합니다! 귀하의 객실 예약으로는 무료입니다. 언제 하고 싶으신지 알려주시면 저희 가이드와 함께 준비하겠습니다.

어휘 nature preserve 자연보호구역   cabin 객실   book 예약하다   reservation 예약   accommodate 수용하다   available 이용 가능한   complimentary 무료의   make arrangements 준비하다, 정하다

Cabin Rates	
North cabin (2 people)	$100
East cabin (3 people)	$120
South cabin (4 people)	$135
[63]West cabin (5–7 people)	$150

객실 요금	
북쪽 객실 (2인실)	100달러
동쪽 객실 (3인실)	120달러
남쪽 객실 (4인실)	135달러
[63]서쪽 객실 (5–7인실)	150달러

62

When will the man stay at the resort?

(A) On Monday night
(B) On Tuesday night
(C) On Wednesday night
(D) On Thursday night

남자는 리조트에 언제 투숙할 것인가?

(A) 월요일 밤
(B) 화요일 밤
(C) 수요일 밤
(D) 목요일 밤

해설 세부 사항 관련 – 남자가 리조트에 투숙할 시점

남자가 두 번째 대사에서 여전히 월요일 밤에 투숙하고 싶은데 더 큰 객실을 원한다(we still want to stay on Monday night, but we'd like a bigger cabin)고 말하고 있으므로 정답은 (A)이다.

63

Look at the graphic. Which cabin does the man agree to reserve?

(A) North cabin
(B) East cabin
(C) South cabin
(D) West cabin

시각 정보에 의하면, 남자는 어떤 객실을 예약하는 데 동의하는가?

(A) 북쪽 객실
(B) 동쪽 객실
(C) 남쪽 객실
(D) 서쪽 객실

해설 시각 정보 연계 – 남자가 예약하는 데 동의한 객실

여자가 네 번째 대사에서 더 큰 객실이 딱 하나 있다(there's only one larger cabin available)면서 150달러다(It costs 150 dollars)라고 하자 남자가 그걸로 하겠다(That's fine—we'll take it!)고 말하고 있고, 차트에 따르면 150달러인 객실은 서쪽 객실이므로 정답은 (D)이다.

64

What can cabin guests receive free of charge?

(A) Shuttle rides
(B) Swimming pool access
(C) A hot breakfast
(D) A guided tour

투숙객은 무엇을 무료로 받을 수 있는가?

(A) 셔틀 탑승
(B) 수영장 이용
(C) 따뜻한 아침식사
(D) 가이드 투어

어휘 free of charge 무료로   access 이용, 접근

해설 세부 사항 관련 – 투숙객이 무료로 제공받는 것

남자가 마지막 대사에서 자연보호구역 개인 투어를 제공하는지(do you offer private tours of the nature preserve?)를 묻자, 여자가 제공한다(We do!)는 긍정의 답변과 함께 귀하의 객실 예약으로는 무료(It's complimentary with your cabin booking)라며 언제 하고 싶은지 알려주면 가이드와 함께 준비하겠다(Just let me know when you'd like to do it, and I'll make arrangements with our guide)고 말하고 있으므로 정답은 (D)이다.

> **Paraphrasing** 대화의 complimentary
> → 질문의 free of charge

65-67 대화 + 지도

W-Br Can I help you find something, Lee?

M-Cn Please! **65 One of the tractors just broke down out in the cornfield,** and Kyle sent me back for a toolbox. I just started working here, though, so I'm still getting used to the layout of this place.

W-Br Oh, **66 you'll want to go to the toolshed. It's right across the road, next to the pond.**

M-Cn Alright. Which way is that?

W-Br Actually, **67 I'll head over there with you.** I need to grab a wheelbarrow.

여 리, 찾는 거 도와줄까요?

남 도와주세요! **옥수수밭에서 트랙터 한 대가 고장 났는데** 카일이 연장통을 가지고 오라고 저를 보냈어요. 그런데 저는 이제 막 일을 시작해서 아직 이곳 배치를 익히는 중이거든요.

여 아, **공구 창고로 가고 싶으신 거네요. 길 건너편 연못 옆에 있어요.**

남 알겠습니다. 어떤 길인가요?

여 실은, **제가 같이 가 드릴게요.** 손수레를 가져와야 해서요.

어휘 break down 고장 나다   toolbox 연장통   get used to ~에 익숙해지다   layout 배치   toolshed 공구 창고   grab 붙잡다, 움켜잡다   wheelbarrow 외바퀴 손수레

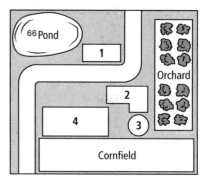

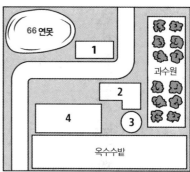

65

What problem does the man mention?
(A) A worker has not yet arrived.
(B) Some tools have been misplaced.
(C) A tractor is not working.
(D) Some crops are damaged.

남자는 어떤 문제점을 언급하는가?
(A) 인부가 아직 도착하지 않았다.
(B) 공구를 제자리에 두지 않아 찾을 수 없다.
(C) **트랙터가 작동하지 않는다.**
(D) 일부 농작물이 손상을 입었다.

어휘 misplace 제자리에 두지 않다   crop 농작물   damaged 손상을
입은

해설 세부 사항 관련 – 남자가 언급한 문제
남자가 첫 대사에서 옥수수밭에서 트랙터 한 대가 고장 났다(One of the
tractors just broke down out in the cornfield)고 말하고 있으므로
정답은 (C)이다.

> Paraphrasing 대화의 broke down → 정답의 is not working

66

Look at the graphic. Where does the woman tell the
man to go?
(A) To building 1
(B) To building 2
(C) To building 3
(D) To building 4

시각 정보에 의하면, 여자는 남자에게 어디로 가라고 말하는가?
(A) **1번 건물**
(B) 2번 건물
(C) 3번 건물
(D) 4번 건물

해설 시각 정보 연계 – 여자가 남자에게 가라고 말하는 장소
여자가 두 번째 대사에서 공구 창고로 가야 한다(you'll want to go to
the toolshed)면서 길 건너편 연못 옆에 있다(It's right across the
road, next to the pond)고 말하고 있고, 지도에 따르면 연못 옆에 있는
것은 1번 건물이므로 정답은 (A)이다.

67

What does the woman offer to do?
(A) Complete the man's work shift
(B) Go with the man
(C) Move some boxes
(D) Unlock a gate

여자는 무엇을 하겠다고 제안하는가?
(A) 남자의 교대 근무 시간 끝내기
(B) **남자와 동행하기**
(C) 상자 옮기기
(D) 문 열기

어휘 complete 완료하다   unlock 열다

해설 세부 사항 관련 – 여자의 제안 사항
여자가 마지막 대사에서 같이 가 주겠다(I'll head over there with you)
고 말하고 있으므로 정답은 (B)이다.

> Paraphrasing 대화의 head → 정답의 Go

68-70 대화 + 작업 리스트

M-Au	A client just called. **68 I need to check on a large batch of tablecloths, napkins, and linens that we're cleaning.**
W-Am	What's the job number?
M-Au	Um. **69 Seventeen. They requested that everything be ready tonight instead of tomorrow.** Let's make this a priority.
W-Am	OK. I see their initial order came in at eleven thirty this morning. Their items haven't been placed in the washer yet. When do they need this rush work done?
M-Au	By five P.M.
W-Am	**70 We can do it if we put them ahead of job sixteen.**
M-Au	Sounds good.
W-Am	So I'll just hold sixteen back then. That will help free up some washing machines and dryers.

남	한 고객이 막 전화했어요. **세탁할 대량의 테이블보, 냅킨, 리넨 제품을 확인해야 해요.**
여	작업번호가 뭐죠?
남	음. **17번이요. 내일 말고 오늘 밤에 모두 준비해 달라고 요청했어요.** 이 일을 최우선 순위에 두도록 하죠.
여	알겠어요. 첫 주문이 오늘 오전 11시 30분에 들어왔네요. 그들의 물품은 아직 세탁기에 들어가지 않았어요. 이 급한 작업은 언제까지 마쳐야 하나요?
남	오후 5시까지요.
여	**16번 작업 앞으로 넣으면 가능해요.**
남	좋아요.
여	그럼 16번은 보류할게요. 그럼 세탁기와 건조기 몇 대가 비어요.

어휘 batch (일괄적으로 처리되는) 집단, 무리   linen (식탁보,
침구류 등) 리넨 제품   instead of ~ 대신   priority 우선
사항   initial 최초의, 처음의   ahead of ~ 앞에   free up
해방하다, 풀어주다

Job Number	Time Received	Business Name
15	9:30 A.M.	Larkston Hotel
16	10:00 A.M.	Trissler Hotel
69 17	11:30 A.M.	Benchlal Restaurant
18	12:00 P.M.	Cho Fine Dining

작업 번호	수령 시간	업체명
15	오전 9시 30분	라크스턴 호텔
16	오전 10시	트리슬러 호텔
69 17	오전 11시 30분	벤치럴 레스토랑
18	오후 12시	조 파인 다이닝

68

Where do the speakers most likely work?
(A) At a fabric store
(B) At an employee staffing service
(C) At a health-inspection department
(D) At a commercial laundry facility

화자들은 어디서 일하겠는가?
(A) 직물 매장
(B) 직원 채용 서비스 업체
(C) 건강 검진 부서
(D) 상업 세탁 시설

어휘 fabric 직물, 천 staffing 직원 채용 inspection 점검, 검사
commercial 상업의 laundry 세탁 facility 시설

해설 전체 내용 관련 – 화자들의 근무지
남자가 첫 대사에서 세탁할 대량의 테이블보, 냅킨, 리넨 제품을 확인해야
한다(I need to check on a large batch of tablecloths, napkins,
and linens that we're cleaning)며 세탁과 관련된 내용을 언급하고
있으므로 정답은 (D)이다.

69

Look at the graphic. Which business did the man
receive a request from?
(A) Larkston Hotel
(B) Trissler Hotel
(C) Benchlal Restaurant
(D) Cho Fine Dining

시각 정보에 의하면, 남자는 어떤 업체에서 요청을 받았는가?
(A) 라크스턴 호텔
(B) 트리슬러 호텔
(C) 벤치럴 레스토랑
(D) 조 파인 다이닝

해설 시각 정보 연계 – 남자가 요청받은 업체
남자가 두 번째 대사에서 17번 작업 업체가 내일 말고 오늘 밤에 모두
준비해 달라고 요청했다(Seventeen. They requested that everything
be ready tonight instead of tomorrow)고 말하고 있고, 작업
리스트에 따르면 17번 업체명이 벤치럴 레스토랑이므로 정답은 (C)이다.

70

How does the woman suggest resolving an issue?
(A) By issuing a refund
(B) By consulting with a supervisor
(C) By explaining a policy to a customer
(D) By adjusting the order of some work

여자는 어떻게 문제를 해결하자고 제안하는가?
(A) 환불 처리함으로써
(B) 관리자와 상의함으로써
(C) 고객에게 정책을 설명함으로써
(D) 작업 순서를 조정함으로써

어휘 issue a refund 환불해 주다 consult 상담하다, 상의하다
supervisor 관리자, 감독관 policy 정책 adjust 조정하다

해설 세부 사항 관련 – 여자가 제안하는 문제 해결 방법
여자가 세 번째 대사에서 16번 작업 앞으로 넣으면 가능하다(We can do
it if we put them ahead of job sixteen)고 말하고 있으므로 정답은
(D)이다.

PART 4

71-73 공지

W-Am Attention, all Curious Minds shoppers.
71 During our going-out-of-business sale, all of our
hardcover books are being deeply discounted.
72 From now until the end of the week, they will
be sold at an 80 percent discount. In addition,
all paperbacks will be 50 percent off this week.
And 73 please remember—while this store will be
shutting down soon, you will still be able to shop
in person at our Lawrenceville location, which is
just a fifteen-minute drive from here.

큐리어스 마인즈 쇼핑객 여러분께 알립니다. 저희 폐업 세일 중에는 모
든 양장본 도서를 많이 할인해 드립니다. 지금부터 이번 주말까지 80퍼
센트 할인 판매됩니다. 또한 페이퍼백 도서는 이번 주 50퍼센트 할인합
니다. 본 매장은 곧 문을 닫지만 저희 로렌스빌 지점에서는 계속 직접
구입하실 수 있다는 걸 기억해 주세요. 여기서 차로 15분 거리입니다.

어휘 attention 알립니다, 주목하세요 going-out-of-business
sale 폐업 세일 in addition 게다가 in person 직접

71

Where is the announcement most likely being made?
(A) At a clothing shop
(B) At a bookstore
(C) At a hardware store
(D) At an auto dealership

공지는 어디서 이루어지겠는가?

(A) 의류 매장
(B) 서점
(C) 철물점
(D) 자동차 대리점

해설 전체 내용 관련 – 공지 장소

화자가 초반부에 폐업 세일 중에는 모든 양장본 도서를 많이 할인해 준다(During our going-out-of-business sale, all of our hardcover books are being deeply discounted)고 도서 할인과 관련된 내용을 말하고 있는 것으로 보아 공지가 나오는 장소는 서점이라는 것을 알 수 있다. 따라서 정답은 (B)이다.

72

What does the speaker say is happening this week?

(A) Discounts are being offered.
(B) An area is being remodeled.
(C) New merchandise is arriving.
(D) Interviews are being conducted.

화자는 이번 주에 무슨 일이 있다고 말하는가?

(A) 할인이 제공된다.
(B) 한 구역에 리모델링을 한다.
(C) 신상품이 도착한다.
(D) 면접이 진행된다.

어휘 merchandise 상품, 물품   conduct 하다

해설 세부 사항 관련 – 이번 주에 일어날 일

화자가 중반부에 지금부터 이번 주말까지 80퍼센트 할인 판매된다 (From now until the end of the week, they will be sold at an 80 percent discount)고 말하고 있으므로 정답은 (A)이다.

Paraphrasing	담화의 From now until the end of the week → 질문의 this week
	담화의 they will be sold at an 80 percent discount → 정답의 Discounts are being offered.

73

What does the speaker remind the listeners about?

(A) A return policy
(B) A rewards program
(C) An updated Web site
(D) An additional location

화자는 청자들에게 무엇을 상기시키는가?

(A) 반품 정책
(B) 보상 프로그램
(C) 웹사이트 업데이트
(D) 또 다른 지점

어휘 policy 정책   rewards 보상   additional 추가의

해설 세부 사항 관련 – 화자가 청자들에게 상기시키는 것

화자가 후반부에서 본 매장은 곧 문을 닫지만 로렌스빌 지점에서는 계속 직접 구입할 수 있다는 걸 기억해 달라(please remember—while this store will be shutting down soon, you will still be able to shop in person at our Lawrenceville location)고 말하고 있으므로 정답은 (D)이다.

74-76 회의 발췌

M-Cn **74 Before we wrap up this meeting, I wanted to discuss the picnic our department has been planning for next Saturday.** I've already purchased most of the decorations, and Lorenzo has volunteered to bring a cake. **75 Actually, Lorenzo, there's a great bakery not far from the park that you could order from. It's cash only, but** there's a bank across the street. We still need other food and supplies, though. **76 I've posted a list of what we still need in the break room, so write your name next to the item you'll bring.**

이 회의를 마치기 전에, 우리 부서에서 다음 주 토요일로 계획한 야유회에 대해 이야기하고 싶습니다. 장식품 대부분은 제가 이미 구입했고, 로렌조가 케이크를 가져오겠다고 자원했어요. 사실, 로렌조, 공원에서 멀지 않은 곳에 당신이 주문할 수 있는 훌륭한 제과점이 있어요. 현금만 받지만, 길 건너편에 은행이 있어요. 그래도 다른 음식과 물품이 필요합니다. 휴게실에 아직 필요한 물품 목록을 게시해 뒀으니 가져올 물품 옆에 자신의 이름을 적어주세요.

어휘 wrap up 마무리하다   department 부서   purchase 구입하다   decoration 장식   actually 사실, 실은   post 게시하다   break room 휴게실

74

What is the speaker discussing?

(A) A vacation schedule
(B) A professional-development opportunity
(C) A department's social event
(D) A marketing campaign

화자는 무엇에 대해 이야기하는가?

(A) 휴가 일정
(B) 직무 능력 개발 기회
(C) 부서 친목 행사
(D) 마케팅 캠페인

어휘 professional development 전문성 신장, 직무 능력 개발   opportunity 기회   social 사교적인, 사회적인

해설 전체 내용 관련 – 회의의 주제

화자가 도입부에 우리 부서에서 다음 주 토요일로 계획한 야유회에 대해 이야기하고 싶다(I wanted to discuss the picnic our department has been planning for next Saturday)고 말하고 있으므로 정답은 (C) 이다.

TEST 9

75

Why does the speaker say, "there's a bank across the street"?
(A) To request assistance
(B) To make a suggestion
(C) To provide driving directions
(D) To complain about a location

화자가 "길 건너편에 은행이 있어요"라고 말하는 이유는?
(A) 도움을 요청하려고
(B) 제안하려고
(C) 길 안내를 제공하려고
(D) 위치에 대해 불만을 제기하려고

어휘 assistance 도움 suggestion 제안 directions 길 안내
complain 불평하다, 항의하다

해설 화자의 의도 파악 – 길 건너편에 은행이 있다는 말의 의도
앞에서 로렌조에게 공원에서 멀지 않은 곳에 주문할 수 있는 훌륭한 제과점이 있는데 현금만 받는다(Lorenzo, there's a great bakery not far from the park that you could order from. It's cash only)고 말한 후, 인용문을 언급하고 있으므로 은행에 가서 현금을 찾은 후 이 제과점을 가라고 제안하려는 의도로 한 말임을 알 수 있다. 따라서 정답은 (B)이다.

76

What does the speaker ask the listeners to do?
(A) Fill out a sign-up sheet
(B) E-mail agenda items
(C) Attend an additional meeting
(D) Complete an evaluation form

화자는 청자들에게 무엇을 하라고 요청하는가?
(A) 신청서 작성하기
(B) 의제를 이메일로 보내기
(C) 추가 회의에 참석하기
(D) 평가지 작성하기

어휘 fill out 작성하다, 기입하다 sign-up sheet 신청서 agenda 의제, 안건 evaluation form 평가지

해설 세부 사항 관련 – 화자의 요청 사항
화자가 마지막에 휴게실에 아직 필요한 물품 목록을 게시해 뒀으니 가져올 물품 옆에 자신의 이름을 적어줄 것(I've posted a list of what we still need in the break room, so write your name next to the item you'll bring)을 요청하고 있으므로 정답은 (A)이다.

77-79 방송

W-Br In local news, **77Malton Supermarket is throwing a party today to celebrate its one-year anniversary. 78I spoke with owner Antonella Lambert about the store's success. She told me that Malton strives to offer products from all over the world to meet the needs of the city's diverse population.** And customers have responded with enthusiasm, happy to find familiar products from their countries of origin. **79As for her vision for the future, Lambert said she's already started raising money from investors so that she can open more Malton Supermarkets in adjacent towns.**

지역 소식입니다. 몰튼 슈퍼마켓이 오늘 창립 1주년을 기념해 파티를 개최합니다. 매장의 성공에 관해 안토넬라 램버트 사장과 말씀을 나눴는데요. 그녀의 말에 따르면, 몰튼은 다양한 시민들의 수요에 맞춰 전 세계에서 온 물품을 제공하는 데 힘쓰고 있다고 합니다. 고객들은 자신의 고국에서 온 친숙한 물건을 찾아 기뻐하며 열정적으로 반응하고 있습니다. 램버트는 미래 자신의 비전에 관해, 인접한 지역에 몰튼 슈퍼마켓을 더 많이 열 수 있도록 이미 투자자들로부터 기금을 모으기 시작했다고 말했습니다.

어휘 throw a party 파티를 열다 celebrate 축하하다, 기념하다 anniversary 기념일 strive 분투하다 meet the needs of ~의 요구에 부응하다 diverse 다양한 population 인구, 모든 주민 respond 대응하다, 반응하다 enthusiasm 열정, 열의 familiar 익숙한 raise money 기금을 모으다 investor 투자자 adjacent 인접한, 가까운

77

Why is Malton Supermarket hosting a party?
(A) To welcome a new manager
(B) To celebrate an anniversary
(C) To thank local suppliers
(D) To promote new products

몰튼 슈퍼마켓은 왜 파티를 여는가?
(A) 새 관리자를 환영하려고
(B) 기념일을 축하하려고
(C) 지역 공급업체에 감사를 전하려고
(D) 신제품을 홍보하려고

어휘 local 지역의 supplier 공급업체 promote 홍보하다, 촉진하다

해설 세부 사항 관련 – 몰튼 슈퍼마켓이 파티를 여는 이유
화자가 도입부에 몰튼 슈퍼마켓이 오늘 창립 1주년을 기념해 파티를 개최한다(Malton Supermarket is throwing a party today to celebrate its one-year anniversary)고 말하고 있으므로 정답은 (B)이다.

78

According to Antonella Lambert, why is Malton Supermarket successful?

(A) It is open 24 hours a day.
(B) It is near public transportation.
(C) It offers international products.
(D) It provides friendly service.

안토넬라 램버트에 따르면, 몰튼 슈퍼마켓은 왜 성공을 거뒀는가?
(A) 하루 24시간 영업한다.
(B) 대중교통을 이용하기에 가깝다.
(C) 해외 제품을 제공한다.
(D) 친절한 서비스를 제공한다.

어휘 public transportation 대중교통

해설 세부 사항 관련 – 안토넬라 램버트가 말하는 몰튼 슈퍼마켓이 성공을 거둔 이유

화자가 초반부에 매장의 성공에 관해 안토넬라 램버트 사장과 말씀을 나눴는데(I spoke with owner Antonella Lambert about the store's success) 몰튼은 다양한 시민들의 수요에 맞춰 전 세계에서 온 물품을 제공하는 데 힘쓰고 있다(She told me that Malton strives to offer products from all over the world to meet the needs of the city's diverse population)고 말하고 있으므로 정답은 (C)이다.

> **Paraphrasing** 담화의 products from all over the world
> → 정답의 international products

79

Why is Antonella Lambert raising funds?

(A) To open additional locations
(B) To remodel a space
(C) To increase advertising
(D) To support a charity

안토넬라 램버트는 왜 기금을 모으는가?
(A) 추가 지점을 열려고
(B) 공간을 개조하려고
(C) 광고를 늘리려고
(D) 자선 단체를 지원하려고

어휘 increase 늘리다 advertising 광고 charity 자선 단체

해설 세부 사항 관련 – 안토넬라 램버트가 기금을 모으는 이유

화자가 마지막에 인접한 지역에 몰튼 슈퍼마켓을 더 많이 개장할 수 있도록 이미 투자자들로부터 기금을 마련하기 시작했다고 밝혔다(Lambert said she's already started raising money from investors so that she can open more Malton Supermarkets in adjacent towns)고 말하고 있으므로 정답은 (A)이다.

> **Paraphrasing** 담화의 open more Malton Supermarkets
> → 정답의 open additional locations

80-83 담화

> M-Au Hi, everyone. ⁸⁰**I'd just like to say that I'm aware of the issues you're experiencing with Internet speed and connectivity in the office.** I realize how difficult it is to get your work done with the interruptions. We're fixing it as fast as we can—⁸¹**a technician is coming in an hour or two.** ⁸²**I know the sales reports are due on Wednesday,** but I've talked to your team leads about the issue. As always, thanks for your hard work.

> 안녕하세요, 여러분. 사무실 인터넷 속도와 연결에 관해 겪고 계신 문제점을 제가 알고 있다는 사실을 말씀드리고 싶네요. 중간에 이런 문제가 끼어들면 업무를 완수하기가 얼마나 어려운지 압니다. 최대한 빨리 고치려고 합니다. 기술자가 한두 시간 후에 올 겁니다. 매출 보고서 마감이 수요일인 것으로 알고 있는데요. 해당 문제에 대해 여러분의 팀장들에게 이야기해 두었어요. 여러분의 노고에 늘 감사드립니다.

어휘 be aware of ~을 알다 experience 경험하다, 겪다 connectivity 연결 realize 인식하다, 깨닫다 interruption 중단

80

What is not working properly?

(A) The lighting
(B) The plumbing
(C) A payment portal
(D) An Internet connection

무엇이 제대로 작동하지 않는가?
(A) 조명
(B) 배관
(C) 급여 사이트
(D) 인터넷 연결

어휘 payment 지급, 지불 connection 연결

해설 세부 사항 관련 – 제대로 작동하지 않는 것

화자가 도입부에 사무실 인터넷 속도와 연결에 관해 겪고 있는 문제점을 알고 있다(~ I'm aware of the issues you're experiencing with Internet speed and connectivity in the office)고 말하고 있으므로 정답은 (D)이다.

> **Paraphrasing** 담화의 Internet speed and connectivity
> → 정답의 An Internet connection

81

According to the speaker, what will happen in the next few hours?

(A) A technician will come in.
(B) A complaint will be filed.
(C) A Web site will be updated.
(D) An office will close.

화자에 따르면, 앞으로 몇 시간 동안 어떤 일이 있을 것인가?

(A) 기술자가 올 것이다.
(B) 항의가 제기될 것이다.
(C) 웹사이트가 업데이트될 것이다.
(D) 사무실이 문을 닫을 것이다.

어휘 file a complaint 항의를 제기하다

해설 세부 사항 관련 – 앞으로 몇 시간 동안 있을 일

화자가 중반부에 기술자가 한두 시간 후에 올 것(a technician is coming in an hour or two)이라고 말하고 있으므로 정답은 (A)이다.

Paraphrasing	담화의 in an hour or two → 질문의 in the next few hours

82

What does the speaker mean when he says, "I've talked to your team leads about the issue"?
(A) The team leads will take over a project.
(B) A deadline will be adjusted.
(C) New teams will be formed.
(D) An extra expense will be approved.

화자가 "해당 문제에 대해 여러분의 팀장들에게 이야기해 두었어요"라고 말하는 의도는 무엇인가?

(A) 팀장들이 프로젝트를 맡을 예정이다.
(B) 마감 기한이 조정될 것이다.
(C) 팀을 새로 구성할 것이다.
(D) 추가 지출이 승인될 것이다.

어휘 take over 인계받다　adjust 조정하다, 조절하다　form 형성하다, 구성하다　approve 승인하다

해설 화자의 의도 파악 – 해당 문제에 대해 여러분의 팀장들에게 이야기해 두었다는 말의 의도

앞에서 매출 보고서 마감이 수요일인 것으로 알고 있다(I know the sales reports are due on Wednesday)고 한 후, 인용문을 언급하고 있으므로 마감 기한 연장과 같은 조치가 있을 것이라는 의도로 한 말임을 알 수 있다. 따라서 정답은 (B)이다.

83-85 전화 메시지

W-Am Hi, Ling. 83**I just received a call from a group asking to reserve the tearoom for tomorrow.** They would like us to decide on the entire menu for the tea party, from the tea selection to the food options. 84**I'd like you to handle the preparations. I know you've never been in charge of a tea party before,** but you've worked here for five months now. By the way, there will be children at the party. 85**Please make sure some low tables and chairs are set up for them. You'll find them in the back room.**

안녕하세요, 링. 내일 티룸 예약을 요청하는 단체의 전화를 받았는데요. 차 선택부터 음식 메뉴까지 티파티 메뉴 전체를 우리 보고 정해달라고 하네요. 그 준비를 맡아 주셨으면 해요. 티파티는 전에 맡아보신 적이 없는 걸로 알지만, 이제 일하신 지 다섯 달이 되니까요. 그런데 파티에 아이들도 참석할 거예요. 아이들을 위해 낮은 탁자와 의자를 놓아주세요. 안쪽 방에 있을 거예요.

어휘 reserve 예약하다　decide 결정하다　entire 전체의　selection 선택　preparation 준비　in charge of ~을 맡아서, 담당해서　by the way 그런데

83

What type of business does the speaker own?
(A) A tea shop
(B) A childcare center
(C) A pottery studio
(D) A party supply store

화자는 어떤 종류의 업체를 가지고 있는가?

(A) 찻집
(B) 탁아소
(C) 도자기 공방
(D) 파티용품 매장

해설 전체 내용 관련 – 화자가 소유하고 있는 업종

화자가 초반부에 내일 티룸 예약을 요청하는 단체의 전화를 받았다(I just received a call from a group asking to reserve the tearoom for tomorrow)고 말하고 있으므로 화자는 찻집을 소유하고 있다는 것을 알 수 있다. 따라서 정답은 (A)이다.

84

What does the speaker imply when she says, "you've worked here for five months now"?
(A) The listener is capable of doing a task.
(B) The listener should apply for a promotion.
(C) The speaker is ready to retire.
(D) A training period is too short.

화자가 "이제 일하신 지 다섯 달이 되니까요"라고 말하는 의도는 무엇인가?

(A) 청자는 업무를 완수할 능력이 있다.
(B) 청자는 승진 신청을 해야 한다.
(C) 화자는 은퇴할 준비가 됐다.
(D) 교육 기간이 너무 짧다.

어휘 be capable of ~을 할 수 있다, ~할 능력이 있다　apply for ~을 신청하다　promotion 승진　retire 은퇴하다, 퇴직하다

해설 화자의 의도 파악 – 이제 일한 지 다섯 달이 된다는 말의 의도

앞에서 준비를 맡아 주셨으면 한다(I'd like you to handle the preparations)면서 티파티는 전에 맡아보신 적이 없는 걸로 안다(I know you've never been in charge of a tea party before)고 말한 뒤 인용문을 언급하고 있으므로, 청자가 티파티 운영 경험은 없지만 근무 경력이 있으므로 업무를 완수할 수 있을 것이라는 의미로 한 말임을 알 수 있다. 따라서 정답은 (A)이다.

85

What does the speaker say is located in the back room?
(A) Some decorations
(B) A video projector
(C) Some furniture
(D) Some dishes

화자는 안쪽 방에서 무엇을 찾을 수 있다고 말하는가?
(A) 장식품
(B) 비디오 프로젝터
(C) 가구
(D) 접시

해설 세부 사항 관련 – 안쪽 방에서 찾을 수 있는 것
화자가 마지막에 아이들을 위해 낮은 탁자와 의자를 놓아 달라(Please make sure some low tables and chairs are set up for them)고 하면서 안쪽 방에 있을 것(You'll find them in the back room)이라고 말하고 있으므로 정답은 (C)이다.

> Paraphrasing   담화의 tables and chairs
> → 정답의 Some furniture

86-88 회의 발췌   ▶ 동영상 강의

W-Br Peak travel season is almost here. And, as everyone knows, [86]**we don't have enough baggage handlers, ground crew, or ticketing agents to handle the demand. Passengers are experiencing longer lines and flight delays.** Therefore, [87]**hiring more staff is our top priority.** Now, we already have an incentive program for employees to refer friends for open positions. Please continue referring your friends to apply to work for us. And, [88]**for our current staff, we're now going to start offering complimentary meals in all employee lounges starting this month.** We want you to know that you're valued and appreciated.

여행 성수기가 거의 다가왔습니다. 다들 아시는 대로 **수요를 처리할 수하물 담당자, 지상직 직원, 발권 담당자가 충분치 않습니다. 승객들은 오랜 대기와 항공편 지연을 겪고 있어요.** 따라서 **직원을 더 채용하는 것이 우리의 최우선 사항입니다.** 자, 직원이 공석에 지인을 추천하면 보상을 주는 인센티브 프로그램이 이미 있어요. 계속해서 지인들에게 우리 회사에 지원하라고 추천해주세요. 또한 **현 직원들을 위해 이번 달부터 모든 직원 라운지에서 무료 식사를 제공해 드리려고 합니다.** 여러분을 소중하게 생각하고 감사한다는 점을 알아주시기 바랍니다.

어휘 baggage 수하물 handle 처리하다 demand 요구 passenger 승객 experience 경험하다, 겪다 delay 지연 priority 우선 사항 incentive 장려책, 우대책 refer 추천하다 complimentary 무료의 meal 식사 value 소중하게 생각하다 appreciate 감사하다

86

What industry does the speaker most likely work in?
(A) Transportation
(B) Health care
(C) Hospitality
(D) Entertainment

화자는 어떤 업계에서 일하겠는가?
(A) 운수업계
(B) 의료업계
(C) 접객 서비스 업계
(D) 연예계

해설 전체 내용 관련 – 화자의 근무 업종
화자가 초반부에 수요를 처리할 수하물 담당자, 지상직 직원, 발권 담당자가 충분치 않다(we don't have enough baggage handlers, ground crew, or ticketing agents to handle the demand)고 하면서 승객들은 오랜 대기와 항공편 지연을 겪고 있다(Passengers are experiencing longer lines and flight delays)고 말하는 것으로 보아 화자는 항공사, 즉 운수업계에 종사하고 있다는 것을 알 수 있다. 따라서 정답은 (A)이다.

87

What does the speaker say is a priority?
(A) Upgrading some equipment
(B) Promoting an industry event
(C) Hiring more staff
(D) Increasing inventory

화자는 무엇이 우선 사항이라고 말하는가?
(A) 장비 업그레이드
(B) 업계 행사 홍보
(C) 직원 추가 채용
(D) 재고 확대

어휘 equipment 장비 promote 홍보하다 increase 늘리다, 증가시키다 inventory 재고, 물품 목록

해설 세부 사항 관련 – 화자가 우선 사항이라고 말하는 것
화자가 중반부에 직원을 더 채용하는 것이 우리의 최우선 사항(hiring more staff is our top priority)이라고 말하고 있으므로 정답은 (C)이다.

88

What change does the speaker mention?
(A) A shuttle bus will be provided.
(B) Free meals will be available.
(C) A work schedule will be reduced.
(D) An additional branch has opened.

화자는 어떤 변화를 언급하는가?
(A) 셔틀버스가 제공될 것이다.
(B) 무료 식사가 제공될 것이다.
(C) 업무 일정이 줄어들 것이다.
(D) 추가 지점을 열었다.

어휘 available 이용할 수 있는   reduce 감소하다   additional 추가의

해설 세부 사항 관련 – 화자가 언급하는 변화

화자가 후반부에 현 직원들을 위해 이번 달부터 모든 직원 라운지에서 무료 식사를 제공한다(for our current staff, we're now going to start offering complimentary meals in all employee lounges starting this month)고 말하고 있으므로 정답은 (B)이다.

> **Paraphrasing**   담화의 start offering complimentary meals → 정답의 Free meals will be available.

89-91 회의 발췌

M-Au **⁸⁹Some quick announcements before we start the assembly-line machines for the day.** First, I need to tell you about a new safety standard for everyone working on the factory floor. Starting immediately, rings, earrings, and jewelry of any kind will not be allowed on the floor during your shift. **⁹⁰Sorry—I know some of you will find this regulation inconvenient.** **⁹¹As a reminder, keep your belongings safe during your shift.** I recommend you put a lock on your designated locker in the break room. If you need one, I have a few in my office.

오늘 조립 라인 기계를 가동하기에 앞서 간단히 공지할 것이 있습니다. 첫째, 공장 작업 현장에서 일하시는 모든 분께 새로운 안전 기준을 말씀드릴 필요가 있습니다. 지금부터 근무 시간에는 작업장에서 반지, 귀걸이 및 어떤 종류의 장신구도 허용하지 않습니다. **이 규정이 불편한 분들도 있으실 것 같아 죄송합니다.** 혹시나 해서 말씀드리자면, 근무 시간에는 소지품을 안전하게 보관하십시오. 휴게실에 있는 지정된 사물함에 자물쇠를 채우실 것을 권합니다. 필요하시면 제 사무실에 몇 개 있습니다.

어휘 announcement 발표, 공지   assembly 조립   safety 안전   standard 표준, 기준   factory floor 공장 작업 현장   immediately 즉시   allow 허락하다, 허용하다   regulation 규정   inconvenient 불편한   reminder 상기시키는 것   belongings 소지품   designated 지정된

89

Where do the listeners most likely work?
(A) At a jewelry store
(B) At a security company
(C) At a factory
(D) At a university

청자들은 어디서 일하겠는가?
(A) 귀금속 매장
(B) 보안업체
(C) 공장
(D) 대학교

해설 전체 내용 관련 – 청자들의 근무지

화자가 도입부에 오늘 조립 라인 기계를 가동하기에 앞서 간단히 공지할 것이 있다(Some quick announcements before we start the assembly-line machines for the day)고 한 것으로 보아 청자들은 공장에서 일하고 있음을 알 수 있다. 따라서 정답은 (C)이다.

90

Why does the speaker apologize?
(A) A wait time increased.
(B) A hiring was delayed.
(C) A new rule may be unpopular.
(D) Some items cannot be stored on-site.

화자는 왜 사과하는가?
(A) 대기 시간이 늘어났다.
(B) 채용이 지연됐다.
(C) 새 규칙이 인기가 없을 수 있다.
(D) 일부 품목은 현장에 보관할 수 없다.

어휘 increase 늘어나다, 증가하다   unpopular 인기 없는, 평이 나쁜   store 보관하다, 저장하다   on-site 현장의

해설 세부 사항 관련 – 화자가 사과하는 이유

화자가 중반부에 이 규정이 불편한 분들도 있으실 것 같아 죄송하다(Sorry—I know some of you will find this regulation inconvenient)고 말하고 있으므로 정답은 (C)이다.

> **Paraphrasing**   담화의 regulation → 정답의 rule

91

What are the listeners reminded to do?
(A) Secure their belongings
(B) Verify their appointment time
(C) Provide detailed information
(D) Arrive early

청자들에게 무엇을 하라고 상기시키는가?
(A) 소지품 안전하게 보관하기
(B) 약속 시간 확인하기
(C) 상세 정보 제공하기
(D) 일찍 도착하기

어휘 secure 안전하게 지키다   verify 확인하다   appointment 약속   detailed information 상세 정보

해설 세부 사항 관련 – 청자들에게 상기시키는 것

화자가 중반부에 혹시나 해서 말씀드리자면 근무 시간에는 소지품을 안전하게 보관하라(As a reminder, keep your belongings safe during your shift)고 주의를 주고 있으므로 정답은 (A)이다.

> **Paraphrasing**   담화의 keep your belongings safe → 정답의 Secure their belongings

92-94 공지

▶ 동영상 강의

W-Br Good morning, all. I have a quick announcement about some staff shifts. **92 Starting next week, everybody will see their evening hours adjusted.** Since summer is ending and people are having dinner earlier, we're going to be closing at eight instead of ten P.M. on weekdays. **93 It doesn't make financial sense for our kitchen to stay open late.** This is a seasonal adjustment that we make every year. **94 There's no reason for you to worry. We still have plenty of customers in the winter.**

안녕하세요, 여러분. 직원 교대 근무 시간에 대해 간단히 안내 드립니다. **다음 주부터 모든 직원의 저녁 근무 시간이 조정되어 있을 겁니다.** 여름이 끝나가고 다들 저녁을 일찍 먹으니 평일에는 밤 10시 대신 8시에 마감할 예정입니다. **우리 식당이 늦게까지 영업하는 건 경제적인 측면에서 말이 안 돼요.** 매년 있는 계절성 조정 사항입니다. **걱정하지 않으셔도 됩니다. 겨울철에도 손님은 많으니까요.**

어휘 announcement 발표, 공지 adjust 조정하다, 조절하다 instead of ~ 대신 make sense 이치에 닿다 financial 재정의, 금융의 adjustment 조정, 수정 plenty of 많은

92

What is the speaker announcing?
(A) A security update
(B) A menu adjustment
(C) A mandatory uniform
(D) A schedule change

화자는 무엇에 관해 공지하는가?
(A) 보안 업데이트
(B) 메뉴 조정
(C) 의무 착용 유니폼
(D) 일정 변경

어휘 mandatory 의무적인

해설 전체 내용 관련 – 공지의 주제
화자가 초반부에 다음 주부터 모든 직원의 저녁 근무 시간이 조정될 것(Starting next week, everybody will see their evening hours adjusted)이라고 말하고 있으므로 정답은 (D)이다.

Paraphrasing	담화의 evening hours adjusted → 정답의 A schedule change

93

Where do the listeners most likely work?
(A) At a farm
(B) At a restaurant
(C) At a public park
(D) At an electronics store

청자들은 어디서 일하겠는가?
(A) 농장
(B) 음식점
(C) 공원
(D) 전자 제품 매장

해설 전체 내용 관련 – 청자들의 근무지
화자가 중반부에 식당이 늦게까지 영업하는 건 경제적인 측면에서 말이 안된다(It doesn't make financial sense for our kitchen to stay open late)고 말하고 있으므로 청자들은 음식점에서 근무 중임을 알 수 있다. 따라서 정답은 (B)이다.

94

What does the speaker reassure the listeners about?
(A) They will be paid overtime.
(B) They will receive annual bonuses.
(C) Their paycheck mistake will be corrected.
(D) There will still be work available.

화자는 청자들에게 무엇에 대해 안심시키는가?
(A) 초과 근무 수당을 받을 것이다.
(B) 연간 보너스를 받을 것이다.
(C) 급여 오류를 바로잡을 것이다.
(D) 일이 계속 있을 것이다.

어휘 be paid overtime 초과 근무 수당을 받다 paycheck 급료 correct 바로잡다 available 이용할 수 있는, 구할 수 있는

해설 세부 사항 관련 – 화자가 청자들을 안심시키는 것
화자가 마지막에 걱정하지 않아도 된다(There's no reason for you to worry)면서 겨울철에도 손님은 많다(We still have plenty of customers in the winter)고 말하고 있으므로 정답은 (D)이다.

95-97 녹음 메시지 + 활동 일정표

M-Au You've reached Hayberry Farm in Millville. **95 We're excited to announce that we're now under new management.** Even with the management change, the farm will still be offering a full schedule of summer activities. **96 We're now accepting registrations for our popular cooking class!** This class focuses on making delicious meals with fresh ingredients. You can find more information on our Web site. Also, **97 be aware that our Western Road entrance is closed until the end of June because of road construction. Visitors should use our entrance on Anderson Road.**

밀빌의 헤이베리 농장입니다. **저희 운영진이 새로 바뀐 것을 알리게 되어 기쁩니다.** 운영진은 바뀌었지만 저희 농장은 계속해서 여름 활동 일정을 모두 제공합니다. **지금 인기 많은 요리 강좌 등록을 받고 있습니다!** 본 강좌는 신선한 재료로 맛있는 요리를 만드는 데 중점을 두고 있

TEST 9

어요. 저희 웹사이트에서 더 많은 정보를 보실 수 있습니다. 또한, **도로 공사로 인해 6월 말까지 웨스턴 로 입구는 폐쇄됨을 알려드립니다. 방문객들은 앤더슨 로 입구를 이용하셔야 합니다.**

어휘 management 경영진 activity 체험 accept 받아주다, 수락하다 registration 등록 ingredient 재료, 성분 be aware 알다 entrance 입구 construction 공사, 건설

96Cooking Class	June 2
Starting a Garden	June 9
Music with Larry Bowen	June 16
Harvest Festival	June 23

96요리 강좌	6월 2일
정원 시작하기	6월 9일
래리 보웬 음악 수업	6월 16일
수확제	6월 23일

어휘 harvest 추수, 수확

95

According to the speaker, what has changed at the farm?
(A) The prices
(B) The type of crops
(C) The management
(D) The hours of operation

화자에 따르면, 농장에 어떤 변화가 있는가?
(A) 가격
(B) 농작물 유형
(C) 운영진
(D) 운영시간

해설 세부 사항 관련 – 농장의 변화
화자가 초반부에 운영진이 새로 바뀐 것을 알리게 되어 기쁘다(We're excited to announce that we're now under new management)고 말하고 있으므로 정답은 (C)이다.

96

Look at the graphic. When does the mentioned activity take place?
(A) On June 2
(B) On June 9
(C) On June 16
(D) On June 23

시각 정보에 의하면, 언급된 활동은 언제 진행되는가?
(A) 6월 2일
(B) 6월 9일
(C) 6월 16일
(D) 6월 23일

해설 시각 정보 연계 – 언급된 활동의 진행 시점
화자가 중반부에 지금 인기 많은 요리 강좌 등록을 받고 있다(We're now accepting registrations for our popular cooking class)고 말하고 있고, 활동 일정표에 따르면 요리 강좌는 6월 2일에 예정되어 있으므로 정답은 (A)이다.

97

What are visitors to the business advised to do?
(A) Come on weekdays
(B) Park in a designated area
(C) Bring reusable containers
(D) Use an alternate entrance

업체 방문객에게 무엇을 하라고 조언하는가?
(A) 평일에 방문하기
(B) 지정된 구역에 주차하기
(C) 재사용할 수 있는 용기 가져오기
(D) 대체 입구 이용하기

어휘 designated 지정된 reusable 재사용할 수 있는 container 용기 alternate 대체의, 대체 가능한

해설 세부 사항 관련 – 업체 방문객에게 조언하는 것
화자가 마지막에 도로 공사로 인해 6월 말까지 웨스턴 로 입구는 폐쇄됨을 알린다(be aware that our Western Road entrance is closed until the end of June because of road construction)면서 방문객들은 앤더슨 로 입구를 이용하라(Visitors should use our entrance on Anderson Road)고 말하고 있으므로 정답은 (D)이다.

98-100 방송 + 지도

M-Cn This is Yun Kang with local information for Greenville residents. **98Your taxes have increased significantly this year—I know you've noticed,** and you want to know what your money's being spent on! The city is going ahead with four major projects to improve your library, parkland, firehouse, and streets. **99Work on the firehouse is currently in progress,** while the other projects will be started in coming months. Remember: the election for mayor is approaching, and your vote affects what projects become future priorities in the community. **100The candidates are holding a debate in our studios this Wednesday,** and you're all encouraged to attend.

그린빌 주민 여러분께 지역 정보를 전해드리는 윤 강입니다. **올해 세금이 상당히 올랐죠. 이미 아시겠지만요.** 여러분의 돈이 어디에 쓰이는지 알고 싶으실 겁니다! 시에서는 도서관, 정원, 소방서, 도로를 개선하는 네 개의 주요 프로젝트를 추진하고 있습니다. **소방서 프로젝트가 현재 진행 중이고,** 다른 프로젝트는 향후 몇 개월 내에 시작될 것입니다. 시장 선거가 다가오고 있다는 걸 기억하세요. 여러분의 표는 지역사회에

서 향후 어떤 프로젝트에 우선 순위를 두게 될지에 영향을 줍니다. **후보자들이 이번 주 수요일 저희 스튜디오에 나와 토론을 펼치는데요.** 여러분 모두 참석하셔도 좋습니다.

어휘 local 지역의 resident 주민 significantly 상당히
go ahead with ~을 추진하다 improve 개선하다, 향상시키다
currently 현재 in progress 진행 중인 election 선거
mayor 시장 approach 다가오다 vote 표 affect 영향을 주다 priority 우선 사항 candidate 후보자 debate 토론
encourage 장려하다, 권장하다

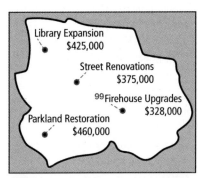

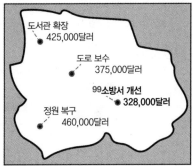

어휘 expansion 확장 renovation 개조, 보수 restoration 복원, 복구

98

What does the speaker say residents have noticed?
(A) Rising fuel prices
(B) Limited housing options
(C) Traffic congestion
(D) Increased taxes

화자는 주민들이 무엇을 알아챘다고 말하는가?
(A) 유류비 상승
(B) 한정적인 주택 선택의 폭
(C) 교통 혼잡
(D) 세금 증가

어휘 fuel price 유류비 limited 제한된, 한정된 congestion 혼잡

해설 세부 사항 관련 – 주민들이 알아챘다고 말하는 것
화자가 초반부에 올해 세금이 상당히 올랐다며 이미 아실 것(Your taxes have increased significantly this year—I know you've noticed)이라고 말하고 있으므로 정답은 (D)이다.

99

Look at the graphic. What is the cost of the project currently being worked on?
(A) $425,000
(B) $375,000
(C) $328,000
(D) $460,000

시각 정보에 의하면, 현재 진행 중인 프로젝트 비용은 얼마인가?
(A) 425,000달러
(B) 375,000달러
(C) 328,000달러
(D) 460,000달러

해설 시각 정보 연계 – 현재 진행 중인 프로젝트의 비용
화자가 중반부에 소방서 프로젝트가 현재 진행 중(Work on the firehouse is currently in progress)이라고 말하고 있고, 지도에 따르면 소방서 개선 비용은 328,000달러이므로 정답은 (C)이다.

100

What is scheduled for Wednesday?
(A) A fund-raiser
(B) A festival
(C) An election
(D) A debate

수요일로 예정된 일은 무엇인가?
(A) 모금 행사
(B) 축제
(C) 선거
(D) 토론회

해설 세부 사항 관련 – 수요일로 예정된 일
화자가 마지막에 후보자들이 이번 주 수요일 스튜디오에 나와 토론을 펼친다(The candidates are holding a debate in our studios this Wednesday)고 말하고 있으므로 정답은 (D)이다.

TEST 9

1 (D)	**2** (B)	**3** (C)	**4** (A)	**5** (C)
6 (A)	**7** (A)	**8** (B)	**9** (C)	**10** (A)
11 (C)	**12** (C)	**13** (A)	**14** (C)	**15** (C)
16 (A)	**17** (A)	**18** (A)	**19** (B)	**20** (B)
21 (A)	**22** (C)	**23** (B)	**24** (C)	**25** (C)
26 (A)	**27** (B)	**28** (C)	**29** (A)	**30** (B)
31 (C)	**32** (B)	**33** (C)	**34** (C)	**35** (D)
36 (D)	**37** (B)	**38** (D)	**39** (B)	**40** (A)
41 (C)	**42** (D)	**43** (C)	**44** (C)	**45** (A)
46 (B)	**47** (C)	**48** (B)	**49** (A)	**50** (C)
51 (A)	**52** (B)	**53** (A)	**54** (C)	**55** (C)
56 (C)	**57** (A)	**58** (B)	**59** (A)	**60** (D)
61 (D)	**62** (A)	**63** (B)	**64** (C)	**65** (A)
66 (B)	**67** (A)	**68** (C)	**69** (D)	**70** (B)
71 (B)	**72** (A)	**73** (C)	**74** (A)	**75** (A)
76 (D)	**77** (C)	**78** (D)	**79** (B)	**80** (A)
81 (D)	**82** (B)	**83** (C)	**84** (A)	**85** (A)
86 (C)	**87** (C)	**88** (A)	**89** (C)	**90** (A)
91 (B)	**92** (A)	**93** (C)	**94** (D)	**95** (B)
96 (A)	**97** (D)	**98** (C)	**99** (A)	**100** (D)

PART 1

1　W-Am

(A) The man is reaching above a shelf.
(B) The man is adjusting his glasses.
(C) The man is paying for an item.
(D) The man is trying on gloves.

(A) 남자가 선반 위로 손을 뻗고 있다.
(B) 남자가 안경을 고쳐 쓰고 있다.
(C) 남자가 물건값을 치르고 있다.
(D) 남자가 장갑을 착용해 보고 있다.

어휘 reach 손을 뻗다, 내밀다　adjust (매무새를) 바로잡다, 정돈하다
　　　pay 지불하다　try on 입어[신어] 보다

해설 1인 등장 사진 – 사람의 동작/상태 묘사
(A) 동사 오답. 남자가 선반 위로 손을 뻗고 있는(is reaching above a shelf) 모습이 아니므로 오답.
(B) 동사 오답. 남자가 안경을 고쳐 쓰고 있는(is adjusting his glasses) 모습이 아니므로 오답.
(C) 동사 오답. 남자가 물건값을 치르고 있는(is paying for an item) 모습이 아니므로 오답.

(D) 정답. 남자가 장갑을 착용해 보고 있는(is trying on gloves) 모습이므로 정답.

2　W-Br

(A) She's opening an umbrella over a dining area.
(B) She's standing on a patio near a house.
(C) She's taking a tool out of a storage cupboard.
(D) She's picking up some cushions off the ground.

(A) 여자가 식사 구역 위로 파라솔을 펴고 있다.
(B) 여자가 집 근처 테라스에 서 있다.
(C) 여자가 수납장에서 연장을 꺼내고 있다.
(D) 여자가 땅에서 쿠션을 줍고 있다.

어휘 dining 식사　tool 연장, 도구　storage 보관　cupboard 찬장

해설 1인 등장 사진 – 사람의 동작/상태 묘사
(A) 동사 오답. 여자가 파라솔을 펴고 있는(is opening an umbrella) 모습이 아니므로 오답.
(B) 정답. 여자가 집 근처 테라스에 서 있는(is standing on a patio near a house) 모습이므로 정답.
(C) 동사 오답. 여자가 수납장에서 연장을 꺼내고 있는(is taking a tool out of a storage cupboard) 모습이 아니므로 오답.
(D) 동사 오답. 여자가 땅에서 쿠션을 줍고 있는(is picking up some cushions off the ground) 모습이 아니므로 오답.

3　M-Au

(A) They're raking some leaves.
(B) They're shoveling soil into a bag.
(C) They're working in a garden.
(D) They're watering some flowers.

(A) 사람들이 나뭇잎을 갈퀴로 모으고 있다.
(B) 사람들이 흙을 삽으로 떠서 봉투에 넣고 있다.
(C) 사람들이 정원에서 일하고 있다.
(D) 사람들이 꽃에 물을 주고 있다.

어휘 rake 갈퀴로 모으다　shovel 삽질하다

해설 2인 이상 등장 사진 – 사람의 동작/상태 묘사
(A) 동사 오답. 사람들이 나뭇잎을 갈퀴로 모으고 있는(are raking some leaves) 모습이 아니므로 오답.
(B) 동사 오답. 사람들이 흙을 삽으로 떠서 봉투에 넣고 있는(are shoveling soil into a bag) 모습이 아니므로 오답.

(C) 정답. 사람들이 정원에서 일하고 있는(are working in a garden) 모습이므로 정답.

(D) 동사 오답. 사람들이 꽃에 물을 주고 있는(are watering some flowers) 모습이 아니므로 오답.

4 M-Cn

▶ 동영상 강의

(A) Some food has been laid out on platters.
(B) Some chairs are lined up against the wall.
(C) Some floor tiles are being installed.
(D) Some dinner plates have been placed in a sink.

(A) 음식이 접시 위에 놓여져 있다.
(B) 의자들이 벽에 기대어 늘어서 있다.
(C) 바닥 타일이 설치되고 있다.
(D) 정찬용 접시들이 개수대에 놓여 있다.

어휘 lay out 펼치다 platter 접시 line up 줄을 서다 install 설치하다 place 놓다, 두다

해설 사물/풍경 사진 – 사물 묘사
(A) 정답. 음식(Some food)이 접시 위에 놓여져 있는(has been laid out on platters) 모습이므로 정답.
(B) 상태 오답. 의자들(Some chairs)이 벽에 기대어 늘어서 있는(are lined up against the wall) 모습이 아니므로 오답.
(C) 동사 오답. 바닥 타일(Some floor tiles)이 설치되고 있는(are being installed) 모습이 아니므로 오답.
(D) 사진에 없는 명사를 이용한 오답. 사진에 개수대(a sink)의 모습이 보이지 않으므로 오답.

5 W-Br

(A) A worker is changing a lightbulb.
(B) A worker is handing a box to a customer.
(C) A worker is crouching down behind a counter.
(D) A worker is cleaning a window.

(A) 직원이 전구를 갈고 있다.
(B) 직원이 손님에게 상자를 건네고 있다.
(C) 직원이 카운터 뒤에서 몸을 웅크리고 있다.
(D) 직원이 유리창을 닦고 있다.

어휘 lightbulb 전구 hand 건네다 crouch down 몸을 웅크리다

해설 2인 이상 등장 사진 – 사람의 동작/상태 묘사
(A) 동사 오답. 전구를 갈고 있는(is changing a lightbulb) 직원의 모습이 보이지 않으므로 오답.

(B) 동사 오답. 손님에게 상자를 건네고 있는(is handing a box to a customer) 직원의 모습이 보이지 않으므로 오답.
(C) 정답. 카운터 뒤에서 몸을 웅크리고 있는(is crouching down behind a counter) 직원의 모습이 보이므로 정답.
(D) 동사 오답. 유리창을 닦고 있는(is cleaning a window) 직원의 모습이 보이지 않으므로 오답.

6 M-Au

(A) Some potted plants are on both sides of an entrance.
(B) An awning is shading a parking area.
(C) Some signs are posted on a brick building.
(D) Some furniture is propping open a door.

(A) 입구 양쪽으로 화분에 심은 식물들이 있다.
(B) 차양이 주차장에 그늘을 드리우고 있다.
(C) 벽돌 건물에 표지판이 내걸려 있다.
(D) 가구로 받쳐서 문이 열려 있다.

어휘 potted plant 화분에 심은 식물 entrance 입구 awning 차양 shade 그늘지게 하다 brick 벽돌 prop open 받쳐서 열어 두다

해설 사물/풍경 사진 – 풍경 묘사
(A) 정답. 화분에 심은 식물들(Some potted plants)이 입구 양쪽으로 있는(are on both sides of an entrance) 모습이므로 정답.
(B) 사진에 없는 명사를 이용한 오답. 사진에 주차장(a parking area)의 모습이 보이지 않으므로 오답.
(C) 사진에 없는 명사를 이용한 오답. 사진에 표지판(Some signs)의 모습이 보이지 않으므로 오답.
(D) 동사 오답. 가구(Some furniture)로 받쳐서 문이 열려 있는(is propping open a door) 모습이 아니므로 오답.

PART 2

7

W-Am When will you deliver the furniture I ordered?

M-Au (A) By Tuesday at the latest.
(B) To several clients.
(C) I bought a trailer.

제가 주문한 가구를 언제 배달해 주실 건가요?
(A) 늦어도 화요일까지요.
(B) 여러 고객에게요.
(C) 저는 이동식 주택을 구입했어요.

어휘 at the latest 늦어도 trailer 이동식 주택

해설 가구의 배송 시기를 묻는 When 의문문
(A) 정답. 가구의 배송 시기를 묻는 질문에 늦어도 화요일까지라고 알려 주고 있으므로 정답.
(B) 연상 단어 오답. 질문의 ordered에서 연상 가능한 clients를 이용한 오답.
(C) 연상 단어 오답. 질문의 ordered에서 연상 가능한 bought를 이용한 오답.

8

W-Br Is your flight tomorrow or this afternoon?

M-Cn (A) In-flight snacks.
(B) It's this afternoon.
(C) At baggage claim.

당신이 탈 항공편은 내일인가요, 아니면 오늘 오후인가요?
(A) 기내 간식이요.
(B) 오늘 오후예요.
(C) 수하물 찾는 곳에서요.

어휘 in-flight 기내의 baggage claim 수하물 찾는 곳

해설 항공편 시간을 묻는 선택 의문문
(A) 단어 반복 오답. 질문의 flight를 반복 이용한 오답.
(B) 정답. 이용할 항공편의 시간이 내일과 오늘 오후 중 언제인지 묻는 질문에 오늘 오후라며 둘 중 하나를 선택해 응답하고 있으므로 정답.
(C) 연상 단어 오답. 질문의 flight에서 연상 가능한 baggage를 이용한 오답.

9

M-Cn How often does the research team schedule training sessions?

W-Br (A) The team leader, I think.
(B) Some new software.
(C) Every other week.

연구팀은 얼마나 자주 교육 시간을 잡나요?
(A) 팀장인 것 같아요.
(B) 새로운 소프트웨어요.
(C) 2주에 한 번이요.

어휘 every other 하나 걸러서

해설 교육 일정의 빈도를 묻는 How often 의문문
(A) 단어 반복 오답. 질문의 team을 반복 이용한 오답.
(B) 연상 단어 오답. 질문의 training sessions에서 연상 가능한 new software를 이용한 오답.
(C) 정답. 연구팀의 교육 일정 빈도를 묻는 질문에 2주에 한 번이라며 구체적인 빈도를 제시하고 있으므로 정답.

10

W-Am Can I pay my bill with a credit card?

M-Au (A) Sure, that's fine.
(B) I don't believe him either.
(C) The gas station on your right.

신용카드로 계산해도 될까요?
(A) 그럼요, 됩니다.
(B) 저는 그를 믿지 않아요.
(C) 오른쪽에 있는 주유소요.

어휘 pay a bill 계산서를 지불하다

해설 부탁/요청의 의문문
(A) 정답. 신용카드로 계산해도 되는지 묻는 질문에 그럼요(Sure)라고 수락한 뒤, 된다며 긍정 답변과 일관된 내용을 덧붙이고 있으므로 정답.
(B) 연상 단어 오답. 질문의 bill을 사람 이름 Bill로 잘못 들었을 경우 연상 가능한 him을 이용한 오답.
(C) 질문과 상관없는 오답.

11

M-Cn The project proposal still needs work.

W-Br (A) The other office.
(B) No, it's still not working.
(C) I can help you with it.

프로젝트 제안서는 아직 작업이 필요해요.
(A) 다른 사무실이요.
(B) 아니요, 아직 작동되지 않아요.
(C) 제가 도와드릴 수 있어요.

어휘 proposal 제안, 제안서

해설 의사 전달의 평서문
(A) 연상 단어 오답. 평서문의 work에서 연상할 수 있는 office를 이용한 오답.
(B) 파생어 오답. 평서문의 work와 파생어 관계인 working을 이용한 오답.
(C) 정답. 프로젝트 제안서가 아직 작업이 필요하다는 평서문에 도와줄 수 있다며 호응하고 있으므로 정답.

12

W-Am Where do you plan to stay during your visit to the city?

M-Cn (A) I thought the building had twelve floors.
(B) Oh, just to present at a conference.
(C) At a friend's house.

그 도시를 방문하는 동안 어디서 묵을 계획이에요?
(A) 그 건물은 12층이라고 생각했어요.
(B) 아, 학회에서 발표하려고요.
(C) 친구 집에서요.

어휘 present 발표하다 conference 회의, 학회

해설 도시에서 묵을 장소를 묻는 Where 의문문
(A) 연상 단어 오답. 질문의 city에서 연상 가능한 building을 이용한 오답.
(B) 질문과 상관없는 오답. Why 의문문에 대한 응답이므로 오답.
(C) 정답. 도시를 방문하는 동안 묵을 장소를 묻는 질문에 친구 집에서라며 구체적인 장소를 알려 주고 있으므로 정답.

13

M-Au How did you improve the processing speed?

W-Br (A) That's a question for Silvia.
(B) What's the speed limit?
(C) I don't like to swim.

처리 속도를 어떻게 향상시키셨나요?
(A) 그건 실비아한테 물어보세요.
(B) 제한 속도가 얼마인가요?
(C) 저는 수영을 좋아하지 않아요.

어휘 improve 개선하다, 향상시키다 processing 처리 speed limit 제한 속도

해설 처리 속도를 향상시킨 방법을 묻는 How 의문문
(A) 정답. 처리 속도를 향상시킨 방법을 묻는 질문에 실비아한테 물어보라고 답변해 줄 수 있는 사람을 알려 주고 있으므로 정답.
(B) 단어 반복 오답. 질문의 speed를 반복 이용한 오답.
(C) 질문과 상관없는 오답.

14

W-Br Do you take exercise classes too, or just dance classes?

M-Cn (A) The instructor teaches in the mornings.
(B) These shoes fit perfectly.
(C) I only take dance.

운동 강좌도 듣나요, 아니면 그냥 춤 강좌만 듣나요?
(A) 그 강사는 오전에 가르쳐요.
(B) 이 신발은 딱 맞네요.
(C) 저는 춤만 들어요.

어휘 instructor 강사 fit 맞다 perfectly 완벽하게

해설 수강 강좌를 묻는 선택 의문문
(A) 연상 단어 오답. 질문의 classes에서 연상 가능한 instructor를 이용한 오답.
(B) 연상 단어 오답. 질문의 exercise에서 연상 가능한 shoes를 이용한 오답.
(C) 정답. 운동 강좌도 수강하는지 아니면 춤 강좌만 수강하는지 묻는 질문에 춤만 듣는다며 하나를 선택해 응답하고 있으므로 정답.

15

M-Cn When will the new coffee machine be installed in the lobby?

W-Am (A) No, it wasn't expensive.
(B) The front door is unlocked.
(C) Within the next few days.

새 커피 머신은 언제 로비에 설치될 예정이죠?
(A) 아니요, 그건 비싸지 않았어요.
(B) 앞문은 잠겨 있지 않아요.
(C) 며칠 이내로요.

어휘 install 설치하다 expensive 비싼 unlocked 잠겨 있지 않은

해설 새 커피 머신의 설치 시기를 묻는 When 의문문
(A) Yes/No 불가 오답. When 의문문에는 Yes/No 응답이 불가능하므로 오답.
(B) 연상 단어 오답. 질문의 lobby에서 연상 가능한 The front door를 이용한 오답.
(C) 정답. 새 커피 머신의 설치 시기를 묻는 질문에 며칠 이내라고 알려 주고 있으므로 정답.

16

W-Am The new marketing director will be hired soon, won't she?

M-Cn (A) Didn't you check your e-mail?
(B) It's about ten minutes from here.
(C) No, a little lower.

곧 신임 마케팅 이사를 채용하죠, 그렇죠?
(A) 이메일 확인 안 하셨나요?
(B) 여기서 약 10분 거리예요.
(C) 아니요, 약간 더 낮아요.

해설 신임 마케팅 이사의 채용 여부를 확인하는 부가 의문문
(A) 정답. 신임 마케팅 이사의 채용 여부를 확인하는 질문에 이메일 확인 안 했는지 물으며 이메일을 보면 채용 여부를 알 수 있음을 우회적으로 알려 주고 있으므로 정답.
(B) 연상 단어 오답. 질문의 soon에서 연상 가능한 about ten minutes를 이용한 오답.
(C) 연상 단어 오답. 질문의 hired를 발음이 비슷한 higher로 잘못 들었을 경우 연상 가능한 lower를 이용한 오답.

17

M-Au I really need some help with the presentation graphics.

W-Br (A) Insook can do those for you.
(B) A conference in Chicago.
(C) No, in Research and Development.

발표 시각 자료에 도움이 절실히 필요해요.
(A) 인숙이 해 드릴 수 있어요.
(B) 시카고에서 열리는 학회요.
(C) 아니요, 연구 개발에서요.

어휘 presentation 발표 conference 회의, 학회 research and development 연구 개발

해설 부탁/요청의 평서문
(A) 정답. 발표 시각 자료에 도움이 절실히 필요하다는 평서문에 인숙이 해 줄 수 있다며 도와줄 수 있는 사람을 알려 주고 있으므로 정답.
(B) 연상 단어 오답. 평서문의 presentation에서 연상 가능한 conference를 이용한 오답.
(C) 연상 단어 오답. 평서문의 presentation에서 연상 가능한 research를 이용한 오답.

18

W-Am Who can I talk to about scheduling a haircut?

W-Br (A) Will you be available tomorrow afternoon?
(B) Not too short on the sides, please.
(C) Thanks, the scheduling software has been helpful!

헤어컷 시간을 잡는 건 누구에게 얘기하면 되나요?
(A) 내일 오후에 시간 되세요?
(B) 양 옆은 너무 짧지 않게 해 주세요.
(C) 감사합니다. 일정 예약 소프트웨어는 유용했어요!

어휘 schedule 일정을 잡다　available 시간이 되는, 이용 가능한

해설 헤어컷 일정 담당자를 묻는 Who 의문문
(A) 정답. 헤어컷 시간 잡는 것을 누구에게 얘기해야 하는지 묻는 질문에 내일 오후에 시간 되는지 물으며 본인이 처리해 줄 수 있음을 우회적으로 알려 주고 있으므로 정답.
(B) 연상 단어 오답. 질문의 haircut에서 연상 가능한 too short on the sides를 이용한 오답.
(C) 단어 반복 오답. 질문의 scheduling을 반복 이용한 오답.

19

W-Br Did you already prepare the agenda for the department meeting?

M-Au (A) We should close the windows.
(B) It was postponed.
(C) I bought them at the department store.

부서 회의 안건을 이미 준비하셨나요?
(A) 우리는 창문을 닫아야 해요.
(B) 그건 연기됐어요.
(C) 그것들은 백화점에서 샀어요.

어휘 agenda 의제, 안건　department 부서　postpone 연기하다　department store 백화점

해설 부서 회의 안건의 준비 완료 여부를 묻는 조동사(Did) 의문문
(A) 질문과 상관없는 오답.
(B) 정답. 부서 회의 안건의 준비 완료 여부를 묻는 질문에 연기됐다며 회의 안건을 준비할 필요가 없음을 우회적으로 알려 주고 있으므로 정답.
(C) 단어 반복 오답. 질문의 department를 반복 이용한 오답.

20

M-Cn Do you take your coffee with or without milk?

W-Am (A) The coffee shop on Bayview Avenue.
(B) I prefer drinking tea.
(C) We'll need to place an order for paper.

커피에 우유를 넣으시겠어요, 넣지 않으시겠어요?
(A) 베이뷰 가에 있는 커피숍이요.
(B) 저는 차를 마시고 싶어요.
(C) 종이를 주문해야 할 거예요.

해설 커피에 우유 넣을지 여부를 묻는 선택 의문문
(A) 단어 반복 오답. 질문의 coffee를 반복 이용한 오답.
(B) 정답. 커피에 우유를 넣을지 안 넣을지를 묻는 질문에 차를 마시고 싶다고 두 선택지를 제외한 제3의 안을 제시하고 있으므로 정답.
(C) 연상 단어 오답. 질문의 take your coffee에서 연상 가능한 place an order를 이용한 오답.

21

M-Au Why are you installing new software?

M-Cn (A) Because our current software is outdated.
(B) We rented a large stall.
(C) I'm going to wear a jacket.

왜 새 소프트웨어를 설치하고 있어요?
(A) 현재 소프트웨어가 오래돼서요.
(B) 우리는 큰 가판대를 빌렸어요.
(C) 저는 재킷을 입을 거예요.

어휘 current 현재의　outdated 구식의　rent 빌리다　stall 가판대

해설 새 소프트웨어 설치 이유를 묻는 Why 의문문
(A) 정답. 새 소프트웨어 설치 이유를 묻는 질문에 현재 소프트웨어가 오래돼서라고 이유를 제시하고 있으므로 정답.
(B) 유사 발음 오답. 질문의 installing과 부분적으로 발음이 유사한 stall을 이용한 오답.
(C) 유사 발음 오답. 질문의 software와 부분적으로 발음이 유사한 wear를 이용한 오답.

22

▶ 동영상 강의

W-Am When will next month's cost projections be ready?

W-Br (A) That portable projector was recently replaced.
(B) An unexpected surplus.
(C) I sent an e-mail a few minutes ago.

다음 달 비용 추산은 언제 준비되나요?
(A) 저 휴대용 프로젝터는 최근에 교체됐어요.
(B) 예상치 못한 흑자예요.
(C) 제가 몇 분 전에 이메일을 보냈어요.

어휘 projection 예상, 추정　portable 휴대용의　replace 교체하다　unexpected 예상치 못한, 뜻밖의　surplus 흑자

해설 비용 추산의 준비 완료 시간을 묻는 When 의문문
(A) 파생어 오답. 질문의 projections와 파생어 관계인 projector를 이용한 오답.
(B) 연상 단어 오답. 질문의 cost projections에서 연상 가능한 unexpected surplus를 이용한 오답.
(C) 정답. 다음 달 비용 추산의 준비 완료 시간을 묻는 질문에 몇 분 전에 이메일을 보냈다며 이메일을 보면 알 수 있음을 우회적으로 알려 주고 있으므로 정답.

23

M-Au Would you ask Tae-Joon to help set up the product display?

M-Cn (A) Several kinds of headsets.
(B) No, I can do it myself.
(C) I can't see the bottom line of the chart.

태준에게 제품 진열을 도와 달라고 요청하시겠어요?
(A) 여러 종류의 헤드셋이요.
(B) 아니요, 제가 할 수 있어요.
(C) 도표의 하단이 안 보이네요.

어휘 display 전시, 진열   bottom line 하단, 핵심

해설 제안/권유의 의문문
(A) 유사 발음 오답. 질문의 help set과 부분적으로 발음이 유사한 headsets를 이용한 오답.
(B) 정답. 제품 진열을 태준에게 도와 달라고 요청할 것인지 묻는 질문에 아니요(No)라고 대답한 뒤, 자신이 할 수 있다며 부정 답변과 일관된 내용을 덧붙이고 있으므로 정답.
(C) 질문과 상관없는 오답.

24

W-Am Which version of the contract do you have?

M-Au (A) He's a general contractor.
(B) On the second floor.
(C) The final one.

계약서 어떤 버전을 갖고 계세요?
(A) 그는 원도급자예요.
(B) 2층에요.
(C) 최종본이요.

어휘 contract 계약   general contractor 원도급자, 종합 건설업자

해설 계약서 버전을 묻는 Which 의문문
(A) 파생어 오답. 질문의 contract와 파생어 관계인 contractor를 이용한 오답.
(B) 질문과 상관없는 오답. Where 의문문에 대한 응답이므로 오답.
(C) 정답. 계약서 버전을 묻는 질문에 최종본이라고 알려 주고 있으므로 정답. Which 의문문은 the ~ one을 사용한 응답의 정답률이 높다는 점을 알아 두자.

25

W-Br Why isn't Ms. Pérez here yet?

W-Am (A) No, I can't hear anything.
(B) Company headquarters.
(C) Because she's meeting with her manager.

페레즈 씨는 왜 아직 안 왔나요?
(A) 아니요, 아무 소리도 안 들려요.
(B) 본사요.
(C) 관리자와 면담 중이라서요.

어휘 headquarters 본부

해설 페레즈 씨가 아직 오지 않은 이유를 묻는 Why 의문문
(A) 유사 발음 오답. 질문의 here와 발음이 유사한 hear를 이용한 오답.
(B) 질문과 상관없는 오답.
(C) 정답. 페레즈 씨가 아직 오지 않은 이유를 묻는 질문에 관리자와 면담 중이라고 이유를 제시하고 있으므로 정답.

26

M-Au I heard that our company might be merging with another one.

M-Cn (A) Oh, I didn't know that.
(B) A good-selling product.
(C) Akira told me to put it there.

우리 회사가 다른 회사와 합병할 수도 있다고 들었어요.
(A) 아, 저는 몰랐어요.
(B) 잘 팔리는 제품이요.
(C) 아키라가 저에게 거기에 두라고 했어요.

어휘 merge 합병하다

해설 정보 전달의 평서문
(A) 정답. 우리 회사가 다른 회사와 합병할 수도 있다고 들었다는 평서문에 자신은 몰랐다며 호응하고 있으므로 정답.
(B) 연상 단어 오답. 평서문의 company에서 연상 가능한 product를 이용한 오답.
(C) 평서문과 상관없는 오답.

27

W-Br Could you ask the next patient to come in?

M-Au (A) It's in the cabinet.
(B) The waiting room is empty.
(C) They're both studying nursing.

다음 환자에게 들어오라고 해 주시겠어요?
(A) 캐비닛 안에 있어요.
(B) 대기실이 비어 있는데요.
(C) 둘 다 간호학을 전공하고 있어요.

어휘 patient 환자   waiting room 대기실   empty 비어 있는
nursing 간호학, 간호직

해설 부탁/요청의 의문문
(A) 질문과 상관없는 오답.
(B) 정답. 다음 환자에게 들어오라고 해 달라는 요청에 대기실이 비어 있다며 다음 환자가 없음을 간접적으로 알려 주고 있으므로 정답.
(C) 연상 단어 오답. 질문의 patient에서 연상 가능한 nursing을 이용한 오답.

28

M-Au Are the blueberries ready to harvest?

W-Am (A) I'll try the strawberry flavor.
(B) We have a view of the beach.
(C) It's not summertime yet.

블루베리를 수확할 때가 됐나요?
(A) 딸기맛을 먹어 볼게요.
(B) 해변 전망이에요.
(C) 아직 여름이 아니잖아요.

어휘 harvest 수확하다 flavor 맛, 풍미 have a view of ~이 보이다

해설 블루베리를 수확할 때가 됐는지 묻는 Be동사 의문문
(A) 유사 발음 오답. 질문의 blueberries와 부분적으로 발음이 유사한 strawberry를 이용한 오답.
(B) 질문과 상관없는 오답.
(C) 정답. 블루베리를 수확할 때가 됐는지 묻는 질문에 아직 여름이 아니라며 수확할 때가 아님을 간접적으로 알려 주고 있으므로 정답.

29

 동영상 강의

M-Cn How long will it take us to get to the theater?

W-Br (A) Tickets for the performance are sold-out.
(B) At seven o'clock, I think.
(C) Actually, I don't have a preference.

우리가 극장까지 가는 데 얼마나 걸릴까요?
(A) 공연 티켓이 매진됐어요.
(B) 7시인 것 같아요.
(C) 사실 전 딱히 선호하는 것이 없어요.

어휘 performance 공연 sold out 매진된, 품절된 preference 선호

해설 극장까지 소요 시간을 묻는 How long 의문문
(A) 정답. 극장까지 가는 데 걸리는 시간을 묻는 질문에 공연 티켓이 매진됐다며 극장에 갈 필요가 없음을 간접적으로 알려 주고 있으므로 정답.
(B) 질문과 상관없는 오답. When 의문문에 대한 응답이므로 오답.
(C) 질문과 상관없는 오답. 선택 의문문에 대한 응답이 될 수 있는 오답.

30

M-Au Are you going to send a report or give a presentation to our clients?

M-Cn (A) We enjoyed their talk.
(B) I'll probably do both.
(C) Twenty people attended.

고객에게 보고서를 보내실 건가요, 아니면 발표를 하실 건가요?
(A) 그들의 이야기를 잘 들었어요.
(B) 아마 둘 다 할 것 같아요.
(C) 20명이 참석했어요.

어휘 give a presentation 발표하다

해설 보고서 송부와 발표 중 원하는 방식을 묻는 선택 의문문
(A) 연상 단어 오답. 질문의 presentation에서 연상 가능한 talk를 이용한 오답.
(B) 정답. 보고서 송부와 발표 중 원하는 방식을 묻는 선택 의문문에 아마 둘 다 할 것 같다고 알려 주고 있으므로 정답.
(C) 연상 단어 오답. 질문의 clients에서 연상 가능한 Twenty people을 이용한 오답.

31

W-Am When should we hang up the posters for our conference?

W-Br (A) Sure, my car will be fixed soon.
(B) Next to the main entrance.
(C) The design still needs to be finalized.

언제 학회 포스터를 내걸어야 해요?
(A) 그럼요, 제 차는 곧 수리될 거예요.
(B) 정문 옆이요.
(C) 아직 디자인을 마무리해야 해요.

어휘 main entrance 정문 finalize 마무리를 짓다, 완결하다

해설 학회 포스터를 내걸 시기를 묻는 When 의문문
(A) Yes/No 불가 오답. When 의문문에는 Yes/No 응답이 불가능한데, Sure도 일종의 Yes 응답이라고 볼 수 있으므로 오답.
(B) 질문과 상관없는 오답. Where 의문문에 대한 응답이므로 오답.
(C) 정답. 학회 포스터를 내걸 시기를 묻는 질문에 아직 디자인을 마무리해야 한다며 시간이 더 필요하다는 것을 간접적으로 알려 주고 있으므로 정답.

PART 3

32-34

M-Cn Welcome to the Firelamp Bistro. [32]**How many for dinner?**

W-Br There'll be five of us, but [32]**I'm afraid I forgot to make a reservation.**

M-Cn No problem. But I should mention that [33]**we'll be closing earlier than usual this evening for a private event.** If you'd like to sit outdoors on the patio while you wait, I'll send a server to get you started with drinks and appetizers. We'll get you seated as soon as possible.

W-Br That sounds fine. Thank you. And if possible, [34]**we'd like to sit in a quieter part of the restaurant.** We have some business to discuss.

남 파이어램프 비스트로입니다. **몇 분이 저녁 식사를 하시나요?**

여 저희 다섯 명인데요. **예약하는 걸 깜빡했어요.**

남 괜찮습니다. 그런데 말씀드려야 할 것이, **오늘 저녁에는 개인 행사 건으로 평소보다 일찍 닫을 예정입니다.** 기다리시는 동안 야외 테라스에 앉고 싶으시면 서빙 직원을 보내 음료와 애피타이저로 시작하실 수 있게 할게요. 최대한 빨리 좌석을 드리도록 하겠습니다.

여 좋아요. 감사합니다. 그리고 가능하다면 **조용한 구역에 앉고 싶어요.** 상의할 일이 있어서요.

32

What did the woman forget to do?
(A) Ask about menu choices
(B) Reserve a table
(C) Invite a colleague
(D) Bring a parking permit

여자는 무엇을 잊었는가?
(A) 메뉴에 대해 물어보는 것
(B) 자리를 예약하는 것
(C) 동료를 초대하는 것
(D) 주차 허가증을 가져오는 것

어휘 colleague 동료 permit 허가증

해설 세부 사항 관련 – 여자가 잊은 일
남자가 첫 대사에서 몇 분이 저녁 식사를 할지(How many for dinner?)
묻자, 여자가 예약하는 걸 깜빡했다(I'm afraid I forgot to make a
reservation)고 말하고 있으므로 정답은 (B)이다.

Paraphrasing | 대화의 make a reservation
→ 정답의 Reserve a table

33

What does the man say about the restaurant?
(A) There are more customers than usual.
(B) There is an upstairs area for parties.
(C) The business hours are different today.
(D) The waitstaff is new.

남자는 식당에 대해 뭐라고 말하는가?
(A) 평소보다 손님이 많다.
(B) 위층에 파티를 위한 공간이 있다.
(C) 오늘 영업시간이 다르다.
(D) 종업원들이 새로 왔다.

어휘 upstairs 위층 business hours 영업시간

해설 세부 사항 관련 – 남자가 식당에 대해 하는 말
남자가 두 번째 대사에서 오늘 저녁에는 개인 행사 건으로 평소보다 일찍
닫을 예정(we'll be closing earlier than usual this evening for a
private event)이라고 말하고 있으므로 정답은 (C)이다.

Paraphrasing | 대화의 closing earlier than usual this
evening → 정답의 The business hours are
different today.

34

What does the woman request?
(A) A group discount
(B) A special menu item
(C) To be seated in a quiet area
(D) To be seated near a window

여자는 무엇을 요청하는가?
(A) 단체 할인
(B) 특별 메뉴
(C) 조용한 구역 착석
(D) 창가 근처 착석

해설 세부 사항 관련 – 여자의 요청 사항
여자가 마지막 대사에서 가능하다면 조용한 구역에 앉고 싶다(we'd like
to sit in a quieter part of the restaurant)고 말하고 있으므로 정답은
(C)이다.

Paraphrasing | 대화의 a quieter part of the restaurant
→ 정답의 a quiet area

35-37 3인 대화

W-Br | Hi, Suresh. **35 Office World Incorporated is thrilled about this collaboration with your company.** Your signature line of office products looks great, and we believe they'll sell quite well. We're looking forward to partnering with you.

M-Cn | Thanks. **35 I look forward to a good working partnership as well.** And **36 I'm proud of the fact that all my products are made with recycled materials.** I want to promote environmental responsibility.

W-Br | I'm impressed! Ah, and **37 here is Vedika with her camera equipment.**

W-Am | Hello— **37 I'm here to take some promotional photos.** I'd like to get some shots of you with your products, Suresh. We want to post them online.

여1 | 안녕하세요, 슈레쉬 씨. **오피스 월드 주식회사는 귀사와의 이번 협업에 대해 매우 기쁘게 생각합니다.** 귀사의 대표 사무용품이 훌륭해서 꽤 잘 팔릴 것으로 확신합니다. 귀사와의 협업을 고대하고 있어요.

남 | 감사합니다. **저도 좋은 업무 협력 관계를 기대하고 있습니다. 저희 전 제품이 재활용 소재로 만들어졌다는 점이 자랑스럽습니다.** 환경에 책임지는 자세를 홍보하고 싶어요.

여1 | 감명 받았어요! 아, **베디카가 카메라 장비를 가지고 왔어요.**

여2 | 안녕하세요. **홍보용 사진을 찍으러 왔습니다.** 제품을 들고 계신 사진을 찍고 싶어요, 슈레쉬 씨. 온라인에 게시하고자 합니다.

35

What is the conversation mainly about?
(A) A company training initiative
(B) A factory relocation plan
(C) A business collaboration
(D) An upcoming press conference

대화는 주로 무엇에 관한 것인가?
(A) 회사 교육 계획
(B) 공장 이전 계획
(C) 사업 협력
(D) 다가오는 기자 회견

어휘 initiative 계획 relocation 이전 upcoming 다가오는, 곧 있을
        press conference 기자 회견

해설 전체 내용 관련 – 대화의 주제
첫 번째 여자가 첫 대사에서 오피스 월드 주식회사는 귀사와의 이번 협업
에 대해 매우 기쁘게 생각한다(Office World Incorporated is thrilled
about this collaboration with your company)고 하자 남자가 좋은 협
력 관계를 기대한다(I look forward to a good working partnership
as well)고 말하며 업무 협력에 대한 대화를 이어 가고 있으므로 정답은
(C)이다.

> Paraphrasing   대화의 this collaboration with your company
>   → 정답의 A business collaboration

36

What does the man emphasize about some products?
(A) They have a low price point.
(B) They can easily be customized.
(C) They are designed to be durable.
(D) They are made of recycled materials.

남자는 제품에 대해 무엇을 강조하는가?
(A) 가격대가 낮다.
(B) 쉽게 주문 제작할 수 있다.
(C) 내구성이 있도록 디자인한다.
(D) 재활용한 소재로 만든다.

어휘 price point 가격대 customize 주문 제작하다 durable
        내구성이 있는, 오래가는 be made of ~으로 만들어지다

해설 세부 사항 관련 – 남자가 제품에 대해 강조하는 것
남자가 전 제품이 재활용 소재로 만들어졌다는 점이 자랑스럽다(I'm
proud of the fact that all my products are made with recycled
materials)며 제품이 재활용 소재로 만들어진 것에 대해 강조하고
있으므로 정답은 (D)이다.

37

Why has Vedika joined the meeting?
(A) To discuss sales results
(B) To take some photographs
(C) To conduct an interview
(D) To go over customer feedback

베디카는 왜 회의에 참석했는가?
(A) 판매 결과를 논의하려고
(B) 사진을 촬영하려고
(C) 인터뷰를 하려고
(D) 고객 피드백을 검토하려고

어휘 conduct 하다 go over 검토하다, 조사하다

해설 세부 사항 관련 – 베디카가 회의에 참석한 이유
첫 번째 여자가 두 번째 대사에서 베디카가 카메라 장비를 가지고 왔
다(here is Vedika with her camera equipment)고 말하자 두 번
째 여자 베디카가 홍보용 사진을 찍으러 왔다(I'm here to take some
promotional photos)고 말하고 있으므로 정답은 (B)이다.

> Paraphrasing   대화의 take some promotional photos
>   → 정답의 take some photographs

38-40

M-Au	Hi, Lirong. Thanks for meeting with me. **38 I'd like to consider advertising strategies for our bicycle shop during the annual charity bicycle race.**
W-Br	Well, like last year, as one of the sponsors of the event, we'll have our company name printed on the banner.
M-Au	Great, **39 but this year, I'd also like us to donate our top-of-the-line bicycle to the winner of the race to show how much we care about our community.**
W-Br	That's a nice idea, but **40 sponsoring the race is already going to be costly. I'm worried about the added expense of donating a bicycle as well.**

남	안녕하세요, 리롱. 만나주셔서 감사합니다. **연례 자선 자전거 대회 동안 우리 자전거 매장을 위한 광고 전략을 생각해 보고 싶어요.**
여	글쎄요, 작년과 마찬가지로, 행사 후원업체 중 한 곳으로서 우리 회사의 이름을 플래카드에 인쇄하려고 해요.
남	좋아요. **그런데 올해는 우리 최고급 자전거를 대회 우승자에게 기증해서 지역사회를 얼마나 생각하는지도 보여주고 싶어요.**
여	좋은 생각이네요. 그런데 **대회 후원에 이미 돈이 많이 들고 있어요. 자전거 기부 비용이 추가되는 게 걱정되네요.**

38

What event are the speakers discussing?

(A) An annual sales promotion
(B) A company picnic
(C) An office health fair
(D) A charity bike race

화자들은 어떤 행사에 대해 이야기하는가?

(A) 연례 판촉 행사
(B) 회사 야유회
(C) 직장 보건 박람회
(D) 자선 자전거 대회

어휘 sales promotion 판촉　fair 박람회

해설 전체 내용 관련 – 화자들이 논의 중인 행사

남자가 첫 대사에서 연례 자선 자전거 대회 동안 우리 자전거 매장을 위한 광고 전략을 생각해 보고 싶다(I'd like to consider advertising strategies for our bicycle shop during the annual charity bicycle race)고 대화를 시작하고 있으므로 정답은 (D)이다.

> **Paraphrasing** 대화의 bicycle → 정답의 bike

39

What does the man suggest doing this year?

(A) Hiring a caterer
(B) Donating a prize
(C) Changing a location
(D) Updating a logo

남자는 올해 무엇을 하자고 제안하는가?

(A) 케이터링 업체 고용
(B) 상품 기부
(C) 장소 변경
(D) 로고 업데이트

해설 세부 사항 관련 – 남자가 올해 제안하는 것

남자가 두 번째 대사에서 올해는 우리 최고급 자전거를 대회 우승자에게 기증해서 지역사회를 얼마나 생각하는지도 보여주고 싶다(but this year, I'd also like us to donate our top-of-the-line bicycle to the winner of the race to show how much we care about our community)고 상품 기부를 제안하고 있으므로 정답은 (B)이다.

> **Paraphrasing** 대화의 donate our top-of-the-line bicycle
→ 정답의 Donating a prize

40

What concern does the woman express?

(A) A proposal may be too costly.
(B) An employee needs further training.
(C) A guest speaker is not available.
(D) A shipment has been delayed.

여자는 어떤 우려를 표하는가?

(A) 제안에 비용이 너무 많이 들 것 같다.
(B) 직원에게 교육을 더 해야 한다.
(C) 객원 연설자를 구할 수 없다.
(D) 배송이 지연됐다.

어휘 proposal 제안　further 더 이상의, 추가의　guest speaker 객원 연설자　available 구할 수 있는, 이용 가능한　shipment 수송

해설 세부 사항 관련 – 여자의 우려 사항

여자가 마지막 대사에서 대회 후원에 이미 돈이 많이 들고 있다(sponsoring the race is already going to be costly)며 자전거 기부 비용이 추가되는 게 걱정된다(I'm worried about the added expense of donating a bicycle as well)고 기부 비용에 대한 우려를 나타내고 있으므로 정답은 (A)이다.

41-43

M-Cn　Welcome, Farida, and here's your identification badge. My name's Malik Aljohani. **41 I'm a senior engineer**, and during your first 60 days at Tilmer Tech, I'll be mentoring you throughout the new-employee onboarding process.

W-Am　I'm glad to be here—**42 your company's one of the top manufacturers of robotic vacuum cleaners in the country.** Since I just graduated from university, it's exciting to be applying all that theory directly to this engineering job.

M-Cn　Absolutely! **43 And right now we're headed to your first activity for today. Like all new engineers here, you'll be tasked with taking apart and reassembling our top-selling product.** It's a first step in helping you become knowledgeable about how our product functions.

남　어서 오세요, 파리다. 여기 신분 확인 명찰이 있습니다. 저는 맬릭 알조하니라고 해요. **수석 엔지니어이고**, 틸머 테크에서 일하시는 첫 60일 동안 신입사원 온보딩 과정에서 제가 멘토링을 해 드릴 예정입니다.

여　이곳에 올 수 있게 되어 기뻐요. **전국 최고의 로봇 진공청소기 제조업체 중 하나잖아요.** 이제 막 대학을 졸업해서, 모든 이론을 이 엔지니어링 일에 직접 적용해 볼 수 있다니 기대가 되네요.

남	물론이죠! **이제 오늘 첫 번째 활동을 하러 갑니다. 여기 있는 다른 신입 엔지니어들처럼 우리 최다 판매 제품을 분해하고 재조립하는 일을 하게 될 겁니다.** 우리 제품이 어떻게 작동하는지 아는 데 도움이 될 첫 번째 단계예요.
어휘	identification 신원 확인 onboarding 온보딩(조직 내 새로 합류한 사람이 빠르게 조직 문화를 익히고 적응하도록 돕는 과정) process 과정, 절차 manufacturer 제조업체 vacuum cleaner 진공청소기 graduate 졸업하다 apply 적용하다 theory 이론 directly 직접 absolutely 전적으로, 틀림없이 task (일, 과제 등을) 맡기다 take apart 분해하다 reassemble 재조립하다 knowledgeable 아는 것이 많은 function 기능하다, 작용하다

41

Who is the man?
(A) A security guard
(B) A photographer
(C) An engineer
(D) A safety inspector

남자는 누구인가?
(A) 보안 요원
(B) 사진작가
(C) 엔지니어
(D) 안전 감독관

해설 전체 내용 관련 – 남자의 직업
남자가 첫 대사에서 수석 엔지니어(I'm a senior engineer)라고 본인을 소개하고 있으므로 정답은 (C)이다.

42

What product does the company manufacture?
(A) Drones
(B) Sound systems
(C) Car engines
(D) Vacuum cleaners

회사는 어떤 제품을 제조하는가?
(A) 드론
(B) 음향 시스템
(C) 자동차 엔진
(D) 진공청소기

해설 세부 사항 관련 – 회사가 제조하는 제품
여자가 첫 대사에서 전국 최고의 로봇 진공청소기 제조업체 중 하나(your company's one of the top manufacturers of robotic vacuum cleaners in the country)라고 말하고 있으므로 정답은 (D)이다.

43

What will the woman most likely do next?
(A) Report a lost badge
(B) Tour a facility
(C) Work on an assigned task
(D) Fill out some paperwork

여자는 다음으로 무엇을 하겠는가?
(A) 분실된 명찰에 대해 신고하기
(B) 시설 견학하기
(C) 주어진 업무에 착수하기
(D) 서류 기입하기

어휘 assign 맡기다, 배정하다 fill out 작성하다, 기입하다

해설 세부 사항 관련 – 여자가 다음에 할 일
남자가 마지막 대사에서 이제 오늘 첫 번째 활동을 하러 간다(And right now we're headed to your first activity for today)면서 우리 최다 판매 제품을 분해하고 재조립하는 일을 하게 된다(~ you'll be tasked with taking apart and reassembling our top-selling product)고 안내하고 있으므로 정답은 (C)이다.

44-46

M-Au	Hey, Jyoti. I can't believe it. **⁴⁴You know how I told you that I won some tickets to my favorite basketball team's championship for this weekend?** Well, **⁴⁵now I can't go.**
W-Am	Why? **⁴⁵What happened?** You look really disappointed.
M-Au	**⁴⁵One of my clients has requested a rush on their order. ⁴⁶I'll need to do a quality check on all the products so we can ship by Monday morning.**
W-Am	Well, I'm free this weekend. **⁴⁶Why don't I take over for you?** Just let your supervisor know that I can do the quality check. You can help me out next weekend.

남	안녕하세요, 죠티. 믿을 수가 없네요. **제가 가장 좋아하는 농구팀의 이번 주말 선수권 대회 입장권을 어떻게 구했는지 말했죠?** 음, 갈 수가 없어요.
여	왜요? **무슨 일이죠?** 무척 실망스러워 보여요.
남	**고객 한 명이 주문 건을 서둘러 달라고 요청했어요. 모든 제품에 대한 품질 검사를 해서 월요일 오전에 배송할 수 있도록 해야 해요.**
여	음, 제가 이번 주말에 시간이 있어요. **제가 일을 대신 맡으면 어때요?** 관리자에게 제가 품질 확인을 할 수 있다고 알려 주기만 하세요. 다음 주말에 저를 도와주시면 되잖아요.

어휘	disappointed 실망한 quality 품질 take over for ~의 일을 대신 맡다 supervisor 감독관, 관리자

44

What was the man hoping to do this weekend?
(A) Go on a camping trip
(B) Perform in a local band
(C) Attend a sports competition
(D) Volunteer at a community center

남자는 이번 주말에 무엇을 하고 싶어 했는가?
(A) 캠핑 여행 가기
(B) 지역 밴드에서 공연하기
(C) 운동 경기에 참석하기
(D) 커뮤니티 센터에서 자원봉사하기

어휘 perform 공연하다　competition 대회, 시합　volunteer
자원봉사하다; 자원봉사자

해설 세부 사항 관련 – 남자가 주말에 하고 싶어 한 일
남자가 첫 대사에서 이번 주말에 있을 가장 좋아하는 농구팀 선수권 대회 입장권을 구했다(~ I won some tickets to my favorite basketball team's championship for this weekend?)고 말하고 있으므로 정답은 (C)이다.

> Paraphrasing　대화의 basketball team's championship
> → 정답의 a sports competition

45

Why does the man need to cancel his plans?
(A) A client has made a request.
(B) An event has been postponed.
(C) A coworker is unavailable.
(D) A flight was canceled.

남자는 왜 계획을 취소해야 하는가?
(A) 고객이 요청을 했다.
(B) 행사가 연기됐다.
(C) 동료가 시간이 안 된다.
(D) 항공편이 취소됐다.

어휘 postpone 연기하다　coworker 동료　unavailable 시간이 안
되는

해설 세부 사항 관련 – 남자가 계획을 취소해야 하는 이유
남자가 첫 대사에서 갈 수 없다(now I can't go)고 말했고 여자가 무슨 일인지(What happened?) 묻자 남자가 고객 한 명이 주문 건을 서둘러 달라고 요청했다(One of my clients has requested a rush on their order)고 갈 수 없는 이유를 설명하고 있으므로 정답은 (A)이다.

> Paraphrasing　대화의 requested → 정답의 made a request

46

What does the woman offer to do?
(A) Change a reservation
(B) Check some products
(C) Speak to the man's supervisor
(D) Give the man a ride

여자는 무엇을 하겠다고 제안하는가?
(A) 예약 변경하기
(B) 제품 검수하기
(C) 남자의 관리자에게 이야기하기
(D) 남자를 차에 태워주기

어휘 reservation 예약　give ~ a ride ~을 차에 태워주다

해설 세부 사항 관련 – 여자의 제안 사항
남자가 두 번째 대사에서 모든 제품에 대한 품질 검사를 해서 월요일 오전에 배송할 수 있도록 해야 한다(I'll need to do a quality check on all the products so we can ship by Monday morning)고 하자 여자가 일을 대신 해주겠다(Why don't I take over for you?)고 제품 품질 검사를 제안하고 있으므로 정답은 (B)이다.

47-49

W-Br	**47, 48 I understand that you've found a good candidate to deliver the keynote speech at our conference.**
M-Cn	I have. Dr. Murad Jebreen. **48 He's a specialist in sports medicine,** and he's developed new surgical techniques for athletes with knee injuries. **49 His new book on the topic will be published later this month, actually.**
W-Br	Oh, yes. I've heard of him. **49 I wonder if we have enough money to give copies to everyone who comes to the conference.**
M-Cn	I can check our budget.

여	**우리 학회에서 기조연설을 해 줄 좋은 후보자를 찾으셨다고요.**
남	네. 무라드 제브린 박사예요. **그는 스포츠 의학 전문가이고** 무릎 부상을 입은 운동선수들을 위한 새로운 수술 기법을 개발했어요. **실은 이 주제에 관한 그의 새로운 저서가 이번 달 말에 출간될 거예요.**
여	아, 네. 얘기는 들어봤어요. **학회에 오는 모든 사람들에게 책을 나눠줄 자금이 충분한지 궁금하네요.**
남	제가 예산을 확인해 볼게요.

어휘	candidate 후보자　deliver a speech 연설하다 keynote speech 기조연설　specialist 전문가 medicine 의학　develop 개발하다　surgical 수술의, 외과의　athlete 운동 선수　injury 부상　publish 출판하다　budget 예산

47

What was the man asked to do in preparation for a conference?
(A) Choose a caterer
(B) Book the conference rooms
(C) Find a keynote speaker
(D) Make travel arrangements

남자는 학회 준비를 위해 무엇을 하라고 요청받는가?

(A) 케이터링 업체 선정

(B) 회의실 예약

(C) 기조연설자 물색

(D) 출장 준비

어휘 make arrangements 준비하다

해설 세부 사항 관련 – 남자가 학회 준비를 위해 요청받은 일

여자가 첫 대사에서 우리 학회에서 기조연설을 해 줄 좋은 후보자를 찾았다는 것을 알고 있다(I understand that you've found a good candidate to deliver the keynote speech at our conference)고 말하고 있으므로 정답은 (C)이다.

48

Who is the conference intended for?

(A) Baseball coaches

(B) Medical doctors

(C) Accountants

(D) Publishers

학회는 누구를 위한 것인가?

(A) 야구 코치

(B) 의사

(C) 회계사

(D) 출판업자

해설 세부 사항 관련 – 학회의 대상

여자가 첫 대사에서 우리 학회에서 기조연설을 해 줄 좋은 후보자를 찾았다는 것을 알고 있다(I understand that you've found a good candidate to deliver the keynote speech at our conference)고 하자, 남자가 그는 스포츠 의학 전문가(He's a specialist in sports medicine)라고 언급하고 있는 것으로 보아, 학회의 참가 대상자들은 의학과 관련된 사람들임을 알 수 있다. 따라서 정답은 (B)이다.

49

What does the woman want to hand out to conference attendees?

(A) Books

(B) Tote bags

(C) Tickets to a sports event

(D) Copies of a speech

여자는 학회 참석자들에게 무엇을 나눠주고 싶어 하는가?

(A) 책

(B) 토트백

(C) 스포츠 행사 입장권

(D) 연설 사본

어휘 hand out 나눠주다   attendee 참석자

해설 세부 사항 관련 – 여자가 참석자들에게 나눠주고 싶어 하는 것

남자가 실은 이 주제에 관한 그의 새로운 저서가 이번 달 말에 출간된다(His new book on the topic will be published later this month, actually)고 하자, 여자가 학회에 오는 모든 사람들에게

책을 나눠줄 자금이 충분한지 궁금하다(I wonder if we have enough money to give copies to everyone who comes to the conference)고 말하고 있으므로 여자는 참석자들에게 책을 나눠주고 싶어 한다는 것을 알 수 있다. 따라서 정답은 (A)이다.

50-52

W-Br	Hi. I'm calling about your advertisement. ⁵⁰**I currently rent a space downtown where I build and repair furniture,** but the owners just sold the building, and I have to be out by the end of the month.
M-Au	Well, my space is quite large—enough to fit two cars or a work truck. ⁵¹**It also has a dock in the back to load large containers**, if that would be useful to you.
W-Br	Ideally, yes. I build large items, and a loading dock would make pickup and delivery easier.
M-Au	Would you like to see it this afternoon? ⁵²**Currently, there's no electricity, but I could call and have it turned on today.**

여	안녕하세요. 광고 보고 전화했어요. **저는 현재 도심에 가구를 만들고 고치는 공간을 임대하고 있는데요.** 소유주들이 건물을 팔아서 이번 달 말까지 나가야 하거든요.
남	아, 저희 공간은 꽤 넓어요. 자동차 두 대 또는 작업 트럭이 충분히 들어가요. **또한 뒤쪽에는 대형 컨테이너를 싣기 위한 적하장이 있습니다,** 쓸모가 있으시다면요.
여	완벽하네요. 저는 크기가 큰 물건도 만들거든요. 그래서 적하장이 있으면 픽업과 배송이 더 쉬워질 거예요.
남	오늘 오후에 보시겠어요? **현재 전기가 안 들어오는데 오늘 전화해서 들어오게 할 수 있어요.**

어휘	advertisement 광고 dock 적하장 load 싣다, 적재하다 ideally 완벽하게, 이상적으로 electricity 전기

50

Who is the woman?

(A) A truck driver

(B) A plumber

(C) A furniture maker

(D) A mechanic

여자는 누구인가?

(A) 트럭 운전기사

(B) 배관공

(C) 가구 제조업자

(D) 기계공

여자가 첫 대사에서 현재 도심에 가구를 만들고 고치는 공간을 임대하고 있다(I currently rent a space downtown where I build and repair furniture)고 말하는 것으로 보아 여자는 가구 제조업자임을 알 수 있다. 따라서 정답은 (C)이다.

51

What does the man highlight about a work space?
(A) It has a loading dock.
(B) It is close to the city center.
(C) It has an assigned parking space.
(D) It has fast Internet service.

남자는 작업 공간에 대해 어떤 점을 강조하는가?
(A) 적하장이 있다.
(B) 도심과 가깝다.
(C) 배정받은 주차 공간이 있다.
(D) 빠른 인터넷 서비스를 갖추고 있다.

어휘 assign 배정하다

해설 세부 사항 관련 – 남자가 작업 공간에 대해 강조하는 점
남자가 첫 대사에서 뒤쪽에 대형 컨테이너를 싣기 위한 적하장이 있다(It also has a dock in the back to load large containers)고 말하고 있으므로 정답은 (A)이다.

> **Paraphrasing** 대화의 a dock ~ to load large containers
> → 정답의 a loading dock

52

What does the man offer to do for the woman?
(A) Print out a contract
(B) Activate a utility
(C) Replace some lights
(D) Apply a discount

남자는 여자를 위해 무엇을 하겠다고 제안하는가?
(A) 계약서 출력하기
(B) 공공 서비스 작동시키기
(C) 조명 교체하기
(D) 할인 적용하기

어휘 contract 계약, 계약서 activate 작동시키다, 활성화시키다 utility (수도, 전기, 가스 등의) 공공 서비스 replace 교체하다 apply 적용하다

해설 세부 사항 관련 – 남자의 제안 사항
남자가 마지막 대사에서 현재 전기가 안 들어오는데 오늘 전화해서 들어오게 할 수 있다(Currently, there's no electricity, but I could call and have it turned on today)고 말하고 있으므로 정답은 (B)이다.

> **Paraphrasing** 대화의 electricity → 정답의 a utility
> 대화의 have ~ turned on → 정답의 activate

W-Am	Waseem, I know this is last-minute, but **53,54is there any chance we can add another section to the workbook for tomorrow's seminar?**
M-Au	Oh. The workbook's already been printed.
W-Am	I see. I just learned that the company added a new policy about working with clients that we need to include.
M-Au	Well, **55why don't we just add an insert to each copy of the workbook before we pass them out?** Then everyone will be informed of the change.

여	와심, 막바지란 건 알지만 **내일 세미나 워크북에 혹시 섹션 하나를 더 추가할 수 있을까요?**
남	아, 워크북은 이미 출력됐는데요.
여	알겠어요. 회사에서 고객 응대 업무 관련 새 정책을 추가했다는 걸 이제 알았어요. 그걸 포함해야 해요.
남	**나눠주기 전에 워크북마다 삽지를 추가하면 어때요?** 그럼 모두가 변경 사항에 대해 알 수 있을 거예요.

어휘	last-minute 막판의, 막바지의 policy 정책 include 포함시키다 insert (따로 인쇄하여) 끼워 넣은 페이지 pass out 나눠주다

53

What are the speakers preparing for?
(A) A seminar
(B) A trade show
(C) A client meeting
(D) A book launch

화자들은 무엇을 준비하는가?
(A) 세미나
(B) 무역 박람회
(C) 고객 회의
(D) 도서 출시

어휘 launch 출시, 개시

해설 세부 사항 관련 – 화자들이 준비하는 것
여자가 첫 대사에서 내일 세미나 워크북에 섹션 하나를 더 추가할 수 있는지(is there any chance we can add another section to the workbook for tomorrow's seminar?) 물었고, 관련 대화를 이어 가고 있는 것으로 보아 화자들은 세미나를 준비하고 있다는 것을 알 수 있다. 따라서 정답은 (A)이다.

54

What does the man imply when he says, "The workbook's already been printed"?
(A) He is not sure enough copies were ordered.
(B) He is expecting a delivery.
(C) A change cannot be made.
(D) A task was completed on schedule.

남자가 "워크북은 이미 출력됐는데요"라고 말하는 의도는 무엇인가?
(A) 책이 충분히 주문됐는지 잘 모르겠다.
(B) 배송을 기다리고 있다.
(C) 변경이 이뤄질 수 없다.
(D) 업무가 예정대로 완료됐다.

어휘 on schedule 예정대로, 예정한 시간에

해설 화자의 의도 파악 – 워크북은 이미 출력됐다는 말의 의도

앞에서 여자가 내일 세미나 워크북에 섹션 하나를 더 추가할 수 있는지(is there any chance we can add another section to the workbook for tomorrow's seminar?)를 묻자 인용문을 언급한 것으로 보아, 워크북을 이제는 수정할 수 없다는 의도로 한 말임을 알 수 있다. 따라서 정답은 (C)이다.

55

What does the man suggest?
(A) Contacting a presenter
(B) Using a catering service
(C) Adding a page to a book
(D) Revising an invitation

남자는 무엇을 제안하는가?
(A) 발표자에게 연락하기
(B) 케이터링 서비스 이용하기
(C) 책에 페이지 추가하기
(D) 초대장 수정하기

어휘 presenter 발표자 revise 수정하다 invitation 초대(장)

해설 세부 사항 관련 – 남자의 제안 사항

남자가 마지막 대사에서 나눠주기 전에 워크북마다 삽지를 추가하는 것(why don't we just add an insert to each copy of the workbook before we pass them out?)을 제안하고 있으므로 정답은 (C)이다.

> **Paraphrasing** 대화의 add an insert to each copy of the workbook
> → 정답의 Adding a page to a book

56-58

M-Cn	Hi, Astrid. Thank you for meeting with me.
W-Am	Of course. ⁵⁶ I have an open-door policy for all my employees here at the factory.
M-Cn	So, ⁵⁷ I'd like to talk about changing my work schedule to the day shift.

W-Am	Well, we've had a lot of requests for that lately.
M-Cn	I see. But remember, I've been working the night shift for over ten years.
W-Am	That's true. Let me look into it. ⁵⁸ I'll check the schedule and see what I can do. No promises though.

남	안녕하세요, 아스트리드. 만나주셔서 감사합니다.
여	물론 그래야죠. 저는 이곳 공장에 있는 모든 제 직원들에게는 항상 소통을 위한 문을 열어 놓자는 주의예요.
남	저, 제 업무 시간을 주간 근무로 바꾸는 것에 대해 말씀드리고 싶어요.
여	음, 최근 그 요청을 많이 받았어요.
남	알겠습니다. 그런데 제가 10년 넘게 야간 근무로 일했다는 걸 기억해 주세요.
여	맞아요. 한번 보죠. 시간표를 확인해서 제가 무엇을 할 수 있을지 볼게요. 약속을 드리지는 못합니다.

어휘 open-door (자유로운) 의사소통을 장려하는 day shift 주간 근무 lately 최근 promise 약속

56

Who most likely is the woman?
(A) A career counselor
(B) A sales representative
(C) A factory supervisor
(D) A computer programmer

여자는 누구이겠는가?
(A) 진로 상담사
(B) 영업 담당자
(C) 공장 관리자
(D) 컴퓨터 프로그래머

해설 전체 내용 관련 – 여자의 직업

여자가 첫 대사에서 이곳 공장에 있는 자신의 모든 직원들에게는 항상 소통을 위한 문을 열어 놓자는 주의(I have an open-door policy for all my employees here at the factory)라고 말하는 것으로 보아 여자는 공장에서 직원들을 관리하고 있음을 알 수 있다. 따라서 정답은 (C)이다.

57

Why does the woman say, "we've had a lot of requests for that lately"?
(A) To express doubt about a possibility
(B) To request assistance with a task
(C) To explain a delay
(D) To compliment a colleague

여자가 "최근 그 요청을 많이 받았어요"라고 말하는 이유는?

(A) 가능성에 대해 의구심을 표현하려고
(B) 업무에 대해 도움을 요청하려고
(C) 지연에 대해 설명하려고
(D) 동료를 칭찬하려고

어휘 express doubt 의구심을 표명하다   possibility 가능성
assistance 도움   compliment 칭찬하다

해설 화자의 의도 파악 – 최근 그 요청을 많이 받았다는 말의 의도
앞에서 남자가 업무 시간을 주간 근무로 바꾸는 것(I'd like to talk about changing my work schedule to the day shift)을 요청하자 여자가 인용문을 언급한 것으로 보아, 주간 근무로 변경을 요청하는 인원이 많아서 해결이 쉽지 않다는 의도로 한 말임을 알 수 있다. 따라서 정답은 (A)이다.

58

What does the woman say she will do?
(A) Attend a meeting
(B) Check a schedule
(C) Take inventory
(D) Hire more employees

여자는 무엇을 하겠다고 말하는가?
(A) 회의 참석하기
(B) 시간표 확인하기
(C) 재고 조사하기
(D) 더 많은 직원 고용하기

어휘 take inventory 재고 조사하다

해설 세부 사항 관련 – 여자가 할 일
여자가 마지막 대사에서 시간표를 확인해서 자신이 무엇을 할 수 있을지 보겠다(I'll check the schedule and see what I can do)고 말하고 있으므로 정답은 (B)이다.

59-61 3인 대화

W-Br	⁵⁹**I have bad news. Ife just sent me a text message.** Her car won't start. The battery seems to be dead. ⁵⁹**She won't be here in time to lead her tour group.**
M-Cn	Oh no. Well, ⁶⁰**I'm leading a tour of the seaport this morning.**
W-Br	⁶⁰**Rajeev, you're available.** ⁶¹**I know you're technically still in training, but I think you can handle it.**
M-Au	Hmm. ⁶¹**The historic warehouse district, right? I'm a little nervous about that.**
M-Cn	You did a great job when you shadowed me on that tour last week. You even answered questions from the group.

여	안 좋은 소식이 있어요. 이페가 문자 메시지를 보냈는데요. 차가 시동이 안 걸린대요. 배터리가 나간 것 같아요. 제시간에 와서 투어 단체를 인솔하지 못할 것 같네요.
남1	저런. 저는 오늘 오전에 항구 도시 투어를 인솔해요.
여	라지브, 시간이 되시네요. 엄밀히 말하면 아직 교육 중이지만 처리하실 수 있을 것 같아요.
남2	음… 역사적인 창고 지역 맞죠? 좀 긴장되네요.
남1	지난주 그 투어를 저와 함께 했을 때 잘하셨어요. 단체에서 나온 질문에 대답도 하셨잖아요.

어휘	lead 이끌다 seaport 항구 도시 available 시간이 되는 technically 엄밀히 말하자면 handle 처리하다, 다루다 historic 역사적인 warehouse 창고 district 지역, 구역 nervous 긴장되는 shadow (배우기 위해) 함께 하다

59

What news does the woman share?
(A) A colleague will be late to work.
(B) An item cannot be found.
(C) A form has a mistake in it.
(D) An order has been canceled.

여자는 어떤 소식을 공유하는가?
(A) 동료가 지각할 것이다.
(B) 물품을 찾을 수 없다.
(C) 서식에 실수가 있다.
(D) 주문이 취소됐다.

어휘 colleague 동료

해설 세부 사항 관련 – 여자가 공유하는 소식
여자가 첫 대사에서 안 좋은 소식이 있다(I have bad news)면서 이페가 문자 메시지를 보냈는데(Ife just sent me a text message) 제시간에 와서 투어 단체를 인솔하지 못할 것 같다(She won't be here in time to lead her tour group)며 동료가 늦을 것이라고 말하고 있으므로 정답은 (A)이다.

Paraphrasing	대화의 She won't be here in time → 정답의 A colleague will be late to work.

60

Who are the men?
(A) Auto mechanics
(B) Factory workers
(C) Boat captains
(D) Tour guides

남자들은 누구인가?
(A) 자동차 정비공
(B) 공장 근로자
(C) 선장
(D) 투어 가이드

TEST 10

해설 전체 내용 관련 – 남자들의 직업
첫 번째 남자가 첫 대사에서 오늘 오전에 항구 도시 투어를 인솔한다(I'm leading a tour of the seaport this morning)고 했고, 여자가 두 번째 남자에게 당신이 시간이 된다(Rajeev, you're available)고 말하는 것으로 보아 남자들은 투어 가이드임을 알 수 있다. 따라서 정답은 (D)이다.

61

Why is Rajeev nervous?
(A) He made a mistake on his paperwork.
(B) He recently asked for a salary increase.
(C) He cannot reach someone by mobile phone.
(D) He has not completed his training yet.

라지브는 왜 긴장하는가?
(A) 서류 작업에서 실수를 했다.
(B) 최근 급여 인상을 요구했다.
(C) 휴대전화로 누군가에게 연락을 할 수 없다.
(D) 아직 교육을 마치지 않았다.

어휘 paperwork 서류 작업, 문서 업무 increase 증가, 인상 reach (특히 전화로) 연락하다 complete 마치다, 완료하다

해설 세부 사항 관련 – 라지브가 긴장한 이유
여자가 두 번째 대사에서 라지브에게 엄밀히 말하면 아직 교육 중이지만 처리할 수 있을 것 같다(I know you're technically still in training, but I think you can handle it)고 말하자 라지브가 역사적인 창고 지역이 맞는지(The historic warehouse district, right?)를 확인하며 좀 긴장된다(I'm a little nervous about that)고 말하고 있으므로 정답은 (D)이다.

62-64 대화 + 차선 도안

M-Cn ⁶²We need to check with the project manager about today's construction schedule.

W-Am I already did—⁶²I just came from his office. He said we're going to close off multiple lanes to create a safe work zone.

M-Cn Got it. ⁶³Which ones are we closing?

W-Am ⁶³All of them except for the passing lane.

M-Cn Wow, this closure is really going to affect the morning commute.

W-Am You're right. ⁶⁴I'm going to ask for extra personnel to help manage the traffic volume.

남 오늘 공사 일정에 대해 프로젝트 관리자와 확인해야 해요.
여 이미 했어요. 그의 사무실에서 오는 길이에요. 안전 작업 구역을 만들기 위해 우리가 차선 여러 개를 폐쇄할 거라고 하던데요.
남 알겠어요. 어떤 차선들을 폐쇄하나요?
여 추월 차선만 빼고 전부요.
남 와! 이번 폐쇄로 아침 출근길에 영향을 크게 주겠군요.
여 맞아요. 교통량을 관리하는 데 도움을 줄 추가 인원을 요청할 거예요.

어휘 construction 공사, 건설 multiple 다수의, 많은 except for ~을 제외하고 passing lane 추월 차선 closure 폐쇄 affect 영향을 주다 commute 통근 personnel 직원들, 인원 manage 감당하다, 관리하다 traffic volume 교통량

어휘 shoulder 갓길 travel lane 주행 차선

62

Where has the woman just come from?
(A) A manager's office
(B) A police station
(C) A rental facility
(D) An equipment storage area

여자는 어디서 오는 길인가?
(A) 관리자 사무실
(B) 경찰서
(C) 임대 시설
(D) 장비 보관 구역

어휘 facility 시설 equipment 장비 storage 보관, 저장

해설 세부 사항 관련 – 여자가 다녀온 곳
남자가 첫 대사에서 오늘 공사 일정에 대해 프로젝트 관리자와 확인해야 한다(We need to check with the project manager about today's construction schedule)고 하자, 여자가 그의 사무실에서 오는 길(I just came from his office)이라고 말하고 있으므로 여자는 프로젝트 관리자 사무실에서 오는 길임을 알 수 있다. 따라서 정답은 (A)이다.

63

Look at the graphic. Which lane will stay open today?
(A) Lane 1
(B) Lane 2
(C) Lane 3
(D) Lane 4

시각 정보에 의하면, 오늘 어떤 차선이 그대로 열려 있는가?

(A) 1번 차선
(B) 2번 차선
(C) 3번 차선
(D) 4번 차선

해설 시각 정보 연계 – 오늘 그대로 열려 있는 차선

남자가 두 번째 대사에서 어떤 차선들을 폐쇄하는지(Which ones are we closing?)를 묻자 여자가 추월 차선만 빼고 전부(All of them except for the passing lane)라고 말하고 있고, 차선 도안에 따르면 추월 차선은 2번 차선이므로 정답은 (B)이다.

64

What does the woman say she will ask for?
(A) A pay raise
(B) Extra supplies
(C) More personnel
(D) A safety barricade

여자는 무엇을 요청하겠다고 말하는가?

(A) 임금 인상
(B) 추가 물품
(C) 추가 인원
(D) 안전 방어벽

어휘 supply 보급품, 용품   barricade 바리케이드, 방어벽

해설 세부 사항 관련 – 여자가 요청할 것

여자가 마지막 대사에서 교통량을 관리하는 데 도움을 줄 추가 인원을 요청하겠다(I'm going to ask for extra personnel to help manage the traffic volume)고 말하고 있으므로 정답은 (C)이다.

> Paraphrasing   대화의 extra personnel
> → 정답의 More personnel

65-67 대화 + 일정표

M-Au	**65 Let's start planning the annual employee retreat.**
W-Br	Yes. **65 I think we should hold it outside.** We're at our desks all day, so it would be really great to spend some time in the sun.
M-Au	I agree. **66 There's a place, Oliver's Orchard, that lets you pick your own fruit. We could have the event there.**
W-Br	**66 Great idea. The retreat's in June.** Is it open then?

M-Au	According to the Web site, they are.
W-Br	Perfect. **67 I'll call the orchard to make a reservation for our group.**

남	**연례 직원 야유회를 계획해 봅시다.**
여	네. **야외에서 해야 한다고 생각해요.** 하루 종일 책상 앞에 있으니 햇빛 아래 시간을 보내는 게 정말 좋을 것 같아요.
남	맞아요. **올리버 오차드라는 장소가 있는데 각자 과일을 딸 수 있어요. 거기서 행사를 할 수 있겠네요.**
여	**좋은 생각이네요. 야유회는 6월이죠.** 그때 문을 여나요?
남	웹사이트에 따르면 열어요.
여	좋아요. **제가 과수원에 전화해서 단체 예약을 할게요.**

어휘	annual 연례의, 매년의 retreat 수련회 orchard 과수원 make a reservation 예약하다

Oliver's Orchard: Picking Dates
Strawberries: May
66 Black Cherries: June, July
Blueberries: August
Green Apples: September, October

올리버 오차드: 과일 따기 날짜
딸기: 5월
66 블랙 체리: 6월, 7월
블루베리: 8월
풋사과: 9월, 10월

65

What does the woman suggest about an event location?
(A) It should be outdoors.
(B) It should be inexpensive.
(C) It should be local.
(D) It should offer lunch.

여자는 행사 장소에 대해 뭐라고 제안하는가?

(A) 야외여야 한다.
(B) 비싸지 않아야 한다.
(C) 지역 내에 있어야 한다.
(D) 점심 식사를 제공해야 한다.

어휘 inexpensive 비싸지 않은   local 지역의

해설 세부 사항 관련 – 여자가 행사 장소에 대해 제안한 것

남자가 첫 대사에서 연례 직원 야유회를 계획해 보자(Let's start planning the annual employee retreat)고 하자 여자가 야외에서 해야 한다고 생각한다(I think we should hold it outside)고 말하고 있으므로 정답은 (A)이다.

> Paraphrasing   대화의 outside → 정답의 outdoors

66

Look at the graphic. Which fruit will be picked during the event?

(A) Strawberries
(B) Black cherries
(C) Blueberries
(D) Green apples

시각 정보에 의하면, 행사 중 어떤 과일을 딸 것인가?

(A) 딸기
(B) 블랙 체리
(C) 블루베리
(D) 풋사과

해설 시각 정보 연계 – 행사 중 딸 과일
남자가 두 번째 대사에서 올리버 오차드라는 장소가 있는데 각자 과일을 딸 수 있다(There's a place, Oliver's Orchard, that lets you pick your own fruit)면서 거기서 행사를 할 수 있겠다(We could have the event there)고 말하자 여자가 좋은 생각(Great idea)이라면서 야유회는 6월(The retreat's in June)이라고 했고, 일정표에 따르면 6월은 블랙 체리를 따는 시기이므로 정답은 (B)이다.

67

What does the woman say she will do?

(A) Contact a business
(B) Draft an invitation
(C) Recruit some volunteers
(D) Prepare a budget

여자는 무엇을 하겠다고 말하는가?

(A) 업체에 연락하기
(B) 초대장 초안 작성하기
(C) 자원봉사자 모집하기
(D) 예산 준비하기

어휘 draft 초안을 작성하다 invitation 초대 recruit 모집하다
budget 예산

해설 세부 사항 관련 – 여자가 할 일
여자가 마지막 대사에서 과수원에 전화해서 단체 예약을 하겠다(I'll call the orchard to make a reservation for our group)고 말하고 있으므로 정답은 (A)이다.

> **Paraphrasing** 대화의 call the orchard
> → 정답의 Contact a business

68-70 대화 + 지도   ▶ 동영상 강의

> **M-Au** Hi. **68 I'm looking for an apartment, and I saw your advertisement. Do you have any two-bedroom apartments available in May?**
>
> **W-Am 68 Yes. In fact, we've just finished construction on a new complex.**

M-Au Does the complex have a lot of outdoor space? I'd like to have an area to entertain guests outside.

W-Am Yes, there's plenty of green space. **69 The building in the back corner, farthest from the office, has the most space and a lot of shade.**

M-Au I'd be interested in that.

W-Am And **70 for an extra 80 dollars per month, you can get a reserved parking space right in front of your unit.**

> 남 안녕하세요. **아파트를 찾고 있다가 광고를 봤어요. 5월에 이용 가능한 침실 2개 아파트가 있나요?**
>
> 여 **네. 사실 새로운 단지 공사가 막 끝났어요.**
>
> 남 단지에 실외 공간이 많이 있나요? 바깥에서 손님 접대를 할 공간이 있었으면 해요.
>
> 여 네, **녹지가 많아요. 사무실에서 가장 먼 뒤쪽 모퉁이 건물은 공간이 가장 넓고 그늘이 많습니다.**
>
> 남 그곳에 관심이 가네요.
>
> 여 **월 80달러를 추가로 내시면 해당 세대 바로 앞에 지정 주차 공간을 받으실 수 있어요.**

어휘 look for ~을 찾다 advertisement 광고 available 이용 가능한, 구할 수 있는 in fact 사실 construction 공사, 건설 complex 복합 건물, 단지 entertain 접대하다 farthest 가장 먼 be interested in ~에 관심이 있다, 흥미가 있다 reserve (자리 등을) 따로 잡아 두다

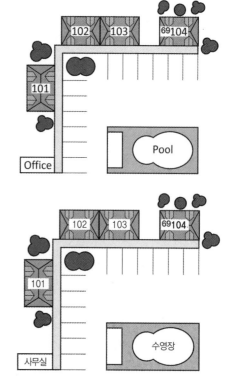

68

Who most likely is the woman?
(A) A landscape worker
(B) A taxi driver
(C) An apartment manager
(D) An interior decorator

여자는 누구이겠는가?
(A) 조경 인부
(B) 택시 기사
(C) 아파트 관리인
(D) 실내 장식가

어휘 landscape 조경, 풍경 decorator 장식가

해설 전체 내용 관련 – 여자의 직업
남자가 첫 대사에서 아파트를 찾고 있다가 광고를 봤다(I'm looking for an apartment, and I saw your advertisement)면서 5월에 이용 가능한 침실 2개 아파트가 있는지(Do you have any two-bedroom apartments available in May?)를 묻자, 여자가 네(Yes)라고 답한 뒤 새로운 단지 공사가 막 끝났다(~ we've just finished construction on a new complex)고 아파트 단지에 대한 내용을 덧붙이고 있으므로 여자는 아파트 단지 관리인임을 알 수 있다. 따라서 정답은 (C)이다.

69

Look at the graphic. Which location is the woman referring to?
(A) 101
(B) 102
(C) 103
(D) 104

시각 정보에 의하면, 여자는 어떤 장소를 언급하고 있는가?
(A) 101
(B) 102
(C) 103
(D) 104

해설 시각 정보 연계 – 여자가 언급하고 있는 장소
여자가 두 번째 대사에서 사무실에서 가장 먼 뒤쪽 모퉁이 건물은 공간이 가장 넓고 그늘이 많다(The building in the back corner, farthest from the office, has the most space and a lot of shade)고 했고, 지도에 따르면 사무실에서 가장 먼 뒤쪽 모퉁이 건물이 104동이므로 정답은 (D)이다.

70

What might the man pay extra for?
(A) A pool membership
(B) A reserved parking space
(C) Monthly maintenance
(D) Laundry facilities

남자는 무엇을 위해 추가 지불을 할 수 있는가?
(A) 수영장 회원권
(B) 지정 주차 공간
(C) 월 유지보수
(D) 세탁 시설

어휘 maintenance 유지보수 laundry 세탁

해설 세부 사항 관련 – 남자가 추가 지불을 할 수 있는 것
여자가 마지막 대사에서 월 80달러를 추가로 내면 해당 세대 바로 앞에 지정 주차 공간을 받을 수 있다(for an extra 80 dollars per month, you can get a reserved parking space right in front of your unit)고 말하고 있으므로 정답은 (B)이다.

PART 4

71-73 회의 발췌

M-Cn ⁷¹Some of you have been accidentally skipping some of your closing duties, so I've called this meeting to clarify what is expected. ⁷²After you've sanitized all the food preparation areas in the kitchen, make sure the pantry and walk-in refrigerator doors are shut and locked. There are a few other tasks to complete before you leave. ⁷³I know the current checklist isn't up-to-date, so I'll make the necessary revisions to it.

몇몇 분들이 실수로 마감 업무를 빠뜨렸어요. 그래서 해야 할 일을 명확히 하기 위해 이 회의를 소집했습니다. 주방의 음식 준비 구역을 모두 소독한 후에는 식료품 저장실과 대형 냉장실 문을 반드시 닫고 잠가야 합니다. 퇴근하기 전에 완료해야 할 몇 가지 다른 작업들이 있습니다. 현재 점검 목록은 최신 정보가 아니니 필요한 수정을 해 두겠습니다.

어휘 accidentally 뜻하지 않게, 우연히 skip 건너뛰다 clarify 명확하게 하다 sanitize 위생 처리하다, 살균하다 preparation 준비 walk-in refrigerator 대형 냉장실 current 현재의 up-to-date 최신의, 최근의 revision 변경, 수정

71

What is the purpose of a meeting?
(A) To prepare staff for a special event
(B) To review some closing procedures
(C) To introduce some staff members
(D) To resolve an issue with inventory

회의의 목적은 무엇인가?
(A) 특별 행사를 위해 직원들을 준비시키려고
(B) 마감 절차를 검토하려고
(C) 직원들을 소개하려고
(D) 재고 관련 문제를 해결하려고

어휘 procedure 절차 introduce 소개하다 resolve 해결하다 inventory 재고, 물품 목록

해설 전체 내용 관련 – 회의의 목적

화자가 도입부에 몇몇 분들이 실수로 마감 업무를 빠뜨려서 해야 할 일을 명확히 하기 위해 이 회의를 소집했다(Some of you have been accidentally skipping some of your closing duties, so I've called this meeting to clarify what is expected)고 한 것으로 보아, 이 회의의 목적은 업무 마감 절차를 검토하려는 것임을 알 수 있다. 따라서 정답은 (B)이다.

72

What type of business do the listeners most likely work for?
(A) A restaurant
(B) A library
(C) An appliance store
(D) A manufacturing facility

청자들은 어떤 종류의 업체에서 일하겠는가?
(A) 식당
(B) 도서관
(C) 가전제품 매장
(D) 제조 시설

해설 전체 내용 관련 – 청자들의 근무지

화자가 중반부에 주방의 음식 준비 구역을 모두 소독한 후에는 식료품 저장실과 대형 냉장실 문을 반드시 닫고 잠가야 한다(After you've sanitized all the food preparation areas in the kitchen, make sure the pantry and walk-in refrigerator doors are shut and locked)고 한 것으로 보아, 청자들은 식당에서 근무하고 있다는 것을 알 수 있다. 따라서 정답은 (A)이다.

73

What does the speaker say he will do?
(A) Sign a contract
(B) Mail an invoice
(C) Edit a document
(D) Change a schedule

화자는 무엇을 하겠다고 말하는가?
(A) 계약서에 서명하기
(B) 청구서 발송하기
(C) 문서 수정하기
(D) 일정 변경하기

어휘 contract 계약, 계약서 invoice 청구서, 송장

해설 세부 사항 관련 – 화자가 할 일

화자가 마지막에 현재 점검 목록은 최신 정보가 아니니 필요한 수정을 해 두겠다(I know the current checklist isn't up-to-date, so I'll make the necessary revisions to it)고 말하고 있으므로 정답은 (C)이다.

Paraphrasing	담화의 make the necessary revisions → 정답의 Edit
	담화의 the current checklist → 정답의 a document

74-76 전화 메시지

M-Au Hi, Melissa. It's Hiroki from *Ecology Now Magazine*. **74I just read your article about protecting old-growth forests in Europe and how important these conservation efforts are to the local communities.** First of all, **75I loved your descriptions of the mushroom-hunting social groups.** Readers will feel like they're there! However, your article mainly presents the views of people who use the forests for recreation. **76We need to hear from the lawmakers responsible for the new regulations impacting land use.** And be sure to include some photos. Aside from that, great job. Call me back if you want more guidance.

안녕하세요, 멜리사. 〈에콜로지 나우 매거진〉의 히로키입니다. 유럽의 오래된 숲을 보호하는 것과 이러한 보존 노력이 지역사회에 얼마나 중요한지에 관해 쓰신 기사를 막 읽었어요. 무엇보다 버섯 채취 동아리에 대한 설명이 아주 좋았습니다. 독자들은 그곳에 있는 것처럼 느낄 거예요! 그런데 기사가 휴양을 위해 숲을 이용하는 사람들의 견해를 주로 보여주고 있군요. 토지 사용에 영향을 미칠 새 규정을 책임지는 입법가들의 이야기를 들어봐야 합니다. 그리고 사진도 넣어 주세요. 그것 외에는 훌륭해요. 지침이 더 필요하시면 전화 주세요.

어휘 protect 보호하다 conservation 보호, 보존 effort 노력 first of all 우선 description 기술, 묘사 present 보여주다, 나타내다 recreation 휴양, 취미 lawmaker 입법가 responsible for ~에 책임이 있는 regulation 규정, 규제 impact 영향을 주다 include 포함시키다 aside from ~ 외에는 guidance 지침, 안내

74

What topic did the listener write an article about?
(A) Forest conservation
(B) Travel recommendations
(C) Bird-watching
(D) Social media usage

청자는 어떤 주제에 대해 기사를 썼는가?
(A) 숲 보호
(B) 여행 추천
(C) 들새 관찰
(D) 소셜 미디어 이용

어휘 recommendation 추천 usage 사용

해설 세부 사항 관련 – 청자가 작성한 기사의 주제

화자가 초반부에 유럽의 오래된 숲을 보호하는 것에 관해 청자가 쓴 기사를 막 읽었다(I just read your article about protecting old-growth forests in Europe ~)고 말하고 있으므로 정답은 (A)이다.

Paraphrasing	담화의 protecting old-growth forests → 정답의 Forest conservation

75

What does the speaker like about the article?
(A) The descriptions
(B) The photographs
(C) The organization
(D) The use of statistics

화자는 기사의 어떤 점을 마음에 들어 하는가?
(A) 설명
(B) 사진
(C) 구성
(D) 통계 이용

어휘 organization 구성, 구조 statistics 통계

해설 세부 사항 관련 – 회자가 마음에 들어 하는 기사의 부분
화자가 중반부에 버섯 채취 동아리에 대한 설명이 아주 좋았다(I loved your descriptions of the mushroom-hunting social groups)고 말하고 있으므로 정답은 (A)이다.

76

Who does the speaker want the listener to interview?
(A) Restaurant chefs
(B) Park rangers
(C) Biologists
(D) Government officials

화자는 청자가 누구를 인터뷰하기를 바라는가?
(A) 식당 요리사
(B) 공원 관리인
(C) 생물학자
(D) 공무원

해설 세부 사항 관련 – 화자가 바라는 청자의 인터뷰 대상
화자가 후반부에 토지 사용에 영향을 미칠 새 규정을 책임지는 입법가들의 이야기를 들어봐야 한다(We need to hear from the lawmakers responsible for the new regulations impacting land use)고 말하고 있으므로 정답은 (D)이다.

> **Paraphrasing** 담화의 lawmakers
> → 정답의 Government officials

77-79 담화

> **W-Am** Welcome, everyone, to this workshop on artificial intelligence technologies. [77]**Though I know everyone's been enjoying the coffee and conversation, we have a lot of speakers on the schedule.** [77,78]**To start things off, we're delighted to invite Dr. Haruka Adachi to the stage.** [78]**She'll demonstrate some ways computer systems can simulate human intelligence.** Even if you're not a computer programmer, I'm sure you'll find this demonstration easy to follow. [79]**Please feel free to raise your hand to ask questions at any time.** We want these sessions to be interactive.

> 인공 지능 기술 워크숍에 오신 여러분을 환영합니다. **모두 커피와 대화를 즐기고 계시는 걸 알지만 예정되어 있는 연설자가 많습니다.** 시작하기 위해 하루카 아다치 박사님을 무대로 모시겠습니다. 박사님께서 컴퓨터 시스템이 인간 지능을 모방하는 몇 가지 방법을 보여주실 겁니다. 컴퓨터 프로그래머가 아니더라도 이 시연은 쉽게 이해하실 수 있을 겁니다. **언제든 자유롭게 손을 들고 질문해 주세요.** 강좌에 상호 작용이 있었으면 합니다.

> **어휘** artificial intelligence 인공 지능 delighted 아주 기뻐하는 demonstrate 실례를 들어 보여주다, 시연하다 simulate ~인 체하다, 흉내 내다 follow 따라가다, 이해하다 raise 올리다, 들다 interactive 상호작용을 하는

77

What does the speaker imply when she says, "we have a lot of speakers on the schedule"?
(A) The listeners should check the schedule.
(B) An advertisement was popular.
(C) An event will begin right away.
(D) More refreshments will be needed.

화자가 "예정되어 있는 연설자가 많습니다"라고 말하는 의도는 무엇인가?
(A) 청자들은 일정을 확인해야 한다.
(B) 광고가 인기 있었다.
(C) 행사가 바로 시작될 것이다.
(D) 다과가 더 필요할 것이다.

어휘 advertisement 광고 refreshment 다과

해설 화자의 의도 파악 – 예정되어 있는 연설자가 많다는 말의 의도
화자가 앞에서 모두 커피와 대화를 즐기고 계시는 걸 알지만(Though I know everyone's been enjoying the coffee and conversation)이라고 한 뒤 인용문을 언급하고, 시작하기 위해 하루카 아다치 박사님을 무대로 모시겠다(To start things off, we're delighted to invite Dr. Haruka Adachi to the stage)고 하는 것으로 보아, 바로 연설이 시작된다는 것을 알리기 위해 한 말임을 알 수 있다. 따라서 정답은 (C)이다.

78

What industry does Dr. Adachi most likely work in?
(A) Filmmaking
(B) Interior design
(C) Construction
(D) Computer science

아다치 박사는 어떤 업계에서 일하겠는가?
(A) 영화 제작
(B) 실내 디자인
(C) 건설
(D) 컴퓨터 과학

해설 세부 사항 관련 – 아다치 박사의 근무 업종

화자가 중반부에 하루카 아다치 박사를 무대로 모시겠다(we're delighted to invite Dr. Haruka Adachi to the stage)면서 박사가 컴퓨터 시스템이 인간 지능을 모방하는 몇 가지 방법을 보여줄 것(She'll demonstrate some ways computer systems can simulate human intelligence)이라고 말하고 있으므로 아다치 박사는 컴퓨터 시스템을 전문적으로 다루는 업계에서 근무하고 있다는 것을 알 수 있다. 따라서 정답은 (D)이다.

79

What does the speaker encourage the listeners to do?

(A) Complete a survey
(B) Ask questions
(C) Introduce themselves
(D) Work in small groups

화자는 청자들에게 무엇을 하라고 권하는가?

(A) 설문 작성하기
(B) 질문하기
(C) 자기소개하기
(D) 소그룹으로 작업하기

해설 세부 사항 관련 – 화자가 청자들에게 권하는 것

화자가 후반부에 언제든 자유롭게 손을 들고 질문해 줄 것(Please feel free to raise your hand to ask questions at any time)을 권하고 있으므로 정답은 (B)이다.

80-82 공지

M-Au Attention, everyone: **80 the home bathroom showcase will begin in an hour in Hall D.** The showcase will feature the latest designs for showers and bathtubs, as well as a variety of materials for home customization. **81 Exhibitors, please be at your designated booth at least 30 minutes before the showcase opens to the public.** If you need assistance, any staff member can direct you to your booth. Attendees, don't forget to bring your tickets to the showcase. **82 We will be running a raffle with a chance to win a new bathtub. You'll need your ticket to participate.**

여러분께 알립니다. 주택 욕실 쇼케이스가 한 시간 뒤 D홀에서 시작됩니다. 쇼케이스에서는 샤워기와 욕조의 최신 디자인뿐 아니라 맞춤 제작을 위한 다양한 자재를 선보입니다. 전시업체 여러분, 행사가 대중에게 공개되기 최소 30분 전까지 지정된 부스에서 대기해 주세요. 도움이 필요하실 경우, 직원이 여러분의 부스로 안내해 드릴 수 있습니다. 참석자 여러분, 쇼케이스 입장권을 잊지 말고 가져오세요. **추첨을 통해 새 욕조를 얻을 수 있는 기회를 드립니다. 참가하시려면 입장권이 필요합니다.**

어휘 attention 알립니다, 주목하세요 feature 특별히 포함하다 latest 최신의 a variety of 다양한 material 재료, 소재 customization 주문 제작 designate 지정하다 at least 최소한 assistance 도움 direct (길을) 안내하다 attendee 참석자 raffle 추첨 participate 참가하다

80

What type of event is most likely taking place?

(A) A trade show
(B) A museum exhibit
(C) A food festival
(D) A gardening workshop

어떤 종류의 행사가 열리고 있겠는가?

(A) 무역 박람회
(B) 박물관 전시회
(C) 음식 축제
(D) 정원 가꾸기 워크숍

어휘 exhibit 전시

해설 전체 내용 관련 – 행사의 종류

화자가 초반부에 주택 욕실 쇼케이스가 한 시간 뒤 D홀에서 시작된다(the home bathroom showcase will begin in an hour in Hall D)면서 쇼케이스에서는 샤워기와 욕조의 최신 디자인을 선보일 것(The showcase will feature the latest designs for showers and bathtubs ~)이라고 안내하고 있으므로 정답은 (A)이다

81

What are exhibitors asked to do?

(A) Wear identification badges
(B) Distribute samples
(C) Obtain parking passes
(D) Arrive at a location early

전시업체들은 무엇을 하라고 요청받는가?

(A) 신분 확인 명찰 착용하기
(B) 견본 배포하기
(C) 주차권 받기
(D) 장소에 일찍 도착하기

어휘 identification 신원 확인 distribute 분배하다, 배포하다 obtain 얻다, 획득하다

해설 세부 사항 관련 – 전시업체들이 요청받은 일

화자가 중반부에 전시업체 관계자에게 행사가 공개되기 최소 30분 전까지 지정된 부스에서 대기해 줄 것(Exhibitors, please be at your designated booth at least 30 minutes before the showcase opens to the public)을 요청하고 있으므로 정답은 (D)이다.

> Paraphrasing 담화의 be at your designated booth at least 30 minutes before the showcase opens to the public
> → 정답의 Arrive at a location early

82

What does the speaker say attendees can do with their tickets?

(A) Receive a discount
(B) Enter a contest
(C) Access a special area
(D) Purchase refreshments

화자는 참석자들이 입장권으로 무엇을 할 수 있다고 말하는가?

(A) 할인 받기
(B) 경합에 참가하기
(C) 특별 구역 입장하기
(D) 다과 구입하기

어휘 enter a contest 대회에 참가하다 access 접근하다, 입장하다 refreshments 다과

해설 세부 사항 관련 – 참석자들이 입장권으로 할 수 있는 것

화자가 마지막에 추첨을 통해 새 욕조를 얻을 수 있는 기회를 준다(We will be running a raffle with a chance to win a new bathtub)면서 참가하려면 입장권이 필요하다(You'll need your ticket to participate)고 말하고 있으므로 정답은 (B)이다.

> **Paraphrasing** 담화의 a raffle → 정답의 a contest
> 담화의 participate → 정답의 Enter

83-85 전화 메시지

 동영상 강의

> **W-Br** Hi, Andrew. I'm calling about the Dearborn Hotel account—⁸³**the clients that we're producing the television commercial for.** I just heard from them, and they said they've been very satisfied with how you're addressing their needs for the project. ⁸⁴**It's always great to get such positive feedback from our clients,** and this is your first account. ⁸⁵**They also mentioned that they'd like to make some adjustments to the project timeline. Could you e-mail me the most recent copy of it?** Thanks!

> 안녕하세요, 앤드류. 디어본 호텔 건 관련해서 전화했어요. **우리가 TV 광고를 만들어 주는 고객이요.** 방금 그들한테 들었는데 당신이 그들의 프로젝트 요구 사항을 해결하는 방식에 굉장히 만족했다고 하네요. 고객으로부터 그런 긍정적인 피드백을 받는 건 항상 멋진 일이에요. 게다가 당신의 첫 번째 고객이잖아요. 또한 프로젝트 일정표를 조정했으면 한다고도 언급했어요. 제게 가장 최근 것으로 이메일을 보내주실 수 있을까요? 감사합니다!

어휘 account 고객 produce 제작하다 commercial 광고 satisfied 만족한 address (문제, 상황 등에 대해) 고심하다, 다루다 positive 긍정적인 mention 언급하다 adjustment 조정, 수정 recent 최근의

83

What industry does the speaker most likely work in?

(A) Hospitality
(B) Finance
(C) Advertising
(D) Technology

화자는 어떤 업계에서 일하겠는가?

(A) 접객 서비스
(B) 금융
(C) 광고
(D) 기술

해설 전체 내용 관련 – 화자의 근무 업계

화자가 초반부에 우리가 TV 광고를 만들어 주는 고객(the clients that we're producing the television commercial for)이라고 말하고 있으므로 정답은 (C)이다.

84

What does the speaker mean when she says, "this is your first account"?

(A) She is impressed by some work.
(B) She is available to answer questions.
(C) A mistake is understandable.
(D) A process will take a long time.

화자가 "당신의 첫 번째 고객이잖아요"라고 말하는 의도는 무엇인가?

(A) 업무에 좋은 인상을 받았다.
(B) 질문에 답할 수 있다.
(C) 실수가 당연하다.
(D) 절차에 시간이 오래 걸릴 것이다.

어휘 impressed 인상 깊게 생각하는, 감명을 받은 understandable (특정 상황에서) 당연한, 이해할 수 있는 process 과정, 절차

해설 화자의 의도 파악 – 당신의 첫 번째 고객이라는 말의 의도

앞에서 고객으로부터 그런 긍정적인 피드백을 받는 건 항상 멋진 일(It's always great to get such positive feedback from our clients)이라고 말한 뒤 인용문을 언급하고 있으므로, 첫 고객으로부터 긍정적인 피드백을 받은 것이 훌륭하다는 의도로 한 말임을 알 수 있다. 따라서 정답은 (A)이다.

85

What does the speaker ask the listener to send?

(A) A timeline
(B) An address
(C) Some sales figures
(D) Some meeting notes

화자는 청자에게 무엇을 보내 달라고 요청하는가?

(A) 일정표
(B) 주소
(C) 매출액
(D) 회의 메모

해설 세부 사항 관련 - 청자에게 보내 달라고 요청하는 것

화자가 마지막에 그들이 프로젝트 일정표를 조정했으면 한다고 언급했다(They also mentioned that they'd like to make some adjustments to the project timeline)면서 가장 최근 일정표를 이메일로 보내줄 것(Could you e-mail me the most recent copy of it?)을 요청하고 있으므로 정답은 (A)이다.

86-88 담화

W-Am Hi, everyone. **86As farm employees, we have all come across various issues with our equipment. 87Today I'm going to talk about what to do when you find liquid leaking from any of our farm equipment.** Our mowers and tractors mainly use fluids like water, or oil to control steering. When you find fluid leaking from a broken tube or valve, don't try to fix it yourself. **88Please let me know, and I'll contact the manufacturer for a replacement part.** Otherwise, the warranty will be voided.

안녕하세요, 여러분. 우리 모두는 농장 직원으로서 장비와 관련된 다양한 문제를 마주치게 됩니다. 오늘 저는 여러분이 농장 장비에서 액체가 새는 것을 발견했을 때 어떻게 해야 하는지에 대해 이야기할 겁니다. 잔디 깎는 기계와 트랙터는 조종 장치 제어를 위해 주로 물이나 기름 같은 액체를 쓰는데요. 고장 난 튜브나 밸브에서 액체가 새는 것을 발견했을 때 스스로 수리하려고 하지 마십시오. 저에게 알려 주시면 제가 제조업체에 연락해서 교체 부품을 구해보겠습니다. 그렇지 않으면 품질 보증서가 무효화됩니다.

어휘 come across 마주치다 various 다양한 equipment 장비 liquid 액체 leak 새다 mower 잔디 깎는 기계 fluid 액체, 유동체 steering 조종 장치 manufacturer 제조업체 replacement 교체 otherwise 그렇지 않으면 voided 무효로 된

86

Where do the listeners most likely work?
(A) At a public park
(B) At a landscaping company
(C) At a farm
(D) At a supermarket

청자들은 어디에서 일하겠는가?
(A) 공원
(B) 조경업체
(C) 농장
(D) 슈퍼마켓

해설 전체 내용 관련 - 청자들의 근무지

화자가 초반부에 우리 모두는 농장 직원으로서 장비와 관련된 다양한 문제를 마주치게 된다(As farm employees, we have all come across various issues with our equipment)고 하므로 청자들은 농장에서 일하고 있음을 알 수 있다. 따라서 정답은 (C)이다.

87

What is the speaker mainly discussing?
(A) Purchasing some tools
(B) Training cleaning staff
(C) Repairing some equipment
(D) Arranging transportation

화자는 주로 무엇에 대해 이야기하는가?
(A) 연장 구매
(B) 청소 직원 교육
(C) 장비 수리
(D) 교통편 마련

어휘 arrange 마련하다, 주선하다 transportation 운송, 수송

해설 전체 내용 관련 - 담화의 주제

화자가 중반부에 농장 장비에서 액체가 새는 것을 발견했을 때 어떻게 해야 하는지에 대해 이야기할 것(Today I'm going to talk about what to do when you find liquid leaking from any of our farm equipment)이라고 말하며 장비 수리에 대한 이야기를 하고 있으므로 정답은 (C)이다.

88

What solution does the speaker suggest?
(A) Contacting a manufacturer
(B) Decreasing a budget
(C) Renting some tents
(D) Extending hours of operation

화자는 어떤 해결책을 제안하는가?
(A) 제조업체에 연락하기
(B) 예산 줄이기
(C) 텐트 임대하기
(D) 영업시간 늘리기

어휘 decrease 줄이다, 감소시키다 extend 늘리다, 연장하다 hours of operation 영업시간

해설 세부 사항 관련 - 화자가 제안하는 해결책

화자가 후반부에 자신에게 알려 주면 제조업체에 연락해서 교체 부품을 구해보겠다(~ I'll contact the manufacturer for a replacement part)고 말하고 있으므로 정답은 (A)이다.

89-91 공지

M-Au Good afternoon, and thanks for visiting Eastgate Art Museum. **89This month, we're delighted to offer a special exhibit of Johann Weber's paintings. 90In just a few minutes, our museum director will be giving a talk in the museum theater about the artist's life and work. 91While you're here, please consider becoming a member of the museum. To sign up, stop by the information desk.** Members will receive advance notice about educational events, like the one today.

안녕하세요. 이스트게이트 미술관을 방문해 주셔서 감사합니다. **이번 달에는 요한 웨버의 그림 특별전을 제공해 드리게 되어 기쁩니다.** 몇 분 후 미술관 극장에서 우리 미술관 관장님이 해당 화가의 삶과 작품에 대해 이야기해 드릴 겁니다. 여기 오신 김에 미술관 회원이 되는 것에 대해 고려해 주십시오. 신청하시려면 안내 데스크에 들러 주세요. 회원은 오늘 같은 교육 행사에 대해 사전 공지를 받을 수 있습니다.

어휘 art museum 미술관 delighted 아주 기뻐하는 exhibit 전시 give a talk 강연하다, 이야기하다 consider 고려하다 sign up 신청하다 stop by 잠시 들르다 advance notice 사전 통고, 예고 educational 교육적인

89

Who is Johann Weber?
(A) A musician
(B) A librarian
(C) A painter
(D) A journalist

요한 웨버는 누구인가?
(A) 음악가
(B) 사서
(C) 화가
(D) 기자

해설 세부 내용 관련 – 요한 웨버의 직업
화자가 초반부에 이번 달에는 요한 웨버의 그림 특별전을 제공한다(This month, we're delighted to offer a special exhibit of Johann Weber's paintings)고 말하고 있으므로 정답은 (C)이다.

90

What will take place momentarily?
(A) A director will give a talk.
(B) A facility tour will begin.
(C) A group photo will be taken.
(D) A meal will be served.

곧 어떤 일이 있을 것인가?
(A) 관장이 강연할 것이다.
(B) 시설 견학이 시작될 것이다.
(C) 단체 사진을 촬영할 것이다.
(D) 식사가 제공될 것이다.

어휘 momentarily 곧, 금방 meal 식사

해설 세부 사항 관련 – 곧 있을 일
화자가 중반부에 몇 분 후 미술관 극장에서 미술관 관장이 해당 화가의 삶과 작품에 대해 이야기해 줄 것(In just a few minutes, our museum director will be giving a talk in the museum theater about the artist's life and work)이라고 말하고 있으므로 정답은 (A)이다.

Paraphrasing	담화의 In just a few minutes → 질문의 momentarily

91

According to the speaker, what can the listeners do at the information desk?
(A) Pick up a newsletter
(B) Sign up for a membership
(C) Enter a contest
(D) Register for a workshop

화자에 따르면, 청자들은 안내 데스크에서 무엇을 할 수 있는가?
(A) 소식지 가져가기
(B) 회원 가입하기
(C) 대회 참가하기
(D) 워크숍 등록하기

어휘 newsletter 소식지 enter a contest 대회에 참가하다 register 등록하다

해설 세부 사항 관련 – 청자들이 안내 데스크에서 할 수 있는 것
화자가 후반부에 여기 오신 김에 미술관 회원이 되는 것에 대해 고려해 줄 것(While you're here, please consider becoming a member of the museum)을 요청하면서 신청하려면 안내 데스크에 들러 달라(To sign up, stop by the information desk)고 말하고 있으므로 정답은 (B)이다.

92-94 회의 발췌

W-Am **92 This chart shows the clinic's average monthly expenses. Our wages for dental hygienists, assistants, and other staff members are about 25 percent of the budget, which is right on target. 93 Even though our rent has gradually increased over the years, it still doesn't take up a large part of our budget. However, look at the costs of our supplies.** You know, we haven't looked at other suppliers recently. Any savings we might find could be used for marketing to help bring in more business. So, **94 where could we focus our marketing efforts?**

이 차트는 병원의 평균 월간 지출을 보여줍니다. 치위생사와 조수, 다른 직원들 임금이 예산의 약 25퍼센트로, 예상과 정확히 일치합니다. 임대료가 몇 년간 점점 인상되고 있지만 여전히 예산의 많은 부분을 차지하지는 않아요. 그런데 물품 비용을 보세요. 아시다시피 최근 다른 공급업체를 생각해 본 적이 없습니다. 절약할 수 있는 부분을 찾아 마케팅에 투입하면 손님을 더 유치하는 데 도움이 될 거예요. 그럼 마케팅 활동은 어디에 중점을 두면 좋을까요?

어휘 average 평균 expense 경비, 비용 wage 임금 dental hygienist 치위생사 assistant 조수 budget 예산 on target 예상대로 gradually 점차 increase 인상되다, 오르다 take up 차지하다 supply 보급품, 물자 savings 절약 금액 focus 초점을 맞추다 effort 노력, 수고, 활동

92

Where does the speaker most likely work?
(A) At a dental office
(B) At a commercial bank
(C) At an equipment rental company
(D) At an employment agency

화자는 어디서 일하겠는가?
(A) 치과
(B) 상업 은행
(C) 장비 대여업체
(D) 직업소개소

해설 전체 내용 관련 – 화자의 근무지
화자가 초반부에 이 차트는 병원의 평균 월간 지출을 보여준다(This chart shows the clinic's average monthly expenses)고 말한 뒤, 치위생사와 조수, 다른 직원들(dental hygienists, assistants, and other staff members)에 대해 언급하고 있는 것으로 보아 화자는 치과에서 근무하고 있음을 알 수 있다. 따라서 정답은 (A)이다.

93

What does the speaker imply when she says, "we haven't looked at other suppliers recently"?
(A) She is unfamiliar with a task.
(B) She is asking for volunteers.
(C) More affordable options may be available.
(D) Some information needs to be corrected.

화자가 "최근 다른 공급업체를 생각해 본 적이 없습니다"라고 말하는 의도는 무엇인가?
(A) 업무가 익숙하지 않다.
(B) 자원봉사자를 요청하고 있다.
(C) 가격이 더 알맞은 선택지를 구할 수 있을 것이다.
(D) 정보를 바로잡아야 한다.

어휘 unfamiliar with ~에 익숙하지 않은 affordable 가격을 감당할 수 있는, 가격이 알맞은 available 이용 가능한, 구할 수 있는 correct 바로잡다

해설 화자의 의도 파악 – 최근 다른 공급업체를 생각해 본 적이 없다는 말의 의도
앞에서 임대료가 몇 년간 점점 인상되고 있지만 여전히 예산의 많은 부분을 차지하지는 않는다(Even though our rent has gradually increased over the years, it still doesn't take up a large part of our budget)고 하면서 물품 비용을 보라(However, look at the costs of our supplies)고 말한 뒤 인용문을 언급한 것으로 보아, 임대료와 달리 물품 비용은 공급업체를 변경함으로써 절약할 수 있다는 의도로 한 말임을 알 수 있다. 따라서 정답은 (C)이다.

94

What will most likely be discussed next?
(A) A relocation plan
(B) A staff-recruitment drive
(C) Some changes to a work policy
(D) Some marketing ideas

다음으로 무엇을 논의하겠는가?
(A) 이전 계획
(B) 직원 모집 운동
(C) 근로 정책 변경
(D) 마케팅 아이디어

어휘 relocation 이전 recruitment 모집 policy 정책

해설 세부 사항 관련 – 다음에 논의할 것
화자가 마지막에 마케팅 활동은 어디에 중점을 두면 좋을지(where could we focus our marketing efforts?)에 대해 묻고 있으므로 정답은 (D)이다.

95-97 전화 메시지 + 차트

M-Cn Hi. I'm calling to purchase some backpacks for my company. We recently started selling textbooks, and our employees will be traveling regionally to sell them. **95I'd like to provide the backpacks to our customers as promotional gifts**, but I'd like them to be sturdy—so **96I'd like something with padded straps to make them comfortable. And there should be easy access to a water bottle as well.** If you have what we need, we plan to order 50 of these. So, **97can you tell me if there is a bulk discount?** Please call me back at 555-0198.

안녕하세요. 저희 회사를 위한 배낭을 구입하려고 전화했어요. 저희가 최근 교과서 판매를 시작했는데 직원들이 이를 판매하러 지역 출장을 가야 합니다. **고객에게 판촉 선물로 배낭을 제공하고 싶은데**, 견고했으면 해요. **그래서 매기 편하도록 푹신한 끈이 있었으면 좋겠어요. 물병도 쉽게 넣을 수 있어야 하고요.** 저희가 필요로 하는 물건을 갖고 계시면 50개 주문할 계획입니다. **대량 구입 할인이 있나요?** 555-0198로 전화해 주세요.

어휘 textbook 교과서 regionally 국지적으로, 지역에서 promotional 홍보의, 판촉의 sturdy 튼튼한, 견고한 padded 속을 채워 넣은, 푹신한 comfortable 편안한 access 접근 bulk discount 대량 구입 할인

Backpack Features

	Laptop Sleeve	Water Bottle Pocket	Padded Straps
96 The Outsider		✓	✓
Modern Traveler			✓
Road Bound	✓	✓	
Elite Pro	✓		✓

배낭 특징

	노트북 커버	물병 주머니	푹신한 끈
96 아웃사이더		✓	✓
모던 트래블러			✓
로드 바운드	✓	✓	
엘리트 프로	✓		✓

어휘 feature 특징, 기능   sleeve 재킷, 커버

95

Why does the speaker want to purchase backpacks?
(A) To make a donation to a local school
(B) To give to clients as gifts
(C) To help employees carry materials at conferences
(D) To advertise a company logo

화자는 왜 배낭을 구매하고 싶어 하는가?
(A) 지역 학교에 기부하려고
(B) 고객에게 선물로 주려고
(C) 직원들이 학회에서 자료를 옮기는 데 도움을 주려고
(D) 회사 로고를 광고하려고

어휘 make a donation 기부하다   local 지역의   material 자료
　　advertise 광고하다

해설 세부 사항 관련 – 화자가 배낭을 구매하고 싶어 하는 이유
화자가 초반부에 고객에게 판촉 선물로 배낭을 제공하고 싶다(I'd like to provide the backpacks to our customers as promotional gifts)고 말하고 있으므로 정답은 (B)이다.

> **Paraphrasing** 담화의 customers → 정답의 clients

96

Look at the graphic. Which backpack fits the speaker's needs?
(A) The Outsider
(B) Modern Traveler
(C) Road Bound
(D) Elite Pro

시각 정보에 의하면, 어떤 배낭이 화자의 요구에 맞는가?
(A) 아웃사이더
(B) 모던 트래블러
(C) 로드 바운드
(D) 엘리트 프로

해설 시각 정보 연계 – 화자의 요구에 맞는 배낭
화자가 중반부에 푹신한 끈이 있었으면 좋겠다(I'd like something with padded straps)고 하면서 물병도 쉽게 넣을 수 있어야 한다(there should be easy access to a water bottle as well)고 말하고 있고, 차트에 따르면 푹신한 끈과 물병 주머니가 있는 것은 아웃사이더뿐이므로 정답은 (A)이다.

97

What does the speaker ask about?
(A) Photographs
(B) Expedited shipping
(C) A return policy
(D) A discount

화자는 무엇에 대해 물어보는가?
(A) 사진
(B) 신속 배송
(C) 반품 정책
(D) 할인

해설 세부 사항 관련 – 화자가 질문하는 것
화자가 후반부에 대량 구입 할인이 있는지(can you tell me if there is a bulk discount?)를 묻고 있으므로 정답은 (D)이다.

98-100 회의 발췌 + 표지판   동영상 강의

W-Br Hi, everyone. As most of you know, **98 I opened this grocery store five years ago.** I'm happy that we are the main supplier of fruits and vegetables in the neighborhood, and the demand for our products has increased. To meet this need, **99 we've received a loan that will allow us to expand our operations!** These additional funds will allow us to make an important change: **100 effective immediately, we'll be open seven days a week!** That means we'll have extra shifts available—if you'd like to work one of these extra shifts, please let me know.

안녕하세요, 여러분. 대부분 아시겠지만 **저는 5년 전 이 식료품점을 열었습니다.** 인근 지역 내 과일과 채소 주요 공급업체이며 저희 제품에 대한 수요가 증가했다는 사실에 기쁩니다. 이러한 요구에 부응하기 위해, **사업을 확장할 수 있는 대출을 받았습니다.** 이 추가 자금은 우리가 중요한 변화를 꾀할 수 있게 해 줄 것입니다. **오늘부터 주 7일 문을 열 것입니다!** 추가 교대 근무를 할 수 있다는 뜻입니다. 이 추가 교대 근무를 하고 싶으시면 알려 주세요.

Hours of Operation

Monday–Wednesday: 9:30 A.M.–7:00 P.M.

Thursday: 9:30 A.M.–9:00 P.M.

Friday: 9:30 A.M.–9:00 P.M.

Saturday: 10:00 A.M.–5:00 P.M.

100 Sunday: Closed

영업시간

월요일–수요일: 오전 9시 30분–오후 7시

목요일: 오전 9시 30분–오후 9시

금요일: 오전 9시 30분–오후 9시

토요일: 오전 10시–오후 5시

100일요일: 휴무

98

What type of business does the speaker run?
(A) A hair salon
(B) A bookstore
(C) A grocery store
(D) An appliance store

화자는 어떤 종류의 업체를 운영하는가?
(A) 미용실
(B) 서점
(C) 식료품점
(D) 가전제품 매장

어휘 run 운영하다 appliance (가정용) 기기

해설 전체 내용 관련 – 화자가 운영하는 업체
화자가 초반부에 5년 전 이 식료품점을 열었다(I opened this grocery
store five years ago)고 말하고 있으므로 정답은 (C)이다.

99

According to the speaker, what did the business
receive?
(A) A loan
(B) An award
(C) Some sample products
(D) Good customer reviews

화자에 따르면, 업체는 무엇을 받았는가?
(A) 대출
(B) 상
(C) 견본 제품
(D) 좋은 고객 후기

해설 세부 내용 관련 – 업체가 받은 것
화자가 중반부에 사업을 확장할 수 있는 대출을 받았다(we've received
a loan that will allow us to expand our operations!)고 말하고
있으므로 정답은 (A)이다.

100

Look at the graphic. Which day will the business hours
change?
(A) Thursday
(B) Friday
(C) Saturday
(D) Sunday

시각 정보에 의하면, 영업시간이 변경되는 요일은 언제인가?
(A) 목요일
(B) 금요일
(C) 토요일
(D) 일요일

어휘 business hours 영업시간

해설 시각 정보 연계 – 영업시간이 변경되는 요일
화자가 후반부에 오늘부터 주 7일 문을 열 것(effective immediately,
we'll be open seven days a week!)이라고 말하고 있고, 표지판에
따르면 일요일은 휴무로 되어 있으므로 일요일 영업시간이 변경된다는
것을 알 수 있다. 따라서 정답은 (D)이다.